FOURTH EDITION

Creating Effective Organizations

FOURTH EDITION

Creating Effective Organizations

Essentials of Organizational Behavior, Human Resource Management, and Strategy

David J. Cherrington

W. Gibb Dyer

Brigham Young University

KENDALL/HUNT PUBLISHING COMPANY
4050 Westmark Drive   Dubuque, Iowa 52002

Cover image copyright © 2004 by Rubberball

Copyright © 2004 by David J. Cherrington and W. Gibb Dryer

ISBN 0-7575-1095-7

Library of Congress Control Number: 2004107670

Printed in the United States of America
10 9 8 7 6 5 4 3 2

CONTENTS

Preface, vi

SECTION I

What are effective organizations and how do you create them? **1**

Chapter 1   *Effective Organizations,* **2**
Chapter 2   *Strategy,* **33**

SECTION II

How do you attract and train an effective workforce? **57**

Chapter 3:   *Human Resource Planning, Recruitment, and Selection,* **58**
Chapter 4:   *Socialization, Training, and Development,* **87**
Chapter 5:   *Employee Relations and Equal Employment Opportunity,* **107**

SECTION III

How do you motivate employees to accomplish the organization's goals? **129**

Chapter 6:   *Analyzing Individual Behavior,* **130**
Chapter 7:   *Motivation,* **159**
Chapter 8:   *Work Design,* **195**
Chapter 9:   *Performance Management,* **219**
Chapter 10: *Employee Discipline,* **245**

SECTION IV

How do you create a productive work environment? **265**

Chapter 11: *Effective Groups,* **266**
Chapter 12: *Intergroup Behavior and Conflict,* **295**
Chapter 13: *Organizational Design,* **327**
Chapter 14: *Organizational Culture,* **353**

SECTION V

What are the key processes leading to organizational effectiveness? **373**

Chapter 15: *Communication and Interpersonal Skills,* **374**
Chapter 16: *Decision Making,* **399**
Chapter 17: *Leadership,* **421**
Chapter 18: *Power and Influence,* **445**

SECTION VI

How do you improve organizational effectiveness? **471**

Chapter 19: *Organizational Change,* **472**
Chapter 20: *Organizational Development,* **493**
Chapter 21: *Improving Your Own Effectiveness,* **515**

Index, 543

This book focuses on what you need to know to create effective organizations. It explains principles that come from organizational behavior, human resource management, strategy, group dynamics, and leadership. This book represents a work in progress as we continue to select the most significant core principles that will help you manage or work with organizations.

We live in an organizational world and we are surrounded by countless organizations, including business organizations, government agencies, family businesses, and churches. We participate in many groups at work, at church, and in our neighborhoods. Some organizations and groups are more effective than others. Effective organizations make a great contribution to society because they produce valuable products and services and provide meaningful opportunities for self expression and fulfillment. Organizations that have direction and purpose, whose strategies are aligned with their structures and processes, and whose leaders make careful and sensitive decisions are a blessing to the lives of organizational members. Ineffective organizations tend to reduce the quality of life and waste environmental resources.

As a society we need people who know how to create effective organizations. We need transformational leaders and entrepreneurs who know how to manage organizations. A major difference between a healthy, thriving society and a struggling society is the existence or absence of a coordinated network of effective organizations that provide goods and services for consumers and work opportunities for citizens.

This text presents the basic principles of organizational effectiveness and explains how to apply them. It focuses more on practical applications than on statistical surveys and empirical research. Some of the major research studies in organizational behavior are included when they illustrate or explain important principles. As a general rule, only the most essential ideas have been included, while ideas that are interesting but not essential have been deleted. We welcome feedback on the material presented here. We are grateful for the editorial assistance of those who eliminated many errors and made the text more readable. Royalties for this text will be contributed to the William G. Dyer Institute for Leading Organizational Change in the Marriott School of Management at Brigham Young University.

David J. Cherrington and W. Gibb Dyer
Department of Organizational Leadership and Strategy
Brigham Young University
Provo, Utah

What are effective organizations and how do you create them?

If all the world is a stage, it is a stage filled with organizations. Regardless of the part we play—student, manager, customer, employee, or entrepreneur—we act our parts on an organizational stage. The quality of our lives is influenced by our interactions with organizations, and by whether these interactions are satisfying and fulfilling. Many of our emotional gratifications and physical comforts depend on the products and services of organizations. Whether we participate as members, managers, or customers, we need to understand organizational behavior and what makes an organization effective. We need to know how organizations influence us and how we influence organizations.

CHAPTER 1
Effective Organizations

CHAPTER 2
Strategy

Section I explains how organizations are created from the mission and strategy of a founder. People who start organizations to fulfill their economic dreams need to understand the characteristics of effective organizations. Chapter 1 describes the central characteristics of organizations, and explains the concepts of efficiency and effectiveness. Chapter 2 explains the concept of strategy, and discusses the advantages of the different competitive strategies that organizations use to succeed.

Effective Organizations

Chapter Outline

Understanding Organizations
Managers, Leaders, and Entrepreneurs
Six Concepts for Creating an Effective Organization
Levels of Analysis

Open System Theory
Defining an Organization
Organizational Subsystems

Organizational Effectiveness
Organizational Goals
Measuring Organizational Effectiveness
Creating Ethical Organizations

Developing and Testing Theories
Analyzing Organizational Events
Developing Theories
Testing Theories

UNDERSTANDING ORGANIZATIONS

Managers, Leaders, and Entrepreneurs

Do you know what an organization is and how to create one? If you needed to start your own company, would you know how to do it? This book explains how to create an organization and how to make it more effective by knowing how to diagnose problems, formulate new policies, and implement change. At one time or another we will all serve as leaders in some kind of organization, whether it is a business, a family, a church, a neighborhood, or a political organization. Consequently, we need to know what organizations are and how to make them function effectively.

How important are healthy organizations? Organizations have an enormous impact on the lives of individuals and societies; almost everything we do is done in the context of an organization. Organizations provide the essential goods and services that benefit society, and they have the potential to greatly improve the quality of our lives. Healthy organizations produce healthy members by providing valuable opportunities for self-expression and fulfillment, plus jobs that provide an income. Conversely, ineffective organizations can damage the self-esteem of their members and cause frustration and unhappiness. Although every organization has the potential to injure people, ineffective organizations can be especially abusive by destroying feelings of self-worth, cheating customers, or wasting resources.

This book adopts a managerial perspective; it is designed to teach you what you need to know to create an effective organization and manage it. Managers and leaders have a large influence on the success of organizations. Studies on the reasons why organizations succeed or fail typically point to the significant role of managers. Key managerial decisions in formulating strategic plans and organizational policies primarily account for the survival or the demise of organizations. Effective managers make things happen. They are largely responsible for establishing organizations that create new jobs and produce useful products and services. Dynamic leaders who have the vision and foresight to create an enterprise and who can excite the minds of followers to coalesce around their vision are a valuable national treasure.

Entrepreneur:
A person who creates a new company and is willing to bear the financial risks of creating a company for the chance to make a profit.

An *entrepreneur* is someone who creates a new organization to produce a product or service. The word *entrepreneur* means *risk bearer*, and an entrepreneur is willing to bear the financial risk of creating a company for the opportunity of making a profit. To be successful, entrepreneurs need to have a vision about producing something new that is better or cheaper than what is currently available. This vision becomes the driving passion that helps them succeed. This entrepreneurial spirit is not only valuable for the wealth of the person, but it is also a vital resource for any society that is fortunate enough to possess it. It is a great economic blessing to nations where it is found. Underdeveloped countries are often rich in natural resources, but lack the entrepreneurial spirit and managerial talent needed to create effective organizations that produce vital products and services.

Six Concepts for Creating an Effective Organization

This book is organized into six sections that explain the six major concepts involved in building and maintaining an effective organization.

1. What is an effective organization and how do you create one? The first step is to know what an effective organization is. Most people define an organization as a group of people working together to achieve a common goal. But this is not an accurate definition for three reasons: (1) the people are not clearly defined, since some participate more than others; (2) they are not all working together, if by that we mean doing the same thing; and (3) they usually have their own personal goals. A much better definition is to view an organization as a system of patterned activities in an open social system that is constantly adapting to its environment. Organizations are goal-directed entities that originate from the vision and mission of a founder, and their survival depends on following a successful strategy. The characteristics of an organization are explained in this chapter, and strategy in chapter 2. These ideas provide a vital foundation for understanding organizational structures and processes that appear in later chapters.

2. How do you attract and train an effective workforce? The most important resource in almost every company is its workforce. Every organization must succeed in attracting talented people who are willing to join the company and contribute to its goals while satisfying their personal goals. Effective human resource management involves recruiting and selecting the right people for the right jobs and giving them the kind of training they need to perform well. People must also be treated fairly, and several laws have been passed to prohibit discrimination. These human resource functions are explained in chapters 3 through 5.

3. How do you motivate employees to accomplish the organization's mission and goals? Once people join an organization, they must be willing to stay for at least some minimum time and make a dependable contribution to its mission and goals. People decide to join organizations for many reasons, and there are even more reasons to explain why they are willing to work. Chapters 6 through 10 explain the major theories of motivation—how effective managers can use intrinsic and extrinsic rewards, as well as punishment, to motivate employees.

4. How do you create a productive work environment? Leaders are responsible for creating a productive work environment. Poorly designed work environments can prevent employees from being productive, regardless of their motivation. Working conditions need to be carefully designed at the individual, group, and organizational levels. Chapters 11 through 14 explain how to design effective work teams, organizational structures, and organizational cultures.

5. What are the key processes leading to organizational effectiveness? Effective organizations are held together by four key processes: communication, decision making, leadership, and power. These processes determine the way information is created and shared, how decisions are made and who makes them, and how influence is exerted to keep the organization functioning smoothly. Good leadership makes people want to contribute and be productive.

6. How do you improve organizations and keep them from becoming obsolete? In many ways, our modern organizations are very different from organizations fifty or even five years ago. Today's organizations are characterized by much greater diversity and technological advancements than in earlier years, and the amount of change in organizations seems to increase each year. Many factors contribute to the growing diversity of the labor force, including an increase in the percentage of female and minority employees and a larger number of ethnic groups represented in the labor force. Scientific discoveries have made dramatic changes in technology, especially in the transmission of information. New products emerge almost instantaneously, making old products obsolete. The world has increasingly become one global economy requiring organizations to interact as competitors and partners across national and cultural boundaries. To survive, many organizations have had to change their orientation from being a product-producing organization to a service-producing organization. Chapters 19 through 21 explain how change occurs and how we can improve the effectiveness of both people and organizations in the midst of such rapid change.

Levels of Analysis

To understand organizational effectiveness, you must be able to analyze organizational events and have a framework for organizing your observations. These events can be examined from three distinct levels of analysis—the individual, the group, and the organization—and they are also embedded in a distinct environment. What we observe depends on which level we use for examining it. For example, a dispute between a purchasing supervisor and a warehouse superintendent would be analyzed quite differently depending on whether it was viewed as a conflict between personalities at the individual level, a problem between members of a task force at the group level, or a conflict between two division heads at the organizational level. All three levels should be considered in order to perform a proper diagnosis of the problem, as illustrated in Exhibit 1.1.

Individual Level of Analysis: Examines such issues as personality, perception, attitudes, motivation, and values.

Individual Level. At the individual level, events are diagnosed in terms of the behaviors and personalities of the people interacting in the situation. Each individual brings to the organization a unique history of attitudes, values, and past experiences. If an organization announced that it was sponsoring a competitive incentive program, the program would be greeted enthusiastically by people with a high need for achievement, while employees with a low need for achievement would feel threatened. When the warehouse superintendent and the purchasing supervisor debate the merits of a proposed change, their comments reflect their own personal attitudes and values. How forcefully they express their attitudes is influenced by their own self-esteem and assertiveness. Whether the proposed change is accepted may depend on which individual has the better negotiation skills or aggressiveness.

Exhibit 1.1   Three Levels for Analyzing Organizational Events

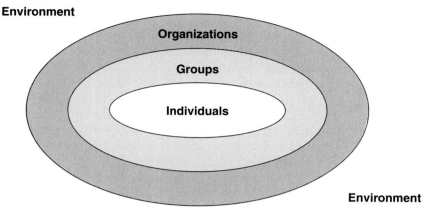

Group Level
of Analysis:
Examines such issues
as group roles, group
norms, conformity, and
status.

Group Level. Although groups are made of individuals, the events that occur within a group are not simply the sum of individual behaviors. Groups develop their own norms of acceptable behavior and these general expectations may be shared by members of the group, even though none of them would be willing to accept the same norms outside the group. The behavior of group members is influenced by group dynamics, group roles, and status. For example, in a task-force meeting, the warehouse superintendent could suggest a superior solution to a critical problem. But because of group dynamics, the task force may select an inferior suggestion that protects the interests of the purchasing supervisor, who is chairing the task force.

Organizational
Level of Analysis:
Examines such issues
as organizational
structure, decision
making, authority, re-
porting relationships,
and span of control.

Organizational Level. Organizations are more than just individuals and groups. Events occur within the context of an organizational structure. This structure, and the location of people within it, have an impact on virtually every social interaction, including casual conversations. For example, secretaries and production workers do not speak to the president of the company with the same candor and ease that they have when they speak with each other.

An organizational structure with hierarchical reporting relationships gives certain individuals the power to influence others. This structure affects the way information is communicated and the way decisions are made. A decentralized organizational structure, for example, allows lower-level mangers to participate in making decisions, thereby raising their status and providing greater variety in their jobs. Let us return to the previous example: The purchasing supervisor is opposed to the warehouse superintendent's recommendation to adopt a computerized inventory system because the people in the warehouse would then have immediate access to all inventory information. In the past this information was controlled by purchasing supervisors, who used it as a source of power to influence other areas of the organization, particularly accounting.

Environment:
All of the external
forces that impact
individuals, groups,
and organizations.

Environment. Organizational events do not occur in isolation; external forces may exert a powerful influence on what is observed at each of these three levels. For example, low productivity, careless work, excessive absenteeism, and high tardiness are serious problems that need to be analyzed at more than just the individual, group, and organizational levels. The seriousness of these problems becomes evident when we realize that the environment includes both consumers who demand high-quality products, and competing firms in Korea, China, or Singapore with workers willing to produce high-quality items for considerably lower wages.

Returning to our earlier example: The purchasing supervisor's desire to maintain control of the inventory data may be inconsistent with the organization's need to install a computerized inventory system. The survival of the organization may be threatened by other organizations who use "just-in-time" manufacturing and require less working capital for raw materials and finished goods. Organizations face many environmental forces that influence their effectiveness, including changes in the labor force, evolving social customs, fluctuating economic conditions, and the enactment of laws by federal or state legislatures.

OPEN-SYSTEMS THEORY

This book uses open-systems theory to describe organizations and explain what makes them effective. Open-systems theory explains the characteristics that all social organizations have in common, including manufacturing companies, service organizations, government agencies, religions, and voluntary associations.

The concept of an organization is usually rather difficult to understand, because we are not accustomed to thinking at an organizational level of abstraction. We can see individual differences and we have observed group dynamics, but organizational processes and structure are more abstract and more unfamiliar. Furthermore, organizations are not physical objects that we can touch or feel. They are systems of activities with subsystems that perform essential functions that enable them to survive and grow. If they consisted of physical objects, like buildings, organization charts, machines, or people, they would be easy to observe. But because they are nonphysical they are more difficult to understand.

We are surrounded by organizations, and we interact with them in almost everything we do. We are largely unaware of the complex organizations that provide the basic goods and services we have come to expect in our society. The food we buy at the supermarket is not provided by just one chain of food stores, but by a complex combination of corporate farms, food-processing companies, transportation companies, and government agencies. Likewise, the gas we buy at the corner station depends on a complex web of national and international organizations that manufacture oil-drilling equipment, drill for oil, transport it, refine it, and market the products. Even simple activities like registering a car or renewing a driver's license require the coordinated efforts of large public organizations.

How well these organizations function has a significant influence on the quality of our lives. Effective organizations make life happier; poorly structured organizations can create enormous inconvenience and unhappiness. Consider the problem of a secretary who wants to purchase a metal bookshelf for her office similar to the one she bought for herself on sale for $39. Since the cost exceeds $25, she cannot simply take the money out of petty cash and buy it herself. But following the correct procedure is almost impossible. Because the bookshelf is capital equipment and has not been budgeted, the purchasing department cannot accept her purchase order until another form with three signatures is obtained authorizing the exception through the accounting department. Finally, in frustration, the secretary takes $25 from petty cash and pays the remainder herself to get the bookshelf before the sale ends. The hassle of buying a new bookshelf is so unpleasant that the secretary believes the accounting and purchasing staffs are consciously refusing to cooperate. In reality, however, both staffs are only trying to follow the proper procedures. The problem isn't a lack of cooperation or motivation; the problem is a rigid organizational structure.

Defining an Organization

An organization is an open social system that consists of the patterned activities of a group of people that tend to be goal directed.[1] Viewing an organization as a system of structured activities is especially useful when diagnosing organizational problems or analyzing the competitive advantages of a firm. Effective organizations consist of smoothly functioning patterned activities that occur at predictable times and require minimal guidance or direction. Thinking of an organization as a system of patterned activities prepares us to improve organizational effectiveness and to identify organizational problems and opportunities.

System:
The set of interrelated or interacting elements that form an entity, such as the solar system, the human body, the public transportation for a city, or a clock.

Open Social Systems. A *system* is a set of interrelated elements that acquires inputs from the environment, transforms them into some form of useful output, and discharges the outputs to the external environment. Social systems can be compared with biological systems: both have subsystems and interact with the environment. A useful analogy is the human body, which consists of a series of subsystems that support the body and help it function, such as the respiratory, digestive, excretory, muscular, and skeletal systems. These subsystems interact in predictable ways that allow the organism to survive. The circulatory system, for example, obtains oxygen from the respiratory system and delivers it throughout the body for the muscular system to use. A breakdown in any system could result in serious illness or even death. But social systems are more complex than biological systems, and this complexity explains why organizations cannot be designed like machines that are simply turned on and allowed to run without further direction. Social systems exist in a changing social environment that requires them to adapt to new demands.

All social systems are open systems, as illustrated in Exhibit 1.2. A closed system would not depend on its environment; it would be autonomous and isolated from the outside world. Plus, it would have all the energy it needed and it would function without consuming external resources. Many studies have examined the internal functioning of organizations as if they were closed systems isolated from their environments. Many industrial-engineering studies, for example, have used a closed-system logic by assuming the environment was constant, that organizational effectiveness depended only on improving internal efficiency, that the organization had a constant supply of incoming resources, and that the products were automatically consumed by a receptive public.

Unfortunately, this closed-system logic is seriously flawed, because there are no closed social systems. Even organizations that try to minimize contact

Exhibit 1.2 Open-Systems Model of Organizations

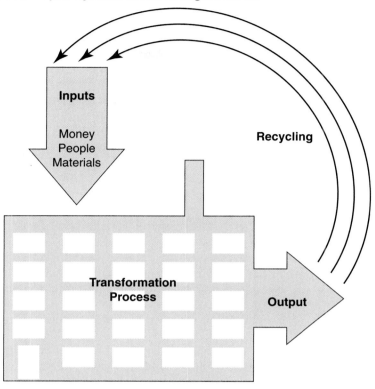

with society, such as prisons and some religious communities, still exist within an environment that influences the availability of resources and the acceptability of outputs.

An *open system* must interact with the environment to survive. It must obtain resources from the environment and export products back to the environment. It cannot isolate itself or seal itself off from the environment; nor can it ignore environmental change. It must continuously adapt to the demands of a changing environment. Organizations must continue to obtain the necessary inputs and produce acceptable products despite an uncertain environment and fluctuations in the availability of resources or demand for the product. The human body is an open system, and so are churches, the military, businesses, cities, and the federal government.

Patterned Activities. The best way to think about an organization is to view it as a series of patterned activities—relatively stable and predictable events that continue to occur with regularity. These patterned activities are complementary and interdependent with respect to a common goal; that is, they are organized and coordinated to achieve a conscious purpose or objective. To analyze an organization we want to first analyze these repeated, relatively enduring patterned activities.

If an activity pattern occurs only once or at unpredictable intervals, we could not speak of an organization. A mob or a protest group, for example,

Open Social System:
A system that is open to the environment in the sense that it depends on the environment to obtain resources and consume its products. All organizations are open social systems.

Patterned Activities:
The relatively stable and predictable events that continue to occur with consistency and regularity. These enduring activities are necessary to form an organization.

would not be considered an organization until some type of structure emerged to provide stability and a recurrence of the activities. The patterned activities in a hospital include such activities as admitting patients, conducting diagnostic tests, performing operations, and providing health care. A significant patterned activity for a university consists of the hundreds of classes where students and teachers meet to share ideas. The patterned activities of a religion consist of worship services and other social events.

Describing an organization as a sequence of patterned activities explains why organizations are difficult to understand. Patterned activities are not objects that we can touch or feel; they are events that can only be viewed one at a time as they occur.

Negative Entropy. According to open-systems theory, organizations are best analyzed in terms of the resources and energy inputs they acquire from the environment, the transformation of energies within the system, the resulting product or output, and the translation of these products into new energy to reactivate the system. In an open social system, products are recycled within the environment and transformed into more resources and energy to perpetuate the cycle of activities. Consumer goods are sold, and the money is used to purchase additional raw materials and to compensate employees. In a voluntary organization, the satisfaction from participating is the output, and it must be great enough to create the expectation that future participation will continue to be satisfying.

In a successful organization this recycling allows the organization to grow and prosper, a condition called *negative entropy*. The process of entropy is a universal law of nature in which all forms of organization move toward disorganization or death. The organization, however, by acquiring more energy from its environment than it uses to produce its products, can store energy and achieve negative entropy. Business organizations hope to sell their products for more than the cost of producing them. These retained earnings and profit represent a form of negative entropy, because they allow the organization to grow.

An illustration of entropy is when a research institute uses a research grant (energy) to study a problem and fails to produce any results. When all the money has been spent on salaries, supplies, and other research costs and the energy is exhausted, entropy has occurred and the institute dies. But the institute can achieve negative entropy if it produces reports or discoveries that it can sell for more than the initial grant. Negative entropy allows it to survive and even grow.

Differentiation and Integration. Open systems move in the direction of greater differentiation and elaboration; not every individual performs every function. Instead, specialized activities are identified and assigned to individuals and departments. In a hospital's emergency center, for example, different people are responsible for admitting patients, cleaning wounds, taking blood samples, inserting IVs, setting bones, taking X-rays, and transporting patients. *Differentiation* is the development of specialized functions and a division of labor.

As organizations become more differentiated, they require some sort of coordinating process, called *integration*, to combine the various activities and

Negative Entropy:
While entropy refers to the dissolution or wearing down of energy and resources and moving to a state of balance, negative entropy refers to the reversal of this process and allows for the growth and increase in energy and resources.

Differentiation:
The process of creating a division of labor by creating specialized functions that are performed by different people and departments.

Integration:
The process of coordinating all of the various specialized functions and events so that a system can continue to operate smoothly.

bring the system together for unified functioning. As organizations become more highly differentiated, the need for integrating activities increases. In living organisms, integration is achieved by the hormonal and nervous subsystems. In organizations, it is achieved by setting priorities, establishing routines, synchronizing functions, and scheduling events. In a university, for example, the two major coordinating instruments are the class schedule, which announces when and where each course will be taught, and the university catalogue, which describes the degree requirements, the courses, and the faculty.

Organizations must receive feedback to know when changes are needed and what must be done to adapt to a changing environment. Without feedback mechanisms to help the organization stay on course, it would lose its ability to survive and continue as a system. Customer satisfaction, new-product information, and employee opinions are essential forms of feedback. As we will see later, the communication and decision-making mechanisms that organizations use to collect, analyze, and disseminate knowledge largely determine how work teams and organizations should be structured.

Social organizations are essentially contrived systems. Because they are made by people, they are imperfect systems. They can come apart at the seams overnight, but they can also outlast by centuries the people who originally created them. Some organizations, such as Freemasonry and the Catholic Church, have survived for centuries in spite of dramatic social and cultural changes. Other organizations essentially disappear overnight, such as the political organization of an unsuccessful candidate. Until election night, the campaign organization may be a rapidly growing and thriving organization. By the next morning, however, the organization is essentially dead, since all the speeches, campaigning, and rallies that represented its patterned activities have come to an end.

The cement that holds organizations together is psychological rather than biological. Social organizations are anchored in the attitudes, beliefs, motivations, and expectations of human beings. Some organizations can continue to survive and even flourish in spite of very limited individual involvement. Such is the case with many political and volunteer associations, for example, parent-teacher associations (PTAs), where most members contribute only a few minutes per year. An organization can have a very high rate of turnover and still persist. The relationships of people, rather than the people themselves, provide the constancy of an organization.

Organizational Subsystems

As an open system, an organization is composed of several subsystems. These subsystems represent the patterned activities that design, produce, market, and deliver a firm's products. Each of these subsystems can also be viewed as a system in its own right; it receives inputs from other subsystems and transforms them into outputs for use within the organization. Six subsystems necessary for any organization to survive and grow are procurement, production, disposal, maintenance, adaptive, and managerial. Although these subsystems are largely associated with particular departments, they could involve patterned activities performed in multiple departments.

Procurement subsystem:
Acquires the energy and resources from the external environment.

1. The *procurement subsystem* acquires energy and resources from the external environment, including human resources, raw materials, financial

**Production
subsystem:**
The operations and ac-
tivities that produce the
product or service of
the organization.

**Disposal
subsystem:**
The activities that are
involved in delivering
the organization's prod-
ucts or services to the
next users in the value
chain, such as cus-
tomers or purchasers.

**Maintenance
subsystem:**
The activities that are
associated with moti-
vating people to con-
tinue to participate
in the organization,
especially evaluating
and rewarding
performance.

**Adaptive
subsystem:**
The activities associ-
ated with making
adaptive changes in
the organization or its
products, especially
research and develop-
ment activities.

**Managerial
subsystem:**
The decision-making
activities associated
with directing and su-
pervising the events
within an organization.

Value chain:
Organizations are
linked together in a
value chain to produce
their products and ser-
vices. Each organiza-
tion receives inputs
from organizations
upstream, adds value
to them, and passes
them on to downstream
organizations.

resources, status, recognition, satisfaction, or future expectations. New
employees and venture capital are important resources for a new enterprise, whereas satisfaction and future expectations may be the most
important resources for a religion or a sorority. The procurement subsystem includes all of the inbound logistics associated with receiving and
storing materials, handling and controlling inventory, and securing energy
and other resources from the environment. The procurement subsystem
tries to guarantee a stable source of future inputs. These activities are typically performed by the purchasing department in most organizations.

2. The ***production or operations subsystem*** creates the products and services of the organization and represents the primary transformation activities. In a manufacturing firm, this subsystem consists largely of the
activities of the production department; in an auto assembly plant, it consists of transforming raw materials into vehicles; in a university, it consists of seminars and classes; and in a driver's license bureau, it consists
of administering tests and issuing licenses. In most organizations, the
production subsystem serves as the foundation around which other subsystems are organized.

3. The ***disposal subsystem*** includes all marketing and sales efforts to dispose of the product in the environment. These activities include all out-
bound logistics, such as processing orders and distributing the product to
the buyer; marketing and sales activities, such as advertising and pricing;
and service activities, including installing and repairing the product and
training customers. Most manufacturing organizations have sales departments that specialize in performing the disposal function. In universities, this function is performed by placement offices and alumni
associations.

4. The ***maintenance subsystem***, sometimes called the human resource subsystem, involves bringing people into the organization and motivating
them to perform. Therefore, maintenance activities include recruiting
and selecting new employees, compensating them fairly, providing attractive benefits, creating favorable work conditions, rewarding outstanding performance, and providing other forms of recognition that
satisfy human needs.

5. The ***adaptive subsystem*** is responsible for helping the organization respond to a changing environment. Adaptive subsystem activities include
developing new products, adopting new technology, gathering information about problems and opportunities, and developing creative innovations. Most of the activities of a research and development department
would be considered part of the adaptive subsystem.

6. The ***managerial subsystem*** is responsible for directing the other subsystems of the organization. Management determines the strategy, goals,
and policies that direct the entire organization. It also allocates resources
and resolves disputes between people and departments. The managerial
subsystem is also responsible for designing the organizational structure
and directing the tasks within each subsystem.

Understanding how these subsystems are linked with each other and to the external environment is essential to analyze a firm's competitive advantages (as
in the following chapter). The competitive position of each firm depends on its

Boundary-spanning activities:
Activities that occur between one organization and other organizations in its environment, such as purchasing new materials, gathering consumer information, evaluating customer satisfaction, and merchandising the products.

Institutional function:
Activities that help an organization to be accepted within its environment, such as public relations, lobbying, and protective legislation.

ability to create value through a *value chain*.[2] Each firm represents a link in a chain of value: it receives inputs from suppliers, adds value to them, and passes them on to buyers. Within each firm, this value chain consists of strategically relevant activities that accomplish the firm's essential subsystem activities. This value chain concept can be used to determine whether a firm has the potential to provide a differentiated product and whether it can add value at each stage of the chain.

Procurement and disposal subsystem activities are sometimes called *boundary-spanning activities*, since they involve transactions at the organization's boundaries. Boundary-spanning activities regulate interactions between organizations and coordinate organizational demands with the environment. They may also include lobbying efforts that create a favorable climate for the organization. This activity, called the *institutional function*, protects the institution and creates a friendly environment that supports the organization. Most public-relations activities, such as lobbying efforts and political action committee activities, are part of the institutional function, because these activities try to obtain favorable legislation that guarantees the survival and protects the special interests of the organization.

ORGANIZATIONAL EFFECTIVENESS

Organizational effectiveness refers to how well the organization is performing and whether it is achieving its goals. When we study organizations, we need a method to measure organizational performance. Performance measures allow us to assess how well the organization is functioning and whether decisions are good or bad. Unfortunately, most organizations do not have clear and concise goals.

Organizational Goals

Effective organizations have clearly defined goals that are widely shared among all members. Clearly defined goals help to focus the efforts of members and give meaning and purpose to the organization. Organizations that have unclear goals usually struggle with high levels of employee frustration and low levels of productivity.

Official versus Operative Goals:
Official goals define the general mission of the organization, while operative goals describe more specifically what the organization is actually trying to accomplish. For example, Dell Computers' official goal is to be a leading computer manufacturer through a direct sales strategy, while one of its operative goals might be to develop and market a new printer.

Organizations have *official goals* that define the general mission of the organization and *operative goals* or *objectives* that are more specific and describe what the organization is actually trying to accomplish. Having clearly defined goals provides several benefits for the organization.

1. *Legitimacy.* The official goals of an organization provide a symbol of legitimacy both to employees and to external constituencies. Goals describe the purpose of the organization, so people know what it stands for and accept its existence.
2. *Employee direction and motivation.* Operative goals provide a sense of direction and motivation for employees. Research on goal setting has shown that the performance of employees can be significantly increased by realistic goals.
3. *Decision guidelines.* Goals provide a standard for evaluating performance. Organizational goals can serve as guidelines for individual behavior and

decisions. The goals can serve as the criteria against which management decisions are made.

4. *Reduction of uncertainty.* The process of goal setting tends to reduce uncertainty for members of the organization, especially top management. The process of arriving at a set of mutually acceptable goals helps to focus the energies and efforts of the entire organization.

Organizations exist for a purpose; therefore, they are considered goal-directed social entities. Some have argued, however, that organizations *per se* do not have goals—only people have goals. Technically this criticism is correct. Organizations and other social entities do not have goals or other human properties, such as a soul, a memory, or feelings. However, most organizations have a goal that is commonly shared by many individuals, and there is sufficient agreement among people about the organization's goals to unite them in a common purpose. Therefore, it is appropriate to conclude that an organization and its members are trying to achieve a particular goal. Participants may have goals different from the organization's goals, and the organization may have several goals, but organizations exist for one or more purposes without which they would cease to exist. Therefore, it is meaningful to talk about organizational goals because of the consensual validation supporting them. The term *consensual validation* refers to a common belief or consensus that is so widely shared among a group of people that most of the people accept it as true, even though it may not match their own personal feelings.

Developing a list of goals and objectives is a valuable process that contributes to an organization's effectiveness, especially when many members participate in the process and the goals are widely shared. Goals tend to be general statements about what the organization hopes to achieve, while objectives tend to be more specific and short-range. The best objectives are measurable, and relate directly to the central mission and goals of the organization. Goal setting activities contribute enormously to organizational success, and the principles associated with goal setting are discussed in later chapters.

Measuring Organizational Effectiveness

How we measure organizational effectiveness depends on the time frame we use to measure it. The most popular short-run criteria are job satisfaction and productivity; productive companies that provide pleasant jobs are considered highly effective. In the long run, however, the survival of the organization is the ultimate measure of organizational effectiveness. If an organization survives for several centuries, we say it is effective because it has acquired resources from the environment, transformed them into usable products, and adapted to changing environmental demands. Although survival is the ultimate measure of organizational effectiveness, we need more immediate measures on a monthly or yearly basis to evaluate managerial decisions.

Efficiency:
A measure of how well the organization translates inputs to outputs.

Effectiveness:
A measure of how well an organization can convert inputs into outputs and then recycle them within the environment to produce new inputs.

Efficiency versus Effectiveness.   *Efficiency* refers to how well the organization converts inputs into outputs, whereas *effectiveness* measures how well products are produced plus how well they are recycled in the environment back into usable inputs for the organization.

Efficiency usually contributes to effectiveness, but not always. An organization could be extremely efficient in transforming inputs into outputs, and yet be ineffective because its products are obsolete. Conversely, an organization could be extremely effective because of innovations or a unique market strategy, even though it is not particularly efficient.

Organizations use a variety of efficiency measures, such as labor costs, productivity per employee hour, costs per unit, and tons per employee hour. These numbers are interpreted by examining historical trends or by making industry comparisons, and managers use this information to improve their organizational efficiency. In some industries the performance of different companies demonstrates wide variations in efficiency ratios, such as the auto industry, where there is considerable variation in the ratios of cars produced per year per employee.

Open-systems theory provides a useful model for evaluating organizational effectiveness. Effectiveness can be measured in terms of inputs, transformation, outputs, stakeholders, and recycling. These processes identify the most frequently used criteria of effectiveness, as illustrated in Exhibit 1.3.

Resource Acquisition Approach:
Measuring organizational effectiveness in terms of how many resources it can attract.

Resource Acquisition Approach. How well does the organization acquire resources? The most effective organizations acquire the most resources. This approach is often used by organizations in the early stage of development: new businesses measure their success by their ability to acquire venture capital.

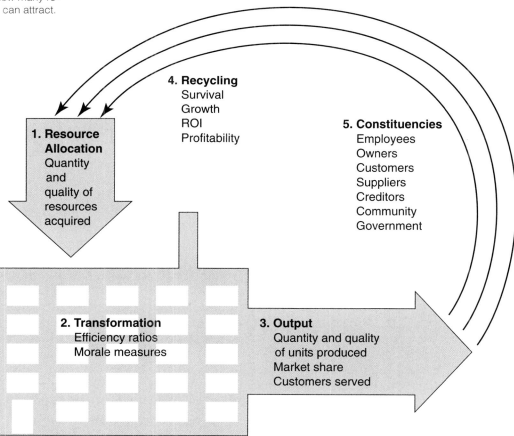

Exhibit 1.3 Approaches to Measuring Organizational Effectiveness

Other organizations use resource acquisition to measure effectiveness because other measures are difficult to obtain. For example, voluntary organizations, such as the March of Dimes or the Muscular Dystrophy Association, frequently report their success in terms of the contributions they receive from society. The number of new converts and new members is an important measure of effectiveness for religious and social organizations. Some government agencies measure their effectiveness by the size of their budget or the amount of office space allocated to them. Along with the ability to attract new faculty or students, universities frequently use allocations from the state legislature as a measure of effectiveness. In their commercials, car dealerships often emphasize how many cars the manufacturers sent to them and consider this number an indication of their effectiveness.

The value of the resource acquisition approach is that it considers the relationship of the organization to its environment and can be used to compare organizations that have different goals. However, it has a very limited perspective. An athletic team that acquires many star players would not be considered effective if the team loses its games. Similarly, a research institute that fails to find new discoveries with the money it receives would not be considered effective.

Transformation Approach:
Measuring organizational effectiveness by how efficient it is in converting inputs into outputs.

Transformation Approach. How efficiently does the organization convert inputs into outputs? The transformation approach includes both quantitative measures of economic efficiency and perceptual measures of internal health. Some examples of quantitative measures include rate of return on capital or assets, unit cost, scrap and waste, down time, cost per patient (or student or client), and occupancy rates.

Many questionnaires have been developed to measure the attitudes of employees concerning internal organizational health. These questionnaires measure the amount of confidence, trust, and communication among workers and management; how well decisions are made; whether there is a feeling of teamwork, loyalty, and commitment; whether the reward system is fair and adequate; and whether the organization is properly structured. These evaluations measure only internal processes and overlook the interaction between the organization and its environment; however, they may be valuable when used to compare internal processes within different companies.

Output Approach:
Measuring organizational effectiveness in terms of how many products and services it can produce.

Output Approach. How many outputs does the organization produce? Some of the most popular measures of output include profit, sales, market share, patients released, documents processed, clients served, students graduated, and the number of arrests or citations issued. The output approach is generally viewed as the most relevant criterion of organizational effectiveness, since it appears to measure goal accomplishment. This approach seems logical because organizations try to maximize their outputs. But unless the output is consumed by the public, the organization will not survive. In using the output approach, it is also important to remember that organizations have multiple goals and multiple outcomes. High achievement on one goal may mean low achievement on another. Therefore, measuring effectiveness on only one dimension could oversimplify the objectives of the organization and produce misleading conclusions.

Recycling Approach:
An overall measure of organizational effectiveness that assesses how well the organization is able to convert inputs into outputs and translate them into new resources to repeat the cycle.

Recycling Approach. How well are the outputs adopted by the environment? The recycling approach concerns how well the goods produced by the organization are consumed by society and translated into essential inputs. Unlike the earlier approaches, the recycling approach involves a long-term perspective and is more abstract. Three dimensions of the recycling approach include adaptability, development, and survival.

Adaptability refers to how well the organization responds to internal and external changes. To the extent that the organization cannot or does not adapt to its environment, its survival is in jeopardy. Changes in consumer taste and foreign competition are two environmental forces that have had a profound influence on many organizations. Some organizations measure their adaptability by examining their growth over time or the number of new products they have produced.

Development includes organizational restructuring, to improve the organization, and training, to help the employees. Organizations need to invest in themselves through organizational development and training programs. By helping their employees develop new skills, organizations hope to adapt to a changing environment with less resistance and difficulty.

Survival is the ultimate measure of organizational effectiveness. Organizations that fail to respond to a changing environment, or that lose their ability to produce viable products and transform them into new inputs, do not survive, and by definition, they are not effective. Accordingly, the final test of effectiveness is whether the organization is able to sustain itself in the environment. However, this criterion is not very useful for managers who want more immediate feedback on the effectiveness of their decisions.

Constituency Approach:
A measure of organizational effectiveness that is based on how well it serves its stakeholders.

Stakeholders:
The people who have a relevant interest in the success of an organization, including employees, owners, customers, suppliers, and members of the community.

Constituency Approach. How well do stakeholders value the organization? The constituency approach involves obtaining feedback from the organization's various constituencies. A constituency is a group either inside or outside the organization that has a stake in the organization's performance. These groups are also called **stakeholders**. Employees, owners, customers, suppliers, and stockholders are all constituencies whose assessment of the organization can serve as a measure of the organization's performance. Each constituency has a different criterion of success, because it has a different interest in the organization. The effectiveness of the organization can be evaluated by surveying the attitudes of each constituency. Seven of the most important constituencies and the effectiveness criteria used by each are listed here.

Constituency	Effectiveness Criterion
1. Employees	Satisfaction with pay, supervision, and the work itself
2. Owners	Financial return on investment
3. Customers	Quality of goods and services produced by the company
4. Suppliers	Satisfactory transactions
5. Creditors	Creditworthiness
6. Community	Social responsibility
7. Government	Compliance with laws and regulations

The strength of the constituency approach is that it uses a broad view of effectiveness and examines both internal and external factors. The concepts of social responsibility and community involvement, absent in the other approaches, are also included here. The constituency approach recognizes that there is no single measure of effectiveness and that the achievement of one criterion may be just as important as another. The well-being of employees, for example, is just as important as achieving the goals of the owners.

The recognition of multiple constituencies and their multiple goals should influence major organizational decisions, such as whether to close a factory or where a new community hospital should be built. The constituency approach also calls attention to the fact that effectiveness criteria reflect the values of different people. The organization must decide which values it wishes to pursue and which values it will exclude. Organizations cannot simultaneously satisfy all criteria. The leaders of organizations are required to balance difficult ethical dilemmas.

Creating Ethical Organizations

Organizations are expected to contribute to the quality of life and the betterment of society. Effective organizations provide avenues for people to develop their talents and skills, and to pursue self-actualization. Some people discover great meaning and fulfillment in life because of the work they perform in organizations, and their relationships with coworkers are highly satisfying. Unfortunately, this is not always the case. Some organizations are a great detriment to society because they pollute the environment, destroy natural resources, create hazardous work conditions, or mistreat workers.

Unfair Policies. Organizations have the power to abuse individuals. The balance of power is clearly in the hands of the organization in power struggles over wages, benefits, and working conditions. Although disgruntled employees are free to quit, the consequences of quitting are clearly more costly to the individuals than to the organization. The loss of a job to an employee is more catastrophic than is the loss of an employee to an organization.

Although the Bill of Rights guarantees certain freedoms to citizens in society, employees in organizations do not enjoy many of the same rights. For example, freedom of speech is sometimes constrained by company regulations that limit what they may say. The rights of privacy and security guaranteed to citizens are also not extended to most employees at work. Although employees' homes are protected from arbitrary search and seizure, their lockers, desks, and files at work can be inspected without warning or permission.

In some situations employees face moral dilemmas because they are asked to perform unethical or illegal acts. For example, employees are sometimes told to falsify reports, to dump toxic wastes in streams, to use substandard materials in construction, or to fire employees because of their age or race. These orders are immoral and illegal, and employees should never be expected to obey them. Even minor violations, such as telling a secretary to say that a manager is out when the manager is really in, can create an uncomfortable situation in which the secretary is forced to compromise personal standards of integrity.

Unintended Abuse. When organizations condone illegal or immoral activities, the potential for abuse is obvious. However, organizations also abuse employees in subtle ways that may be entirely unintended. Every organization has the

Organizational Abuse:
Organizational policies or events that injure or mistreat employees even though they are neutral and not intended to create harm.

potential to abuse individuals—even benign organizations that sincerely try to help and support their employees.

Organizations do not have a heart and a mind or a soul. Employees who have contributed years of faithful service may be forced to find a new job or a new career because of forces beyond the control of the organization, such as a technological advance or an economic collapse. A new management team often has little knowledge about the devoted service of long-term employees who deserve to be protected.

Organizations cannot control the expectations of employees, and there are natural tendencies for employees to develop false expectations. Employees are often seduced into thinking that someone in top management is looking after them and that they should just quietly serve the organization. When their jobs are eliminated because of a merger or new technology, these people feel abused and mistreated. The real irony here is that the most employee-friendly organizations with active career development programs have the greatest potential for abuse because they create the greatest expectations.

Job opportunities—even those that employees typically value, such as promotions, transfers, and sales contests—can result in unintended abuse. Marriages can be damaged by long separations or pressure to relocate. Families may suffer because parents miss important events like graduations and Little League games, or they are not available to provide guidance and support at critical times. Excessive job stress may impair health and leave employees too emotionally exhausted to cope with other demands. It is natural for employees in large and powerful organizations to succumb to the belief that the organization's goals are inherently right and that the interests of the organization are more important than their personal welfare.

The hierarchal authority structure in organizations creates a natural opportunity to adversely influence employees, because they tend to develop a distorted concept of authority. When a person is promoted to a higher-level position, the promotion somehow seems to imply moral superiority, innate goodness, or some other virtuous quality. As a result, employees do not question the decisions of upper-level managers and they give too much relevance to managers' opinions. The blind obedience that results is often a disservice to the employee, the manager, and the organization.

A partial solution to organizational abuse is to change the policies and programs that cause unfair treatment. But more practically, individuals should be taught how to protect themselves from organizational influences. Protecting employees and helping them achieve their goals are basic ethical concerns of leaders.

DEVELOPING AND TESTING THEORIES

Good managers rely on good theories to help them know what to do. It has been said that nothing is as practical as a good theory.[3] To some extent, we are all behavioral scientists as we observe the events around us and try to make sense out of them. We develop our own working theories to help us interpret what is happening and what the consequences of our behavior will be. We rely on informal theories to guide our actions. If our theories are wrong, we can make serious mistakes without realizing that the problem stems from a bad theory. The skills of a good behavioral scientist—observing, interpreting, generalizing, and explaining—are essential for managers, since they are required to collect data, analyze it logically, and act on it. We all need to learn how to develop good theories and use them.

Analyzing Organizational Events

When we analyze organizational events, we typically use this information for one of three purposes: to describe what happened, to explain why it happened, or to control it in the future. Our knowledge of organizational behavior and our ability to use this information to create effective organizations have been acquired over the years through the sequential process of description, explanation, and control.

Description. When we see something occur with regularity we first try to identify it and develop a way to discuss it. This requires that we label and define organizational events. For example, if the comments of women in a mixed committee are consistently ignored, the first goal is to describe what is happening and identify the problem of sexism.

Explanation and Prediction. After we describe recurring events, we need to identify the forces contributing to them. This allows us to predict what will happen in the future when the same conditions are present, thereby making our world more stable and secure. We develop our own informal theories to explain the relationships between events and the motives that cause people to behave the way they do. Even though we may not think of ourselves as behavioral scientists, we can generate our own theories to explain the world around us. For example, we have our own working theories to explain why some people refuse to accept welfare, why supervisors get angry, why people play lotteries, why students are so concerned about grades, and why people quit their jobs.

Control. The third goal of organizational analysis is to control the behavior that occurs in organizations. If behavior has been carefully explained, and we know what causes it, we can create situations that elicit desirable behaviors and eliminate undesirable behaviors. Organizational leaders can use a variety of techniques and interventions to change the behaviors of individuals, groups, and organizations. Controlling behavior, however, creates a difficult ethical problem: some people are firmly opposed to the idea of using organizational behavior knowledge to control the behavior of people at work. Organizational control is criticized as a form of bribery, coercion, or manipulation. It is true that organizations can harm people and society. However, they can also provide excellent opportunities for personal growth and self-fulfillment. This issue points to the continuing need to study the ethics of organizational behavior.

Some organizations do much more than others to control behavior. The military is well known for its structured environment that controls, to a great extent, both thoughts and behaviors. The control process in the military is apparent from the very first minute new recruits begin basic training. Other organizations, especially fraternities and sororities, also use social pressures and rigorous initiation rituals to influence the attitudes and behaviors of new members, and some of these practices have led to public censure when they have become extreme. Smoking is a behavior that is becoming increasingly controlled by organizations. Some companies, such as U.S. Gypsum, use a combination of rewards, punishments, and counseling to induce their employees to completely stop smoking both on and off the job.

Attempts to control behavior are not necessarily unethical. Essentially all managerial actions are designed to influence individual behavior and control what occurs in organizations. Organizations control behavior whether we like it or not, so it seems reasonable that we should try to design them to enhance the quality of life. As an ethical concern, managers should attempt to control behavior in a way that contributes to both individual growth and organizational goal achievement.

Developing Theories

Experiential learning:
Learning that comes from analyzing and observing everyday experiences.

Being an effective manager requires a combination of knowledge and experience; neither one alone is sufficient. *Experiential learning* refers to learning from our own experiences. As we observe the consequences of our behavior and discover how others respond to what we do, we gain new insights into human behavior and learn how to be more effective when working in groups and organizations. Being able to learn from our own experience is a valuable skill. However, experience alone is not enough. We do not adequately learn from our own experiences because life is so complex and our experiences are so limited. We are not exposed to enough information to make broad generalizations about any more than a few topics. Consequently, we must use the insights of others to broaden our knowledge.

Theory:
A statement of functional relationships that helps us explain what is happening in the world we observe.

Behavioral science research involves developing and testing theories. A *theory* consists of a statement of functional relationships among variables; we are stating a theory when we attempt to explain a recurring event. Some theories are very simple, involving only two variables, while other theories are extremely complex. Theories are useful because they direct our observations and tell us what to look for, they help us interpret and explain our observations, and they help us predict future behavior.

Many valuable insights have come from formal theories in the behavioral science literature. However, we also develop our own informal theories to help us organize and interpret our observations. These are some examples of theories:

1. Dissatisfied employees are more likely than satisfied employees to steal from their employers.
2. How people dress influences their career success.
3. Students do not learn very well when they study with the television on.
4. People who have the most power can manipulate situations so they get more power.

In our day-to-day activities, we develop a large repertoire of theories similar to these, and use them to guide our thinking. By making careful observations to test our theories, we can refine them and improve the accuracy of our predictions and the likelihood of behaving effectively. There are no perfect theories in organizational behavior; each theory has advantages and limitations. Good theories generally contain the following characteristics.

1. A good theory is *parsimonious*, that is, stated in simple terms. A theory that explains things simply is superior to one that requires complex relationships to explain the event.

2. Good theories are testable. Although we cannot prove that a theory is true, a testable theory allows us to estimate the probability of its truth. If a theory cannot be confirmed or disproved we cannot assess its accuracy.
3. A good theory should be logically consistent with itself and other known facts, and build on what has already been learned.
4. The conditions when a theory is relevant need to be clearly defined so that the theory is not erroneously applied in situations where it was never intended.

Most of the theories presented in this book do not satisfy all of these criteria. None of the theories has been so extensively researched that it can be pronounced conclusively true. Rather, the theories that have been the most extensively studied are usually the most qualified. Extensive research helps to identify the conditions in which the theory applies and the conditions in which it does not. Although students usually want to know only whether a theory is true or false, this is not the best question to ask. Rather than asking whether a theory is true or false, it is better to ask when it is useful.

Occasionally the development of new knowledge produces a dramatic shift in the way a problem is analyzed and in the way the situation is perceived. This change, which is called a *paradigm shift*, results in a total restructuring of the way we think about a situation and the kinds of assumptions we make about former observations. A *paradigm* refers to an approach to a problem or situation and the kinds of assumptions, values, and attitudes associated with thinking about the situation.[4]

The most dramatic illustration of a paradigm shift was the shift from the Ptolemaic (geocentric) theory of seeing the earth as the center of the universe to the Copernican (heliocentric) theory which saw the sun as the center of the universe. Another illustration of a paradigm shift in management theory was the shift from scientific management to the human relations movement during the 1930s. The focus of scientific management from about 1880 to 1930 was on task efficiency; consequently, the development of time-and-motion studies, piece-rate incentives, and division of labor were analyzed and evaluated according to the criteria of how they influenced task efficiency. On the other hand, the human relations movement, from about 1930 to 1950, focused on personal feelings of satisfaction and worth. Therefore, all corporate policies and management practices were evaluated with respect to how well employees were treated.

Paradigm shift: A new way of thinking about a situation or problem using different assumptions and models.

Testing Theories

Managers need to understand the scientific method and use it to avoid the rampant proliferation of management myths and cures. The management literature is filled with innovative theories, training programs, and consulting advice that are usually nothing more than nice-sounding speculation. The scientific method is a systematic, objective process of discovering and verifying new knowledge. The greatest advantage of the scientific method that distinguishes it from other methods is its capacity for self-correction. The scientific method contains built-in checks to control extraneous explanations and verify the conclusions. This method tries to minimize the effects of the scientist's own biases and preconceptions.

The scientific method's approach to developing and testing new ideas is quite different from experiential learning. Basically, it consists of stating a proposition or theory and testing whether it is true. Some of the major characteristics of the scientific method that distinguish it from experiential learning are the use of hypothesis, constructs, and observations.[5]

Hypothesis:

A provisional statement describing the potential relationship between two or more variables that we can test.

Hypothesis. A hypothesis is a provisional statement describing the potential relationship between two or more variables. In the scientific method, hypotheses are rigorous and precise, whereas in literature and daily events our hypotheses are intuitive and general, and therefore not testable. An example of a testable hypothesis is: "If meat cutters are offered a financial incentive to work safely, then their accident rates will decrease." This hypothesis could be tested by randomly assigning meat cutters to two groups, offering safety incentives to one group, and then measuring the safety records of both groups. Because the hypotheses in science are testable, the procedures are open to the public. Both the methods and the results are clearly described, and other researchers have the opportunity to replicate the results.

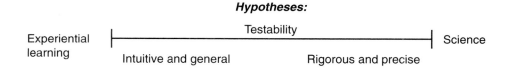

Constructs:

Words and concepts that help us identify the phenomena we want to study.

Constructs. A *construct* is a word or concept that refers to relationships between objects or events, such as intelligence, company loyalty, job satisfaction, and commitment. In literature, the constructs purposely contain surplus meaning to evoke a variety of feelings. In science, however, constructs must be operationally defined to make them very specific and empirical. An *operational definition* consists of defining a construct by specifying the operation or activity involved in measuring it. An IQ test, for example, is an operational definition of intelligence. "Bright" students could be operationally defined as those with grade point averages in the top 10 percent. Job satisfaction has been operationally defined in a variety of ways, including responses on an attitude questionnaire, number of grievances submitted, turnover rates, and percent of negative comments expressed during staff meetings.

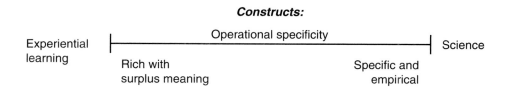

Observations. *Observations* vary in the degree of control and in whether extraneous factors can influence them. In experiential learning, no attempt is made to control the environment in which observations are made. In science, however, observations are carefully controlled through a variety of experimental methods.

Observations:

Experiential learning |————————— Control —————————| Science

Loosely controlled and ambiguous   Experimental

The theory that corporate mergers destroy company loyalty can be used to illustrate the difference between the scientific method and intuition. A newspaper article describing the angry feelings of a worker whose job was terminated after a corporate merger supports the theory that mergers destroy corporate loyalty. However, this newspaper article would be classified as experiential learning, since the hypothesis is not operationally defined and the observation comes from one randomly selected person rather than a representative sample of the affected population. The scientific method requires that a testable hypothesis using operationally defined constructs be stated and examined in a controlled setting. An example of a testable hypothesis would be "If one company acquires another company through a leveraged buyout, the average organizational commitment scores of the employees in the acquired company will decline after the acquisition." Here, loyalty is operationally defined by responses to the organizational commitment questionnaire. The observations could come from administering the questionnaire to randomly selected groups of employees at designated times before and after the merger.

Research Methods. Behavioral scientists use a variety of research methods to obtain knowledge about organizations, including observational studies, field surveys, field experiments, and laboratory experiments.

1. Observational studies. Most of our common sense views about organizations and people come from *observational studies* in which we examine the natural activities of real people in an organizational setting. Behavioral scientists are trained to describe the behavior they see using specific terms that can be confirmed by others. They try to avoid drawing unwarranted conclusions about things they cannot observe, such as motives and attitudes.

Observational studies:
Case studies that are based on the careful observation of the events and relationships that we see transpire.

   Case studies are a form of observational study that examine numerous characteristics of one or more people, usually over an extended period of time. Occasionally an experimenter will join a group and actively participate in group activities in what is called *participant observation*. This method has often been used by anthropologists who study the customs and norms of various cultures by actually living among them.

   Case studies are often used to help students learn how to diagnose organizational problems and formulate possible solutions. Although they are useful for educational purposes, a case study is not a good research method. The insights and conclusions from a case study depend entirely on the skill of the observer. Although a trained researcher may be able to make valuable observations, the results are based on a sample of one (N=1), meaning that they cannot be generalized to other situations; rarely can case studies be repeated or their findings verified.

Field studies:
Research studies that involve collecting data from people in actual work settings and examining the relationships between the variables that are measured.

2. Field studies. Field studies allow us to examine a few characteristics of a large number of people in actual organizational settings, but they do not allow

Exhibit 1.4 The Continuum of Scientific Research Methods

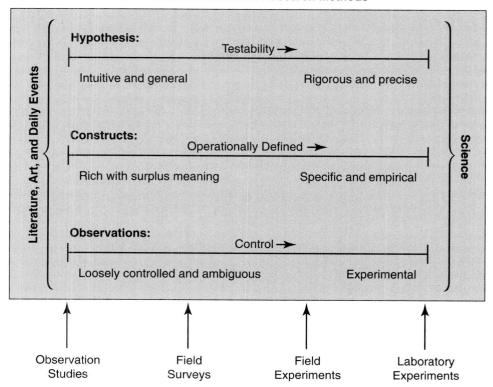

us to make causal inferences. Most field surveys are **correlational studies** that measure two or more variables and then test whether they are related, such as a test of the relationship between office size and job satisfaction. A correlation coefficient could be computed between job satisfaction, as measured by a questionnaire, and office space, measured in square feet. A positive correlation would indicate that office space and satisfaction seem to be related, but we could not conclude that increased office space *caused* greater satisfaction.

Field experiments: Research studies that occur in natural work situations in which an independent variable is changed and its effects on one or more dependent variables are assessed.

3. Field experiment. In a field experiment, we attempt to manipulate and control variables in the natural setting of the organization. Here the subjects being observed continue to work as employees in an ongoing organization, and certain important organizational variables are manipulated or changed to examine their effects on behavior. An illustration of a field experiment is offering a select group of employees a financial incentive for every day they work without a recordable accident and then measuring the reduction in their accidents.

The advantage of a field experiment is that the individuals continue to interact in a real situation under relatively normal circumstances. The effects of different variables can be assessed by varying them one at a time. The results of a field experiment allow researchers to draw causal inferences, such as a change in variable A caused a change in variable B. The disadvantages of a field experiment are that the results cannot always be generalized to other organizations, and some experiments disrupt the organization.

Laboratory experiment:
A research study that is conducted in a behavioral science laboratory that serves to control extraneous variables while the effects of an independent variable are assessed regarding its impact on one or more dependent variables.

Hawthorne effect:
A change in the behavior of people that occurs when they know they are being evaluated.

Nondirective interviews:
Interviews that encourage the person to determine the flow of the discussion rather than following a scheduled list of questions.

Patterned interview:
An interview that follows a predetermined list of interview questions.

Unobtrusive measures:
Measures of behavior that are obtained without the participants knowing that their behavior is being evaluated. Often these measures are indirect indications of behavior.

4. Laboratory experiments. In a laboratory experiment, the environment is controlled to eliminate extraneous influences, which is both an advantage and disadvantage. It is an advantage because it eliminates competing explanations for the observed changes, and it is a disadvantage because it creates an artificial environment that does not necessarily represent reality.

In laboratory and field experiments, the variable we control is called the *independent variable,* since we decide when it will be presented, in what form, or how much. The *dependent variables* are the variables that are measured to see if the independent variable had an influence. For example, in a study that tests whether financial incentives influence productivity, the independent variable is the change in financial incentives, while the dependent variable is the level of productivity.

Data Collection Methods. Four of the most frequently used methods of collecting research data include observations, interviews, questionnaires, and archival data. Each of these methods has advantages and disadvantages and is appropriate for a particular type of research.

1. **Observations.** Direct observations allow us to accurately record specific behaviors, but these observations sometimes influence behavior. This problem was recognized in the Hawthorne experiments (1927–1935) and has come to be known as the *Hawthorne effect:* when people know they are being observed, they tend to behave differently.[6]

2. **Interviews.** Interviews can be used to assess personal feelings and attitudes. A *nondirective interview*, in which employees talk about issues important to them, provides a rich and meaningful description for a researcher. This type of interview is particularly helpful when a researcher does not know what to look for and is searching for an explanation. The major disadvantage of nondirective interviews is that they are not reliable. What individuals say in an interview tends to vary from time to time and may be highly influenced by the unique circumstances of the interview. To increase the reliability of interviews, researchers can develop a *patterned interview* schedule, in which they ask specific written questions and the interviewee may even be given a list of alternatives for making a multiple-choice answer. A highly patterned interview, however, fails to generate the richness, diversity, and creative insight that makes interviewing so valuable, and it becomes more like a verbal questionnaire.

3. **Questionnaires.** One of the major advantages of a questionnaire is that it can be used to collect extensive information from a large sample of people at the same time. Furthermore, questionnaire data can be conveniently analyzed using a variety of statistical procedures. Most well-developed questionnaires are usually reliable and valid measures of specific variables.

4. **Archival Data.** Archival data are the information contained in the personnel files and historical records of a company, such as financial reports, attendance records, accident reports, application forms, grievance statements, exit interviews, and performance evaluations. Sometimes this information is referred to as *unobtrusive measures*, since the nature of the data and the way they are obtained do not influence how employees behave.[7] The advantages of using archival data are that they already exist

and they provide a long-term perspective. Unobtrusive measures may also be more accurate than direct measures in some situations. For example, adults may not be willing to admit their interest in the hatching-chick display at the National Museum of Science and Industry in Chicago. Therefore, a better measure showing the public's great interest in this display is a record of how frequently the linoleum must be replaced in front of this display. Likewise, to assess the interest of students in different library books, an alternative to asking them about their interest is measuring the accumulated dust on the top of each book or counting how many times each book has been checked out.

Discussion Questions

1. What do we mean when we say that an organization is an *open social system* that consists of *goal-directed behaviors* and *patterned activities*? Identify an organization of which you are a member and describe specific activities that illustrate these three characteristics.
2. A group of friends who play string instruments get together every Thursday night to practice and play together; occasionally they perform at wedding receptions and funerals. Would this group be considered an organization? What are its patterned activities, inputs, transformation process, and outputs? How are its outputs recycled to provide additional inputs?
3. What are some illustrations of the differences between organizational *efficiency* and *effectiveness*? What are the potential consequences of confusing these two terms?
4. What is a theory? Describe two informal theories you have created to explain things you have observed, and explain your thinking.

Notes

1. Daniel Katz and Robert L. Kahn, *The Social Psychology of Organizations*, 2nd ed. (New York: Wiley, 1978).
2. Michael E. Porter, *Competitive Strategy: Techniques for Analyzing Industries and Competitors* (New York: Free Press, 1980); Michael E. Porter, *Competitive Advantage: Creating and Sustaining Superior Performance* (New York: Free Press, 1985).
3. Kurt Lewin, "The Research Center for Group Dynamics at the Massachusetts Institute of Technology," *Sociometry*, vol. 8 (1945), pp. 126–135.
4. Thomas S. Kuhn, *The Structure of Scientific Revolutions* (Chicago: University of Chicago Press, 1952).
5. Melvin H. Marx. "The General Nature of Theory Construction," *Theories of Contemporary Psychology*, Melvin H. Marx, ed. (New York: McMillan, 1963), 4–46.
6. Fritz J. Roethlisberger and William J. Dickson, *Management and the Worker* (Cambridge: Harvard University Press, 1939, 1967).
7. Eugene J. Webb, Donald T. Campbell, Richard D. Schwartz, and Lee Sechrist, *Unobtrusive Measures: Non-Reactive Research in the Social Sciences*. (Chicago: Rand-McNally, 1966).

Harmony Psychiatric Center

Harmony Psychiatric Center (HPC), was founded in the 1980s by Dr. Sigmund Frank, a prominent psychiatrist from New York City. Located in a renovated nursing home along the banks of the Hudson River, HPC was one of the first private psychiatric hospitals in the state. HPC was the brainchild of Herbert Hofstadter, one of Dr. Frank's friends. The center prided itself on individualized treatment, and quickly gained a reputation as the place for wealthy socialites to recover from mental stress.

In its early years, the Center was very profitable as a solely owned partnership. Dr. Frank, the only MD, maintained a tight rein on all medical services. The employees of HPC were well trained and most had advanced degrees in psychology or social work. They usually received sizable year-end pay increases plus bonuses of as much as $3000. Mr. Hofstadter held a Master of Social Work degree and managed the center's business affairs, although he had no formal business training. He spent most of his time talking to employees and keeping everyone happy. Gradually, other MDs were added to the staff, but Dr. Frank retained a tight control of medical services.

Eventually the founding partners decided that the Center had outgrown the renovated nursing home and they needed to build a new facility. The construction was completed after two years, but the costs exceeded their estimates by $1 million. For the first time, the partners were forced to borrow money.

Everyone was excited to move into the new building, including the patients. The new center differed in several ways from the old renovated nursing home. At the old facility, the MDs shared one large office and used the same secretary, while the psychologists had small individual offices for personal therapy. The social workers had no offices, but freely circulated throughout the facility, conducting group therapy and informal individual counseling.

The new facility provided all the MDs, psychologists, and social workers with their own offices. The offices of the founding partners were rather lavish and well equipped, and the psychologists' offices were almost as nice. In addition, the MDs were each assigned a personal secretary to help them record information. The only employees without their own offices were the nurses and psychiatric technicians, who were still required to circulate through the facility.

The patients loved the new facility. Each one had a private room that was tastefully decorated and furnished with new furniture. The new center also had an indoor spa with weight training equipment, exercise bicycles, and two large hot tubs. Mr. Hofstadter thought the spa would add a nice touch to the center and the employees were allowed to use it when it was not being used by the patients.

After a mild heart attack, Mr. Hofstadter decided to retire and move his family back to Germany. He was replaced by Tom, a recent Harvard MBA and Dr. Frank's son. Tom made several changes at the Center: the spa was off limits to all employees; the MDs were required to increase their patient load by 20 percent; the psychologists and social workers were required to keep detailed records in the center's new computer system; and the nursing staff was drastically reduced, making it necessary for the psychologists and social workers to perform routine patient care, such as monitoring behavior modification programs.

Dr. Frank was startled to receive a notice from the bank that a loan payment was past due. When he asked Tom about it, he was informed that the Center had a cash flow problem. He was also surprised to learn from one of the psychologists that the occupancy rate had declined from 85 percent during the previous year to 35 percent now. This psychologist also said that many of the employees had been offered jobs at a new psychiatric hospital scheduled to open soon in Hyde Park.

Dr. Frank decided to talk to some of the other employees to learn how they felt. In a group meeting with ten employees, the following recurring complaints emerged:

- We can't use the spa anymore
- The nursing staff is overworked
- The psychologists don't have time to conduct necessary therapy
- The social workers are not being treated fairly
- Things were much better at the old facility
- I wish Mr. Hofstadter had not retired
- Your son, Tom, should get a job somewhere else
- You can't expect MDs to meet quotas
- Many employees will take competing job offers if things don't change
- We haven't received a bonus or salary increase since we moved into the new building

Questions

1. Is HPC an effective organization? Why or why not? What criteria should be used to judge the effectiveness of HPC?
2. What is HPC's current strategy? What should HPC's strategy be in the future?
3. If you were a consultant to HPC, what recommendations for change would you give to Dr. Frank?

Exercise Office Building Construction Exercise

Purpose. As you begin your study of organizational effectiveness it is useful for you to experience the problems of planning, organizing, decision making, leadership, implementation, communication, and other aspects of group dynamics. It is easier to appreciate organizational problems after you have experienced and discussed them with an actual task. This exercise is also designed to acquaint you with other class members.

Objective. The objective of your group is to build an attractive and structurally sound two-story office building using only cards (5 x 7 cards or computer cards, if you can still find them) and tape. The building should have floors and a roof. Windows, walls, and other design features are optional.

Activity. The class should be divided into groups of four to seven members. Your group will have 40 minutes to plan and then 10 minutes to construct your office building. The group will receive one free card during the planning period to assist with the design. Other cards and tape should be obtained before the construction period, although additional supplies may be requested. All construction must occur during the construction period. The instructor will start and stop the planning and construction periods.

Evaluation. Your group will be awarded one point per cubic inch of office space in your building (based on outside dimensions) subject to the following costs: each card costs 10 points and tape costs 1 point per inch. After your building has been constructed and tested for structural stability, it will be judged by an impartial committee according to two criteria; aesthetic beauty and structural stability. For aesthetic beauty you can receive up to plus or minus 50 percent of your initial points. For structural stability you may also receive up to plus or minus 50 percent of your group points. There are two tests of structural stability. First, it must be dropped from an elevation of six feet to the floor without falling apart. Second, a textbook will be dropped on it from a height of three feet and, again, your building should not be destroyed. (Before you think this is impossible, you should know that one group built a structure using computer cards that supported the weight of a 95-pound student.)

Discussion Questions

1. How well did your group succeed in this task? Did your group have a clear vision about what it was trying to do and did everyone have a shared understanding of this vision?
2. How effective was your group? What were your goals and how well did you achieve them? Did everyone cooperate, and if so, how did a group of strangers succeed in obtaining the immediate cooperation of all members?
3. How were decisions made—by consensus, by majority rule, by a powerful leader, or by default? Did anyone make a suggestion that was ignored?
4. Which members exerted the greatest influence? Who was the informal leader? Was there a power struggle? Did coalitions emerge? Does everyone agree which member exerted the greatest influence?

5. How were people treated? Did everyone participate equally, or were some more quiet? Was there a difference in the participation of men and women? Were the ideas of females received with as much consideration as the ideas of males?
6. What was the climate of the group? Were the members serious and task oriented, happy and friendly, sarcastic and critical, competitive, or apathetic? Did the group members enjoy their interactions?

2

Strategy

Chapter Outline

Discovering a Mission

The Value of Mission Statements

Writing Mission Statements

Selecting a Strategy

The Role of Strategy

Three Grand Strategies

Strategy Formulation

Analyzing the Firm

Aligning the Organization

Firm Resources and Core Competencies

Analyzing the Environment

Environmental Sectors

Industry Analysis

Competitor Analysis

Environmental Uncertainty

DISCOVERING A MISSION

If you want to be an entrepreneur and create your own company, what are the first steps you must take? This chapter describes the concept of strategy and explains the kinds of decisions you need to make to create a successful company. An effective organization begins with a mission that identifies what it is striving to become and a strategy that explains how it plans to succeed. Organizations are created for a purpose and they function more effectively when all stakeholders clearly understand the organization's mission and strategy. *Strategy* refers to the goals and set of policies designed to achieve competitive advantage in a particular marketplace. *Competitive advantage* refers to the ability to transform inputs into goods and services at a maximum profit on a sustained basis, better than competitors.

Strategy:
The set of goals and policies designed to achieve competitive advantage in a particular marketplace.

Competitive advantage:
Having the ability to transform inputs into goods and services at a maximum profit on a sustained basis, better than one's competitors.

The central insight of this chapter can be stated simply: To create a successful company, you must identify a product or service that you can provide in a competitive market and do it better than your competitors. The probability that your company will be profitable increases as you have a clear vision about the product or service you want to provide and how it will benefit people, other companies, and society; you choose an attractive industry in which to compete; you provide a superior product or service in terms of cost and/or quality; you have few, or no, competitors; your product or service cannot be easily imitated by competitors; and few, if any, substitutes can replace the demand for your product or service.

The Value of Mission Statements

An organization is formed when someone has a vision or idea about the kind of product or service the company ought to provide, and this becomes the firm's mission. Even nonprofit organizations have a shared understanding of what the organization is trying to accomplish and how it will improve the lives of people. The vast majority of organizations are started as small, family-run businesses by a founder who has such a vision. Even large corporations started as small companies with a vision of a founder. Effective organizations depend on the existence of a powerful shared vision that evolves and is refined through wide participation. It is the power of a shared mission that usually inspires and unites people more than does the charisma of a leader.

Mission statement:
A statement that explains what an organization is trying to accomplish and why it exists.

A *mission statement* explains the essence of an organization – why it exists, what it wants to be, who it serves, and why it should continue. It is based on the organization's assumptions about its purpose, its values, its distinctive competencies, and its place in the world. Effective organizations usually have a written mission statement that defines success for the company. The focus of a mission statement should be realistic and credible, the language should be well articulated and easily understood, and the direction should be ambitious and responsive to change. It should orient the group's energies and serve as a guide to action. It should also be consistent with the organization's values.

Written mission statements help to focus the energies of their members by answering such questions as: Why does our organization exist? What business are we in? What values will guide us? Organizational goals and objectives are usually derived from the mission statement, but they are more specific. While mission statements are not measurable, goals and objectives ought to be.

Writing Mission Statements

Although there are no commonly accepted guidelines for writing mission statements, the following elements are usually found in carefully crafted statements:

1. A *purpose statement*: This statement explains what the organization seeks to accomplish and why it deserves the commitment of members and support of the public. Purpose statements try to answer such questions as "How is the world going to be different?" and "What is going to change?" and "How will things be better?"
2. The *business statement*: This statement identifies the organization's business activities or functions, such as to produce and transport alfalfa (for a ranch) or to construct affordable housing for first-time home owners (for a construction firm).
3. *Values statements*: These statements explain the values and beliefs that members hold in common and try to follow. Some of the most common values statements include a commitment to customer service, innovation, diversity, creativity, integrity, and personal development.

Useful mission statement should:

1. identify the purposes of the organization clearly enough that measurable objectives can be derived from them; a clear formulation of the firm's objectives will enable progress toward them to be measured;
2. differentiate the firm from other companies in the industry and establish its individuality and uniqueness;
3. define the business of the company with respect to its activities and products;
4. identify and explain the firm's relationships and obligations to all relevant stakeholders; and
5. explain how it will contribute to society and the betterment of people well enough to be exciting and inspiring.

Example

A segment of Hewlett-Packard's mission statement illustrates these characteristics:

"Hewlett-Packard Company designs, manufactures, and services electronic products and systems for measurement, computing, and communication used by people in industry, business, engineering, science, medicine, and education. HP's basic business purpose is to accelerate the advancement of knowledge and improve the effectiveness of people and organizations. The company's more than 25,000 products include computers and peripheral products, electronic test and measurement instruments and systems, networking products, medical electronic equipment, instruments and systems for chemical analysis, handheld calculators, and electronic components."[1]

SELECTING A STRATEGY

Organizations operate in a dynamic environment; external and internal forces change continually. To use a sports metaphor, both the playing field and the rules of the game are constantly being revised for organizations. Products that were popular yesterday may be obsolete today; reliable customers who were satisfied last week may buy from a competitor this week; and last month's suppliers may have gone out of business.

Strategy involves the combination of goals and plans to achieve competitive advantage and the methods of implementing them. To use another sports metaphor, a strategy is a game plan. Strategy has generally been used in a military context to refer to the coordinated action plans a military unit intends to use to defeat its enemy. The deployment of troops, the timing of the attack, and the means of deception are all part of military strategy.

Organizations create generic strategies to help them succeed in a dynamic and competitive environment. These generic strategies share several important characteristics:

- They promote the mission and goals the organization is striving to achieve.
- They have a long-term focus that extends beyond the immediate time horizon.
- They define the action plans the organization intends to follow to achieve its mission and goals.
- They recognize explicitly the impact of the external environment, especially the reactions of competitors.

The Role of Strategy

An organization's strategy determines the direction it will go and serves to coalesce the energies of many people and departments in a unified effort. Good strategies help organizational leaders make consistent and effective decisions. They also communicate expectations and coordinate the actions of the members. For example, decisions about product quality and where they will be marketed are important strategic decisions. An organization that decides to produce high-quality products and compete in the markets of industrialized nations is pursuing a much different strategy from a company that decides to produce inferior products and sell them in underdeveloped countries. Such was the case with the Korean company Daewoo Group, which decided to focus its markets in the Third World because of criticism regarding its poor quality and poor after-sales service.[2]

Strategy is about winning and succeeding. In a business organization, strategy is about profits; it explains how the firm plans to make money now and in the future. A good strategy helps it to remain profitable and continue to grow. Firms that have a sustained competitive advantage are able to provide above-average profits for their investors; firms that do not have a sustained competitive advantage or that are not competing in an attractive industry earn at best only average profits, and seldom survive. Strategies are also important to nonprofit companies, such as hospitals, universities, and government agencies, since they compete with other organizations for clients and resources. Every organization needs to have a strategy that is consistent with its mission. Managers try to position their companies so that they can gain a relative advantage over their rivals. This positioning requires a careful evaluation of the competitive forces that dictate the rules of competition in each industry.

The goal of strategy is to find a competitive environment where a company has *imperfect competition*. As shown in Exhibit 2.1, such an environ-

Imperfect competition:
An economic condition that allows an organization to achieve a competitive advantage because there are few competitors, numerous suppliers and buyers, asymmetric information, heterogeneous products, and barriers to entry.

Exhibit 2.1 The Goal of Strategy: Imperfect Competition

Perfect Competition	Imperfect Competition
■ Numerous sellers and buyers	■ Few competitors, numerous suppliers and buyers
■ Perfect information	■ Asymmetric information
■ Homogeneous products	■ Heterogeneous Products
■ No barriers to entry or exit	■ Barriers to entry
Average or below-average profits	Supernormal Profits

ment occurs when there are few, if any, competitors (allowing one firm to operate as a monopoly); numerous suppliers and buyers (making it easy to obtain supplies and sell products at advantageous prices); asymmetric information (preventing the dissemination of information to all parties); heterogeneous products (allowing a firm to specialize in specific products); and barriers to entry (making it difficult for other firms to provide competitive products). Firms that have the good fortune to compete in markets that have imperfect competition are generally able to obtain supernormal profits. This situation is much more favorable than one with perfect competition: numerous sellers and buyers, perfect information, homogeneous products, and no barriers to entry or exit. Firms that compete in conditions of perfect competition have difficulty earning anything more than average or below-average profits.

Example
Wal-Mart has succeeded in earning supernormal profits through imperfect competition with a strategy of locating stores in small towns where customers can purchase many low-cost, high-quality items in one location. Wal-Mart's competitive advantage is sustainable primarily because of its natural geographic monopoly and positioning, and secondarily because of its operational efficiencies. Competitors rationally decline to enter towns where Wal-Mart stores are located because Wal-Mart is already there with an optimally efficient store, there is no feasible way to increase local demand, and a second store would create substantial overcapacity such that neither store would make money.

Example
A fast-food restaurant that sells hamburgers near a college campus would not likely earn above-average profits if there were dozens of other fast-food outlets within a short distance. Although this location might have many potential customers, they tend to be price-sensitive and informed; they will buy wherever they can get the best value for their money. If any restaurant started to earn significant profits, other restaurants would imitate it and new restaurants would be waiting to enter the same market. Other competitors also have access to the same suppliers.

Three Grand Strategies

Michael Porter, one of the leading strategy theorists, has identified three grand strategies to maintain a competitive edge: cost leadership (being the low-cost producer), differentiation (having a unique product in a large market), and focus (having a unique product in a narrow market).[3]

Cost leadership:
A competitive strategy
that depends on being
able to sell more prod-
ucts because they are
less expensive.

Cost Leadership. Gaining a competitive advantage through *cost leadership* involves selling your products and services at a lower cost. This is usually achieved by technological innovations that improve the efficiency of operations or using low-cost labor that reduces the costs of production. Success with this strategy requires that the organization be the cost leader, not merely one of the contenders for that position. Furthermore, the products and services being offered must be perceived as comparable to or better than those offered by rivals. Companies that have used this strategy successfully include Southwest Airlines, Wal-Mart, and Canadian Tire.

> **Example**
> Southwest Airlines has achieved a significant competitive advantage in the airline industry by offering low-cost fares to customers. Other airlines have been forced to match these low-cost fares, but in doing so they have not achieved the same level of profitability. Southwest has been able to sustain its competitive advantage because it has lower costs (by eliminating reservations, check-in, and baggage handling) and higher revenues per plane (by faster turnaround times that keep the planes flying longer).

Differentiation:
A competitive strategy
that depends on sell-
ing higher-priced
products that are
distinguished by
such things as higher
quality.

Differentiation. A *differentiation* strategy involves providing unique products and services in ways that are widely valued by buyers. This can be achieved by providing exceptionally high quality, extraordinary service, innovative designs, technological capability, or an unusually positive brand image. Whatever attribute the company chooses to establish its uniqueness must be different from those offered by rivals, and significant enough to justify its price premium. Exaggerated advertising claims and the customary hyperbole that borders on sheer deceit provide evidence that many firms rely on this strategy. Firms that have succeeded in finding a unique differentiating factor include Maytag on reliability, Mary Kay Cosmetics on distribution, and Nordstrom on customer service.

> **Example**
> Toyota Motors has succeeded in differentiating itself from its competitors by gaining a reputation of exceptional quality in its cars. The Toyota Camry, for example, is widely recognized as a very well-built car with excellent reliability and dependability. Consequently, it sells at a substantial premium above other cars of similar size, and the depreciation on the price of a used Camry is also much less than normal.

> **Example**
> In the mid-1980s, Delta Airlines's market researchers found that customers, particularly business customers, were strongly influenced to choose a particular airline by the airline's frequent flyer program. Consequently, Delta tried to differentiate itself within the airline industry by offering a special program. To motivate customers to choose Delta, they established an exclusive arrangement with American Express that allowed customers to receive triple miles when they flew on Delta with tickets purchased with an American Express card. Unfortunately, Delta failed to anticipate how easily and quickly this strategy could be imitated by its competitors.

Focus strategy:
A competitive strategy that depends on selling a unique product within a segmented niche of the market.

Focus Strategy. A *focus strategy* aims at either a cost advantage or a differentiation advantage in a narrow market segment. Companies that use this strategy select a defined segment of an industry, such as a particular product, a specific kind of end-use buyer, a defined distribution channel, or a limited geographical location, and target its strategy to serve them to the exclusion of others. This strategy is also known as a *niche strategy*, since the firm seeks to compete in a niche of the larger market. The goal is to exploit a narrow segment of a market by appealing specifically to it. The success of a focus strategy may depend on how narrow the segment is. If the segment is too large, the strategy may suffer because of a lack of focus and uniqueness. But an extremely small segment may limit a company's success until it expands to other segments.

Example

Benmark Inc. of Atlanta, Georgia specializes in providing unique medical and life insurance benefits for the banking industry, because that industry has liquid assets that can be used advantageously for insurance, tax reduction, and investment purposes. Focusing on one industry allows Benmark to develop targeted services and a social network that facilitates sales. Since bankers tend to know and interact with each other, many sales leads come from referrals. Bank executives tend to make deliberate and rational decisions based on careful cost analyses. Consequently, Benmark uses complex financial data that executives in other industries avoid.

Strategy Formulation

Selecting the right competitive strategy is vital to a firm's success. This decision determines how it is positioned in its industry. Strategy formulation is not a systematic process that advances sequentially from one action plan or objective to another, although it is less chaotic in some organizations than others. Strategy formulation is a dynamic process that is evolutionary in nature and subject to change as external forces change. Since strategy focuses on the future and the future is uncertain, strategy needs to be flexible and ready to respond to revised conditions.

SWOT Method of strategy development:
A method of developing a firm's strategy by examining its strengths, weaknesses, opportunities, and threats.

The *strategic management process* involves an analysis of both internal and external factors to identify sources of competitive advantage. This popular approach to strategy development is often called the **SWOT method**, which stands for Strengths, Weaknesses, Opportunities, and Threats. Decision makers should examine the organization's competitive advantages relative to its internal strengths and weaknesses, its external opportunities and threats, and potential competitor actions. The six steps of the strategic management process are illustrated in Exhibit 2.2.

1. The first step is to identify the organization's mission and decide "What business are we in?" This step forces management to identify carefully the scope of its products or services. Sometimes it is just as important to know what businesses they do not want to pursue as what they do want to pursue.

2. The second step is to analyze the environment and identify the opportunities it wants to pursue and threats it wants to avoid. This process, called

Exhibit 2.2   Strategic Management Process

**Environmental
Scanning:**
Examining the condi-
tions in the external
environment that might
have an impact on
the economic success
of the firm, such as
economic conditions,
the supply of labor,
and governmental
regulations.

Core Competency:
The unique skills and
resources that give an
organization a compet-
itive edge.

environmental scanning, involves anticipating and interpreting changes in the environment and usually requires screening diverse information to detect emerging trends. There is some evidence that companies that scan the environment achieve higher profits and revenue growth than companies that don't.

3. The third step is to analyze the organization's resources and identify its strengths and weaknesses. What are its skills and abilities? What unique knowledge and patents does it possess? Has it been successful at developing new and innovative products or services? What is its reputation for quality? Unique skills or resources that give an organization a competitive edge are called its *core competency.* Conversely, those resources an organization lacks or activities the firm does not do well are its weaknesses.

4. The fourth step is to combine the external and internal analyses and formulate an overall generic strategy for the organization to follow, plus functional strategies for each organizational function. These functional strategies need to be aligned with the generic strategy so that the entire organization is united.

5. The fifth step is implementation. Even good strategies must be implemented properly or they will not succeed. Good implementation usually requires competent leaders who have the vision to know which direction to pursue, and the trust of the members to encourage their involvement.

6. The sixth step is to evaluate and monitor the organization's results and maintain its competitive advantage. Long-term success with any strategy requires that the advantage be sustainable. That is, it must withstand both the actions of competitors and the evolutionary changes in the industry. This is a difficult challenge, since technology changes continually, customer preferences are not stable, and competitors continually imitate successful organizations.

The SWOT approach to strategy formulation assumes that decision makers carefully analyze an organization's strengths, weaknesses, opportunities, and threats as they decide its future. This approach is a very proactive way to develop a strategy and it appears very clean and logical. However, it is not characteristic of the reactive way most organizational strategies develop.

Rather than creating a unified strategy based on a systematic analysis of the environment, most organizations formulate their strategies in response to problems. For example, a competitive threat, such as the sudden introduction of inexpensive competing products, might first cause a company to reduce its price, then segment itself as a quality producer, then pursue a different product line, or finally seek to enter a different market.

Both proactive and reactive methods of strategy formulation are appropriate, depending on the circumstances. In a stable environment, a proactive method can be used effectively to move the organization toward its long-term objectives. In an unstable environment, however, strategies need to be more flexible and responsive to change. There is a fine line between weak strategies that fail to proactively set the future course of the organization versus rigid strategies that are inflexible and unable to reactively adapt to change.

Example

The history of U.S. Steel illustrates how one company failed to adapt to competitive forces. When foreign steel companies began selling cheaper steel in the United States, U.S. Steel adopted a series of strategies to help it survive, but each one failed. First it relied on the loyalty of its customers to continue buying higher-priced steel. Next it lowered its prices. Then it lobbied for protective tariffs and embargoes. Then it tried various cost-cutting and technological improvements. Then it merged with Marathon Oil and became USX. Finally, it abandoned making steel. The demise of U.S. Steel, which reigned for many years in the early twentieth century as America's largest company, represents a significant strategy failure.

ANALYZING THE FIRM

Aligning the Organization

To survive in a dynamic environment, organizations must be prepared to diagnose their opportunities and revise their strategies. Choosing the right strategy usually makes the difference between success or failure. But good strategies depend on good alignment and implementation; new strategies require corresponding changes throughout the organization. Exhibit 2.3 shows how the events that transpire within an organization are a consequence of its mission and strategy. If we want to make organizations more effective, the mission and strategy must be aligned with four organizational characteristics: structure, systems, culture, and processes.

Many strategies have failed because the organization's structure, control systems, and reward systems were not adequately designed to implement the strategies. The vital relationship between strategy and organizational structure has been recognized at least since 1920, when DuPont and General Motors implemented innovative multidivisional structures that created separate product divisions. Each product division acted like an independent profit center. These multidivisional structures were needed to match the strategic changes in the organizations due to their size, managerial control, and reward systems.

Structure:
The fixed relationships in an organization that describe which jobs are assigned to which departments, who has authority to make decisions, who reports to whom, and how many people each leader supervises.

Structure. *Structure* refers to the fixed relationships of the organization, such as how jobs are assigned to departments, who reports to whom, and how the jobs and the departments are arranged in an organizational chart. Strategies and structures must be aligned. An intended strategy has a substantial impact on how a firm is structured, which in turn affects its strategy. For example, a strategy that attempts to diversify responsibility for decision making by creating independent profit centers or autonomous work teams requires a multidivisional structure. However, a multidivisional structure would be highly inappropriate for a firm that had a strategy requiring central coordination and tight control. Likewise, a small firm following a single-business strategy requires a simple structure in which the owner-manager makes all major decisions and monitors all activities, while the staff merely serve as an extension of the manager's authority. The impact of different organizational structures on profitability and effectiveness are examined in chapter 13.

Systems:
The patterned activities of the various subsystems in an organization that keep it functioning.

Systems. *Systems* refer to the patterned activities that keep an organization operating. Chapter 1 identified six essential subsystem activities: procurement, production, disposal, human resource, adaptive, and managerial. Organizational strategies need to be aligned with their subsystem activities, as illustrated in Exhibit 2.4. The strategy of the corporation must be aligned with the strategies of each business unit, which in turn should be aligned with the functional strategies of each subsystem.

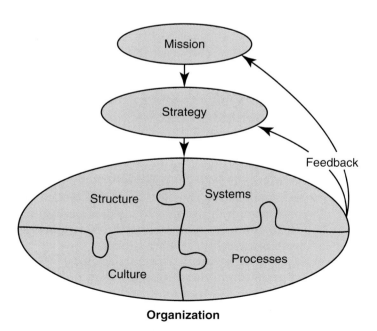

Exhibit 2.3 **Designing Effective Organizations**

Example

A bank in the southeast made the strategic decision to change from an institutional bank to a consumer bank. This decision required the bank to establish numerous branch offices in neighborhoods to make banking services more convenient. This generic strategy of growth for the bank had to be aligned with human resource strategies that included aggressive recruiting, careful selection procedures, rapidly rising wages, job creation, and expanded orientation and training.

Example

A tire company discovered that its foreign competitors were manufacturing tires with a new technology that increased productivity, improved quality, and reduced costs. This new technology required fewer workers, which meant that some workers had to be terminated or retired early. But more important, the workers who remained had to be well educated and highly trained. The human resource strategies at this tire manufacturer focused on reducing the size of the labor force and retraining those who stayed. High school and college classes were used to help them acquire quantitative skills and learn how to operate computers. The compensation system was also revised to pay workers for their knowledge, and to reward new learning.

Culture:

The system of shared values and beliefs in an organization that influence the attitudes and behaviors of members and make each organization unique.

Culture. Organizational *culture* refers to the system of shared values and beliefs that influence worker behavior. Each organization creates its own distinctive culture much as people have distinctive personalities. This culture is based on the values that seem to be widely shared among members of the organization, and they are reflected in the rituals and ceremonies that are held, the traditions that are celebrated, and the stories and myths that are circulated among workers. In times of uncertainty, an organization's culture guides the

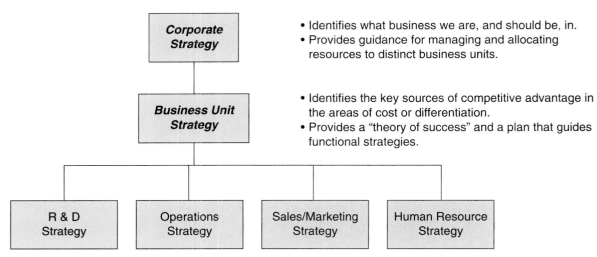

Strategies and tactics of the functional units should align with
and support the overall business unit strategy.

Exhibit 2.4   **Multiple Levels of Strategic Analysis**

behavior of members and creates a sense of stability and direction. How culture influences organizational effectiveness is explained further in chapter 14.

Processes:
The interactions among members of an organization, especially the communication, leadership, decision making, and power.

Processes. Organizational *processes* refer to the interactions among members of the organization. Some of the major organizational processes are the human resource functions of recruiting and staffing that provide the right people in the right jobs at the right time. Other important organizational processes include communication, decision making, leadership, and power. A major consideration in designing an effective structure is ensuring that these processes are accomplished efficiently. For example, effective methods for collecting and communicating useful information need to be integrated within the organizational structure.

Example

Two electronics firms, N.V. Philips (Netherlands) and Matsushita Electric Industrial (Japan) have followed very different strategies and emerged with different organizational capabilities. Philips used a geographic structure to build a worldwide federation of national organizations that are largely autonomous in each country. Product development and production were based on local market conditions and were unique to each country. For example, the furniture-encased televisions sold in the United States were very different in color and style from the TVs sold in other nations. Each national organization took major responsibility for its own financial, legal, and administrative functions

To overtake Philips as the world leader in consumer electronics, Matsushita maintained a centralized structure and leveraged its highly efficient operations in Japan as it expanded overseas. Matsushita adopted a divisional structure: each product line formed a separate division that operated almost like an independent corporation. Product development and engineering occurred in each of the product divisions, spurred by competition among them. As the company expanded overseas, its production, marketing, and sales facilities maintained the culture of a Japanese firm. The company also relied on hundreds of expatriate managers sent from Japan to facilitate communication and leadership processes in the overseas subsidiaries.

Firm Resources and Core Competencies

Resource-based theory of the firm:
A strategy theory that focuses on examining the resources of a firm to find a competitive advantage rather than on the external environment.

Although strategy focuses mostly on the external environment, internal conditions also play a major role in strategy formulation and implementation. This view, referred to as the *resource-based theory of the firm*, provides a very different focus on the sources of competitive advantage. According to Jay Barney, the person most frequently credited for the resource-based view, sustained competitive advantage results from the ownership and control of resources that are rare, nontradable, nonsubstitutable, valued by the market, and difficult or impossible to imitate.[4] Such resources include physical assets, intangible resources, and organizational capabilities.

Some organizations are able to achieve a sustained competitive advantage and earn above-average profits because they possess unique resources or they have capabilities that provide a competitive edge and cannot be easily imitated. Many inputs to a firm's production process might act as unique resources, such as capital equipment, the skills of individual employees, patents, venture capital, and talented managers. These resources are often categorized as human resources, physical resources, and organizational capital resources. This capability is referred to as its *distinctive competence* or *core capability*.

Core capability:
Unique resources that provide an organization with a distinctive competence or unique competitive advantage.

Example

An illustration of a distinctive resource that is rare, nonsubstitutable, and virtually impossible to imitate is Walt Disney's animated characters. Although competitors have attempted to develop their own sets of animated characters, Mickey Mouse, Donald Duck, and other Disney characters are well recognized, very distinctive, and highly admired. Furthermore, Disney has exploited its capability to use these resources in producing universal and timeless entertainment in both animated films and theme parks. For Disney, this capability represents a distinctive competence.

Example

Hayes International is a consulting firm started by Jack L. Hayes, an expert in loss prevention. Although Hayes International hires other consultants and clerical employees, the core competence of this firm is Jack Hayes' forty years of experience in studying employee theft and designing loss-prevention systems. When Jack retires and wants to sell his firm, the purchase price will depend largely on how much of his knowledge and experience he has been able to transfer to others. The core asset of this company is the intellectual property that resides in its founder.

When an organization considers a diversification strategy, it needs to have a clear understanding of its distinctive competence. If the new diversification is able to leverage an existing skill base, the organization will likely achieve high performance. But if the diversification requires acquiring a significantly different skill and knowledge set, it will not likely achieve high performance.

ANALYZING THE ENVIRONMENT

All organizations must interact with their environment. Organizations depend on the environment to provide the necessary resources and to consume its products. The products must be acceptable to society, and the organization needs to obtain a favorable exchange so that it can recycle the products and convert them into new resources.

The survival of an organization can be threatened by public disapproval. Organizations can be terminated or drastically restricted if society disapproves of the organization's products, the way they are produced, or the organization's failure to comply with social expectations, such as safety requirements, environmental pollution standards, tariff agreements, and other legal requirements. The environment of tobacco companies, for example, has become increasingly hostile because of adverse scientific research, changing social customs, and antismoking laws.

Environmental Sectors

Domain:
The sectors or sub-environments surrounding each organization that impact how it interacts with its environment.

In a broad sense, an organization's environment is infinite, and includes everything outside the organization. It is more useful, however, to focus on specific elements that influence it, called the organization's *domain*, which can be

Exhibit 2.5 The Environmental Sectors of an Organization

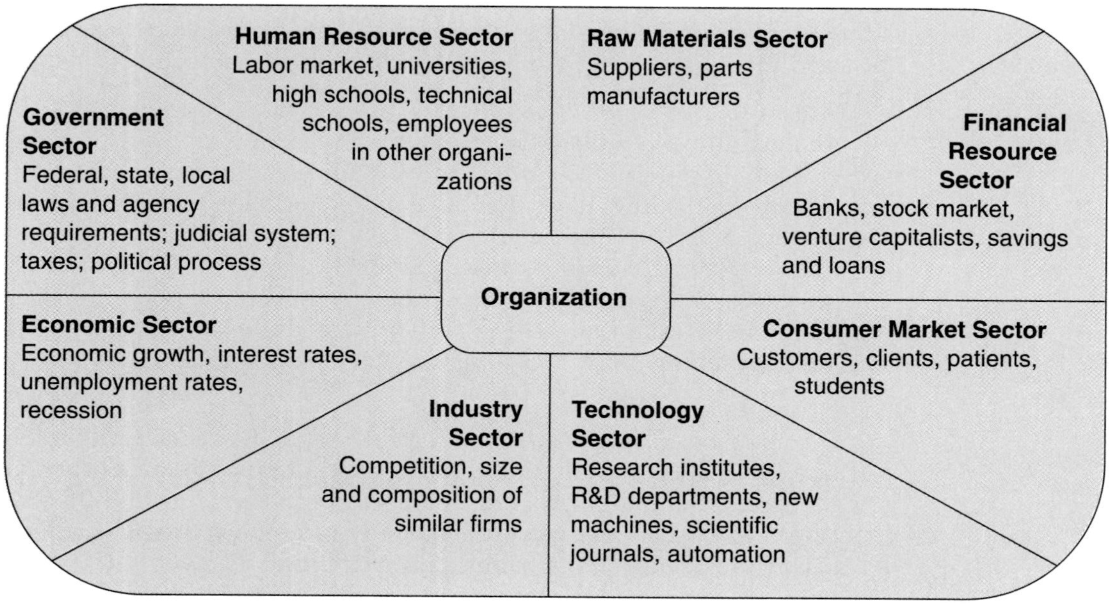

divided into sub-environments or *sectors* that contain similar elements.[5] Each sector represents an important segment of the environment that has the potential to influence the survival and effectiveness of the organization. Eight of the most important sectors are shown in Exhibit 2.5.[6] In strategic planning, a firm would want to examine each of these sectors to discover any competitive advantages it could adopt or weaknesses it should avoid.

1. *Human resources sector.* The human resources sector includes the labor market and all the sources from which potential employees may be obtained, including employment agencies, universities, technical schools, and other educational institutions. Employees can also be pirated from other organizations.

2. *Raw materials sector.* Raw materials must be obtained from the external environment. These materials include everything from paper and students for a university, patients for a hospital, iron ore for a steel mill, and insecticide for a farm. The raw materials sector for the auto industry includes a large number of suppliers and parts manufacturers.

3. *Financial resources sector.* Money is an essential input for most organizations, especially new companies. The financial resources sector includes places where needed money can be obtained, such as banks, savings and loan institutions, stock markets, and venture capitalists.

4. *Consumer markets.* The outputs produced by the organization must be consumed by customers who purchase the goods and services. This market sector includes the customers, clients, and potential users of the organization's products and services. For example, hospitals serve patients, schools serve students, supermarkets supply homemakers, airlines move travelers, and government agencies serve the public.

5. *Technology sector.* Technology is the use of available knowledge and techniques to produce goods and services. The technology sector includes scientific research centers, universities, and the research-and-development efforts of other organizations that contribute to new production techniques and the creation of new knowledge.

6. *Industry sector.* An industry encompasses all the organizations in the same type of business, most of which act as competitors to an organization. The size of the industry and the number of other competing firms create a unique industry sector for each organization. An industry dominated by one or two major corporations, such as heavy-equipment manufacturing, is much different from an industry characterized by hundreds of small companies, such as the fast-food industry.

7. *Economics sector.* Organizations are not isolated from economic conditions. The success and effectiveness of an organization are influenced by the health of the overall economy and by such factors as whether the economy is expanding or contracting. Some of the most important aspects of this sector include economic growth, unemployment rates, recessions, inflation rates, and the rate of investment.

8. *Government sector.* The government sector includes all the federal, state, and local laws plus the regulatory agencies that administer these laws, and the judicial system that resolves disputes. This sector also includes the political system, and political action committees and lobbyists who try to change the laws and obtain favorable legislative treatment.

Industry Analysis

We live in a global economy. Every nation participates in the production and consumption of goods and services that move around the globe, crossing economic, cultural, and political boundaries. Globalization has encouraged international integration. For example, financial resources from one country may be used to buy natural resources from another country and be manufactured in still another country and distributed worldwide. But it has also led to intense competitive pressures for companies everywhere in the world. These conditions force global companies to think seriously about the strategies required to sustain their competitive advantage.

One strategy model focuses on helping firms identify their competitive niche in the external environment by selecting a profitable industry and competing effectively in it. The ***industrial organization model***, or I/O model, suggests that the conditions and characteristics of the external environment are the primary determinants of successful strategies that will help firms earn above-average profits.[7]

Firms face the challenge of finding the most attractive industry in which to compete. Because most firms are assumed to have equal access to similar resources that are mobile across companies, competitiveness generally can be increased only when they find the industry with the highest profit potential and learn how to use their resources to formulate and implement the strategy required by that industry. Michael Porter has developed a ***five forces model of competition*** that identifies the major environmental forces of an industry analysis, as illustrated in Exhibit 2.6.[8] This five forces model suggests that an industry's profit potential is a function of the interactions among these five

Industrial organization model:
A strategy theory that focuses on identifying the competitive advantage of each organization within its industry.

Five Forces Model:
A model that is used to examine a firm's competitive advantage within its industry by examining suppliers, buyers, rival firms, substitutes, and new entrants.

forces. Organizations can use this analysis to examine an industry's profit potential and to establish a defensible competitive position, given the industry's structural characteristics. The five forces are suppliers, buyers, rival firms, product substitutes, and the threat of new entrants.

1. *Suppliers.* Firms depend on their suppliers for materials to which they provide added value. The power of suppliers depends on such factors as how many suppliers are available, whether there are satisfactory substitute supplies, and whether a supplier might choose to integrate forward, such as a bakery deciding to open its own retail outlet.

2. *Buyers.* Firms seek to maximize their revenues, while buyers want to purchase goods at the lowest possible price. The power of buyers increases when there are many competing products, when the products are similar, or when only one or a few buyers purchase the entire output.

3. *Rival firms.* Competition among rivals is stimulated when one or more firms identifies an opportunity to improve their market position or when they feel competitive pressures. Since the firms in an industry are mutually dependent on each other, a competitive advance by one (such as frequent flyer mileage in the airline industry) usually precipitates corresponding moves by all of the others. Rivalry is especially strong when most of the firms are equally balanced and feel a need to distinguish themselves, when the market is not expanding and firms fear a loss of market share, and when the products are not unique and can be easily replaced.

4. *Substitute Products.* Firms compete against other firms that offer substitute products. Therefore, substitute products place an upper limit on the prices firms can charge, since substitutes will be used whenever the price of the product exceeds the price of the substitute. The threat of substitute products is strong when customers can easily switch to the substitute and when the substitute's quality is high and its costs are low. For example, Nutrasweet is a substitute for sugar, since it performs similar functions, and the price of Nutrasweet provides an upper limit on the price of sugar.

   Substitutes do not need to be other products; they can also be other processes or activities that eliminate the need. For instance, the companies that manufacture water meters would discover that the demand for their product could be eliminated if a city decided to charge users a flat monthly fee rather than according to the number of gallons they used. Likewise, California's lawyers who were representing workers in industrial accidents found that the lucrative incentives they anticipated disappeared when that state's supreme court ruled that plaintiffs were not eligible to receive punitive damages for worker's compensation injuries.

5. *New entrants.* New entrants threaten existing competitors by providing additional production capacity. Unless there is a corresponding increase in the demand for additional production, there will likely be price cuts and a corresponding loss of revenues and profits for all firms. Existing competitors try to develop barriers to new entrants, while new entrants seek markets where the barriers are relatively weak. Some of the most challenging entry barriers are inefficient economies of scale for new entrants (small operations do not benefit from large production runs), unrecognized product differentiation (customers are not familiar with the new product), insufficient starting capital (significant funds are needed

Exhibit 2.6 The Five Force Model

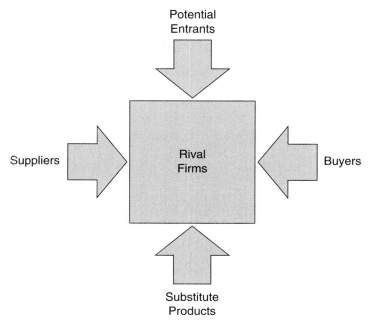

Source: Adapted from Michael Porter, *Competitive Strategy*, (New York: Free Press, 1980), p. 4.

for a firm's initial resources in physical facilities and inventory), limited access to distribution channels (new firms do not have established relationships with distributors), and historical cost disadvantages (the established competitors have already acquired the most favorable locations, proprietary product technology, and favorable access to raw materials).

Competitor Analysis

Competitor analysis:
An examination of the strengths and weaknesses of a firm's competitors.

In addition to analyzing the overall industry, firms also need to analyze each company with which they directly compete. This assessment, called a *competitor analysis*, is especially critical for firms facing one or a few powerful competitors. In the airline industry, for example, each airline is vitally interested in what other airlines are doing. Are they changing their routes or prices? Are they purchasing new planes or increasing their work force? Are they providing new or improved services or benefits?

Successful companies perform a competitor analysis for each competing firm in their industry. This analysis involves examining each competitor's future objectives, current strategy, assumptions, and capabilities. The kinds of questions involved in this analysis are:[9]

1. *Future objectives*: How do our goals compare to our competitors' goals? What will we emphasize in the future? What are our attitudes and the attitudes of others toward risk?
2. *Current strategy*: How are we currently competing? Does this strategy support changes in the competitive structure?

3. *Assumptions*: Do we assume the future will be volatile or stable? Are we operating under a status quo or are we advancing? What assumptions do our competitors hold about the industry and about themselves?
4. *Capabilities*: What are the strengths and the weaknesses of each competitor? How do we rate compared to our competitors?

Competitor intelligence:

Information regarding the strengths and weaknesses of one's competitors and their strategic decisions.

An effective competitor analysis requires gathering needed information and data, referred to as *competitor intelligence*. Information needs to be obtained about each competitor's customers, distribution channels, marketing, sales, advertising, finances, operations, organizational structure, research and development, and strategic plans. Analysts have an obligation to obtain this information in ways that are ethical. Stealing drawings or documents, eavesdropping, and trespassing are unethical and illegal methods of collecting information. However, techniques that are generally considered both legal and ethical include (a) obtaining publicly available information, such as court records, help-wanted ads, annual reports, financial reports of publicly held corporations, and Uniform Commercial Code filings; and (b) attending trade fairs and shows to obtain brochures and advertisements, view the exhibits, and listen to discussions about their products.

The ethics of several intelligence-gathering techniques is questionable even though they are technically legal, such as paying someone to serve as an impostor (such as a student, a management consultant, or a reporter) to obtain inside information, conducting job interviews for jobs that don't exist in hopes that a competitor's employees will apply and volunteer inside information, hiring a competitor's key employees to obtain knowledge about technological innovations, and purchasing a competitor's trash to obtain documents and other inside information. As a general rule, information-gathering techniques ought to respect the right of competitors not to reveal information about their products, operations, and strategic intentions that they do not want divulged. When evaluating the ethics of such cases, the Golden Rule should serve as a useful moral guideline.

Environmental Uncertainty

All organizations function in an uncertain environment, but the uncertainty is much greater for some organizations than others. Reducing this uncertainty may be important to an organization's effectiveness and survival.

Environmental complexity:

Refers to the number of external organizations an organization is required to interact with and the nature of these interactions.

Complexity and Stability. When the environment is uncertain, managers have difficulty predicting external changes and they have to make decisions with insufficient information. Producing viable products requires good information about such things as consumer interests and the availability of resources. Uncertainty also increases the risk of failure, and makes it difficult to compute the costs and probabilities associated with different decisions.

Organizational uncertainty is determined by two dimensions: complexity and stability, as shown in Exhibit 2.7.[10] *Environmental complexity* concerns the number of external elements relevant to an organization. In a simple environment, the organization interacts with only a small number of external elements. For example, a family-operated chicken farm that sells most of its eggs to one food chain has a very simple environment. In a complex environment,

Exhibit 2.7 Framework for Evaluating Environmental Uncertainty

	ENVIRONMENTAL COMPLEXITY	
	Simple	**Complex**
Stable	**Simple + Stable = Low Uncertainty**	**Complex + Stable = Low Moderate Uncertainty**
	Examples: Soft drink bottlers, beer distributors, container manufacturers, agricultural farms, auto repair shops.	*Examples:* Universities, hospitals, insurance companies, government agencies
Unstable	**Simple + Unstable = High Moderate Uncertainty**	**Complex + Unstable = High Uncertainty**
	Examples: Software companies, fashion clothing, music industry, toy manufacturers	*Examples:* Airline companies, oil companies, computer firms, aerospace firms, auto industry

(ENVIRONMENTAL STABILITY)

Source: Adapted from Duncan, R., "Characteristics of Organizational Environments and Perceived Environmental Uncertainty," *Administrative Science Quarterly* 17 (1972): 320.

however, the organization must interact with a large number of diverse external elements. Automobile companies, for example, interact with hundreds of parts suppliers located in many different countries, plus hundreds of dealerships scattered throughout the world. Furthermore, they interact with countless elements in the human resources sector in acquiring new employees, plus dozens of agencies from the government sector.

Environmental stability:

Refers to how much change occurs in a firm's products and the stability of its suppliers and buyers.

How rapidly the environment changes is called ***environmental stability,*** and it is stable when it remains relatively unchanged for several years. Some organizations enjoy a very stable environment, such as lead pipe manufacturers, whose pipe and connecting joints have remained virtually unchanged for many years. Other organizations have a very unstable environment, such as the electronics industry, whose products may become obsolete overnight because of technological advances and new scientific discoveries. The actions of competitors and the unpredictability of the market also contribute to making the electronics industry a very unstable environment.

Reducing Uncertainty. Because uncertainty threatens organizational survival and reduces its effectiveness, organizations use a variety of strategies to reduce environmental uncertainty. Most of these efforts focus on gaining greater control over environmental resources. The first two strategies listed here, however, involve internal changes within the organization.

1. *Changing the organizational structure.* As the environment becomes more complex, the organization needs more buffering departments and boundary spanners. In a stable environment, the internal structure can be centralized, and can operate according to fixed rules and procedures. When the environment is unstable, however, the organization's structure must be informal, decentralized, and coordinated by the efforts of many individuals whose specific responsibility is to facilitate this control.

2. *Planning and forecasting.* Organizations can increase their capacity to respond to an unstable environment by forecasting environment changes and creating contingency plans. Planning can soften the adverse impact of external shifts. Organizations that have unstable environments frequently create separate planning departments to help the organization adapt successfully. For example, economic forecasting may not change the economy any more than weather forecasting can change the weather. However, a good economic forecast may be as helpful to organizational planning as a weather forecast is to scheduling a company picnic. An interesting paradox regarding economic forecasts is that their accuracy increases as the environment becomes more stable, but their usefulness increases as the environment becomes more unstable. Although forecasts in an unstable environment are not as accurate, they are nevertheless more useful because they identify the important contingencies and the relationships among them, and forecasts can always be updated.

3. *Mergers and acquisitions.* An effective method to control environmental resources is to buy a controlling interest in an upstream or downstream company that serves as a supplier or consumer. If there is uncertainty about the source of a crucial raw material, this uncertainty can be removed by buying the supplier. For example, steel companies have acquired iron and coal mines, and soft-drink manufacturers have acquired bottle makers. A similar method of controlling environmental resources is through joint ventures and contracts that create a legal and binding relationship between two or more firms. In a joint venture, organizations share the risks and costs associated with large projects. Contracts are designed to provide long-term security for both the supplier and the consumer of raw materials by tying the consumer and the supplier to specific amounts and prices. For example, McDonald's Corporation will sometimes acquire an entire crop of potatoes to be certain of its supply of french fries.

Cooptation:
Including members of an outside group within the organization to secure their compliance and assistance.

4. ***Cooptation. Cooptation*** is any strategy of bringing outside people into the organization and making them feel obligated to contribute because of their organizational involvement. Cooptation occurs when leaders of important environmental sectors are brought into the organization by having them serve on an advisory committee or a board of directors. Cooptation explains why organizations in more uncertain environments tend to have larger boards of directors—a larger board can reduce uncertainty to a greater degree.[11] Some organizations reduce their resource uncertainty by creating a formal linkage called an *interlocking directorate*, in which the members of the board of directors of one company sit on the board of directors of another company. These individuals influence the policies and decisions of each organization in ways that guarantee interfirm cooperation. Another form of cooptation is to recruit executives from another interdependent organization. For example, companies in the aerospace industry hire retired generals and executives from the Department of Defense, to obtain better information about technical specifications and to improve their chances of obtaining defense contracts.

5. *Public relations and advertising.* Organizations spend enormous amounts of money to influence consumer tastes and public opinion. Advertising

and public relations activities are designed to reduce uncertainty by providing a stable demand for the company's outputs or a constant level of inputs. Press reports and other news media shape the company's image in the minds of suppliers, customers, and government officials. Hospitals, for example, have begun to advertise their services to attract more patients.

6. *Political activity.* Since government legislation and agency enforcement can exert such a powerful influence on organizations, many of them spend a considerable amount of money on lobbyists and political action committees. These individuals strive to protect the interests of the organization by making members of governing bodies aware of the interests of the organization and the consequences of a proposed bill. Many organizations have formed trade associations for similar purposes, such as the National Association of Manufacturers. By pooling their resources, organizations expect the associations to have a larger voice in lobbying legislators, influencing new regulations, developing public relations campaigns, and blocking unfair competition.

7. *Illegal activities.* Although it is wrong, many organizations resort to illegal activities to control environmental uncertainty. Scarce environmental resources and pressures to succeed, especially from top managers, often lead managers to behave in illegal ways. Some examples of illegal behaviors include payoffs to foreign governments, illegal political contributions, promotional gifts, illegal kickbacks, price fixing, illegal mergers, franchise violations, refusals to bargain in good faith with a union, and espionage in market development and innovations.

Although organizations usually try to adapt to the environment, some try to change and control the environment. This is especially true of large organizations that command large resources. The environment is not fixed. Organizations can adapt when necessary, but they can also neutralize or alter a problematic sector in the environment. Although the potential of significantly influencing the environment is small when organizations act alone, a group of organizations can make a noticeable change within the environment when they are united.

Discussion Questions

1. What benefits come from written mission statements? Write a mission statement for an organization or group with which you are affiliated, or for your own personal life.
2. Explain the differences among these three strategies: cost leadership, differentiation, and focus. Describe a company in which you have worked, and explain which strategy it was using to compete. Also discuss how effectively you think it was following its strategy.
3. What makes some organizational environments more uncertain than others? Identify two contrasting organizations that have very different environments, and describe their situations. Explain what the organization in the uncertain environment can do to reduce some of its uncertainty.

Notes

1. Http://www.hp.com
2. Steve Glain, "Strategic Move: Daewoo Group Shifts Its Focus to Markets In the Third World," *The Wall Street Journal*, October 11, 1993, p. A1.
3. Michael E. Porter, *Competitive Advantage* (New York: Free Press, 1985).
4. Jay B. Barney, "Organizational Culture: Can it be a Source of Sustained Competitive Advantage?" *Academy of Management Review* 11, (1986): 656–65; Jay B. Barney, "Firm Resources and Sustained Competitive Advantage," *Journal of Management* 17 (1991): 99–120.
5. Richard L. Daft, *Organization Theory and Design*, 2nd ed. (Saint Paul, Minn.: West, 1986), ch. 2.
6. Ibid., 49–55.
7. Michael A. Hitt, R. Duane Ireland, and Robert E. Hoskisson, *Strategic Management: Competitiveness and Globalization*. (Minneapolis: West Publishing, 1995), ch. 1.
8. Michael E. Porter, *Competitive Strategy: Techniques for Analyzing Industries and Competitors* (New York: Free Press, 1980); Michael E. Porter, *Competitive Advantage* (New York: Free Press, 1985).
9. Michael E. Porter, *Competitive Strategy: Techniques for Analyzing Industries and Competitors* (New York: Free Press, 1980), 49.
10. Ibid., 67.
11. Jeffrey Pfeffer, "Size and Composition of Corporate Boards of Directors: The Organization and Its Environment," *Administrative Science Quarterly* 17 (1972): 218–28

Developing a Strategy for the Acme Corporation

John Phillips, founder of the Acme Corporation, has a difficult decision to make. His family business has lost money for the second straight year. He is operating four different businesses under the umbrella of the Acme Corporation, and only two are profitable. He needs to make each business profitable to provide an income for him and his children, and to create a savings for his retirement. The four businesses include a supermarket, two motels, and a used-car dealership.

Supermarket: This store is located in a small community where it is the only store in town for people to buy groceries and other goods. This highly profitable store is the original business founded by John. He works at the store 10 to 12 hours a day, but at age 60, his health is beginning to decline. Fortunately, he has several good hourly employees who help him run the store successfully and contain costs. Net income from this business is about $100,000 after taxes.

Motel A: The first motel is located in the city, close to the supermarket, and is managed by John's son Bill. Bill is a good manager and able to market the motel to tourists who come to the area to visit the local parks and canyons. Occupancy for the motel is typically 90 percent during the summer months and about 60 percent during the winter. With this level of occupancy, net income from this motel is $40,000 annually after taxes.

Motel B: The second motel, located about 200 miles from Bill's hotel, is managed by a nonfamily employee, Fred. Since this motel was originally designed to serve business travelers, all the rooms are small and contain only one bed, which prevents families from staying at the motel. The occupancy rate for this motel is about 50 percent, which only allows it to break even. John isn't sure whether he should try to remodel the motel, sell it, or find another way to attract a larger portion of the business traveler market.

Used-Car Dealership: John's son, Bob, runs the family's used-car dealership. Bob has had difficulty keeping a job, and John feels that giving Bob an opportunity to run his own business will help him become more independent. Unfortunately, Bob is not a very good salesman and manager, and the car dealership has lost over $50,000 during the past two years. His salespeople turn over at a rate of 100 percent per year. John is using the profits from the supermarket to subsidize the losses from the car dealership. John realizes that Bob does not know how to attract customers and make sales, and there is stiff competition in this market from a number of dealerships that sell both new and used cars. John would like Bob to succeed and does not want to hurt his feelings, but he feels that he cannot continue to support the car dealership indefinitely. Bob, however, says he just needs a little more time to turn the business around and make it profitable.

Questions

1. What should John do? What strategies could he use to make his businesses profitable?
2. Should John sell or close the unprofitable motel or the used car dealership? Why or why not?
3. How much should John consider the feelings of his children in making his decision?

How do you attract and train an effective workforce?

The first requirement of every organization is to attract and train an effective workforce. Once you have identified the vision, mission, and strategy of your organization, your next responsibility is to find other people to help you achieve your goals.

An organization's first opportunity to create an effective workforce occurs during the staffing process. Hiring competent employees and placing them in jobs that are suited to their interests and abilities are important strategic functions. An effective staffing process significantly improves the attitudes and expectations of new employees. The process requires careful planning, including the development of procedures for training and promoting present employees. The professionalism of the staffing process can even influence employees' feelings of pride and loyalty.

CHAPTER 3
Human Resource Planning, Recruitment, and Selection

CHAPTER 4
Socialization and Training

CHAPTER 5
Employee Relations

Section II contains three chapters that focus on human resource management. Chapter 3 explains how companies recruit and hire new employees who will likely become outstanding employees. Chapter 4 explains the role-transition process that helps new employees acquire the skills and attitudes they need to succeed. Chapter 5 summarizes the major employment laws that regulate the hiring process and protect employees. Because the employment processes used in earlier years often discriminated against certain members of society, federal regulations have been passed to restrict what employers can do.

Human Resource Planning, Recruitment, and Selection

Chapter Outline

Human Resource Functions

Strategic Alignment of HRM

Relationships Between HR and Line Management

Human Resource Policies

Human Resource Planning

HR Planning Model

Forecasting Employment Needs

Succession Planning and Development

Recruitment

Recruitment Planning

Recruiting Sources

Selection

Selection Process

Selection Decisions

HUMAN RESOURCE FUNCTIONS

Human resource management (HRM) is responsible for how people are treated in organizations – it is responsible for bringing people into the organization, helping them perform their work, compensating them for their labors, and solving problems that arise. Human resource management plays a central role in organizational effectiveness.

Since people are a company's most important asset, all managers should be vitally concerned with human resource management. Furthermore, in one sense, *all* managers are human resource managers because they share with human resource specialists the responsibility for most human resource functions.

Strategic Alignment of HRM

Human resource activities must fit the mission and structure of each organization. Organizations face unique challenges, and they need to develop human resource functions that are consistent with their unique situations. The major human resource functions include staffing, performance evaluations, compensation and benefits, training and development, employee relations, and safety and health. These functions are necessary for every organization, regardless of size and organizational structure, and the responsibility for them is typically assigned to a human resource department. Small organizations with fewer than 50 to 80 employees typically do not have a human resource manager; these functions are assigned to other departments. Large organizations may delegate them to separate departments. For example, a large organization may have a separate safety department, while a small organization delegates safety responsibilities to its line managers.

Strategic alignment of HRM: Establishing human resource policies and functions that are coordinated with and supportive of the organization's overall strategy and other organizational functions, such as production, marketing, and finance.

Strategic alignment refers to the development of specific action plans that support the overall mission and direction of the organization. These action plans help the organization achieve its goals. The generic strategy of the organization must be aligned with the human resource strategies and all other functional strategies, such as marketing, finance, and production. If the action plans of all these groups are not coordinated to form a unified thrust, the strategy disintegrates and the organization falls into confusion and frustration.

A human resource plan is *strategic* when it helps management anticipate and manage increasingly rapid and tumultuous change. As an organization's generic strategy is revised to adapt to change, the human resource strategies must also be revised. The following examples illustrate how human resource strategies are derived from generic corporate strategies.

Cost Reduction. To compete in a competitive international environment, a steel company modernized its production process and upgraded its marketing and distribution systems. An analysis indicated that even with these changes, the company would still need to reduce other costs to achieve a satisfactory profit picture. This cost-reduction strategy required corresponding human resource strategies that focused on eliminating unnecessary positions, renegotiating labor agreements, controlling benefits expenses, and doing a careful cost-benefit analysis of all training activities.

Improving Quality. A hotel chain adopted a strategy of quality service to improve its competitive position with customers. As part of its desire to be a "provider of choice" it focused on concierge services, video checkout, frequent flier points, weekend rates, and customer-satisfaction cards for feedback. Its generic strategy of being a provider of choice had to be aligned with human resource strategies to make it an "employer of choice." These strategies included offering employees training programs, providing career opportunities, developing joint-venture internship programs with local high schools or colleges, and experimenting with ways to give employees feelings of ownership and responsibility for their work areas.

Mergers and Acquisitions. When two companies are combined, regardless of the strategic reason for combining them, there are inevitable conflicts. Each company brings to the merger its own organizational culture and history of human resource practices. A smooth transition to becoming one unified company requires appropriate human resource strategies that create consistent policies and practices. Effective strategies establish unity in compensation, benefits, layoffs, transfers, appraisal, promotion, discipline, vacations, and employee services.

Retrenchment. Several companies (such as GM, GE, and IBM) have discovered that they cannot sustain their previous production levels and realize they must reduce their capacity and workforce. This economic reality means reducing work hours, idling assembly lines, or possibly closing entire plants. The human resource strategies supporting this retrenchment typically focus on layoffs, early retirements, wage reductions, productivity increases, job redesign, and renegotiated labor agreements.

Relationships between HR and Line Management

Human resource managers are required to interact constantly with other managers in an organization. These interactions may produce conflict, unless the managers have a clear understanding of their relationships and shared expectations about their responsibilities and authority.

Most organizations make a distinction between line and staff authority. *Line authority* refers to the right to make decisions and give orders to subordinates regarding production, sales, or finance. Line managers supervise the employees who produce the organization's products and services; they are responsible for making operating decisions, and the units supervised by line managers have the ultimate responsibility for the successful operation of the company.

Staff authority is the responsibility to advise or assist those who possess line authority. Staff members are expected to help line managers accomplish the objectives of the enterprise by giving advice and service when it is requested. However, staff members also have the responsibility to give advice and service even when not requested if necessary. The human resource department is considered a staff department, as are quality control, engineering, and accounting. As they work with other managers to help them deal with human resource issues, human resource managers may perform three very different roles in the organization: an advisory or counseling role, a service role, and a control role.

Line authority: The right to make decisions and give orders to subordinates regarding activities that are directly involved in producing the organization's products and services.

Staff authority: The responsibility to advise and assist those who possess line authority.

1. *The advisory or counseling role*: In the advisory or counseling role, staff personnel are seen as internal consultants who gather information, diagnose problems, prescribe solutions, and offer assistance and guidance in resolving human resource problems. This relationship is similar to the relationship between a professional consultant and a client. It is the responsibility of the human resource manager to give advice regarding staffing, performance evaluation, training programs, and job redesign. In these situations, the human resource department provides input that assists line managers in making decisions.

2. *The service role*: HR managers must also play an active role in helping the company choose its people well, invest in them, support their growth, and respect their needs, while fostering innovations needed to achieve the company's strategic business objectives. In this role, staff personnel perform activities that can be provided more effectively through a centralized staff than through the independent efforts of several different units. These activities are a direct service for line management or for other staff departments. Recruiting, orientation training, record keeping, and reporting duties are examples of the human resource department's service role.

3. *The control role*: The human resource department is required to control certain important policies and functions within the organization. This staff role is sometimes called *functional authority*. In performing this role, the human resource department establishes policies and procedures, and monitors compliance with them. The human resource staff members are seen as representatives or agents of top management. Because of legislation, the control role has become increasingly important in the areas of safety, equal employment opportunity, labor relations, and compensation. When the human resource department places hiring quotas on another department to achieve affirmative action goals, it exercises its control role.

A critical issue in the relationship between line and staff is whether the line managers are required to follow the recommendations of the staff. Traditionally, line managers have had the authority to accept staff advice, modify it, or reject it. In recent years, however, greater authority for certain areas of management has been delegated to staff units. In these areas, accepting staff advice is compulsory for line managers, subject only to appeal to higher authority. The expanded authority of a human resource department is illustrated by the limitations that have been placed on a supervisor's authority to terminate an employee. To protect the organization from expensive wrongful-discharge suits, an employee cannot be terminated until the supervisor has followed the human resource department's termination guidelines.

In recent years, the emphasis of human resource management has moved away from the traditional support role toward becoming a bottom-line decision maker and strategic partner. Being a strategic partner means being able to contribute unique information to the strategic decision making of the company. Participating in these strategic discussions requires HR managers to have a clear understanding about the company's mission, its competitive advantages, the interests of its customers, what it takes to make a profit, and how it should be positioned to compete effectively in the market.

Economic Contribution of HRM. Human resource activities should be evaluated to determine whether they are simply proliferating programs and reports or making a positive contribution to the economic success of the organization. Some corporations are not content to view the human resource function as an overhead expense; they require their human resource departments to measure the contribution they make to both employee attitudes and organizational effectiveness.

The economic contribution of human resource management to increased sales, greater profitability, and reduced turnover was demonstrated in a study of 968 firms. Each firm was evaluated on the proportion of its workforce that participated in "high performance work practices," such as formal job analysis, employee attitude surveys, quality of work-life programs, formal performance appraisals, company incentive and gain-sharing plans, preemployment testing, and promotion by performance rather than seniority. The results indicated that a one-standard-deviation increase in high performance work practices was associated with a $27,044 increase in annual sales per employee, and a $3,814 increase in annual profits per employee, and a 7.05 percent decrease in turnover.[1]

HR Practices and the Balanced Scorecard. Companies need to balance the interests of their stakeholders. Two important stakeholders are a firm's owners and customers, and the expectations of these two groups are typically incompatible. Owners and stockholders expect an organization to be run efficiently using sound management practices, and everything should contribute to the profitability of the organization, including training and development activities, bonuses and benefits, and employee relations programs. For example, stockholders and owners may question the value of programs designed to help employees with alcoholism or financial problems, since these programs may not contribute to the profitability of the organization.

Customers and clients, on the other hand, believe the organization should provide useful products and services, and also be socially responsible by improving the quality of society. To fulfill its social responsibility, an organization is often expected to recruit and train disadvantaged members of society and provide a work environment that contributes to the overall quality of life for all employees. Customers and clients also demand high-quality products and competent service.

Balancing the demands of these stakeholders requires a great deal of skill. Managers should be prepared to justify their actions with respect to both short-term profits and long-term growth. This may require managers to demonstrate the financial impact of their programs and also prove that their activities are socially responsible in contributing to the quality of work-life for employees.

The ***balanced scorecard*** refers to the idea that there are three important stakeholders for every company—the stockholders, the customers, and the employees.[2] This concept explains what it takes for a company to succeed, and there are two key premises underlying it: (1) For businesses to succeed in the long run, the expectations of all three stakeholders need to be simultaneously satisfied; and (2) the interests of all three stakeholders are interrelated. Employee attitudes and behaviors impact the level of customer satisfaction and retention. In turn, customer attitudes and behaviors influence shareholder

Balanced scorecard:
Balancing the interests and economic returns of all stakeholders, including employees, owners, and customers by being fair, profitable, and socially responsible.

satisfaction and retention, since customers are essential to profitability. Shareholder satisfaction affects employee satisfaction through bonuses, stock options, and further investment in employee growth and development. Although a business that ignores the expectations of one of the stakeholders may succeed in the short run, in the long run its business performance will suffer.

Human Resource Policies

Human resource policies refer to standing plans that furnish broad guidelines and direct the thinking of managers about human resource issues. These policies are typically formed under the direction of top-level managers, with input from first-level supervisors who are primarily responsible for administering them. Some of the most common issues treated in human resource policies are (a) discipline problems, such as absenteeism, tardiness, insubordination, and horseplay; (b) promotions, transfers, and layoffs; (c) compensation, pay increases, and benefits; (d) holidays, vacations, and sick leave; and (e) termination. Human resource policies serve three major purposes:

1. They reassure employees that they will be treated fairly and objectively.
2. They help managers make rapid and consistent decisions.
3. They give managers the confidence to resolve problems and defend their decisions.

To achieve these purposes, human resource policies should be written and available for everyone to examine. Written policies are more authoritative than verbal ones and serve as valuable aids in orienting and training new employees, in administering disciplinary actions, and in resolving grievance issues. These policies are usually explained in employee handbooks that are distributed to each employee.

Implied promise: A statement, usually in an employee handbook, that can be construed as a promise of continued employment, such as calling employees "permanent".

Employee handbooks create problems for employers if they contain *implied promises* of continued employment. For example, some handbooks have called full-time employees "permanent" to distinguish them from temporary or part-time employees. Some courts have construed this label to constitute a promise of continued employment, and companies have been forced to reinstate terminated employees. Due to an increase in the number of wrongful-discharge lawsuits being won by employees, employers need to review carefully the language and intent of their human resource policies.

An employee handbook should not promise anything the employer is not willing to deliver. For example, a statement that "employees can be terminated only for just cause" requires an employer to demonstrate good and sufficient reason for terminating an employee. If an employee handbook contains a progressive disciplinary system, the employer is obligated to follow it when taking disciplinary action. Employers are better off not having employee handbooks if they are not willing to follow them.

Employers have attempted to protect themselves from wrongful termination claims by requiring employees to sign a disclaimer when they receive their handbooks. A typical disclaimer is:

> This handbook is not a contract of employment. Employment in this organization is at-will, and either party may terminate employment without

cause and without having to use any prescribed procedure. I understand that I am an at-will employee and that I can be terminated at any time and for any reason without advanced notice. Signed: _____

Although these disclaimers help employers avoid charges of wrongful termination, they are not an absolute protection. If the handbook contains statements promising continued employment, or stating that specified procedures will be followed, the courts are likely to decide that employees have a legitimate expectation that these promises will be fulfilled.

HUMAN RESOURCE PLANNING

Organizations can achieve a competitive advantage by having a highly trained and skilled workforce. Planning for a firm's human resources is as important as planning for its capital and financial resources.

HR Planning Model

HR planning should coincide with a company's business planning; to reach its long-term goals, a company must have the proper mix of employees with the necessary knowledge, skills, and abilities. HR planning precedes recruitment and selection, and provides the foundation for personnel staffing. Before new employees are recruited, someone needs to decide what kinds of employees are needed and how many, and these decisions need to be aligned with the organization's strategic business plans. Hiring new employees should be based on the projected staffing requirements. If the projection indicates a demand for new employees, recruiting activities should be initiated; if it indicates a surplus of personnel, early retirements, layoffs, or other actions may be necessary.

Strategic HR planning contains three time frames—long-range, middle-range, and short-range—that simultaneously consider both business plans and human resource plans. As shown in Exhibit 3.1, *long- range business planning* involves a strategic analysis of a firm's competitive advantages, and this analysis should include an examination of the availability of human resources. This analysis, called ***environmental scanning***, examines the composition of the labor force and changes in the labor supply, including demographic changes, immigration, birth rates, educational training, social and cultural changes, and changes in laws and regulatory agencies. Each of these changes could have a significant influence on the availability and preparation of potential human resources.

Middle-range business planning consists of setting specific goals the organization expects to achieve within the next two to five years. These plans need to be coordinated with forecasts of how many employees will be needed in each job category to achieve them; achieving these goals requires the proper mix of people. Since some of the present workforce will leave because of turnover, these plans need to consider both attrition rates and productivity changes. Some organizations maintain five-year forecasts that are updated annually, so that an organization always has a five-year plan and separate yearly plans leading toward its long-range objectives.

Short-range business planning typically produces annual operating plans and budgets that should simultaneously plan for adequate human resources to achieve them. Operating officers are responsible for projecting their own hu-

Environmental scanning:
An examination of factors in the external environment that could have a significant impact on the future labor force, especially demographic changes, educational opportunities, and government legislation.

Exhibit 3.1 Staffing Model

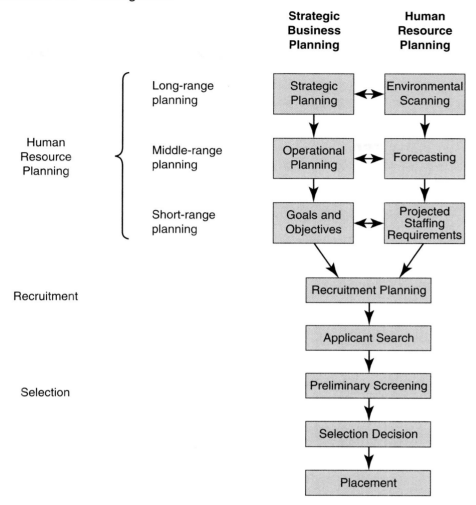

man resource needs. If more employees are needed, staffing authorizations should be prepared and sent to the people responsible for recruiting. If a surplus of employees is forecast, administrators must decide how the workforce should be reduced. The short-range human resource plan also should include an analysis of promotions and transfers, which is called *succession planning*, and should project whether these changes will require additional training.

Human Resource Planning System. A formal human resource planning system is not essential for small organizations. Until a company has more than two or three hundred employees, one or two top executives generally can list all of the supervisors and managers, predict when they are likely to leave, and name the most likely replacements. As organizations become larger, however, a more sophisticated human resource planning system is needed.

A human resource planning system consists of a series of defined activities for collecting and analyzing information. Forms must be developed to obtain the relevant information from numerous individuals, including supervisors, managers, and corporate planners. The system also determines how the information is processed, since several individuals are involved in collecting and synthesizing it. Decision rules are established so that each manager knows when specific information calls for an action plan and where the action plan should be sent. For example, information about training needs is sent to the training and development office, projected staffing requirements are relayed to the recruiting office, an analysis of the forecasted employment levels is submitted to top management, and an analysis of replacement needs is sent to the managers who make replacement decisions. All of this information needs to be integrated and available on organizational replacement charts, personnel files, or computer databases. The vehicles that are typically used to integrate these activities are the annual performance-evaluation process and the compensation system. These activities require that managers complete the relevant forms and process the necessary information to create career paths, succession plans, and other human resource plans.

Human Resource Information
System, HRIS:
A compilation of personnel information regarding employees that is usually stored on the Internet or in a company's computer system.

Human Resource Information Systems. Effective human resource planning requires an inventory of the people working for the organization, called a *human resource information system (HRIS)*. A carefully designed HRIS that contains current and reliable data helps managers anticipate replacement needs, plan for promotions, evaluate training needs, conduct personnel research, submit EEO reports, analyze compensation costs, examine pay equity issues, and find employees with unique skills to fill unique needs, such as someone who speaks a particular language to serve as an interpreter or who has musical talent to participate in a performance. In large companies, this information is typically available on an Internet system that integrates the company's HR, payroll, and accounting functions.

The major purpose for collecting this information is to make staffing and promotion decisions. For example, a construction company considering a project in Mexico might want to know how many of its employees speak Spanish and if there is a potential project manager who has an MBA, has experience in construction, and also speaks Spanish.

The following kinds of data are useful in an employee profile: (1) present job category or current position; (2) skills, including areas of knowledge and experience; (3) educational level, including degrees and certificates; (4) geographical location and preference; (5) employment history; (6) health and accident insurance and other benefit options; (7) vacation and sick leave availability, including Family and Medical Leave Act status; (8) potential for development and interest in promotion; (9) wage and salary history; (10) performance evaluations; (11) attendance record; and (12) disciplinary actions. For research and EEOC reporting purposes, the HRIS should also contain information about each employee's age, race, religion, sex, national origin, marital status, and number of dependents; but this information must not be illegally used for selection, promotion, training, compensation, or evaluation.

The information contained in an HRIS is typically obtained from application forms, performance evaluations, personnel change notices, disciplinary action reports, payroll data, and skills inventories. Some companies give their employees passwords and usernames that provide them with limited access to their own files, and expect them to update their personal information.

Forecasting Employment Needs

Forecasting a company's human resource needs involves answering these three questions: (1) How many employees will be needed in the future? (2) What kinds of skills and talents will they need? (3) When will they be needed? When forecasting employment needs, the forecaster is required to make assumptions about economic conditions, productivity changes, technological improvements, and the future of the organization. Forecasting is more accurate in organizations that have a stable environment, but they are usually more valuable for those in volatile environments, even if they are not as accurate.

Employment forecasting need not produce exact estimates of future employment to be useful. The forecasting process itself facilitates HR planning by requiring managers to think about the future and anticipate the kinds of events that might occur. Having a forecast that is wrong is usually better than having no forecast at all, since an incorrect forecast can be modified as conditions change and new assumptions become necessary. The value of a forecast should be judged not so much by how close it was to the actual needs, but by the degree to which it caused managers to think about and anticipate future situations. Some of the most popular methods of forecasting employment include the following:

1. *Budgeting.* In many organizations, short-term employment forecasting is part of the budgeting process. Managers are expected to identify the kinds of resources that they will need for the coming business period. If they will need additional personnel to fill new positions demanded by their unit's objectives, then this information should be included in their budgets. Managers often use rules of thumb to assist them, such as three sales associates per cash register.

2. *Workload Analysis.* A workload analysis uses ratios and standard staffing guidelines to identify human resource needs. For example, a company can estimate what its total output will be and how many hours will be required to produce it, and then calculate how many people it will need.

3. *Unit Demand.* Unit demand forecasting requires that supervisors estimate the number of employees they expect to need in each of the coming years to achieve their units' goals. These estimates are compiled to form an overall projection for the company.

4. *Expert Opinion.* Long-term employment needs can be forecast from the subjective estimates of experts based on their intuition or past experience. Combining the estimates of multiple forecasters increases one's confidence in their accuracy.

5. *Trend Projections.* Trend projections are based on a relationship between employment levels and a factor related to employment, such as sales, production, or types of services provided. If such a relationship exists, the human resource planner can use the forecasted levels of sales, production, or services to estimate how many employees will be needed in each job category. Some form of informal trend projection is typically involved in unit demand and expert opinion. The most sophisticated way to use historical information is to do a ***regression analysis***, which is a statistical technique showing how one variable (employment) can be predicted by other variables (e.g., sales, production, occupancy rates, patients, etc.).

Succession Planning and Development

Succession planning refers to the process of deciding how management vacancies will be filled. Effective succession planning occurs when qualified replacements are identified and prepared to fill vacancies in all key positions.

Succession planning:
Identifying potential replacements for managerial and other key positions and creating developmental opportunities so these replacements will be ready for promotion when they are needed.

Succession Planning. The traditional approach to succession planning has been for managers to groom their own replacements, but this process is not always adequate. Managers frequently need more training than their mentors can provide. Especially important are developmental job assignments in which managers receive special training by serving as managers of other departments.

Effective succession planning involves identifying potential replacements for each key job, assessing the interest and preparation of each replacement, and determining what developmental experiences they need to prepare for promotion. This managerial review and discussion represents the heart of succession planning.

Replacement planning has been formalized in some organizations with the aid of replacement charts showing key management positions and the availability of replacements. For example, Exhibit 3.2 indicates that a vacancy will soon occur in the store manager's position and that the two possible candidates for this position are the human resource director and the furniture

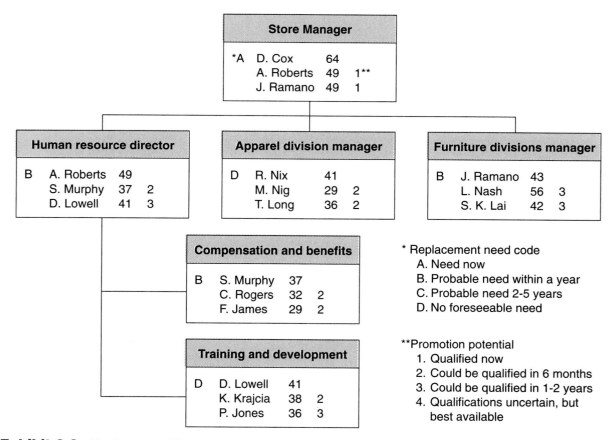

Exhibit 3.2   Replacement Chart

division manager. Since the human resource director is the most likely replacement for the store manager, it is important that replacements for the human resource director be carefully considered.

A detailed position-replacement chart is shown in Exhibit 3.3. In completing this form, managers are forced to carefully consider not only the abilities of each replacement but also the specific training experience that a replacement needs before filling a vacancy.

Succession planning is useful to the extent that it contributes to the development of new managers and facilitates the promotion process. If promotion decisions continue to be based on subjective, ill-defined criteria, then the planning process loses much of its effectiveness. Succession planning is a waste of time if it only results in static charts. The objective of succession planning is not to create added paperwork but to provide for developmental experiences in preparing managers to fill potential vacancies.

Position: _Human Resource Director_   Date: _July 1, 20xx_

Incumbent: _A. Roberts_   Overall Performance Rating: _9_

Age: _49_   Years in Position: _6_

Present Salary: _$59,500_

Replacement Need: _B (Probably next January)_

Comments: _A. Roberts may be promoted to replace D. Cox within the next year_

Most Qualified Replacement: _S. Murphy_   Age: _37_

Title: _Compensation and benefits director_   Salary: _$47,000_

Years in Position: _2_   Years with Company: _11_

Promotional Potential: _2_   _Could be qualified in 3-6 months_

Overall Performance Rating: _8_

Training Needed: _Needs to learn how to prepare the personnel budget and to control expenditures_

Second Most Qualified Replacement: _D. Lowell_   Age: _41_

Title: _Training and development director_   Salary: _$46,400_

Years in Position: _6_   Years with Company: _12_

Promotional Potential: _3_   _Could be qualified in 1-2 years_

Overall Performance Rating: _7_

Training Needed: _Needs some experience in labor relations and college recruiting_

Exhibit 3.3   **Detailed Position-Replacement Chart**

Surplus Personnel. Occasionally, projected staffing requirements indicate a surplus of personnel. This situation can be much more painful to managers than having inadequate personnel, since it is usually more difficult to reduce the size of the workforce than to increase it. The primary methods for reducing the number of personnel include layoffs, attrition, reduced hours, and early retirements.

1. *Layoffs.* The employees who are to be laid off are typically given advance notice. The Worker Adjustment and Retraining Notification Act requires companies with 100 or more employees to give 60-day advance notice of layoffs or plant closings that affect large numbers of employees (50 or more employees who comprise at least 33 percent of the workforce at one site, or 500 or more employees regardless of the percent). In a union organization, layoff decisions are typically based on seniority as specified in the labor agreement. In a nonunion organization, layoff decisions may be based upon a combination of seniority and ability.

2. *Attrition.* Attrition, sometimes called *restrictive hiring*, refers to reducing the workforce by failing to replace individuals who leave. If enough advance planning has been done, an organization may avoid layoffs simply through attrition; only essential replacements are made.

3. *Reduced Hours.* If the labor surplus appears to be a short-term problem, many organizations prefer to reduce the number of hours each employee works and keep all of the employees. Instead of continuing a forty-hour workweek, management may decide to cut each employee's wages and hours by a fixed percentage.

4. *Early Retirements.* If an organization has a number of employees who are nearing retirement age, it may be able to reduce its workforce by encouraging older employees to take early retirement. To encourage early retirement, however, an organization must frequently offer financial incentives that may offset the savings that might have been accrued by reducing the workforce. Nevertheless, if the rewards are sufficient, an organization can significantly reduce its workforce through voluntary early retirement. The Age Discrimination in Employment Act allows employers to offer early retirement incentives, but the employees should be fully informed about the offer and there should be no coercion to accept it.

Attrition:
The practice of not replacing employees who leave in an effort to reduce the size of the workforce.

Recruitment

Effective organizations are able to attract sufficient job candidates with the requisite talents to help the organization achieve its objectives. Recruitment is a prerequisite for effective selection. Outstanding job candidates cannot be selected if they are not included in the applicant pool. The recruitment process basically consists of (1) formulating a recruiting strategy, (2) searching for job applicants, (3) screening those who are obviously unfit, and (4) maintaining an applicant pool.

Recruitment Planning

In planning recruiting activities, an organization needs to know how many applicants must be recruited. Since some applicants may not be satisfactory and

Yield ratios:
A ratio that shows how many job applicants at one stage of the recruitment process advance to the next stage.

others may not accept job offers, an organization must recruit more applicants than it expects to hire. *Yield ratios* help organizations decide how many employees to recruit for each job opening. These ratios express the relationship between the number of people at one step of the recruiting process relative to the number of people who will move to the next step. For example, the overall yield ratio for a major oil company is 60:1 because the yield ratio of interviews to invitations is 6:1, the yield ratio of invitations to offers is 5:1, and the yield ratio of offers to acceptances is 2:1. Therefore, 60 college students must be interviewed for every person who accepts a position.

Internal versus External Recruiting. Vacancies in upper-level management positions can be filled either by hiring people from outside the organization or by promoting lower-level managers. Both strategies have advantages and disadvantages.

Promotion from within:
The practice of selecting from among current employees and promoting them into higher-level positions that become vacant.

A major advantage of a *promotion-from-within* policy is its positive effect on employee motivation. Opportunities for promotion tend to improve performance, increase satisfaction with the company, and solidify feelings of loyalty to the company. Moreover, having extensive information about present employees reduces the likelihood of making a poor decision. Employees who are promoted from within also are knowledgeable about the organization, and thus little time is lost in orienting them to their new positions. The major disadvantage of a promotion-from-within policy is that it creates narrowness of thinking, a condition sometimes referred to as "inbreeding."

The major advantage of external hiring is that new people bring new ideas and new insights into an organization. They also are able to make changes in the organization without having to please constituent groups. However, some risk is involved in hiring someone from outside the organization because the person's skills and abilities have not been assessed on a first-hand basis. Hiring someone from outside the organization also involves an opportunity cost, because of the time lost while the person becomes oriented to the new job.

Attracting Recruits. An organization has to decide how it plans to attract job applicants and what enticements it has to offer. It may have difficulty attracting the people it wants, especially highly skilled employees in competitive markets. During the recruiting process, it is forced to walk a fine line between conveying a positive image and conveying an unrealistic image. Recruiters often fear that if they "tell it like it is," no one will be interested in applying for a position. However, when recruiters paint only a one-sided, positive view of an organization, new recruits often undergo reality shock because of unmet expectations, disillusionment, surprise, anxiety, and other feelings of not being fully prepared for the day-to-day activities and problems of the work environment.

Realistic Job Previews:
Telling new recruits both the positive and negative features of a job so that they have a realistic understanding of what it will be like.

Reality shock can be reduced by providing job applicants with realistic views of what an organization is like, and the kind of working conditions that they will experience on the job. Research has shown that when new recruits are given realistic information about a job, (1) the number of applicants does not decrease and (2) turnover rates decrease significantly.

When they are competing for applicants, most employers assume new applicants are attracted by money, so they offer high starting salaries, and sometimes signing bonuses, to entice employees. Although high starting salaries help to attract applicants, other factors are also important, especially the requirements of the job, the attractiveness of the industry, the reputation of the company, the job's location, and other non-wage benefits.

Recruiting Sources

Internal Recruiting. The first place an organization should look to fill a job vacancy is within. Qualified employees should be considered for promotion as a reward for their service and commitment. Furthermore, the organization should have useful performance information to predict whether they will succeed. Recruiting among present employees is generally less expensive than recruiting from outside the organization. The major forms of internal recruiting include promotion from within, job posting and bidding, and contacts and referrals.

1. *Promotion from within.* Promoting entry-level employees is an excellent way to fill job vacancies when companies have a good human resource planning system that includes succession plans and replacement charts. An effective promotion-from-within policy requires that companies hire entry-level employees who may be overqualified for their initial job but are capable of being trained for more responsible positions. Skills inventories are useful in identifying individuals who have the potential for advancement.

2. ***Job Posting and Bidding.*** An organization that does not have a good human resource planning system and does not know who wants to be considered for promotion can use a job-posting-and-bidding system. In a ***job-posting*** system, the organization notifies its present employees about job openings through the use of bulletin boards, company publications, or personal letters. ***Job bidding*** allows individuals who believe they have the required qualifications to apply for the available jobs.

3. *Contacts and Referrals.* Before going outside to recruit new employees, many organizations ask present employees to encourage friends or relatives to apply for job openings. Contacts and referrals from present employees are valuable sources of job recruits that are relatively inexpensive and usually produce quick responses. However, some organizations are concerned about problems that result from hiring friends of employees. The practice of hiring friends and relatives increases the likelihood of ***nepotism***, which refers to favoritism that is shown to friends and relatives. Hiring friends and relatives also is more likely to create cliques, causing some individuals to feel excluded from informal group associations. Since friends and relatives tend to be of the same race and gender as present employees, relying on contacts and referrals for finding new employees also can create an imbalance in equal employment opportunity and affirmative action goals.

External Recruiting. Numerous methods are available for external recruiting, some of which are listed below. Organizations should select an appropriate method to reach potential applicants. For example, major newspapers, such as the *Wall Street Journal*, are generally good for recruiting executives; Internet

Job posting and bidding:
The practice of filling a job vacancy by advertising the opening and allowing current employees to apply for it.

Nepotism:
The practice of showing unfair favoritism to family members or friends in the employment process.

postings are good for recruiting computer services employees; and help-wanted posters serve well for recruiting fast-food employees.

1. Direct applications from help-wanted posters or Internet postings
2. Public employment agencies
3. Private employment agencies, including executive search firms and "headhunters"
4. Placement offices in schools and colleges
5. Former employees
6. Advertisements in newspaper, television, and radio
7. Summer internships

Professional Employer Organization, (PEO):
A separate private company that manages the human resource functions, such as employment, performance evaluation, compensation, and employee relations for the employees in another company.

Contingent Labor Force:
Workers who are temporary or on-call, and not regularly employed on a full-time basis by a company.

Alternatives to Recruiting. When an organization decides to increase its staff, it makes a significant financial investment. Recruitment and selection costs are high, and benefits are usually about 40 percent of payroll. Furthermore, once employees are placed on the payroll, removing them may be difficult, even if their performances are below standard. Consequently, before an organization decides to recruit new employees it ought to consider the feasibility of other alternatives. Four alternatives to recruiting are subcontracting some of the work to outside contractors, having present employees work overtime, using temporary employees, and employee leasing. Leasing employees from a *professional employer organization (PEO)* that provides benefits and other HR services is especially popular for small employers.

Some employers have experimented with flexible staffing and creative scheduling to solve their employment needs in a tight labor market. These staffing alternatives include developing an on-call pool, hiring employees who work only during peak hours, telecommuting from a home computer attached to the Internet, and permanent part-time work. These alternatives often appeal to people who do not want a full-time position.

People who work for temporary agencies or in-house company pools, workers on short-term contracts, and some part-time employees, form what is called the *contingent labor force*. *Contingent workers* are people who have little or no attachment to the workplace where they are employed. When and how much they work depends on the employer's immediate need for them. The employer incurs no obligation to them beyond paying them for the time they work. The use of contingent labor has grown significantly in recent years.

SELECTION

Making an informed selection decision depends largely on two basic principles of selection. The first principle is that *past behavior is the best predictor of future behavior*. Knowing what an individual has done in the past is the best indication of what the individual is likely to do in the future. This principle is not deterministic: an employee who has been outstanding in previous jobs may be only mediocre in a new position. A student who did very poorly as a freshman can have an outstanding sophomore year. Knowing what people have done in the past is not an absolutely accurate indication of what they will do in the future. Nevertheless, in making selection decisions it is best to assume that past behavior is the best predictor of how an individual will perform in the future.

Reliability:
Repeatability or con-
sistency of measure-
ment.

Validity:
Capable of measuring
what it is expected to
measure, such as suc-
cessfully predicting job
performance.

The second principle is that *organizations should collect as much reliable and valid data as is economically feasible and use it to select the best applicants.* *Reliability* refers to repeatability or consistency of measurement. If we obtain similar scores every time we interview or test an applicant, we would say that the data are reliable. *Validity* refers to predicting job success: Does the data measure what it is supposed to measure? Valid data indicates how well employees will perform their jobs.

Very little information needs to be collected for jobs that are simple and can be performed by almost any applicant, or when the cost of making a bad hiring decision is negligible. However, as jobs become increasingly difficult to staff with competent employees, and as the cost of making a poor hiring decision increases, the collection of reliable and valid information becomes very important. The selection of good managers is especially important, and some organizations have prospective managers spend several days in assessment center activities from which reliable and valid information can be obtained.

Selection Process

The selection process is a sequential procedure involving some or all of the steps illustrated in Exhibit 3.4. Organizations may have all applicants go through the entire selection process, waiting until the end to choose the best candidate, or they may treat each step in the process as a hurdle that systematically screens the number of employees advancing to the next step. Either

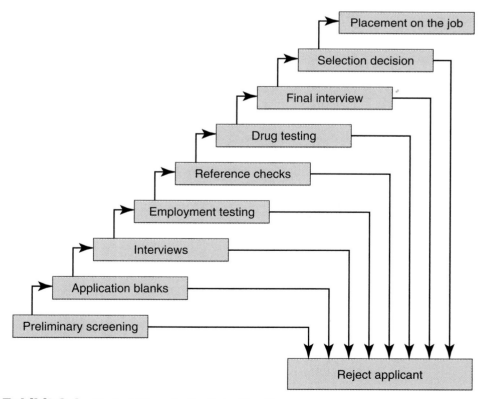

Exhibit 3.4 **Typical Steps in the Selection Process**

way, each step in the selection process should be designed to obtain specific, useful information for making a hiring decision.

Preliminary Screening Interviews. The first step in the selection process is a preliminary screening interview that typically occurs as part of the recruiting process. Applicants who are obviously not qualified for the job opening, usually because of inadequate education, training, or experience, should be immediately eliminated from the applicant pool. Arbitrary standards that have no relationship to an individual's ability to perform the job should not be used to disqualify an applicant, especially age, race, religion, sex, national origin, and disability.

Application Blanks. Completing an application blank is a basic step in almost every selection process; all but the very smallest companies have job seekers complete some type of application form. The primary purpose of an application blank is to provide meaningful employment information that helps employers make accurate hiring decisions. The usefulness of most application forms is relatively limited, however, because they have not been adequately developed to provide relevant data. Nevertheless, a carefully designed application blank that requests relevant past experience can be scored and used to predict job performance. These forms are typically referred to as *weighted application blanks*, *biodata forms*, or *biographical information blanks*, and experience has demonstrated that when they are properly designed they can be reliable and valid predictors of performance.

Weighted application blank:
A job application form that can be scored and used to predict which applicants have a high likelihood of succeeding.

Interviews. Employment interviews are used by virtually every organization to hire employees at all job levels, and they are very influential. The results of a survey conducted by the Bureau of National Affairs indicated that 56 percent of the participating companies believed that interviews were the most important aspect of the selection procedure, and that 90 percent of the hiring managers had more confidence in interviews than in other sources of information.[3]

Unfortunately, research evidence does not support the value of employment interviews. Interviews are conducted by individuals who have different orientations, different levels of competence, and different perceptual biases. The interview process generally is not consistent—each interview is conducted differently depending on what is said—and the evaluations of the interviewer are essentially random observations. Although interviewers believe their conclusions are the most important step in the decision process, research shows that most interview data are generally neither reliable nor valid.[4] However, interviews are used for more than just selection purposes. They also are used to recruit employees and answer their questions.

Behavioral interviews:
A type of interviewing that involves asking applicants to describe specific behaviors associated with the critical dimensions of the job for which they are applying.

Some types of interviews are more useful than others. *Behavioral interviews*, for example, focus on the critical dimensions of a job and how well an applicant's past performance demonstrates the necessary skills. The first step in preparing for a behavioral interview is to identify the essential dimensions of the job through a careful job analysis, and the next step is to develop questions that require applicants to describe situations when they have demonstrated these skills. Applicants are expected to describe the **S**ituation or **T**ask they performed, the **A**ction they took, and the **R**esult they achieved. This *STAR* interviewing technique is used frequently because it tends to be more reliable and valid than normal, semi-structured interviews.

Employment Testing. Personnel testing can be a highly reliable and valid way to predict job performance. Hundreds of tests have been developed to measure numerous dimensions of human behavior, including paper-and-pencil tests, performance tests, performance simulations, graphology, and honesty tests. Personnel tests provide objective and standardized measures of such human characteristics as aptitudes, interests, abilities, and personalities. Test results measure how much of a given characteristic individuals possess relative to other individuals, and, if the characteristics being measured are important to successful job performance, personnel tests represent a valuable selection device.

Like other selection devices, personnel tests should be used to select applicants for a specific job. Deciding which tests to use to predict performance on a given job requires a careful job analysis. Someone who knows each job very well or who has examined the job descriptions and job specifications should identify the abilities and attitudes essential for effective job performance. Thus, the necessary skills for a secretarial position might be the ability to type, proofread, and work cooperatively with others. Once the critical skills and abilities have been identified, personnel tests can be examined to identify those that predict these characteristics. Some of the most popular tests include the following:

1. *Honesty tests*: Honesty tests measure a person's orientation toward the issues of honesty and integrity, and they are used more frequently in industry than all other personnel tests combined. These tests contain questions regarding such situations as whether a person who has taken company merchandise should be trusted in another job that involves handling company money or whether taking damaged goods without permission from a company is acceptable if the merchandise would be disposed of otherwise. An individual's responses to the test statements indicate the individual's attitudes toward theft, embezzlement, and dishonest practices. Extensive research has shown that some of these instruments not only produce reliable information that validly predicts dishonest behavior but that they also are free from biases of age, race, and sex.[5] These honesty tests represent a valuable selection tool for choosing employees who will occupy positions that involve handling company money.

2. *Aptitude tests*: Aptitude tests measure the capacity for learning. Aptitude and ability tests are typically used to indicate which individuals will learn best during training and which will perform best after they have been trained. Although there are hundreds of ability tests, most can be grouped into three major categories: mental abilities, mechanical abilities, and psychomotor abilities. Aptitude and ability tests are frequently combined into a test battery and then used to predict different jobs within organizations. Many organizations have been successful in validating various parts of their test batteries to predict successful performers on various jobs. Aptitude tests have been found to have broad applicability in predicting performance on a wide variety of jobs.[6]

3. *Achievement tests*: Achievement tests measure how much individuals have learned about a broad content area, such as an academic discipline, or knowledge regarding a general trade, such as carpentry or financial in-

vesting. Achievement tests have been validated for jobs that require specific information. For example, if an organization needs to hire plumbers and several applicants claim to have previous experience in plumbing, a written trade test on plumbing might be useful.

4. *Personality tests and interest inventories*: Many personality tests have been used to predict good employees, such as the Minnesota Multiphasic Personality Inventory (MMPI), the California Psychological Inventory (CPI), and the Sixteen Personality Factor Questionnaire (16PF). These tests are lengthy, and numerous scoring keys have been developed to predict dozens of mental disorders or personality profiles. Although validity studies have shown that specific scoring keys are occasionally correlated with how well people perform on certain jobs, most of the correlations have been too low to be considered very useful. Personality tests have probably demonstrated their best predictive success for hiring sales representatives.[7] Interest inventories show how well a person's interests compare with those of people in various professions. Although interest inventories are useful for diagnostic and counseling purposes, most organizations have found that the validity coefficients of these instruments are generally too low for selection purposes.[8]

5. *Job knowledge and job sample tests*: A job knowledge test measures whether applicants have the specific knowledge that is required to perform a unique job. These tests are not too difficult to construct for someone who has a clear understanding of the relevant body of knowledge. A job sample test, also called a job tryout test, consists of a small, well-defined portion of the actual job that applicants are asked to perform. These tests are also not too difficult to construct. Job knowledge and job sample tests are generally reliable and valid when they are carefully constructed.

Job sample tests:
A test that usually consists of a small, well-defined segment of the actual job that can be standardized for all applicants.

Reference Checks. Before employers make a selection decision, they should investigate the backgrounds of prospective employees. These background investigations, usually called reference checks, may include an investigation of previous employment, educational credentials, criminal activities, credit records, and general character.

Many organizations, including graduate schools, ask applicants to provide letters of recommendation from former employers and acquaintances. These letters of recommendation generally constitute the most useless form of reference check, since applicants do not ask someone to write a letter unless they are certain that the person will make a favorable evaluation. Since letters of recommendation generally represent a very biased form of information, employers usually disregard such letters unless they contain negative information. The value of letters of recommendation has decreased in recent years because of a growing concern among employers that they could be sued for reporting adverse information. To protect themselves from potential law suits, many employers simply confirm the individual's employment, the dates of employment, and salary information.

A better means of obtaining information about an applicant's previous employment history is to phone the applicant's previous employer and request a reference. While a letter of recommendation may simply say that an individual is creative and brilliant, a phone call affords the opportunity to ask the employer how the individual demonstrated creativity and brilliance. Employers are protected against charges of defamation of character by the qualified privilege doctrine when providing job references. The *qualified privilege doctrine* allows previous employers to describe former employees' work records to prospective employers, provided the information is factual and relevant and serves a legitimate business purpose.

Qualified Privilege Doctrine:
The right of employers to share relevant job-related previous work experience about an applicant without being guilty of slander or defamation of character.

Another way for employers to check the backgrounds of prospective employees is to buy investigative reports from a credit reporting agency or private investigative agency. Such agencies specialize in gathering information about applicants for employment, life insurance, and financial credit. When employers request an investigative report, they can specify the length of time to be covered in the report. The information usually concerns an applicant's length of service with previous employers, a salary history, reasons for termination of employment, eligibility for rehire, and other information about the applicant's general reputation, living habits, credit records, criminal records, health, and driving habits. This information is collected by field representatives who are employed in regional offices located throughout the United States and Canada. The Fair Credit Reporting Act requires employers to notify applicants when their applications are rejected either in part or in whole because of the investigative report. An applicant also is allowed to challenge incorrect information and to have it changed.

In some situations an employer may find it useful to examine an applicant's criminal record. Court records are open to the public, and information can be obtained that indicates whether an applicant has been tried for a crime and either convicted or acquitted. Because of the Privacy and Security Act (1976), however, police records are not open to the public.

Employers need to know when an applicant's background indicates a propensity for abusive behavior. Courts have ruled that an employer can be held liable for injuries committed by its employees if the company failed to investigate the applicant's criminal record and medical history. As part of an emerging legal trend, firms are now being held responsible for their employees' wrongdoing, even if the crimes have no connection with the workers' jobs. Injured parties have been successfully advancing the legal theory of *negligent hiring*, claiming that employers knew, or should have known, that an employee was dangerous.

Negligent hiring:
When an employer fails to adequately investigate job applicants and hires someone who the employer knew or should have known had a tendency toward violence or criminal conduct.

Although reference checks are costly and inconvenient, they are increasingly important because there appears to be a growing tendency for applicants to misrepresent information on their resumes and applications. Some impostors have been fired for employee theft multiple times when a simple reference check would have indicated that they were poor hiring risks. In some cases impostors have even changed their names and obtained graduation certificates, grade transcripts, and other supporting documents to pretend they were someone else.

Drug Screening. As part of the selection process, applicants can be required to pass a drug screening test. If the drug test confirms that an applicant is currently using illegal drugs, that person can be disqualified from the applicant pool. The Americans with Disabilities Act (1991) prohibits employers from giving preemployment physical exams, but it specifically allows for preemployment drug testing. Physical exams and other types of health tests cannot occur until after a conditional job offer has been made. Some organizations require that new employees obtain physical examinations, particularly if a job requires heavy physical exertion. Other organizations, especially hospitals and food service concerns, depend on physical examinations to identify applicants with communicable diseases.

Final Interview. The applicant's final interview is usually conducted by the supervisor to whom the applicant will report. This interview usually occurs after the human resource office has narrowed the selection decision to three or four candidates. Although the human resource office may indicate its choice, the ultimate hiring decision is left to the line manager. Since managers usually select whom they like the most and think they would enjoy working with, this step is essentially a personality contest.

Selection Decisions

Clinical judgement:
Making hiring decisions based on a subjective evaluation of each candidate's relative strengths.

Weighted Composite:
Assigning weights to the various predictors and statistically combining them to make a hiring decision.

Multiple cutoff:
Identifying the minimum passing level for each step in the selection process and eliminating job applicants who fail to meet each criterion.

Combining the Information. Three methods are typically used for making selection decisions: (1) clinical judgment, (2) weighted composite, and (3) multiple cutoff. *Clinical judgment* refers to the informal process of examining the information about each individual and making a subjective decision about the most desirable applicant to hire. The *weighted-composite* procedure involves weighing the information and statistically combining it into a composite score. The applicant with the highest composite score is hired. *Multiple cutoff* consists of a sequential process in which applicants are required to achieve satisfactory levels at each successive step. Illustrations of each of these methods are presented in later sections.

When a great deal of information has been collected, clinical judgments are inefficient. Most individuals consider only three or four factors when making a decision, so clinical judgments entail wasted effort when more information is collected than can be used.

The use of a weighted composite avoids this loss of information. Organizations that use the weighted composite keep all applicants in the selection process until data have been obtained on each predictor. This information is then weighted and combined into a composite score, and those with the highest composite scores are hired.

The multiple-cutoff procedure has the advantage of reducing the size of the applicant pool at each step. Organizations that use the multiple-cutoff procedure systematically eliminate applicants who do not achieve satisfactory scores on each predictor.

Both weighted-composite and multiple-cutoff procedures are used by universities to admit students. Some universities establish a minimum composite score as an admission requirement. The students' grade-point averages, test scores, class ranks, and recommendations are combined to form their composite scores, and those who have composite scores above the minimum are admitted to the universities. Other universities establish a minimum cutoff score on each predictor, and reject applicants who are below the cutoff on any specific factor.

Assessment center:
A series of selection activities that usually involve a group of applicants participating in group activities with evaluators observing them and discussing their ratings.

Assessment Centers. An *assessment center* refers to a series of structured activities (not a place) that are used for either selection or training. An assessment center is one of the most powerful methods for identifying management potential. Applicants participate in a series of activities that usually occur over a one- or two-day period and they are evaluated on each activity by a group of trained assessors who unobtrusively observe their performance. After the participants have been observed in many activities, the evaluators discuss their observations and try to achieve a consensus evaluation of each participant. Multiple assessors using consensus decision making tend to produce higher reliabilities and validities for assessment-center data than for typical selection procedures. Although the assessment center technique was first used by the military during World War II, the pioneering work in its development was done by American Telephone and Telegraph.[9] Most assessment centers today are patterned after AT&T's assessment technique, which involves clinical interviews, projective tests, work samples, paper-and-pencil tests, and participation in group problem-solving and leaderless group discussions.

Over time assessment centers have generally been excellent predictors of job performance, because the activities included in them are usually designed to replicate the activities and responsibilities of the actual job. These activities are also structured to provide opportunities for multiple assessors to observe the participants in a broad range of behavior.

Determining the Value of the Selection Procedure. The value of a selection procedure is determined by how well it contributes to hiring successful employees. If most applicants are successful even if they are hired at random, an elaborate procedure would be worthless. But if only a small proportion of randomly selected employees achieve success, then a careful selection procedure would be valuable, especially if the position is important. In any situation, the costs of using a predictor should be weighed against the benefits expected from it. The benefits are determined by three factors: the selection ratio, the validity coefficient, and the base rate of success, as shown in Exhibit 3.5.

1. The *selection ratio* indicates the percent of applicants who are hired for the job, and is influenced by the recruiting strategy. This ratio determines the vertical line in Exhibit 3.5.
2. The *validity coefficient* is the correlation coefficient between the predictor (such as a test or interview scores) and the criteria (job performance). A correlation coefficient of 0 indicates that no relationship exists between the two variables. However, as the correlation coefficient approaches ± 1.00, the relationship between the two variables becomes stronger. A high correlation means that the predictor is useful in identifying outstanding performers. The validity coefficient is illustrated by the ellipse. As the shape of the ellipse becomes longer and narrower, approaching a straight line, the validity coefficient approaches 1.00.

Validity coefficient:
The correlation coefficient showing the relationship between a predictor, such as a mental ability test score, and the criterion, such as performance evaluations.

Exhibit 3.5   **Assessing the Usefulness of a Predictor**

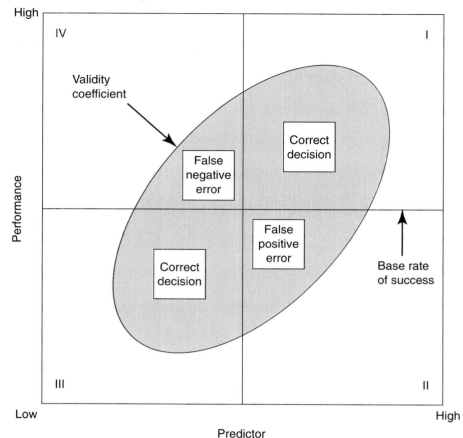

3. The ***base rate of success*** refers to the percentage of employees who would be considered successful if they were hired without the use of the new predictor. A high base rate of success indicates that almost any applicant would be a good performer. The base rate of success determines where the horizontal line is placed. As a smaller percentage of job applicants is considered successful, the horizontal line is raised to a higher level.

False positive error:
An error that occurs when a positive hiring decision has been made, but the new employee is not a satisfactory performer.

False negative error:
A selection error that occurs when an applicant is rejected who would have been a good performer.

In making selection decisions, two kinds of errors may occur. A ***false positive error***, shown in Quadrant II, represents those who were hired but were inadequate performers. They are called false positives because a positive hiring decision was made based on their predictor scores, but it was a false prediction. The individuals in Quadrant IV represent a ***false negative error***. These individuals would have been successful performers if they had been hired, but because of their low predictor scores, they were not hired. The individuals in Quadrant I and Quadrant III represent correct decisions—those who were hired became successful performers and those who were not hired would have been poor performers.

Discussion Questions

1. What is succession planning and why is it useful? Explain how it might be useful to a medium- sized organization with 250 employees, such as an accounting or law firm.

2. Develop a recruitment and selection procedure for selecting just one key person, such as a manufacturing firm that needs to hire a new company president, a female chiropractor who needs to hire a male partner to assist with her practice, or a single 25-year-old who decides it is time to find a spouse.

3. What recruiting methods would you recommend for a construction company planning to build a major project in an isolated wilderness area? Where should the construction company recruit, and what sort of enticements should it offer? Write the recruitment ad.

4. Why are employment interviews so unreliable and what can be done to improve their reliability? What questions would you recommend for interviewing applicants for a job you have held, and how would you use the answers to make a selection decision?

Notes

1. Mark A. Huselid, "The Impact of Human Resource Management Practices on Turnover, Productivity, and Corporate Financial Performance," *Academy of Management Journal* 38 (1995): 635–72.

2. R.S. Kaplan and D. P. Norton, "The Balanced Scorecard— Measures That Drive Performance," *Harvard Business Review* (January-February, 1992): 71–79; R.S. Kaplan and D.P. Norton, "Putting the Balanced Scorecard to Work," *Harvard Business Review* (September-October, 1993): 134–47.

3. Bureau of National Affairs, *Personnel Policies Forum*, Survey No. 114 (September 1976).

4. Michael M. Burgess, Virginia Calkins, and James M. Richards, "The Structured Interview: A Selection Device," *Psychological Reports* 31 (1972): 867–77; Eugene Mayfield, "The Selection Interview—A Reevaluation of Published Research," *Personnel Psychology* (Autumn 1964): 239–60; Donald P. Schwab and Herbert Heneman III, "Relationship Between Interview Structure and Interviewer Reliability in an Employment Situation," *Journal of Applied Psychology* 53 (1969): 214–17; Lynn Ulrich and Don Trumbo, "The Selection Interview Since 1949," *Psychological Bulletin* 63 (February 1965): 110–16; Michael J. Campion, Elliot D. Pursell, and Barbara K. Brown, "Structured Interviewing: Raising the Psychometric Properties of the Employment Interview," *Personnel Psychology* 41 (Spring 1988): 25–42. Richard A. Posthuma, Frederick P. Morgensen, and Michael A. Campion, "Beyond Employment Interview Validity: A Comprehensive Narrative Review of Recent Research and Trends over Time." *Personnel Psychology*, 55 (Spring, 2002): 1–81.

5. Linda A. Goldinger, *Honesty and Integrity Testing: A Practical Guide*, (Impress, 1989); Philip Ash, "Screening Employment Applicants for Attitudes Towards Theft," *Journal of Applied Psychology* 55 (1971): 161–64; Philip Ash, "Predicting Dishonesty with the Reid Report," *Journal of the American Polygraph Association* 5 (June 1075): 139–53; Philip Ash,

"Convicted Felon's Attitudes Towards Theft," *Criminal Justice and Behavior* 1, no.1 (March 1974): 1–8.

6. Hans J. Thamhain, "From Engineer to Manager," *Training & Development* 45 (September 1991): 66–70; see also "Test Validity Yearbook—Volume 2," a special issue of *Journal of Business and Psychology* 7 (Summer 1993).

7. Edwin E. Ghiselli, "The Validity of Aptitude Tests in Personnel Selection," *Personnel Psychology,* 26 (1973): 461–77.

8. Ramon A. Avila and Edward F. Fern, "The Selling Situation as a Moderator of the Personality-Sales Performance Relationship: An Empirical Investigation," *Journal of Personnel Selling and Sales Management* 6 (November 1986): 53–63; G. Gough, "Personality and Personality Assessment," in *Handbook of Industrial and Organizational Psychology,* ed. Marvin Dunnette (Chicago: Rand McNally, 1976); Robert M. Guion and R.F. Gottier, "Validity of Personality Measures in Personnel Selection," *Personnel Psychology* 18 (1965): 135–64; A.K. Korman, "The Prediction of Managerial Performance: A Review," *Personnel Psychology* 21 (1968): 295–322.

9. Douglas W. Bray and Donald L. Grant, "The Assessment Center in the Measurement of Potential for Business Management," *Psychological Monographs* 80, whole no. 625 (1966); Douglas W. Bray, Richard J. Campbell, and Donald L. Grant, *Formative Years in Business* (New York: John Wiley, 1974).

Test Scores versus Letters of Recommendation

Marlin Porter, the hiring officer for Davis Electronics Company, faces a difficult dilemma as he reviews Jody Williams' application. Jody has applied for a position in the filament department, and several openings in that department still remain. However, Marlin does not think Jody will be able to learn the job and do it well.

Jody's application indicates that she is a recent high school graduate who has never held a full-time job. Her best recommendation is a letter from Phil Robbins, the general superintendent for Davis Electronics. Phil described Jody as an excellent worker, a dedicated person, and "the kind of person our company ought to employ." Jody has been a babysitter for the Robbins family and she lives on the same street.

Although Jody's application and letters of recommendation are very positive, Marlin doubts that she will succeed in the filament department because of her low test scores. To work in that department, all candidates are expected to achieve satisfactory scores on tests of eye-hand coordination and finger dexterity. Jody's scores on both tests are well below the normal cutoff levels, and indicate that her chances of surviving the thirty-day probationary training are less than 20 in 100. Jody probably would be a very pleasant and cooperative employee, and hiring her would please Phil Robbins. But can she succeed?

Questions

1. Should Marlin disregard the test scores and hire Jody?
2. Should recommendations from company officers be automatically accepted or given extra consideration?
3. Would it be kinder to hire Jody or to not hire her?

A Behavioral Interview Schedule for a Sales Associate

Behavioral interviewing involves asking applicants to describe their behavior either retrospectively—what they have done in the past—or prospectively—how they would respond in a future situation. Either way, the interviewer must have a list of questions that are designed to assess applicants on critical dimensions of the specific job. An effective interviewer will only ask questions that encourage the applicant to discuss job-related topics and will direct the applicant back to job-related areas when the conversation strays to irrelevant topics.

The first step in developing a behavioral interview is to identify the critical dimensions that are essential to successfully performing the job. This information is typically taken from the job description and job specification. A dimension refers to the kind of knowledge, skill, and ability that a successful worker must possess. A person does not have to be high in every dimension to be successful; some jobs only require average behavior on certain dimensions. But the job requires at least minimal competence in each dimension.

An effective behavioral interview question requires applicants to describe the situation or task they faced, the actions they took, and the results that were obtained. Interviewers should listen carefully to make certain that each response contains all three elements (Situation/Task, Action, and Result) and then use this information to evaluate the applicants on the relevant dimensions. Behavioral interviews are more reliable if the interviewers force themselves to use numerical scales and essay comments to evaluate the applicants. Some questions can be used to assess multiple dimensions, such as evaluating planning and organizing and sensitivity by asking, "What do you do when you have two or more people trying to talk to you at the same time?"

Sales associates are responsible for greeting customers, describing the merchandise, answering questions, closing sales, and maintaining attractive displays of the merchandise. The major dimensions for a successful sales associate are:

- planning and organizing: establishing a course of action to accomplish a specific goal or objective,
- sensitivity: showing actions that indicate a consideration for the feelings and needs of others,
- tolerance for stress: demonstrating emotional stability under pressure or opposition,
- energy: maintaining a high activity level,
- attention to detail: making certain all relevant tasks are accomplished correctly and timely,
- integrity: acting in ways that are moral and ethical,
- oral communication: effective expression in individual and group situations.

Develop a list of behavioral questions for hiring a sales associate that would allow you to evaluate an applicant on these seven dimensions. For example, some questions that could be used to assess planning and organizing are:

1. Tell me what you did last week and how you planned your activities. How well were you able to follow your schedule?
2. Describe a situation when you were required to have multiple things completed at the same time. How did you handle it? What was the result?

CHAPTER 4

Socialization, Training, and Development

Chapter Outline

Socialization

    The Socialization Process

    Role Transition Process

    Stages of Career Development

Training and Development

    Systems Model of Training

    Principles of Training

    Training and Development Techniques

    Orientation Training

SOCIALIZATION

Because a large portion of one's life revolves around work, it is not surprising that people want a fulfilling job. Abraham Maslow found that the effect of one's career on personal identity is especially strong among highly self-actualized people. When Maslow asked the people in his study what they would be if they were not in their respective jobs, many hesitated and had difficulty answering. Others responded with comments such as, "I can't say. If I weren't a _____, I just wouldn't be me, I would be someone else."[1]

The Socialization Process

Socialization:
The process of acquiring socially acceptable attitudes and behaviors that conform to the standards of society or the organization.

The process of molding the attitudes and behaviors of people to socially acceptable standards is called *socialization*. This process is particularly important during the formative years of childhood, but it continues during education and employment. Through the socialization process, individuals acquire the kinds of attitudes and behaviors they need to participate as members of an organization. Socialization teaches people how to behave in socially acceptable ways consistent with social customs and organizational demands.

Organizations have an important stake in the socialization process. To the extent that the goals of the organization are consistent with the members' goals, the organization is more effective and the individuals are more satisfied and successful. The socialization process is a continuous activity throughout an individual's career. As the needs of the organization change, and as jobs are redefined, employees must adapt to these changes; that is, they must be socialized. Socialization is especially important when employees begin their first job, or change jobs.

Organizations use a variety of methods to help individuals conform to the ever-changing needs of the organization. Three of the most prominent socialization processes include new-employee orientations, training and development programs, and performance appraisal. New-employee orientation programs are designed to inform new employees about the mission of the organization and the basic rules and procedures they are expected to follow. Training programs help to socialize employees by teaching specific job skills, plus the proper attitudes and values demanded by the organization. For example, an effective safety training program not only teaches employees how to perform their jobs safely, but it also creates an appropriate attitude about the importance of safety and the need to follow safe procedures. Performance appraisals provide feedback to employees about the appropriateness of their behaviors and attitudes, and serve as a form of reward or punishment for acceptable behavior. Performance evaluations are a powerful socializing influence when they are done properly.

Organizational Integration:
The process of integrating people into the organization by matching their objectives and goals with the objectives and goals of the organization.

Individuals are effectively integrated into an organization when their interests and goals are consistent with the mission of the organization. This consistency, referred to as *organizational integration*, is maximized when the goals of individuals are congruent with the goals of the organization. Occasionally these goals are naturally consistent, such as with most voluntary associations. More frequently, however, individuals are required to go through a relearning process to acquire the necessary values and behaviors. The most

Exhibit 4.1   Balance in Socialization

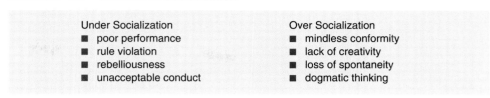

Under Socialization	Over Socialization
■ poor performance	■ mindless conformity
■ rule violation	■ lack of creativity
■ rebelliousness	■ loss of spontaneity
■ unacceptable conduct	■ dogmatic thinking

extreme form of this undoing and relearning process involves debasement techniques designed to eliminate individuality, such as those experienced by fraternity pledges and Marine Corps recruits. Rigorous initiation ceremonies typically increase the perceived value of membership to new recruits and help them acquire the appropriate attitudes and behaviors.

When socializing new employees, organizations need a balance between over-socialization and under-socialization, as illustrated by Exhibit 4.1. If new employees are under-socialized, their behavior will violate the social norms or they will rebel against organizational expectations. If they are over-socialized, however, their behavior will be excessively rigid and conforming—they will suffer a loss of creativity and spontaneity as their behavior adheres to fixed and unquestioned expectations. Between these two extremes, there is a point where individuals are able to display their own creative individuality while still adhering to the social expectations of the organization.

Role Transition Process

A person's life history may be viewed as a series of passages from one role to another—from high school student to college student, to company trainee, to junior partner, to senior partner, and so on. The process of advancing from one stage to another has been termed "rites of passage."[2] Three phases are associated with moving from one stage to another:

- *separation* of the person from the former role,
- *initiation* into the new role, and
- *incorporation* into the new environment.

These three phases are illustrated in Exhibit 4.2. As individuals move from one role to another, they experience a form of identity change. The new role requires them to develop a different self-perception regarding their feelings of competency, responsibility, relationships with others, and status.[3]

Two psychological processes occur between the stages of the role transition process: anticipatory socialization and reality shock. As people begin to separate themselves from their previous environment, they typically experience *anticipatory socialization* as they adopt the attitudes, attributes, and self-perceptions of the new role. For example, as MBA students approach graduation, they begin to anticipate what it will be like to be a manager, and prepare themselves to think and act like professionals in their new role.

The other psychological change occurs as people struggle to accept the new role. The difference between a person's work expectations before and after joining an organization is called *reality shock*. Here, individuals realize

Separation:
The first stage of the role transition process where people begin to disassociate themselves from their former role.

Initiation:
The second stage of the role transition process wherein new members are tested and expected to prove themselves to be accepted in full fellowship.

Incorporation:
The final stage of the role transition process in which people are integrated into the new role.

Anticipatory Socialization:
The process of acquiring the attitudes and behaviors associated with a new role as people anticipate changing from one role to another.

Reality Shock:
Realizing that a new role is not as glamorous as it appeared at first.

Exhibit 4.2   **Role Transition Process: Rites of Passage**

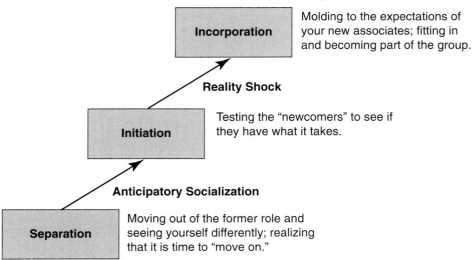

Incorporation — Molding to the expectations of your new associates; fitting in and becoming part of the group.

Reality Shock

Initiation — Testing the "newcomers" to see if they have what it takes.

Anticipatory Socialization

Separation — Moving out of the former role and seeing yourself differently; realizing that it is time to "move on."

that their new role involves much hard work and responsibility and it is not as glamorous as they expected it to be. During the anticipatory socialization period, the self-perceptions of those expecting a promotion are typically more favorable than after they are actually promoted. It is not unusual for new college graduates to feel a sense of disillusionment during their first few months on a new professional job.

Before new employees join an organization, they experience a variety of socialization processes that prepare them for working in an organization. These anticipatory socialization experiences include formal schooling, internships, conversations with recent graduates, and company presentations. Organizations contribute to anticipatory socialization by their recruiting activities and the information they provide to job applicants. Unfortunately, the recruiting activities in many organizations overstate the benefits of working for the company and glorify the job descriptions. The consequence of this strategy is that organizations often create unrealistic expectations that produce a severe reality shock after the individuals join the organization.

A strategy for reducing exaggerated recruiting is called *realistic job previews.* Here, recruits are given a balanced presentation describing both the favorable and unfavorable aspects of the job and the company. For example, a realistic job preview for a school bus driver might include the negative aspects of promptness, rigid scheduling, low pay, and noisy students, plus the positive aspects of serving the students and not being confined to an office. Studies have shown that the recruitment rate is about the same for those who receive realistic job previews as for those who do not. More importantly, however, those who receive realistic previews are more likely to remain on the job and to express greater job satisfaction than those who received one-sided presentations. Realistic information facilitates the socialization process by helping individuals adjust to the job and the work environment.[4]

Realistic Job Previews, (RJPs): A recruiting strategy that involves telling applicants both the favorable and unfavorable aspects of the job so they have a more realistic understanding of it and can make an informed decision.

Stages of Career Development

Young children progress through a sequence of predictable developmental stages. These stages are characterized by both physical and psychological development, and they are remarkably stable across individuals. Thus, we can explain much of the behavior of young children by knowing their chronological age.

Adults, likewise, progress through a sequence of phases associated with their work. However, the adult phases are not as easy to delineate. The stages of transition in childhood, such as entering grade school, graduating from high school, and becoming old enough to drive or to vote are common experiences to almost all youth, while most of the clear advancements of adults are specific to their occupations. Nevertheless, even during adulthood, a series of relatively discrete career stages common to most people can be identified.

Life Stages. Erik H. Erikson is the author of a popular career development model that contains eight developmental stages.[5] According to Erikson, individuals must pass through eight developmental stages on their way to complete maturity. The first four stages—oral, anal, genital, and latency—describe childhood development. The last four stages, which are shown in Exhibit 4.3, describe the process of development from adolescence through maturity. Erikson believes that each stage is characterized by a particular developmental task or crisis that the person must resolve before advancing fully into the next stage.

Adolescent Stage:
The fifth stage of development, when individuals begin to develop their sexual and occupational identify.

During the *adolescent stage*, an individual attempts to establish a personal identity that includes both sexual identity as a male or female and occupational identity as a person who is expected to eventually become a working, functioning adult. Adolescents begin to develop their occupational interests and to solidify their career preferences during this stage. Occupational exploration is an important activity as they solidify their career interests and search for their first employment. High turnover among younger employees reflect their efforts to improve their employment. Young workers try to match their interests and abilities with the demands of a job. When better opportunities are presented, they anxiously pursue them.

Young adulthood stage:
The sixth stage of development when people learn how to work and to love, and how to develop a balance between work and love.

During the *young adulthood stage*, an individual learns how to work and to love, and how to pursue an intensity in both areas without destroying the balance that should exist between them. The developmental task at this stage is to develop involvements that include interpersonal intimacy along with learning how to let oneself become ego-involved with another person, or group, or organization, or cause.

During this stage, individuals strive to create a permanent position within their chosen occupation. There may be some trial and error early in this stage with subsequent career changes, but eventually individuals attempt to create a stable place within the organization to establish their worth and make their contribution. During this period the organization is also attempting to assess the long-term worth of the individual.

Individuals who resolve the crises during the first six stages exceptionally well become trustworthy, autonomous, industrious, highly competent at a variety of tasks, sure of their social and personal roles, and able to identify with and understand the intimate feelings of others. According to Erikson, however,

Exhibit 4.3   **The Last Four Developmental Stages of Erik Erikson**

Stage 5 Adolescence

Identity. Being able to find oneself and establish an accurate self-concept in terms of sexual identity and occupational aspirations.

versus

Role Confusion. Uncertainty regarding one's sexual identity and an inability to plan one's life in the direction of becoming a working, functioning adult.

Stage 6 Young Adulthood

Intimacy. Learning how to become ego-involved with other people, groups, organizations, and causes; learning how to work and love and achieve a balance between them.

versus

Isolation. Becoming absorbed in oneself or afraid to become involved with others; unable to share oneself with others.

Stage 7 Adulthood

Generativity. A concern for establishing and guiding the next generation; having the power to produce things and generate new ideas or new inventions.

versus

Stagnation. Standing still, producing nothing, becoming obsolete.

Stage 8 Maturity

Ego Integrity. Satisfaction with the life one has lived; an acceptance of the character one has acquired.

versus

Despair. Dissatisfaction with the life one has lived; a feeling of despair because time is too short to start another life or to try alternate roads to integrity.

Adulthood stage:
The seventh stage of development, when people are concerned about generativity versus stagnation.

Stagnation:
A condition of becoming unproductive or obsolete; the opposite of generativity.

Generativity:
A positive growth-oriented response of people in the adulthood stage of career development that involves a concern for establishing and guiding the next generation, having the power to produce things, and generating new ideas or new inventions.

Maturity:
The eighth and final stage of development when people face what they have made of their lives and either feel a sense of ego integrity or despair.

very few individuals are fortunate enough to successfully pass through all six stages, and therefore are a mixture of partial successes and failures. Anticipating these challenges and planning how to confront them, however, helps people proactively take charge of their lives and achieve higher levels of career success.

During the **adulthood stage**, an individual is concerned with **generativity**, which involves helping to socialize and establish the next generation. In a work setting, generativity may be achieved through endeavors such as developing creative theories, building organizations, coaching and sponsoring younger colleagues, and teaching and guiding students. The opposite of generativity is what Erikson calls **stagnation**, which means standing still, producing nothing, and becoming obsolete.

During this stage, individuals try to protect themselves and secure their positions within the organization. Leaving the organization to pursue a different career is much more difficult at this stage, and individuals who are laid off or terminated feel very threatened by such actions. The performance levels of individuals in this stage vary considerably. While some individuals continue to develop and grow and are highly productive, others begin to stagnate and deteriorate. Problems of obsolescence become particularly acute during this stage. Although some individuals continue to reach out and grasp new opportunities, others become overly concerned with security and survival.

Erikson's eighth stage—**maturity**—occurs during the final years of life as people face the end of life and thoughts of death. People who are satisfied with their lives and who can accept the character attributes they have developed are able to integrate the inevitability of death into their patterns of existence.

In this declining stage, individuals approach the end of their employment years and enter retirement. Although the decline stage is typically accompanied by a reduction in the physical and mental abilities of older employees, many older individuals are capable of contributing far more to the organization than the organization or society allows. Indeed, many of the great scientific discoveries and contributions to culture have been made by people who were beyond the normal retirement age.

According to Erikson's theory, individuals behave differently depending on which developmental stage they are in and how well they have resolved the crises and tasks of earlier stages. Erikson's theory is particularly useful in understanding career development and career stages. For most people, career stages influence how they perceive organizational events, such as the appointment of a new president or the introduction of a quality-improvement program. Career stages also provide a frame of reference through which organizational events are interpreted.

The concerns of people in the young adulthood stage are not the same as the concerns of those in the adulthood stage. During their early career years, when they are becoming established, people are primarily concerned about opportunities for advancement, social status, prestige, doing something important, recognition by others, opportunities to use special aptitudes, opportunities to be creative, and high salary. Many individuals early in their careers have unrealistically high aspirations and frequently feel a sense of reality shock as they realize their expectations were overly ambitious and unrealistic.

Career success during the young adulthood stage is greatly influenced by the individual's work assignments. The first year is a particularly crucial period, when new employees are susceptible to learning new attitudes and adjusting to the requirements of the job. Competent supervisors who patiently coach and encourage can have a profound influence on the career success of new employees.

During mid-career, when people are in the adulthood stage, they are concerned with a different set of issues than earlier. The aging process creates an awareness of the inevitability of death. People begin to realize that many of their career goals may never be achieved, and some are forced to search for more realistic life goals. During their early 40s, many experience a "mid-life crisis" that can be very traumatic and difficult. A variety of threatening circumstances often contribute to a feeling of anxiety and despair, such as rebellious teenagers at home, financial pressures, a growing sense of obsolescence on the job, and a threat of being replaced by a younger employee. While some people view these problems as challenges that spur them to higher levels of performance and competence, others are thrown into a state of constant defensiveness in which they simply try to endure. During the mid-life decade, which typically occurs between the ages of 35 and 45, individuals tend to appraise their life's accomplishments and ask such questions as, "What have I done with my life? What do I really get from and give to my spouse, children, friends, work, community, and self? What are my real values and how are they reflected in my life?" In one study of men during their mid-career, 80 percent experienced significant struggles over career or family that frequently resulted in moderate or severe crises, forcing these men to question every facet of their lives. To resolve these crises, many individuals were required to make new

Exhibit 4.4   Professional Career Stages

Central Activities, Relationships, and Psychological Issues in the Four Career Stages

	Stage I	Stage II	Stage III	Stage IV
Central Activity	Learning to work and follow directions	Independent contributor	Training Interfacing	Shaping the direction of the organization
Primary Relationship	Apprentice	Colleagues	Mentor	Sponsor
Major Psychological Issues	Dependence	Independence	Assuming responsibility for others	Exercising power

Source: From *Organizational Dynamics* (Summer 1977).

choices about career and family and accept a more realistic view of themselves and their limitations of time and ability.[6]

Apprentice:
A professional in the first career stage, who must learn to follow directions.

Independent Contributor:
A professional in the second career stage, who must learn to work independently.

Mentor:
A professional in the third career stage, who directs the work of apprentices.

Sponsor:
A professional in the fourth career stage, who is expected to shape the future of the company and standards of the profession.

Professional Career Stages. A model of career development that focuses specifically on professionals (engineers, lawyers, and accountants) has been developed by Gene Dalton and Paul Thompson.[7] Their research identified four career stages, as shown in Exhibit 4.4.

Stage I professionals are typically new employees who have recently completed their professional training and must now learn to work under the direction of someone who supervises their activities and evaluates their performance. Here they are expected to demonstrate their abilities to follow directions and perform competently.

Stage II professionals are independent contributors. After proving their competence under the direction of others, they are now ready to work on their own in performing their professional activities.

Stage III professionals are involved in training and directing the work of others, particularly those who are in Stage I. Professionals at this level are evaluated not only on their own performance but on their ability to supervise others.

Stage IV professionals are involved in making strategic decisions that guide the organization and shape its direction. They also perform crucial institutional functions that facilitate the firm's interactions with outside people and organizations.

Dalton and Thompson examined the relationship between career stages and performance, and found that the performance ratings of professionals depended in part on whether they were performing the "right" activities or, in other words, activities that were consistent with their career stage. For example, their data suggested that professionals older than 40 were generally not considered above-average performers unless they had moved into Stages III and IV. Only 18 percent of those over age 40 who were rated as above-average performers were in Stage I or II. Apparently, age and experience are associated with fairly well-accepted expectations about the kinds of activities individuals should be performing. Those who are performing activities inconsistent with their professional career stage generally suffer from a lack of social acceptance.

TRAINING AND DEVELOPMENT

Training and development are important activities in all organizations, large and small. Every organization, regardless of size, needs to have well-trained employees who are prepared to perform their jobs. Approximately three million new employees enter the workforce each year and need to be trained. Even those who have been trained in professional and technical fields require orientation training to help them understand their specific roles in an organization. Present employees also need training. Because of the rapidly expanding technology and the growth of new knowledge, there is a need for continual retraining of experienced workers to perform new and changed jobs.

The terms training, development, education, and learning all refer to a similar process—it is the process that enables people to acquire new knowledge, learn new skills, and perform behaviors in a new way. Although training and education are quite similar, a distinction usually is made between them. *Training* refers to the acquisition of specific skills or knowledge. Training programs attempt to teach trainees how to perform particular activities or a specific job. *Education*, on the other hand, is much more general, and attempts to provide students with general knowledge that can be applied in many different settings.

To illustrate the differences, teaching an employee how to use a specific computer program that has already been written to produce a computerized payroll is an example of training, but teaching an employee how to program a computer using a computer language is an illustration of education. Specific instruction on how to produce a payroll helps the employee perform a specific activity. But learning how to use a computer language helps the employee obtain general skills that can be applied to many different situations.

Another distinction between training and education concerns their effects on the range of responses. Training tends to narrow the range of responses, so that all employees who have been trained will make the same response in a specific situation. Education, on the other hand, tends to broaden the range of responses, so that individuals who have obtained a general education will respond to a particular situation in a variety of different ways.

Training:
The process of acquiring specific information or skills that tend to reduce the variability or range of responses by trainees.

Education:
The process of acquiring general knowledge and information that usually results in a broadening of responses that students are likely to make.

A Systems Model for Training

A model showing how training programs should be developed and implemented is presented in Exhibit 4.5. This exhibit illustrates the three phases of training: (1) an assessment phase, (2) a training and development phase, and (3) an evaluation phase.[8]

In the assessment phase, the need for training and development is examined, as well as the resources available to provide the training both within the organization and in the external environment. The assessment should include a consideration of who should be trained, what sort of training they will need, and how such training will benefit the organization. The objectives of the training program are derived from the assessment. These objectives play a vital role in both the development of the training program and its subsequent evaluation.

Systems Model of Training:
A model that views training as an ongoing cycle of assessing training needs, providing training, and evaluating how well the needs have been met.

Exhibit 4.5   A Systems Model for Training

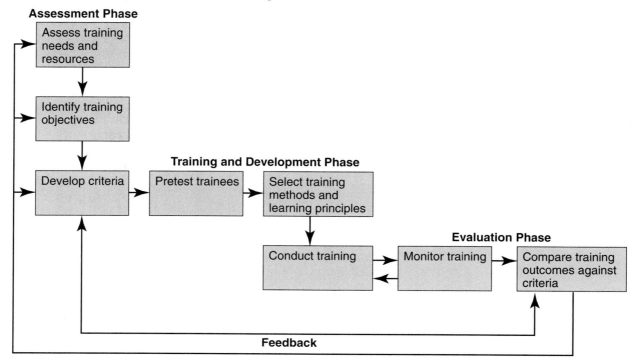

In the training and development phase, the training is designed and presented. The training should contain activities and learning experiences that satisfy the objectives established in the assessment phase. Many different training activities, including both on-the-job and off-the-job activities, can be used, depending on the objectives of the training.

After the training has been conducted, the evaluation occurs. The first step in evaluating the success of a training program is deciding what the evaluation criteria are. These criteria should be based on the initial objectives of the training. For example, was the purpose of the training to disseminate new information, to change certain behaviors, to acquire new skills, or to change specific attitudes? Once the criteria have been established, the trainees can be evaluated to determine whether the training was successful. The evaluation also should assess whether the learning that occurred in the training program transferred to the actual job situation.

The feedback arrow at the bottom of Exhibit 4.5 emphasizes the idea that training should be ongoing. Training does not have a definite beginning and ending—it is an ongoing process of assessing needs, presenting programs, and evaluating results to determine how well organizational needs have been satisfied and what additional training is needed. Because it is an ongoing process, the degree to which a training program has met its objectives cannot really be assessed at one particular point in time. Instead, the effects of training have to be viewed in terms of their short-term and long-term implications.

Principles of Learning

The design and presentation of training programs should be consistent with the two major learning theories: operant conditioning and social cognitive theory. These theories, which are explained in chapter 7, suggest that the following principles of learning are important in designing training programs.

1. *Meaningful organization of training materials.* To facilitate learning, the stimulus should be easily perceived and meaningfully organized. For example, learning calculus is easiest when the text describing how to do it is written logically so that one idea builds on another. Learning to drive is simplified when the visual field of stop signs, intersections, and other objects can be perceived easily. Learning safety procedures is easiest when they are explained in a logical and systematic order.

2. *Practice and repetition.* Rote learning and motor response learning consist of developing stimulus-response associations—when the appropriate stimulus is presented, the trainee should make the correct response. To increase the likelihood that the trainee will make the correct response on future occasions, operant conditioning recommends that the response be rehearsed through extensive practice accompanied by intermittent reinforcement. To gain the full benefit of training, learned behavior must be *overlearned* to ensure smooth performance and a minimum of forgetting at a later date. However, practice is not as necessary for learning ideas and insights. Many human behaviors are performed with little or no practice. Studies of imitative behavior have shown that after watching models perform a novel behavior, observers can later describe the behavior with considerable accuracy, and, given appropriate incentives, the observers are able to reproduce the behavior exactly on the first trial.[9]

3. *Motivation and active participation.* Training programs do not succeed unless trainees are receptive to the instruction and motivated to learn. As a general rule, learning improves as the rewards for learning increase. Active participation and involvement with others are usually highly reinforcing. Both intrinsic satisfaction and extrinsic rewards can be used to facilitate training. Most learning situations are intrinsically reinforcing because of the satisfaction associated with acquiring new knowledge or skills. However, intrinsic satisfaction by itself is not enough to perpetuate new learning.[10] Even safety training to reduce accidents that cause death and disability is not sufficiently self-rewarding to change behavior without additional incentives.[11] Companies are required to provide other forms of rewards or punishment, such as financial incentives, recognition, intergroup competition, or the threat of being fired.

4. *Feedback: knowledge of results.* Performance feedback is a necessary prerequisite for learning.[12] Feedback improves performance not only by helping learners correct their mistakes but also by providing reinforcement for learning. Knowledge of results is a positive form of reinforcement by itself. Learning activities have more intrinsic interest when performance feedback is available. Performance feedback should inform learners whether they were right or wrong and, when possible, explain how they can avoid making mistakes in the future. In general, knowledge of results is an essential feature of learning, and the sooner this knowledge comes after the learner's response, the better. Studies in animal

learning suggest that the ideal timing of the feedback is to have it occur almost immediately after the response has been made.[13]

5. *Transfer of training.* Transfer of training occurs when trainees can apply the knowledge and skills learned in training back to their jobs. If the learning does not transfer, then the training has failed. Three transfer-of-training situations are possible: (1) Positive transfer of training occurs when the training activities enhance performance in the new situation, (2) negative transfer of training occurs when the training activities inhibit performance in the new situation, and (3) no observable effect of training could occur. The conditions that determine whether positive, negative, or no transfer of training will result depend on the similarity of the two environments and how similar the responses learned in training are to the responses required on the actual job.

Training and Development Techniques

Job instruction training:
An extensively used training technique that consists of showing a trainee how to perform a task and supervising the trainee's attempts to learn it.

Apprenticeship:
A training technique in which the trainee, or apprentice, works under the direction of a skilled employee who teaches the apprentice how to perform the job.

Internship:
A learning experience in which students are able to work for a period of time and apply the information they have learned.

Job rotations:
A training technique that involves transferring trainees to different jobs to broaden their focus and to increase their knowledge.

Junior Boards:
A training technique that consists of assigning new trainees to an executive board that is responsible for making a decision.

Training and development techniques are categorized as on-the-job or off-the-job techniques. Some training techniques, such as classroom instruction, are fairly typical, while others are unusual and novel, such as taking a group of executives on a wilderness survival adventure.

On-the-Job Techniques. On-the-job training does not require special space or equipment, and it allows employees to produce and earn while they learn. It also allows employees to practice what they are expected to do after training ends, and to associate with their future coworkers. On-the-job training techniques include the following:

1. *Job instruction training* is the most popular form of training. The trainer explains the purpose of the job and provides a step-by-step demonstration of the job operations. After the trainer has demonstrated the job enough times for the trainee to comprehend the steps, the trainee is given the opportunity to try it alone.
2. *Apprenticeships* allow new workers, called apprentices, to work alongside and under the direction of skilled technicians until they are qualified to become a journeyman.
3. *Internships and assistantships* provide opportunities for students to work in a company under the direction of a supervisor and a faculty member. These internships may be part of what is called a "cooperative education" project. Students are frequently expected to write reports describing their experiences and what they have learned, and they typically receive academic credit toward graduation for such experiences.
4. *Job rotations and transfers* are usually reserved for managerial and technical occupations. Movement from one position to another exposes managers to different job functions, and helps them acquire a broad grasp of the overall purpose of an organization.
5. *Junior boards and committee assignments* provide trainees with the opportunity to interact with other executives and observe how they perform while participating on a committee responsible for making administrative decisions or recommendations.

6. *Coaching and counseling* provide systematic feedback on performance, encouragement by the trainer, and patient explanations of how to perform a job accurately.

Off-the-Job Techniques. Off-the-job training generally focuses more on long-term development and general education than on the skills and information needed to perform a specific job. Because off-the-job programs focus more on learning and less on production, they provide trainees with an environment that is conducive to concentrating on new ideas and engaging in reflective thought. The major disadvantage of off-the-job training is that it does not provide immediate transfer of training to real job situations.

Vestibule training:
Training that occurs in a special training room that is a replication of the actual job situation.

1. *Vestibule training* is similar to on-the-job training except that it occurs in a separate training area equipped like the actual production area. The training that occurs in a vestibule is usually some form of job-instruction training. In vestibule training, however, the emphasis is on learning as opposed to the emphasis on production in job-instruction training. Vestibule training is typically used for teaching specific job skills.
2. A *lecture* is an efficient means of transmitting large amounts of factual information to a relatively large number of people at the same time. A skilled lecturer can organize material and present it in a clear and understandable way. If the trainees are ready to receive it, a well-prepared lecture may succeed in transferring conceptual knowledge. However, a lecture does not allow active participation by the learners, nor does it provide for practice, feedback, or knowledge of results.
3. *Independent self-study* allows learners to train themselves. The most frequent kinds of self-study activities are reading books and professional magazines, taking special courses through a local university, and attending professional meetings. The tremendous increase in new technology has increased the need for employees to train themselves using owners' manuals and other handbooks. Although most employees do not have the motivation to undertake a special study program as an ongoing form of personal development, they can be motivated to do so if there are adequate opportunities for promotion and pay increases.
4. *Visual presentations* include television, films, and video presentations of real-life events or animated cartoons. Real-life photography can make the training seem real and factual, but drawings can emphasize expressions, emotions, and ideas with few conflicting stimuli.
5. *Conferences and discussions* provide forums where individuals are able to learn from one another. A major use of group discussion is to change attitudes and behavior. Numerous studies have shown that individuals are much more inclined to change their attitudes if they are part of a consensus decision than if they listen to a lecture.[14]

Teleconferencing:
A training method that involves the use of televised instruction between trainers and trainees in different locations.

6. *Teleconferencing* makes it possible for a trainer to be in one location while the learners are in many other locations watching the trainer on a television monitor. It requires higher levels of skill for the trainers because they may be speaking only to a video camera and may be unable to observe how well their ideas are being received. Greater demands are also placed on the learners, who are encouraged to ask questions and provide feedback to the trainer.

7. *Case discussions* help students discover underlying principles by discussing specific events or experiences. Most cases do not have a single correct solution. Instead, a trainee is expected to analyze the problem and consider alternative solutions. Even though trainees may not agree on the best solution, a fair amount of agreement about the relevant issues should exist.

8. *Role playing* requires learners to act a particular role in a specific situation. Rather than simply talking about what the solution should be, the participants attempt to solve the situation as if they were the individuals involved. Role playing usually creates a higher level of participation than regular group discussion. It is also an effective method to facilitate attitude change when participants play roles that require them to express attitudes that are the opposite of their own personal feelings, called *counter-attitudinal role playing*. When individuals participate in counter-attitudinal role playing, their private opinions typically shift in the direction of the arguments they present.[15]

9. *Simulations* create an artificial learning environment that approximates the actual job conditions as much as possible; they have been used extensively for learning technical and motor skills. Business simulations also motivate students to learn on their own. Students will voluntarily master even difficult concepts, such as break-even analysis and linear programming, if making an effective decision requires it. Computer simulations allow participants to examine the long-term effects of their business decisions in a relatively short period of time. If they make bad decisions, they can learn from their mistakes without having to suffer the actual consequences.

10. *Programmed instruction* is an application of the principles of operant conditioning to training. It involves dividing the material to be learned into small learning segments, usually called frames, and having the learner make a response after each frame to demonstrate mastery of it. The trainees know immediately whether their responses are correct or incorrect. This feedback has the advantage of giving immediate reinforcement as well as knowledge of results.

11. ***Computer-based training (CBT)*** refers to any form of interactive learning experience between a computer and a learner, in which the computer provides the majority of the stimulus and the learner is required to make some form of response during the learning.

12. ***Experiential exercises*** involve trainees working together in a discussion group to solve a specific problem. Although the problem may be artificial, the participation by each trainee within the group is not artificial. Participants interact with each other as if they were in a real problem-solving situation. After the decision has been reached, participants discuss what occurred, analyze the group processes, and analyze the behavior of each person in the group. Valuable learning occurs not only during the actual exercise but also during the following discussion.

Computer-based training:
Training presented to learners using a computer, and often the Internet, which allows them to study on their own and at their own pace.

Experiential learning:
Learning that usually occurs in groups in which members participate in a group activity and then discuss what they observed and learned.

Since so many different techniques are available, trainers should consider the advantages and disadvantages of each, relative to the situation. The selection should be determined primarily by the objective of the training. For example, a lecture is ideal for disseminating a large amount of information to learners who are already motivated to receive it. But the lecture is not useful for changing attitudes or teaching new motor skills.

The design of an ideal training program should be consistent with the five principles of learning. Job instruction training and vestibule training, for example, are generally very effective techniques because they utilize all five training principles—the stimulus is meaningful, trainees have an opportunity to practice the response, they are motivated by encouragement, they receive immediate feedback on their performance, and the new learning transfers directly back to the job. However, all five principles may not be equally important, depending on the particular training activity. For example, all five principles may not be important in a lecture to a group of sales representatives about changes in the product mix for the coming year. A carefully organized lecture or video-tape presentation of information may be adequate, and therefore, the four principles of active participation, knowledge of results, practice, and transfer of training would not be required.

Orientation Training

Orientation training plays an important role in helping new employees understand the company's culture and their specific job expectations. Good orientation training can reduce turnover, alleviate anxiety, create positive work values, reduce start-up costs, and save the time of supervisors and coworkers.

Effective orientation training contains a brief explanation of the mission of the organization to inspire new employees, plus the basic survival information they need to know to help them get started. The most relevant and useful information is: working hours, including breaks and lunch hours; location of facilities, especially the new employee's office, rest rooms, and eating places; health and safety considerations, such as safe operating procedures, fire escapes, exits, first-aid supplies, and location of the nursing station; and information on whom to contact in case of problems or difficulties.

In designing an orientation program, the trainer should carefully consider the kinds of impressions and expectations that the program should create. Initial expectations have a profound influence on the behavior and values of new employees. Since new employees do not know what to anticipate, the comments made during an orientation program generate rather profound expectations that have a way of becoming a self-fulfilling prophecy. For example, employees who are told that they are expected to become outstanding performers often become just that.

During the orientation program, an attempt should be made to reduce anxiety. Since new employees are usually concerned about being able to perform adequately on the job, they ought to know that their chances of succeeding are very good and that other individuals just like them have succeeded in the past. Anxiety is also reduced by acquainting new employees with their supervisors and coworkers.

New employees should be warned if they are likely to face hazing by coworkers. Hazing refers to the harassment of new employees by senior coworkers, such as laughing at their mistakes, making derogatory comments, asking them to perform impossible tasks, and telling them they don't have what it takes. If it occurs, they should be encouraged to ignore it or accept it in good humor; however, abusive hazing should not be tolerated or permitted.

An experienced coworker or supervisor should be assigned to each new employee as a *sponsor* or *mentor.* The purpose of the sponsor is to provide specific job-related instructions and other information regarding the informal work-group norms and procedures. The sponsor should provide encouragement and advice, and should be available to answer questions as they arise. A major role of the mentor is to help introduce the new employee to other members of the work group. These introductions are generally best if they do not occur all at once. New employees should be introduced to their coworkers gradually.

Organizations often want to present the entire orientation training the first day and get it over with. If they want employees to remember it, however, the training should either be spaced over a period of time, or written instructions should be provided. Written instructions are particularly necessary for detailed information. Although new employees should know about the company's policies, benefits, and work procedures, they should not be expected to remember them if they are presented in one long session. A better procedure is to highlight the most important issues in the training and provide detailed material in an employee handbook that employees can read later as issues arise.

In summary, the guidelines for developing an effective training program include the following:

- Begin with the most relevant information.
- Provide sponsors or mentors to help new employees learn the ropes.
- Gradually introduce new employees to members of the work group.
- Space the orientation training over a period of time rather than concentrating it in one long session.
- Provide both oral and written information. Oral instruction should provide general orientation information, while detailed, specific information should be written.

Discussion Questions

1. Using one of the career development models in the text, describe the various career stages, and indicate which stage you are in. What do you need to do to be successful in this career stage and prepare yourself for the next stage?
2. What is the most important information new employees need to know to begin a job? Describe a time you started a new position (work, school, or church) and describe your orientation experience and how you think it could have been improved.
3. Identify and describe the crucial principles of learning associated with teaching a child to ride a bicycle. Describe a skill or talent you have recently acquired, and explain the learning principles involved in your acquisition.

Notes

1. Abraham A. Maslow, "A Theory of Metamotivation: The Biological Rooting of the Value-Life," *Psychology Today* 2 (July 1968): 38, 39, 58–61.
2. Arnold van Gennep, *The Rights of Passage* (Chicago: University of Chicago Press, 1960).

3. Douglas T. Hall, *Careers in Organizations* (Pacific Palisades, CA: Goodyear Publishing Company, 1976), chapter 5.

4. Robert J. Vandenberg and Vida Scarpello, "The Matching Model: An Examination of the Processes Underlying Realistic Job Previews," *Journal of Applied Psychology* 75, (1990): 60–67.

5. Erik H. Erikson, *Childhood and Society*, 2nd ed. (New York: Norton, 1963).

6. D. J. Levinson, "The Mid-life Transition: A Period in Adult Psychological Development," *Psychiatry* 40 (1977): 99–112.

7. Gene W. Dalton, Paul H. Thompson, and Ray L. Price, "The Four Stages of Professional Careers: A New Look at Performance by Professionals," *Organizational Dynamics* 6 (1977): 19–42; Gene W. Dalton and Paul H. Thompson, *Novations: Strategies for Career Management*, (Glenview, IL: Scott Foresman and Company, 1986).

8. See, for example, Todd Heider, "The Tailored Course: Saving Money and Time," *Training and Development Journal* 43 (February 1989): 42–45.

9. Albert Bandura, ed., *Psychological Modeling: Conflicting Theories* (Chicago: Aldine-Atherton, 1971); J.P. Flanders, "A Review of Research on Imitative Behavior," *Psychological Bulletin* 69 (1968): 316–37.

10. Richard W. Malott, *Contingency Management in Education* (Kalamazoo, MI: Behaviordelia, 1972), chapter 9.

11. "Adding Incentives to Safety Training Cuts Injuries, Boosts Productivity," *Training: The Magazine of Human Resources Development* 17, no. 7 (July 1980): A2–A3. See also A3–A15.

12. Edward L. Thorndike, et al., *The Fundamentals of Learning* (New York: Teachers College, Columbia University, 1932).

13. George S. Reynolds, *A Primer of Operant Conditioning*, rev. ed. (Glenview, IL: Scott, Foresman, 1975), chapters 2–4.

14. Kurt Lewin, "Group Decisions and Social Change," in *Readings in Social Psychology*, 2nd ed., G.E. Swanson, T.M. Newcomb, and E. L. Hartley, eds. (New York: Holt, 1952), 459–73.

15. Alan C. Elms, *Role Playing, Reward, and Attitude Change* (New York: Van Nostrand, 1969)

Japanese Leadership Boot Camp

Business is viewed as a martial art in Japan. Mid-level executives who do not qualify for advancement in many companies are sent to Kanreisha Yosei Gakko on Mt. Fuji, the most famous business school in Japan. Companies such as Nissan and Honda pay $2000 tuition for struggling executives who should be ready for promotion but aren't, to attend this two-week training. This intense executive training program represents a pass-fail opportunity for those who are sent. Those who pass, continue their assent up the corporate ranks. Failure means more than just career derailment, it also brings social disgrace and family dishonor.

The students, who are men and women in their thirties and forties, are expected to prove their dedication to their companies, and ultimately to Japan, through creating profitable businesses. The training is called "Hell Camp" partly because of its physical rigors, but mostly because of its emotional trauma and mental attacks. Like military boot camps, these students are demeaned and re-shaped in preparation for war against global companies like GE and IBM.

This business school does not teach business fundamentals; instead, it focuses on building the confidence and fighting spirit students will need to succeed in global business. The training is intense. Each student receives fourteen ribbons of shame that must be removed one assignment at a time before he or she can graduate. Yelling, assertiveness, and even laughter are part of what they learn as their instructors work to destroy and then rebuild their self-conceptions. Their weaknesses are not overcome by necessarily being the best or the brightest, but in many instances, by being the loudest and the fastest. Students must learn how to be aggressive, have clear pronunciation, be comfortable outside of their comfort zone, and even how to sing, not necessarily well, but loud. Activities include standing in a busy subway station singing the school song, making telephone sales calls, and debating issues with each other. They are evaluated on whether their singing was in full voice, their phone etiquette was commanding and firm, and their arguing was quick and opinionated. Groups of students are sent on rigorous mountain hikes with maps that are inconsistent and inaccurate, to see how they lead, make decisions, and resolve conflicts.

Students who do not remove all fourteen ribbons of shame in the first thirteen days are given three more days of intense work to complete the course. If they fail, their future as a manager is probably over and they return in shame to their families and friends. If they succeed, they return to their companies better socialized and prepared for higher levels of responsibility. This socialization experience produces an immense sense of satisfaction and confidence in their ability to compete in a global market and bring success to their company and, ultimately, Japan.

Questions

1. What are the strengths and weaknesses of rigorous training programs like this that try to intentionally destroy one's self concept and then rebuild it?
2. How well would this intense socialization training be accepted in the United States and elsewhere?
3. Would this type of intense socialization experience be beneficial for other groups, such as a military unit or a police academy?

Rites of Passage or Sex Discrimination?

Since engineering has been a male-dominated profession, Patricia Davis was very pleased when she landed an engineering job with the Streuling Scientific Company, even though she was the only female engineer. Patricia did well in graduate school and expected to be accepted as a competent professional within the company. As a graduate student, Pat often received differential treatment, and she struggled to be accepted as a legitimate student. Pat resolved that on her first job she would not allow anyone to treat her as a second-class citizen. Instead, she would insist on being treated as a professional equal to others in the engineering department.

During her first six weeks, Pat was pleased with how well she was accepted by her colleagues. Her first job assignment was challenging but her colleagues willingly provided assistance. After six weeks she had finished her first project and looked forward to presenting it to the engineering group in a "project defense" meeting.

During lunch the day before Pat was to make her project defense, one of the engineers tried to warn Pat about what she would face the next day. In a hushed voice he said, "You'd better be ready for tomorrow because they will be coming after you with their guns loaded."

Because she was disturbed by this comment, Pat called Carl Mahoney in advertising. Carl was the husband of a former roommate in college, and she trusted him to give her a straight answer. Carl told her he didn't think the comment meant anything, but after he hung up, he decided to check into it. Carl was very disturbed by what he learned.

When junior engineers complete a project, they are expected to present it to a group of senior engineers. Anyone interested is invited to attend these presentations. Normally, only a few people attend, but when it is the first presentation for a new engineer, the custom has developed for many people to attend and ask tough questions. The first project defense for new engineers is viewed as an initiation ceremony during which the work of a new engineer is severely challenged. Many of the engineers referred to their first project defense as "baptism by fire," and it was generally believed that no one was accepted fully as a member of the engineering department until he or she had survived the first project defense. Although the event was extremely threatening and unpleasant, the engineers viewed it as a valuable ritual that helped new engineers understand the importance of thorough and careful work.

Carl learned that the entire engineering department planned to attend Pat's project defense. Realizing how threatening this situation would be, several of the engineers were informally betting on how long Pat would last before she left the room in tears. Carl was told not to warn Pat because there was nothing she could do at this point, and she would probably perform better if she entered the room expecting a positive experience rather than feeling threatened.

Discussion Questions

1. Do you agree that the project defense is a useful rite of passage, and what are the consequences of changing or eliminating it for Patricia Davis?
2. How is this an illustration of sex discrimination?
3. Should Carl say anything to Pat, or should he try to intervene by talking to anyone else in the organization?
4. Do any of the engineers have a moral or social responsibility to protect Pat?

5

Employee Relations and Equal Employment Opportunity

Chapter Outline

Employment Law

Fair Employment Practices

Labor Relations Laws

Organizing a Union

Negotiating an Agreement

Equal Employment Opportunity

Civil Rights Laws

Affirmative Action

Discrimination

Race and National Origin Discrimination

Gender Discrimination

Sexual Harassment

Religious Discrimination

Age Discrimination

Disability Discrimination

EMPLOYMENT LAW

Fair Employment Practices

People deserve to be treated fairly at work. Effective organizations have human resource policies and practices that treat people with respect and protect them from unfair discrimination. The following list of moral principles represents an ethical Bill of Rights for treating people fairly:

1. All employment decisions regarding hiring, promotion, pay increases, training opportunities, and terminations should be based on objective, performance-related criteria rather than on subjective biases or personal whims. This means that employment decisions should be more than just non-discriminatory; they should be based on job-related criteria.

2. Each employee should be treated as a person of worth, with dignity and respect, rather than as an object that can be physically, sexually, or verbally abused. Employees should not be subjected to unwelcome or intimidating acts.

3. Disciplinary actions and criticisms should only occur for good cause, and employees should have the right to due process before any punitive actions are taken.

4. Employees should not be terminated unless their jobs are eliminated or they are unable to perform them. Personal whims and personality clashes are not valid reasons for termination.

5. Performance should be fairly and objectively evaluated against clearly defined standards; the evaluation should not be influenced by subjective biases or irrelevant personality traits.

6. Employees should be fairly and equitably paid for their work on the basis of the job's requirements, the employee's performance, and the employee's knowledge, skills, and abilities. One person should not be paid more than another unless there is a legitimate, job-related reason for it.

7. Employees should be taught how to perform their jobs, and they deserve accurate and timely feedback on their performance.

8. Employees should have a safe and healthy work environment that is free from unnecessary hazards or harmful substances, and they should be informed about anything that could cause health problems.

9. An employee's personal health and family responsibilities have a higher priority than organizational responsibilities; therefore, the organization should make reasonable accommodations to help employees with personal problems and family emergencies.

10. Organizations should not invade employees' personal privacy. Only relevant, job-related information should be disseminated within an organization; nothing personal should be disseminated outside the organization unless the employee authorizes it or the outside party has a legitimate need to know.

If every employer followed these moral principles, employees would be treated fairly, and the plethora of state and federal anti-discrimination laws would be unnecessary. But because of abuses in the past, employers are now required to abide by numerous laws that regulate how employees should be treated.

Although employers may disagree about the need for some of these laws, a careful analysis of the employment conditions at the time they were passed explains why each law was necessary to correct an abusive situation.

Labor Relations Laws

During the 1800s employees were virtually powerless against employers' arbitrary wage cuts and terminations. In some situations, employees' wages were arbitrarily reduced even though the rent for company-owned housing remained unchanged. From 1806 to 1842, employees were guilty of a criminal conspiracy in restraint of trade if two or more of them simultaneously decided to quit. Eventually, employees were allowed to organize unions to protest management actions, and later they were allowed to strike to enforce their demands. Although these were important gains for labor, the strikes were still ineffective; the balance of power was clearly in the hands of employers, who used court injunctions, yellow-dog contracts, union spies, and even violence to destroy the effectiveness of unions. A *yellow dog contract* is a statement that employees were required to sign before they could be hired, stating that they were not union members nor would they join a labor union or encourage others to join. *(Yellow Dog* was a derisive term for a lackey or coward.) These contracts helped employers obtain court injunctions to prevent strikes, and workers who violated the injunctions were held in contempt of court.

The history of labor relations in America demonstrates that employers are much more powerful than individual employees are, and that employees need some form of protective legislation. Congress has passed four major labor relations laws to protect unions and create a better balance of power between employers and employees.

The *Norris-LaGuardia Act* of 1932 limited the use of court injunctions and prevented the courts from interfering in picketing and union meetings.

The *National Labor Relations Act* of 1935 provided for the establishment of unions and declared that labor disputes should be settled peacefully through collective bargaining between the company and representatives of the workers. Settling disputes through collective bargaining became a national policy in all industries. This act also created the *National Labor Relations Board (NLRB)* and charged it with the responsibility of supervising union elections and resolving unfair labor charges.

The *Taft-Hartley Act* was passed in 1947 to create a better balance of power between unions and employers. During the 1940s, the balance of power favored unions; unions grew rapidly and they wanted to exercise their new power. Many strikes were prevented only because of wartime demands. When the war was over, the nation experienced a record number of lost days because of strikes. The Taft-Hartley Act identified and eliminated unfair labor practices, such as forcing employees to join the union, charging excessive dues, or coercing employees to participate in union activities.

The *Landrum-Griffin Act,* passed in 1959, required that unions use democratic procedures. During the 1950s, a congressional investigation revealed a serious misuse of union funds and other abuses by union leadership. As a consequence of these abuses, the act required that union leaders be democratically elected and union policies be approved by the vote of the membership.

Yellow-dog contract:
A statement employees were required to sign in which they agreed not to join a union.

National Labor Relations Board:
The agency created by the National Labor Relations Act that is assigned to resolve charges of unfair labor practices and to conduct fair representation elections.

Some people criticize labor unions for generating restrictive work rules, demanding exorbitant wage rates, disrupting important public services, creating inflationary pressures, protecting incompetent workers, limiting the rights of nonunion workers, and instigating violent acts. Other people praise unions for protecting employees from arbitrary management decisions, providing safe and pleasant working conditions, and increasing wages and benefits so that workers can have a decent standard of living. Union sympathizers claim that unions are necessary to protect employees from arbitrary management actions. They say that unions provide a necessary balance of power in negotiations with large, powerful corporations. Union critics claim that unions abuse their power by disregarding productive efficiency, and that they threaten rather than protect the rights of individual workers to have secure jobs.

Like political issues, these arguments could be debated endlessly. Deciding whether one side is right or wrong, however, is not as important as understanding both sides of the issue. You should be able to appreciate both views regardless of your biases. As a general rule, *companies that are unionized deserve to be* because of how they have treated their employees. And for the same reason, *companies deserve the kind of working relationship they have with their union.*

Organizing a Union

The procedure for organizing a labor union involves electing union officers and gaining recognition as the bargaining representative of the workers. Some employers voluntarily recognize the union; however, most employers require that the union be certified through an NLRB-supervised election.

The typical organizing procedure starts when employees sign authorization cards requesting an NLRB-supervised election. Once 30 percent of the employees have signed authorization cards, the NLRB notifies the company that an election will be held on a given date. The NLRB supervises the election. If a majority of the workers vote in favor of having a union represent them, the union is certified as the bargaining representative of the employees, and the employer is required to negotiate with it in good faith bargaining.

The process for decertifying a labor union follows the same procedure. The NLRB must receive a petition from at least 30 percent of the workers calling for an election. After the usual investigation, an election is held. If less than 50 percent vote in favor of the union, the union is decertified.

The time just prior to an election is an intense period when employers and union representatives campaign for employee support. Both sides need to know the special laws limiting what they can and cannot do. Many activities that are normally legal become illegal prior to a representation election. The Taft-Hartley Act allows unions and employers to express their views and disseminate information, as long as it "contains no threat of reprisal or force or promise of benefit."

The NLRB has established a lengthy list of guidelines for fair elections. The general intent of the board is to provide conditions that are as close to ideal as possible so that the uninhibited desires of the employees can be determined. Any evidence of violence by either management or union is certain to be condemned by the board. Many other actions also are illegal because they violate the employees' freedom of choice. When violations by either side are observed and the guilty party receives a majority vote, the NLRB can order a new election or override the results. For example, the board has ruled that an election is invalid when an employer visits employees in their homes or assembles them in a manager's office for the purpose of urging them to reject the union. Employers cannot single out certain employees and talk with them individually or in small groups, nor can an employer question employees about their union sentiments.

An employer must not threaten economic retaliation if the union wins the election. The employer cannot suggest that there will be a loss in wages or benefits if a union is elected, nor can an employer threaten to divert production to another nonunion facility, threaten to close the plant, or in any other way intimate that the employees might lose their jobs if they vote in favor of a union. However, the employer is not prevented from presenting factual information to employees about the economic effects of union representation or the consequences of increased labor costs.

During an election campaign, employers are generally not free to grant wage increases or benefits improvements unless they can demonstrate that these changes are completely unrelated to the campaign. Normally this means that all wage-and-benefit improvements have to be announced either before or after the election campaign. Nor can an employer announce a wage or benefit improvement that will begin after the election regardless of the outcome. Such an announcement appears to imply an incentive to defeat the union by showing that the union is not needed to obtain better wages.

Employers are allowed to assemble their employees on company time and disseminate information without being required to provide equal time for the union. The meeting place, however, must be a customary meeting place and not a place having a "special impact of awe," such as the company president's office. Since the union is generally not given equal access to a captive audience of employees on company time, union representatives often meet with employees in their homes.

Even though employers are not allowed to threaten employees, promise rewards, or use inflammatory rhetoric during an organizing campaign, they are free to describe aggressively the disadvantages of a unionized company. An employer can remind employees that if they organize a union, they will have to pay union dues. The employer can show employees the union's financial reports, and tell them that if they become union members, most of their dues will be used to pay the salaries and expense accounts of union officials. The employer can explain that collective bargaining and grievances are costly because both sides need to request highly paid experts to settle the disputes and that the company would prefer to see both sides keep their money. An employer can also show that union activities such as strikes, bargaining, and grievances are costly to the employees, the company, and society, because of lost production and lost time during these periods. The employer can present information showing the indirect costs of unionization which the company wants to avoid: executive time spent in bargaining sessions, working time of employees spent on union business, payment of arbitrator's fees, and costs of hiring lawyers and labor relations experts. Money for such costs obviously cannot go to the company as profits or to the employees as higher wages.

An employer also is free to explain how a union can limit the employees' personal freedoms. Employees who join unions have to obey the orders of union officials, within the scope of their authority, which means that the employees will have two bosses instead of one. Once the employees join a union, the union's constitution becomes a binding contract between them and the union, and they will be expected to obey all union rules. An employer is free to explain that a union's constitution contains provisions for punishable union offenses, union trials, suspensions, expulsions, and fines. Finally, the employer can point out that a union represents a threat to job security, since the union may call a strike regardless of a given employee's feelings, and can fine employees who cross its picket line.

Negotiating an Agreement

Collective bargaining basically consists of management and union representatives coming together to reach an agreement that will be acceptable to their constituents. The process can be smooth and uncomplicated if both parties are willing to negotiate cooperatively. However, the process can also be extremely combative and time-consuming. The bargaining process usually consists of four stages:

1. *Opening presentation of demands.* During the first formal bargaining meeting, both sides present their demands, unless they have been exchanged beforehand. The union typically goes first, and the management team asks questions to clarify the issues and to assess the importance of each demand. The first meeting usually determines whether the bargaining will be a combative struggle or a cooperative, problem-solving effort.
2. *Analyzing the demands.* The demands submitted by each side usually include some that absolutely must be fulfilled before an agreement can be reached, others that are desirable but not necessary, and a few that are included just for trading purposes. The negotiators examine each other's lists and try to identify the real issues.
3. *Compromise.* When the interests of both sides are not identical, a compromise must be achieved. Generally, each side continues to make counter-proposals until an agreement is reached.
4. *Informal settlement and ratification.* After both sides have obtained what they feel is their best compromise, their agreement must be ratified. Top management assesses whether the tentative agreement allows them to operate the company efficiently and profitably. The agreement is then presented to the union membership to obtain their ratification.

Two very different strategies for reaching an agreement are distributive bargaining and integrative bargaining.[1]

Distributive bargaining:
A bargaining strategy in which each party tries to maximize its own outcomes at the expense of the other party.

Integrative bargaining:
A bargaining strategy in which both parties work together cooperatively to achieve the best outcome for both.

Distributive bargaining refers to conflictive negotiation, in which each side negotiates aggressively to receive the largest share of the rewards. A win-lose relationship exists in this situation. Each side sees the confrontation as a predicament in which the total rewards to be allocated are fixed, and each is battling to maximize its own share. Getting more is sometimes achieved by threats, deceit, and misinformation.

Integrative bargaining refers to a cooperative, problem-solving form of negotiation. Both parties investigate problem areas and try to reach mutually acceptable solutions. A working relationship of trust, respect, and acknowledged legitimacy exists in this situation. Communication between the parties is open and frequent. The total rewards are not viewed as a fixed amount to be divided but as a variable amount that both sides can increase and share through cooperative teamwork.

The dominant negotiating strategy in American unions has been distributive bargaining. When employers and employees have an open and trusting relationship, the employees generally do not vote to have a union represent them. Where a union exists, distrust, conflict and a "them-versus-us" mentality tend to exist. Consequently, most negotiations are a power struggle between the union and management.

Good-faith bargaining:
The requirement that both parties meet at reasonable times and places and make offers and counter-proposals in an effort to reach an agreement.

Occasionally, negotiations reach an impasse because neither side is willing to give. The Taft-Hartley Act requires that both parties engage in *good-faith bargaining*, or they will be guilty of an unfair labor practice. The conditions for good-faith bargaining, as defined by the courts and the NLRB, involve a willingness to meet at reasonable times, in reasonable places, to discuss each party's bargaining issues. A serious attempt must be made to adjust differences and reach an acceptable common ground. If one side rejects a proposal, it must be willing to make a counter-proposal. This must involve the "give and take" of an auction system. During negotiations, a position on contract terms may not be constantly changed, and evasive behavior is not permitted. Once both sides have agreed to terms on an issue, that issue should be renegotiated only if both sides agree that doing so is necessary to resolve other issues. Finally, there must be a willingness to incorporate oral agreements into a written contract.

Offering a counter-proposal is an important indication of good-faith bargaining, since it demonstrates a bona fide intent to reach an agreement and shows that bargaining is more than empty discussions. Although the law says that the parties must engage in good-faith bargaining, it does not say that they must reach an agreement. The NLRB cannot order the parties to reach agreement, nor can it direct the parties to incorporate a particular provision into their labor agreement. When an impasse occurs, several things might happen, including strikes, lockouts, picketing, boycotts, mediation and conciliation, and arbitration.

A strike occurs when the entire workforce of a company acts in concert and refuses to work. A strike is a union's strongest negotiating weapon because it can exert intense economic pressure on a company. But it must be used carefully. Before going on strike, union members should know why they are striking and what they hope to gain. Although strikes are usually called for economic reasons, they cannot ordinarily be justified economically. More income is usually lost during the strike than the workers can hope to recover through higher wages and benefits in a new contract. Strikes can be costly in other ways, too. If the strike does not succeed in achieving its purpose, union leaders may be voted out of office, the union may be defeated in a decertification election, or the union could lose its public support.

Strike:
When employees refuse to work.

Sit-down strike:
When employees come to work but do not produce anything.

Work Slowdown:
When employees come to work but intentionally work slowly.

Occasionally, workers may engage in other forms of protest. A *sit-down strike* is what happens when they report to work but accomplish nothing. A *work slowdown* occurs when they report to work but accomplish very little. A

Wildcat strike:
When employees walk off the job in violation of a valid labor agreement.

Sickout:
When employees call in sick for work but they are not really sick.

Lockout:
When employers lock the doors and refuse to allow workers to work. This is management's counter-weapon to a strike.

wildcat strike occurs when workers walk off the job in violation of a valid labor agreement and usually against the direct orders of the labor union. Under many labor agreements, the employer has the right to discharge employees who engage in such strikes, or to otherwise penalize them. Those who participate in a wildcat strike also lose their status as employees under the Taft-Hartley Act, which prevents them from voting on a new contract or from being reinstated. A *sickout* occurs when several employees refuse to work and claim they are not working because of illness. Employers dislike paying sick leave to striking workers, but they usually have to pay because it is extremely difficult to prove a *prima facie* case of employee conspiracy.

A *lockout* occurs when an employer refuses to allow employees to work. In some ways a lockout is management's counter-weapon against the union's strike. However, a lockout is not a legal economic weapon if its use is intended to discourage union membership. Like a strike, a lockout is permissible only after a deadlock has been reached on mandatory bargaining items.

EQUAL EMPLOYMENT OPPORTUNITY

Equal opportunity is every American's birthright. The American Dream is based on the belief that everybody can achieve success if they work hard to earn it; success does not depend on being born into a privileged class. Unfortunately, many Americans have not had equal opportunities for employment. Instead, they have been unfairly treated because of their age, race, religion, sex, or disability. The drive to eliminate racial discrimination has progressed very slowly, and at some points very painfully. The Civil War highlighted the issue of whether one individual has the right to own another human being. Following the war, two amendments to the Constitution prohibited slavery and provided equal protection for all citizens within state and local governments.

Section 1981:
The Civil Rights Act of 1866 that guarantees all citizens of the United States the right to make and enjoy the benefits of contracts the same as white citizens.

Five civil rights acts were passed between 1866 and 1875 to eliminate racial discrimination in society. The 1866 act, also known as **Section 1981**, applies to racial discrimination in employment relationships. Section 1981 guarantees all persons of the United States the same right in every state and territory to make and enforce contracts, and to the full and equal benefit of all laws and protections that are enjoyed by white persons. This provision (as amended by the 1991 Civil Rights Act) applies to employment contracts, union or nonunion, and guarantees all employees the right to nondiscrimination in the making, performance, modification, and termination of contracts, as well as the enjoyment of all benefits, privileges, terms, and conditions of the contractual relationship. Section 1981 continues to serve as the legal basis for pressing some charges of discrimination, even though there are more recent civil rights acts.

Civil Rights Laws

Although slavery was abolished after the Civil War and civil rights legislation prohibited discrimination, racial prejudice continued. Minorities in America—blacks, Indians, Asians, Hispanics, and other nationalities—were often treated as second-class citizens and systematically excluded from many areas of society. Finally, a comprehensive civil rights act was passed in 1964 to prohibit dis-

Title VII:
The section of the 1964 Civil Rights Act that prohibits employment discrimination on the basis of race, color, religion, sex, or national origin.

crimination in society. *Title VII* of this act (as amended in 1972 and 1991) prohibits discrimination in employment on the basis of race, color, religion, sex, or national origin. The law applies to employers with 15 or more employees, employment agencies, labor organizations, state and local governments, and educational institutions.

Sec. 703. (a) It shall be an unlawful employment practice for an employer—

1. to fail or refuse to hire or to discharge any individual, or otherwise to discriminate against any individual with respect to his compensation, terms, conditions, or privileges of employment, because of such individual's race, color, religion, sex, or national origin; or
2. to limit, segregate, or classify his employees or applicants for employment in any way which would deprive or tend to deprive any individual of employment opportunities or otherwise adversely affect his status as an employee, because of such individual's race, color, religion, sex, or national origin.

The act expressly prohibits any advertisements or recruiting activities that indicate a preference based on race, color, religion, sex, or national origin unless the preference can be justified as a bona fide occupational qualification for employment. Furthermore, the act requires employers to compile and keep records that can be used to determine whether unlawful employment practices have been or are being committed.

Bona fide occupational qualifications (BFOQ):
Employers are allowed to discriminate on the basis of religion, sex, or national origin only when these attributes are necessary for the operation of their businesses; that is, when they are bona fide occupational qualifications.

Business necessity:
When an otherwise illegal practice can be justified because it is necessary for the efficient operation of a business.

Bona Fide Occupational Qualifications (BFOQ). Title VII specifically states that it is not unlawful for an employer to discriminate on the basis of religion, sex, or national origin if such an attribute is a "bona fide occupational qualification reasonably necessary to the normal operation of that particular business or enterprise." Race is never a legitimate BFOQ.

The concept of *business necessity* has been narrowly defined by the courts. When a practice is found to have a discriminatory effect, it can be justified only by showing that it is necessary to the safe and efficient operation of the business, that it effectively fulfills the purpose it is supposed to serve, and that no alternative policies or practices would serve the same purpose with less discriminatory impact.

Many employers initially assumed that sex was a BFOQ that would make women ineligible for strenuous jobs and males ineligible for traditional female jobs, such as airline flight attendants. Employers were concerned that customers might object when jobs were performed by members of the nontraditional sex. However, the courts have refused to view tradition or customer preference as establishing a BFOQ. The few times when sex has been held to be a legitimate BFOQ include: (1) in order to satisfy basic social mores about modesty, such as the case of a locker-room attendant; (2) when a position demands a particular sex for aesthetic authenticity, as in the case of a fashion model or movie actor; and (3) when one sex is by definition unequipped to do the work, as in the case of a wet nurse.

Equal Employment Opportunity Commission (EEOC). The jurisdiction of the **EEOC** has been broadened since it was first created by Title VII. The EEOC was originally charged with the responsibility of preventing unlawful employment practices through informal methods of conciliation and persuasion. In 1972, Congress gave the EEOC power to bring lawsuits against employers in the federal courts on behalf of an aggrieved person or a class of aggrieved persons. The authority of the EEOC has been further extended to prevent discrimination based on age and physical or mental handicaps.

EEOC inspectors have the power to obtain many kinds of information from the employer, even though it may be costly and difficult to collect. For example, if a Hispanic female who was fired for insubordination claimed that she was terminated because her employer did not want to promote her, the EEOC may request more information than just that relevant to this particular case. The inspector might request a complete census of each job category by race and sex, a record of all promotions and transfers over the past several years, and a record of all disciplinary actions and the bases for them over the past several years. These requests for information can be enforced with a court order if an employer resists providing them.

When an EEOC investigation determines that a charge of discrimination is justifiable, it attempts to resolve the problem through a process called *conciliation*. Conciliation refers to an informal, out-of-court settlement between the employer and the EEOC. Most discrimination charges are settled by conciliation agreements.

If the EEOC and the employer are unable to reach an agreement, the case can be prosecuted in a federal district court either by the EEOC or by the aggrieved individual. If either party appeals the federal court's decision, it can be heard by a court of appeals and ultimately the U.S. Supreme Court. If an employer is found guilty of discrimination, the court decrees can call for drastic remedies, including back-pay, hiring quotas, reinstatement of employees, immediate promotion of employees, elimination of testing programs, or the creation of special recruitment and training programs.

Affirmative Action

In 1965 President Lyndon B. Johnson issued Executive Order 11246 to reverse the effects of racial discrimination. This order, commonly known as Order Number 4, was issued during the Vietnam War and applies to all federal government contractors and subcontractors with 50 or more employees or with contracts exceeding $50,000. This order does more than prohibit discrimination—it requires employers who hold federal contracts or subcontracts to develop written *affirmative action plans* that establish goals and timetables to achieve equal opportunity. Affirmative action plans are reviewed by the *Office of Federal Contract Compliance Programs (OFCCP)* from the Department of Labor.

Preparing an affirmative action plan requires collecting extensive information on the percentages of minorities and females in a company's workforce by job category and comparing them with the availability of minorities and females in the surrounding labor force. If there is an imbalance, the employer

Systemic discrimination: Employment discrimination that results from the normal operation of human resource systems, especially the procedures used for hiring, promoting, compensating, and training employees. Because these practices can create a disparate effect on the employment of minorities and females, EEO laws require their elimination.

Reverse discrimination: Where preferential treatment is shown to females and minorities, often to achieve an affirmative action goal.

must establish goals and timetables for correcting it. Furthermore, the company must communicate internally and externally that it is an equal opportunity employer.

Almost every human resource function must be carefully evaluated to determine whether it systematically discriminates against minorities and females. This form of discrimination is referred to as *systemic discrimination*, meaning that the human resource system itself tends to exclude protected groups. The OFCCP requires employers to have written affirmative action plans available for review and audit.

Many white males have complained that affirmative action plans have made them the victims of *reverse discrimination,* and some court decisions have agreed. Some state and local laws have also prohibited using race as a basis for showing preference for employment or education. The Supreme Court allows employers to give preferential treatment to minorities and females through an affirmative action plan, providing the rights of other workers are not "unnecessarily trammeled," such as violating a negotiated seniority agreement when making layoffs or promotions.[2] However, affirmative action plans that show preferences to minorities or females are not legal unless a company can show that it is correcting a manifest imbalance caused by prior discrimination.[3]

DISCRIMINATION

Experience has demonstrated that without protective legislation many employers tend to discriminate against disadvantaged workers to the detriment of both these people and society. The interests of society are advanced when everyone has an opportunity to participate and contribute without unfair discrimination.

Race and National Origin Discrimination

Recruiting announcements, employment application forms, and preemployment interviews are the traditional instruments that have been used to eliminate minority persons at an early stage of the employment process. The law, interpreted through court rulings and EEOC decisions, prohibits the use of recruiting methods that disproportionately eliminate members of minority groups unless the methods are valid predictors of successful job performance or can be justified by business necessity. Some of the state fair-employment-practice laws also prohibit requesting information that could indirectly reveal race or national origin, such as former name, previous residence, names of relatives, place of birth, citizenship, education, or color of eyes and hair. The EEOC cautions employers about obtaining the following kinds of information unless they can demonstrate a business necessity.

1. *Height and Weight.*
2. *Marital status, number of children, and provisions for child care.* An employer is not allowed to have different hiring policies for men and women with preschool children.
3. *Educational level.* Unless evidence exists that a specific educational level is significantly related to successful job performance, this information

should not be requested, since a high rate of minorities tend to be disqualified on this basis.[4]

4. *English language skill.* Unless skill in the English language is required for the work, it should not be assessed, since minority groups could be discriminated against on this basis. Employers should not have rules that require employees to speak only English at work unless such rules are necessary.

5. *Names of friends or relatives working for the employer.*

6. *Arrest records.* People can be arrested without being convicted.

7. *Conviction records.* Federal courts have held that conviction records should be used as bases for rejection only if their number, nature, and recency indicate that the applicant is unsuitable for the position. If an inquiry is made concerning an applicant's record of convictions, it should be accompanied by a statement that the conviction record will not necessarily be a bar to employment and that factors such as age at the time of offense, seriousness and nature of the violation, and rehabilitation will be taken into account.

8. *Discharge from military service.* Employers should not automatically reject applicants with less-than-honorable discharges from military service. According to the Department of Defense, minority service members receive a higher proportion of undesirable discharges than whites. An applicant's military service record should be used to decide whether further investigation is warranted. As with conviction records, a question regarding military service should be accompanied by a statement that a discharge indicating other than honorable service is not an absolute bar to employment and that other factors also will influence the hiring decision.

9. *Citizenship.* The law clearly protects all individuals, both citizens and noncitizens residing in the United States, against discrimination on the basis of race, color, religion, sex or national origin.

10. *Economic status.* Rejecting applicants because of poor credit ratings can have a disparate impact on minority groups; hence questions about economic status have been found unlawful by the EEOC unless business necessity can be proven. This includes inquiries regarding bankruptcy, car ownership, rental or ownership of a house, length of residence at an address, or past garnishment of wages.

11. *Availability for work on weekends or holidays.* Employers and unions should attempt to accommodate the religious beliefs of employees and applicants unless doing so would cause undue economic hardship.

Although this information should normally not to be used in making an employment decision, some of it may be needed for legitimate business purposes. For example, employers need such information as marital status, number and ages of children, and age of the employee for benefits, insurance, reporting requirements, and other business purposes. The EEOC recommends that this information be obtained after the selection decision has been made.[5]

Although the EEOC guidelines and some state laws restrict employers from asking certain questions, it is important to remember that discrimination does not occur because of the questions that are asked, nor is it prevented by avoiding these questions. Discrimination is a function of how people are treated, not what they are asked. A recruiter who is prejudiced has countless ways to determine age, race, and sex without asking.

Gender Discrimination

Manifestations of gender discrimination have been most frequently observed in five areas:

1. *Hiring*: Women have been typecast into traditionally female jobs, such as secretary, teacher, clerk, teller, flight attendant, and nurse.
2. *Pay*: Women have been paid less than men, a practice that originated when women were viewed as temporary workers earning supplementary income and men were viewed as family breadwinners, who needed a larger income.
3. *Promotion*: Women have often been overlooked for promotions because they are not expected to have the same long-term career orientation that men do, especially if the promotion involves a transfer.
4. *Benefits*: Because of childbirth and child care, women have had different medical benefits and leave policies (such as maternity benefits and mandatory leave following childbirth).
5. *Sexual harassment*: Women have been subjected to a variety of abusive activities that have ranged from sexual assault to verbal harassment.

Protection for women against these types of gender discrimination is provided primarily by two laws: the Equal Pay Act (1963) and the Civil Rights Act Title VII (1964). The Equal Pay Act requires equal pay for equal work. Men and women doing the same or substantially similar work, requiring equivalent skill, effort, and responsibility, must be paid the same.

The Civil Rights Act of 1964 (amended in 1972) prohibits sex discrimination regarding any employment condition, and serves as the basis for prohibiting sexual harassment. Preferential treatment for either gender, male or female, is strictly prohibited unless there is a bona fide occupational qualification (BFOQ) that justifies it.

Glass ceiling: Attitudinal and organizational barriers that inhibit the career advancement of women.

Many women experience subtle forms of discrimination that limit their career advancement. This condition, called the ***glass ceiling***, is created by a host of attitudinal and organizational barriers that prevent women from receiving the information, training, encouragement, mentoring, and other opportunities they need to advance. In recent years, significant progress has been made to eliminate barriers to women's advancement, even though some barriers still exist.

The Civil Rights Act does not protect sexual preference. The federal courts have rejected repeated attempts by homosexuals, transsexuals, and transvestites to shield themselves from unequal treatment by claiming discrimination under Title VII. The EEOC has also concluded that adverse employment actions taken against individuals because of their sexual orientation do not constitute discrimination.[6] The gay rights movement has obtained legislated protection from employment discrimination only at the state and local level.

Sexual harassment:
Any unwelcome sexual advance, requests for sexual favors, or physical contact of a sexual nature, including conduct that interferes with a person's performance or that creates an intimidating or hostile environment.

Quid pro quo harassment:
A form of sexual harassment that requires a person to provide a sexual favor in order to retain a job benefit, ie., "this for that" harassment.

Hostile environment harassment:
Where sexually-oriented activities create an intimidating, hostile, or offensive working environment.

Sexual Harassment

Although Title VII of the Civil Rights Act does not mention sexual harassment, court decisions since 1964 have extended this protection to cases of sexual harassment. The EEOC has issued guidelines that define sexual harassment and explain the employer's responsibility to prevent it. According to the EEOC, unwelcome sexual advances, requests for sexual favors, and other verbal or physical conduct of a sexual nature constitutes sexual harassment when (1) submission to such conduct is made either explicitly or implicitly a term or condition of an individual's employment; (2) submission to or rejection of such conduct by an individual is used as the basis for employment decisions affecting the individual; or (3) such conduct has the purpose or effect of unreasonably interfering with an individual's work performance or creating an intimidating, hostile, or offensive working environment.[7]

Two kinds of sexual harassment have been defined by the courts: quid pro quo and hostile environment. A *quid pro quo* (this for that) charge of sexual harassment occurs when one person offers another person something in exchange for a sexual favor, such as a pay increase, a promotion, or continued employment. A case of *hostile environment* occurs when the discriminatory misconduct is "sufficiently severe or pervasive to alter the conditions of the victim's employment and create an abusive working environment." The Supreme Court has identified several factors for determining whether a work environment is hostile or abusive: (1) the frequency and severity of the conduct; (2) whether the conduct is physically threatening or humiliating, or a mere offensive utterance; (3) whether it unreasonably interferes with an employee's work performance; and (4) its impact on the employee's psychological well-being. The Supreme Court has even ruled that employers are vicariously liable for the actions of supervisors even if the harassment does not result in a tangible employment action.

Employees who are offended by sexual conduct in the work environment, such as touching, jokes, lewd comments, or pornographic pictures, may request that the environment be changed. It is the employee's responsibility to make it known that a sexual advance or the work environment is offensive. If the employer fails to correct the offensive environment, employees can press charges of sexual harassment without having to demonstrate that the harassment caused either physical or psychological damage.

The EEOC holds the employer responsible for the acts of its agents and supervisory employees with respect to sexual harassment, regardless of whether the employer knew or should have known of their occurrence. The employer is also responsible for conduct between coworkers and even responsible for the acts of non-employees, such as vendors or customers. It is the employer's responsibility to take all steps necessary to prevent sexual harassment, such as discussing the subject, expressing strong disapproval, and taking strong, appropriate sanctions when it occurs.

The EEOC guidelines have forced employers to become involved in the romantic entanglements of their employees and the potentially discriminatory impact of these entanglements on employment decisions. The EEOC guidelines state "where employment opportunities or benefits are granted because of an individual's submission to the employer's sexual advances or requests for sexual favors, the employer may be held liable for unlawful sexual discrimination against other persons who were qualified for but denied that employment opportunity or benefit." According to this guideline, if two people are romantically involved and one partner receives preferential treatment, then other members of the work group who did not get promoted can claim that they were the victims of unlawful sex discrimination. Because of the difficulty of knowing when a sexual advance is unwanted or the possibility that it may suddenly become unwanted, employers find that it is wise to have rules similar to their nepotism policies that prevent members of a work group from becoming romantically involved.

To protect themselves with an affirmative defense against liability and damages, employers must be able to demonstrate that (1) they exercised reasonable care to prevent and correct harassing behavior, and (2) the employee failed to take advantage of any corrective opportunities provided by the employer to avoid harm. To demonstrate reasonable care, employers should create and communicate a "zero tolerance" sexual harassment policy, train employees about the policy and what they should do if they witness or experience sexual harassment, and train supervisors about the policy and their obligation to take corrective action.

Religious Discrimination

Under Title VII of the Civil Rights Act, employers are not allowed to hire, promote, train, compensate, discipline, lay off, or terminate on the basis of an individual's religious beliefs or observances. This provision is intended to protect employees from any adverse employment decisions because of their religious beliefs and how they choose to observe them. The most frequent type of accommodation requested is adjustments in an employee's work schedule. If an employee has a legitimate request for time off for religious observances (for Sabbath or holy days), an employer should try to accommodate the employee's request.

Religious discrimination charges typically arise after employees are asked to work overtime or when they are assigned to perform an unpleasant task. However, it may be difficult to know when the charges are frivolous claims because of resistance to change versus legitimate religious conflicts requiring accommodation. According to a Supreme Court case, religious accommodation should not require an employer to (1) sacrifice the rights of other workers to accommodate another employee; (2) breach a collective bargaining agreement to provide benefits or special needs that would not be equally enjoyed by others; (3) suffer a loss in work unit efficiency in their efforts to accommodate; and (4) provide more than *de minimus* action (in other words, the employer should not have to pay overtime for another worker or for a replacement worker).[8]

Age Discrimination

While most cultures show respect and veneration for the elderly, the United States is one of the few cultures that tend to attach a stigma to age. Middle-aged managers and professionals are often considered more competent than older managers and professionals, and older workers are frequently discriminated against because of their age. Some forms of age discrimination are very

Age harassment:
Demeaning comments and actions directed toward older employees, such as age-related jokes, sarcasm, and derisive labels.

visible, such as terminating 60-year-old employees first when there is a reduction in force, and refusing to hire older applicants. Other forms of age discrimination are more subtle, such as not including an older worker on a project team, not listening to the ideas of an older worker in a committee meeting, or demeaning older workers by applying derisive labels (such as "old goat") to them.

The *Age Discrimination in Employment Act (ADEA)*, passed in 1967, originally protected workers between the ages of 40 and 60. Subsequent amendments have eliminated the upper age limit for almost everyone but executives and policymakers, who can still be forced to retire at age 65. The ADEA protects employees over age 40 from arbitrary and age-biased discrimination in hiring, promotion, training, benefits, compensation, discipline, and terminations. Employers are not even allowed to provide different health or medical benefits to older workers than younger workers, nor can they stop making contributions to an employee's pension plan just because that employee has reached retirement age but chooses to continue working. Early retirement programs are allowed under ADEA, but employers must be very careful to avoid using early retirement incentives as a means of forcing older workers to quit.

The EEOC guidelines prohibit age harassment against employees over age 40.[9] Age harassment refers to any form of demeaning behavior associated with age, such as (a) age-inferred remarks having a derogatory connotation; (b) comments that attribute a person's health, attendance, performance, or attitudes to age; (c) age-related jokes and sarcasm; and (d) the use of age-related terms such as "Pops," "the old man," "the old goat," and "dead wood" when they are used in a derisive manner.

Employers who try to induce older workers to quit by making their jobs unpleasant also violate the ADEA. By requiring them to perform difficult, degrading, or boring jobs, older workers can be forced to quit. This action is called *constructive discharge*, because the court constructs from the facts of the situation evidence that the employee was actually discharged. A constructive discharge is deemed to have occurred if a reasonable person would have found the conditions of employment to be intolerable.

Constructive discharge:
A decision constructed by a court that an employee who quit because of intolerable working conditions was essentially discharged.

Occasionally, there are legitimate reasons why a business decision should be based on age. The act itself states that it shall not be an unlawful employment act for employers to base certain decisions on age "where age is a bona fide occupational qualification (BFOQ) reasonably necessary to the normal operation of the particular business." It should be noted, again, that the BFOQ defenses have been very narrowly defined by the courts. The burden of proof is on the employers to show that their business survival depends on employing younger workers in specific jobs, such as a youth counselor, a fashion model, a teen sales clerk, or an actor. If older workers are unable to perform a job because of reduced physical abilities or stamina, they should only be removed from that job after an individual assessment has been made showing they are unable to satisfactorily perform the job. Only a very few mandatory retirement policies have survived the scrutiny of the courts such as an age 55 retirement policy for police officers and an age 60 limit for airline captains. Although airline captains are not permitted to continue beyond age 60, as imposed by FAA regulations, flight engineers are allowed to continue until the airline can demonstrate that their performance is inadequate.

Disability Discrimination

Americans with Disabilities Act:
The 1991 law that protects people with disabilities from employment discrimination and requires employers to provide reasonable accommodations for otherwise qualified individuals.

In 1991, Congress passed the *Americans with Disabilities Act* to protect people with disabilities from job discrimination. The law requires all employers with 15 or more employees to make reasonable accommodations to hire disabled people. A *person with a disability* is defined as (a) an individual who has a physical or mental impairment that substantially limits one or more major life activities (such as caring for oneself, performing manual tasks, walking, seeing, hearing, speaking, learning, and working); (b) a person who has a record of such an impairment (such as cancer or heart disease); or (c) a person who is regarded as having such an impairment (such as a former drug addict or alcoholic). A person who currently uses illegal drugs is specifically excluded from coverage. Although a former addict who has been successfully rehabilitated is protected by the act, those who have used illegal drugs within the past several weeks are excluded.

A physical or mental impairment refers to a condition that weakens, diminishes, or restricts an individual's physical or mental ability. Thus, the definition of a disability is very broad. The Supreme Court has been forced to deal with the question of whether communicable diseases are defined as a disability, and the answer is yes. At least two forms of communicable diseases, tuberculosis (TB) and acquired immune deficiency syndrome (AIDS), have been classified as physical disabilities. Court decisions have also indicated that epilepsy, cancer, heart conditions, and morbid obesity qualify as protected disabilities. However, being too short or left-handed have not been considered disabilities.

Direct threat:
A disease or physical condition that poses a significant risk of substantial harm to the health or safety of the individual or others, such as a highly contagious disease among job holders who work in food preparation. The Americans with Disabilities Act does not protect people who pose a direct threat unless reasonable accommodations can be made to reduce the threat.

People who have disabilities that pose a *direct threat* to the health or safety of themselves or society may be denied employment in those instances where reasonable accommodations cannot eliminate the threat. The direct threat must pose a significant, specific, and current risk of substantial harm rather than a speculative or remote concern for what might happen.

Employers are required to make *reasonable accommodations* to the known physical or mental limitations of people who are otherwise qualified, unless they can show that the accommodation would impose an undue hardship on the business. Reasonable accommodations refer to modifications in the job or changes in the work setting that make it possible for an individual with a disability to work successfully. People are considered *otherwise qualified* if they can perform the essential functions of a job with reasonable accommodations. Employers are encouraged to have written job descriptions listing the essential functions of each job.

Reasonable accommodation:
Efforts by an employer to facilitate the employment of a handicapped person that are not excessively expensive and do not interfere with normal operations.

Otherwise qualified:
A handicapped individual who is capable of performing a job if necessary barriers created by their handicap are eliminated.

Employers are not expected to abandon legitimate job requirements or suffer burdensome sacrifices, however, to make accommodations. Whether an accommodation is reasonable is decided separately for each case. The federal guidelines offer some suggestions, such as making bathrooms and drinking fountains accessible to disabled persons, restructuring jobs, instituting part-time or modified work schedules, modifying equipment, and providing readers or interpreters.

The Americans with Disabilities Act places severe restrictions on the hiring process to prevent discrimination. Employers are not allowed to ask whether an applicant has a disability on application forms, in job interviews, or in background or reference checks. Nor can the employer ask questions about a disability even if it is obvious, such as whether it is temporary or permanent, how long it is expected to last, or if the condition is likely to change. An employer is also prohibited from requiring a preemployment medical examination or from obtaining medical histories until after a conditional offer of employment has been made. However, tests for illegal drugs are not medical examinations under the act and may be given at any time.

In the hiring process, employers are expected to describe the essential functions of the job and then ask the applicants if they can perform them. If an otherwise qualified person needs an accommodation, it is that person's responsibility to request it, and the employer decides whether it is reasonable. With certain limitations, an employer may ask applicants with obvious disabilities to describe or demonstrate how they would perform the essential functions of a job.

After making a conditional job offer and before an individual starts work, an employer may require a medical examination or ask health-related questions, providing that all candidates who receive job offers are treated the same way. A person with a disability can be denied employment only for a valid, job-related reason.

The act also prohibits discrimination against a person who has a known relationship or association with a disabled person. This refers to family relationships and other social or business associations. Therefore, an employer may not refuse to hire an applicant because that person has a spouse, a child, or another dependent who has a disability. The employer may not assume that the individual will be unreliable, have to use leave time, or be away from work in order to care for the family member with a disability.

Discussion Questions

1. What are the arguments for and against voting in favor of a labor union? Explain why you would or would not join a union. Do you think the laws are more supportive of unions or management? Explain.
2. Some people believe that civil rights legislation proves that morality can be legislated. Do you agree that racial prejudice has been significantly reduced in recent years, and if so, would you attribute this in whole or in part to the laws that have been passed?
3. What are the conditions when sex and age are considered bona fide occupational qualifications? Why is race never a BFOQ? Do you think the courts have interpreted the laws too narrowly and are forcing undesirable changes in social customs? Explain.
4. Why is sexual harassment often described as a display of power? How do power and status differences contribute to problems of sexual harassment?
5. Why do we have affirmative action programs, and what are the arguments for and against them? Explain when they are useful and necessary and when they are unfair.
6. Can a company fire or refuse to hire people who smoke? How do the laws regarding discrimination and disability apply to smokers? Aside from the question of what is legal, how should the issue of smoking be treated morally?

Notes

1. Richard E. Walton and Robert B. McKersie, *A Behavioral Theory of Labor Negotiations* (New York: McGraw-Hill, 1965).
2. *Johnson v. Transportation Agency of Santa Clara County*, 480 U.S. 616 (1987).
3. *Regents at the University of California v. Bakke*, 438 U.S. 265 (1978); *Steelworkers v. Webber*, 443 U.S. 193 (1979); *Adarand Constructors, Inc. v. Pena, 93–1841, U.S.C., (1995)*
4. *Griggs v. Duke Power Company*, 401 U.S. 424 (1981).
5. Preemployment Inquiries (Washington, D.C.: Equal Employment Opportunity Commission).
6. Sabrina M. Wrenn, "Gay Rights and Workplace Discrimination," *Personnel Journal* 67 (October 1988): 91–102.
7. 29 Code of Federal Regulations, Part 1604.11.
8. *Hardison v. Trans World Airlines*, 375 F. Supp. 877 (W.D. Mo. 1974).
9. 29 Code of Federal Regulations, Part 1625.

A Timid Asian Female

Because the company was expanding into European and African markets, the international department needed to hire another person to handle its growing workload. The company announced that it was looking for a person who had legal training, international experience, and excellent writing and editorial skills.

Four applicants expressed interest in the position, but three of them withdrew when they learned that the starting salary was only half what they expected. The remaining applicant, Kim Li, assumed she would be offered the job because she met the qualifications, she had an excellent academic record, and she had outstanding previous experience as an editor.

Kim was very disappointed when they refused to hire her. She learned that the company planned to reopen the position and advertise the job more widely. Although Kim was highly qualified, she was short and looked more like a grade school student than a professional lawyer. She also spoke with a distinct accent in spite of her outstanding writing skills.

When Kim asked why she was not hired, the HR manager asked the international director for a written explanation. The director sent a memo that said in part: "This job requires someone who will be able to negotiate sensitive agreements with representatives in European and African companies. Success in this job will depend greatly on assertiveness, deportment, and first impressions and it can't be performed adequately by a timid Asian female."

Questions

1. Is this a situation of illegal discrimination?
2. Since Kim feels she is being treated unfairly, what options should she consider and what are the consequences of each?
3. The director of the international department feels strongly that some of the agreements with clients in Northern Africa can only be successfully negotiated by an African-American male. How should the director staff this position?

Employment Interviewing and the ADA

Evaluate the following interview questions. Indicate whether each question is legal or illegal under the Americans with Disabilities Act. If it is legal, describe when the question would be useful. If it is illegal, explain why.

1. Do you have any disabilities or limitations that would prevent you from being able to perform the essential functions of this job?

   Legal _____ Comment: _____

   Illegal _____ _____

2. Are you able to perform the tasks required by this job with or without an accommodation?

   Legal _____ Comment: _____

   Illegal _____ _____

3. If accommodations are required for you to perform the tasks required by this job, what are these accommodations?

   Legal _____ Comment: _____

   Illegal _____ _____

4. Have you ever been diagnosed as being addicted to drugs or alcohol?

   Legal _____ Comment: _____

   Illegal _____ _____

5. Have you used any illegal drugs within the past month?

   Legal _____ Comment: _____

   Illegal _____ _____

6. Have you ever had a serious injury or accident that required hospitalization?

   Legal _____ Comment: _____

   Illegal _____ _____

7. Have you ever been under the care of a psychiatrist or psychologist? If so, for what condition?

   Legal _____ Comment: _____

   Illegal _____ _____

8. How many days of work have you missed in the past year because of illness?

   Legal _____ Comment: _____

   Illegal _____ _____

9. Have you ever had a job that required you to perform this particular task? What was your performance record?

   Legal _____ Comment: _____

   Illegal _____ _____

10. Do you smoke?

Legal _____ Comment: _____

Illegal _____ _____

11. Are you currently taking any prescribed drugs or medications?

Legal _____ Comment: _____

Illegal _____ _____

12. Will you be required to take time off to receive any type of medical treatment?

Legal _____ Comment: _____

Illegal _____ _____

13. Will you be required to take time off to transport another individual to receive medical treatment?

Legal _____ Comment: _____

Illegal _____ _____

14. Have you ever had an on-the-job injury? If so, did you receive workers' compensation?

Legal _____ Comment: _____

Illegal _____ _____

15. Ninety percent of this job involves driving a car to make sales calls. Do you have a valid driver's license? What is your accident record?

Legal _____ Comment: _____

Illegal _____ _____

How do you motivate employees to accomplish the organization's goals?

After you have hired employees and assigned them to their jobs, your next major challenge is to create conditions that will lead to high levels of motivation. Managers have five primary strategies for motivating people, including individual rewards, such as base pay and incentives; system rewards, such as benefits and vacations; intrinsic satisfaction, such as job enrichment; internalized values, such as job involvement and organizational commitment; and rule compliance, such as enforcing written policies backed by punishment.

CHAPTER 6
Analyzing Individual Behavior

CHAPTER 7
Motivation

CHAPTER 8
Work Design

CHAPTER 9
Performance Management

CHAPTER 10
Employee Discipline

Section III contains five chapters that explain the different methods of motivating employees. Chapter 6 explains perception and how the expectations of others influence behavior. Chapter 7 summarizes the different motivation theories, and explains why people tend to do what they expect to be rewarded for doing. Chapter 8 describes the differences between job specialization and job enrichment, and explains how jobs can be enriched to stimulate greater levels of motivation and commitment. Chapter 9 explains the principles of evaluating and rewarding performance, and describes how compensation systems can be used to motivate employees. Chapter 10 explains how to create and implement programs that balance the rights of individuals and the interests of the company. Every company should have a complaint procedure to protect employees and a discipline system that protects the organization.

CHAPTER 6

Analyzing Individual Behavior

Chapter Outline

Perception

The Perceptual Process

Perceptual Errors

Discrimination and Prejudice

The Self-Fulfilling Prophecy

Personality

Attribution Theory

Personality Dimensions

Maslow's Need Hierarchy

McClelland's Learned Needs Theory

PERCEPTION

An understanding of perception is important because it has such an enormous impact on understanding individual behavior. No two people share the same reality; for each of us the world is unique. We cannot understand behavior unless we understand why two people observing the same event can honestly see something entirely different. Furthermore, we need to understand that through our perceptions we are not simply passive observers of the drama of life, but active participants, helping to write the script and play the roles. The behavior of others is influenced by how you perceive them.

The Perceptual Process

Perception is the process of receiving and interpreting environmental stimuli. In a world filled with complex environmental stimuli, our perceptions help us categorize and organize the sensations we receive. We behave according to our interpretation of the reality we see. What we fail to appreciate is that the reality we see is almost never the same as the reality perceived by others. The perceptual process consists of three major components, as shown in Exhibit 6.1: sensation, attention, and perception. These three components are involved in perceiving both physical objects and social events.

Sensations:
Environmental stimuli that we are capable of receiving through one or more of the five sense mechanisms—sight, smell, taste, touch, and hearing.

Sensation. At any given moment we are surrounded by countless environmental stimuli. We are not aware of most of these stimuli, either because we have learned to ignore them, or because our sense organs—sight, smell, taste, touch, and hearing—are not capable of receiving them. Environmental stimuli can only produce sensations in the human body if the body has developed the sensing mechanism to receive them. Whether you are consciously aware of these sensations, however, depends on the next step in the perception process—attention.

Attention:
Part of the perceptual process in which we acknowledge the reception of sensations from the environment. The major characteristics involved in attending to physical stimuli include size, intensity, frequency, contrast, motion, change, and novelty.

Attention. Although we are capable of sensing many environmental stimuli, we attend to only a very small portion of them and ignore the rest. Numerous factors influence the attention process:

1. *Size.* The larger the size of a physical object, the more likely it is to be perceived.

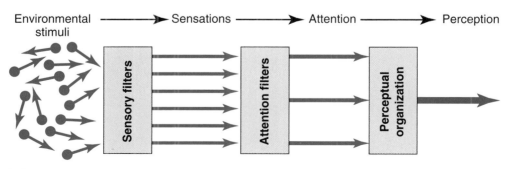

Exhibit 6.1 Perceptual Process

2. *Intensity.* The greater the intensity of a stimulus, the more likely it is to be noticed. A loud noise, such as shouting, is more likely to get attention than a quiet voice.

3. *Frequency.* The greater the frequency with which a stimulus is presented, the greater are the chances you will attend to it. This principle of repetition is used extensively in advertising to attract the attention of buyers.

4. *Contrast.* Stimuli that contrast with the surrounding environment are more likely to be selected for attention than stimuli that blend with the environment. The contrast can be created by color, size, or any other factor that distinguishes one stimulus from others, as shown in Exhibit 6.2.

5. *Motion.* Since movement tends to attract attention, a moving stimulus is more likely to be perceived than a stationary object. An animated sign, for example, attracts more attention than a fixed billboard. An object with lights blinking on and off, such as a Christmas tree or sign, attracts more attention than one without blinking lights.

6. *Novelty.* A stimulus that is new and unique will often be perceived more readily than will stimuli that have been observed on a regular basis. Advertisers use the impact of novelty by creating original packaging or advertising messages.

Perception:
The process of interpreting and organizing the sensations we attend to.

Perceptual inferences:
The process of extrapolating from a small amount of information to form a complete perception about an object or event. Often we are required to act on only limited pieces of information from which we infer what more information might tell us.

Perception. The process of perception involves organizing and interpreting the sensations we attend to. Visual images, sounds, odors, and other sensations do not simply enter our consciousness as pure, unpolluted sensations. As we attend to them, we consciously try to organize or categorize the sensations into a meaningful perception that somehow makes sense to us.

Although we would like to think of ourselves as open-minded, unbiased, and nonjudgmental in our perceptions, the demands of the situation make it impossible; we are forced to draw quick inferences based on very sparse information. If you were a counselor in a college advisement center and a student came for assistance, you would be required to make rapid inferences based on only limited information. Your recommendations on course loads and elective classes would depend on your perception of the student's situation.

We tend to categorize people using limited pieces of information and then act on this information, even though most of our inferences have not been confirmed. This process is called making *perceptual inferences,* since we are required to diagnose our situation and make rapid inferences about it from scanty clues.

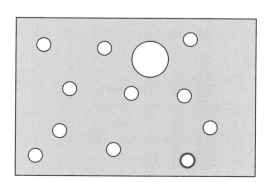

Exhibit 6.2   The Effects of Size, Intensity, and Contrast on Attention

We cannot wait until we have complete information about each individual before we respond. If we waited until we were fully informed about each person's unique personality and problems, we would never respond. Instead, we develop a system of categories based on only a few pieces of information and use this system to organize our perceptions. For example, college students tend to categorize other college students according to sex, marital status, year in school, and major. If you started a casual conversation with another student, your conversation would likely be much different if you thought that student was a married graduate student majoring in engineering, rather than an unmarried freshman majoring in sociology.

The process of grouping environmental stimuli into recognizable patterns is called *perceptual organization*. Rather than just seeing the stimuli as random observations, we attempt to organize them into meaningful, recognizable patterns. Some of the principles we use to organize these sensations include these:

Perceptual organization: The process of organizing our perceptions into recognizable patterns. Four of the principles we use to assist in this effort include figure-ground separation, similarity, proximity, and closure.

1. *Figure-ground.* People tend to perceive objects that stand against a background. In a committee meeting, for example, most people see the verbal conversation as *figure*, and fail to attend to the background of nonverbal messages that may be far more meaningful in understanding the group processes.
2. *Similarity.* Stimuli that have common physical traits are more likely to be grouped together than those that do not. Athletic teams wear uniforms to help players recognize their teammates. Some organizations color-code memos to identify messages about the same topic. Some companies that have open floor plans color-code partitions and other furniture to visually define separate functions and responsibilities. Because of the principle of similarity, the management style of top managers sets the stage for how the feedback and instructions of middle managers will be perceived by their subordinates.
3. *Proximity.* Stimuli that occur in the same proximity, either in space or in time, are often associated. For example, if you see two people together frequently, you will tend to attribute the characteristics you learn about one individual to the other until your perceptions become more accurate. An illustration of proximity in time occurs when the boxes in the hall are removed on the same day that you complain about them. You may assume that your complaints led to their removal without realizing that it would have occurred anyway.
4. *Closure.* Since most of the stimuli we perceive are incomplete, we naturally tend to extrapolate information and project additional information to form a complete picture. For example, a pole placed in front of a stop sign may prevent us from seeing the entire eight-sided figure. But since we have seen many stop signs before, the principle of closure causes us to "see" the complete sign. If we watch an employee work for fifteen minutes and complete the first half of a task, and return twenty minutes later to find the task completed, we attribute the entire task to the employee because of the principle of closure. However, we only saw this person perform half the task, and so our inference about the last half may be incorrect.

Perceiving social events and people is more difficult than perceiving physical objects. If two people disagree about the length of an object, they can measure it. But if they disagree about whether a supervisor is pleased with their work, they may have difficulty verifying which one is right, even if the supervisor's response were filmed. Although the inferences we make about someone's personality should be based upon the behavior we observe, our perceptions are influenced by a variety of physical characteristics, such as appearance and speech.

The appearance of others influences how we perceive and respond to them, as has been amply demonstrated by the dress-for-success literature. Although many people, especially college students, feel somewhat repulsed by the implications of the research, the data nevertheless show that people who dress in conservative business attire are more likely to be hired, be promoted, make a sale, obtain service, and be treated as someone important.[1] We generally assume that people who are dressed in business suits and uniforms are professional or technical employees performing their assigned functions. Therefore, we tend to respond to them with respect and deference, and willingly comply with their requests. On the other hand, we assume that people dressed in work clothes are lower-level employees, who possess little, if any, authority to tell us what to do. We are more likely to treat them in a discourteous manner.

How people speak also influences our perceptions of them. As we listen to people talk, we make rapid inferences about their personalities, backgrounds, and motives. We notice tone of voice to detect whether individuals are happy, sad, angry, or impatient. We notice the precision and clarity in the messages communicated to us, and generally assume that a message spoken in a very emphatic and distinct manner is supposed to be carefully attended to. When individuals speak in a particular dialect or accent, we make inferences about their geographic and cultural background. The topics people choose to discuss not only reveal their educational training, but also their personal interests and ways of thinking. In a leaderless group discussion, a female student with a soft, nonassertive voice frequently has difficulty getting the other group members to listen to her ideas. On the other hand, individuals who speak with a distinct, authoritative tone of voice often receive greater credibility than their contributions deserve. A person speaking less than perfect English may be perceived as unintelligent although he or she may be fluent in many languages.

We also draw numerous inferences from nonverbal communications such as eye contact, hand motions, and posture. Sitting up straight, looking the other person in the eye, and nodding your head in agreement indicate to other people that you are interested, and they will perceive you as being friendly and concerned.

The way we organize and interpret environmental stimuli is also influenced by our own characteristics. How we feel about ourselves has an enormous effect on how we perceive others. When we understand ourselves and can accurately describe our own personal characteristics, we can more accurately perceive others. For example, secure people tend to see others as warm rather than cold, and our own sociability influences the importance we attach to the sociability of others. When we accept ourselves and have a positive self-image, we tend to see favorable characteristics in others. We are not as negative or critical about others if we accept ourselves as we are.

Cognitive complexity:
The degree to which individuals have developed complex categories for organizing information.

Our perceptions are also influenced by our cognitive complexity and our expectations. When we have complex thinking and reasoning structures, we are able to perceive small differences in what we see. *Cognitive complexity* allows us to differentiate people and events using multiple criteria, which increases the accuracy of our perceptions. Furthermore, we tend to see things that our past experience and personal values have taught us to see. If we are prepared and expecting to see something, we might see it even if it is not there.

Theory X versus Theory Y:
A theory proposed by Douglas McGregor that explains two opposite perceptual styles of managers. Managers who espouse Theory X see employees as lazy and refusing to work while managers who espouse Theory Y believe employees are dedicated and willing to work.

McGregor's Theory X versus Theory Y. An excellent illustration of how a perceptual set influences the behavior of managers is provided by Douglas McGregor's theory X versus theory Y.[2] McGregor developed his theory at a time when television commercials were contrasting brand X, the ineffective product, with brand Y, the effective one. According to McGregor, *theory X* represents an outdated, repressive view of human nature that assumes people are lazy, they don't want to work, and management's job is to force or coerce them. Theory X contains three assumptions:

1. The average human being inherently dislikes work and will avoid it if possible.
2. Because they dislike work, most people must be coerced, controlled, directed, and threatened with punishment to get them to achieve organizational objectives.
3. The average human being prefers to be directed, wishes to avoid responsibility, has relatively little ambition, and wants security above all.

McGregor says employees would behave much differently if managers would adopt a different set of assumptions. In contrast to his pessimistic theory X view of human nature, McGregor presents a set of six assumptions, which he calls *theory Y*:

1. The expenditure of physical and mental effort in work is as natural as play or risk. The average human being does not inherently dislike work.
2. External control and the threat of punishment are not the only means of motivating people to achieve organizational objectives. People will exercise self-direction and self-control in the pursuit of objectives to which they are committed.
3. Commitment to objectives is a function of the rewards associated with their achievement. The most significant rewards, the satisfaction of ego and self-actualization needs, can be obtained from effort directed toward organizational objectives.
4. The average human being learns, under proper conditions, not only to accept but to seek responsibility. Avoidance of responsibility, lack of ambition, and an emphasis on security are generally consequences of experience, not inherent human characteristics.
5. The capacity to exercise a relatively high degree of imagination, ingenuity, and creativity in solving organizational problems is widely, not narrowly, distributed in the population.
6. Under the conditions of modern industrial life, the intellectual potentialities of the average human being are only partially utilized.

According to theory X, poor performance can be blamed on the employees' failure to demonstrate initiative and motivation. In contrast, theory Y represents an enlightened view of human nature suggesting that organizational inefficiencies should be blamed on management. If employees are lazy, indifferent, unwilling to take responsibility, uncooperative, or uncreative, these problems indicate that management has failed to unleash the potential of its employees.

These two views of human nature represent significantly different perceptual sets that managers use to perceive the behavior of their subordinates. McGregor explains how these two views cause managers to behave quite differently in response to organizational problems. In his own writing, McGregor uses theory Y to redesign such management practices as performance appraisal, wage and salary administration, profit sharing, promotions, and participative management.

Perceptual Errors

As we observe people and events, we make countless perceptual errors. This section analyzes six of the most frequent perceptual errors.

Halo effect:
One of the perceptual errors in which individuals allow one characteristic about a person to influence their evaluations of other personality characteristics.

Halo Effect. The *halo effect* refers to the tendency to allow one personality trait to influence our perceptions of other traits. For example, if we see a person smiling and looking pleasant, we may conclude, as one study found, that the person is more honest than people who frown. However, there is no necessary connection between smiling and honesty. One potentially serious application of the halo effect is when it occurs in a performance evaluation. If one particular attribute, positive or negative, colors a supervisor's perception of other unrelated attributes, the performance evaluation process can be extremely unfair and misleading.

Selective perception:
A source of perceptual errors caused by people choosing to perceive only the information that they find acceptable.

Selective Perception. The process of systematically screening out information we don't wish to hear is referred to as *selective perception*. This process is a learned response; we learn from past experience to ignore or overlook information that is uncomfortable and unpleasant. Occasionally we face stimuli that are so threatening or embarrassing that we refuse to perceive them, and this process is also called perceptual defense.

Implicit personality theories:
The process of allowing our personal stereotypes and expectations regarding certain kinds of people to create a perceptual set that influences how we respond to other people.

Implicit Personality Theories. Based on our interactions with many people, we create our own system of personality profiles and use them to categorize new acquaintances. To the extent that our personality profiles are accurate, they facilitate our ability to perceive more rapidly and accurately. Since each person is unique, however, our *implicit personality theories* can serve at best as only a rough approximation for categorizing people. If we continue to observe carefully, we may find that many of our expectations were not correct.

Projection:
A form of perceptual bias in which we project our own personal feelings and attitudes onto others as a means of helping us interpret their attitudes and feelings.

Projection. The tendency to attribute our own feelings and characteristics to others is called *projection*. As with other perceptual errors, projection is occasionally an efficient and reasonable perceptual strategy. If we don't like to be criticized, harassed, or threatened, it is reasonable to assume that others would not like it any better. However, projection usually refers to more than just attributing our thoughts and feelings to others. Instead, it is used to describe the dysfunctional process of attributing to others the undesirable thoughts and traits we possess but are not willing to admit. In essence, we attribute or project onto others the negative characteristics or feelings we have about ourselves. Projection serves as a defense mechanism to protect our self-concept and makes us more capable of facing others, whom we see as imperfect.

First Impressions. When we meet people for the first time, we form impressions based on limited information that should be open for correction on subsequent encounters. Research evidence indicates, however, that first impressions are remarkably stable. In recruiting interviews, for example, it has been found that recruiters form a fairly stable impression of the applicant within the first three or four minutes. Negative first impressions seem to require abundant favorable information to change them, and some recruiters are so opinionated that they refuse to perceive contradictory information.[3]

Primacy effect:
The tendency for first impressions and early information to exert a particularly profound influence on our evaluations and judgment.

Allowing first impressions to have a disproportionate and lasting influence on later evaluations is known as the *primacy effect*. The primacy effect explains why the first few days on the job may have a large impact on the attitudes and performance of new employees. Likewise, the opening comments in a committee meeting may have a lasting impact on the remainder of the group discussion because of the primacy effect.

Stereotyping:
The process of using a few attributes about an object to classify it and then responding to it as a member of a category rather than as a unique object.

Stereotyping. The process of *stereotyping* refers to categorizing individuals based on one or two traits and attributing other characteristics to them based on their membership in that category. Stereotypes are frequently based on sex, race, age, religion, nationality, and occupation. Although stereotypes help us interpret information more rapidly, they also cause serious perceptual errors. When we create fixed categories based on variables such as sex, race, and age, and resist looking more carefully to confirm our expectations, we make serious perceptual errors that damage ourselves and others.

Since the passage of the Civil Rights Act (1964), significant progress has been made to reduce the use of stereotypes, particularly in hiring new employees. However, we continue to use stereotypes because they serve a useful purpose: they facilitate our rapid perception of others. Occasionally these stereotypes are very useful, especially age and sex stereotypes. For example, it is reasonable to guess that older workers are not as interested in new training programs and opportunities for promotion as younger workers are, because such differences have indeed been documented. Likewise, it may seem reasonable to think that female employees would be less interested in working overtime, since many women, especially those with small children in the home, find working overtime a particular burden. But, even if these assumptions are true in general, they are not necessarily true for a particular person. Some older workers may be very excited about a new training program, and some mothers may be very anxious to work overtime. Although it is impossible to confirm all our stereotypes, we should constantly question the accuracy of our perceptions, and maintain a flexible system of categories.

Discrimination and Prejudice

Illegal discrimination on the basis of race, religion, or sex typically occurs because of prejudice, which is defined as an unreasonable bias associated with suspicion, intolerance, or an irrational dislike for people of a particular race, religion, or sex. To understand the nature of prejudice, it is important to appreciate the psychological impact of individuality and uniqueness. The simple fact that one or two individuals differ significantly from other members of the group will cause them to be perceived and treated differently regardless of whether the differences are on the basis of race, religion, sex, or any other visible characteristic. This can best be illustrated by looking at the letters below.

X X x x x x x X X x x O X x x X

If you studied this configuration briefly and then attempted to describe it, you would probably say that it consisted of some big and little *X*'s with an *O*. Unless you studied it carefully, you would probably not remember how many big *X*'s and little *x*'s there were or how they were arranged in the configuration, but you would probably remember the *O* and where it was located.

The same process occurs among a group of individuals when one or more individuals differ significantly from the others because of their unique sex or race. They are perceived differently, and they attract more attention regardless of which race or sex constitutes the majority. This perceptual process occurs simply because the minority stands out from the majority. Three perceptual tendencies explain why minorities experience prejudice within the group: visibility, contrast, and assimilation.[4]

Visibility. When a small percent of the group belong to a particular category, these individuals are more visible. Therefore, if a committee consisted of one female and several males, it is likely that everyone will remember where the woman sat in the committee meeting, what she wore, what she said, and how she voted. The minority tend to capture a larger share of the awareness within that group.

Contrast. When one or more individuals who are different are added to a group, their presence creates a self-consciousness among the dominant group about what makes them a separate class. Each group defines itself partly by knowing what it isn't. Consequently, a polarization and exaggeration of differences occurs, highlighting the differences between the minorities and majorities. Both groups become more aware of their commonalities and their differences, and group processes tend to accentuate the differences by creating stereotypes to separate the two groups.

Assimilation. The third perceptual tendency, assimilation, involves the application of stereotypes and familiar generalizations about a person's social category. Minority group members are not perceived as unique individuals but as representatives of a particular category. In essence, their behavior is assimilated into a stereotype of how members of their particular group are expected to behave. An illustration of assimilation is when a Japanese business executive who is meeting with a group of American executives is asked how other Japanese executives would react to a particular proposal. The question assumes that all Japanese executives respond alike, and that one person can represent them all.

Assimilation and contrast appear to be a function of how much effort people are willing to make to form accurate impressions. While some people challenge their assumptions and seek additional information, others label behavior and ignore uniqueness.

Prejudice and discrimination occur in a variety of settings and range in intensity from very innocent and unintended to very injurious and nasty. Some of the most obvious forms of racism and sexism include name-calling and slurs directed toward a specific individual. Such cruel behavior is considered entirely unacceptable in today's organizations; it is both immoral and illegal. Other forms of prejudice and discrimination, however, are much more subtle because the acts are not directed toward a specific individual and are often said in jest. Such behavior, however, is still considered inappropriate. Jokes and other comments that reflect negatively on another person's race or sex are both insulting and demeaning to everyone.

The Self-Fulfilling Prophecy

Pygmalion Effect or Self-fulfilling prophecy:
A process which explains how the expectations in the mind of one person, such as a teacher or researcher, come to influence the behaviors of others, such as students or subjects, such that the latter achieves the former's expectations.

An interesting application of biased perceptions is the self-fulfilling prophecy, also called the *Pygmalion effect*.[5] We are not passive observers of our own social worlds, but active forces in shaping those worlds. To an important extent we create our own social reality by influencing the behavior we observe in others. The self-fulfilling prophecy explains how the expectations in the mind of one person about how others should behave are communicated in a variety of ways, until these individuals actually behave in the way expected. However, the self-fulfilling prophecy involves more than just one person having strong expectancies that influence the behavior of others. It requires that (1) the expectancies have a particular effect on the behavior of the person holding them, (2) this behavior in turn has an effect on the behavior of the other person, (3) the other person's behavior confirms the first person's expectancies, and (4) the first person views this behavior as unsolicited evidence that the expectancy was right all along. This relationship between the perceiver and the target person is illustrated in Exhibit 6.3.

The self-fulfilling prophecy has been demonstrated in several experiments with both children and adults.[6] Four elements have been proposed to explain why the self-fulfilling prophecy occurs:

1. *Input.* Individuals who are expected to do well receive better ideas and suggestions than people who are expected to do poorly. As the quantity and quality of information increase, it helps them perform better and communicates a sense of urgency and importance about the task.
2. *Output expected.* Specific comments about how much individuals are expected to achieve help them establish realistic levels of aspiration and higher performance goals.
3. *Reinforcement.* Individuals from whom high performance is expected tend to be rewarded more frequently when they achieve their performance goals. Individuals from whom low performance is expected usually perform poorly and are not reinforced. *But even if they perform well, they may not be rewarded, because their supervisors feel threatened or irritated that their expectations are disconfirmed.*
4. *Feedback.* Managers who communicate high performance expectations typically provide greater feedback. This feedback occurs more frequently, and usually contains specific suggestions for improvement.

Exhibit 6.3   A Social Interaction Sequence in Which Both Perceptual and Behavioral Confirmation Create the Self-fulfilling Prophecy

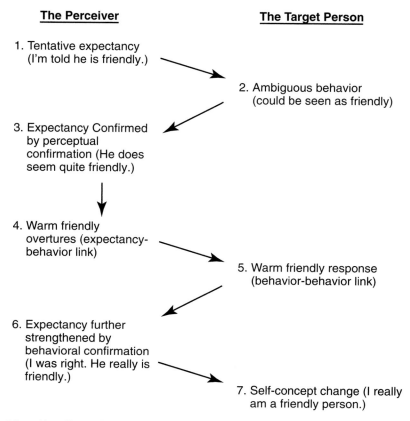

| The Perceiver | The Target Person |

1. Tentative expectancy (I'm told he is friendly.)

2. Ambiguous behavior (could be seen as friendly)

3. Expectancy Confirmed by perceptual confirmation (He does seem quite friendly.)

4. Warm friendly overtures (expectancy-behavior link)

5. Warm friendly response (behavior-behavior link)

6. Expectancy further strengthened by behavioral confirmation (I was right. He really is friendly.)

7. Self-concept change (I really am a friendly person.)

Source: Adapted from Edward E. Jones, "Interpreting Interpersonal Behavior: The Effects of Expectancies." *Science*, Vol. 234, (3 October 1986), p. 43.

The self-fulfilling prophecy normally starts when the expectations are planted in the mind of the leader. However, the expectations can also be communicated directly to the actor. The self-fulfilling prophecy has been recommended as a valuable strategy for improving organizational performance. The key is to start the sequence by creating positive expectations in managers and workers for themselves and the organization. Expectations can originate with upper management or a consultant, and must be both challenging and realistic. This strategy works best with new beginnings—before either the manager or workers have prior expectations about performance.

When new employees are introduced into an organization, the self-fulfilling prophecy contributes importantly to their career success. Some have argued that the expectations of managers may be more important than the skills and training of the new trainees in determining their success.[7] An analysis of management training programs suggests that the self-fulfilling prophecy is particularly crucial to the success of new managers.

PERSONALITY

Personality:
The attributes and pre-dispositions associated with each individual that make that person unique and predict how that person will likely behave in many different situations.

Behavior has traditionally been explained as a combination of personality and environmental forces, as expressed by the formula B = fn (P,E). This formula suggests that our behavior at any given time is a combination of unique personality traits and the demands of the environment.

Personality refers to stable attributes that cause us to behave the same way in many different situations. Several personality traits have been shown to influence behavior. However, research has also shown that situational forces exert a much larger impact on behavior than personality factors. Indeed, several reviews of the research literature suggest that correlation coefficients are almost always less than .30 between any measured personality variable and actual behavior.[8] Most people find this quite surprising because they believe the way we behave is a direct reflection of our personalities—friendly people are friendly, and aggressive people are aggressive. However, the evidence indicates that in a friendly environment everyone will be friendly, and in an aggressive environment even passive people will push back when they are pushed long enough.

This research means that the impact of personality on behavior is usually rather small, but it is not insignificant. Occasionally personality factors are sufficiently strong to overcome all environmental forces, and over time people have an opportunity to create their own situations that match their personalities. Attribution theory examines how we assign responsibility to the person and the situation.

Attribution Theory

Attribution theory:
A theory that explains how we assign responsibility for behavior either to personality characteristics or environmental circumstances.

When we perceive social events, part of the perceptual process includes assigning responsibility for behavior. Are people responsible for their own behavior because of their personal characteristics, or were they forced to behave as they did because of the situation? The assignment of responsibility and the cognitive processes we use to understand why people act as they do are known as *attribution theory*.[9]

According to attribution theory, the assignment of responsibility stems from our observations of people over time. For example, if we observe a group of people attempting to use a word processor and find that many of them have difficulty getting the printer to function properly, we perceive the problem as being caused by the situation. But if only one person has difficulty with the printer, we attribute the cause of the problem to that individual's personal skills or abilities. Studies on attribution theory have generated the following conclusions:

1. When we observe someone else's behavior, we tend to overestimate the influence of personality traits and underestimate situational influences.
2. When we explain our own behavior, we tend to overestimate the importance of the situation and underestimate our own personality characteristics.

The explanation for these contrasting conclusions is that as actors we are more aware of the differing situations we face, and therefore we attribute our behavior to these differing situations. But since we are not as knowledgeable about the variety of situations others face, we overlook the situation and attribute their behavior to their personalities. This explanation has been confirmed by a study showing that when observers had empathy for another person, they were more likely to take the actor's perspective and were better able to notice situational causes for the actor's behavior. Conversely, distant observers tended to only notice personality characteristics.[10]

3. As we observe others in casual situations, we tend to attribute their successes to personality traits, such as effort and ability, and their failures to external factors, such as the difficulty of the task.

It is not clear why we attribute success to the person and failure to the situation in casual situations, but apparently this tendency does not extend to an organizational setting. In fact, studies of attribution in organizations suggest that the results are the opposite.

4. In evaluating the performance of employees, poor performance is generally attributed to internal personal factors, especially when the consequences are serious.

A study of nursing supervisors found that they were more likely to hold their employees accountable for poor performance as performance problems became more serious.[11] The behavior of subordinates reflects on their managers; therefore, when subordinates do well, managers are quick to accept partial credit for success; but when problems occur, they are quick to blame subordinates to exonerate themselves.

5. Employees tend to attribute their successes to internal factors and their failures to external causes.

Because of our need to maintain a positive self-image, we attribute our own successes to our personal skills and abilities. When we fail, however, we blame external causes.

Personality Dimensions

Numerous personality traits have been used to explain the differences in individual behavior. Some of the most well-researched traits include the locus of control, self-esteem, and self-efficacy.

Locus of control:
A personality trait that is determined by whether individuals think the rewards they obtain are based on internal factors such as knowledge, effort, and skill, or external factors such as luck, chance, and fate.

Locus of Control. The locus of control refers to the degree to which individuals believe that their actions influence the rewards they receive in life. Individuals with an *internal locus of control* believe that the rewards they receive are internally controlled by their own actions, whereas individuals with an *external locus of control* believe external forces such as luck, chance, or fate control their lives and determine their rewards and punishments.[12] If an unexpected opportunity for advancement were presented to two people, the externally controlled individual would probably attribute it to luck or being in the right place at the right time. The internally controlled individual would be more inclined to attribute the opportunity to hard work, effort, and knowledge. As with other personality factors, however, people vary along a continuum and cannot be neatly placed into one category or the other.

Individuals behave differently depending on whether they believe their rewards are internally or externally controlled. In contrast to externals, internals believe that how hard they work will determine how well they perform and how well they will be rewarded. Consequently, internals generally perceive more order and predictability in their job-related outcomes and usually report higher levels of job satisfaction.[13] Since managers are required to initiate goal-directed activity, it is not surprising that they tend to be internally controlled.

In times of upheaval and disruption, externals generally experience more frustration and anxiety than internals, and are less able to cope with the situation. A study of how people responded to a flood following a hurricane found that externals were more concerned than internals about coping with their own tension and frustration. They tended to withdraw from the task of rebuilding and to express bitterness and aggression about the "rotten hand" they had been dealt. Internals, on the other hand, went immediately to the task of acquiring new loans, gathering new resources, and rebuilding their homes and businesses. Obviously, no one could have prevented the storm from happening, but the internals had faith that an active, problem-solving response could determine whether the flood would be a conclusive tragedy or only a temporary setback.[14]

The locus of control is determined largely by an individual's past experiences. Internals are the product of an environment where their behaviors largely decided their outcomes, while externals experienced futility in trying to set their own rewards. Child-rearing practices are thought to have an important influence on the development of locus of control: an internal locus of control is created by predictable and consistent discipline, by parental support and involvement, and by parental encouragement of autonomy and self-control. Some evidence also suggests that the locus of control can be influenced over a long period of time by the way employees are reinforced at work. At least one study has shown that the locus of control becomes more internal as a result of exposure to a work environment where important rewards are consistently associated with individual behavior.[15]

Self-Esteem. Our self-concept is presumed to be a particularly human manifestation, and refers to our own conscious awareness of who we are. We see ourselves relative to others, and form evaluative impressions about our skills, abilities, and behaviors. Our self-concept is a collection of the attitudes, values, and beliefs we have acquired about ourselves from our unique experiences. We form opinions about our behavior, ability, appearance, and overall worth as a person from our own observations and the feedback we receive from others.

Over time, our accumulated experiences establish our self-concept. This self-concept determines how we feel about ourselves, and influences how we respond to others. Individuals with high self-esteem are generally more creative, independent, and spontaneous in their interactions with others. Because of their positive feelings about themselves, they can concentrate on the issues at hand and focus on new and original ideas without being as concerned about how people feel about them. On the other hand, people with low self-esteem tend to feel overly concerned about the evaluations of others, which dilutes their ability to concentrate on problems and to think creatively. Their low self-esteem often causes them to withdraw from the task or social situation.

Extensive research has shown that the behaviors of individuals are consistent with their self-concepts. Students, for example, who see themselves as competent academic achievers quite consistently perform better in school than students who don't. Individuals with high self-esteem are generally more accurate in their perceptions of social situations than those with low self-esteem.[16]

Problems of low self-esteem are often attributed to inadequate positive reinforcement from others. Although people with low self-esteem have usually experienced less praise than others, the solution is not to simply give them more praise and recognition. Our self-esteem is greatly influenced by how well we have actually performed. Although the comments of others help us interpret our performance, how well we have actually done has a greater impact on our self-esteem. Therefore, in raising an individual's self-esteem, praise and compliments may not be as effective as actually helping the individual perform better.

Self-efficacy:
A belief in one's ability to perform a specific activity that is determined primarily by how well the person has learned and practiced the task.

Self-Efficacy. Self-efficacy refers to one's belief in one's capability to perform a specific task. In many respects the concept of self-efficacy is similar to the concepts of self-esteem and locus of control. However, self-efficacy is task-specific rather than a generalized perception of overall competence.

Self-efficacy emerged from the research on social cognitive theory (explained in chapter 7) and represents an important personality variable that explains variations in individual performance. Several studies suggest that self-efficacy is a better predictor of subsequent performance than past behavior.[17] Although knowing how well people have performed in the past helps to predict their future performance, an even better predictor is knowing how capable they feel regarding a specific task.[18]

Self-efficacy has three dimensions: magnitude, strength, and generality. *Magnitude* refers to the level of task difficulty that a person believes he or she can attain, and is related to the concept of goal setting. Some people think they can achieve very difficult goals. *Strength* refers to the amount of confidence one has in one's ability to perform, and it can be strong or weak. Some people have strong convictions that they will succeed even when they face difficult challenges. *Generality* indicates the degree to which one's expectations are generalized across many situations or restricted to an isolated instance. Some people believe they can succeed in a variety of situations.

Self-efficacy is a learned characteristic that is acquired by four kinds of information cues:

1. *Enactive mastery*: The most influential stimulus contributing to the development of self-efficacy is enactive mastery, which refers to the repeated performance or practicing of the task. For example, a nurse who has inserted many IV needles should have high self-efficacy in being able to do it again.
2. *Vicarious experience*: Observing the behavior of others (modeling) can be almost as effective as enactive mastery, especially when the person and the model are similar in terms of age, capability, and other characteristics, and when the model's behavior is clearly visible.
3. *Verbal persuasion*: In the development of self-efficacy, verbal persuasion is less effective than practicing or modeling; nevertheless, it can be an im-

portant source of efficacy information, especially if the source has high credibility and expertise, and if there are multiple sources who agree.

4. *Perceptions of one's physiological state*: Efficacy perceptions are influenced by momentary levels of arousal as illustrated by these statements of athletes: "We were ready for them," "They were really up for this game," "I was mentally prepared," and "He was really psyched for this match."

Efficacy perceptions appear to be self-reinforcing. Self-efficacy influences the kinds of activities and settings people choose to participate in, the skills they are willing to practice and learn, the amount of energy they are willing to exert, and the persistence of their coping efforts in the face of obstacles. People with high self-efficacy tend to engage more frequently in task-related activities and persist longer in coping efforts; this leads to more mastery experiences, which enhance their self-efficacy. People with low self-efficacy tend to engage in fewer coping efforts; they give up more easily under adversity and demonstrate less mastery, which in turn reinforces their low self-efficacy.[19]

Self-efficacy can predict performance in a variety of settings, as long as the efficacy measure is tailored to the specific tasks being performed. Consequently, efficacy perceptions are relevant in many organizational settings, such as employee selection, training and development, and vocational counseling. Employees with high self-efficacy would be expected to respond more favorably to most personnel programs, such as performance evaluation, financial incentive, and promotion programs.[20]

Maslow's Need Hierarchy

Maslow's need hierarchy:
A theory of motivation and personality developed by Abraham Maslow that is based on a hierarchy of five human needs.

Abraham Maslow, a clinical psychologist, developed a popular need theory as part of a larger theory of human behavior. From his experience as a therapist and counselor, Maslow formulated a theory that explained human behavior in terms of a hierarchy of five universal needs that were ordered from the lowest-level basic needs to the highest-order needs.[21]

1. *Physiological needs.* Physiological needs, the most basic needs in Maslow's hierarchy, included needs that must be satisfied for the person to survive, including food, water, oxygen, sleep, sex, and sensory satisfaction.
2. *Safety and security needs.* If the physiological needs are relatively satisfied, Maslow claimed that safety and security needs would emerge. These needs include a desire for security, stability, dependency, and protection; freedom from fear and anxiety; and a need for structure, order, and law. Threats of wild animals, physical harm, assault, or tyranny prevent individuals from satisfying their safety needs, and cause them to focus their energies almost exclusively on eliminating these threats.
3. *Social needs.* Originally Maslow referred to this need as the need for belongingness and love. Social needs include the need for emotional love, friendship, and affectionate relationships with people in general, but especially a spouse, children, and friends. Individuals who are unable to satisfy this need will feel pangs of loneliness, ostracism, and rejection.
4. *Ego and esteem.* The need for ego and esteem includes the desire for self-respect and self-esteem, and for the esteem of others, and may be focused either internally or externally. When focused internally, the esteem needs

include a desire for strength, achievement, adequacy, mastery, confidence, independence, and freedom. When focused externally, this need consists of a desire for reputation or prestige, status, fame and glory, dominance, recognition, attention, importance, dignity, and appreciation.

5. ***Self-actualization.*** The highest need in Maslow's hierarchy is for ***self-actualization***, which refers to the needs for self-realization, continuous self-development, and the process of becoming all that a person is capable of becoming.

According to Maslow, these five needs are arranged in a hierarchy that he called ***prepotency***. Higher-level needs are not important and are not manifest until lower-level needs are satisfied. Once lower-level needs are satisfied, needs at the next highest level emerge and influence behavior. The levels of the need hierarchy are not rigidly separated but overlap to some extent. Thus it is possible for a higher-level need to emerge before a lower-level need is completely satisfied. In fact, Maslow estimated that average working adults have satisfied about 85 percent of their physiological needs, 70 percent of their safety needs, 50 percent of their social needs, 40 percent of their self-esteem needs, and 10 percent of their self-actualization needs. Although Maslow never collected data to support these estimates, numerous studies have found that lower-level needs are more completely satisfied than higher-level needs.[22]

Maslow's theory has been widely adopted by organizations and is frequently used as the foundation for organizational development programs such as participative management, job enrichment, and quality of work-life projects. According to his theory, an organization must use a variety of factors to motivate behavior, since individuals will be at different levels of the need hierarchy. A list of the general rewards and organizational factors used to satisfy different needs is illustrated in Exhibit 6.4. Maslow encouraged managers to be more sensitive to the needs of employees; he called the convergence of management and human relations "enlightened management."

Self-actualization. One of Maslow's unique contributions was his description of self-actualization. Self-actualization refers to the process of developing our true potential as individuals to the fullest extent, and expressing our skills, talents, and emotions in the most personally fulfilling manner. Self-actualization is a process, not an end state—individuals do not become self-actualized in the sense that they have finally reached an ultimate goal. Instead, they are continually in the process of becoming more and more of what they are uniquely capable of becoming.

In his later writings Maslow suggested that the need for self-actualization could not be gratified or satiated like the other needs. Instead, the need for self-actualization tends to increase as individuals engage in self-actualizing behaviors. Thus, self-actualization is an ongoing process of becoming that is sustained and intensified as people achieve self-fulfillment.

How self-actualization is manifest varies greatly from person to person. Maslow believed each person has a genetic blueprint that identifies what he or she is uniquely capable of becoming. In one person self-actualization might take the form of becoming an ideal mother, while others could express the same need athletically, musically, artistically, or administratively. Self-actualization does not require that we be the best in the world, only the best we can possibly

---

Self-Actualization:
The highest order need in Maslow's need hierarchy that consists of the need for self-realization, continuous self development, and ever increasing personal fulfillment.

Prepotency:
The idea that human needs are arranged in a hierarchical order and that higher-level needs do not emerge until lower-level needs are mostly satisfied.

Self-actualization:
The tendency for individuals to seek fulfillment and to achieve all that they have the potential to achieve according to their genetic blueprint.

Exhibit 6.4 Applying Maslow's Need Hierarchy

Need Levels	General Rewards	Organizational Factors
1. Physiological	Food, water, sex, sleep	a. pay b. pleasant working conditions c. cafeteria
2. Safety	Safety, security, stability, protection	a. safe working conditions b. company benefits c. job security
3. Social	Love, affection, belongingness	a. cohesive work group b. friendly supervision c. professional associations
4. Esteem	Self-esteem, self-respect, prestige, status	a. social recognition b. job title c. high status job d. feedback from the job itself
5. Self-actualization	Growth, advancement, creativity	a. challenging job b. opportunities for creativity c. achievement in work d. advancement in the organization

be. For example, people expressing their self-actualization athletically do not have to be world-class athletes to develop and enjoy their talents. Fulfillment can be derived from achieving their personal best performances. Although Maslow said self-actualization could not be defined precisely, he suggested that it was associated with such things as greater freshness of appreciation and richness of emotional reaction, improved interpersonal relations, more democratic values and character structure, increased creativity, a carefully designed system of values, and greater frequency of peak experiences.

McClelland's Learned Needs Theory

Learned Needs: Needs that have been acquired by the events individuals have experienced within their culture. David McClelland studied three learned needs, achievement, affiliation, and power and described how these needs are acquired and how they influence behavior.

Another popular theory for examining behavior is the learned needs theory developed by David McClelland and his associates. This theory is closely associated with learning theory, since McClelland believed that needs were learned, or acquired, by the kinds of events people experienced in their culture. These learned needs represented behavioral predispositions that influence the way people perceive and act in each situation. People who acquire a particular need behave differently from those who do not possess it. McClelland and his associates, particularly John Atkinson, investigated achievement, affiliation, and power, abbreviated *"nAch," "nAff,"* and *"nPow,"* respectively.[23]

The Need for Achievement—nAch. The most thorough series of studies conducted by McClelland and his associates concerned the need for achievement, which they measured with a projective test called the Thematic Apperception Test (TAT). This test consisted of showing people a series of pictures and asking them to write an imaginative story about each picture. Their scores measured how many times they referred to achievement-oriented ideas in their stories. McClelland believed that high-need achievers would write achievement-oriented stories about people seeking success and striving to accomplish particular goals. His research identified three characteristics of high-need achievers:

Need for achievement:
A personality trait that reflects the importance of achievement and upward striving in a person's life. High-need achievers are characterized by a desire for personal responsibility, moderate levels of risk, and immediate feedback on their performance.

1. High-need achievers have a strong desire to assume *personal responsibility* for performing a task or finding a solution to a problem. Consequently, they tend to work alone rather than with others. If the task requires the presence of others, they tend to choose coworkers based upon their competence rather than their friendship.
2. High-need achievers are characterized by *moderate risk taking and goal setting*. They tend to set moderately difficult goals and take calculated risks. Consequently, in a ring-toss game in which children tossed rings at a peg at any distance they chose, high-need achievers chose an intermediate distance where the probability of success was moderate, while low-need achievers chose either high or low probabilities of success by standing extremely close to or very far away from the peg.
3. High-need achievers have a strong desire for performance *feedback*. These individuals want to know how well they have done, and they are anxious to receive feedback regardless of whether they have succeeded or failed.

In his research on the need for achievement, McClelland found that money did not have a very strong motivating effect on high-need achievers; they were already highly motivated. In a laboratory study, for example, high-need achievers performed very well with or without financial incentives.[24] Low-need achievers did not perform well without financial incentives, but when they were offered money for their work, they performed noticeably better. This study does not mean that money is unimportant to high-need achievers. Instead, to them, money is a form of feedback and recognition. When high-need achievers succeed, they see monetary rewards as evidence of their success.

High-need achievers are characterized by their single-minded preoccupation with task accomplishment. Consequently, the need for achievement is an important motive in organizations because many managerial and entrepreneurial positions require such a single-minded preoccupation for success. McClelland believed that a high need for achievement was essential to entrepreneurial success. In a series of rather unique and interesting studies, McClelland examined the need for achievement among managers in a number of current societies to show that a high need for achievement correlated with managerial success and economic activity. By examining the literature of earlier civilizations, McClelland showed that the rise and fall of economic activity correlated with the rise and fall of the achievement motive.

This line of research is perhaps best illustrated by a study of the need for achievement in England between A.D. 1500 and 1850. To measure the achievement orientation of the English culture, the researchers analyzed the literature written at various points during this period. The need for achievement was measured by counting the number of achievement themes per 100 lines of literature. The measure of economic activity came from historical records showing the tons of coal exported from England. The results, summarized in

Exhibit 6.6 The Relationship between the Need for Achievement and Economic Activity in England: 1500 to 1850 A.D.

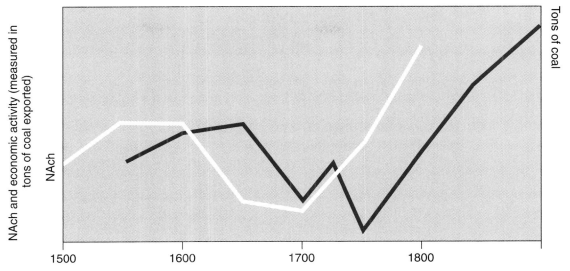

Source: David C. McClelland, *The Achieving Society*, New York: Free Press, 1967, p. 139.

Exhibit 6.6, show that the rise and fall of economic activity followed the rise and fall of the need for achievement by about 50 years.[25]

McClelland concludes from his research that the need for achievement, like other personality characteristics, is apparently learned at an early age and largely influenced by child-rearing practices of parents. Children tend to have a high need for achievement if they have been raised by parents who have fairly strict expectations about right and wrong behavior, who provide clear feedback on the effectiveness of their performance, and who help their children accept a personal responsibility for their actions.[26]

The need for achievement appears to be an important personal characteristic for entrepreneurs. A willingness to take reasonable risks, personal accountability, and a constant striving for goal accomplishment seem to be essential traits for successful entrepreneurs. A review of 23 studies that attempted to link achievement motivation and entrepreneurship found a positive relationship in 20 of the studies.[27]

McClelland argues that economic development and national prosperity are closely related to the need for achievement, and recommends that U.S. foreign aid programs to poorer countries focus on raising the need for achievement rather than on providing financial aid. He argues that the achievement motive can be taught, and explains how to do it. His training focuses on four objectives. First, managers are encouraged to set personal goals and keep a record of their performance. Second, they are taught the language of achievement—to think, talk, and act like people with a high achievement motive. Third, managers are given cognitive or intellectual support—they are taught why the achievement motive is important to success. Fourth, they are provided with group support—a group of budding entrepreneurs met periodically to share success stories. In short, managers are taught how to think and behave as entrepreneurs with a high achievement motive. Their new success-oriented behavior is reinforced verbally and intellectually, and through peer group influences.

Following this model, McClelland conducted a training program for 52 business executives in Hyderabad, India. Six to ten months after the course, many executives had doubled their natural rate of entrepreneurial activity. These findings have important implications for efforts to assist underdeveloped nations because they suggest that beyond giving economic aid lies a greater need to instill the achievement motive in the population.[28]

Need for Affiliation:
The need to associate with other people and obtain their friendship and approval.

The Need for Affiliation—nAff. The need for affiliation is defined as a desire to establish and maintain friendly, warm relations with other individuals. In many ways the need for affiliation is similar to Maslow's social needs. Individuals with a high need for affiliation possess these characteristics:

1. They have a strong desire for approval and reassurance from others.
2. They have a tendency to conform to the wishes and norms of others when they are pressured by people whose friendship they value.
3. They have a sincere interest in the feelings of others.

Individuals with a high need for affiliation seek opportunities at work to satisfy this need. Therefore, individuals with a high nAff prefer to work with others rather than alone, and they tend to have good attendance records. Individuals with a high nAff tend to perform better in situations where personal support and approval are tied to performance.

The implications for organizations are fairly straightforward. To the extent that managers can create a cooperative, supportive work environment where positive feedback is tied to task performance, individuals with a high nAff will be more productive. Such an environment allows individuals with high nAff to satisfy their affiliation needs. Conversely, individuals who have a low need for affiliation should be placed in positions where they can work independently, since they prefer to work alone.

Need for Power:
The desire to influence or control other people either for the sake of personal satisfaction of for the benefit of society.

The Need for Power—nPow. The need for power has been studied extensively by McClelland and others.[29] This need is defined as the need to control others, to influence their behavior, and to be responsible for them. Some psychologists have argued that the need for power is the major goal of all human activity. These people view human development as the process by which people learn to exert control over the forces that exert power over them. According to this view, the ultimate satisfaction comes from being able to control environmental forces, including other people. Individuals who possess a high need for power are characterized by:

1. A desire to influence and direct somebody else.
2. A desire to exercise control over others.
3. A concern for maintaining leader-follower relations.

Individuals with a high need for power tend to make more suggestions, offer their opinions and evaluations more frequently, and attempt to bring others around to their way of thinking. They also tend to seek positions of leadership in group activities, and their behavior within a group, either as leader or member, is described as verbally fluent, talkative, and sometimes argumentative.

Personal Power:
A manifestation of the need for power in which individuals strive for dominance and control over other individuals.

Social Power:
A form of the need for power in which individuals attempt to satisfy their power needs by working with a group to achieve group and organizational goals.

In his research on the need for power, McClelland describes "two faces of power." The need for power can take the form of *personal power*—individuals strive for dominance almost for the sake of dominance—or *social power*—individuals are more concerned with the problems of the organization and what can be done to facilitate goal attainment. Individuals with a high need for personal power tend to behave like conquistadors or tribal chiefs, who inspire their subordinates to heroic performance but want their subordinates to be accountable to the leader, not to the organization. Individuals with a high need for social power, however, satisfy their power needs by working with the group to formulate and achieve group goals. This method of satisfying power needs is oriented toward achieving organizational effectiveness rather than satisfying a self-serving egotism.[30]

Power needs are especially salient when the time comes for an entrepreneur to step aside and place the direction of a company under the control of a successor. A study of succession planning among entrepreneurs found that social power entrepreneurs are likely to have less trouble turning over their positions of power to someone else than do entrepreneurs who need personal power.[31]

McClelland argues that the need for social power is the most important determinant of managerial success. Although a high need for achievement may be necessary for entrepreneurial activity, most managerial positions in today's corporate world require managers who have a strong need for social power. Successful managers also need to have a relatively high need for achievement, but achievement is not as important for corporate managers in large corporations as it is for entrepreneurs.

Although individuals with a high need for social power tend to be more effective managers, McClelland provides some evidence that these individuals pay a fairly high price for their success in terms of their own personal health. McClelland measured the need for power among a group of Harvard graduates and followed their careers over a 20-year period. He found that 58 percent of those rated high in nPow either had high blood pressure or had died of heart failure.[32]

Discussion Questions

1. Explain the concepts of perceptual inferences, stereotyping, and projection, and explain how they are both good and bad. Provide illustrations of them from your own experience.
2. How does the self-fulfilling prophecy occur, and how large a factor do you think it is in determining the success of new employees? Describe a time in your life when the self-fulfilling prophecy impacted your behavior.
3. Describe the locus of control and apply it to your life; i.e., are you more internally or externally directed? How would you expect internals to respond differently than externals to each of these organizational events: a job enrichment program, a profit-sharing plan, a management development program, and a union election?
4. Describe the concept of self-actualization and explain its meaning in Maslow's theory of motivation. Apply it to your career: what do you think you have the unique capacity to do or become?

5. How is the need for achievement learned, and what impact does it have on behavior? How would you rate your personal level of achievement orientation? What experiences have contributed to your need for achievement?

Notes

1. J. T. Malloy, *Dress for Success* (New York: Warner Books, 1975); M. Snyder, E.D. Tanke, E. Berscheid "Social Perception and Interpersonal Behavior: On the Self-Fulfilling Nature of Social Stereotypes," *Journal of Personality and Social Psychology* 35 (1977): 656–66.
2. Douglas McGregor, *The Human Side of Enterprise* (New York: McGraw-Hill, 1960).
3. Eugene Mayfield, "The Selection Interview-A Reevaluation of Published Research," *Personnel Psychology* (Autumn 1964): 239–60. S.W. Constantin, "An Investigation of Information Favorability in the Employment Interview," *Journal of Applied Psychology* 61 (1976): 743–49; O.R. Wright, "Summary of Research on the Employment Interview Since 1964," *Personnel Psychology*, 22 (1969): 391–413; Angelo J. Kinicki, Peter W. Hom, Chris A. Lockwood, Roger W. Griffeth "Interviewer Predictions of Applicant Qualifications and Interviewer Validity: Aggregate and Individual Analyses," *Journal of Applied Psychology* 75, (October 1990): 477–86).
4. Rosabeth Moss Kanter, *Men and Women of the Corporation* (New York: Basic Books, 1977), chapter 8.
5. Robert Rosenthal and L. Jacobson, *Pygmalion in the Classroom* (New York: Holt, Rinehart, and Winston, 1968).
6. Ibid. See also Jack Horn "Pygmalion vs. Golem in a High School Gym," *Psychology Today* 18, (July 1984): 9–10.
7. J. Sterling Livingston, "Pygmalion in Management," *Harvard Business Review* (July-August 1969) 81–89; L. Sandler, "Self-Fulfilling Prophecy: Better Training by Mayle." *Training: The Magazine of Human Resource Development* 23 (Feb. 1986): 60–64.
8. Lee Ross and Richard E. Nisbett, *The Person and the Situation* (New York: McGraw Hill, 1991).
9. F. Heider, *The Psychology of Interpersonal Behavior* (New York: Wiley, 1958); Steven E. Kaplan, "Improving Performance Evaluation," *CMA-The Management Accounting Magazine* 61 (May-June, 1987): 56–59.
10. Jean M. Bartunek, "Why Did You Do That? Attribution Theory in Organizations," *Business Horizons* 24, 5 (1981): 66–71; Edward E. Jones and Richard E. Naisbett, *The Actor and the Observer: Divergent Perceptions of the Causes of Behavior* (Morristown, NJ: General Learning Press, 1971); J. C. McElroy and C. B. Shrader, "Attribution Theories of Leadership and Network Analysis," *Journal of Management* 12 (Fall 1986): 35.
11. Harold H. Kelley and John L. Michela, "Attribution Theory and Research," *Annual Review of Psychology* (1980): 457–501.; Terence R. Mitchell and Robert E. Wood, "Supervisors' Responses to Subordinate Poor Performance: A Test of an Attributional Model," *Organizational Behavior and Human Performance* (1980): 123–28.
12. Julian B. Rotter, "Generalized Expectancies for Internal Versus External Control of Reinforcement," *Psychological Monographs* 80 (1966): 1–28.

13. Virginia T. Geurin and Gary F. Kohut, "The Relationship of Locus of Control and Participative Decision Making Among Managers and Business Students," *Mid-Atlantic Journal of Business* 25, (February 1989): 57–66; Mia Lokman, "Participation in Budgetary Decision Making, Task Difficulty, Locus of Control, and Employee Behavior: An Empirical Study," *Decision Sciences* 18, (Fall 1987): 547–61; Paul E. Spector, "Development of the Work Locus of Control Scale," *Journal of Occupational Psychology* 61 (December 1988): 335–40.

14. C. Anderson, Donald Hellriegel, and John Slocum, "Managerial Response to Environmentally Induced Stress," *Academy of Management Journal* 20 (1977): 260–72; see also Phillip L. Storms and Paul E. Spector, "Relationships of Organizational Frustration with Reported Behaviorial Reactions: The Moderating Effect of Locus of Control," *Journal of Occupational Psychology* 60 (December 1987): 227–34.

15. S. Eitzen, "Impact of Behavior Modification Techniques on Locus of Control of Delinquent Boys," *Psychological Reports* 35 (1974): 1317–18; Charles J. Cox and Gary L. Cooper, "The Making of the British CEO: Childhood, Work Experience, Personality, and Management Style," *Academy of Management Executive* 3 (August 1989): 241–45.

16. R. H. Combs and V. Davies, "Self-Conception and the Relationship between High School and College Scholastic Achievement," *Sociology and Social Research* 50 (1966): 460–71; B. Borislow, "Self-Evaluation and Academic Achievement," *Journal of Counseling Psychology* 9 (1962): 246–54; D. E. Hamachek, ed. *The Self in Growth, Teaching, and Learning* (Englewood Cliffs, NJ: Prentice-Hall, 1965).

17. Albert Bandura, "Self-Efficacy: Toward a Unifying Theory of Behaviorial Change," *Psychological Review* 84 (1977): 191–215; Albert Bandura, "Self-Efficacy Mechanism in Human Agency," *American Psychologist* 37 (1982): 122–47; Albert Bandura, N.E. Adams, A.B. Hardy, G.N. Howells, "Tests of the Generality of Self-Efficacy Theory," *Cognitive Therapy and Research* 4, (1980): 39–66.

18. John Lane and Peter Herriot, "Self-Ratings, Supervisor Ratings, Positions and Performance," *Journal of Occupational Psychology* 63 (March 1990): 77–88; Robert Wood, Albert Bandura, and Trevor Bailey, "Mechanisms Governing Organizational Performance in Complex Decision-Making Environments," *Organizational Behavior and Human Decision Processes* 46 (August 1990): 181–201.

19. Albert Bandura, D.H. Shunk, "Cultivating Confidence, Self-Efficacy, and Intrinsic Interest Through Proximal Self Motivation," *Journal of Personality and Social Psychology* 41 (1981): 586–98.

20. Marilyn E. Gist, "Self-Efficacy: Implications for Organizational Behavior and Human Resource Management," *Academy of Management Review* 12 (July 1987): 472–85.

21. Abraham H. Maslow, *Motivation and Personality* (New York: Harper, 1954).

22. Abraham H. Maslow, "A Theory of Human Motivation," *Psychological Review* 1 (1943): 370–96.

23. David C. McClelland, "Toward a Theory of Motive Acquisition," *American Psychologist* 20 (1965): 321–33.

24. J. W. Atkinson and W. R. Reitman, "Performance as a Function of Motive Strength and Expectancy of Goal-Attainment," *Journal of Abnormal Social Psychology* 53: (1956): 361–66.

25. David C. McClelland, *The Achieving Society* (New York: The Free Press, 1961). However, McClelland's research findings were not confirmed in a follow-up study thirty years later by Christopher J. Gilleard, "The Achieving Society Revisited: A Further Analysis of the Relation Between National Economic Growth and Need Achievement," *Journal of Economic Psychology* 10 (March 1989): 21–34.

26. David C. McClelland, "Achievement Motivation Can be Developed," *Harvard Business Review* (Nov.-Dec. 1965): 6–24.

27. Bradley R. Johnson, "Toward a Multi-Dimensional Model of Entrepreneurship: A Case of Achievement Motivation and the Entrepreneur," *Entrepreneurship: Theory and Practice* 14 (Spring 1990): 39–54; see also Ari Ginsberg and Ann Buchholtz, "Are Entrepreneurs a Breed Apart? A Look At The Evidence," *Journal of General Management* 15 (Winter 1989): 32–40.

28. David C. McClelland, "Business Drive and National Achievement," *Harvard Business Review* 40 (July, 1962): 99–112.

29. David C. McClelland, "The Two Faces of Power," *Journal of International Affairs* 24 (1970): 29–47; Jeffrey Pfeffer, *Power in Organizations* (Marshfield, MA: Pitman, 1981).

30. David C. McClelland, "The Two Faces of Power," *Journal of International Affairs* 24 (1970): 29–47.

31. Roger T. Peay and W. Gibb Dyer, Jr. "Power Orientations of Entrepreneurs and Succession Planning," *Journal of Small Business Management* 27 (January 1989): 47–52.

32. David C. McClelland, "Power is the Great Motivation," *Harvard Business Review* 54 (No. 2, 1976): 100–10.

Using Positive Pygmalion In the Fast Food Industry

The fast food industry is plagued by high turnover and labor shortages. Many entry-level employees leave because they lack the basic interpersonal skills managers expect of all employees. Several Philadelphia fast-food restaurants have found a solution to their turnover and labor-shortage problems by using the Pygmalion effect—the influence that one person's expectations can have on another person's behavior.

Project Transition started when a fast-food chain in Philadelphia hired a consultant to reduce turnover. He suggested that welfare recipients would be a good source of employees for entry-level positions if they could acquire basic interpersonal skills. Project Transition screens and trains welfare recipients, and places them in full-time jobs with participating restaurants. Experience has shown that the managers of the fast-food restaurants adequately explain the technical requirements of the job, but they fail to convey important behavioral expectations.

Therefore, each new employee is paired with a volunteer coach who helps the person make the transition from welfare to employment. The coaches, who are graduate students from business schools, explain to the employees what they are expected to do and how to create a favorable expectation in the manager so the managers will be willing to give them the help they need to succeed. The training is very simple; they tell the employees to smile instead of frown, how they should dress and groom themselves, and that they should use good posture and positive body language.

These simple interventions improve the managers' perceptions of employees, and thus increase their expectations. Because the managers expect them to succeed, they stay and succeed. During the first year of Project Transition, all 57 participants stayed off welfare and remained gainfully employed.

Project Transition aids former welfare recipients by helping them understand how they are perceived by their managers, and what they can do to enhance that perception. As the managers' perceptions improve, their expectations also increase, and consequently, the performance of the employees improves to meet those higher expectations.

Questions

1. What is the Pygmalion effect? How does it function?
2. What are some examples of specific daily events that have to occur for it to happen?
3. How can managers use the Pygmalion effect as a conscious strategy to increase productivity?
4. To what extent can any of your successes and failures be explained as self-fulfilled prophecies?

Source: Barbara Whitaker Shimko, "Using Positive Pygmalion to Build Your Work Force," *Cornell HRA Quarterly*, (November 1989), pp 91-94; Barbara Whitaker Shimko, "The McPygmalion Effect," *Training and Development Journal*, Vol. 44 (June 1990), pp. 64-70.

Locus of Control

This exercise is designed to measure how you think certain important events in our society affect different people. Each item consists of a pair of alternatives lettered A and B. Circle the statement that you more strongly believe to be true. Be sure to mark the one you actually believe to be true rather than the one you think you should choose or the one you would like to be true. This is a measure of personal belief. Obviously, there are no right or wrong answers.

Please answer these items carefully, but do not spend too much time on one item. In some instances, you may discover that you believe both statements or neither. In such cases, select the one you more strongly believe to be the case. Try to respond to each item independently. Do not be influenced by your previous choices.

1. a. Promotions are earned through hard work and persistence.
   b. Getting promoted is really a matter of being a little luckier than the next person.
2. a. Succeeding in your chosen occupation is mainly a matter of social contacts— knowing the right people.
   b. Succeeding in your chosen profession is mainly a matter of personal competence— how much you know.
3. a. Achieving a successful marriage depends on the devotion and commitment of both partners to each other.
   b. The most important element in a happy marriage is being lucky enough to marry the right person.
4. a. It is silly to think that you can really change another person's basic attitudes.
   b. When I am right, I can convince others.
5. a. In our society, future earning power depends on ability.
   b. Making a lot of money is largely a matter of getting the right breaks.
6. a. I have little influence over the way other people behave.
   b. If you know how to deal with people, you can lead them and get them to do what you want.
7. a. I believe the grades I receive are the result of my own efforts; luck has little or nothing to do with it.
   b. Sometimes I feel that I have little control over the grades that I get.
8. a. Marriage is largely a gamble that can end in divorce no matter how hard the partners try.
   b. Most divorces could be avoided if both partners were determined to make the marriage work.
9. a. Success in an occupation is mainly a matter of how much effort you put into it.
   b. Success in an occupation is mainly a matter of luck—being in the right place at the right time.
10. a. Often, the way teachers assign grades seems haphazard to me.
    b. In my experience, I have noticed that there is usually a direct connection between how hard I study and the grades I get.

11. a. People like me can change the course of world affairs if we make ourselves heard.
     b. It is only wishful thinking to believe that you can really influence what happens in society at large.
12. a. A great deal that happens to me is probably a matter of chance.
     b. I am the master of my fate.
13. a. Getting along with people is a skill that must be practiced.
     b. It is almost impossible to figure out how to please some people.

Scoring

For each of the thirteen items, one statement reflects an internal response and the other statement reflects an external response. For the odd items, the internal response is the first statement. For the even items, the internal response is the second statement. After completing the exercise, count how many internal choices you have circled. Your score is the total number of choices.

This questionnaire is adapted from Julian B. Rotter's internal-external control scale, which measures the extent to which individuals believe that the rewards that come to them are controlled by internal forces, such as their own ability and effort, as opposed to external forces, such as luck, chance, fate, or "the system." In this exercise, extreme externals would score between 0 and 3, while extreme internals would score between 10 and 13.

Discussion Question

How would you expect extreme internals to respond differently from extreme externals to the following kinds of personnel activities: job search, performance evaluation, a piece-rate incentive system, training and development activities, safety programs, physical fitness centers?

Source: Adapted from Julian B. Rotter, "Internal Control External Control: A Sampler." *Psychology Today*, vol. 5 (June 1971), p. 42. The actual research scale is reported in Julian B. Rotter, "Generalized Expectancies for Internal vs. External Control of Reinforcement," *Psychological Monographs* (vol. 80, no. 1, Whole no. 609, 1966).

7

Motivation

Chapter Outline

Theories of Learning and Reinforcement

Classical Conditioning

Operant Conditioning

Social Cognitive Theory

Reinforcement

Reinforcers

Reinforcement Contingencies

Reward Schedules

Behavior Modification

Cognitive Motivation Theories

Expectancy Theory

Equity Theory

Goal Setting

Motivating Employees

THEORIES OF LEARNING AND REINFORCEMENT

Motivation is probably the most popular topic in organizational behavior because it involves such critical questions as "Why do people behave the way they do?" and "How can we motivate employees to perform their jobs?" Perhaps the best summary principle explaining human behavior is that people do what they expect to be rewarded for doing. However, we do not always know when a specific outcome will be perceived as a reward, or if it will be the most important reward.

Numerous motivation theories address these basic questions, including both reinforcement theories and cognitive theories. The three major reinforcement theories described in this chapter include classical conditioning, operant conditioning, and social cognitive theory. These theories explain behavior in terms of the reinforcing consequences of behavior, and they are also called learning theories because they explain how individuals acquire new behaviors and why their present behavior is sustained.

The three major cognitive theories of motivation are expectancy theory, equity theory, and goal-setting theory. These theories explain how people analyze their situations and behave in ways that maximize the rewards available to them.

Classical Conditioning

Classical conditioning consists of connecting or pairing a neutral stimulus with a reflexive response. *Reflexive responses*, also called respondent behaviors, consist of responses controlled by the autonomic nervous system, such as blood pressure changes, salivation, and the secretion of adrenaline. These responses are normally caused by specific unconditioned (unlearned) stimuli. For example, the taste of food causes salivation, peeling onions causes the eyes to water, and a state of stress causes the blood pressure to rise. However, these same responses can be conditioned to otherwise neutral stimuli by repeatedly pairing or associating the unconditioned stimuli with the conditioned stimuli.[1]

The pioneering research on classical conditioning comes from Ivan Pavlov, the noted Russian physiologist, who was studying the automatic reflexes associated with digestion in dogs. Pavlov noted that the secretion of saliva and gastric juices were unlearned responses caused by the chemical reactions of food, and he succeeded in training the dogs to salivate not only to the sight of food but also to various other signals, such as rotating disks, a metronome, or the sound of a bell. The training process consisted of presenting meat powder and the sound of a bell at the same time to a dog. After repeated pairings of the food with the bell, the dog became conditioned to salivate to the sound of the bell.[2] Exhibit 7.1 illustrates how a conditioned stimulus (bell) can become paired with an unconditioned stimulus (food) to evoke a conditioned response (salivation).

Classical conditioning is also called *respondent conditioning* or *reflexive conditioning,* because the conditioned responses are innate reflexive responses. Some conditioned responses can be acquired quite rapidly with very few pairings of the conditioned and unconditioned stimuli. Conditioned responses also tend to extinguish rather rapidly. After the dog was conditioned to salivate to the sound of the bell, salivation would occur to the sound of the bell

Classical conditioning: A form of learning involving responses of the autonomic nervous system where a conditioned stimulus is associated with a conditioned response.

Reflexive responses: Responses that are governed by the autonomic nervous system, such as blood pressure, heart rate, salivation, and respiration rate.

Unconditioned Stimulus (UCS): A stimulus that naturally elicits a reflexive response. By associating an unconditioned stimulus with a neutral stimulus, the neutral stimulus becomes a conditioned stimulus that produces the same response, called a conditioned response.

Conditioned stimulus (CS): A neutral stimulus that has become paired with a conditioned response through the process of classical conditioning.

Conditioned response (CR): A response that has been paired with a conditioned stimulus.

Exhibit 7.1   Classical Conditioning Process: Pairing a Conditioned Stimulus with a Conditioned Response

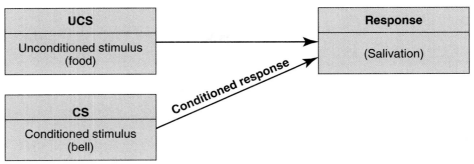

Reflexive conditioning:
Another name for classical conditioning where reflexive behavior governed by the autonomic nervous system is associated with a conditioned stimulus.

Stimulus generalization:
The process of using a slightly different stimulus to elicit a response.

Spontaneous recovery:
The reappearance of a conditioned response that had been created earlier and then extinguished.

alone without the meat powder. However, if the meat powder was not occasionally presented with the sound of the bell, the conditioned response of salivating was soon extinguished. A dog will not endlessly salivate to the sound of the bell if it is not periodically accompanied by meat powder. However, some reflexive responses, especially those associated with pain, are very resistant to extinction.

When a reflexive response is conditioned to one stimulus, other similar stimuli will also elicit the response. If a dog is conditioned to salivate to the sound of a bell producing a tone of middle C, it will also salivate to slightly higher or lower tones without further conditioning. This principle, called *stimulus generalization,* explains how we are able to respond to novel situations because of their similarities to familiar ones.

Extinction does not actually destroy a conditioned response. After a period of time, a conditioned stimulus may elicit the conditioned response again even though it has not recently been paired with the unconditioned stimulus. This return of the conditioned response is called *spontaneous recovery,* and it suggests that extinction is some sort of active inhibition or suppression of the conditioned response, not a permanent forgetting or disappearance of the response.

The most interesting applications of classical conditioning are found in marketing and stress-management programs. Many advertising campaigns attempt to associate a particular product or brand name with a conditioned response. Commercials are designed to associate a neutral stimulus such as a new product or a brand name, with another stimulus, such as the sound of pleasant music or the sight of an exciting activity to evoke a favorable emotion as a conditioned response.[3]

Stress and anxiety are largely responses of the autonomic nervous system that have been classically conditioned to other stimuli. For example, if telephone calls consist of one harassing problem after another, the sound of a ringing telephone can become a conditioned stimulus eliciting high blood pressure. If the telephone continues to ring throughout the day, and the majority of the calls are unpleasant hassles, the consequence could be chronically high blood pressure. Many stress management programs attempt to reduce excessive stress and anxiety by eliminating the association between the stimulus and the conditioned response.

Operant Conditioning

Operant conditioning focuses on learning voluntary behaviors—behaviors that are under the control of the muscle system of the body. Consequently, operant conditioning involves a much wider range of potential behavior than does classical conditioning. The term *operant conditioning* derives from the idea that individuals learn to operate on their environment to achieve desired consequences. Individuals learn to repeat certain behaviors because they are rewarded by the environment; these voluntary behaviors are called *operant responses*.

Stimulus-Response Bonds. Operant conditioning refers to the process of reinforcing a response that is made in the presence of a stimulus. The process is diagramed in this way:

Stimulus-response bonds are created by the consequences of the response. In operant conditioning, an environmental stimulus (S) is followed by a response (R), which is followed by an environmental consequence that can be either a positive or negative reinforcer. The response is said to be "instrumental" in receiving the consequence, which explains why operant conditioning is also referred to as *instrumental conditioning*.

According to operant conditioning, if a response is emitted (occurs) in the presence of a stimulus, and this response is reinforced, this will increase the probability that on future occasions the same response will be emitted in the presence of similar stimuli. An important aspect of this definition is the word *probability*. The stimulus does not cause the response, and it is not certain that an operant response will be emitted after the stimulus is presented. Operant conditioning is a probabilistic model that simply indicates that the probability of a response in a given situation is higher if it has been positively reinforced in the past than if it has not.

The principles of operant conditioning have been amply demonstrated in thousands of experimental studies using many different organisms including humans and animals, especially rats and pigeons. B.F. Skinner pioneered so much of the work on operant conditioning that the experimental chamber where rats and pigeons are tested has come to be known as a Skinner box. A Skinner box typically consists of three glass walls (so the researchers can observe the animal), a fourth wall containing a food box, and a device for making a response (such as a lever for rats to press or a key for pigeons to peck). This experimental chamber allowed the researchers to eliminate extraneous environmental stimuli and carefully reinforce a unique operant response. The basic principles of operant conditioning so amply demonstrated in animal studies have been extensively replicated with human subjects.[4]

Stimulus Generalization and Discrimination. In a typical organization, employees are simultaneously bombarded with dozens of stimuli. Even a relatively calm office environment contains countless stimuli, such as the lighting, the color of the walls, the sound of the keyboard, the conversation at the next desk, the hum of the air conditioning, the odor of perfume, and the feel of clothes that fit too tight.

Within this massive stimulus environment, the telephone rings and the employee is expected to respond to this unique stimulus by making a unique response. In this situation, the ringing of the telephone is considered a ***discriminative stimulus,*** since the individual is required to discriminate the sound of the phone from all the other environmental stimuli and make a differential response. Helping individuals identify the discriminative stimulus is an important part of operant conditioning and a critical part of many training and development programs. For example, basketball players must be trained to recognize a teammate breaking toward the basket as the discriminative stimulus for the response of passing the ball without being distracted by thousands of screaming fans or other distracting stimuli.

Someone who has learned to discriminate the sound of a ringing telephone should be able to recognize a slightly different ringing sound and still make the correct response because of the principle of ***stimulus generalization***. If the new stimulus was radically different, however, then a response would probably not be emitted until the individual learned to associate it with the new response. For example, most people would have difficulty learning to respond to a telephone that ticked like a clock instead of rang when someone phoned.

Operant Responses. Individuals have the capacity to produce a wide variety of potential responses, called a ***response repertoire***. Different organisms have unique response repertoires. For example, rats cannot be trained to fly, and pigeons cannot be trained to dribble a basketball or shoot free throws like humans. Nevertheless, animals have been trained to make remarkable responses that are both astonishing and entertaining. For example, chickens have been trained to play poker, ducks have been trained to play the piano, and porpoises have been trained to sing. People have been entertained by a variety of animal shows starring farm animals, such as pigs, dogs, and horses; and aquatic animals, such as whales, walruses, and porpoises.[5]

Chaining. Most of the responses we make are not simple responses to discriminative stimuli. Many of the things we do are far more complex. We usually make a series of responses, each one altering the environment and setting the stage for the next response. For example, shooting a lay-up consists of dribbling a basketball several times as the player runs toward the basket, jumps, and then shoots. Each response of running, dribbling, jumping, and shooting changes the stimulus environment and calls for the next response. Frequently only the last response of seeing the ball go through the basket is reinforced. This process of stringing together stimulus response bonds is called ***chaining,*** and is diagramed like this:

$$S \longrightarrow R \longrightarrow S \longrightarrow R \longrightarrow S \longrightarrow R \overset{\text{Reinforcement}}{\downarrow}$$

The concept of chaining is particularly important in the design of training programs. Rather than expecting learners to perform a complex series of responses, the task is divided into smaller steps, and each stimulus-response association is

---

Discriminative stimulus:
A specific environmental stimulus that a person has learned to distinguish from other environmental stimuli and to respond to.

Chaining:
The process of combining several stimulus response associations to form a complex behavior.

presented to the learners separately. As the learners practice each response, they are reinforced and receive feedback on their performance. Gradually the responses are combined until the learners can perform the entire complex response, and reinforcement is provided only for the final response.

Shaping:
The process of refining a response by selectively reinforcing closer and closer approximations of the desired response.

Shaping. *Shaping* refers to the process of acquiring a unique response by reinforcing closer and closer approximations of it. This process is also called the ***method of successive approximations***. During the early stages of learning, any response that remotely resembles the correct response is reinforced. However, as learning continues, only the responses that most closely approximate the correct response are reinforced. The process of shaping is used extensively in animal training, such as teaching porpoises to sing, or ducks to play the piano. At first the porpoise is reinforced for making any sound, but gradually the sounds must become closer and closer approximations to the desired sound before reinforcement is given. The process of shaping also occurs in human learning, especially in the development of skills such as learning to ice skate, dance, shoot a jump shot, or operate a machine.

Feedback. Performance feedback is a necessary prerequisite for learning. In one of the early studies on the importance of feedback, blindfolded students were asked to draw a three-inch line.[6] Students who received no feedback regarding the lengths of their lines did not improve in their ability to draw three-inch lines, even after several thousand trials. Although less variability in the lengths of the lines existed after many trials, the students were no closer to the goal after thousands of trials than at the start. However, significant improvements were noted in the lengths of the lines of the blindfolded students who were told whether their lines were too long or too short.

Feedback improves performance not only by helping employees correct their mistakes but also by providing reinforcement for learning. Knowledge of results is a positive form of reinforcement by itself. Learning activities have more intrinsic interest when performance feedback is available. Performance feedback should do more than tell employees whether they were right or wrong; it should also tell them how they can avoid making mistakes in the future. Merely informing individuals of their incorrect responses can be very frustrating for those who want to know why they were wrong. Studies have concluded that feedback is a valuable resource for individuals, and is especially important to employees who are new, who face ambiguous situations, who have ambiguous roles, and who are highly involved in their work.[7]

In general, knowledge of results is essential for learning, and the sooner this knowledge comes after the learner's response, the better. Studies in animal learning suggest that the ideal timing of the feedback is to have it occur almost immediately after the response has been made.[8] Some training programs are able to provide this kind of ideal feedback, but not all. Management development programs typically fail to provide any form of feedback, mainly because the managers are not given opportunities to respond until they are back on the job.

Social cognitive theory:
A major theory of learning based on observational and symbolic learning. Learning is influenced by what is reinforced, either extrinsically or through self-administered reinforcement, especially the anticipations of future events.

Social Cognitive Theory

Social cognitive theory developed during the 1960s and 1970s, primarily as a result of the research of Albert Bandura and others who recognized the need to consider cognitive thought processes in understanding human behavior.[9] Social cognitive theory, which was first called *social learning theory*, also developed in part as a reaction against operant conditioning's refusal to consider thinking processes or any other psychological functions that could not be openly observed.

A basic proposition to both operant conditioning and social cognitive theory is that behavior is influenced by its consequences. Responses that are rewarded are more likely to occur in the future while responses that are punished will probably be terminated.

Reciprocal Determinism. One of the important differences between operant conditioning and social cognitive theory concerns the degree to which individuals are controlled by the environment. According to operant conditioning, behavior is environmentally determined: the environment contains both the cues for responding as well as the reinforcement; and if the environment changes, the behavior of individuals will also change. Although this position, called *environmental determinism*, is a bit oversimplified, it illustrates why so much concern exists about the possibility of cultural engineering used to control the behavior of people, and the loss of freedom and dignity that might accompany it.

Reciprocal determinism:
A basic philosophy of social cognitive theory which suggests that there are reciprocal relationships between personality, behavior, and the environment. The environment influences individual behavior, but individuals also influence their environment and can change it.

According to social cognitive theory, behavior is determined by more than just the environment; the environment, behavior, and personal factors such as skills, values, and physical limitations interact to influence each other. This interaction, called *reciprocal determinism*, is illustrated in Exhibit 7.2. According to reciprocal determinism, behavior, personality, and the environment operate as interlocking determinants of each other. Behavior is influenced by the environment, but the environment is also influenced by behavior. Individuals have the capacity to change their environment if they don't like the effect it is having on their personality and behavior. The strength of these three influences (behavior, personality, and environment) vary over time and in various settings. At times, environmental factors may exercise powerful constraints on behavior while at other times personal factors may override or alter environmental conditions.

Vicarious Learning. Another important difference between operant conditioning and social cognitive theory concerns the analysis of thought processes. Social cognitive theory emphasizes the importance of *vicarious learning*, symbolic thinking, and self-regulatory processes in understanding human behavior. Vicarious learning, also called *imitative learning*, refers to the process of learning by observing others—watching how they behave and seeing the

Vicarious or Imitative learning:
The process of learning new behaviors by observing others and modeling their behavior.

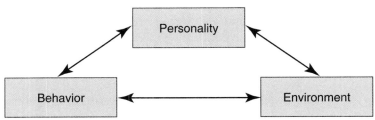

Exhibit 7.2   Reciprocal Determinism

consequences they experience from their behavior. An enormous amount of human learning occurs through observational learning. By observing how other people perform complex behaviors, we learn quickly, and sometimes with very few errors, how to competently perform the same behaviors. Imitative learning is especially superior to trial and error learning when mistakes can produce costly or even fatal consequences. When teaching children to swim, adolescents to drive a car, or novice medical students to perform surgery, a trainer cannot rely on trial and error learning, or simply wait to reinforce correct responses.

Another distinguishing feature of social learning theory is the idea that people can regulate their own behavior. People can effectively control their own behavior by arranging environmental rewards, by generating cognitive supports, and by producing consequences for their own actions. For example, students who think their poor academic performances are caused by a lack of study can decide to do something about it. The student can find a quiet place to study, remove all distracting materials such as magazines and newspapers, record the hours spent each day in studying, set daily study goals, and give a friend six dollars which can be returned at the rate of one dollar per day only if the goals for that day are met. Although individual behavior is influenced by the reinforcers that exist in the environment, people can change their environment both physically and psychologically so that they are reinforced for doing what they want to do.

Symbolic learning:
A process of learning that uses symbols such as words, mental images, and other cognitive associations.

Symbolic Learning. The use of symbols, either as words, pictures, or mental images, greatly facilitates learning. Humans use symbols to represent events, to analyze conscious experiences, to communicate with others at any distance in time and space, to imagine, to create, to plan, and to engage in purposeful action. The use of symbols also contributes to the effectiveness of imitative learning. When a model is present, the trainee can observe the model and immediately try to reproduce the same behavior. But when a model is absent, the trainee must rely on such symbols as mental images, verbal statements, or written descriptions, to reproduce the behavior. Without symbols, humans would be unable to engage in reflective thought or foresightful planning. Even conducting a careful analysis of the present environment requires being able to use symbols to represent objects, events, and relationships. According to social learning theory, symbolic activities cannot be ignored in understanding human behavior.

The use of symbols is also important in training and education. Operant conditioning claims that practice and repetition are necessary to help trainees learn the correct responses; learned behavior must be overlearned to ensure smooth performance and a minimum of forgetting at a later date. Social learning theory, however, claims that practice is not always necessary; thinking is more important than practice in some learning situations. Although practice may be necessary for developing motor skills, it is not important for behavior that is learned symbolically through "central processing" of the response. Learning how to produce an income statement, for example, does not require practicing each component activity. Instead, it involves central processing using symbols to know how to handle cash, accounts receivable, debts, and other items. Many human behaviors are performed with little or no practice.

Studies of imitative behavior have shown that after watching models perform a novel behavior, observers can later describe it with considerable accuracy; and given appropriate incentives, they can often reproduce it exactly on the first trial.

REINFORCEMENT

Reinforcement contingency:
The relationship between behavior its consequences.

Reinforcement theories (both operant conditioning and social cognitive theory) claim that behavior is a function of the consequences associated with the behavior. Put very simply, people tend to do things that lead to positive consequences and avoid doing things that lead to unpleasant consequences. The relationship between behavior and its consequences is called a *reinforcement contingency*. Knowing the reinforcement contingencies associated with a person's behavior allows you to diagnose and predict that person's behavior. To change behavior requires changing the reinforcement contingencies. Five of the major reinforcement contingencies are described here, along with a description of reinforcers.

Reinforcers

The greatest problem in applying reinforcement theory to human behavior is knowing what is reinforcing. People are reinforced by many objects and events, and there are important individual differences in what people find attractive. Efforts to study reinforcers have focused on classifying reinforcers as positive or negative, primary versus secondary, and intrinsic versus extrinsic.

Aversive stimuli:
An unpleasant or punishing stimulus.

Positive and Negative Reinforcers. Positive reinforcers refer to desirable consequences that people normally report as pleasant and enjoyable. Negative reinforcers refer to negative consequences, and are described as undesirable. Negative reinforcers are also referred to as *aversive stimuli*.

While these definitions seem obvious, they are not acceptable to strict behaviorists, who refuse to rely on their own subjective judgments to decide whether a consequence is pleasant or aversive to others. Strict behaviorists define positive and negative reinforcers according to their influence on behavior. Anything that increases the probability of a response is a positive reinforcer, and anything that decreases the probability of a response is called a negative reinforcer or punisher. These operational definitions are especially useful for conducting research on animal behavior, since they do not require behavioral scientists to decide what is pleasant or aversive.

Primary rewards:
Rewards or outcomes that are desirable because of their association with physiological requirements or comforts, especially food, water, sex, rest, and the removal of pain.

Primary and Secondary Reinforcers. *Primary rewards* are those associated with physiological needs such as food, water, sex, sleep, and the removal of pain. These rewards are satisfying because of their association with physical comforts and survival. They do not have to be learned: food is innately satisfying to a hungry person, and sex is innately pleasurable. However, various cultural forces and personal experiences influence the strength and attraction of these primary rewards. For example, the threat of going without food may be more punishing to someone who has experienced periods of starvation than to one who has not.

Secondary rewards:
Learned rewards or outcomes that have a powerful influence on behavior because they are self-administered. They can become increasingly important or valued and they do not become satiated or filled.

Secondary rewards are learned or acquired reinforcers. Examples of secondary reinforcers include social approval, money, recognition, and pride in craftsmanship. These reinforcers are not innate; an individual is not born with a need for recognition or a desire for money. Furthermore these reinforcers may not contribute to physical comfort. In fact, the hard work and effort required to obtain secondary rewards might be physically painful.

Calling them secondary and saying that they are acquired rather than innate do not mean that their influence on behavior is weaker than that of primary rewards. Indeed, just the opposite seems to be true: secondary rewards usually have a much greater influence on day-to-day behavior than primary reinforcers do. Social approval, for example, has been shown to be an extremely powerful secondary reward, especially during adolescence, that has a major impact on behavior, often overriding the effects of other reinforcers.[10] Because of their desire to be approved and accepted by their peers, most teenagers allow peer pressures to guide their behavior, even if it is physically uncomfortable, and sometimes socially illegal. Clothing and jewelry are determined by what is socially approved, not by what is comfortable. Dieting fads and the unhealthy conditions of anorexia nervosa or bulimia occur when the desire for social approval is more important than other primary rewards.

Primary rewards are ineffective motivators after people become satiated. For example, after people have eaten, they are no longer motivated to do something for food. However, secondary rewards do not become satiated; instead, they tend to become increasingly reinforcing the more they are used. Individuals do not get tired of being praised and complimented. In fact, as individuals receive increasing amounts of praise and recognition, they tend to place a higher value on praise and recognition, and they are more influenced by them in the future.

Money is a generalized secondary reinforcer because its effects can be generalized to numerous behaviors. Praise and recognition are generalized secondary reinforcers that have been used extensively to influence job performance. By carefully using these rewards, their strength can be increased and their effects can be generalized to other related behaviors. For example, a 25-year service pin can be a very powerful secondary reinforcer, not because of its economic value, but because of the symbolic meaning attached to it.[11]

Extrinsic and Intrinsic Reinforcers. Another way to classify reinforcers is to distinguish between extrinsic and intrinsic rewards. *Extrinsic rewards* are administered by external sources such as coworkers, supervisors, or the organization. Financial compensation is clearly the most popular form of extrinsic rewards, including wages, salaries, bonuses, profit sharing, and incentive plans. Promotions to higher jobs and recognition from peers are extrinsic rewards, since they too are administered by external sources. Even though these rewards are not physical or tangible, they are classified as extrinsic rewards because they are administered by others. Compliments from friends and supervisors are likewise extrinsic rewards.

Intrinsic rewards are associated with the job itself, and refer to the positive feelings individuals derive from the work they do. Intrinsic rewards are self-administered, based on the personal values of each individual. For example, individuals who have a strong work ethic, will derive satisfaction from successfully performing an outstanding job. Individuals who value courtesy

Extrinsic rewards:
Rewards that are administered by external agents, such as praise, bonuses, and awards.

Intrinsic rewards:
Rewards that are self-administered such as feelings of personal fulfillment or pride and craftsmanship from doing a good job.

and helpfulness will derive intrinsic satisfaction from helping someone in need. Individuals who have a high need for achievement feel rewarded when they achieve challenging goals.

The relationship between extrinsic and intrinsic rewards has been closely examined, because in some situations it appears that extrinsic rewards destroy the effects of intrinsic rewards. For example, in a laboratory study in which students were asked to perform an intrinsically satisfying task of solving puzzles, they tended to persist longer in working on the puzzles after the experiment was over if they were not paid for their participation. It was suggested that extrinsic rewards in the form of money tended to divert the students' interest from the intrinsically rewarding nature of the tasks themselves. The implications of this study were that individuals should not receive pay incentives for performing a job, since pay incentives destroy the intrinsic satisfaction inherent to a job.[12]

Subsequent research, however, has failed to show that extrinsic rewards necessarily inhibit intrinsic rewards, especially on actual jobs where people expect to be paid for their employment. If the extrinsic rewards are exorbitant sums that make people feel bribed or paid off, the extrinsic rewards may contribute to destroying the intrinsic satisfaction. However, if extrinsic rewards appear to be fair and equitable and are based on a careful assessment of performance, the extrinsic rewards do not destroy intrinsic rewards. Instead, the extrinsic rewards combine with intrinsic rewards to create higher levels of motivation and task satisfaction.[13]

People obviously derive numerous rewards from work, most of which are learned rewards. To predict how an individual will behave in a given situation, we must know all of the significant rewards and the attractiveness of each reward. In most instances, however, individuals are confronted with conflicting rewards, which makes it difficult to predict how they will behave.

Reinforcement Contingencies

Positive reinforcement contingency:
When positive reinforcement is presented after the correct response is made.

Positive Reinforcement Contingencies. A positive reinforcement contingency consists of providing a positive reinforcement after the correct response has been emitted (made). When the pigeons made the correct response by pecking at the disk, they were reinforced with a kernel of grain. The effect of a positive reinforcement contingency is to increase the probability of the response. Consequently, the pigeon was more likely to continue pecking at the disk.

Most of the things we do in life are a result of positive reinforcement contingencies; most of our behaviors occur because positive consequences are associated with them. We go to movies, attend sports events, and watch TV because they are entertaining; we attend parties and visit with friends because they are fun; we eat, sleep, and rest because they make us feel better; we study to get good grades; and we work to earn money. When we pass a friend in the hall, we smile and nod, because we have learned that this friendly gesture increases the probability that our friend will also smile and say hello—a pleasant experience. When we carefully examine our behavior, we usually find that most of it can be explained by some form of positive reinforcement.

It is easy to underestimate the effects of positive reinforcement contingencies because so many of the situations where we think they exist do not produce high levels of motivation. A careful examination of these situations usually indicates that the relationship between the behavior and the reward is very weak. Compensation programs illustrate this problem. Although being paid for work is a positive contingency, most employees do no think their pay is closely associated with their performance. Except for a few jobs that use direct incentives, such as commission sales or piece-rate incentives, pay is not directly tied to performance. Consequently, we tend to underestimate the potential effect of compensation on employee performance. Supervisor compliments and the recognition of others are recognized as powerful reinforcers, probably because they are more closely tied to performance.

Punishment contingency:
When negative reinforcement or punishment is associated with a specific response.

Punishment Contingencies. A punishment contingency consists of administering a punisher or an aversive stimulus after the response has been made. In animal studies, punishment contingencies were usually created by administering an electrical shock after the animal made a response. The effect of a punishment contingency is a decrease in the probability that the response will be emitted on future occasions.

Punishment contingencies also occur frequently in everyday life because we are surrounded by many forms of physical or psychological pain. When children touch things they are not supposed to, their parents slap their hands. When employees make mistakes, their supervisors reprimand them. When drivers change lanes without signaling and looking, they may cause either an accident or a blaring horn from another driver. When we run on an icy sidewalk, we may fall down.

Learning theorists claim that punishment is not the most effective method of changing behavior for these reasons.[14]

1. Punishment is effective only when the threat of punishment is present. If the only reason employees do not engage in horseplay is because the supervisor is there to discipline them, the horseplay is likely to begin as soon as the supervisor leaves.
2. Punishment indicates what is wrong but not what is right. One wrong response might be replaced with another wrong response. When students are criticized for coming late to class, they might choose to avoid class altogether the next time they are behind schedule. When individuals are criticized for attempting to resolve interpersonal conflicts, they may decide to quit talking, and the interpersonal conflict continues to smolder.
3. Punishment may eliminate both good and bad behavior if both behaviors are tied together. For example, trying to help a co-worker might be seen as "getting in the way" and result in punishment. Employees may feel as if their helpfulness was punished.
4. Punishment may cause frustrated behavior because the individual's thinking becomes fixed on past errors rather than on searching for a correct solution. For example, a new employee may be so humiliated in a public meeting after incorrectly giving the name of his new department that he makes the same mistake again because the humiliation prevents him from thinking of anything else.
5. Punishment creates a negative feeling toward the punishing agent, such as a supervisor, and interferes with relationships regarding other issues. When supervisors and parents are highly critical and constantly harass

subordinates and children, they tend to create such a negative feeling that even friendly comments and legitimate requests are ignored.

6. Punishment is sometimes a reward, since any form of attention is better than being ignored. Grade school teachers are often surprised to find that rowdy students seem to enjoy being disciplined, because it tends to raise their status in the eyes of their peers.

Escape contingency:
When the person is required to make a correct response in order to terminate a negative condition that is already present in the environment.

Escape Contingencies. An escape contingency refers to a situation in which an aversive stimulus is present, and the person must respond to eliminate it. In animal studies, a loud buzzer or electric shock was presented and the animal had to press a lever to eliminate it. The effect of an escape contingency is to increase the probability of a response; the individual does not like the aversive stimulus and acts to remove it. Escape contingencies are also called *negative reinforcement contingencies*, since a negative reinforcer is removed from the situation following a response.

Escape contingencies are illustrated by many of the little annoying things in life. For example, when the wind is blowing unpleasantly through the window, we close it; we fasten our seatbelts to eliminate the sound of a buzzer; we go to the kitchen to get food to feed a crying baby; we stumble out of bed to turn off an irritating alarm clock; we take antacid to ease stomach discomfort; and we complete a weekly report to silence a nagging supervisor. Advertising that emphasizes the removal of aversive stimuli tries to capitalize on escape contingencies.

Escape contingencies motivate us to act, but only to make the minimal response required to terminate the aversive condition. When employees are demoted or placed on probation for poor performance, for example, they will improve their performance just enough to be promoted or removed from probation. Unless other reinforcers are present, they will not be motivated to achieve outstanding performance; instead they will be content with minimally acceptable performance.

Avoidance contingency:
When a person is required to make a response to avoid an aversive stimulus.

Avoidance Contingencies. An avoidance contingency consists of making a response to avoid an aversive consequence. In animal studies, for example, a light would indicate that within a matter of seconds the animal would receive an unpleasant electrical shock unless it responded by pressing a lever.

Some illustrations of *avoidance contingencies* are taking an umbrella to avoid getting drenched, studying late at night to avoid failing an exam, completing a report to avoid being humiliated by a supervisor, and paying your phone bill to avoid having your phone service cut off. Like an escape contingency, avoidance contingencies are based on a motive of avoiding pain rather than seeking rewards. Therefore, even though avoidance contingencies tend to increase the probability of a response, the response tends to be the least possible effort needed to avoid the unpleasant consequence.

Extinction contingency:
When positive reinforcement is no longer associated with a response. In time the person stops making the response.

Extinction Contingency. An extinction contingency consists of not reinforcing a response. When the response is made, the individual receives no reinforcement, positive or negative. This contingency is based on the premise that people do what they are reinforced for doing. Behaviors that are not reinforced will be extinguished, in other words, not displayed any more. In animal studies, *extinction contingencies* are created by discontinuing any form of reinforcement and observing how long the animal continues to perform without any form of reinforcement. Some responses are much more persistent than others, depending on the schedules of reinforcement. In time, nonreinforced responses are terminated.

Examples of extinction contingencies include ignoring students who talk without raising their hands, failing to notice good performance from employees who have attempted to do a good job, and not responding to written reports. An extinction contingency tends to decrease the probability of a response. If written reports are continually ignored, before long they will no longer be prepared.

These five reinforcement contingencies, summarized in Exhibit 7.3, describe the major approaches to changing behavior. They indicate the kinds of consequences that should follow behavior to increase or decrease the probability of a response in the future.

Reward Schedules

The timing of the reinforcement also influences behavior. Reinforcers are most effective when they occur immediately after a response, but not necessarily after each response. Delayed reinforcement tends to lose its reinforcing effect. If reinforcement is delayed too long, it might be associated with some other response and lose its effect altogether. Immediate reinforcement is especially important for teaching new behaviors. New behavior can be learned faster if the learner receives immediate performance feedback and reinforcement. After the response has been learned, however, every response does not have to be reinforced. In fact, intermittent schedules of reinforcement are often more effective in maintaining high levels of response. The three major reinforcement schedules are continuous, intermittent, and interval.

Continuous reward schedule:
A reward schedule that reinforces every correct response.

Continuous Reward Schedule. A *continuous reinforcement schedule* reinforces each correct response. Most of our day-to-day behavior is maintained on a continuous reinforcement schedule. Every time we push the knob on the drinking fountain, we get a drink; when we push the horn, it honks; if we twist the knob, the door opens; when we turn the key, the car starts; when we pick up the phone, we get a dial tone.

Continuous reinforcement schedules tend to produce a steady rate of performance as long as reinforcement continues to follow every response.

Label	Effect on Behavior	Nature of the Contingency
1. Positive	increases	Correct response is followed by a positive reinforcing stimulus.
2. Punishment	decreases	Behavior is followed by an aversive stimulus.
3. Escape	increases	An aversive stimulus is present and the correct response terminates it.
4. Avoidance	increases	An aversive event will occur unless the correct response is made.
5. Extinction	decreases	The behavior is ignored. No reinforcement is associated with the response.

Exhibit 7.3   **Summary of Reinforcement Contingencies**

However, a high frequency of reinforcement may lead to early satiation. In animal studies, pigeons would develop a fairly consistent rate of response when each response was reinforced; but after many reinforcements, the response declined because the pigeon was apparently no longer hungry.

When reinforcement is terminated, behaviors that have been maintained on a continuous schedule tend to extinguish rapidly. If you twist the knob on the drinking fountain and nothing comes out, you will probably conclude that the water has been turned off, and leave until you think the water has been turned on again.

In training programs, continuous reinforcement schedules are ideal during the early training periods when learners are attempting to acquire a new response. Continuous reward schedules provide immediate feedback on performance to help the learners evaluate their performance and correct their mistakes.

Intermittent reward schedule:
A reward schedule that provides reinforcement for every *n*th response, where *n* is either a fixed or variable number.

Fixed ratio schedule:
A reward schedule that rewards every *n*th response, where *n* is a fixed number.

Intermittent Reward Schedules. An intermittent reinforcement schedule occurs when only a portion of the correct responses are reinforced. Only every *n*th response is reinforced, which explains why they are also called partial reward schedules. However, *n* can be either a fixed or a variable number.

If *n* is a fixed number, the reinforcement schedule is called a *fixed ratio schedule.* Here, a fixed number of responses must be made before a reinforcement occurs. Fixed ratio schedules are easy to construct in animal studies by requiring the pigeon to peck at a disk five times before being reinforced. In organizational life, however, fixed ratio schedules are rarely observed. Some piece-rate incentive plans and commission sales programs are fixed ratio schedules, where 12 units must be produced and submitted by the dozen, or three subscriptions must be sold before the order forms can be submitted.

Fixed ratio schedules tend to produce a vigorous and steady rate of response that is typically a little higher than continuous reward schedules. Since the number of responses being reinforced is less, the individuals tend to perform at a higher rate to obtain higher levels of reinforcement. Like a continuous reinforcement schedule, fixed ratio schedules tend to extinguish quite rapidly when reinforcement is terminated.

Variable ratio schedule:
An intermittent reinforcement schedule in which rewards are administered on the basis of a variable number of correct responses. Variable ratio schedules lead to high rates of responding, and are very resistant to extinction.

If *n* is a variable number, the reinforcement schedule is called a *variable ratio schedule*. Here, a varying or random number of responses must be made before reinforcement occurs. Most social reinforcers are administered on a variable ratio schedule. Employees never know for certain whether their outstanding performance will be recognized, but they have learned from past experience that occasionally it will be. Sales also tend to occur on a random basis, so that sales representatives are reinforced on a variable ratio schedule in making sales.

Variable ratio schedules tend to produce a very high rate of response that is vigorous, steady, and resistant to extinction. Variable ratio schedules are especially effective in maintaining behavior long after the reinforcement has been terminated. Games of chance, such as bingo and slot machines, are excellent illustrations of variable ratio reinforcement schedules. People play slot machines for long periods of time even though they are infrequently reinforced. In fact, most people who play slot machines know they will go broke if they play long enough. To comprehend the power of variable ratio schedules, remember that playing slot machines is a very repetitive (i.e. boring) activity, according to industrial engineering standards. Nevertheless, many people pay to play them in an atmosphere where the noise and air pollution might not meet acceptable industrial requirements.

Interval Schedules. In some situations, the timing of a reinforcer is based on an interval of time which can be either a fixed or variable length.

With a *fixed interval schedule*, responses are not reinforced until after a fixed period of time. In animal studies, a pigeon may be required to wait for a period of time, such as one minute, before any responses are reinforced. Responses made before the minute ends are ignored. The most popular example of a fixed interval schedule is a weekly or monthly paycheck. However, this illustration has to be treated somewhat cautiously, because even though the pay only comes after a specified interval of time, employees are expected to perform during that period. A failure to perform might result in being fired. Therefore, a weekly salary only partially illustrates a fixed interval schedule.

Fixed interval schedules tend to produce an uneven response pattern that varies from a very slow, lethargic response rate immediately after being reinforced to a very fast, vigorous response rate immediately preceding reinforcement. This pattern of responding can be illustrated by a monthly board of directors meeting. The reinforcements to managers occur on a fixed interval schedule once each month. Before each board meeting, managers are frantically gathering data, preparing reports, and supervising their staffs as they work ten and twelve hours per day. After the board meeting, however, their rate of activity declines precipitously—they work only two or three hours each day to answer their mail. The same response pattern is observed in the study habits of students. Much more reading occurs just before each exam than right after.

When the interval varies in length of time, the reinforcement schedule is called a *variable interval schedule*. Again, responses made during the interval of time are ignored, and only the first correct response after the end of the variable interval is reinforced. Conceptually, variable interval schedules are different from variable ratio schedules, but to the person being reinforced they are essentially the same. Reinforcements, such as promotions, are delivered on an irregular and unpredictable schedule—new college graduates are often told that after a year or two they will probably be promoted, but it is uncertain.

Like variable ratio schedules, variable interval schedules are capable of producing very high rates of response that are vigorous, steady, and resistant to extinction. Individuals who have been maintained on a variable interval schedule tend to persist in their performance long after the reinforcement has been terminated. Gamblers will tend to continue playing slot machines long after the machines have quit paying off. Sales representatives continue to make sales calls long after the product has stopped selling. Managers continue to operate outdated companies and produce obsolete products even though they are consistently losing money. The effects of these reinforcement schedules on behavior are illustrated in Exhibit 7.4.

Behavior Modification

One of the earliest applications of reinforcement theories to individual behavior is called behavior modification. Through behavior modification, the be-

Fixed interval schedule:
A reward schedule in which no reinforcement is given during a pre-determined period of time, but after the end of that time interval, the first correct response is reinforced.

Variable interval schedule:
A reinforcement schedule based on an interval of time. However, the length of the interval is not constant; it varies on a random basis.

Exhibit 7.4   Schedules of Reinforcement and Their Effects on Behavior

1. *Continuous reinforcement schedule.* Reinforcement follows every correct response.
   - Produces a steady rate of performance as long as reinforcement continues to follow every response.
   - High frequency of reinforcement may lead to early satiation.
   - Behavior extinguishes rapidly when reinforcement is terminated.
   - Best schedule for teaching new behavior.

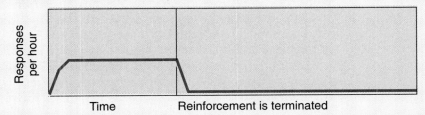

2. *Fixed ratio (FR).* A fixed number of responses must be made before a reinforcement occurs.
   - Tends to produce a vigorous and steady rate of response that is higher than continuous reinforcement.
   - Tends to extinguish rapidly when reinforcement is terminated.
3. *Variable ratio (VR).* A varying or random number of responses must be made before reinforcement occurs.
   - Capable of producing a very high rate of response that is vigorous, steady, and resistant to extinction.
4. *Variable interval (VI).* The first correct response after a varying or random interval of time is reinforced.
   - Capable of producing a very high rate of response that is vigorous, steady, and resistant to extinction.

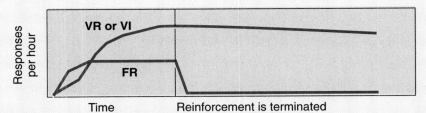

5. *Fixed interval (FI).* The first response after a fixed period of time is reinforced.
   - Produces an uneven response pattern that varies from a very slow, lethargic response rate immediately following reinforcement to a fast, vigorous response rate immediately preceding reinforcement.

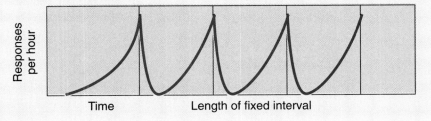

havior of individuals is modified by analyzing the antecedents (environmental cues) and consequences of behavior and changing them as necessary. Individuals are assisted in acquiring desirable behaviors by creating positive rewards for good behavior and by designing appropriate reward contingencies. For example, a high school student was so shy and self-conscious that she had difficulty making friends. She requested help from a school counselor, who developed a behavior modification program that taught her three simple responses: smiling and nodding her head, introducing herself by telling her name, and asking the question "What do you like most about school?" The girl wore a simple counter on her wrist that looked like a watch, which she used to record how many times she made a response each day. Reinforcement came first from the counselor's praise, then from the counter recording her new behavior, and eventually from the acceptance of her new friends. Simple behavior modification programs such as this have proved to be very effective at helping individuals change their behavior and make the kinds of responses they want to make.

Using behavior modification in organizations is called *organizational behavior modification,* or *OB Mod.* Principles of reinforcement are applied within organizations to change and direct the behavior of members toward the attainment of organizational and societal objectives.[15]

OB Mod focuses on observable and measurable behaviors instead of needs, attitudes, or even general organizational goals. OB Mod separates performance problems into three levels of analysis that vary along a continuum from specific actions, to intermediate outcomes, to general outcomes:

1. Behavioral events—specific acts people perform while working.
2. Performance—behaviors that contribute to the intermediate goals of the organization.
3. Organizational consequences—measures of organizational effectiveness associated with the long-range survival and success of an organization.

An example of a behavioral event is cleaning up an oil spill on the shop floor. At the performance level, cleaning up oil spills improves safety, and the organizational consequence is a reduction in accidents. Another behavioral event is punching in on time and getting to the work station by 8 a.m. These events result in dependable attendance at the performance level, and the organizational consequence is reduced absenteeism and tardiness.

The identification of behavioral events is important in OB Mod, because these are the specific acts that are measured and reinforced. Desirable organizational consequences are pursued by obtaining the desired behavioral events that create them. The process of implementing OB Mod, called *behavioral contingency management,* consists of a five-step process for solving performance problems:

1. *Identify performance-related events.* The first step is to identify the specific behaviors that contribute to effective performance. These behaviors must be observable and countable. For example, if the performance problem is late reports, the behavioral event might be the number of reports submitted by a specified date.
2. *Measure the frequency of response.* Before trying to change a behavior, a baseline measure of its frequency must be established. When measuring

Organizational Behavior Modification: (OB Mod)
The application of reinforcement theories to organizational behavior.

Behavioral events:
The basic unit of OB Mod, which consists of a specific act or response.

Behavioral contingency management (BCM):
The process of implementing an OB Mod program in which behavioral events are specified and the conditions to achieve them are created.

the frequency of a response, all responses can be counted if they are infrequent, such as absenteeism and tardiness. But if the responses are frequent, only samples of behavior need to be counted, such as the number of correct strokes of a data entry operator during a five-minute sample every two hours.

3. *Identify existing contingencies through a functional analysis.* A functional analysis refers to an examination of the antecedents and consequences of behavior. The antecedents consist of the environmental conditions surrounding the behavior, and any actions that occurred immediately prior to the behavior. The consequences consist of all the outcomes associated with the behavior, both positive and negative. Since human behavior is so complex, identifying all of the antecedents and consequences is extremely difficult, but very important.

4. *Select an intervention strategy.* The first three steps provide a foundation for altering behavior by changing the reinforcement contingencies. The success of OB Mod depends on selecting and implementing an appropriate intervention strategy. The basic strategies involve the use of positive reinforcement, punishment, escape, avoidance, and extinction contingencies, or a combination of these. Once the strategy is applied, the results are monitored and charted. The goal of the intervention is to change the frequency of the identified behavior.

5. *Evaluate.* The final step is to assess whether behavior has changed and is improving the organizational consequences. Several successful applications of OB Mod have been reported in various organizations, including industry, government, and military.

Although studies show that OB Mod has been highly successful in increasing productivity and helping organizations function more effectively, it has been criticized for threatening individual freedom. Because behavior modification programs have been so successful in changing behavior, their success has raised questions about the morality of changing another person's behavior. Does OB Mod cause people to lose their individuality, forcing them to behave differently?

OB Mod programs are not necessarily unethical simply because they change individual behavior. Like other social influence processes, the determination of whether they are unethical depends on a variety of circumstances, particularly on how they are developed and implemented. An OB Mod program is not considered unethical in these situations: (1) when it helps individuals pursue their own personal and social ideals, (2) when it uses positive rather than negative techniques, (3) when the participants are fully aware of the methods and goals used in the program, (4) when there is a clearly established need and widespread agreement that change is necessary, and (5) when those who design the program openly discuss the consequences of the program and its potential side effects. There is a dramatic difference in the ethical implications of an OB Mod program designed to force employees to behave in ways they consider immoral or illegal versus an OB Mod program designed to help employees to succeed in an organization or pursue their own personal goals. While one program is viewed as an invidious form of manipulation, the other is viewed as constructive assistance.

COGNITIVE MOTIVATION THEORIES

Some theories of motivation depend on what people think and how they reason. These theories are called cognitive theories of motivation, and they include expectancy theory, equity theory, and goal setting theory.

Expectancy Theory

Expectancy Theory:
A decision-making theory of motivation in which people decide what to do by subjectively estimating the probability of being able to perform an activity and whether that activity will be rewarding. The three components of Expectancy Theory include expectancy, instrumentality, and valence.

Expectancy theory is a decision-making model of motivation that explains how individuals decide what to do by evaluating the likely outcomes of their behavior and the probabilities associated with them. Several disciplines have contributed to the development of expectancy theory, including economics, decision theory, and psychology.[16] Consequently, many different models of expectancy theory have been presented in the literature, and it has been called expectancy/valence theory, instrumentality theory, and valence-instrumentality-expectancy (VIE) theory.

The Determinants of Effort. The basic idea of expectancy theory is that motivation is determined by the outcomes people expect as a result of their actions. These elements are outlined in the diagram below: the amount of effort an individual is willing to exert depends on (1) the perceived relationship between effort and performance (expectancy), (2) the perceived relationship between performance and the outcomes (instrumentality), and (3) the value of the outcomes (valence).

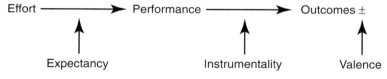

Expectancy
(E ➤ P):
The subjective probability that one's performance depends on the amount of effort exerted.

Expectancy refers to the probability that effort will lead to performance. "If I really try hard, can I do this job?" "If I exert enough effort, can I perform well?" This relationship is viewed as a probability, and in research on expectancy theory, individuals are asked to estimate the perceived probability that a certain level of effort will achieve a particular level of performance. Workers who are highly skilled and have direct control over their work normally report a high expectancy, since they know they can perform well if they try. Expectancies are much lower on jobs where employees see little relationship between their effort and performance, such as sales jobs where sales depend more on the customer's needs than the efforts of the sales representatives.

Instrumentality:
(P ➤ R):
The perceived correlation between performance levels and possible rewards. The association can be positive or negative.

Instrumentality refers to the relationship between performance and outcomes. "If I perform well, will I be rewarded?" "What are the consequences of performing well?" Most situations produce a variety of consequences, and some are more likely than others. Since several outcomes are possible, individuals subjectively calculate several instrumentalities to decide what to do—one for each outcome. Instrumentalities are typically viewed as a correlation coefficient showing the relationship between two variables. An instrumentality of +1.0 implies a direct relationship between performance and outcomes, such as piece-rate incentives. Individuals who are paid a fixed salary regardless of their performance, however, would report an instrumentality close to 0, indicating no relationship between pay and performance. Instrumentalities can also be negative. For example, leisure time would probably be negatively associated with performance, since employees are forced to relinquish some of their leisure time to increase their performance.

Valence:
The desirability or perceived worth of the various work outcomes, either positive or negative.

Valence refers to the value of the outcomes and the extent to which they are attractive or unattractive to the individual. Some rewards are almost universally valued, such as praise, recognition, and compliments from others, while other outcomes may only appeal to certain employees, such as promotions or opportunities to work overtime. Research studies measuring expectancy theory typically use an arbitrary scale, such as one that ranges from +10 to –10, to measure the valence of various outcomes. Pay increases, feelings of pride in craftsmanship, and feelings of being helpful to others typically have positive valences, while being fired, being criticized by your supervisor, and feeling fatigue typically have negative valences.

Effort or force is the combination of expectancy, instrumentality, and valence. Individuals who expect to receive highly valued outcomes if they perform well, and who expect to perform well if they exert sufficient effort, should be highly motivated employees. The components of expectancy theory—expectancy, instrumentality, and valence—can be multiplied together to measure individual effort. Because the components are multiplied together, expectancy theory is sometimes described as a multiplicative model.[17] The formula for measuring effort is expectancy multiplied by the sum of the products of instrumentality times valence for all relevant outcomes.

$$\text{Effort} = \text{Exp} \, \Sigma(\text{I} \times \text{V})$$

Although expectancy theory appears rather complex, the central ideas underlying it can be simply stated in a way that is easily understood. People are motivated to exert effort if by doing so they can perform well and attain desired outcomes. It is important to remember that expectancy theory is based on personal perceptions. Two workers placed in an identical situation may not exert equal effort, because they perceive different expectancies, instrumentalities, or valences. These perceptions are influenced by past experiences, observations of the rewards others receive, and future anticipations.

Extensive research has examined expectancy theory, and most studies have produced positive results in spite of some difficult methodological problems. Although various modifications have been proposed, the basic concepts have remained unchanged: Effort is determined by the combination of expectancy, instrumentality, and valence. The correlations between the levels of effort predicted by expectancy theory and actual job performance have generally ranged between .20 and .70. These correlations are quite encouraging, since performance is determined by variables other than just individual effort.

Applying Expectancy Theory. Expectancy theory provides a convenient and practical model for diagnosing performance problems and motivating employees. When supervisors analyze poor performance, they often use phrases like "lacks initiative," "insufficient dedication," "no commitment," or "bad attitude." Unfortunately, these explanations do not help supervisors know what to do differently to obtain greater motivation.

Rather than attributing motivation problems to a lack of initiative or other personality traits, expectancy theory provides specific recommendations for improving motivation. Motivation problems are solved by altering the components of expectancy theory: expectancy, instrumentality, and valence:

1. Examine the effort-performance relationships. Employees are not willing to put forth much effort if they think their efforts are unproductive. They need to see a strong relationship between their efforts and how well they perform. Low expectancies are usually an indication that supervisors need to provide job training to help employees make their efforts more productive.
2. Examine the performance-reward relationships. Since people do what they are reinforced for doing, the performance-reward relationships should be revised to ensure that significant rewards are closely tied to performance.
3. Use highly valued rewards to reinforce good performance. The consequences of good performance should be highly valued. Money is a positive reward for most employees, but it is not the only valuable reward. Intrinsic rewards, such as achievement and feelings of pride in craftsmanship, can also reinforce outstanding performance.

Equity Theory

Equity Theory:
A motivation theory derived from social comparison theory in which people compare their input-output ratios with the input-output ratios of others.

Equity theory comes from the field of social psychology and is based on a series of studies examining social comparison processes. According to social comparison theory, people evaluate their social relationships in much the same way that economists describe economic exchanges in the marketplace.

Comparison Processes. According to equity theory, people evaluate their inputs to the job relative to the outputs they receive, and then they compare them to the inputs and outputs of others.[18] "Did I get as much from my inputs as my co-workers received for theirs?" Inputs refer to all the relevant factors individuals bring to the exchange, such as effort, performance, education, skills, time, and opportunity costs. Outcomes include all of the rewards individuals receive from the exchange. Although pay is the most obvious organizational outcome, many other positive and negative outcomes may also be viewed as relevant, such as working conditions, social interactions, stress, and fatigue. It is important to note that the value attached to both inputs and outcomes is based on the person's *perception* of its value, rather than its objective worth.

The basic comparisons of equity theory can be illustrated by the following formula, which compares the input-output ratios of a person relative to the input-output ratios of others.

$$\frac{O_p}{I_P} \stackrel{?}{=} \frac{O_o}{I_o}$$

O = Outputs   I = Inputs   o = others   p = person

In this formula, O_p divided by I_p refers to the ratio of a person's outcomes-to-inputs, while O_o divided by I_o refers to the outcomes-to-inputs ratio of others. A state of equity exists when the two ratios are essentially equal. But this state of equity can be destroyed by changing any of the four values. For example, you could feel underpaid because your outcomes were decreased ("My shift differential was eliminated"), because your inputs were increased ("I have to travel farther to get to work"), because the outcomes of the others were increased ("Sam got a production bonus"), or because the inputs of others were decreased ("Sam's new machine is easier to operate than mine").

A state of inequity exists whenever the two ratios are unequal, which can be caused by either ratio being greater than the other. In other words, inequity can exist because people are either overpaid or underpaid. The available research suggests that people are more easily upset by underpayment than by overpayment; people are more willing to accept overpayment in a social exchange than underpayment. Nevertheless, according to equity theory, both conditions of inequity motivate individuals to establish a more equitable exchange.

Equity theory explains why employee performance is often poorer than expected. Many employees have inflated perceptions of a "fair wage" because high wages are mentioned more frequently in the popular literature. Since their actual wages are generally less than what they think is fair, these workers do not work to their full potential.

Equity theory seems to apply slightly more to men than women. Research has shown that men are more prone than women to distribute outcomes to other individuals in direct proportion to their inputs. Women, however, are more apt to adopt an equality norm in which outcomes are distributed equally regardless of inputs.[19]

Consequences of Inequity. When a perceived state of equity exists, individuals tend to feel satisfied, and they report that the conditions are fair. When a perceived condition of over reward exists, however, individuals tend to feel guilty and dissatisfied, and they are motivated to correct the imbalance. Likewise, when a perceived state of underreward exists, individuals tend to feel dissatisfied and angry, and again they are motivated to do something about it. According to equity theory, a perceived state of inequity creates tension within individuals that is proportionate to the magnitude of the inequity.

Six methods have been proposed to explain how individuals attempt to reduce inequity:

1. People may alter their inputs. Underpaid workers could reduce their level of effort, while overpaid workers could increase theirs.
2. People may alter their outcomes. Individuals who feel overrewarded can share their rewards with others (although they usually don't), while underrewarded people will try to obtain greater rewards by increasing prices, requesting a raise, or joining a union.
3. People may cognitively distort their inputs and outcomes. Individuals who are underrewarded may cognitively distort their inputs ("I don't really work that hard, after all"), or their outcomes ("Besides, I get a lot of satisfaction living in this community"). Cognitive distortion is especially likely for overrewarded people who may distort either their inputs ("I bring a lot of experience and leadership from my earlier jobs") or their outcomes ("Even though I get more money, I pay more taxes").
4. People may distort the inputs or outcomes of others. It is just as easy for individuals to distort their perceptions of others' outcomes and inputs as it is to distort their own.

5. People may change objects of comparison. Sometimes the easiest adjustment is to adopt a different comparison group. For example, if a group of executive secretaries were to receive a substantial pay increase, an easy way for them to rationalize it would be to think of themselves more as executives and less as secretaries.

6. People may leave the field. If they can't change the actual inputs or outcomes, and cognitive distortion becomes too difficult or painful, individuals may choose to leave the situation by transferring to another job or quitting.

The object of these methods is to reestablish a condition of equity and reduce the tension created by the former inequitable state. Since equity theory is a cognitive theory of motivation, it is frequently rather difficult to predict which method of tension reduction an individual may adopt. It is likely that over time individuals use them all.

Research on Equity Theory. Equity theory has generated a substantial body of research to assess the validity of the theory. Most of this research has focused on equity theory's predictions of how employees react to pay. These studies focused on two types of pay inequity, overpayment and underpayment; and two methods of compensation—hourly pay and piece-rate pay. The results of several studies generally support these conclusions:[20]

1. When individuals are underpaid on a piece-rate system, they tend to increase the quantity of their work while the quality declines. Since they get paid only for what they produce, they try to correct for their underpayment by producing more units while allowing the quality to decline.

2. Individuals who are underpaid on an hourly rate tend to respond by reducing their effort and allowing both the quantity and quality of their work to decline. Since they can't change their hourly rate of pay, their outcomes are fixed. Therefore, they attempt to correct the underpayment by reducing their inputs of effort.

3. Individuals who are overpaid on a piece-rate system tend to reduce the quantity of their work and increase their quality. Since overpayment is created by more outputs than inputs, they tend to reduce their pay by producing fewer units, but invest significantly greater effort, thereby raising the quality.

4. Individuals who are overpaid on an hourly rate tend to increase both the quantity and quality of their performance. Since their outcomes are set at a fixed hourly rate they can correct the imbalance only by increasing their inputs. Consequently, by exerting greater effort they increase both the quantity and quality of their work.

Applying Equity Theory. The most significant implication of equity theory for managers is that perceived underpayment will have a variety of negative consequences for the organization such as low productivity, turnover, grievances, absenteeism, and dissatisfaction. When evaluating and rewarding employees, managers need to remember that the objective reality of how much individuals are paid is not as important as the subjective perceptions of equity. Rewarding one individual is not an isolated event. A sizable bonus awarded to one employee may cause that individual to feel rewarded, but it may create intense dissatisfaction among many others because of their perceived state of inequity.

According to equity theory, individuals should increase the quantity and quality of their performance when they feel overpaid. Overpayment can be created by actually paying employees more than they are worth, or by manipulating them to believe they receive more than they are worth, such as by down-grading the quality of their inputs. Overpayment is not really an effective long-term strategy to increase productivity, however, since feelings of overpayment appear to be extremely temporary. Individuals have the ability to cognitively change their perceptions very rapidly. Rather than continuing to feel overpaid and working harder to compensate, they very quickly come to believe that their efforts are worth what they receive.

Goal Setting

Individuals perform significantly better when they are attempting to achieve a specific goal such as: complete a project before noon, increase productivity by 5 percent, work for the next hour without making a mistake, maintain 100 percent attendance, or get a research paper submitted on time.

Goal Setting Theory. In 1968 Edwin A. Locke first presented a theory of goal setting and a series of studies showing the effects of goal setting on performance. Continuing research in both laboratory and field studies supports Locke's theory and shows that goal setting has a powerful impact on motivation.[21] Reinforcement theory explains why goal setting has such a powerful influence on behavior.

A goal is simply a standard of performance that an individual tries to achieve. For example, completing a project before noon or increasing productivity by 5 percent describes specific actions individuals must perform in a specified period of time. Some of the earliest work on goal setting was performed by Frederick W. Taylor in his work on scientific management. Taylor attempted to identify appropriate goals for workers, using time-and-motion studies and a careful task analysis. The methods and procedures by which employees were to perform their assigned tasks, such as tools, pacing, and physical movement, were specified in great detail. Rather than referring to them as goals derived from a goal setting process however, Taylor referred to them as standards derived from a time-and-motion study.

The basic elements of goal setting theory are illustrated in Exhibit 7.5. The goals we seek are determined by our values. After examining our present circumstances, we compare our actual conditions with our desired conditions. If we are achieving success, we feel satisfied and continue on the same course. But if there is a discrepancy, we go through a goal setting process.

Students go through the goal-setting model frequently during their educational program. Based on their personal values, students have an idea of what they want, such as graduating from college, going on to graduate school, or securing an attractive job. As they assess their present conditions, however, they often discover that their test scores are low, their class attendance is down, and their term papers are behind schedule. These discrepancies between their desired and actual conditions frequently cause students to initiate a goal setting process. They establish such goals as raising their next test score

Exhibit 7.5 Goal Setting Model

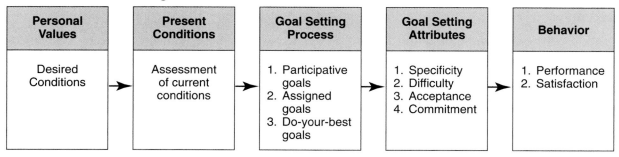

from a C+ to an A–, attending every lecture, and having a first draft of that term paper written within the next two weeks.

Goal setting occurs in three ways. *Participative goals* allow employees to participate in the process of setting goals by providing information and contributing to the goal selection. If they believe the goals are too high or too low, they can express their opinions and try to influence the goal statements. *Assigned goals* are determined by management and simply assigned to the employees. In scientific management, the standards of performance are determined by industrial engineers with almost no input from the employees. *Do-your-best goals* allow employees to control their own goals; management simply asks the employees to do their best, without getting involved in approving or vetoing their goals.

Applying Goal Setting Theory. The effects of goal setting on behavior are influenced by four major goal setting attributes: goal specificity, goal difficulty, goal acceptance, and goal commitment.

Goal specificity:
A measure of how clearly defined and measurable the goals are.

Goal Specificity. Numerous studies have found a direct relationship between *goal specificity* and increased performance. When employees are working toward specific goals they consistently perform at higher levels than they do when they are simply told to do their best or are allowed to work at their own rate with no instructions at all. Since do-your-best goals are only loose guidelines rather than specific goals, they have approximately the same effect on performance as no goals at all. Studies indicate that when workers are simply told to do their best, this instruction is considered equivalent to not having goals. A review by Locke and his associates of field experiments using a wide variety of jobs found that 99 out of the 110 studies they reviewed concluded that specific goals led to better performance than vague goals.[22]

Goal difficulty:
A measure of the amount of effort required to achieve the goal.

Goal Difficulty. Studies on the effects of *goal difficulty* have found a direct linear relationship, showing that an increase in goal difficulty is associated with an increase in task performance. In other words, higher goals lead to higher performance. These results have been observed for brief one-time tasks lasting as little as one minute, and for ongoing tasks lasting as long as seven years.[23] Again, these studies investigated a wide variety of jobs with participants ranging in age from four years to adulthood.[24] The relationship between goal difficulty and task performance however, does not hold for unreasonably difficult goals. When the goals are so high that they become unreasonably difficult or impossible, individuals tend to ignore the goals, and performance may be only slightly better than it would have been with no goals at all. When a goal is perceived as so difficult that it is virtually impossible to attain, the result is often frustration rather than achievement. Dreaming the impossible dream does not improve performance as much as a difficult but realistic goal. Research on the achievement motive found that the optimum levels of motivation occurred when the probability of success (.5) was equal to the probability of failure (.5).[25] Other combinations of probabilities produce lower numbers (e.g. $.3 \times .7 = .21$, which is less than $.5 \times .5 = .25$). Therefore, to obtain high performance levels, goals should be difficult and challenging, but the difficulty should not be so great that individuals believe their chances of succeeding are less than 50/50.

Goal acceptance:
The degree to which individuals accept a specific goal as their own.

Goal Acceptance. *Goal acceptance* refers to the degree to which individuals accept the goal as their own. Individuals need to feel that the goal belongs to them: "This is my goal." Goals are typically resisted or ignored when they are too difficult and out of reach. They can also be rejected for a variety of other reasons, such as when the employees distrust management, when they feel they are being exploited by the organization, when the goals are not fair and consistent, or when the activity is meaningless and irrelevant. Unrealistically high goals are not always entirely rejected. There is some indication that unreachable goals are reinterpreted by employees rather than rejected altogether.[26] For example, if a music student has only been practicing 15 minutes a day, and then is told that he should be practicing four hours daily, rather than totally disregard the four-hour goal, he may adopt a compromise position and practice two hours per day.

Goal commitment:
The degree to which individuals are dedicated to reach the goals they have adopted.

Goal Commitment. *Goal commitment* is determined by both situational variables (goal origin and public announcement) and personal variables (need for achievement and locus of control). The evidence suggests that commitment to difficult goals is higher when (1) goals are self-set rather than assigned, (2) goals are made public rather than private, (3) the person has an internal locus of control, and (4) the person has a high need for achievement.[27] High levels of goal commitment can also be expected regarding goals associated with one's self-esteem. To the extent that individuals become ego-invested in achieving a goal, their level of goal commitment can be expected to be very high.

Motivating Employees

Motivation is a complex issue and each theory contributes to our understanding of how to motivate employees. A model summarizing how the various theories of motivation contribute to the practical problems of motivating employees is shown in Exhibit 7.6. According to this model, managers need to examine seven issues to create high levels of motivation.

1. *Are employees motivated to produce high levels of effort?* According to expectancy theory, effort is produced by expectancy, instrumentality, and valence.

Exhibit 7.6   Summary Motivation Model

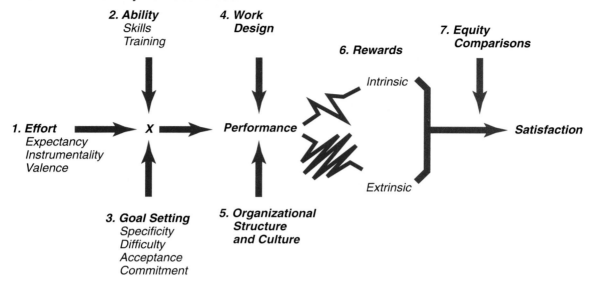

2. *Do employees have the ability to perform their jobs*? Ability includes both the physical and intellectual skills they need to do their work, which is largely a selection issue, as well as the knowledge they require, which is primarily a training issue.

3. *Do employees have clear job expectations that come from carefully established goals*? Goal setting theory suggests that goals should be specific, challenging, and acceptable.

4. *Is the work designed efficiently so that the efforts of employees are not wasted on unproductive activities*? Poorly designed jobs can prevent employees from being productive regardless of their efforts.

5. *Does the organizational environment contribute to a productive work setting*? Uncooperative work groups and inefficient structures can destroy productive efficiency as much as poorly designed work.

6. *Are meaningful rewards contingent on performance*? Are the reinforcement contingencies and reward schedules designed to reward people for high performance? People are motivated by many possible reinforcers, but some are much more effective than others, especially intrinsic rewards that serve as internalized values.

7. *Are the rewards fair*? Whether they are fair is a subjective decision that is based on equity comparisons relative to what others receive. Equity theory explains the way these comparisons are made, and the consequences of inequity.

This model suggests that effort, ability, and goal setting attributes combine in a multiplicative fashion to produce performance. A multiplicative model means that if any of the three factors is zero, or missing, there is no performance. This idea ought to seem quite reasonable, since zero effort should produce zero performance regardless of a person's ability. Similarly, nothing will be produced if the person has no ability or does not understand what to do. Likewise, it suggests that the work design and the organizational environment influence performance, since people cannot perform well if their jobs or the organization prevent them from translating their efforts into productive outcomes. Later chapters will examine work design and the kinds of organizational environments that contribute to outstanding motivation.

Rewards should be based on performance. The wavy lines between performance and rewards suggest that the relationship for intrinsic rewards is more direct than for extrinsic rewards, since people administer their own intrinsic rewards, while extrinsic rewards depend on uncertain organizational practices. Job satisfaction is determined largely by the kinds of rewards people receive from their work; however, their perceptions of whether their rewards are fair and equitable are important considerations.

Discussion Questions

1. What are the differences between positive reinforcement, punishment, escape, and avoidance contingencies? What are some examples of each that might be found in organizations?
2. If variable ratio schedules are so effective in maintaining a high and steady rate of responding, why are they not used more frequently in organizations? Identify some illustrations of variable ratio schedules, and explain how they could be used to reward employee performance.
3. Describe the components of the expectancy theory. If you were a supervisor, explain how you would use each component of expectancy theory to motivate the employees you supervise.
4. What are the principles of goal setting theory? Identify a goal you would like to achieve, and describe how you could apply these principles to your challenge.

Notes

1. Fred S. Keller, *Learning: Reinforcement Theory* (New York: Random House, 1967).
2. Ivan P. Pavlov, *Conditioned Reflexes* (New York: Oxford University Press, 1927).
3. C. T. Allen and T. J. Madden, "A Closer Look at Classical Conditioning," *Journal of Consumer Research* 12 (December, 1985): 30+; Elnora W. Stuart, Terrence A. Shimp, Randall W. Engle, "Classical Conditioning of Consumer Attitudes: For Experiments in an Advertising Context," *Journal of Consumer Research* 14 (December 1987): 334–49.
4. B. F. Skinner, *Contingencies of Reinforcement: A Theoretical Analysis* (Englewood Cliffs, NJ: Prentice-Hall, 1969). B. F. Skinner, *Science and Human Behavior* (New York: Macmillan, 1953).
5. Beth Nissen, "Can A Chicken Play Poker? Maybe If Its Been to Hot Springs," *Wall Street Journal*, February 1, 1979.
6. Edward L. Thorndike, et. al. *The Fundamentals of Learning* (New York: Teachers College, Columbia University, 1932).
7. S. J. Ashford and L. L. Cummings, "Proactive feedback seeking: The instrumental use of the information environment," *Journal of Occupational Psychology* 58 (1985): 67–79.

8. George S. Reynolds, *A Primer of Operant Conditioning, Revised Edition* (Glenview, IL: Scott Foresman, 1975), chapters 2-4.

9. Albert Bandura, *Social Learning Theory* (Englewood Cliffs, NJ: Prentice-Hall, 1977); Albert Bandura, *Principles of Behavior Modification* (New York: Holt, Rinehart, and Winston, 1969); Albert Bandura, *Self-efficacy: The Exercise of Control* (New York: Cambridge University Press, 1997).

10. Richard W. Mallott, *Contingency Management in Education* (Kalamazoo, MI: Behaviordelia, 1972), ch. 9.

11. D. J. Cherrington and B. J. Wixom "Recognition is still a top motivator," *Personnel Administrator* (May 1983): 87–91; David J. Cherrington, "Designing an Effective Recognition Award Program: Dispelling the Myths," *Clinical Laboratory Management Review* 7 (May-June 1993): 106–11.

12. Edward L. Deci, "Intrinsic Motivation, Extrinsic Reinforcement, An Inequity," *Journal of Personality and Social Psychology* 22 (1972): 113–20.

13. H.J. Arnold, "Effects of Performance Feedback and Extrinsic Reward upon High Instrinsic Motivation," *Organizational Behavior and Human Performance* 17 (1976): 275–88; also, Barry M. Staw, *Intrinsic and Extrinsic Motivation* (Morristown, NJ: General Learning Press, 1976); Thomas C. Mawhinney, Alyce M. Dickinson, Lewis A. Taylor III, "The Use of Concurrent Schedules to Evaluate the Effects of Extrinsic Awards on 'Intrinsic Motivation'," *Journal of Organizational Behavior Management* 10 (Number 1, 1989): 109–29; Thomas C. Mawhinney, "Decreasing Intrinsic 'Motivation' With Extrinsic Rewards: Easier Said Than Done," *Journal of Organizational Behavior Management* 11, 1 (1990): 175–91.

14. W. K. Estes, "An Experimental Study of Punishment," *Psychological Monograph* 57, 263 (1944).

15. Fred Luthans and Robert Kreitner, *Organizational Behavior Modification* (Glenview IL: Scott Foresman, 1975).

16. Victor Vroom, *Work and Motivation* (New York: Wiley, 1964).

17. Lyman W. Porter and Edward E. Lawler, *Managerial Attitudes and Performance* (New York: Irwin Dorsey, 1968).

18. J. S. Adams, "Injustice in Social Exchange," in Leonard Berkowitz (ed.), *Advances in Experimental Social Psychology* 2 (New York: Academic Press, 1965); Karl E. Weick, "The Concept of Equity in the Perception of Pay," *Administrative Science Quarterly* 11 (1966): 414–39.

19. Joel Brockner and Laury Adsit, "The Moderating Impact of Sex on the Equity-Satisfaction Relationship," *Journal of Applied Psychology* 71 (1986): 585–90.

20. R. T. Mowday, "Equity Theory Predictions of Behavior in Organizations," in Richard M. Steers and Lyman W. Porter (eds.), *Motivation and Work Behavior*, 2nd ed., (New York: McGraw-Hill, 1979).

21. Edwin A. Locke, "Toward a Theory of Task Performance and Incentives," *Organizational Behavior and Human Performance* 3 (1968): 157–89; "The Motivational Effects of Knowledge of Results: Knowledge or Goal Setting?" *Journal of Applied Psychology* 51 (1967): 324–29.

22. Edwin A. Locke, Karyll N. Shaw, Lise M. Saari, and Gary P. Latham, "Goal Setting and Task Performance: 1969–1980," *Technical Report*, GS-1, Office of Naval Research, Washington, D.C., June 1980.

23. Edwin A. Locke and Gary P. Latham, *Goal Setting: A Motivational Technique That Works!* (Englewood Cliffs, NJ: Prentice-Hall, 1984).

24. Christopher P. Earley, Cynthia Lee, and Alice L. Hanson, "Joint Moderating Effects of Job Experience and Task Component Complexities: Relations Among Goal Setting, Task Strategies, and Performance," *Journal of Organizational Behavior* 11 (January 1990): 3–15; John P. Meyer and Ian R. Gellatly, "Perceived Performance Norm as a Mediator in the Effect of Assigned Goal on Personal Goal and Task Performance," *Journal of Applied Psychology* 73 (August 1988): 410–20.

25. John W. Atkinson, *An Introduction to Motivation* (Princeton, NJ: Y. Van Nostrand, 1964, Chapter 9); Zur Chapira, "Task Choice and Assigned Goals as Determinants as Task Motivation and Performance," *Organizational Behavior and Human Decision Processes* 44 (October 1989): 141–65.

26. H. Garland, "Influence of Ability-Assigned Goals, and Normative Information of Personal Goals and Performance: A Challenge to the Goal Attainability Assumption," *Journal of Applied Psychology* 68 (1983): 20–30; D. J. Cherrington and J. O. Cherrington, "Appropriate Reinforcement Contingencies in the Budgeting Process," *Empirical Research in Accounting: Selected Studies* (1973): 225–53.

27. John R. Hollenbeck, Charles R. Williams, and Howard J. Kline, "An Empirical Examination of the Antecedents of Committment to Difficult Goals," *Journal of Applied Psychology* 74 (February 1989): 18–23

Free Turkey Dinners

For the past several years, the employees at Wright's Furniture Manufacturing Company have received free turkey dinners on Wednesday before Thanksgiving. The free dinners were intended as an expression of appreciation by the company to its employees. Management viewed the dinner as an important event to build company loyalty and improve job motivation.

Last year, however, there were several complaints about the dinner: The meal was not ready on time, service was too slow, the lines were too long, the food was not as good at the end because all the good pieces of turkey had been taken, and the food was cold. Douglas Wright, the president of the company, was very irritated by the employees' criticisms because he thought they showed a total lack of gratitude for the company and a self-centered disregard for the problems associated with feeding 200 people at the same time.

Mr. Wright decided that this year the company would distribute free turkeys the day before Thanksgiving and let the employees prepare their own meals. Giving each employee a full-size turkey was considerably more expensive for the company, but Mr. Wright thought it was a good solution to the problem of trying to feed a large crowd.

Unfortunately, some of the employees did not think getting a free turkey was all that great. Representatives of the union threatened to submit the issue as a grievance, complaining that it altered a condition of employment. The most negative reactions came from the six employees in the machine shop. Four of them, who were all single men, did not take their turkeys home and one left an anonymous note: "Give my bird to Mr. Wright and tell him to stuff it!" The most offensive reaction, however, was an obscene caricature drawn on a bathroom wall of Mr. Wright as a turkey.

Mr. Wright was so incensed by the picture that he ordered the personnel director to fire the entire department. "If they don't appreciate what we do for the employees, we'll get someone who does. How can anyone be so ungrateful?"

Questions

1. How should this episode be interpreted? Does it mean that employees dislike gifts or that they just dislike turkeys?
2. Should companies give rewards to all employees, or just some employees? What kinds of rewards should they give, or does it matter?
3. What theories of human behavior can be used to answer these questions, and do all of these theories produce similar conclusions?

Contingency Management

If people do what they are reinforced to do, why do people have so much trouble accomplishing some of their cherished goals? Why do some people have so much trouble trying to quit smoking? Why do students have so much trouble studying to get good grades? Why do overweight people have so much difficulty losing weight?

One of the useful insights of learning theory that explains why large reinforcers such as losing weight, quitting smoking, and passing a course are ineffective is the following principle:

> "Our behavior is more easily influenced by small, immediate, and definite reinforcers than it is by large, distant, and uncertain reinforcers."

The problem is not that getting good grades is unimportant—getting a degree is a large, significant reinforcer. But at a given moment in the life of a college student, receiving a degree is a distant and uncertain reinforcer. The student thinks, "I'm not going to graduate today, and hanging out with my friends for a few minutes will not keep me from getting a degree." This principle is illustrated in the diagram below:

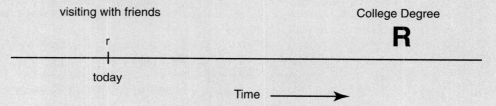

Since behavior is more easily influenced by small, immediate, and definite reinforcers than by large, distant, and uncertain reinforcers, how can individuals achieve long-term goals? The answer is to bring some of the large reinforcers from the future into the present in the form of small, immediate reinforcers. This process is called ***contingency management***. New reinforcement contingencies are created to reinforce small, specific steps leading to the attainment of a large, distant objective. The following examples illustrate the principles of contingency management:

- Four students who shared an apartment found that their academic performance was suffering because of inadequate study. They spent too much time visiting and not enough time studying. To reinforce their studying they used a small financial incentive. On Sunday evening, each roommate prepared a list of daily study assignments for the coming week and put five quarters into a jar. Each day they completed their assignments, they were allowed to remove one of their quarters from the jar. If someone didn't achieve his daily goal, his quarter remained in the jar that day. At the end of the week, any money that remained was used to buy snacks.

- A graduate student who was an avid football fan made an agreement with his wife that he could watch Monday night football if he studied enough the week before. He put a chart above his desk at home, and each day he recorded the number of hours he spent either in class or studying. Unless he had 64 hours of study or class time the previous week, he could not watch Monday night football.

Steps of Contingency Management

Since behavior is a function of the reinforcement contingencies that maintain it, the best way to change behavior is to change the reinforcement contingencies. The following six steps describe the procedure.

1. *Identify the undesirable behavior that you want to eliminate or change.* Focus on the specific behavior that needs to be changed, such as spending time at the snack bar or visiting with friends, rather than on a personality characteristic.

2. *Identify the consequences that maintain the undesirable behavior.* What are the rewards that maintain the present behavior? For example, going to the snack bar and discussing politics with friends is a form of social affiliation, which is a powerful reinforcement.

3. *Specify the desired behavior.* Identify the specific actions you need to perform to achieve your long-range goal. For example, reading a chapter from a textbook is a specific behavior needed to pass a course and obtain a college degree.

4. *Design new contingencies to reinforce the desired behavior.* In the beginning, reward each step of the behavioral sequence. For example, instead of waiting until mid-semester to experience the consequences of reading ten chapters, establish immediate consequences for each chapter. Relying on natural consequences, in which the behavior itself provides the reinforcement, is sometimes not enough and artificial consequences must be created to reward each step. Productivity charts, gold stars, recognition awards, and other secondary reinforcers can be used effectively to reward good performance.

5. *Devise a method to observe and measure the new behavior.* Set deadlines for specific observable behaviors that can be easily measured. The measuring process should not be so inconvenient that it defeats its purpose.

6. *Arrange for the new reinforcement contingency to be administered.* Getting others involved in administering the rewards, such as roommates or friends, helps to keep the program running and keep it honest. After the new reinforcement contingencies have been designed and the behavior is evaluated, consequences must be administered consistently. To illustrate, a student who was leaving for college promised her parents she would write to them each week. The parents also said they would write to her each week, and they agreed to include a check for $50 only if they received a letter from her the previous week. The letter did not have to be long, but it should at least contain a brief description of how she was doing in school and a specific request for $50. The parents wrote each Sunday afternoon, and if they had not heard from their daughter, they did not include the check. On one occasion, the daughter's letter did not

arrive until Monday. The following Sunday, the parents thanked her for sending two letters that week, enclosed one check for $50, and expressed regret that she had missed receiving a check the week before.

Directions. Identify a behavior in your own life that you would like to change, and use the six steps of contingency management to develop an effective change program. Some illustrations of the kinds of behaviors you may choose to develop include adopting better study habits, exercising regularly, losing weight, writing to parents, and maintaining a personal journal. Use your creativity to design reinforcement contingencies to support your new behavior. As you try to arrange for the new reinforcement contingencies to be administered, try to involve others who can help to keep you honest and increase the probability of a successful change.

8

Work Design

Chapter Outline

Job Specialization, Job Enlargement, and Job Enrichment
Job Specialization
Job Enlargement and Job Enrichment
Job Characteristics
Job Characteristics Model of Job Enrichment

Effects of Job Enrichment
Organizational Effectiveness
Criticisms of Job Enrichment

Alternative Work Schedules
Flextime
Permanent Part-Time
Job Sharing
Compressed Workweek
Telecommuting

JOB SPECIALIZATION, JOB ENLARGEMENT, AND JOB ENRICHMENT

While financial incentives provide extrinsic motivation, job design programs try to provide intrinsic rewards from the job itself by creating optimal levels of variety, responsibility, autonomy, and interaction. Carefully designed jobs that minimize wasted effort and maximize employee motivation improve productivity, attendance, and organizational effectiveness. Job satisfaction and overall life satisfaction are greatly influenced by the job demands and whether they match one's abilities and interests. Sometimes a very simple job change can make a big difference to employees.

The history of organizational behavior contains a continuous stream of job redesign programs, each with its own distinctive focus. For example, the construction of galleys (ships) as they were towed through the canals in the Arsenal of Venice (1104–1796) demonstrated the efficiency of assembly-line construction and specialized craft jobs. The cottage industry of the fifteenth and sixteenth centuries allowed workers to produce at home as independent contractors, occasionally with the assistance of family members. During the eighteenth and nineteenth centuries, self-directed teams of skilled craftsmen worked together as autonomous groups in craft guilds such as the barrel makers, the hat makers, and the cordwainers (boot makers).[1]

Elements of these early job design programs are visible in recent programs such as "flexible manufacturing systems" that require workers with broad skills to work on alternating product lines, flexible work scheduling that allows workers to select their own working hours, and sociotechnical redesign, where workers participate in redesigning both their social interactions and the work they do.

Other recent job design programs also use strategies of earlier periods, such as job rotation (moving employees from one job to another), job enlargement (combining previously fragmented tasks into one job), job enrichment (increasing job responsibility and the variety of tasks performed), self-directed work teams (delegating a task to a work group and letting them decide how to do it), job sharing (having two people share one job), and telecommuting (allowing workers to work at home with a computer and telephone).

Two major strategies of job redesign are *job specialization* (sometimes called job simplification), and *job enlargement*. These two strategies are almost exact opposites. Job specialization involves simplifying a job by reducing the number of elements performed by a single worker. Job enlargement involves making a job more complex by combining elements to increase the number of activities performed by each worker.

Job Specialization

Job specialization:
Simplifying a job by reducing the number of elements or activities performed by a job holder. Job specialization normally involves more repetitive activities with short work cycles.

The job specialization versus job enlargement controversy has a long history. One of the major themes of the Industrial Revolution was task specialization: complex jobs were divided into separate tasks and assigned to separate individuals. Indeed, the history of the Industrial Revolution was the history of task specialization. When the production process was separated into many highly specialized tasks, manufacturing was taken out of the craft shops and brought into the factories. One of the earliest descriptions of the advantages of task specialization was Adam Smith's book, *The Wealth of Nations*, published in

1776. Smith described how one person could make twenty ordinary pins per day, whereas ten specialized workers could make forty-eight thousand per day.[2]

Scientific Management. Although the modern factory system existed throughout most of the nineteenth century, the development of highly specialized jobs became much more widespread at the end of that century, thanks to the scientific management movement. Under the leadership of Frederick Winslow Taylor, *scientific management* significantly changed the practices of management from traditional "handed down" methods to carefully analyzed tasks, methods, and piece-rate incentives.[3]

Scientific management involves a detailed analysis of each task to identify the best way of performing it. The goal is to find the ideal method for reducing fatigue, eliminating wasted motions, and maximizing productive efficiency. The ideal timing of rest periods is studied to reduce fatigue, changes are made in the equipment, such as large shovels for loading light materials and small shovels for loading heavy materials. The workers are "scientifically" selected to match job requirements with their abilities. Piece-rate incentives are established to motivate employees to perform highly specialized, repetitive tasks.

One of the most popular illustrations of Taylor's work was the study of pig-iron handling at Bethlehem Steel Company in the 1890s. For years Bethlehem Steel had been dumping pig-iron in an open field as a byproduct of its smelting process. During the Spanish-American War, however, the price of pig-iron increased enough to create a market for it, and the mountains of pig-iron needed to be loaded onto railroad cars. When Taylor first analyzed the task, he found a group of 75 men working at the rate of 12½ tons per man per day. By calculating the ideal walking speed and the percent of time a worker needed to be free of a load to avoid excessive fatigue, Taylor designed a method of increasing productivity almost fourfold. By following Taylor's instructions of when to lift, how fast to walk, and when to rest, the workers succeeded in loading 47¼ tons per day. Even though they were performing three or four times the volume of work, the workers reported less fatigue because, Taylor claimed, they followed his procedures and observed the prescribed rest pauses.

To gain the cooperation of workers, Taylor proposed a differential piece-rate incentive system that paid a low piece-rate for substandard workers and a higher piece-rate for those who exceeded the standard performance. Taylor argued that scientific management was in the best interest of the company, since it reduced labor costs; it was in the best interest of the workers, since it increased their wages; and it was in the best interest of society, since it increased the production of consumer goods and improved the overall economy.[4]

Although Taylor is frequently criticized for ignoring the feelings of workers and focusing only on task efficiency, this criticism is unjust; it overlooks the breadth of his strategic vision for scientific management. Taylor clearly recognized the need for a cooperative relationship between managers and workers, and the powerful influence of cohesive group norms. Indeed, the Taylor Society's mission statement, the *Aims of Scientific Management,* published in 1929, suggests that he also recognized the importance of analyzing competitive market forces and the need for strategic alignment.[5]

Scientific Management:
The industrial engineering movement started by Frederick W. Taylor that used time-and-motion studies to simplify work processes, and differential piece rates to improve productivity.

Therblig:
A basic body movement as defined by two colorful pioneers of scientific management, Frank and Lillian Gilbreth.

Perhaps the most colorful contributors to scientific management were Frank B. and Lillian M. Gilbreth, the parents of twelve children and the topic of a popular movie and book, *Cheaper by the Dozen*.[6] Their work focused on improving task efficiency by using motion films with a clock or a stop watch to time basic motions, called *therbligs* (Gilbreth spelled backwards). For example, after studying bricklaying Frank Gilbreth developed an improved method that reduced the number of motions required to lay interior brick from eighteen to four and a half motions per brick, which increased the rate of brick laying from 120 to 350 bricks per hour.[7]

The principles of scientific management significantly increased manufacturing productivity in the early 1900s. Many of these same principles are still used in job redesign, such as time-and-motion studies, work simplification, piece-rate incentives for individuals or groups, and error analysis to improve quality. After Taylor participated in Interstate Commerce Commission hearings in 1911, knowledge of scientific management quickly spread to other countries, especially France, Italy, Germany, Holland, Russia, and Japan.

Ergonomics:
The application of technology and engineering to the way people are able to move and function while working. Sometimes called biotechnology, it considers the mutual adjustment of people and machines, and how to create greater comfort and efficiency.

Ergonomics. The professional disciplines that study job design include industrial psychology, human factors engineering, and *ergonomics*, sometimes called *biotechnology*. Ergonomics is that aspect of technology concerned with the application of biological and engineering factors to problems relating to the mutual adjustment of people and machines. Professionals in ergonomics are concerned with the adaption of technology to the betterment of productive efficiency and human life.

An application of ergonomics is research on the health problems associated with working at a computer terminal. People who work long, continuous hours at a computer terminal often experience a variety of problems, such as carpal tunnel syndrome, arm and shoulder muscle cramps, back strain, and eye fatigue. Concern has also been expressed about the possibility that radiation from the video display terminal causes birth defects, cancer, or eye cataracts. Although research indicates that the radiation from the video display terminal is no more harmful than emissions from an ordinary electrical appliance, the physical problems caused by repetitive motions can be quite serious, especially back and wrist problems. Through ergonomic research, keyboards have been redesigned, wrist braces have been developed to reduce the incidence of carpal tunnel syndrome, and special chairs have been designed to reduce back strain by providing lumbar support, adjustable arm rests, and an adjustable front edge.

Advantages of Specialization. The advantage of job specialization is greater efficiency. Since the early writings of Adam Smith and Charles Babbage, specialized jobs have been known for substantially increasing both quantity and quality performance for the reasons summarized in Exhibit 8.1.

The advantages of job specialization can be seen in companies that use assembly line procedures. In the sewing industry, for example, one company has 425 employees; only 120 of these employees are sewing machine operators, and the remainder work in other departments such as shipping, receiving, and cutting. All the jobs in this company are highly specialized, and each worker performs the same repetitive activity hundreds of times each day.

Exhibit 8.1 Advantages of Job Specialization

1. *Learning time.* Training time is dramatically reduced, since the worker only masters a small segment of the job. Complex and highly sophisticated products can be produced by relatively unskilled workers who are required to master only the skills needed for their particular job rather than the entire production process.
2. *Time spent changing jobs.* Workers performing highly specialized jobs are able to perform the same repetitive motions without losing time changing from one activity to another. Workers who are required to perform a variety of tasks are less efficient because of the time required to change their physical position, move from one station to another, or pick up different tools.
3. *Increased proficiency.* By performing the same repetitive activity, workers are able to develop greater proficiency and speed in their work. Practicing the same motions time after time helps workers develop habits and work more rapidly.
4. *Development of technology.* Highly specialized jobs are more conducive to the development of new machines and unique tools to help workers eliminate wasted motions, perform several activities simultaneously, or perform each activity more rapidly.
5. *Greater precision and control.* When each worker performs a small definable task, it is easier for management to observe the quantity and quality of performance, detect errors, and pay each worker for the exact amount produced. Supervisors have better control over workers, since deviations from standards can be easily recognized and corrected.

Rather than using scissors to cut cloth, a cutter rolls several dozen layers of material onto a large table and uses a specialized tool to cut all the fabric simultaneously. The materials then go from operator to operator along an assembly line. For example, one operator sews two button holes on the back of each dress and is paid $.38 per dozen dresses. Each bundle of one dozen dresses is then passed to the next operator, who sews two buttons adjacent to the holes and receives $.39 per dozen. Two operators tend a row of specialized machines that are guided by a computer program as they make ruffles and special design markings.

Using highly specialized jobs, this sewing company produces an average of 7,000 dresses per day. If job specialization were eliminated, and each worker had to design, cut, and sew an entire dress, even experienced workers could not make two dresses per day. These data illustrate the advantages of job specialization. With job specialization, the employees produce over seven thousand dresses per day; without it, they could produce less than seven hundred dresses, and these dresses would lack the ruffles, special design markings, and periodic design changes. The enormous advantages of job specialization have led some to conclude that the real reformers of our society, who have significantly improved the quality of life, are not the leaders of revolts to overthrow oppressive governments, but the leaders of industry who mass-produce inexpensive consumer goods that raise the standard of living.

Disadvantages of Specialization. The major disadvantage of task specialization is that highly specialized jobs are extremely repetitive, causing workers to feel bored and alienated. Workers are expected to perform like machines; they do not see the final product, and they never have the satisfaction of pointing to a finished product and saying, "I made that myself."

The disadvantages of specialization—boredom and worker dissatisfaction—were apparent from the beginning. These problems were ignored, however, as the productive efficiency and increased profitability of task

Exhibit 8.2   **Disadvantages of Job Specialization on Assembly Lines**

1. *Mechanical pacing.* The production rate is determined by the speed of the conveyor line rather than by the workers' natural rhythm or inclination.
2. *Repetitiveness.* Workers are required to perform the same short work cycle over and over each day. Most work cycles are less than one minute, and workers may be required to perform the same activity over five hundred times a day.
3. *Low skill requirements.* Highly specialized jobs prevent workers from developing and displaying a variety of skills and talents.
4. *Concentration on only a fraction of the product.* Each job represents only a small fraction of the total product, and workers cannot see the final product.
5. *Limited social interaction.* Even though they work as a team, the workers feel socially isolated because they are physically separated along an assembly line. The speed of the line and the noise levels prevent workers from interacting or developing meaningful relationships.
6. *Elimination of the need to think.* The production processes, equipment design, and use of tools are determined by staff specialists to maximize operating efficiency.

Source: See C. R. Walker and R. Guest, *The Man on the Assembly Line* (Cambridge, Mass.: Harvard University Press, 1952) pp. 71–83.

specialization led to the widespread adoption of assembly line manufacturing. During the 1950s, a large-scale study of assembly line work, particularly in the auto industry, identified a list of criticisms, as shown in Exhibit 8.2.

The effects of depersonalization and loss of control in auto assembly lines was dramatically highlighted in 1972 by a wildcat strike at the General Motors assembly plant in Lordstown, Ohio. This new plant was an engineering showplace in which jobs had been carefully designed using the latest information in engineering technology, even using computers. This unauthorized strike lasted 22 days and attracted public attention to the workers' dissatisfaction with assembly line work. The issues were not pay, benefits, or any of the traditional grievances; the workers went on strike over what they called dehumanizing work. Chevrolet Vegas were coming off the assembly line at the rate of 101.6 per hour—a pace that required each worker to perform the same specialized task every thirty-six seconds. The assembly line had been recently designed to represent the best in engineering knowledge, and the workers were mostly young employees who had the health and stamina to make Lordstown the most productive assembly line in the world. But for 22 days they produced nothing. The initial complaint was that the line was moving faster than it should. Further examination, however, concluded that the problem was the very existence of a line. All assembly line work was condemned as monotonous, boring, and dehumanizing.[8]

Job Enlargement and Job Enrichment

During the 1940s the trend toward highly specialized jobs was countered by a trend toward job enlargement. Proponents of job enlargement argued that it created greater satisfaction and productivity. Even though enlarged jobs were less efficient than specialized jobs, the proponents argued that increased motivation more than compensated for the loss in efficiency. Job enlargement gradually came to be seen as the solution to many organizational problems. By the 1970s, job enlargement was being proposed as the primary cure for such diverse forms of worker discontent as job dissatisfaction, labor grievances, careless work, and drug abuse.[9]

Job enlargement:
Making a job larger by adding more of the same kinds of elements.

Job Enlargement. *Job enlargement* consists of making a job larger in scope by combining additional task activities into each job through what is called *horizontal expansion* or *horizontal loading*. An example of job enlargement would be to allow a sewing machine operator to sew both sleeves onto a piece of clothing rather than just one. Job enlargement is an attempt to increase task variety by extending the length of the work cycle, or the length of time required to complete a task from start to finish before the worker begins the same activity again.

Job enrichment:
Changing a job to significantly increase the level of variety, autonomy, and responsibility. Job enrichment involves changing the content of the job, rather than just adding more of the same activities.

Job Enrichment. The greatest criticism of job enlargement is that it does not really change the essential nature of the task; sewing two sleeves is not materially different from just sewing one. A noticeable change in the job requires vertical rather than horizontal loading; the job must be redesigned to include functions performed by management. To enrich an assembly line job, workers might be allowed to determine their own pace of work (within limits), serve as their own inspectors by giving them responsibility for quality control, repair their own mistakes, be responsible for their own machine setup and repair, and select their own work procedures.

Herzberg's motivator-hygiene theory:
A motivation theory that claims the factors in a work setting can be separated into two lists of motivator factors and hygiene factors. Motivators create satisfaction and motivation but do not create dissatisfaction, while hygienes can create dissatisfaction but do not create motivation or satisfaction.

Many job enrichment programs rely extensively on **Frederick Herzberg's hygiene-motivator theory.** Herzberg classifies work characteristics as either hygienes or motivators and suggests that the only way to make meaningful changes in work design is to improve the motivator factors rather than the hygiene factors.

In his research, Herzberg found that workers used different lists of job characteristics to describe times when they felt good versus bad at work. When describing what made them feel bad about their jobs they usually mentioned factors in the context surrounding the job, such as company policy and administration, supervision, salary, interpersonal relations, and working conditions. These factors are called *maintenance factors* or *dissatisfiers* because they had the potential to make employees unhappy with their jobs, but lacked the potential to make them satisfied. Herzberg labels them *hygienes* to emphasize their preventive nature. When these context factors were present they prevented dissatisfaction. Thus, context factors = dissatisfiers = hygienes.

Hygienes:
Job factors associated with the job context, such as pay, working conditions, interpersonal relationships, and company policies.

When employees described the times they felt especially good about their jobs, they tended to identify factors directly associated with the content of the job: achievement, recognition, the work itself, responsibility, and advancement. These content factors were directly associated with the task itself and were called *satisfiers* or *motivators*. Herzberg claims that they were effective in motivating the individual to superior performance and effort. Thus, content factors = satisfiers = motivators. Herzberg argues that meaningful job changes can occur only if the job is redesigned to include more of these seven motivator factors.[10]

Motivators:
Job factors associated with the content of a job such as achievement, recognition, the work itself, responsibility, advancement, and the possibility of growth.

1. *Accountability*. Workers should be held responsible for their own performance.
2. *Achievement*. Workers should feel that they are accomplishing something worthwhile.

3. *Control over resources.* If possible, workers should have control over their resources and costs. Cost and profit centers should be delegated to lower levels in the organization.

4. *Feedback.* Workers should receive direct and timely information from the job itself regarding their performance.

5. *Personal growth and development.* Workers should have the opportunity to learn new skills.

6. *Work pace.* Within constraints, workers should be able to set their own work pace and have the flexibility to schedule rest pauses and work breaks.

7. *Client relationships.* When possible, workers should develop a relationship with the customers who use the products they produce, to know whether they are satisfied.

Herzberg's theory guided the job enrichment and job redesign programs in many companies, such as AT&T, which conducted a series of 19 generally successful experiments in job enrichment.[11] Job enrichment can make a significant change in a job. Unlike simple job enlargement, job enrichment seeks to improve both task efficiency and personal satisfaction by building into a job a greater scope for personal achievement and its recognition, more challenging and responsible work, and more opportunity for individual growth and advancement.

Job Characteristics

Job scope:
The characteristics or attributes associated with a job, as defined by its breadth and depth.

Job breadth:
One of the dimensions of job scope which refers to the number of different activities performed by a job holder.

Job depth:
One of the dimensions of job scope that refers to the degree of decision making or control the worker exercises over how the job is to be performed.

In job redesign projects, managers need to analyze the characteristics of each job, called the *job scope*, and decide which characteristics to change. This analysis involves reviewing the range of activities performed by the worker and the types of decisions a job holder must make.

Job scope is defined by the breadth and depth of the job. *Breadth* refers to the number of different activities performed on the job. Jobs are said to have a greater breadth if the individual is required to perform a wide range of different activities. In general, the greater the number of tasks performed and the longer it takes to complete the job, the greater is the job breadth.

Job *depth* refers to the degree of discretion or control the worker has over how these tasks are to be performed. Workers who have control over when they do the job, how it is to be done, and the order in which the activities are to be performed, are said to have jobs with greater depth.

Assembly line work is the classic example of jobs with low depth and low breadth. Assembly line workers perform repetitive activities, with little variation and no control over when or how they perform them. Other jobs vary from organization to organization in the depth and breadth of the job. For example, in some hospitals nursing jobs are highly specialized, creating very limited job breadth. At other hospitals, the nurses perform a wide variety of tasks, making for greater job breadth. The nurses in intensive care units typically have greater job depth than the nurses in other units, since they have greater discretion in the care of patients. These combinations of job depth and job breadth are illustrated in Exhibit 8.3.

Exhibit 8.3 Job Scope of a Nursing Job

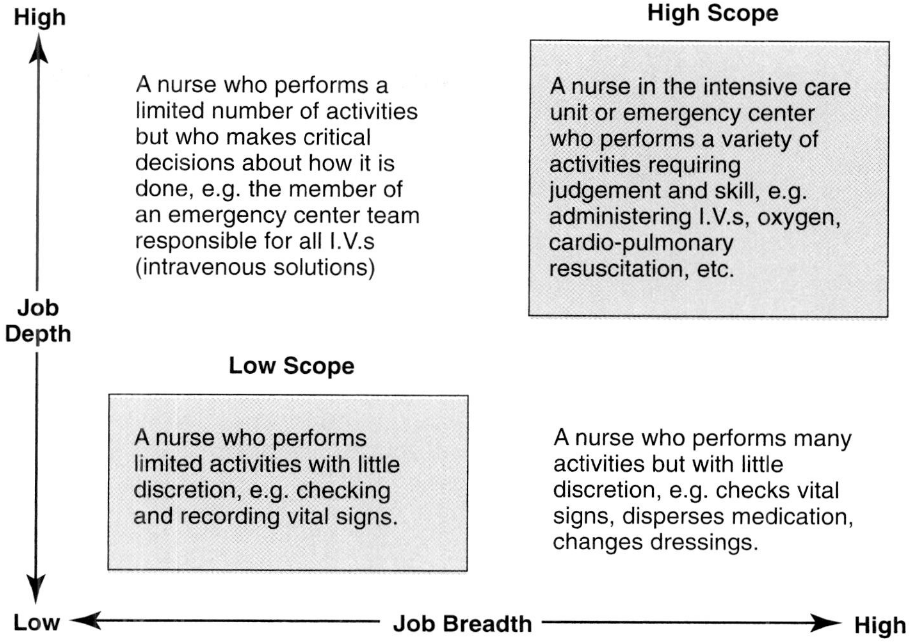

Job Characteristics Model of Job Enrichment

Job characteristics model:

A model explaining how job enrichment programs change the core dimensions of the job, which in turn influence the psychological states of workers, which in turn influence the work outcomes.

The best conceptual framework for examining the effects of job enrichment on work attitudes and behavior is the job characteristics model.[12] This model explains the psychological impact of various job characteristics, and predicts what effect the resultant psychological states will have on work attitudes and performance. The usefulness of a job enrichment program can be predicted from this model by analyzing how the program changes the core dimensions of the job, thereby influencing the behavior of the worker. Questionnaires measuring each concept in the model have been developed and tested in numerous companies. The results indicate that the interactions specified in the model, as shown in Exhibit 8.4, are generally correct.[13]

Work Outcomes. The model is explained best by starting at the outcome end and working backwards. Organizations desire four important outcomes from each worker.[14]

1. *Dependable performance:* high quantity and quality work.
2. *Good attendance:* low absenteeism and low tardiness.
3. *High satisfaction with work:* positive feelings about the job, the company, and the treatment received at work.
4. *Spontaneous and innovative behaviors:* doing more than what is called for in one's formal job description, such as showing initiative, making creative suggestions, cooperating with fellow workers, and pursuing self-development and training.

These four outcomes are clearly in the organization's best interests. An organization that can elicit such behavior from its members will be more effective than an organization that cannot. Generally, these outcomes are also in the individual's best interest, since pay and other rewards are usually associated with good performance.

Psychological States. The desired work outcomes result from three psychological states, as shown in Exhibit 8.4. These three states represent the motivating force behind all activity (including nonwork activity, such as practicing a golf swing at a driving range).

1. *Meaningful.* The activity must have a purpose and be perceived as important and worthwhile.
2. *Responsibility.* Employees must believe that they are personally accountable for results, and that their efforts will influence the outcome.
3. *Knowledge of results.* Employees need systematic and timely information about how well they are performing so they can make corrective adjustments if necessary.

When these three conditions are present, individuals are expected to feel good about their activities and perform well because of their own internal motivation. They are willing to continue performing the activity because of the positive internal feelings created by the activity itself. If any one of the three psychological states is missing, motivation will decline significantly. When all three are present, however, employees demonstrate dependable performance, good attendance, high satisfaction, and spontaneous and innovative behaviors.

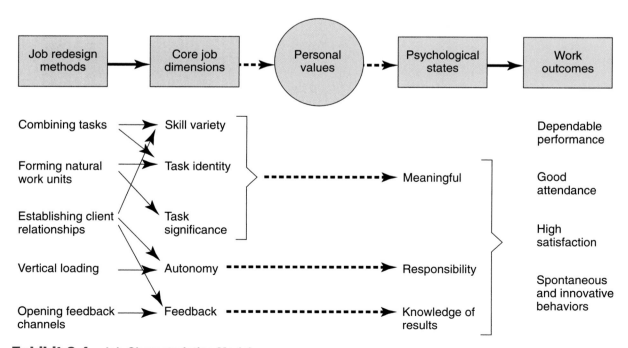

Exhibit 8.4 Job Characteristics Model

Core Job Dimensions. The three psychological states are created by five core job dimensions, as shown in Exhibit 8.4. However, the relationships between the core dimensions and the psychological states are influenced by the personal values of the worker, as indicated by the dashed arrows. The five core dimensions include the following:

1. *Skill variety:* the degree to which a job allows workers to develop and use their skills and to avoid the monotony of performing the same task repeatedly.
2. *Task identity:* the degree to which a task consists of a whole or complete unit of work as opposed to a small, specialized, repetitive act.
3. *Task significance:* the degree to which a task impacts the organization, the community, or the lives of other people.
4. *Autonomy:* the degree to which workers are free of the direct influence of a supervisor and can exercise discretion in scheduling their work and in deciding how it will be done.
5. *Feedback:* the degree to which workers obtain evaluative information about their performance in the normal course of doing their jobs.

According to the model, skill variety, task identity, and task significance make a meaningful job, as indicated by the arrows in Exhibit 8.4. Responsibility and personal accountability are created by autonomy, which comes from allowing workers to schedule their own work and decide how it will be done. Performance feedback provides employees with knowledge about the results of their efforts.

A questionnaire, called the Job Diagnostic Survey, is used to measure each of these core job dimensions using 7-point scales where 1 = low and 7 = high for each dimension. The motivating potential of various jobs can be compared by algebraically combining the scores for the five core characteristics into a ***motivating potential score (MPS).*** The MPS provides a single score measuring how well a job provides high internal work motivation. The formula for the MPS is:

Motivating Potential Score:
A score measuring the degree of job enrichment that is obtained by algebraically combining the scores for the job's five core dimensions.

$$\text{MPS} = \frac{\text{variety} + \text{identity} + \text{significance}}{3} \times \text{autonomy} \times \text{feedback}$$

According to the job characteristics model, a job high in motivating potential will create a higher state of internal work motivation than a job with a low motivating potential score.

Job Redesign Methods. Five job enrichment programs are proposed to improve the core job dimensions.

Horizontal loading:
A form of job enrichment where the job is enlarged by combining additional tasks or elements into a job. On an assembly line horizontal loading involves combining elements from the preceding or following jobs to enlarge a particular job.

1. Combine tasks to eliminate highly specialized jobs and to make larger work modules, called *horizontal loading*.
2. Form natural work units—work teams—in which each person feels part of the team, and jobs can be rotated among team members. Job rotation increases the variety of skills workers can use and contributes to greater task identity. Rotation can occur informally, such as when workers trade assignments, or it can be a formal program, such as when workers are assigned to a new department.
3. Establish client relationships so workers will know who uses the products or services they produce and how the clients feel about their work.

Vertical loading:
A form of job enrich-
ment in which higher
level administrative
and supervisory re-
sponsibilities are in-
cluded in the job to
create greater levels of
responsibility.

4. Give workers greater authority and discretion by allowing them to perform functions previously reserved for higher levels of management,
   called *vertical loading*.
5. Open feedback channels so that information about the quality of performance goes directly to the employee performing the job.

This model provides a useful framework for diagnosing jobs. The core dimensions represent the important areas of each job that need to be examined. If
the decision is made to redesign a job, the model suggests some of the most
appropriate changes that ought to be considered. In recent years, a broad assortment of changes have been tried and are frequently referred to as *quality of
work-life* programs.

Which is the best way to enrich a job? A review of 30 job enrichment
studies where productivity was measured suggested that the most effective redesign method was opening feedback channels so that workers could learn
how well they were doing from the job itself rather than from someone's description of how well they were doing. A comparison of the studies that opened
feedback channels with those that didn't found that more feedback led to increased productivity, higher quality of work, and a decrease in absenteeism.
Although opening feedback channels appeared to have the greatest impact,
other redesign methods were also effective, especially if they were used in
combination. This review also revealed that the productivity increases were related to the number of redesign methods that were used. All five redesign
methods were used in eight studies, three or four methods were used in another eight studies, and only one or two methods were used in the remaining
fourteen studies. The median increases in productivity were 10.2 percent, 7.7
percent, and 2.5 percent, respectively.[15]

Personal Values. The job characteristics model recognizes that not everyone
will respond equally to the core job dimensions. According to the model, skill
variety, task identity, and task significance should contribute to the meaning-
fulness of a job. But whether an activity is actually perceived as meaningful depends on an employee's personal values. Some people (such as social workers
and school teachers who complain of burnout) think their jobs are meaningless, even though they contain extensive variety, identity, and significance. The
same principle applies to assembly line work. Sewing pockets inside the waist-
bands of tennis shorts is a meaningful activity if you perceive it as a necessary
step in producing a useful product. But if you think tennis shorts are worthless
products consumed by a self-indulgent group of idlers in society, the same activity could be perceived as meaningless.

The job characteristics model, as it was originally proposed, claims that
the effects of the core dimensions on the psychological states is moderated (or
influenced) by a person's growth need strength. This moderator, derived from
Maslow's need hierarchy, refers to whether the individual is primarily interested in satisfying lower-level survival needs or higher-level growth needs.
People who are striving to satisfy their growth needs should respond more favorably to an enriched job. It is reasonable to expect, however, that many other
personal values will also serve as moderator variables. Whether workers perceive a task as meaningful, and whether they feel a sense of accountability or

responsibility for it, depend not only on the core job dimensions but also upon their own personal values.[16]

EFFECTS OF JOB ENRICHMENT

Many studies have examined the effects of job enrichment programs on both organizational effectiveness and individual responses. The results have been both positive and negative, and part of this inconsistency seems to be explained by individual differences.

Organizational Effectiveness

Most of the early studies of job enrichment programs reported positive results. Although these reports were usually case studies that relied extensively on subjective impressions, more recent studies using better experimental designs have been almost as supportive. Higher levels of satisfaction and productivity are often achieved by adding variety, responsibility, and other enriching characteristics to specialized jobs.

A review of 32 job enrichment studies found that job redesign programs typically contribute to organizational effectiveness. The studies included in this review all assessed the impact of job redesign in terms of either measurable productivity, production quality, or absenteeism.[17] In 30 studies where productivity was measured, the median result was a 6.4 percent increase in production. In 11 of these 30 experiments, however, the results were zero or negative. The effects on quality were more encouraging; 21 studies measured quality and only 1 of these experiments reported a decline. The median result was a 28-percent increase in production quality. Absenteeism was measured in only 9 experiments, and the median result was a decrease of 14.5 percent in absenteeism. All in all, the evidence suggests that job redesign frequently improves production quality, modestly reduces absenteeism, and occasionally increases productivity.

The effects of job redesign, however, are not permanent. At least one study found that the desirable results that were so encouraging after the first 5 months had essentially disappeared at the end of 14 months.[18] Escalating levels of challenge may be required to prevent boredom and frustration. The temporary nature of these results underscores the disturbing question asked by those who have tried job enrichment: "What can we do next to keep our employees challenged and interested in their work?"

Criticisms of Job Enrichment

Some reviews of job enrichment are not favorable. One review harshly criticizes job enrichment as an attempt by behavioral scientists to impose their values on others. A statement in a union newspaper denounces General Electric's job enrichment program: "Makes no difference how you slice it, it's still monotony and more speedup."[19]

Some of the strongest criticisms of job enrichment come from labor unions. One union leader makes the following statement: "If you want to enrich the job, enrich the paycheck . . . If you want to enrich the job, do something about the nerve-shattering noise, the heat, the fumes . . . Worker dissatisfaction diminishes with age and that's because older workers have accrued more of the kinds of job enrichment that unions have fought for—better wages, shorter hours, vested pensions, a right to have a say in their working conditions, the right to be promoted on the basis of seniority, and all the rest. That's the kind of job enrichment that unions believe in."[20]

Another criticism of job enrichment programs is that some jobs are already too enriched. "When I read this stuff on job enrichment it makes me shake my head. My job is already too enriched for me or anyone else. Everyday I'm being called on to make decisions I'm not prepared to make. I don't have enough time and I've got too many things to do. It's frustrating to be spread so thin."[21]

Many of these criticisms of job enrichment are well deserved. The success of a job enrichment program depends not only on its design, but also on how well it is implemented. Even if appropriate job changes are made, the change may be resisted if it is not implemented properly. Some job enrichment projects tried to enrich jobs that did not need to be changed, because they were already adequately enriched. In other projects, the improvements in one area created dysfunctional consequences elsewhere in the company. Many job enrichment failures could have been avoided through better diagnosis and implementation.

There are limits to how much some jobs can be improved; work is still work, even in an enriched job. Ford Motor Company produced a film called *It Ain't Disney* to help its workers recognize the limits of their job redesign programs. The central message of the film was "Listen folks, we've really tried to enrich the jobs and improve the working conditions. But there is only so much we can do. The jobs are still hard work with much repetition and we can't eliminate it all."

ALTERNATIVE WORK SCHEDULES

Since the Great Depression, the typical workweek for most employees has been a five-day, forty-hour week. Five eight-hour days from Monday to Friday have generally represented the standard workweek in the minds of most people. However, numerous exceptions to the standard workweek have always existed, particularly in the farming and transportation industries. In recent years, many employees enjoy considerable flexibility in scheduling the hours they work. Demographic changes (increased participation of women, minorities, elderly, and dual-career couples) and the desire for more leisure time have spurred interest in alternative work schedules.

Five of the most popular alternatives to the standard workweek include flextime, permanent part-time, job sharing, the compressed workweek, and telecommuting. These five alternative patterns of work have both advantages and disadvantages. They are not universally desirable to all workers, and they are not feasible for some jobs. But the fact that they are being implemented in so many companies indicates the concern of top managers for improving the quality of life at work. The major reason for trying these alternatives is that they contribute to the quality of life by being more consistent with the unique circumstance of workers and the non-work demands of their lives.

Flextime:
An alternative work schedule that allows employees to set their own work hours, subject to specific constraints, such as requiring them to work a specific number of hours per day or per week, and to be at work during the core period.

Core period:
The period of time during the work day when employees on flexible working hours must be at work.

Flextime

An attractive alternative to the standard workweek is the concept of flexible working hours, or flextime. Under flexible work hours, employees choose when to arrive at work and sometimes when to depart, subject to limits set up by management. Most companies have a *core period* when all employees are expected to be at work, with flexible hours at both ends of the workday.

Flextime is not appropriate for jobs that require continuous coverage, such as receptionist, switchboard operator, or bus driver, unless employees cover these jobs during their core hours and perform discretionary activities during their flexible hours. Flextime is also not appropriate for interdependent jobs, such as assembly line jobs. Some of the major advantages and disadvantages of flextime are presented in Exhibit 8.5.

Studies on the effects of flextime indicate that it creates favorable job attitudes. Employees say that flextime makes them feel more trusted, and they report higher levels of satisfaction. The effects on productivity are not as clear. Most studies have indicated that flextime either increases productivity or has no effect. However, these studies generally relied on employees' perceptions of their performance rather than objective measures of productivity. There is no reason to expect productivity to improve. Nevertheless, very few companies that have tried flextime have reported undesirable results.[22]

Many companies have found that most employees do not make extensive use of flextime when the option is offered to them. Even on jobs where flextime is appropriate and employees are free to set their own work hours, companies find that employees tend to follow the standard workday and generally vary their starting times by fewer than plus or minus thirty minutes. The typical response of most employees is to start work a few minutes earlier, but even if employees do not use flextime much, they like having the option of flexible hours.

Advantages
1. Tardiness is virtually eliminated since employees are not tardy unless they miss the core hours.
2. Absenteeism is reduced, especially the one-day absences caused by employees deciding to miss work rather than come to work late.
3. It is easier to schedule personal appointments and personal time.
4. Employees can schedule their work to match their biorhythm or internal clock. Some people work best early in the day, and others work better late in the day.
5. It reduces traffic congestion and creates less stress on getting to work on time.
6. It provides greater flexibility in handling uneven workloads and reducing idle time.
7. It provides increased customer service because the company is open longer.

Disadvantages
1. Communication problems increase since employees frequently need to communicate during the flexible hours.
2. Keeping attendance records can become a problem. Employees do not like time clocks, but some tend to misrepresent their hours when they are on their own.
3. If administrative decisions need to be made throughout the day, providing supervision for twelve to fifteen hours a day can become a problem.
4. Legislation presents some obstacles to the use of flextime, since overtime pay is required for certain jobs that exceed the standard workweek.
5. Utility and administrative costs may be higher with flextime because of longer operating hours.
6. Security risks arise, such as theft and violence, as employees tend to work alone during early or late hours.

Exhibit 8.5 Advantages and Disadvantages of Flextime

Permanent part-time:

A work arrangement permitting employees to work less than 35 hours per week. This arrangement is considered a permanent, rather than a temporary, part-time job.

Permanent Part-Time

Part-time employment is defined as a job consisting of less than 35 hours per week and is usually considered temporary work. However, many part-time employees do not consider themselves temporary. Working less than 35 hours per week is a permanent position for them. In recent years the part-time work force has increased significantly; more people are choosing to work less than full-time.

One of the reasons for the growth of permanent part-time employment is that it fits the needs of people who prefer working shorter hours. Mothers who have children at home and older employees who have low stamina are two groups who especially prefer part-time employment. Part-time positions have increased the size of the work force. Many individuals who are unable to work full-time are attracted to part-time work. The advantages of part-time employment include (1) greater job satisfaction for those who need to work but do not want to work full-time, and (2) greater flexibility in hiring employees to meet erratic work requirements.[23]

One disadvantage of part-time employment is that it creates additional administrative and scheduling difficulties—half-time employees require almost as much supervision as full-time employees. The greatest problem, however, concerns benefits coverage. Although some part-time workers are covered by their spouses' benefit programs, those who are not covered cannot afford their own coverage, and it is very costly for companies to provide full coverage for part-time workers.

Job sharing:

A work arrangement whereby two workers split one job; each worker is responsible for his or her share of the job; they split the salary, the benefits, and the responsibilities.

Job Sharing

One of the most popular variations of permanent part-time employment is *job sharing*. Here a full-time position is divided into two part-time positions, and the duties and responsibilities of the job are assigned to two employees. In some cases the job functions of the two individuals may be distinctly different, since each may be responsible for separate activities. Accountability for the total job may be divided between the two sharers, or both may assume equal and full accountability. Job sharing usually involves a splitting of the responsibilities and the accountability between the sharers. When both part-time employees are held responsible for the whole job it is sometimes called *job pairing*.

Job sharing has been tried successfully among many different employees, including clerical and office workers, elementary school teachers, district attorneys, librarians, and various production-level workers. In most instances job sharing has been initiated by two individuals who submitted a proposal to split a job in response to a job opening. Two mothers, for example, prepared a proposal to split the job of an elementary school teacher. They convinced the school district that their combined efforts and unique contributions were superior to what was offered by any of the alternative full-time applicants for the job. Some of the major advantages of job sharing include these:[24]

1. Productivity is usually higher because two people sharing one job have higher levels of energy and enthusiasm than one full-time person. Companies gain two sets of skills and ideas for the price of one full-time employee. In an early study of job sharing among social workers, half-time social workers handled 89 percent as many cases as full-time workers

did.[25] Other studies have also reported greater productivity for job sharers. However, most of the evidence relies on subjective perceptions.

2. Increased flexibility in scheduling work assignments allows for better coverage during peak periods.
3. Reduced absenteeism and turnover have resulted from job sharing. One of the major causes of absenteeism is the need for more personal time than a 40-hour workweek allows. Job sharing not only provides more personal time but also provides the option of trading hours between partners during times of crisis or illness. Reduced turnover rates are probably an indication that part-time work is more consistent with the personal needs of employees as they try to balance competing responsibilities and interests.
4. Job sharing improves job training and reduces turnover costs. When one member of a team quits, the remaining partner provides on-the-job training for the new employee. The remaining partner also provides continuity during the transition period.
5. Job sharing provides better employment options for people who cannot perform a full-time job. Job sharing provides greater employment opportunities not only for parents but also for individuals who are older, handicapped, or disabled. Part-time employment in the form of job sharing may provide meaningful employment to people who might otherwise be unable to work.

Job sharing has similar disadvantages to part-time employment. The most serious problem again concerns the allocation of benefits. Generally benefits are prorated to each partner according to the percentage of the job that each performs. If they want full benefits, job sharers are sometimes allowed to pay the additional costs themselves; however, job sharers are usually surprised at the cost of benefits and sometimes prefer to take fewer benefits. A growing number of companies have decided to provide full benefits to job sharers.

Compressed Workweek

Compressed work week:
An alternative work schedule in which employees work fewer days per week by working more hours on the days they work. The most typical compressed work week schedule is four ten-hour days called the 4/40 plan.

The compressed workweek consists of scheduling a full-time job in fewer than five workdays per week. The most typical compressed workweek consists of four workdays of ten hours per day. This alternative is usually referred to as the 4/40 alternative. A workweek that is further compressed consists of three twelve-hour days; however, this 3/36 alternative has not been very popular except in some hospitals.

The idea of a compressed workweek was quite exciting when it was first tried in a few companies. Working a couple of extra hours each day did not seem like much of an added burden, since many employees frequently worked overtime anyway. The trade-off was a free day with no work. The compressed workweek was typically scheduled to free either a Friday or a Monday to provide an extended weekend. The advantages of a compressed workweek include these:

1. It reduces the time and costs of commuting to work.
2. It increases the leisure time of employees.
3. It creates greater job satisfaction and morale for employees who like it.
4. It reduces the setup and cleanup costs on certain jobs.

In a field experiment, the initial enthusiasm for a 4/40 workweek led to increased employee satisfaction and performance. After two years, however, the novelty and enthusiasm for change disappeared and performance had returned to original levels.[26]

The disadvantages of a compressed workweek usually outweigh the advantages. The early proponents of the compressed workweek expected it to increase productivity and lead to higher quality work. The results have suggested just the opposite. Working more than eight hours per day generally increases fatigue. An extended schedule of ten-hour days (beyond two or three weeks) often results in less total productivity during a ten-hour day than during a regular eight-hour day. Heavy physical work or taxing mental work is generally not suited to a compressed workweek. Accidents and safety violations are likely to increase with a compressed workweek schedule, because of fatigue and carelessness.[27] Further, some state labor laws require employers to pay overtime compensation when workers work more than eight hours per day.

The compressed workweek is not popular with some employees. Even though the initial response to a compressed schedule is usually favorable, many dislike it after a short time. This schedule is not convenient for working parents who want a steady daily routine that enables them to handle family responsibilities, for older employees who are prone to fatigue, or for young employees who do not want long work schedules to interfere with their social lives. A compressed workweek appears to be most suitable for middle-aged males, especially those who want to hold a second job. Compressed workweeks usually lead to increased moonlighting, which tends to divert an employee's interest and commitment.

Compressed workweeks are best suited for jobs where the responsibility to initiate action comes from the job itself rather than from the worker. Security guards, hospital nurses, and refinery workers who monitor dials are examples of jobs where actions are made in response to a job demand. These jobs are better suited for compressed workweeks than physically tiring jobs that require the worker to initiate action, such as most construction jobs.

Telecommuting

Telecommuting:
A work arrangement that allows employees to work from home using a computer, facsimile machine, email, and the Internet.

For some people, the epitome of flexible work is *telecommuting*—working at home or at a satellite office and communicating with the home office electronically. Technological advances have made it possible for many jobs to be performed at home more effectively than at the office, using laptops with dial-up Internet connections, cell phones, and other telecommunication means. It is estimated that over 15 percent of the workforce work from their homes rather than travel to work.[28] Working at home eliminates the disadvantages of lengthy commutes to work, and reduces the number of unnecessary interruptions, unless other family members are present. Some companies have found that telecommuters actually work more hours, they are more productive, and they are easier to manage. The disadvantage of telecommuting is the loss of social and intellectual stimulation that come from person-to-person communication. Face-to-face conversations satisfy affiliation needs, and help employees feel part of a group; creative ideas and improved work procedures occasionally come from such casual conversations. Employers also worry about maintaining corporate culture, containing administrative costs, and resolving worker compensation issues for employees who have accidents at home.

Discussion Questions

1. Describe the advantages and disadvantages of job specialization. Are repetitive jobs necessarily boring? Why are some tasks with a short work cycle, such as bingo and playing slot machines, not perceived as boring? Describe a repetitive activity you perform and explain your reactions to it.
2. What are the benefits of job enrichment? Identify a job you have done in the past and use the Job Characteristics Model to explain how you would redesign and possibly enrich that job.
3. How important is it to you to have a job with flexible work hours? Which jobs are particularly well suited for flextime, permanent part-time, job sharing, compressed workweek, and telecommuting? Which jobs are poorly suited for each of these alternative patterns of work?

Notes

1. Frederic C. Lane, *Venetian Ships and Shipbuilders of the Renaissance* (Baltimore: Johns-Hopkins Press, 1934); John J. Norwich, *Venice: The Rise to Empire* (New York: Penguin Books, Ltd., 1977); Alvise Zorzi, *Venice: The Golden Age, 697–1797,* (New York: Abbeville Press Publishers, 1980); Herbert G. Gutman, *Work, Culture, and Society in Industrializing America* (New York: Vintage Books, 1977); Daniel T. Rodgers, *The Work Ethic in Industrial America: 1850–1920* (Chicago: The University of Chicago Press, 1978).
2. Adam Smith, *An Inquiry Into the Nature and Causes of the Wealth of Nations* (First published in five books, 1776. Reprinted in London: W. Lewis, Printer, 1811 in 3 volumes). See vol. 1, chapter 1.
3. Frederick W. Taylor, *The Principles of Scientific Management* (New York: Harper and Brothers, 1911).
4. Frederick W. Taylor, *Shop Management* (New York: Harper and Brothers, 1911).
5. Taylor Society, "Thirteen Aims of Scientific Management." *Scientific Management in American Industry*. Harlow S. Person, ed. (New York: Harper & Row, Publishers, 1929): 16–17.
6. Frank B. Gilbreth, Jr. and Ernestine Gilbreth Carey, *Cheaper by the Dozen* (New York: T. Y. Crowell Company, 1949).
7. Claude S. George, Jr., *The History of Management Thought, 2nd ed.* (Englewood Cliffs, NJ: Prentice-Hall, Inc., 1972): 99–101.
8. See Paul Dickson, *The Future of the Work Place* (New York: Weybright and Talley, 1975): 14.
9. See *Work in America: a Report of a Special Task Force to the Secretary of Health, Education, and Welfare.* (Cambridge MA: The MIT Press, 1973) especially chapter 4; Stephen M. Pittell, "Addicts in Wonderland: Sketches for a Map of a Vocational Frontier," *Journal of Psychedelic Drugs* 6 (April–June, 1974): 231–41; Arthur S. Grecham and Yoash Wiener, "Job Involvement and Satisfaction as Related to Mental Health and Personal Time Devoted to Work," *Journal of Applied Psychology* 60 (1975): 521–23.

10. Frederick Herzberg, *Work and the Nature of Man* (Cleveland, OH: World Publishing Company, 1966); Frederick Herzberg "The Wise Old Turk," *Harvard Business Review* (September–October 1974): 70–80.

11. Robert N. Ford, "Job Enrichment Lessons From AT&T," *Harvard Business Review* 51 (January–February 1973): 96–106.

12. J. Richard Hackman and Greg R. Oldham, "Motivation Through the Design of Work: Test of a Theory," *Organizational Behavior and Human Performance* 7 (1976): 250–79; J. Richard Hackman, Greg R. Oldham, Robert Janson, and Kenneth Purdy, "A New Strategy for Job Enrichment," *California Management Review* 17 (Summer 1975): 57–71.

13. Brian T. Loher, Raymond A. Noe, Nancy L. Moeller, and Michael P. Fitzgerald, "A Meta-analysis of the Relation of Job Characteristics to Job Satisfaction," *Journal of Applied Psychology* 70 (1985): 280–89; Thomas C. Head and Peter F. Sorenson, "A Multiple Site Comparison of Job Redesign Projects: Implications for Consultants," *Organizational Development Journal* 3 (Fall 1985): 37–44.

14. According to the job characteristics model the fourth outcome is "internal work motivation." Since this is really a personal value it has been replaced with a more general outcome that has been described in the literature by Daniel Katz and Robert Kahn, *The Social Psychology of Organizations* (New York: John Wiley and Sons, 1965), chapter 12.

15. Richard E. Kopelman, "Job Redesign and Productivity: A Review of the Evidence," *National Productivity Review* 4 (Summer 1985): 237–55.

16. John P. Wanous, "Individual Differences and Reactions to Job Characteristics," *Journal of Applied Psychology* 59 (1974): 67–622; David J. Cherrington and J. Lynn England "The Desire for an Enriched Job as a Moderator of the Enrichment—Satisfaction Relationship," *Organizational Behavior and Human Performance* 25 (1980): 139–59.

17. Richard E. Kopelman, op. cit.

18. Charles N. Greene, "Some Effects of a Job Enrichment Program: A Field Experiment," *Proceedings*, 41st Annual Academy of Management Meetings, 1981, pp. 281–282.

19. Mitchell Fein, "Job Enrichment: A Re-evaluation," *Sloan Management Review* 15, 2, (Winter 1974): 69–84. Quote is on page 75.

20. W. Winpisinger, "Job Satisfaction: A Union Response," *AFL-CIO American Federationist* (February 1973): 8–10.

21. David J. Cherrington and J. Lynn England, op. cit., p. 156.

22. Sarah F. Gale, "Formalized Flextime: the Perk That Brings Productivity," *Workforce* (February 2001): 39–42; David A. Ralston, "The Benefits of Flex-Time: Real or Imagined?" *Journal of Organizational Behavior* 10 (October 1989): 369–73; Pam Silverstein and Jozetta H. Srb, *Flex-Time: Where, When, and How* (Ithaca, NY: Cornell University Press, 1979).

23. Frank W. Schiff, "Short-Time Compensation: Assessing the Issues," *Monthly Labor Review* 109 (May 1986): 28–30; Robert N. Lussier, "Should Your Organization Use Job-Sharing?" *Supervision* 51 (April 1990): 9–11; Diane E. Schmidt and Gilbert Duenas, "Incentives to Encourage Worker-Friendly Organizations," *Public Personnel Management* 31 (Fall 2002): 293–308.

24. David Clutterbuck, "Why a Job Shared is not a Job Halved," *International Management* 35 (October 1979): 45–47; Gretel S. Meier, *Job Sharing: A New Pattern for Quality of Work Life* (Kalamazoo, MI: W. E. Upjohn Institute for Employment Research, 1978); Barney Olmstead, "Job Sharing: A New Way to Work," *Personnel Journal* 56 (February 1977): 78–81; Christina Scordato and Julie Harris, "Workplace Flexibility," *HRMagazine* 35 (January 1990): 75–78.

25. S. Greenwald, and Judith Liss, "Part-Time Workers can Bring Higher Productivity," *Harvard Business Review* 51 (September–October 1973): 20–22.

26. John M. Ivancevich and H.C. Lyon, "The Shortened Workweek: A Field Experiment," *Journal of Applied Psychology* 62 (1977): 41–55.

27. "Effect of Scheduled Overtime," in *Coming to Grips with Some Major Problems in the Construction Industry* (New York: Business Round Table Report, 1974): 1–14; Boris B. Baltes, et al., "Flexible and Compressed Workweek Schedules: A Meta-analysis of Their Effects of Work-related Criteria," *Journal of Applied Psychology* 84 (1999): 496–513.

28. Department of Labor, 2001

McDonaldization: An American Menace?

Frederick Taylor's early studies in scientific management were done in the steel industry at Bethlehem Steel, and reports of their impressive gains in efficiency soon caused scientific management to spread to other industries and other countries. Automobile assembly lines have usually represented the classic application of Taylor's principles, where new cars have been known to roll off the assembly line as fast as one car every 36 seconds.

In recent years, the principles of scientific management have revolutionized the fast-food industry. Because of the demand for fresh, fast food, the food preparation process has been scrutinized and streamlined to eliminate every unnecessary second in filling a customer's order. McDonalds Corporation has probably streamlined their preparation process as much or more than any other fast-food chain, and their success has led to a new term called *McDonaldization*, which refers to the process by which the principles of the fast-food industry dominate the entire labor force.

McDonald's efficiency principles are contained in a 14-volume set of three-ring binders that every franchise is expected to follow. Customer's orders are input into registers and immediately communicated to the appropriate work stations where the food is prepared. Everything is designed to move the food forward toward the customer without having to backtrack. Exact times are established for every activity, such as fifteen seconds for toasting the buns: two seconds for putting the buns into the toaster, eleven seconds for the toasting, and two seconds for retrieving the buns. Automatic timers and equipment are used for preparing the fries and operating the drink dispensers. A special dispenser that is suspended from the ceiling to make it immediately accessible is used to squirt catsup on the hamburgers in four evenly distributed and exactly measured amounts.

McDonaldization represents all that is negative with task specialization even though McDonalds did nothing to invent it. The process is condemned for replacing human labor, eliminating the need to think, destroying social relationships, and subjecting workers to technological controls. It is viewed by some as an American disease that is spreading to other global economies. For example, a survey in Holland reported that 40 percent of all jobs in that country were certainly not McDonaldized yet. "However, for the Dutch labor market the threatening American menace of McDonaldization is certainly present."

Questions

1. Is McDonaldization anything new? Is this something that should cause great concern?
2. What are the effects of job specialization on the quality of life and is this something that developing nations should fear?

Source: G. Ritzer, *The McDonaldization of Society: An Investigation into the Changing Character of Contemporary Social Life*, Thousand Oaks: Pine Forge Press, 1993; A. J. Steijn and M. C. deWitte, "The Dutch Labor Market: Threatened by McDonaldization. *Sociale Wetenschappen*, 1996, jrg. 39, nr. 4, p. 45-58.

Measuring the Motivating Potential of a Job

According to the job characteristics model, a job high in motivating potential will create a higher state of internal work motivation than a job with a low motivating potential score. To measure the motivating potential of a given job, the five core characteristics can be combined algebraically into a "motivating potential score" (MPS). The MPS provides a single summary index of the degree to which the objective characteristics of a job will provide high internal work motivation. The formula for the MPS score is:

$$MPS = \frac{variety + identity + significance}{3} \times autonomy \times feedback$$

Think of your job, or a job you have performed in the past, and answer the questions below. Then calculate your MPS score using the above formula.

Selected Questions from the Job Diagnostic Survey

Please describe your job as objectively as you can.

1. How much *variety* is there in your job? That is, to what extent does the job require you to do many different things at work, using a variety of your skills and talents?

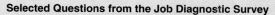

1 ——— 2 ——— 3 ——— 4 ——— 5 ——— 6 ——— 7

| Very little; the job requires me to do the same routine things over and over again. | Moderate variety | Very much; the job requires me to do many different things, using a number of different skills and talents. |

2. To what extent does your job involve doing a *"whole" and identifiable piece of work?* That is, is the job a complete piece of work that has an obvious beginning and end? Or is it only a part of the overall piece of work, which is finished by other people or by automatic machines?

1 ——— 2 ——— 3 ——— 4 ——— 5 ——— 6 ——— 7

| My job is only a tiny part of the overall piece of work; the results of my activities cannot be seen in the final product or service. | My job is a moderate-sized "chunk" of the overall piece of work; my own contribution can be seen in the final outcome. | My job involves doing the whole piece of work, from start to finish; the results of my activities are easily seen in the final product or service. |

3. In general, how *significant or important* is your job? That is, are the results of your work likely to significantly affect the lives or well-being of other people?

1 ——— 2 ——— 3 ——— 4 ——— 5 ——— 6 ——— 7

| Not very significant; the outcomes of my work are not likely to have important effects on other people. | Moderately significant. | Highly significant; the outcomes of my work can affect other people in very important ways. |

4. How much *autonomy* is there in your job? That is, to what extent does your job permit you to decide on your own how to go about doing the work?

1 ——— 2 ——— 3 ——— 4 ——— 5 ——— 6 ——— 7

| Very little; the job gives me almost no personal "say" about how and when the work is done. | Moderate autonomy; many things are standardized and not under my control, but I can make some decisions about the work. | Very much; the job gives me almost complete responsibility for deciding how and when the work is done. |

5. To what extent does *doing the job itself* provide you with information about your work performance? That is, does the actual *work itself* provide clues about how well you are doing–aside from any "feedback" coworkers or supervisors may provide?

1 ——— 2 ——— 3 ——— 4 ——— 5 ——— 6 ——— 7

| Very little; the job itself is set up so I could work forever without finding out how well I am doing. | Moderately; sometimes doing the job provides "feedback" to me; sometimes it does not. | Very much; the job is set up so that I get almost constant "feedback" as I work about how well I am doing. |

Source: J. Richard Hackman and Greg R. Oldham, "The Job Diagnostic Survey: An Instrument for the Diagnosis of Jobs and the Evaluation of Job Redesign Projects," Technical Report No. 4, Department of Administrative Sciences, Yale University, May 1974, pp. 2-3.

Performance Management

Chapter Outline

Evaluating Performance

Multidimensionality of Performance

Role of Performance Evaluation

Criticisms of Performance Evaluation

Performance Evaluation Methods

Results-Oriented Appraisals

Performance Feedback

Evaluation Process

Who Should Evaluate Performance?

Performance Interviews

Rewarding Performance

Base Pay

Financial Incentives

Recognition Awards

Intrinsic versus Extrinsic Rewards

EVALUATING PERFORMANCE

Performance evaluation programs represent a significant application of motivation theory. The process of evaluating an individual's performance contains elements of both positive and negative reinforcement. How well people perform is largely determined by whether their performance is evaluated and rewarded.

Multidimensionality of Performance

What are the behavioral requirements of effective organizations and how do organizations want their members to behave? Effective organizations require three basic types of behavior:[1]

1. *Attracting and retaining people.* The first requirement of every organization is to attract people and persuade them to stay for at least a reasonable period of time. Every organization (other than the military when the draft is in effect) depends on its ability to attract members; the failure to attract a sufficient number of new members could prevent it from functioning effectively and even cause it to die. High turnover and absenteeism are very costly, and as a general rule, organizations that are more successful in attracting and retaining people are more effective.

2. *Dependable role performance.* Members are assigned to perform their individual roles, they are expected to know their responsibilities and achieve minimal levels of quantity and quality performance. Organizations are more effective when workers are motivated to do their jobs well.

3. *Spontaneous and innovative behaviors.* In addition to the formal task requirements, many other behaviors profoundly influence the effectiveness of an organization. These are called spontaneous and innovative behaviors because they are not stated in the formal task requirements. Since an organization cannot foresee all contingencies in its operations, its effectiveness is influenced by the willingness of its employees to perform spontaneous and innovative behaviors as the need arises. Some of the most important spontaneous and innovative behaviors include these:

   ■ *Cooperation:* assisting coworkers and helping them achieve the organization's goals.
   ■ *Protective acts:* safeguarding the organization by removing hazards or eliminating threats.
   ■ *Constructive ideas:* contributing creative ideas to improve the organization.
   ■ *Self-training:* improving one's skills to fill the organization's ever-present need for better-trained workers.
   ■ *Favorable attitudes:* expressing positive comments about the organization to other employees, customers, and the public, thus facilitating recruitment, retention, and sales.

Role of Performance Evaluation

Whether a company should formally evaluate employees is an important philosophical question. Many organizations, especially smaller ones, do not

Dependable Role Performance:
The requirement that employees do their assigned jobs dependably in terms of acceptable quantity and quality performance.

Spontaneous and Innovative Behaviors:
Behaviors that are important for organizational effectiveness but are not typically considered part of an employee's formal job description, such as performing cooperative acts, making creative suggestions, and protecting the company.

have formal evaluation programs because they do not see a need for them. However, performance evaluation programs serve at least five important organizational functions.

1. *To reward and recognize performance.* Evaluation information allows high performers to be rewarded and recognized. Merit pay programs, for example, base the size of pay increases on performance. Without performance data, everyone has to be rewarded equally, or rewards must be distributed subjectively—conditions that are perceived as inequitable by the recipients. Performance appraisals also provide intrinsic rewards, since outstanding performers receive positive recognition for their efforts.

2. *To guide personnel actions such as hiring, firing, and promoting.* Performance information is necessary for making rational decisions about whom to promote or terminate. When this information is not available, personnel decisions are made by subjective impressions. It is more desirable to make careful, defensible decisions based on good performance data. Organizations that fail to have a formal evaluation program are vulnerable to costly legal challenges, because without accurate performance data, they cannot show that their personnel decisions are free from illegal discrimination on the basis of race, religion, sex, national origin, or age.

3. *To provide individuals with information for their own personal development.* Individuals need performance feedback to help them improve; accurate and timely feedback facilitates the learning of new behavior. Furthermore, most people want to know how well they are doing and where they need to improve.

4. *To identify training needs for the organization.* A well-designed performance evaluation system identifies who could benefit from training, and what abilities and skills are needed for each job.

5. *To integrate human resource planning and coordinate other personnel functions.* The information obtained from a performance evaluation is essential for individual career planning and for organizational staffing. Performance information is used to identify high potential people, who are known as "fast-track" employees.

Criticisms of Performance Evaluation

In spite of its importance, the evaluation process has been severely criticized, and these criticisms have prompted many managers to abandon performance evaluation as a useless and perhaps harmful practice. Many people, especially low performers and people who dislike work, simply dislike being evaluated. They are opposed to having anyone evaluate their performance because they are threatened by it.

The process of evaluating performance can also be threatening to supervisors. Evaluating the performance of subordinates is a basic supervisory responsibility, and a supervisor who lacks the skills to provide performance feedback simply cannot be a good supervisor. Nevertheless, some supervisors do not like to evaluate their subordinates, and they feel threatened by having to justify their evaluations. These supervisors argue that having to evaluate subordinates creates role conflict by forcing them to be a judge, coach, and friend at the same time. Many supervisors do not have adequate interpersonal skills to handle evaluation interviews.

On some jobs, performance is difficult to define, especially jobs that do not produce a physical product. Managers provide leadership, engineers create new ideas, and trainers present information, but these products cannot be meaningfully counted. So how do we know what to measure? While some argue that intangible products such as new ideas, leadership, and training cannot be reliably measured, others argue that everything can be measured, even if it is only by a subjective rating scale. If an evaluator has an attitude about an employee's performance, this attitude can be evaluated like any other attitude, regardless of how subjective it is. Organizations need to make certain that these subjective judgments are job-related, however. Because subjective evaluations can give rise to discrimination against protected groups, the federal courts have not been willing to accept evaluation procedures that allow "unfettered subjective judgments." In some instances, organizations have been required by the courts to establish objective guidelines for evaluation, promotion, and transfer.[2]

Evaluating performance and assigning a number to represent it often create feelings of anxiety in both the evaluator and the person being evaluated. Eight of the most frequent criticisms of performance evaluation are described in Exhibit 9.1. Although these criticisms represent legitimate problems, they should be treated as problems to resolve rather than insurmountable obstacles.

Performance Evaluation Methods

Performance evaluations occur whether or not a formal evaluation program exists. The demands to hire, fire, promote, and compensate necessitate some form of evaluation. Supervisors have always evaluated their subordinates and formed impressions about each employee's work, and these informal, subjective evaluations have influenced personnel decisions just as much as formal written evaluations. The advantage of an informal system is that it is easier to design and administer; the advantage of a formal program is that it is more unbiased, defensible, and open to inspection.

The popular proverb, "what you evaluate is what you get," emphasizes the importance of evaluating behaviors that are essential to organizational effectiveness. The importance of evaluating relevant behaviors was illustrated by the experience of a military officer who included "orderliness" as one of the criteria for evaluating a unit of clerk-typists.[3] The officers who conducted the evaluation defined orderliness in terms of how clear and uncluttered the clerk-typists kept their desks. The clerk-typists responded by removing everything from the tops of their desks and keeping it in their desk drawers. Although the procedure was inefficient, and the volume of work dramatically declined, the clerk-typists obtained high performance evaluations.

Deciding what to evaluate is in part a value judgment; the personal values of those who design the evaluation system will be reflected in it. In deciding what to evaluate, an important issue is whether the evaluation should focus on outcomes (results) or behaviors (activities). For example, the performance evaluation of a salesclerk could focus on the number of products sold per hour, or it could focus on the behaviors required to produce the sale, such as de-

Exhibit 9.1 Criticisms of Performance Appraisals

1. **Halo Effect:** Sometimes one characteristic about a person, positive or negative, strongly influences all other attitudes about that person.
2. **Leniency-Strictness Effect:** Some evaluators give mostly favorable ratings, while other evaluators evaluate the same performance more unfavorably.
3. **Central Tendency Effect:** Some evaluators give average ratings to everyone to avoid sticking their necks out to identify marginal or outstanding performance.
4. **Interrater Reliability:** Two evaluators seeing the same behavior may disagree and give different ratings.
5. **Contrast Effect:** The evaluation of one employee's performance may be influenced by the relative performance of the preceding individual.
6. **Zero-Sum Problem:** Some appraisal systems require supervisors to balance high ratings given to some employees with low ratings given to others.
7. **Numbers Fetish:** An excessive focus is sometimes placed on numbers, which may be treated as though they possess unquestioned accuracy.
8. **Recency Effect:** Recent events are unduly reflected in the appraisal, to the exclusion of events earlier in the year.

scribing the product, arranging for financing, and making repeat calls. When asked, most people say outcomes are more important to measure than behaviors; they are primarily interested in measuring results. However, most performance evaluations focus more on behaviors than on results, especially when evaluating managers and supervisors.

The major advantage of focusing on outcomes is that attention is directed toward producing specific results. The primary objective of all employees should be to produce results, not behaviors. Unfortunately, some employees perform many of the right behaviors and still fail to produce results. This situation can be illustrated by examining the behaviors of a student writing a research paper. The right behaviors include finding references, reading articles, making notes, and studying the materials. A student can perform all these activities very well and still fail to get the paper written.

A potential problem with exclusively evaluating outcomes is that results can sometimes be achieved by unethical or undesirable means. By exerting excessive pressure on subordinates, supervisors can increase performance, but over time, excessive pressure leads to turnover, dissatisfaction, and unethical conduct. In managing people, the way it is done (behavior) is just as important as the result (outcome).

Good performance evaluation programs depend more on the competence of the evaluator than on the specific evaluation technique. Nevertheless, some appraisal techniques are considerably better than others, depending on the purpose of the evaluation and the nature of the work being done. The primary techniques include ranking procedures, classification procedures, graphic rating scales, behaviorally anchored rating scales, and descriptive essays.

Ranking procedures: Arranging employees along a scale from best to lowest performer.

Ranking Procedures. The objective of a ranking procedure is to order a group of employees from highest to lowest along some performance dimension, usually overall performance. Ranking is frequently used when making promotion decisions, and occasionally used when making compensation decisions, to decide which employees should get the largest financial bonuses. However, ranking is not helpful for providing personal feedback.

Classification procedures:
Classifying employees into set categories, such as outstanding, excellent, good, average, fair, and poor.

Graphic Rating Scales:
A performance evaluation method that identifies various job dimensions and contains scales that are used to rate each employee on each dimension.

Classification Procedures. *Classification procedures* simply assign individuals to one of several categories based on their overall performance. Many evaluation systems classify employees as "greatly exceeds expectations," "exceeds expectations," "meets expectations," "below expectations," and "fails to meet expectations."

Graphic Rating Scales. *Graphic rating scales* are the most frequently used method of evaluating performance for nonmanagerial workers. Some of the most popular characteristics measured by graphic rating scales include quantity of work, quality of work, cooperativeness, job knowledge, dependability, initiative, creativity, and overall performance. The scales used to measure these characteristics are typically seven- or ten-point scales that are described by such words as *high* versus *low*, or *exceeds job requirements* versus *needs improvement*, as shown in Exhibit 9.2. The accuracy of graphic rating scales and their freedom from bias and subjectivity improve as the points along the scale are more accurately described in behavioral terms. Ideally, each point along the scale should be defined by a specific behavioral description.

Behaviorally based rating scales:
A performance evaluation method that uses scales that are anchored by observable behavior to reduce the subjectivity and bias associated with ordinary graphic rating scales.

Descriptive essays:
A method of evaluating employee performance that requires evaluators to write free-form essays describing the employee's performance.

Behaviorally Based Rating Scales. When the points along a graphic rating scale are clearly defined by specific behavioral descriptions, as shown in Exhibit 9.3, these scales are called behaviorally anchored rating scales (BARS). Research indicates that these scales are superior to regular graphic rating scales because they are more reliable, less ambiguous, and less biased; furthermore, they are more accurate measures of performance and provide better feedback to employees.[4] The disadvantage of using behaviorally based rating scales is that they require more time and effort to develop.

Descriptive Essays. Some performance evaluation forms simply provide a blank space for the evaluator to write a descriptive essay summarizing the employee's performance. New and inexperienced evaluators find this procedure extremely challenging and unpleasant; however, experienced evaluators use it quite effectively. The essay description typically identifies the employee's job responsibilities on one side of the page, and the other side of the page contains a description of how well these duties have been performed. If they want to, evaluators are free to construct and use their own scales to facilitate their essay descriptions. One of the major benefits of a descriptive essay procedure is that it provides valuable feedback to help employees improve their performance. The major disadvantage is that the information cannot be used readily to make comparisons among employees.

Management by Objectives:
A philosophy of management that reflects a positive, proactive way of managing. MBO requires all employees to establish written, measurable objectives that can later be used to evaluate performance.

Results-Oriented Appraisals

Many organizations emphasize individual accountability through a results-oriented approach to performance evaluation. Less emphasis is placed on the activities employees perform and more emphasis is placed on the results they are expected to produce. Many labels have been attached to these results-oriented evaluations. The most popular label is *management by objectives (MBO)*.

Peter Drucker is credited with first publicizing MBO in his 1954 book *The Practice of Management*.[5] Drucker noted the advantages of managing people by "objectives" rather than by "drives." The advantages are that each manager

Exhibit 9.2   Illustration of a Graphic Rating Scale

Name of Employee   Job Title
Department   Rated By
Date

Instructions: Rate this employee on the basis of the actual work he or she is now doing.
Read the definitions very carefully. Compare this employee with others in the same occupation
in this company or elsewhere. In the space before each number, rate the employee according to
the following scale.

1	2	3	4	5	6	7	8	9
Fair				Average				Excellent

[ ] 1. **Quantity of Work:** How does the quantity of this employees work compare with what you
expect? Is this employee energetic and industrious, or does he or she waste time?

[ ] 2. **Quality of Work:** How does the quality of this employee's work compare with what you
expect? Consider the degree of completeness and the number of errors and mistakes.

[ ] 3. **Dependability and Responsibility:** Habits of punctuality and attendance. Can this employee be trusted to complete work with a minimum of supervision?

[ ] 4. **Initiative, resourcefulness, and leadership:** Consider the employee's ability to proceed
without supervision and achieve results without being told. How does this employee affect
the output of coworkers? Does he or she have the ability to direct and train others and utilize company resources and properties effectively?

[ ] 5. **Judgement:** Does the employee impress you as a person whose judgment would be dependable, even under stress? Is the employee likely to be excitable or hasty when making
decisions in an emergency? Are decisions objective and rational, or swayed by feelings
and the opinions of others?

[ ] 6. **Ability, training, skill, and experience:** Does the employee have sufficient job knowledge to perform satisfactorily? Does the employee need additional training on the job?

[ ] 7. **Personal appearance and speech:** Does the employee make a good first impression? Is
the employee well-groomed, or slovenly? Does the employee have a pleasant speaking
voice? Does he or she express thoughts and ideas well?

from the highest level to the lowest level has clear objectives that reflect and
support the objectives of the organization. All managers participate in the
goal-setting process and then exercise self-control over their own performance;
that is, they monitor their own performance and take corrective actions as
necessary. To do this, their performance is measured and compared with their
objectives. The measurements do not need to be rigidly quantitative or exact,
but they must be clear and rational.

MBO is primarily a philosophy of management that reflects a positive,
proactive way of managing, rather than a reactive way. The focus is on (1) predicting and shaping the future of the organization by developing long-range
organizational objectives and strategic plans, (2) accomplishing results rather
than performing activities, (3) improving both individual competence and organizational effectiveness, and (4) increasing the participation and involvement of employees in the affairs of the organization.

MBO is also a process consisting of a series of integrated management
functions: (1) the development of clear, precise organizational objectives; (2)
the formulation of coordinated individual objectives designed to achieve the
overall organizational objectives; (3) the systematic measurement and review

Exhibit 9.3   Illustration of a Behaviorally-Anchored Rating Scale

Cooperation and dependability refer to spontaneous and innovative behaviors beyond the formal job description that contribute significantly to the effectiveness of the company, e.g., dependability, willingness to accept assignments, cooperation in working with others, initiative in seeing what needs to be done and doing it willingly.

Excellent attitude	7	Positive and enthusiastic approach to work. Always pleasant, helpful, and cooperative. A self-starter. Strives to further the company's interests.
Good attitude	6	Excellent and enthusiastic worker, willing to do more than expected. Always pleasant and cooperative unless criticized or mistreated.
Slightly good attitude	5	Performs assigned work but seldom goes beyond the normal job expectations.
Average attitude	4	Adequate worker, but occasionally allows personal problems to influence work much of the day.
Slightly poor attitude	3	Sometimes resistive; expresses a dislike for being asked to assist others.
Poor attitude	2	Openly resistive; may even resist performing tasks that are part of the normal job. Argumentative and sometimes nasty to coworkers.
Very poor attitude	1	Occasionally acts belligerently or hostile to supervisors

of performance; and (4) the use of corrective action as needed to achieve the planned objectives.

MBO programs are typically implemented in three phases. The first phase focuses on evaluating managers by having them identify measurable objectives and recording how well they have achieved them at the end of a period. In phase two, MBO programs are integrated into an organization's planning-and-control processes so that the objectives are coordinated with the strategy and objectives of the company. Phase three fully integrates the MBO system with other organizational functions, including the development of strategic plans, budgeting and financial planning, staffing, performance evaluations, compensation, human resource development, and management training. This integration is achieved by emphasizing teamwork and flexibility during the goal setting process, and by emphasizing individual growth and development during the performance review process.

Performance Feedback

The importance of performance feedback is emphasized in learning theory. Operant conditioning explains that feedback is essential for acquiring new responses and that learning cannot occur without timely feedback. Feedback is also central to goal setting theory, since goals are meaningless when feedback is absent. There is no uncertainty about the importance of feedback, but there are questions about the most helpful way to give it.

Some recommendations for giving feedback are inconsistent with empirical research. For example, learning theory recommends that feedback occur immediately after the response for optimal learning. However, supervisors are cautioned to postpone telling employees what they did wrong until they can do so privately, to avoid public humiliation. Another popular recommendation is that supervisors should limit their feedback to positive comments and avoid criticism. Studies on discipline have shown, however, that criticism is useful and even necessary to improve performance.[6] The interesting paradox regarding criticism is that those who need it most are usually the most threatened by it and the least capable of benefitting from it. Research on the effects of performance feedback has produced these conclusions:

1. Supervisors give subordinates feedback more often after instances of good performance than after instances of poor performance. People dislike being criticized, and negative feedback creates an uncomfortable discussion. Consequently, many supervisors avoid giving negative feedback.[7]

2. When they are compelled to give negative feedback, supervisors tend to distort the feedback to make it less negative or convey the feedback in very specific terms in order to convince the subordinate that the evaluation was not biased.[8] While distorting the feedback is dysfunctional, giving specific comments is generally beneficial and helps the recipient know how to improve.

3. Supervisors are traditionally told that discussions about performance levels and pay increases should be separate. Research does not support this, however. Discussions about pay increases represent a significant form of feedback that clarifies and reinforces other comments about performance. Therefore, performance reviews should include information about the recommended pay increase that accompanies a given performance level.[9]

4. Feedback tends to improve performance to the extent that it indicates that prior performance levels are inadequate for reaching the goal. Therefore, negative feedback that implicitly calls for greater effort tends to improve performance more than positive feedback that endorses current performance levels.[10]

5. Individuals who have high self-efficacy and self-esteem can respond more adaptively to criticism than can individuals who are low. People with high self-efficacy and high self-esteem are likely to use the feedback to diagnose their performance and make adaptive changes, while people who are low are inclined to coast or quit.[11]

Performance interviews are usually uncomfortable experiences for both supervisors and subordinates, but they are also significant events that have an enormous impact on employee motivation, personal development, and job satisfaction. Good performance reviews require good interpersonal skills, accurate performance information, and careful preparation. The feedback is most helpful when supervisors describe behavior in a way that is direct, specific, and nonpunishing.

EVALUATION PROCESS

Who Should Evaluate Performance?

In most instances, the immediate superior should be responsible for evaluating an employee's performance, although information can also be obtained from subordinates, peers, clients, and customers. When data come from all of

360 Degree appraisals:
A method of evaluating employees that involves gathering performance feedback from people above them, below them, and beside them on an organizational chart.

these sources, the appraisal is referred to as a *360 degree appraisal*. As a general rule, performance appraisals are most accurate and useful when the evaluations come from sources closest to the person being rated.

Supervisors. The hierarchical arrangement of formal authority in most organizations gives the supervisor the legitimate responsibility to evaluate subordinates. Generally there is a shared expectation that the superior has the right and obligation to evaluate performance. To behave otherwise would seem unnatural and inappropriate. Furthermore, since supervisors administer the rewards and punishments, they should be responsible for evaluating performance.

Subordinate appraisals:
Evaluating the performance of supervisors and managers by asking subordinates to evaluate their superior's performance.

Subordinates. Although evaluations of superiors by subordinates might seem backward, they can be useful in some circumstances. Subordinates are being asked frequently to evaluate corporate officers in what are sometimes called *upward appraisals* or *subordinate appraisals*, and this information may be used to decide pay increases and promotions. There are at least three good reasons for using subordinate appraisals: (1) subordinates possess unique information about superiors that ought to be included in the evaluation process, (2) feedback from subordinates provides a powerful impetus for change, and (3) evaluations by subordinates tend to equalize the power differentials in organizations and make the workplace more democratic and responsive to human needs. Power equalization improves the flow of communication.

Subordinate evaluations of superiors have certain limitations. Subordinates can only evaluate what they observe, and so they generally evaluate their superiors based on their interactions with them. This means that supervisors are primarily evaluated on the basis of interpersonal skills rather than on organizational effectiveness. Some administrative decisions are not popular, and a desire to please their subordinates could cause managers to make bad decisions. Subordinate evaluations also have the potential to undermine the legitimate authority of superiors and reduce their organizational effectiveness. For a two-way evaluation process to function effectively, both superiors and subordinates must have adequate maturity to make responsible evaluations and accept feedback from one another.

Peers. In some situations, the most knowledgeable and capable evaluators are an employee's peers. Co-workers are sometimes in a better position than supervisors to evaluate each other's performance. Research on peer evaluations has found them to predict success and correlate with both objective and subjective ratings of success in numerous situations. A review of many studies examining the use of peer ratings in the military found that peer ratings were more valid predictors of leadership performance than were ratings by superiors. Peer ratings also have yielded good reliability and validity.[12]

The conditions required for good peer appraisals are (1) a high level of interpersonal trust, (2) a noncompetitive reward system, and (3) opportunities for peers to observe each other's performances. When these conditions are not met, the usefulness of peer appraisals is severely restricted. Peer appraisals are most frequently used among professional and technical employees in organizations that meet these conditions. The use of peer appraisals has the potential to increase the interaction and coordination among peers.

Self. People are always evaluating themselves; the question is how formally and systematically these self-evaluations should be recorded and acted on. In recent years a decline in authoritarian leadership has contributed to an increase in self-evaluations in both large and small companies. Some of the arguments in favor of self-evaluation are that self-evaluation results in (1) more satisfying and constructive evaluation interviews, (2) less defensiveness regarding the evaluation process, and (3) improved job performance through greater commitment to organizational goals.

On the other hand, the arguments opposing self-evaluations center on the fact that low agreement usually exists between self- and supervisory evaluations. Because of the systematic biases and distortions that can appear, self-evaluations must be used very carefully. Self-evaluations are very valuable for personal development and the identification of training needs, but they are not useful for evaluative purposes. Asking employees to evaluate themselves for purposes of promotions or pay increases is like asking students to grade themselves. It puts individuals in the awkward and uncomfortable situation of trying to guess how biased others will be in rating themselves.

Clients. As a general rule, everyone who can observe the behaviors or outcomes of an individual should be included in the evaluation process. According to this principle, there are occasions when clients and customers ought to be asked for their observations. This information could come from casual complaints or letters of appreciation, or companies could systematically survey their clients and consumers.

Performance Interviews

Performance evaluation interviews can be uncomfortable experiences for both superiors and subordinates. Managers complain about the difficulties they encounter in the appraisal interview, such as explaining poor performance to marginal employees, providing feedback to poor performers who think they are doing a good job, and trying to find something fresh to say about an experienced employee's performance. They are especially threatening to insecure supervisors and new employees. Some supervisors tend to postpone interviews indefinitely, which means that the employees do not receive adequate feedback on their performance. If the interview occurs but is handled poorly, feelings of disappointment, anger, and resentment may result. Rather than increasing performance and improving personal development, poor evaluation interviews can destroy initiative, creating feelings of defeat and despair. The effectiveness of evaluation interviews will be enhanced if managers and subordinates follow some simple guidelines:

1. Evaluators should develop their own styles so they feel comfortable in an interview. If the evaluator feels uncomfortable, the employee being evaluated probably will feel uncomfortable too. An evaluator should not try to copy someone else or follow a rigid format if it does not feel comfortable and natural.

2. Both parties should prepare for the interview beforehand. Employees should review their performance, and document how well they have done. Evaluators should gather relevant information and compare it

against the objectives for the period. Lack of preparation for the interview by either party is an obvious indication of lack of interest.

3. The evaluator should begin by clarifying the purpose of the interview. The employee should know whether it is a disciplinary session, a contributions appraisal that focuses on employee results, or a personal development appraisal. In particular, the employee should understand the possible consequences of the interview, so that he or she can prepare appropriate responses. For example, an employee's responses during a contributions appraisal can appropriately be a bit guarded and defensive, but in a personal development appraisal, such responses would greatly reduce the effectiveness of the interview.

4. Neither party should dominate the discussion. The superior should take the lead in initiating the discussion, but the employee should be encouraged to express opinions. The superior should budget time so that the employee has approximately half the time to discuss the evaluation.

5. The most popular format for the interview is the "sandwich" format—criticism sandwiched between compliments. The rationale for the *sandwich interview* format is that positive comments made at the beginning and end of the interview create a positive experience. The opening compliments should put the employee at ease and the closing compliments should leave the employee feeling good about the interview and motivated to do better. However, most employees dislike the sandwich interview format and report that it makes them feel manipulated.

6. An alternative format is to identify and discuss problems, then talk about future improvements, and finally express appreciation for good behaviors. This approach is very direct and to the point. The supervisor begins by saying, "There are ＿＿ problems I'd like to talk with you about: ＿＿ , ＿＿ , and ＿＿." Each problem is briefly identified at the beginning before the supervisor discusses the problems in detail. An employee immediately knows what the "charges" are and does not sit in uncertainty waiting for the next bomb to fall. After the problems have been discussed by both superior and subordinate, the discussion focuses on accomplishments for which the employee deserves recognition. The superior should describe specific actions that deserve recognition and be as complimentary as the behavior merits. The interview should not end until the superior and subordinate have discussed plans for future performance. Future goals and objectives should be clarified, and plans for improvement should be discussed.

Employees should be encouraged to take an active role in the performance-evaluation process. Most employees wait until their superior initiates action and schedules an interview. Then they sit through the interview feeling as though they are being "chewed out," manipulated, or run over. Instead, employees should take an active role by anticipating their evaluations, collecting data about their performance, scheduling interviews with their superior, taking the lead in interviews to discuss their strengths and weaknesses, and asking for feedback. An active role makes the evaluation process a dramatically different experience for subordinates. Rather than dreading the interviews, subordinates consciously plan for them and anticipate the experience.

Sandwich interviews:
A format for a performance evaluation interview in which negative comments are sandwiched between positive comments at the beginning and end of the interview.

The evaluation interview should focus on behaviors and results rather than on personality factors. Performance feedback helps employees achieve better results, while discussions about personality characteristics are usually dysfunctional. Because personality factors are poorly defined, discussing them usually creates unnecessary conflict. Personality changes are difficult to achieve and are usually not necessary anyway. When supervisors think a personality change is needed, what they are actually concerned about are the behaviors caused by the personality. To correct such problems, the supervisor should describe the improper behaviors and help the employee change his or her behavior. If a personality change is indeed required, feedback about the specific behavior that needs to be changed is still the best approach to changing personality.

Some have suggested that appraisal interviews should include only the outstanding and poor performers, while the middle group should be excluded. Not only are the ones in the middle more difficult to evaluate, but it appears that telling people they are average is dysfunctional. Most people resent being labeled as average when they think they are members of an above-average group. Employees report a significant drop in organizational commitment when they are told that their performance is satisfactory, but below average.

REWARDING PERFORMANCE

Compensation systems influence the overall strategy of an organization because pay has such a strong influence on job satisfaction, productivity, and labor turnover. Compensation also has an enormous impact on all human resource functions, especially staffing, performance evaluation, training and development, and employee relations.

All employers have similar compensation objectives: attract qualified employees, retain them, and motivate them to perform their duties in the most effective manner. Employers want their employees to feel financially secure, but they also want them to be highly motivated. To achieve security they must provide a predictable monthly income, regardless of performance; to motivate their employees they must pay for performance. Employees are more highly motivated if at least some of their pay depends on their performance. Achieving an appropriate balance between security and motivation, called *fine tuning*, requires an appropriate balance between base pay and incentives.

Base Pay

Compensation Maxim:
An ethical principle regarding compensation that can be examined to determine whether it is morally right or wrong.

Employees deserve to be paid an amount that is considered just and fair. An ethical principle regarding compensation, called a ***compensation maxim***, is that *employees should be compensated first according to the requirements of the jobs they perform and how well they perform them, and second by labor market conditions (supply and demand) and the organization's ability to pay.* Ethical issues concerning compensation are especially sensitive because money is such an important reason why people work. People expect to be treated fairly, and our concept of fairness is greatly influenced by such issues as why managers deserve more than laborers, why older workers should be paid more than younger workers, and whether people who need more should get it. The development of a sound wage-and-salary system requires three basic decisions.

Each decision answers a critical question regarding an organization's compensation program.

Wage-level Decision. The first decision concerns the overall level of an organization's compensation. It answers this question: How much money do members of this organization receive relative to people in other organizations who perform similar work? This decision reflects the values of the leaders of a company and expresses their desire to be wage leaders, to be wage followers, or to pay the going market rate. In a firm that has an average profit picture for its industry, the most compelling definition of an equitable wage is usually the "going market wage," as determined by a wage survey. Both employees and managers are inclined to accept such a wage level as equitable. The primary instruments for making *wage-level decisions* include surveys conducted by the Bureau of Labor Statistics, surveys conducted by professional organizations, and surveys conducted by individual companies. Wage surveys report data regarding wages and benefits for jobs in various industries and geographic areas.

Wage-structure Decision. The second decision concerns the pay associated with different jobs in an organization: how much money is paid for one job relative to other jobs in the same company? People typically receive more pay if their job requires greater skill, effort, and responsibility. Companies generally use either a classification system or the point method to make decisions about the wage structure. *Classification systems* classify jobs from simple to complex by describing different levels of skill, effort, and responsibility, and a pay range is associated with each classification. Classification systems are used extensively in public organizations, such as the GS system used by the United States government. The *point method* evaluates job descriptions and assigns points to different degrees of skill, effort, and responsibility; the pay for each job is determined by how many points it receives. The point method is very useful for determining and defending the base pay assigned to jobs that may be very different.

Individual Wage Decision. The third decision concerns individual pay rates and incentives. It answers this question: How much money does one employee receive relative to others who perform similar work? As a general rule, employees receive more money if their performance increases or if they have been with the company longer. Companies use a variety of incentive systems to reward employees for their performance, including individual, group, and company-wide incentive systems.

These three wage decisions illustrate the kinds of wage comparisons employees make when they evaluate their wages. Accountants in Company A, for example, compare their wages with the wages of accountants in other organizations, to see whether Company A has a higher or lower level of wages. The accountants also compare their wages with the pay of bookkeepers, computer programmers, and other members of Company A to learn whether the internal wage structure offers higher pay to jobs that involve more responsibility and greater difficulty. Finally, the accountants discuss their wages among themselves to determine whether each person's wage is the same, or whether

Wage level decision:
How much does one company pay relative to other companies for the same jobs?

Wage structure decision:
How much does one job pay relative to other jobs within the same company? How does a company justify paying some jobs more than others?

Individual Wage Decision:
How much money should people who all perform the same job receive? What criteria should be used to pay one person more than another, such as seniority and performance?

differences in wages are related to productivity, seniority, education, or something else.

Financial Incentives

The effects of money on motivation depend primarily on whether pay is based on performance. Companies that use direct financial incentives, such as piece-rates or commission sales, discover that they have a greater impact on performance than any other variable. In spite of this relationship, however, it is surprising to observe how seldom pay is based on performance. For example, when employees are asked what would happen if they doubled their efforts and produced twice as much, very few say they would receive additional income. Some say their supervisors would recognize their efforts and commend them, and a few think they might eventually receive a pay increase. Most say that the consequences of doubling their effort would be negative: it would disrupt the flow of work, their coworkers would hassle them, and they would eventually be expected to work at that rate all the time without additional compensation.

Companies use a variety of incentive plans to motivate employees. Incentive compensation can be granted on the basis of individual performance, group performance, or company-wide performance.

Individual Incentives. The most popular forms of individual incentive pay include merit pay, piece-rate incentives, and commission sales. *Merit pay plans* are based on a subjective assessment of each employee's performance, and the merit pay is typically awarded by increasing base pay for the coming year. An effective merit pay plan requires that companies have an effective performance evaluation program. To the extent that performance is more difficult to evaluate, the potential problems associated with tying pay to performance increase.

Merit Pay:
Increases in an employee's basic wage level based on performance levels.

Merit pay increases are relevant to all jobs paid a fixed wage or salary. The most important requirement for an effective merit pay incentive program is the ability to measure performance against clearly defined objectives. For an effective merit pay plan to function smoothly, supervisors and managers must have the competence to evaluate employee performance and provide meaningful feedback. But even when performance can only be evaluated subjectively, most employees still believe that pay increases should be related to performance.

Piece-rate incentives:
An incentive system that pays employees a specific amount of money for each unit of work they produce.

The most direct relationship between pay and performance generally appears in the form of *piece-rate incentives*, where workers receive a specified amount for each unit of work. The effectiveness of piece-rate incentives has been studied for many years. Frederick W. Taylor defended his recommendations of piece-rate incentives on the basis of research showing that workers paid on a piece-rate basis produced more work and earned more money. Taylor argued that piece-rate incentive programs would increase productivity by at least 25 percent. Surveys of piece-rate plans over the past 80 years have suggested that Taylor underestimated the actual results. Most surveys have found that productivity under piece work has increased by 30 to 40 percent, and in some cases by greater than 60 percent.[13]

Although piece-work incentive systems predictably increase productivity, there is some question whether the increase is due to financial incentives alone or to other changes that accompany piece-work plans. Two variables that accompany piece-work programs are (1) changes in the design of the work, and (2) higher performance goals. Before a piece-work plan is installed, a careful analysis of the job is usually conducted to ensure that it is being performed efficiently. A careful job analysis often identifies more efficient methods of performing the task. Moreover, when the task is being timed to establish pay rates, a goal setting process occurs, followed by performance feedback. The question, then, is whether goal setting, measurement, and job redesign are more responsible than pay incentives for increasing productivity. Studies generally show that each factor alone has a positive influence on productivity, but that the impact is far greater when all three factors are present. Thus, incentive systems contribute to productivity increases because of improved work methods, higher performance goals with specific performance feedback, and monetary incentives that induce greater effort.[14]

An alternative to paying people for what they do is to pay them for what they are capable of doing. *Skill-based pay* encourages employees to acquire additional skills. Companies identify a list of valuable skills they would like to encourage their workers to acquire, and as the workers demonstrate mastery of each skill, they receive an increase in their base pay. Skill-based compensation plans reinforce employees for their growth and development, and hopefully result in more creative ideas, organizational flexibility, and quality performance.

Another alternative, called *pay for knowledge*, provides incentives for employees to learn new information and demonstrate it by taking achievement tests. Specific dollar amounts are associated with each test, and employees receive an increase in their base pay after successfully passing each test. Pay for knowledge and skill-based pay systems are vital elements in the change strategies of organizations that experience rapid change and need to adapt to an uncertain environment.

Group Incentives and Bonuses. Although piece-work plans are typically based on individual performance, they can also be based on group production, with all members of the group sharing the money earned by the group. Group incentive plans have some important advantages over individual incentive plans, since they create greater cooperation among co-workers. This climate of cooperation usually reduces the need for direct supervision and control, since workers are supervised more by their co-workers than by their supervisors. In such a climate, slow workers are pressured by their co-workers to increase their productivity. Moreover, group incentives greatly facilitate the flow of work and flexibility in job assignments. When the normal work routine is disrupted because of unique problems such as illness or broken machines, individuals paid on a group incentive plan are willing to adapt to the problem and solve it themselves rather than complain to a manager or wait for the problem to solve itself.

Group incentives have certain limitations, however. When their jobs are independent, group members feel responsible only for their own jobs and think they should be paid individually. In this situation, group incentives provide little extra incentive to produce, since extra efforts by one worker will only result in a small increase in that worker's weekly pay. As the group gets larger, this problem becomes more severe. Thus, group incentives are most useful

Skill-based pay:
A pay system in which an employee's pay level is partially determined by the employee's skills as a means of motivating them to acquire greater skills.

Pay for knowledge:
A pay system in which an employee's pay level is determined in part by how many knowledge tests the employee has successfully completed.

when jobs are interdependent, when the output of the group can be counted, and the group is small.

The powerful influence of group pressure explains why piece-rate incentives are sometimes not effective. Although many studies have shown that incentive pay systems increase productivity, other studies have found examples where groups restrict output to arbitrarily low levels. Group norms restricting productivity are very troublesome to managers, and they are particularly perplexing because they seem to be so irrational. Why should a group of workers collectively decide to restrict their productivity when they are paid only for what they produce? This behavior is not so irrational when it is examined from the workers' perspective. The problem centers on how the performance standards are established. Workers know that performance standards are somewhat arbitrary. They believe that if they consistently produce more than the standard, the industrial engineer will return and re-time the job; then they will be expected to produce more work for the same amount of pay.

Management has been guilty of re-timing jobs often enough in some organizations to justify the workers' fears. Several interesting case studies have described the games played by workers and industrial engineers in setting performance standards. Since industrial engineers know that workers intentionally work slowly, they arbitrarily tighten the standards above the measured times. The workers know the industrial engineer suspects them of working slowly, so they add unnecessary and inefficient movements to look busy, which the industrial engineers expect and try to disregard.

Company-wide Incentives. In some organizations, financial incentives are based on the performance of the entire organization. Three of the most popular forms of company-wide incentives include profit-sharing plans, Scanlon plans, and gainsharing.

Profit sharing is the most popular company-wide incentive, and in some companies the employees have been highly motivated to perform as a result of a generous profit-sharing plan. A typical *profit-sharing plan* distributes 25 percent of the pretax profit to the employees according to an allocation formula that combines years of service and base wages. For example, in some plans, employees receive points for their base pay, such as one point for every $1000 of annual salary, and points for length of service, such as one point for every year of service. Profit-sharing money is then distributed to employees according to their percentage of the total points.

Profit-sharing plans can be either *cash plans* or *deferred plans*. Cash plans are more directly tied to performance because employees are paid annually. However, deferred plans are more popular because of tax considerations. Under a deferred plan, an employee's share of the profit is held in an individual account where it grows without being taxed until it is received later, usually at retirement. Some deferred plans provide enormous wealth to their participants.

Profit-sharing plans generally reduce the conflict between managers and workers. Many companies claim that their plans have created a sense of partnership between employees and management, and have increased employee interest in the company. Profit-sharing plans typically increase productivity by increasing motivation; however, the impact of profit sharing is typically less than that for piece-rate plans, since each individual's profit share is not directly

Profit-sharing plan: A program that allows employees to share in the profits of a company based on the profitability of the company and an allocation formula determining each employee's share.

Cash versus Deferred Plans: Profit-sharing money can be distributed as cash at the end of each period or placed in a deferred fund that grows tax-free until retirement.

tied to individual productivity. Immediate rewards that are directly tied to specific individual behaviors are more effective than profit-sharing plans, especially for motivating employees who have short attention spans and cannot delay gratification. Deferred compensation plans, for example, are more effective for older workers than they are for younger workers, since retirement is not so distant.

Scanlon plans:
A company-wide incentive plan that combines profit sharing, based on a wages to revenue ratio, with a suggestion plan.

Scanlon plans were named after their founder, Joseph Scanlon, an accountant and union steward in a steel mill. While negotiating a new labor agreement, Scanlon proposed that the percent of revenue allocated to labor costs be maintained at a fixed ratio of what it had been over the past few years. Scanlon believed that the employees would be highly motivated to increase their productivity if they knew that a fixed percent of the revenue would be paid in wages. Scanlon believed that significantly higher revenues could be obtained without an increase in the number of employee hours by motivating the employees to work harder and submit suggestions of how to improve productivity. Since 1941, when Scanlon first proposed his idea, Scanlon plans have grown in popularity, and the results have shown that they tend to increase both company profits and employee wages.

Gainsharing:
A pay-for-performance plan that shares some of the economic gains with employees according to improvements in specific performance measures.

Gainsharing is a company-wide incentive program similar to profit sharing, but the bonuses are based on improved productivity rather than a percent of the profit. An effective gainsharing program requires managers to tie specific incentives to the strategic factors that determine a company's economic success, called *business drivers*. Some examples of business drivers are occupancy rates for hotels, turn-around time and vacant seats for airlines, and inventory shrinkage for retail companies. A successful gainsharing program at an oil refinery identified targeted goals for seven business drivers and promised to share the proceeds with the workers if they exceeded these goals. The goal for safety was an incident rate of 0.5, and for each accident that didn't happen the company would put $18,000 (the average cost of an accident) into the fund to be divided among employees. Gainsharing plans normally reward employees on a monthly or quarterly basis, depending on how productivity is measured, whereas profit sharing is usually paid annually.

Bonuses. Executives and managers often participate in an additional bonus program designed specifically for them. The basic philosophy behind executive bonuses is to reward managers for good performance. When they are tied to the overall performance of a company, the bonuses are expected to create greater creativity and better cooperation among managers.

Executive bonuses are typically larger for upper-level managers than for middle-level managers, even when expressed as a percentage of salary. At upper levels of a company, a typical bonus might be 80 to 120 percent of salary. At lower levels of the company, supervisors typically receive bonuses that add only 15 to 40 percent of their salaries, if they receive bonuses at all.

The bonus plans of many companies are not carefully designed and administered. Although bonuses are intended to improve the performance of individual managers and the organization as a whole, the research evaluating bonuses does not entirely support their effectiveness.[15] Because management performance is difficult to evaluate, most bonus plans distribute money based on the manager's position rather than on the manager's performance. Consequently, these plans typically do little to motivate greater performance.

Even though they are very expensive and the research evidence regarding their effectiveness is mostly negative, they are still widely used.

Fine-Tuning the Compensation Plan. In designing an effective compensation program, organizations need to find the proper balance between base pay and incentive pay, including individual incentives, group incentives, and company-wide incentives. The process of balancing the various incentives is called *fine-tuning the compensation system*. Compensation managers must fine-tune the compensation system, just as a mechanic fine-tunes an engine. The engine needs to be adjusted for the load it must pull, the quality of fuel it will use, and even the altitude at which it will operate. Similarly, a compensation system needs to be fine-tuned to balance the employees' needs for security, equity, and motivation.

Employees who have a sizable base pay feel secure, but not motivated. However, if their total compensation consists of incentive pay without adequate base pay, several problems could develop, such as increased turnover because of inadequate security, dissatisfaction over inaccurate performance evaluations, and dysfunctional competition between co-workers.

The fine-tuning process consists of adjusting base pay, individual incentives, group incentives, and profit sharing to create feelings of security and motivation. Stable base pay that provides a dependable weekly or monthly income provides security. Equity and motivation, however, are provided through incentive plans. Some organizations choose to pay large base salaries and give small bonuses, while other organizations do just the opposite.

Fine-tuning compensation:
Balancing the relative percentages of base pay, individual incentives, group incentives, and company-wide incentives to create a balance between motivation and security for employees.

Recognition Programs

Nonmonetary reward systems have been used effectively to improve employee motivation. Every motivation theory agrees that praise and recognition are effective rewards. Companies have created a variety of nonmonetary reward programs to recognize employees, and some have been more effective than monetary incentives. The following illustrations demonstrate the diversity of recognition rewards.

- A storage company paneled one of its walls inside the warehouse, and used it to display the photographs of the employee with the best safety record each month. The number of accidents in the warehouse was greatly reduced, and the forklift operators were pleased with the recognition they received, even though the public could not see their photographs.
- Sewing machine operators receive silver stars on their nameplates if they exceed 120 percent of their production quotas every day for a week. After they get ten silver stars, they receive a purple seal. Ribbons are awarded for high-quality production, and the operators display them with pride.
- A hospital gives five-, ten-, fifteen-, twenty-, and twenty-five-year service pins to recognize employees for their years of service. The pins are top-quality jewelry made with diamonds and gold that show the hospital's logo. When the price of gold increased, the hospital decided to give savings bonds rather than pins, but the administrators abandoned the idea

when they discovered that the pins were far more important and valued by the employees than were the savings bonds.

- To reduce absenteeism and tardiness, a small apparel manufacturer decided to give gifts of ten to fifteen dollars to randomly selected employees who had perfect attendance. At the end of each week, the names of those who had perfect attendance records were placed in a drawing. For every 20 names in the drawing, one name was selected to receive a gift. After three months, tardiness was only a third of what it had been, and absenteeism was cut in half.

Recognition awards, such as silver stars, purple seals, and photographs hung on a wall, are not inherently rewarding. Primary rewards such as food, water, rest, and the removal of pain are reinforcing because of their relationship to the innate physiology of the body. Secondary rewards such as recognition awards do not directly satisfy physiological needs. Instead, they become powerful reinforcers as people come to place value on them. Consequently, social approval, recognition, status, and feelings of pride and craftsmanship are secondary or learned rewards, because their reinforcing properties are acquired through experience with them. Although a person may not immediately see the secondary reinforcer as a highly motivating award, over time it can become a powerful form of reinforcement. Recognition awards are often inconsequential to new employees, but as new workers observe their co-workers participate in meaningful recognition experiences, the reward comes to be a highly valued reinforcer. For example, a 25-year service pin can be an extremely motivating reward, not because of its financial worth but because of the symbolic meaning associated with it. In some organizations the service pins are distributed at an annual awards banquet where the recipients are recognized individually. Employees who observe this ritual year after year come to appreciate the ceremony and see the pin as a highly valued reward.[16]

Intrinsic versus Extrinsic Rewards

Some scholars are opposed to using any form of monetary incentives to motivate workers. Indeed, they adamantly condemn all extrinsic reward programs that are designed to motivate people or change their behavior, including piece-rate incentives in industry, grades in education, and gold stars in child rearing. Their argument is not that incentives do not work, because they admit that well-designed incentive programs can have an immediate and substantial impact on behavior. Their claim is that they work for all the wrong reasons. Six of the most important reasons are:[17]

1. *Rewards are used to control behavior.* Rather than encourage people to direct their lives according to their personal values, rewards manipulate and control them. Rewards are effective only for people who are dependent on them, and they only work if they continue to be received.
2. *Rewards punish.* Rewards and punishment are both elements of a common psychological model that views motivation as nothing more than the manipulation of behavior. To not be rewarded, or to be rewarded less than last time, is to be punished.
3. *Rewards rupture relationships.* Competition for rewards within a group tends to destroy group cohesiveness. Likewise, the relationships between

the person giving the rewards and the recipients are also damaged because of the unequal status inherent in the situation.

4. *Rewards ignore reasons.* Successful performance is determined by both personal and situational factors, and when rewards are based strictly on performance, the uncontrolled situational factors that may have prevented success are ignored.
5. *Rewards discourage risk taking.* When people are competing for rewards, they focus primarily on customary methods that have worked in the past, and overlook new opportunities and creative insights for improving performance.
6. *Extrinsic rewards destroy intrinsic satisfaction.* The good feelings people have for performing a task or helping others are destroyed when they are given extrinsic rewards.

Since people must be paid to work, and rewards do serve many useful purposes, those opposed to the use of extrinsic rewards offer the following suggestions to minimize the damage caused by extrinsic rewards:

1. *Get rewards out of people's faces.* Encourage people to perform well without continually talking about the potential rewards. Focus on the intrinsic satisfaction of providing service and assistance.
2. *Offer rewards after the fact, as a surprise.* Rewarding excellence with unexpected rewards prevents people from feeling that they were only motivated by the rewards.
3. *Never turn the quest for rewards into a contest.* Contests reward some at the expense of others. Only have contests in which people compete against their own personal records.
4. *Make rewards as similar as possible to the task.* The best reward for good behavior is the opportunity to do it again and feel good about it.
5. *Give people as much choice as possible about how rewards are used.* If possible, let people suggest what will be given, to whom, and when.

Discussion Questions

1. Since employees dislike being evaluated and supervisors dislike evaluating them, why should companies evaluate employee performance? Students also dislike being graded. What would most likely happen and how would you respond if grading were eliminated or if all students received A grades?
2. Describe the conditions that contribute to effective performance appraisal interviews. Identify a time when someone has evaluated your performance, discuss what you liked and disliked about it, and assess whether it was helpful.
3. Which organizational conditions are best suited for using individual, group, and company-wide incentives? Identify a specific job and explain what percent of the pay for that job should come from base pay, individual incentives, group incentives, and company-wide incentives to balance the objectives of motivation versus security.
4. Do you agree that extrinsic rewards, such as money, destroy intrinsic motivation? Describe a time when you received an extrinsic reward and explain its impact on your intrinsic motivation. What are the effects of financial in-

centives on motivation, and how do you recommend that employers use money to increase motivation?

Notes

1. Daniel Katz and Robert L. Kahn, *The Social Psychology of Organizations*, 2nd ed. (New York: John Wiley and Sons, 1978), 402–5.

2. *Baxter v. Savannah Sugar Refining Corp.*, 495 F2d 437 (1974); *Brito v. Zia Co.*, 478, F2d, 1200 (1973); *Albemarle Paper Company v. Moody*, 95 SCt 2362 (1974); *Rowe v. General Motors Corp.*, 457 F2d 348, 1972; *Wade v. Mississippi Cooperative Extension Service*, 528 F2d 508 (1976).

3. Personal communication from the commanding officer.

4. John P. Campbell, R. Darvey, Marvin D. Dunnette, and L. V. Hellervik, "The Development and Evaluation of Behaviorally Based Rating Scales," *Journal of Applied Psychology*, 57, 1(1973); Donald P. Schwab, Herbert G. Heneman, and T. A. DeCotis, "Behaviorally-Anchored Rating Scales: A Review of the Literature," *Personnel Psychology*, 28, 4 (Winter, 1975): 549–62; Aharon Tziner and Richard Kopelman, "Effects of Rating Format on Goal-Setting Dimensions: A Field Experiment," *Journal of Applied Psychology*, 73(May 1988): 323–6; Aharon Tziner and Gary P. Latham, "The Effects of Appraisal Instrument, Feedback and Goal-Setting on Worker Satisfaction and Commitment," *Journal of Organizational Behavior*, 10 (April 1989): 145–53.

5. Peter F. Drucker, *The Practice of Management*, (New York: Harper and Row, 1954).

6. Stephen G. Green, Gail T. Fairhurst and B. Kay Snavely, "Chains of Poor Performance and Supervisory Control," *Organizational Behavior and Human Decision Processes* 38 (1986): 7–27.

7. James R. Larson, Jr., "Supervisors' Performance Feedback to Subordinates: The Impact of Subordinate Performance Valence and Outcome Dependence," *Organizational Behavior and Human Decision Processes* 37 (1986): 391–408.

8. C.D. Fisher, "Transmission of Positive and Negative Feedback to Subordinates: A Laboratory Investigation," *Journal of Applied Psychology* 64 (1979): 533–40; Daniel R. Ilgen and W.A. Knowlton, "Performance Attributional Effects on Feedback From Superiors," *Organizational Behavior and Human Performance* 25 (1980): 441–56.

9. J. Bruce Prince and Edward E. Lawler, III, "Does Salary Discussion Hurt the Developmental Performance Appraisal?" *Organizational Behavior and Human Decision Processes* 37 (1986): 357–75.

10. Tamao Matsui, Akinori Okada, and Osamu Inoshita, "Mechanism of Feedback Affecting Task Performance," *Organizational Behavior and Human Performance* 31 (1983): 114–22.

11. Albert Bandura, "Self-Efficacy Mechanism in Human Agency," *American Psychologist* 37 (February 1982): 122–47.

12. Glenn M. McEvoy, Paul. F. Buller and Steven R. Rognaar, "A Jury of One's Peers," *Personnel Administrator* 33 (May 1988): 94–101; E.P. Hollander, "Buddy Ratings: Military Research and Industrial Implications," *Personnel Psychology* 7, 3 (Autumn 1954): 385–93; E.P. Hollander, "Peer Nominations as a Predictor of the Pass-Fail Criterion in Naval Air

Training," *Journal of Applied Psychology* 38 (1954): 150–53; Harry E. Roadman, "An Industrial Use of Peer Ratings," *Journal of Applied Psychology* 48, 4 (1964): 211–14.

13. Surveyed by Allan N. Nash and Stephen J. Carroll, Jr., *The Management of Compensation*, (Monterey, CA: Brooks-Cole, 1975), 199.

14. James S. Devlin, "Wage Incentives: The Aetna Plan," Presented at the LOMA work measurement seminar (April 1975).

15. J. Perham, "What's Wrong with Bonuses?" Dun's Review of *Modern Industry* 98 (1981): 40–44.

16. David J. Cherrington and B. Jackson Wixom, Jr., "Recognition is Still a Top Motivator," *Personnel Administrator* (May 1983): 87–91.

17. Alfie Kohn, *Punished by Rewards: The Trouble with Gold Stars, Incentive Plans, A's, Praise, and Other Bribes*. (Boston: Houghton Mifflin, 1993); Mark R. Lepper and David Greene, *The Hidden Costs of Rewards: New Perspectives on the Psychology of Human Motivation* (Hillsdale, NJ: Erlbaum, 1978).

Supervising an Obnoxious Employee

Michelle Boyd is the supervisor of the customer support department and she wants to fire one of her six staff members, Donald Harrison. She thinks Don's behavior is rude and obnoxious and she wants to terminate him. Michelle is required to evaluate the performance of her staff and she thinks this is a good time to get rid of him.

Don has more seniority than Michelle; he has been with the company for two and a half years while Michelle was hired two years ago. She has been a supervisor for nine months. Don is probably the most technically competent member of the staff and he is usually the one who solves the most difficult customer problems. But he is also very arrogant and self-centered, and he brags about the difficult problems he solves.

Between customer calls, Don dominates the group conversation with discussions of politics, current events, or personal feelings. Some staff members enjoy listening to him, but Michelle finds him argumentative and abrasive. What she objects to most is his teasing and questions about personal topics. While some staff members seem to enjoy discussing intimate feelings and personal opinions, Michelle finds it very threatening and does not like being questioned. Don is a master of practical jokes that are harmless but usually embarrassing.

When she announced to the human resource manager her decision to terminate Don he did not support her decision. The human resource manager says Don has a record of excellent performance reviews, including the one Michelle submitted six months ago as a new supervisor. According to the company's human resource policies, Don should not be terminated without a warning and a hearing.

Michelle's supervisor also disagrees with firing Don for a different reason: she thinks Don's conversations are interesting and intellectually stimulating. She thinks Don should only be fired if he is incompetent. Since Don is highly competent, her supervisor thinks Michelle should either tolerate Don's personality and teasing, or get him to change.

Questions

1. Should Michelle be allowed to fire Don? Since she also recommends semi-annual pay increases, should she withhold Don's pay increase to punish Don?
2. Is being obnoxious a legitimate reason to fire an employee? What process should a company follow to terminate employees who deserve to be fired?
3. Can supervisors change the personality of subordinates? If so, how?

Deciding Pay Increases

In the College of Business, all salary changes, including merit increases and cost-of-living adjustments, are decided by the department heads. This year, the dean's office has allocated $16,000 for salary increases to the six members of one department. The six faculty members and information about their performances are shown in the following table.

Professor	Present Salary	Years of Teaching	Performance Information
Brooks	$64,800	15	Students say he is a horrible teacher. Never keeps his office hours, spends most of his time doing outside consulting, and hasn't written anything but consulting project reports for nine years.
Falk	$52,100	3	Excellent researcher; good teacher of graduate classes; receives mixed evaluations from undergraduate students because most class activities are used to collect research data. Published six articles last year in leading journals.
Hunter	$65,100	12	Students say she is a very good teacher and is very helpful to students; a member of the College Advisory Council; published three articles last year in practitioner journals and one article in an academic journal.
Moore	$50,200	2	New to the job; students say she is entertaining in class, but her lectures are weak because she lacks experience; spent first year finishing dissertation and has been working on other research projects since then, but nothing is finished.
Stephens	$75,600	28	Former associate dean and department head, influential in college politics but is not on any committees; author of three books, including a textbook that he revised eight years ago. Has written nothing in the last four years. Students complain that his lectures are boring and obsolete. He spends much of his time at his hobby, training dogs.
Walker	$72,200	26	Considered an outstanding teacher at both graduate and undergraduate levels. Served on several thesis committees last year; involved in two major research projects; has authored two and coauthored six research articles; wrote about 40 percent of a textbook last year; serves on the editorial review board for a research journal.

In the past, pay increases have largely been tied to the rate of inflation, and everyone has received about the same percentage increase. The rate of inflation this year has been about 3 percent, and everyone would normally receive a cost-of-living adjustment of at least that amount. However, during its fall retreat, the college executive committee decided that pay increases should be based primarily on performance rather than on cost-of-living increases. The committee concluded that greater efforts should be made to reward outstanding faculty members for teaching, research, and professional service to the university or to society. When this decision was announced, some of the faculty members objected. The dean said publicly that everyone would probably receive some increase, but that weak faculty members might not keep up with inflation.

Directions

Decide how you would allocate the $16,000 salary increases. After you have made your own decisions, discuss your recommendations with four or five other students and try to reach a group consensus based on similar arguments. Imagine that you are the department head who must justify these decisions to the faculty members.

10

Employee Discipline

Chapter Outline

Grievance and Complaint Systems

Grievance Procedures in Union Companies

Complaint Procedures in Nonunion Companies

Rule Enforcement and Discipline

Compliance to Rules

Punishment

Progressive Discipline

Wrongful Discharge

Solving Performance Problems

Describing the Situation

Diagnosing Problems: Ability versus Motivation

Solving Ability Problems

Communicating Consequences for Motivation Problems

Dealing with Emergent Problems

GRIEVANCE AND COMPLAINT SYSTEMS

To maintain fair and effective employee relations, every organization needs both a grievance procedure and a discipline procedure. *Grievance procedures*, which are more frequently called complaint procedures in nonunion companies, provide a systematic process for hearing and evaluating employees' complaints. They tend to be more highly developed in union companies than in nonunion companies because they are guaranteed by the labor agreement. But they are also needed in nonunion companies. These procedures protect the rights of employees, and eliminate the need for strikes or slowdowns every time a disagreement occurs. They also increase upward communication in organizations and make top management decisions more sensitive to employee feelings.

Discipline procedures provide a systematic process for handling problem employees. The goal of a good discipline system is to help employees perform better. If employees fail to respond, a procedure is needed for terminating them as a last resort. A good discipline system can make terminations "stick" so that fired employees will not be reinstated.

Grievance Procedures in Union Companies

Most union agreements grant employees the right to submit grievances and explain how their complaints will be resolved. The agreement assures employees that they can express their complaints freely without jeopardizing their jobs, and obtain a fair hearing through appeals to progressively higher levels of management. Most unions follow a procedure similar to the one illustrated in Exhibit 10.1.

Most grievance procedures specify time limits for each stage. Failure to make a timely response may result in forfeiture of the grievance by the union or in the company's granting the grievance to the union. To resolve a grievance, both management and union representatives must be willing to discuss the issue rationally and objectively. A grievance should not be treated as a form of competition in which each side keeps track of its win-loss record. Instead, each side should seek to resolve conflict and remove inequities.

Most grievances are resolved at the first step of the process by competent supervisors who are willing to listen and act fairly. To reduce the number of grievances that are appealed, supervisors are encouraged to follow these recommendations:

- Treat all complaints seriously.
- Investigate and handle each case as though it may eventually result in arbitration.
- Talk with an employee as soon as possible about his or her grievance and give the employee a full hearing.
- Correct the problem if the company is wrong.
- Examine the labor agreement carefully, and obtain clarification from the human resource office if necessary.
- Collect evidence and determine whether there were any witnesses.
- Remain calm.
- Carefully examine all the evidence before making a decision.
- Avoid lengthy delays. When all the information is in, make a decision and communicate it.

Exhibit 10.1   Grievance Process

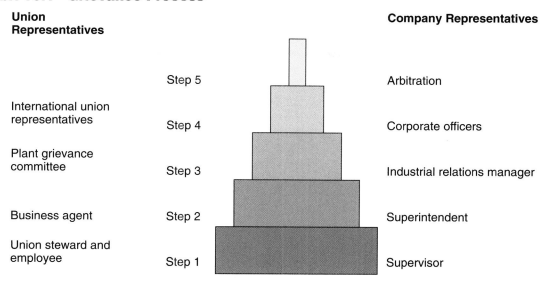

Union Representatives   **Company Representatives**

Union Representatives		Company Representatives
	Step 5	Arbitration
International union representatives	Step 4	Corporate officers
Plant grievance committee	Step 3	Industrial relations manager
Business agent	Step 2	Superintendent
Union steward and employee	Step 1	Supervisor

Step 1. The first step in most labor agreements calls for the complaint to be submitted to the supervisor, sometimes with the help of a union steward. Most grievances are settled at this step by a simple discussion.

Step 2. If the employee is not satisfied with the actions of the supervisor, the grievance can be appealed to a superintendent or division manager. At this point the grievance is almost always written. In smaller companies, this step is usually bypassed.

Step 3. If the union is not satisfied with the decision, the grievance can be appealed to the plant manager or director of industrial relations. Grievances that are not settled at this step may go directly to arbitration.

Step 4. Large corporations that have multi-employer agreements may have a fourth step if the issue is one that has general interest to the union and corporation.

Step 5. The final step in the grievance process is binding arbitration by an outside third party acceptable to both the management and the union. Both parties agree beforehand to abide by the arbitrator's decision.

Binding arbitration:
The final step in most grievance procedures. The dispute is submitted to a neutral third party who has the authority to decide the issue and both parties agree beforehand to accept the decision.

Submission Agreement:
A statement prepared by both management and union that describes the dispute and the potential solutions the arbitrator can decide.

Sometimes a supervisor is not in a good position to resolve a grievance because it concerns a company policy. Such a dispute may have to be appealed to the second, third, or even fourth step of the grievance procedure before the appropriate people who can change or interpret the policy become involved.

Issues that cannot be resolved satisfactorily through mediation or discussion are submitted to binding arbitration by an outside third party. Anyone acceptable to both sides is eligible to serve as an arbitrator, such as a local minister or a member of the local school board; however, in most instances a professional arbitrator is selected from a list maintained by the Federal Mediation and Conciliation Service.

After an arbitrator has been chosen, the arbitrator is presented with a *submission agreement*, which is a statement that formally outlines the issues for arbitration and grants final authority to the arbitrator to settle the issue. The arbitration hearing may be as formal as a civil court hearing and involve written testimony, signed statements and affidavits, the swearing in of witnesses, cross examination, and a recorded transcript of the proceedings; or the hearing might be very informal, with just an opening statement by each side and then questioning by the arbitrator. To save time, most testimony of witnesses is obtained in advance and presented to the arbitrator. Normally, the hearing does not last more than one day.

Most arbitrators stipulate that the burden of proof is on the party that initiates the complaint. If the union alleges violation of the agreement, it must provide evidence of what happened and describe how the agreement was violated. If an employee was disciplined or discharged, the company must provide evidence showing that the action was legitimate.

After all of the evidence has been presented, the hearings are adjourned. The arbitrator reviews the evidence, examines the labor agreement, and usually looks at previous arbitration awards in similar cases before reaching a decision. Arbitrators are not bound by the decisions of other arbitrators but, like federal judges, most arbitrators have tried to render decisions that are consistent with a body of "case law" that has emerged over the years. Within 30 days, the arbitration award is usually announced to both parties along with a written review of the case.

The enormous time and expense associated with litigating disagreements have prompted employers to pursue other methods for resolving disagreements. These methods, known generally as alternative dispute resolution, include negotiation, mediation, binding arbitration, and even rent-a-judge services. When two parties are unable to negotiate an acceptable solution, the next step may be to ask for the services of a mediator. The mediator examines both sides of the dispute and tries to help both parties find an acceptable compromise. If mediation fails, the parties can agree to submit the issue to binding arbitration and promise to live by the arbitrator's decision.

Complaint Procedures in Nonunion Companies

The complaint procedures in nonunion companies are more informal than in union companies. Employees are encouraged to express their complaints and most executives believe their organizations have adequate procedures for solving employee problems. Nevertheless, many employees have two fears: first, that they will be fired if they complain, and second, that their complaint will not receive adequate attention. The procedures used in nonunion companies to overcome these concerns include an ombudsman, a grievance committee, a grievance appeal procedure, an open-door policy, and fact finding.

Ombudsman:
An impartial person (male or female) designated by an organization to hear complaints from members who feel powerless and unable to obtain a fair hearing on their own.

Grievance Committee:
A committee assigned to hear complaints from employees and recommend a solution, usually in nonunion companies.

Ombudsman. The term *ombudsman* originally referred to a politically neutral and independent person who represented ordinary citizens in their disputes with government officials. The concept first originated in Sweden and Finland in 1809. In recent years, numerous organizations have appointed one of their employees to be an ombudsman. Such an individual is charged with investigating and settling employee complaints. The ombudsman reports to the president, who is the only person with the authority to reverse the ombudsman's decision.

Grievance Committee. Some nonunion organizations have established a grievance procedure that allows individuals to submit their grievances to a grievance committee. The members of the committee may be appointed by top management or elected by employees. These committees hear the evidence and issue a judgment. In most companies, the grievance committee makes a recommendation to the president rather than making a binding decision on its own.

Grievance Appeal Procedure. Some companies allow employees to submit grievances to successively higher levels in the organization, as explained in Exhibit 10.2. In some cases, the aggrieved employee is represented by an attorney, a peer, or a member of the personnel office. This procedure is similar to the appeal process in a union agreement, with two exceptions. First, it is usually an informal appeal system that can be stopped at any time at management's discretion without a guarantee that the appeal will reach the top officers. Second, ultimate appeal is usually made to top management and does not go to arbitration.

Open-door policy:
An invitation by top management for employees who have complaints to visit them in their offices and discuss their grievances.

Open-Door Policy. The most popular procedure for responding to employee complaints is an open-door policy. All employees, regardless of their positions, are encouraged to discuss their complaints with a top executive without being forced to go through a chain of command. After the executive investigates the complaint, the aggrieved employee is informed of the outcome. Although open-door policies provide an avenue for employees to express their complaints, they do not always function effectively, because of the perceived social distance between executives and workers. The open-door policy needs to exist throughout the organization so that complaints can also be taken to lower-level managers. Many complaints concern day-to-day issues that are far removed from the top officers.

Fact Finding:
Gathering information about employee complaints and sharing it with people who can resolve them.

Fact Finding. Employee complaints can be investigated by an impartial fact finder. The investigation is normally conducted by a human resource executive or by an assistant to the president, and then a report is submitted to top management. Fact finders are usually authorized to examine problems without

---

Problem-Solving Procedure

Objective: The purpose of this problem-solving procedure is to provide a formal process for solving problems and protecting the rights of employees.

Step 1: Your supervisor is responsible for hearing and resolving work-related problems. You should fully discuss the problem with your immediate supervisor. However, in unusual cases or because of personal conditions between you and your supervisor, you may want to discuss the problem directly with the Employee Relations Office.

Step 2: If your supervisor does not resolve the problem to your satisfaction, you can appeal it to your functional manager. This manager will explore all the facts of the case and render a decision.

Step 3: If you are still dissatisfied with the resolution of your problem, you can discuss it with the plant manager. The employee relations manager will make the appointment for you. After the discussion, the plant manager's decision will be considered final.

The following time limits have been established:

Step 1 - five working days

Step 2 - two to five working days

Step 3 - three to five working days

Exhibit 10.2 **Complaint Procedure for a Retail Store**

conducting formal hearings. Informal investigations give fact finders access to information that a complaining party might be reluctant to share in a formal hearing, such as instances of sexual harassment. Fact finders are usually expected to prepare a recommendation such as discipline, transfer, compensation for the victim, or training. The advantages of fact finding are that problems can be addressed quickly and privately.

RULE ENFORCEMENT AND DISCIPLINE

Rule enforcement and the threat of punishment are an important part of motivation theory. Although most motivation theories focus on rewards to elicit desired behaviors, the effects of punishment and rule enforcement for eliminating undesirable behavior should not be overlooked. Rule enforcement and punishment are used far more frequently than rewards in influencing everyday behavior.[1]

Compliance to Rules

Much of our behavior in organizations can be explained by examining the organization's rules. We obey organizational rules partly because of the threat of punishment, but mostly because we accept the rules as legitimate expectations. Most of us believe we have an obligation to follow the rules. If the company wanted to change behavior, it would simply need to change the rules.

Legal compliance is effective in creating acceptable levels of performance, especially when the tasks are routine and are paced by some type of mechanical control, such as an assembly line, and all that is needed is steady, perfunctory performance. However, legal compliance and rule enforcement are notoriously poor for motivating performance beyond the minimum standard. An emphasis on rule compliance tends in practice to mean that the minimum standard eventually becomes the maximum standard. A minimum standard of sixty units per hour, for example, soon becomes interpreted by employees to be the maximum required, and the speed of work is gauged to achieve that standard but never higher.

Another problem with relying excessively on rule compliance is that it is largely ineffective at motivating spontaneous and innovative behaviors that go beyond the call of duty. Since these acts are not part of the formal job description, they are not included in the rules. Organizations cannot stimulate innovation by decreeing it. In general, when there is greater emphasis on rule compliance, there is less motivation for individuals to do more than is specified by their job descriptions.

Punishment

Punishment has the effect of reducing the probability of a response. Some managers are opposed to the use of punishment for moral reasons, although it can be used very effectively to improve performance, and some forms of punishment are unavoidable.

Types of punishment. Punishment occurs when an aversive stimulus follows a response. An aversive stimulus refers to something unpleasant, and whose removal is reinforcing. Physical pain, criticism, and being fired are examples of aversive stimuli; we try to avoid doing things that elicit these consequences. Punishment plays a major role in shaping the behavior of people in organizations. Some managers argue that there is no justification for the use of punishment in organizational settings. Others believe that there are times when punishment is the most effective way to change behavior. Three different kinds of punishment occur in organizations: natural consequences, logical consequences, and contrived consequences.[2]

Natural consequences occur when behavior violates the laws of nature or society, such as being injured because you followed unsafe work procedures, or being excluded from a lunchroom clique because you have body odor. Virtually every form of misbehavior creates some form of undesirable natural consequence, although some consequences are difficult to recognize immediately.

Logical consequences refer to punishment that contains a logical relationship to the violated rule. An example of a logical consequence is requiring employees to wait for an assigned secretary to make copies for them because they misuse the copy machine or fail to record the number of copies when they use it themselves.

Contrived consequences refer to punishment for wrongdoing where the punishment is unrelated to the misbehavior. Fining a football player $100 for missing practice and revoking an employee's use of a company privilege for a late report are examples of contrived punishments.

Because no one has to initiate action to create natural consequences, nor can anyone really prevent them from occurring, the following discussion focuses largely on logical and contrived punishment. In organizational leadership, as in parenting, the use of logical consequences is probably much more effective in changing behavior than the use of contrived consequences.

A highly recommended procedure for administering punishment is called the "hot stove rule." A hot stove with its radiating heat provides a warning that it should not be touched. Those who ignore the warning and touch it, like employees who violate a rule, are burned. The punishment, in this case the burn, is immediate and directly associated with violating the rule. Like the hot stove, which immediately burns anyone who touches it, an established rule for employees to follow should be consistently enforced and applied to all employees. The pain of a hot stove is administered in a rigid and impersonal way to everyone who touches it.[3]

Punishment does not need to be experienced personally in order to change behavior. Just as we learn vicariously from observing others what will be rewarding, we also learn through vicarious punishment what we should avoid. We are less likely to imitate those behaviors for which we see others punished. Studies of punishment have shown that individuals who have observed others being punished change their behavior almost as much as those who were actually punished.[4]

Conditions for the Effective Use of Punishment. The most severe criticisms against the use of punishment are that it is effective only when the punishing agent is present, it creates a negative attitude toward the punishing agent, it only tells people what they did wrong and not what they should do right, and it creates a negative emotional feeling. In spite of these criticisms, however,

---

Natural consequences: Outcomes that occur naturally without anyone having to make them happen.

Logical consequences: Punishment that is logically related to the violation of a rule.

Contrived consequences: Punishment that is imposed by an agent and not related directly to the misbehavior.

Hot-stove rule: A guideline for administering punishment in a way that is direct, impartial, and immediate.

there are appropriate times when punishment should be used, and there is considerable evidence that punishment can be an effective tool if the conditions are right. Seven conditions have been proposed for the effective use of punishment:[5]

1. Punishment is more effective when it occurs immediately after the mistake. The longer the delay, the more likely that it will be perceived as arbitrary, unfair, and unrelated to the undesired behavior.
2. Punishment should be unpleasant, but not severe. If it is too mild, it will be ignored; but if it is too severe, those who are punished will think too much about the pain and not enough about how they must change their behavior to avoid it in the future.
3. Punishment should focus on a specific act, not on a person or on general behavior patterns. Punishment should not be a means of revenge or a way of venting frustrations. Instead, it should be tied to a specific act that can be described.
4. Punishment should be consistent across persons and across time. Whether punishment is administered should not depend upon who misbehaved, how they get along with the manager, or whether things are running smoothly.
5. Punishment should be administered in a way that informs people what they did wrong and also how they must change. Simply knowing that what they did was wrong without knowing how to change can be very frustrating.
6. Punishment is most effective when it occurs in the context of a loving and nurturing relationship. Since punishment naturally creates a negative feeling toward the punishing agent, it is essential that on other occasions a warm and supportive relationship be developed to withstand the strain of punishment. When the relationship between a person and the punishing agent is already strained or distant, the punishment tends to be perceived as a personal attack that creates a feeling of hatred rather than an indication of a wrongdoing that needs to be changed.
7. Punishment should not be followed by undeserved rewards. Although greater efforts should be made after punishment to reestablish an interpersonal relationship, these efforts should not include showering the person with undeserved rewards, because it encourages them to misbehave again.

There are many reasons why punishment cannot be administered as quickly or as intensely in organizations as reinforcement theory would recommend. Many undesirable behaviors such as leaving the work station, sleeping on the job, fighting, stealing, and damaging equipment cannot be punished as immediately or as severely as the hot-stove rule recommends. Furthermore, most managers prefer to delay punishment until an appropriate time in order to avoid publicly humiliating an employee. Since punishment is often delayed, it is important for the person administering punishment to explain the importance of the rules and provide what is called ***cognitive structuring***. Evidence has shown that clear, reasonable explanations for punishment significantly increase the effectiveness of punishment and produce desirable behavior.[6] Reasonable explanations help individuals understand why their behavior was wrong and how their behavior needs to change in the future.

Progressive Discipline

Progressive discipline:
A formal discipline procedure that contains progressively severe penalties for misbehavior.

Discipline refers to the use of some form of punishment or sanction when employees deviate from the rules. The overall objective of a disciplinary action is to remedy a problem and help employees behave acceptably in their work. Although some organizations have lists of rules and unacceptable behavior, the disciplinary processes in most organizations are based upon two concepts of administrative justice: due process and just cause.

Due process:
Telling people who have misbehaved what they did wrong and allowing them to defend themselves in an impartial setting.

Due process means that disciplinary actions may be taken only after an accepted procedure that protects employees from arbitrary, capricious, and unfair treatment. Due process normally involves providing individuals with written statements of the charges against them, as well as the reasons for the penalties. The charged employees must then have full opportunity to defend themselves and use a formal grievance procedure if one exists. After all relevant information has been fairly evaluated, a decision should be rendered by an impartial person. The employer is normally expected to bear the burden of proof; that is, the employer must show both the evidence of wrongdoing and the need for discipline.

Just cause:
Taking disciplinary action only for good and sufficient reason.

Just cause means that disciplinary actions will be taken only for good and sufficient reasons. Discipline should not be administered for trivial matters or for obscure and irrelevant rules. However, every employee is expected to know that certain behaviors are never tolerated, such as insubordination, theft, alcoholism, drug use, sexual harassment, and violence.

The disciplinary procedures in most organizations follow a process called *progressive discipline*, in which the disciplinary actions become increasingly severe. Most progressive discipline procedures include these five steps:

1. *Verbal warning:* a simple comment, usually by a supervisor, warning employees that certain acts are not acceptable.
2. *Verbal reprimand:* a verbal discussion, usually by a supervisor, informing employees that the situation is not acceptable and that improvement is required. This reprimand is more than a casual comment, and both the misbehavior and the desired change must be carefully described.
3. *Written reprimand:* a written record summarizing the history of the problem, and identifying the kinds of changes required and the consequences of failing to make them. This step is more formal than the first two steps. The company may need to use this written record to defend itself in court on a case of wrongful discharge.
4. *Suspension:* a mandatory absence dictated by a supervisor. Employees who fail to improve may be suspended for a few days to think about whether they are willing to change their behavior to keep their job.
5. *Discharge:* the last resort. Those who have failed to respond to previous disciplinary actions and persist in wrongdoing are terminated.

Demotions and transfers are sometimes used as disciplinary actions, although they are not highly recommended. Personal problems such as drug abuse, embezzlement, and habitual tardiness are problems that demotion and transfer are not likely to correct. Consequently, demotions and transfers are usually recommended only for problems of unsatisfactory performance when employees have been promoted to a job that is too demanding for them to handle.

Even then, demotion may not be a viable form of discipline because of the stigma attached to it.

Wrongful Discharge

Employers are generally free to fire employees for good reasons, bad reasons, or even immoral reasons, without being guilty of breaking the law. This philosophy, called the *employment-at-will doctrine*, allows both the employer and the employee the mutual right to terminate the employment relationship at any time, for any reason, and with or without advance notice to the other.

Although there are no federal laws that specifically address employment-at-will, an employer's freedom to terminate employees has gradually eroded since about 1980 because a variety of tort claims have identified various public policy violations leading to *wrongful discharge*. Here are four recognized limitations:

1. Many federal statutes prohibit employers from firing employees in retaliation for helping to enforce the statute. For example, the National Labor Relations Act prohibits firing employees for organizing a union, striking, or testifying before the NLRB. Likewise, many state statutes protect employees from retaliation for filing claims or participating in proceedings under workers' compensation laws, disability laws, and unemployment insurance laws.
2. Employers may be prevented from firing employees if they have an *implied contract* for employment. An example of an implied contract is a salary memo promising to pay employees an annual salary spread over the next twelve months.[7] Some courts have declared that terminating employees before the end of the year is a violation of this implied contract. Another example of an implied contract is a statement in an employee handbook that employees will not be terminated except for just cause.[8]
3. An employer may be guilty of improper discharge and liable for punitive damages if his or her breach of an employment agreement is fraudulent, oppressive, or malicious. An example of a fraudulent promise was an offer to give an employee a favorable recommendation if she agreed to quit. The employer had no intention of giving a recommendation; he only wanted to avoid unemployment compensation payments.[9]
4. Employers have been sued by employees and subjected to tort liability because they dismissed employees for reasons that violated public policy. These improper dismissals have been labeled "wrongful discharges," "abusive discharges," or "retaliatory discharges." Some examples of public policy violations include: (a) firing an employee for choosing to serve on a jury when she could have been excused because of her job[10] and (b) firing an agent for refusing to give false testimony before a legislative committee.[11]

SOLVING PERFORMANCE PROBLEMS

You need to know how to solve performance problems without letting small problems grow into big problems or allowing big problems to destroy a working relationship. The following model presents an effective procedure for han-

Employment-at-will: The right to terminate an employment relationship for any reason.

Wrongful discharge: Terminating an employee for reasons that are judged to be unfair because they violate the law or public policy.

Implied contract: A statement, either verbal or written, that can be construed as a promise of continued employment.

dling disciplinary problems. You would do well to memorize this model and practice using these skills.

1. Describe the situation.
2. Diagnose whether it is an ability or motivation problem.
3. Use joint problem solving for ability problems.
4. Communicate consequences for motivation problems.
5. Handle emergent problems.
6. Decide who will do what by when and then follow up.[12]

Describing the Situation

The first skill in solving disciplinary problems is learning how to describe the situation properly. When you observe something wrong, your first response should be to describe the situation before taking action. The correct procedure for describing the situation is to

- Be direct.
- Be specific.
- Be non-punishing.

Communicate the problem:
Be direct, specific, and nonpunishing.

The reason you should be direct, specific, and non-punishing can be illustrated by examining some of the incorrect methods supervisors typically use. For example, many supervisors respond to problems by pretending they are a grand inquisitor with an endless string of questions. Most of the questions don't make much sense, and they frequently don't deserve an answer. When employees are late, for example, they are often asked "Can't you tell time?" or "Do you know what time it is?" They have been telling time successfully for several years; why should they forget now? Getting angry and shouting at a co-worker is also not a good way to respond to problems.

The opposite response is to ignore problems. Many supervisors confuse ignoring problems with being patient. Supervisors certainly can't expect to discipline employees for every trivial problem, but many supervisors ignore serious problems until the problems get too big or they can't stand it any longer. Then they realize that rather than ignoring the problem, they have been stockpiling their anger. At the top of their voice they finally begin to yell, "I've had it with you! I'm not going to stand this any longer!"

Another approach used by some supervisors who attempt to be a bit more sophisticated is a smoothing approach, sometimes called sandwiching. Here supervisors begin and end by saying something sweet, such as, "I know you want to be a good performer," or "Usually you're such a good worker," but in the middle they torpedo the employee with criticism and complaints. Supervisors think this sandwiching technique resolves the problem and leaves the employee's self-esteem untouched. Most employees feel, however, that they have been subjected to a patronizing and insincere attack.

Be Direct. In learning how to solve problems, you need to learn to be direct. When a problem exists, you need to discuss it openly and intentionally without beating around the bush. For example, suppose you are concerned about an employee completing a safety report. You could attempt to diagnose the problem using an indirect approach, which some supervisors confuse with being tactful. "Did you get all the information you needed for that report?" "Are you pressed for time?" If you ask enough questions you may ultimately get the information you are after, but employees will probably feel as though they are being set up or manipulated. If you want to know whether an employee has completed the report, you ought to simply ask if it is finished. "I need to talk with you about a missing safety report."

Learning how to be direct helps you to be less punishing. It is easier to discuss problems when you are direct. By discussing problems directly, there are no hidden agenda and no hidden motives. The atmosphere of the discussion is more open and honest. Problems can be resolved faster because both parties know where they stand and what the other person's feelings and motives are. A very simple phrase that helps you learn to be direct is, "I'd like to talk with you about the problem of . . ." This phrase helps you convey to the other person, simply and directly, the idea that there is a problem that needs to be solved.

Be Specific. When describing problems, you need to be specific in your description. Being specific teaches others what they did wrong and helps them avoid unnecessary arguments. The two elements of being specific include (1) stating a standard of acceptable performance, and (2) describing the actual behavior. Both of these elements can be seen in the following statement: "Ken, you were supposed to have the report submitted by noon, and you didn't get it submitted until 4:00 p.m." The advantages of being specific can be clearly illustrated by comparing specific and nonspecific descriptions. "Ken, your report was late yesterday. Why are you always late?" "Ken, why can't you be more responsible? You're always so slow." Most of the contentious arguments during disciplinary discussions result from failing to describe problems specifically.

As you describe the problem, you should provide sufficient detail so that the nature of the problem is accurately presented, but not so many details that the description becomes patronizing or punishing.

Be Non-Punishing. When you describe the situation, you should avoid being punishing in the description. If punishment or discipline is needed, it should occur later, after the problem has been adequately described and diagnosed. Some of the typical forms of punishment include making emotional outbursts or displays of anger, shouting, using derogatory names or sarcasm, speaking in a nasty tone of voice, and using condemning facial expressions or other nonverbal behaviors. There are times when it may be appropriate to show emotion, but not until after the problem has been diagnosed.

Diagnosing Problems: Ability versus Motivation

Diagnose the problem:
Determine whether the problem is caused by a lack of motivation or ability.

After the situation has been described in a way that is direct, specific, and non-punishing, you need to diagnose the nature of the problem. The purpose of the diagnosis is to determine whether the problem is caused by a lack of ability or a lack of motivation. You need to respond differently to problems that are caused by a lack of ability from those caused by a lack of motivation. Therefore, after the problem has been described, you should ask for a response from the other person, "What happened?" "What went wrong?" "Am I right?" "Is there a reason for this that I don't understand?"

Knowing whether the problem was caused by a lack of ability or a lack of motivation is sometimes a very difficult decision. A motivation problem is caused by a lack of effort on the part of the employee—the person could have done the job with enough effort, but didn't. An ability problem is caused by something beyond the person's control—the person was inadequately trained or lacked the proper materials and equipment.

Most problems are a combination of inadequate motivation and inadequate ability. Supervisors generally think the problem was a lack of motivation, while employees are more inclined to say they were willing, but the difficulty or inconvenience of the job prevented them from doing it. Some supervisors have the attitude that hard things take a little while to accomplish; the impossible takes only a little longer.

Some situations appear to be such obvious motivation problems that it seems absurd to ask for an explanation of the problem after describing it. Swearing and insubordination are good illustrations of such problems. When an employee uses bad language or refuses a work assignment, it seems silly for the supervisor to ask whether this behavior is a motivation or an ability problem. Nevertheless, even when the behavior appears to stem from an obvious lack of motivation, the description of the problem could still conclude with a simple question asking the employee to acknowledge the problem. "Is there any reason for this behavior that I don't understand?" or "Is there any good reason why you should continue to talk this way in the future?" Asking for a simple acknowledgment forces the employee to objectively assess his or her behavior and think about its appropriateness. This type of objective self-assessment helps to make employees more responsible for analyzing their behavior and correcting it where it is wrong. Furthermore, supervisors are sometimes surprised to discover that what they assumed was clearly a motivation problem was not as simple as they thought.

Solving Ability Problems

Solving Ability Problems:
Use joint problem solving to find an acceptable solution.

When the problem is an ability problem, the supervisor needs to engage in joint problem solving with the employee. Even when the problem is largely a motivation problem, it may still be useful for supervisors to engage in joint problem solving.

During a joint problem solving session, both the supervisor and the employee should participate in discussing ways that the job can be accomplished. People who do not know how to perform a job successfully will usually ask for training. If they do not have adequate resources, they will probably ask for them. At the conclusion of the joint problem solving session, both of you should agree on how to solve the problem and who does what by when. After you have determined this, set a follow-up time when the task should be completed and then follow up.

Communicating Consequences for Motivation Problems

Two kinds of problems are classified as motivation problems: (1) the person was capable of doing a task and yet failed to accomplish it, and (2) the person knowingly did something wrong. In both situations the person could have behaved properly but for some reason chose not to do so.

Solving motivation problems:
To solve motivation problems, communicate consequences first to the task, second to others, and third to you as the supervisor. Finally, if compliance has not been reached, communicate imposed consequences.

Serious motivation problems occur when the problem has been appropriately described and the person essentially responds with an attitude of "So what?" or "I don't want to." Now comes the real task of motivating behavior, and there is a correct procedure for doing so. If a group of supervisors participated in a brainstorming session they could probably identify hundreds of techniques for motivating stubborn employees. A common element in all of these techniques is that they involve some form of consequence. The consequences might be positive in the form of financial incentives, special privileges, or treats; or negative in the form of verbal harangues, denial of privileges, or removal of rewards. All of these consequences have the potential to influence behavior, but they are not equally effective as long-term solutions to solving motivation problems.

In handling motivation problems there is a proper procedure for communicating consequences for misbehavior. Following this order teaches positive values and helps to maintain a pleasant relationship between you and the other person. Communicating consequences in this order also helps others learn to be intrinsically motivated to behave properly, and reduces the need to monitor their performance.

Motivation problems are solved by communicating consequences in this order:

1. Natural consequences
   a. to the task
   b. to others
   c. to you
2. Imposed consequences

Natural consequences refer to outcomes that occur naturally because of the demands of the situation. Imposed consequences, on the other hand, refer to consequences that bear no necessary relationship to the behavior of the person; they are created by people.

In communicating consequences, you should communicate only as many consequences as are needed to obtain compliance. Natural consequences should be communicated at all three levels before imposed consequences are communicated. This order is just the reverse of what most people are inclined to do. In fact, many people are quick to communicate imposed consequences before they have even described the problem or diagnosed the possibility that it could have been caused by an ability block. Before imposing consequences, however, you should carefully and systematically go through all three levels of the natural consequences. If the other person willingly complies after the problem has been properly described, you will not need to describe any consequences. The objective is to solve the problem and get the job done rather than harass the other person or damage feelings.

Second- and third-level natural consequences first to others and then to you should be communicated only if the person fails to respond to the natural consequences to the task. To illustrate, suppose you told the other person, "You are expected to come to work at 8:00 and you have not been arriving until 8:30. Is there any good reason for this?" Hopefully this reminder will help the other person resolve to be on time. But suppose he says "Others come late and it is no big deal." The first consequence you should communicate is the consequence to the task: "If you are late, there is no one to answer the phone." This explanation will probably sound reasonable and the employee will willingly comply. But suppose instead that he or she responds by saying, "So what difference does it make if the phone gets answered? They will call back." Next, you should communicate the consequences to others: "If you are not there to answer the phone, other co-workers have to interrupt their work to answer the phone for you." If the response is the same "Who cares?" attitude, you should communicate the third level of consequences: "It is my responsibility to have someone there to staff the office and answer the phone, and when you are late it reflects on my performance."

After the natural consequences have proved to be ineffective, then begin to use your list of imposed consequences. "If you continue to come late, I will have to issue a written reprimand." When using imposed consequences, you should remember two basic principles: you ought to *be consistent* in administering the imposed consequences, and the consequences should *be fair.*

Although most of us are inclined to use imposed consequences at the first sign of disobedience, we should appreciate the natural consequences associated with using natural consequences. In other words, using natural consequences as a discipline technique produces desirable outcomes. When you use natural consequences, the other person learns why the correct behavior is correct. Therefore, natural consequences are a useful mechanism for teaching. As a result of learning that natural consequences are associated with their behavior, people are able to acquire intrinsic rewards and personal values that improve their work habits. Since natural consequences are not meant to be threatening, a pleasant environment can be created and maintained between you and the other person. People are less likely to become resistive when they realize that the consequences occur naturally and are not intended to injure or restrict them. An important advantage of using natural consequences is that the natural outcome occurs without anyone having to be there to administer it.

As you communicate consequences to solve motivation problems, you need to remember to stop communicating consequences as soon as the person agrees to comply. If you continue to communicate consequences after compliance is achieved, the other person will interpret this behavior as harassment and punishment. After the other person agrees to comply, the final three steps in the problem solving process are to decide who will do what by when, set a follow-up time, and then follow up.

The problem solving process as it has been described so far has focused primarily on obtaining compliance. The most difficult problem, however, is not getting compliance but getting results. How should you respond if the other person agrees to do something and then fails to follow through?

If the other person fails to follow through as agreed, this failure represents a new problem that should be handled with the same problem solving procedure used with the first problem. The problem now, however, is the person's failure to follow through. "I need to talk to you about coming to work on time again. Yesterday you said you would be here on time, but you weren't. I thought we had an agreement."

As with the first problem solving discussion, your goal is once again to obtain compliance from the other person to correct his or her behavior. This time, however, there are simultaneous problems that have to be solved: the original behavioral problem, and the failure to follow through as promised. Once again you should communicate consequences—natural consequences first and then imposed—until the other person agrees to comply. Again, the purpose of the discussion is to obtain compliance rather than harass, criticize, or condemn them.

A difficult question is what you should do if the person continually agrees to perform the task but never does. This situation normally indicates that you have not adequately clarified who should do what by when or arranged for the person to report back. Some people need to have very specific goals and timetables to focus their attention, and frequent feedback and reinforcement to maintain their motivation. This is especially true for young workers who are just entering the labor force.

Another question is how many times should you let the person fail before taking additional disciplinary action. This question challenges you to exercise your greatest judgment. Although the procedure outlined here is excellent for gaining cooperation and maintaining a pleasant interpersonal relationship, there is no guarantee that it will work in every case. At some point employees who continually come late probably need to be terminated.

Dealing with Emergent Problems

Emergent problems:
When the other person raises other difficulties, deal with them before proceeding.

Many times as you are trying to describe the problem and diagnose whether it is an ability or motivation problem, the other person will introduce a totally different issue. While you are trying to talk about coming to work on time, the other person begins to complain about being assigned an unpleasant task. These types of problems are referred to as *emergent problems*. They occur when the other person feels he or she has a problem that is more important than the problem you are discussing. Occasionally the other person may try to intentionally divert you by raising emergent problems. However, most people are sincere when they raise emergent problems, and in essence they are saying "If you're going to clear the air and talk about something that's bothering you, then I want to talk about something that's bothering me." Although you may feel frustrated by this diversion, you should remember that their problems are as important to them as your problems are to you.

When an emergent problem arises you should first assess whether the other person has a genuine interest in it, to avoid being sidetracked by trivial issues. If the emergent problem is indeed a serious problem, you need to detour and resolve it before solving your own problem. Before discussing the emergent problem it may be useful to acknowledge that you are being sidetracked and indicate that you will return to the original problem once the new problem has been discussed.

Discussion Questions

1. What are the advantages and disadvantages of the different complaint systems? Which one would you recommend for a small family business? Identify a problem you have experienced in an organization. What kind of complaint procedure would have helped you?
2. Identify the natural consequences, logical consequences, and contrived consequences associated with these acts: missing class, coming to class late, submitting a term paper late, and missing an exam.

3. Explain how you would use the problem solving procedure with your supervisor to resolve a problem caused by your supervisor's failure to share vital information (or another problem of your choice).

Notes

1. Dennis W. Organ and Thomas Bateman, *Organizational Behavior: An Applied Psychological Approach*, 3rd ed. (Plano, TX: Business Publications Inc., 1986), p. 320.
2. Rudolf Dreikurs and Loren Grey, *Logical Consequences: A New Approach to Discipline*, (New York: Hawthorn Books, Incorporated, 1968).
3. This principle is attributed to Douglas McGregor. See George Strauss and Leonard Sayles, *Personnel: The Human Problems of Management* (Englewood Cliffs, NJ: Prentice-Hall, 1967); Walter Kiechel, III, "How to Discipline in the Modern Age," *Fortune* 121 (May 7, 1990): 179–80.
4. R. Di Giuseppe, "Vicarious Punishment: An Investigation of Timing," *Psychological Reports* 36 (1975): 819–24; Charles A. O'Reilly, III, and Sheila M. Puffer, "The Impact of Rewards and Punishments in a Social Context: A Laboratory and Field Experiment," *Journal of Occupational Psychology* 62 (March 1989): 41–53.
5. Dennis W. Organ and Thomas Bateman, *Organizational Behavior: An applied psychological approach*, op. cit., Chapter 11; Robert A. Baron, "Negative Effects of Destructive Criticism: Impact on Conflict, Self-efficacy, and Task Performance," *Journal of Applied Psychology* 73 (May 1988): 199–207; Appa Rao Korukonda and James G. Hunt, "Pat on the Back vs. Kick in the Pants: An Application of Cognitive Inference to the Study of Leader Reward and Punishment Behaviors," *Group and Organizations Studies* 14 (September 1989): 299–324.
6. Martin L. Hoffman, "Moral internalization, Parental Power, and the Nature of Parent-Child Interaction," *Developmental Psychology* 11, 2 (1975): 228–39.
7. *Greuer v. Valve & Primer Corp.*, 361 N.E. 2d 863 (Ill. App.2d 1977).
8. *Toussaint v. Blue Cross & Blue Shield of Michigan*, 292 NW 2d 880, 884 (Mich. 1980); Gerard Panaro, "Don't Let Your Personnel Manual Become A Contract," *Association Management* 40 (August 1988): 81–84; Gerard P. Panaro, "The Legal Tentacles of Wrongful Discharge Suits," *Security Management* 31 (July 1987): 98–106.
9. *Gates v. Life of Montana Insurance Co.*, 668 P. 2d 213 (Mont. 1983).
10. *Nees v. Hocks*, 536 P. 2d 512, 516 (Ore. 1975).
11. *Petermann v. International Brotherhood of Teamsters*, 344 P. 2d 25 (Cal. Appl. 1959); Steven H. Winterbauer, "Wrongful Discharge in Violation of Public Policy: A Brief Overview of an Evolving Claim," *Industrial Relations Law Journal* 13 (1991/1992): 386–415.
12. Kerry Patterson, "Performance Skills For Managers: Problem Solving" (Interact Performance Systems, 1981).

Rewards or Punishments: Which Works Best?

GTE Corporation in California tells employees to be customer-oriented, but they pay them to be fast. They talk about the importance of good customer service, but they continue to press employees for productivity and efficiency gains. This inconsistency is confusing to employees.

GTE executives were surprised to learn from a company survey that most customer service representatives thought speed was more important than customer service. To change this impression, GTE invested $170,000 in weekend seminars for 850 employees who were paid to attend. The events featured actors, singers, and a motivational speaker who preached the concept that when you pick up the phone to help a customer, you own the problem. Asking the customer to call another department is not an acceptable solution. Instead, you should put the caller on hold and make the call yourself.

Although the training was entertaining, the message was still muddled. GTE says both speed and quality count, but only speed is measured. GTE continues to time how long workers talk on the phone. The only reward for customer service is the intrinsic satisfaction that comes from helping customers; but helping a customer with a problem takes time.

Scott DeGarmo, the manager of *Success* magazine, does not use incentives. Instead, he imposes monetary fines on his six senior editors for printing articles containing typographical errors and grammatical mistakes. Most typos and misplaced commas cost $25, while misspelling the name of the main person in a story costs $500. The fines are deducted from the next year's pay raises for the six editors.

Although the fines seem excessive to some, DeGarmo considers them rather lenient. On his first newspaper job, writers who made serious misspelling errors were automatically fired. Mr. DeGarmo instituted his system of fines when other strategies failed to reduce the frequency of errors. He says he tried all the positive things to no avail, such as praising perfect copy and gently citing mistakes.

The system of fines immediately reduced the number of errors. During the first six weeks after the penalties started, fines costing $625 were assessed for one misspelled name, 3 misspelled words, and two grammatical errors. Mr. DeGarmo finds that when employees are motivated by the threat of punishment they seem to quickly learn to do it right.

Questions

1. Why are fines working so well at *Success* magazine? In which situations would you expect fines to function effectively?
2. How could GTE use incentives to improve customer service? What fines could they use?
3. What has the greatest impact on behavior, incentives or fines and when would you recommend each?

Source: Joan E. Rigdon, "More Firms Try to Reward Good Service, But Incentives May Backfire in Long Run," *Wall Street Journal*, December 5, 1990, B1, B4; Gilbert Fuchsberg, "Now You Know What We Know About How Most Writers Write," *Wall Street Journal*, 18 December 1990, B1.

Constructive Discipline

Daniel Salazar, age 23, is the son of an immigrant family of seven children. Despite the family's financial poverty, Dan stayed in school and graduated from technical school in drafting. His father has been dead for seven years. His mother receives welfare and is raising the four youngest members of the family. It is well known at the company that part of Dan's earnings helps to support the family.

During his schooling, Dan denied himself the ordinary social activities because he was required to work part-time to help his family. Within the past year, however, he has made several remarks suggesting that he has felt a little resentful at having to spend so many hours working and would now like to have more social contacts.

Dan's performance at work has been outstanding. Both his supervisors and his co-workers were impressed with how rapidly he learned his job. Recently, however, his supervisor has become concerned about an attendance problem. On one occasion, Dan called his supervisor and requested a substitute because of illness. A substitute was not available and the other members of his department decided to complete Dan's work. That evening the supervisor called to see how Dan was feeling and found that he was on a date. The supervisor noted the incident on Dan's record and warned him that a similar occurrence would lead to disciplinary action. In the past Dan has maintained a good relationship with the other members of the department, although some of them felt irritated when they learned that Dan was not actually ill and they had to cover for him.

Two months later it was again learned that in a period of claimed illness, Dan was not at home. He was reprimanded by the supervisor, but he claimed he was helping an older sister take care of a family emergency. In the past week it has come to the attention of the supervisor that a similar breech of conduct has occurred. The supervisor consulted with the area supervisor, who contacted the plant manager. The plant manager decided that the other area supervisors should be involved in the development of a general policy.

The plant manager has accordingly called a meeting involving all the area supervisors plus Dan's supervisor. The purpose of the meeting is to determine what course of action should be taken regarding Dan's problem.

Alternatives: What are the arguments for and against each of these alternatives:

1. Be supportive of Dan and try for the time being to overlook his misbehavior.
2. Counsel with Dan regarding both his personal and family problems and help him to manage them more effectively so that they do not interfere with his work.
3. Make it very clear to Dan that he has violated the standards of the plant, and help him see the difficulty that his absence creates for others. Make arrangements for him to make up the time.
4. Tell Dan that he is now on probation and that another incident of this nature will lead to his dismissal.

5. Tell Dan that since he has been warned about missing work he is now terminated, but give him a favorable recommendation to help him find another job.
6. Since Dan has ignored two previous warnings and continued in the same pattern, he should be terminated from the plant and this termination should appear on any recommendation for future employment.

IV

How do you create a productive work environment?

Managers need to create a work environment that encourages workers to perform their jobs effectively. Poorly designed work environments can limit worker productivity, regardless of how highly motivated and cooperative they are. When an organization is poorly structured, people can waste countless hours performing worthless activities. On the other hand, a productive work environment allows motivated and talented workers to work efficiently, like a well-oiled machine that runs flawlessly and without interruption.

CHAPTER 11
Effective Groups

CHAPTER 12
Intergroup Relations

CHAPTER 13
Organizational Design

CHAPTER 14
Organizational Culture

Section IV identifies the characteristics of a productive work environment and explains how to create one. A productive work environment is characterized by effective groups and a carefully designed organization whose structure and culture match its strategy. Chapter 11 describes high-performance work teams and explains why some groups are better at getting things done than others. Chapter 12 examines the relationships between groups and explains the causes and consequences of intergroup conflict. Conflict is not always bad, but it usually is, and it often occurs naturally. Chapter 13 describes the design concepts that comprise organizational structure and explains how these concepts form different structures that fit with the organization's environment. Chapter 14 explains the concept of organizational culture and describes how culture influences everything that occurs in organizations. Although group dynamics, organizational structure, and organizational culture are not physical objects that you can see and touch, they are important elements that have an enormous impact on organizational effectiveness.

CHAPTER 11

Effective Groups

Chapter Outline

Group Formation
Group Development
Characteristics of Effective Groups

Group Structure
Group Size
Social Density
Nature of the Task

Group Roles
Typical Group Roles
Role Episode

Group Norms
Development of Norms
Generally Accepted Norms
Norm Violation

Conformity
Pressures to Conform
Levels of Conformity
Factors Influencing Conformity

Effects of the Group on Individual Behavior
Social Facilitation
Social Loafing
Deindividuation

GROUP FORMATION

Groups are a central part of our everyday lives, and at any given time we are members of many groups, such as work groups, student clubs, church groups, professional associations, dormitory groups, political parties, and our families. At any one time the average individual belongs to five or six groups. The study of group dynamics is important for two reasons:

1. Groups exert an enormous influence on the attitudes, values, and behaviors of individuals. Groups teach us how to behave and help us understand who we are. Unique behavior occurs within groups because of group roles and norms.
2. Groups have a powerful influence on other groups and organizations. Much of the work that gets done in organizations is done by groups within the larger organization, and the success of an organization is limited by the effectiveness of its groups.

The collective action of a group of individuals can be much greater than the sum of individuals acting alone. Therefore, we need to know how to build effective teams.

Group Development

A group consists of two or more people interacting interdependently to achieve a common goal or objective. The principal characteristics of this definition are people, face-to-face interaction, and at least one common goal. A collection of people who use the same copy machine are not a group, even though they have face-to-face contact, because they are not interacting interdependently. Members of a group must think they belong together; they must see themselves as forming a single unit. This feeling of self-awareness usually happens because the group members share common beliefs and attitudes, and accept certain group norms.

Why People Join Groups. Formal groups, such as work teams and committees, are typically created to satisfy a particular organizational objective or to solve a specific problem. However, informal groups, such as friendship groups and reference groups, are created for personal reasons, and these reasons explain why people maintain their membership in them.

When individuals join a group, they voluntarily surrender part of their personal freedom, since they must be willing to accept the standards of the group and behave in prescribed ways that are sometimes very restrictive. Musical groups and athletic teams, for example, place heavy demands on members regarding attendance at practices and performances, dressing in the proper attire, and behaving in prescribed ways, even outside the group. Although the loss of freedom varies from group to group, every individual voluntarily relinquishes at least some personal freedom as a member of a group. Why then do individuals want to join a group and sacrifice part of their personal freedom? People form groups for four primary reasons:

1. **Goal Accomplishment.** People work together in groups because they need the help of others to achieve important goals. Physical goals, such as building a high-rise tower, extinguishing a forest fire, and playing a

basketball game, require the cooperative efforts of other group members. Intellectual goals may also require help from others, such as developing a new consumer product, restructuring the production process, and evaluating applications for college scholarships.

2. **Personal identity.** Membership in a group helps us know more about ourselves. Comments of peers generally have a great impact on our self-esteem because they come from people we respect; therefore, we have confidence in what they say. Their comments are also more credible because we assume they know us well and are concerned about our well-being.

3. **Affiliation.** People like to associate with other people, particularly if they have something in common. The mere presence of others provides friendship, social stimulation, and personal acceptance. College students and factory workers alike form informal peer groups simply to avoid the discomfort of being alone.

4. **Emotional Support.** To handle the pressures of daily living, and especially when situations are threatening or uncertain, people rely on others for emotional support. A person facing a stressful situation is comforted by the physical presence of another person facing the same stress.[1]

Stages of Group Development. Most groups experience similar conflicts and challenges that need to be resolved as they strive to become effective. Groups do not immediately function as highly effective teams until they have gone through various stages of development and addressed the kinds of issues that separate effective from ineffective groups. Every work group, whether it is a surgical team, a quality control circle, or a production crew, has to resolve similar issues, and the way it resolves these issues determines the group's effectiveness.

Although the developmental process is not highly standardized, most effective groups go through four stages: orientation, confrontation, differentiation, and collaboration, as shown in Exhibit 11.1.[2] A useful mnemonic for

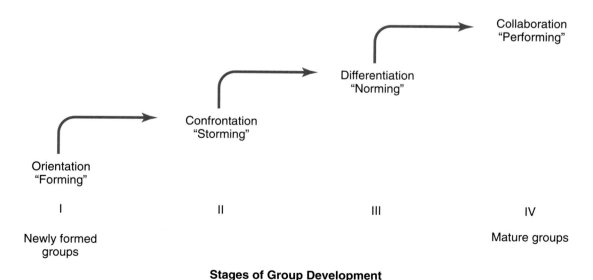

Stages of Group Development

Exhibit 11.1   Stages of Group Development

remembering these developmental stages is forming, storming, norming, and performing. Groups may not necessarily advance through each of these four stages; indeed, some groups never advance to the later stages because of internal conflicts.

Orientation:
The first stage of group development, when members are getting to know each other.

Orientation ("Forming"). The first stage for almost every group is an *orientation* stage when members learn about the purposes of the group and the roles of each member. This stage is marked by caution, confusion, courtesy, and commonality. Individual members must decide how the group will be structured and how much they are willing to commit themselves to the group. The formal leader, or the person who assumes the leadership role, typically exerts great influence in structuring the group and shaping member expectations. Members strive to discover the rules of the game, and the biases and motives of other group members. During this stage, members should get acquainted with each other and share their expectations about the group's goals and objectives. Efforts to rush this process by expecting members to be fully open and express their real feelings can be very destructive, both to the individuals and the group. The trust and openness necessary for members to feel willing to share intimate details comes in later stages of development.

Confrontation:
The second stage of group development, when members resolve issues regarding conflicting roles and expectations.

Confrontation ("Storming"). Although conflict is not a necessary phase of group development, the purposes of the group and the expectations of group members are eventually challenged in most groups. This stage contains conflict, *confrontation*, concern, and criticism. Struggles for individual power and influence are common. Challenging the group's goals can be a healthy process if the conflict results in greater cohesiveness and acceptance. If the conflict becomes extremely intense and dysfunctional, the group may dissolve, or continue as an ineffective group that never advances to higher levels of group maturity.

Differentiation:
The third stage of group development, when members divide the work to be done and perform their assigned tasks.

Differentiation ("Norming"). The major issues at this stage of development are how the tasks and responsibilities will be divided among members and how members will evaluate each other's performance. Individual differences are recognized, and task assignments are based on skills and abilities. If a group can resolve its authority conflicts and create shared expectations regarding its goals and task assignments, it can become a cohesive group and achieve its goals. At this stage, the members often feel the group is successful as they pursue their group goals, and indeed their short-term effectiveness may look rather impressive. As unique situations arise that violate personal expectations, however, the long-term effectiveness of the group will require additional maturity in resolving conflicts and reestablishing shared expectations.

Collaboration:
The fourth stage of group development when group members form a cohesive relationship and are committed to the group's success.

Collaboration ("Performing"). The highest level of group maturity is the stage of collaboration, where there is a feeling of cohesiveness and commitment to the group. Individual differences are accepted without being labeled good or bad. Conflict is neither eliminated nor squelched, but is identified and resolved through group discussion. Conflict concerns substantive issues relevant to the group task rather than emotional issues regarding group processes. Decisions are made through rational group discussion, and no attempts are made to force decisions or to present a false unanimity. The members of the group are aware of the group's processes and the extent of their own involvement in the group.

Separation ("Adjourning"). Some groups go through an "adjourning" stage by consciously deciding to disband, usually because the group has completed its tasks or because members choose to go their separate ways. This stage is typically characterized by feelings of closure and compromise as members prepare to leave, often with sentimental feelings.

Characteristics of Effective Groups

Some groups are considerably more successful than others in accomplishing their goals and satisfying the needs of their members. Douglas McGregor identifies 11 dimensions of group functioning and argues that these dimensions make the difference between highly effective groups and ineffective groups.[3] Each dimension presents a continuum showing the differences between effective groups on the right and ineffective groups on the left.

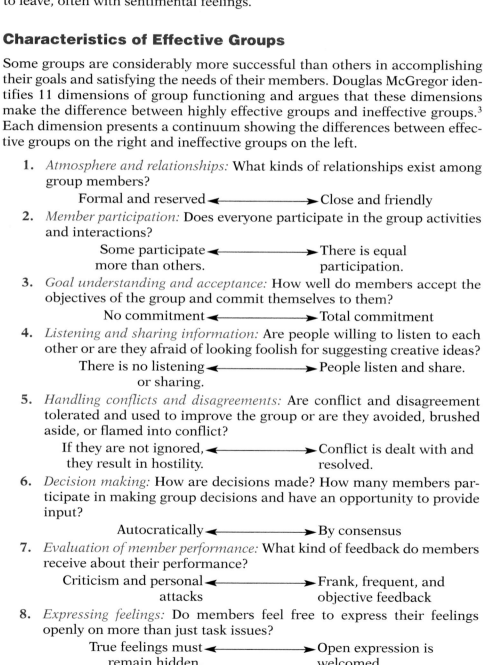

1. *Atmosphere and relationships:* What kinds of relationships exist among group members?

    Formal and reserved ←—————→ Close and friendly

2. *Member participation:* Does everyone participate in the group activities and interactions?

    Some participate ←—————→ There is equal
    more than others.   participation.

3. *Goal understanding and acceptance:* How well do members accept the objectives of the group and commit themselves to them?

    No commitment ←—————→ Total commitment

4. *Listening and sharing information:* Are people willing to listen to each other or are they afraid of looking foolish for suggesting creative ideas?

    There is no listening ←—————→ People listen and share.
    or sharing.

5. *Handling conflicts and disagreements:* Are conflict and disagreement tolerated and used to improve the group or are they avoided, brushed aside, or flamed into conflict?

    If they are not ignored, ←—————→ Conflict is dealt with and
    they result in hostility.   resolved.

6. *Decision making:* How are decisions made? How many members participate in making group decisions and have an opportunity to provide input?

    Autocratically ←—————→ By consensus

7. *Evaluation of member performance:* What kind of feedback do members receive about their performance?

    Criticism and personal ←—————→ Frank, frequent, and
    attacks   objective feedback

8. *Expressing feelings:* Do members feel free to express their feelings openly on more than just task issues?

    True feelings must ←—————→ Open expression is
    remain hidden.   welcomed.

9. *Division of labor:* Are task assignments clearly made and willingly accepted?

Poorly structured ◄──────► Effective job
job assignments　　　　　specialization

10. *Leadership:* How are the leaders selected? Are the leadership functions shared?

Leadership is lacking or ◄──────► Leadership is shared
dominated by one person.　　　and effective.

11. *Attention to process:* Is the group conscious of its own operations? Can it monitor and improve its own processes?

Unaware of group ◄──────► Aware of operations
operations　　　　　and monitors them

Effective groups share several important characteristics: the atmosphere is close and friendly; all members participate in the group; all members are committed to the group's goals; members listen to each other and share information; decisions are made by consensus; conflict is dealt with openly and resolved; members receive frank and objective feedback, and feel free to express their feelings openly; there is a division of labor with shared leadership; and the group is aware of its own operations, and able to monitor itself.

GROUP STRUCTURE

As a group develops, a structure emerges that influences what it does and how effectively it performs. Group structure is not an easy concept to explain because it does not refer to specific, observable objects. Group structure is the stable pattern of relationships among group members that maintain the group and help it achieve its goal. The major variables defining group structure are group roles and group norms. ***Group roles*** are the task activities and responsibilities the group members perform; and ***group norms*** are general expectations about how members ought to behave. Situational factors also influence group structure by influencing the relationships among group members. This section examines three of these situational factors: group size, social density, and nature of the task. Later sections examine group roles, group norms, and status in greater detail.

Group Size

Perhaps the most visible factor influencing group structure is the size of the group. Groups vary enormously in size, from a dyad (two-person group) or a triad (three-person group) to as large as 400 to 500 members (such as the House of Representatives).

Size and Participation. Small groups provide each member with an opportunity to be actively involved in the group. As the group gets larger, however, participation declines rather rapidly. A small graduate seminar with four students, for example, allows each student to participate freely in the discussion. In large classes, however, students have limited opportunities to participate. Large, informal groups must develop a method that allows members to participate in an orderly manner so that everyone doesn't speak at once. When an informal group gets to be larger than eight to twelve individuals, a significant part of the time, called ***process time***, can be wasted simply trying to decide who should participate next.

Size and Satisfaction. As the size of a group increases, the satisfaction of the group members with the group and their involvement in it tend to increase up to a point—"the more the merrier." A five-person group provides twice as many opportunities for friendly interaction as a three-person group. Beyond a certain point, however (probably fewer than 10 to 15 members), increasing size results in reduced satisfaction. Members of an extremely large group cannot identify with the group's accomplishments nor experience the same degree of cohesiveness and participation as members of a smaller group.[4]

Size and Performance. The relationship between group size and performance depends on whether the task is an additive task, conjunctive task, or disjunctive task.

On ***additive tasks*** the final group product is the sum of the individual contributions. Additive tasks are sometimes referred to as ***pooled interdependence***, since the individual contribution of each member simply adds to the group product. Interviewing customers leaving a store as part of a consumer survey is an example of an additive task. In additive tasks, the group's performance will almost always be better than the performance of a single individual, even though the average performance of each individual may be small in the group. For example, three interviewers working together will survey more customers than one interviewer working alone, but the three working together in one location will probably not conduct as many interviews as they would have if they had been working alone in separate locations.

Conjunctive tasks are those that can be divided into interdependent subtasks and then assigned to various group members. The overall performance depends on the successful completion of each subtask. The group's maximum performance is limited by the capacities of the least capable member. A chain, for example, is only as strong as its weakest link. An example of a conjunctive task is a TV news team filming an event. A mistake by any member means failure for the whole group, whether it is a bad interview, a bad picture, or bad sound.

Disjunctive tasks are decision-making tasks that require the group to select the best solution. An early study on the performance of individuals and groups in performing a disjunctive task asked individuals working alone or groups working together to arrive at a solution to the following problem: "On one side of a river are three wives and three very jealous husbands. All of the men but none of the women can row. Get them all across the river in the smallest number of trips by means of a boat carrying no more than three people at one time. No man will allow his wife to be in the presence of another man unless he is also there."[5]

Disjunctive tasks require at least one individual with sufficient insight to solve the problem. As a group gets larger, there is a greater probability that the group will contain at least one person with superior insight. In the study just mentioned, correct solutions to the problem of the three couples were pro-

Additive tasks:
An independent group task in which the contributions of all members are simply summed or pooled to form the group product.

Conjunctive tasks:
A group task that is divided into interdependent subparts, and the successful completion of each subpart is necessary for overall task accomplishment.

Disjunctive tasks:
A group task involving some form of decision making or problem analysis that requires a yes or no decision.

duced by 60 percent of the groups, but only 14 percent of the individuals who worked alone.

On disjunctive tasks, therefore, the potential performance of the group depends on the performance of its best member. The term *potential performance* is used here instead of *actual performance* because the actual performance is usually something less than the potential performance. Although the potential performance of a group performing a disjunctive task increases with group size, the actual performance is typically less because the group suffers from process losses. *Process losses* are the inefficiencies that arise from having to organize and coordinate larger groups. Large groups tend to restrict communication, inhibit creative thought processes, and reduce the personal commitment of group members. Therefore, actual performance equals potential performance minus process losses.

Process losses:
Inefficiencies that arise from having to coordinate the contributions and activities of group members.

Social Density

The interactions among group members are influenced by the physical or spatial locations of group members—whether they are physically separated or close together. Consequently, considerable interest has been expressed in the effects of modern architectural arrangements. Many modern offices use an open office plan with many desks in a large open room or small cubicles separated by partitions rather than separate rooms connected by long hallways. The concentration of people within an area is called *social density*, which is measured by square feet per person or the number of group members within a certain walking distance. Walking distance is used rather than straight-line distance, since it is the distance someone must go to have face-to-face contact that is important.

Social density:
The number of people physically located within a confined area.

Some organizational studies have found that greater social density improves performance because of greater accessibility. In a research-and-development organization, for example, reducing the distance between desks tended to improve performance by increasing the flow of technical information. In another technical organization, engineers reported less stress and tension when colleagues and other authority figures were located in close proximity. Likewise, the employees of a petroleum company reported greater feedback, friendship opportunities, and satisfaction with work when their social density was increased because of a relocation.[6]

Obviously, the performance of a group will not endlessly increase as the level of social density increases. At some point, the conditions become too crowded and people get in each other's way. The optimal social density depends on the nature of the task, the amount of feedback members need from each other, and their needs for privacy. Most studies of open office plans have found that employees generally dislike open office plans because of a lack of privacy. A large number of studies have shown that high levels of social density in organizations produce feelings of crowdedness, intentions to quit, high levels of stress, and low levels of satisfaction and performance. Although high social density normally has only a small effect on performance, the effects appear to be larger among employees who have a high need for privacy and complex tasks that require intense concentration.[7]

Nature of the Task

Since the interactions among group members are influenced by the nature of the task, the group structure needs to adapt to the demands of the task. Three types of tasks have already been described: additive, conjunctive, and disjunctive tasks. The need for coordination among group members is much greater for conjunctive tasks than it is for additive or disjunctive tasks. For example, if five students decided to sell tickets by telephone, they could divide the student directory into five sections, and each one could call the students in one section. Since this is an additive task, the need for coordination is minimal, and the performance of the group would simply be the sum of each individual's sales. Deciding how to divide the student directory would be a disjunctive task, and it, too, requires minimal coordination. With a conjunctive task, however, the need for coordination increases as the task becomes more complex. Organizing and presenting a new product development conference is a conjunctive task that would require the coordinated efforts of many people from several departments, including research, sales, training, production, and finance. Playing basketball, another conjunctive task, is an even more complex activity that requires team members to constantly coordinate their efforts and even anticipate each other's moves.

The relationships between group structure, the nature of the task, and task difficulty help to determine the best organizational structure. This topic will be discussed again in chapter 13. There we will see that the organizational structure needs to vary depending on the nature of the task and how much coordination is required to keep everyone working cooperatively. Organizations that have highly specialized tasks require special efforts to coordinate the activities of employees, especially when the activities change frequently. The same general conclusion applies here in the study of groups. Groups that perform complex conjunctive tasks require greater coordination among group members than groups performing simple additive or disjunctive tasks. With a basketball team, for example, as the team develops more complex offensive and defensive plays and assigns team members to perform specialized activities, the need for constant coordination among team members during the game increases.

GROUP ROLES

Assigned roles:
Group roles that are formally assigned to group members.

Emergent roles:
Group roles that are voluntarily performed by group members without being formally assigned.

A *role* refers to the expected behaviors attached to a position or job. In organizations, roles are briefly described by position titles and more extensively described by job descriptions. In athletic teams, these positions that have designated titles, such as point guard, power forward, middle linebacker, and goalie. Informal groups usually do not have explicitly stated roles; one group member may perform several roles or several members may alternate performing the same role. In formal groups, however, roles are usually designated or assigned. These ***assigned roles*** are prescribed by the organization as a means of dividing the labor and assigning responsibility. ***Emergent roles*** develop naturally to meet the needs of group members or assist in achieving formal goals. The dynamics in many groups often result in emergent roles replacing assigned roles as people express their individuality and assertiveness.

Work roles:
The activities performed by one or more group members that help the group accomplish its task and pursue its goals, for example, structuring the tasks, delegating assignments, and initiating action.

Maintenance roles:
The activities performed by one or more group members that are designed to maintain the members' willingness to participate in the group.

Blocking roles:
Group roles that prevent the group from functioning effectively because they attack other group members or divert the group's attention.

Work Roles and Maintenance Roles

Group members may be expected to perform a variety of different behaviors. Exhibit 11.2 makes a distinction between three major kinds of group roles: work roles, maintenance roles, and blocking roles.[8]

- *Work roles* are task-oriented activities involved in accomplishing the work and achieving the group objective. Work roles include such activities as clarifying the purpose of the group, developing a strategy for accomplishing the work, delegating job assignments, and evaluating progress.
- *Maintenance roles* are the social-emotional activities of group members that maintain their involvement and personal commitment to the group. These roles include encouraging other members to participate, praising and rewarding others for their contributions, reconciling arguments and disagreements, and maintaining a friendly group atmosphere.
- *Blocking roles* are activities that disrupt or destroy the group, such as dominating the discussion, attacking other group members, disagreeing unreasonably with other group members, and distracting the group with irrelevant issues or unnecessary humor. Deciding whether someone is performing a blocking role is sometimes difficult because the behavior may not be intentional. For example, a member may question a conclusion to force the group to think more carefully about an issue. Other group members may feel that this person is stubbornly resisting the

Work Roles	Maintenance Roles	Blocking Roles
1. *Initiator:* Proposing tasks or actions; defining group problems; suggesting a procedure.	1. *Harmonizer:* Attempting to reconcile disagreements; reducing tension; getting people to explore differences.	1. *Aggressor:* Deflating another's status; attacking the group or its values; joking in a barbed or semi-concealed way.
2. *Informer:* Offering facts; giving expression of feeling; giving an opinion.	2. *Gatekeeper:* Helping to keep communication channels open; facilitating the participation of others; suggesting procedures that permit sharing remarks.	2. *Blocker:* Disagreeing and opposing beyond reason; resisting stubbornly the group's wish for personal reasons; using a hidden agenda to thwart the movement of a group.
3. *Clarifier:* Interpreting ideas or suggestions; defining terms; clarifying issues for the group.	3. *Consensus tester:* Asking if a group is nearing a decision; assessing whether there is agreement on a possible conclusion.	3. *Dominator:* Asserting authority or superiority to manipulate the group; interrupting contributions of others; controlling by means of flattery or patronizing behavior.
4. *Summarizer:* Pulling together related ideas; restating suggestions; offering a decision or conclusion for the group to consider.	4. *Encourager:* Being friendly, warm, and responsive to others; indicating by facial expression or remark the acceptance of others' contributions.	4. *Comedian:* Making a comical display of others or one's lack of involvement; using sarcasm and humor to disrupt the group; seeking recognition in ways not relevant to the group task.
5. *Reality tester:* Making a critical assessment of the situation and problem; testing an idea against data to see if it would work.	5. *Compromiser:* Offering a compromise that yields status; admitting error; modifying an interest of group cohesion or growth.	5. *Avoidance behavior:* Pursuing special interests not related to task; staying off the subject to avoid commitment; preventing group from facing controversy.

Source: Kenneth D. Benne and Paul Sheats, "Functional Roles of Group Members," *Journal of Social Issues,* 2 (1948), pp. 42–47.

EXHIBIT 11.2 Group Roles

emerging consensus, simply trying to disrupt its progress. Likewise, a good joke may help to relieve tension and keep the group working together, or it may disrupt the group discussion and prevent the group from returning to a crucial issue.

Both work roles and maintenance roles are necessary for effective group functioning and they can be performed either by a designated leader or as emergent roles by someone else. These two group roles will be discussed again in chapter 17, where they will be used to examine leader behaviors.

Role Episode

Role expectations are communicated to individuals during a *role episode*, which is the interaction between role senders and the person receiving the role.[9] A role episode is diagrammed in Exhibit 11.3. A *role sender* may be anyone attempting to change the behavior of another individual, called the *focal person*. In formal groups, the most legitimate role senders are generally supervisors, project directors, and other organizational leaders responsible for delegating assignments. In reality, however, every group member participates as a role sender to other group members. Even subordinates tend to communicate how they expect their superiors to behave.

Role senders typically communicate only a small percentage of their role expectations. Some expectations are so self-evident that they do not need to be communicated (such as answering your telephone when you hear it ring), while others are not communicated because of uncertainty on the part of the role sender (such as whether the supervisor should say anything to group members involved in horseplay).

The focal person may or may not respond to the role sender. Communication problems may create a discrepancy between the sent role and the received role. But even if the expectations are accurately received, the focal person may not respond because of a lack of motivation or inadequate ability. The feedback loop, going from the focal person back to the role sender, illustrates the ongoing nature of a role episode. A role episode is a continuous process of evaluating each other's behavior and communicating expectations, both overtly and covertly.

An important factor influencing how well the focal person will respond to a sent role is the focal person's state of role readiness. *Role readiness* concerns the focal person's ability and willingness to accept the responsibility associated with a new role. For example, a new employee who has had a broad background of relevant experience and is prepared to immediately perform a new job would have a high degree of role readiness. A lack of role readiness occurs when union stewards resist promotions to supervisory positions because they have difficulty changing their thinking from hourly wages, seniority, and job security to salary, merit pay, and raising productivity.

Role Ambiguity. Role ambiguity concerns the discrepancy between the sent role and the received role, as shown in Exhibit 11.3. Ambiguity often comes from confusion when delegating job responsibilities. Many jobs do not have written job descriptions and when employees are told what to do, their instructions are often unclear. Supervisors may contribute to the ambiguity because they may not understand how the job should be done, what the standards of

Role episode:
An encounter between a role sender and the focal person in which role expectations are sent, received, and evaluated.

Focal person:
The person in a role episode to whom the role expectations are communicated.

Role readiness:
An individual's preparation to perform a group role by possessing the appropriate motivation and/or ability.

Exhibit 11.3 The Role Episode: Role Ambiguity and Role Conflict

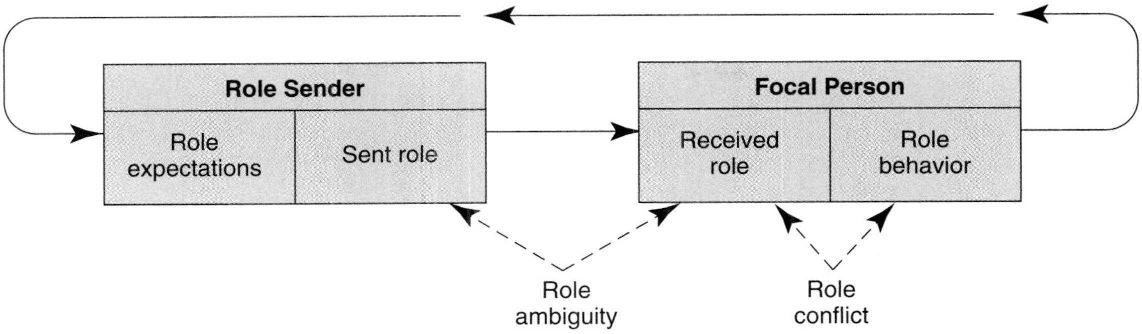

Source: Adapted from Daniel Katz and Robert Kahn, *The Social Psychology of Organizations*, 2nd ed. (New York: Wiley, 1978), p. 196.

acceptable performance are, how performance will be evaluated, or the limits of the employees' authority and responsibility. Even when supervisors know this information, the instructions usually overwhelm new employees.

The consequences of role ambiguity are frustration and other signs of stress. Moderate levels of ambiguity may be tolerable and even desirable, since some employees like to structure their own environment. However, extreme role ambiguity creates an unhealthy condition that contributes to dissatisfaction and turnover.[10]

Role Conflict. Role conflict comes from inconsistency between the received role and role behavior, as shown in Exhibit 11.3, but role conflict is not the same as role ambiguity. The conditions that create role conflict and the amount of discomfort it creates seem to be unique to each person. The same situation may cause more stress for one person than for another. There are four major types of role conflict.[11]

Intrasender role conflict:
Role conflict created by incompatible demands of a single role sender.

Intersender role conflict:
Role conflict created by incompatible demands and expectations of two or more role senders.

1. *Intrasender role conflict* occurs when a single role sender communicates incompatible role expectations to the focal person. For example, a manager could tell the staff members that they are each expected to perform the role of critical evaluator and challenge every decision, but they are also expected to work together cooperatively and be team players.

2. *Intersender role conflict* occurs when two or more role senders communicate incompatible expectations to the focal person. The first-line supervisors in most organizations typically experience rather intense intersender role conflict. Upper management expects them to tighten the controls to increase productivity, reduce errors, and eliminate wasted time. In contrast, their subordinates send messages that the supervisors need to loosen the controls and be less interested in productivity, quality, and wasted time. Boundary role occupants, those who straddle the boundary between the organization and its clients and customers, are also prone to experience intersender role conflict. For example, salespeople, schoolteachers, and purchasing agents often receive incompatible instructions from people within the organization and external clients or customers.

Person-role conflict:
Role conflict created by asking people to behave in ways that violate their personal values.

3. *Person-role conflict* occurs when people are asked to behave in ways that are inconsistent with their personal values. An administrative aide, for example, may be told that a report must be completed before going home, even if it means several hours of overtime. But working overtime would mean missing the school play, and the aide's daughter is the star of the play. Employees experience person-role conflict when they are asked to do something illegal or unethical, such as falsifying reports or lying to customers.

Role overload:
Role conflict caused by too many demands on a person.

4. *Role overload* is caused by the conflicting demands of too many roles (also called inter-role conflict). People fill a variety of roles, both within the organization and in their personal lives. We cannot be in two places at one time, and conflicting time schedules often create severe role overload, forcing us to reassess which role should take precedence. A personnel director, for example, may experience role overload because of the inconsistent demands accompanying numerous roles, such as affirmative action officer, safety director, facilitator of a quality control circle, career development counselor, and manager of the human resource planning system. In addition to the roles she fills in the organization are her roles outside the organization as a wife, mother, and fund raiser for the United Way campaign. These multiple roles contain conflicts of time, interests, and loyalty, because they cannot all be filled simultaneously.

GROUP NORMS

Group Norms:
General expectations of a demand nature regarding acceptable group behavior.

Group norms are the commonly held beliefs of group members about appropriate conduct. As such, they represent general expectations or codes of conduct that imply a duty or obligation. Group norms identify the standards against which the behavior of group members will be evaluated and help group members know what they should or should not do. *Group norms* typically develop around the 11 issues presented earlier regarding group effectiveness.

Every group creates its own norms and standards for evaluating the appropriateness of individual behavior. To illustrate, the members of a fraternity created a group norm that it wasn't "cool" to act like dedicated students—a little studying was OK, but it should not interfere with social activities. To get good grades, several fraternity members had to lie about how they spent their time and not admit that their dates and weekend trips were actually to the library. Similarly, the members of an engineering firm created the norm that no one should leave until after the supervisor had left. None of the engineers actually accomplished very much after the regular working hours; but even though they quit working, they did not leave.

Group norms are essential to group effectiveness. Although norms limit individuality and restrict the creativity of individuals, they create greater predictability within the group by structuring its activities. In a typical classroom, for example, most students adhere to the norm of raising their hands when they want to comment. This hand-raising norm prevents some class members from making insightful comments, but it also provides for an orderly class discussion.

Development of Norms

Over time, groups develop a variety of norms regarding many aspects of behavior. The most crucial group norms are those regarding issues of central concern to the group. In general, groups tolerate less deviation from norms regarding important group concerns. For the offensive unit of a football team, for example, a highly enforced norm is that no one talks in the huddle but the quarterback. Accuracy in listening to the quarterback's instructions is vital to the success of the team. Wearing wristbands or putting stickers on helmets, however, are not closely enforced norms because they are not as important to the team's success.

Group norms are typically created and enforced for four reasons: (1) they facilitate group survival, (2) they simplify the membership requirements and make the behavior of group members more predictable, (3) they help the group avoid embarrassing situations, and (4) they express the central values of the group and clarify what is distinctive about its identity.[12]

Two almost opposite theories are used to explain how group norms are developed.[13] In one explanation, norms are viewed as the product of the shared attitudes and beliefs of group members that exist prior to behavior. These shared attitudes result from either a group consensus after the group discusses the issue or from a dominant group member who simply voices an opinion. If no one expresses a dissenting view, the group may adopt the dominant member's viewpoint. For example, a norm of no smoking during the weekly planning meetings was created when one of the division managers took the ashtray off the table, put it on the shelf behind her, and said, "There's no need to get lung cancer." Her action went uncontested and no one said anything; thereafter, a no-smoking norm existed.

Another explanation for how group norms are created is that they are post-hoc justifications. After the group has been functioning for a while, we observe certain patterns of behavior and explain them as being a group norm. Many performance norms are simply justifications for what has happened in the past, such as stopping the machines 20 minutes early to wash up, or considering 38 pallets a full day's work. These standards were never part of a labor agreement; this was just how the employees behaved from the start.

Generally Accepted Norms

Our day-to-day behavior is influenced by so many general social norms that we often fail to recognize them. Most people are members of numerous groups, and these multiple memberships generate a lengthy list of norms, lending regularity and predictability to our behavior.

Social Conduct. Social conduct norms are designed to create a pleasant social atmosphere, such as smiling when you pass a friend in a hallway, answering the phone when it rings by saying hello, and saying goodbye before you hang up. When we are introduced, we shake hands and say, "I'm pleased to meet you," whether it's true or not. If someone asks, "How are you?" the norm is to say "Fine!" not to give a full medical report. Walking away while someone is talking to you is considered a norm violation, and leaving in the middle of a lecture or public address is generally considered impolite.

Dress Codes. Some organizations have formal dress standards for their members, such as the military, police, hospitals, restaurants, and hotels. The dress codes in other organizations may be more informal and unwritten, but just as powerful. Many organizations, especially banks and insurance companies, expect employees to wear conservative dresses, shirts, ties, and suits.

Performance Norms. How fast group members are expected to work and how much they should produce are important issues to most groups. Therefore, performance norms are created to guide individual efforts. Supervisors can become very frustrated with a group's performance norms when they are unreasonably low or inconsistent with the organization's goals. Sometimes they appear to be very irrational because they are not in the worker's best interests either. In the bank-wiring experiment of the Hawthorne Studies, for example, a group of men maintained an arbitrarily low production norm that restricted productivity even though the workers were paid according to how much work they did, and this study was conducted during the Great Depression when the workers needed additional income. In many work groups, productivity is determined more by the group's performance norms than by the ability and skill of the employees.

Reward Allocation Norms. Groups develop norms governing how rewards should be distributed to the group members. The most commonly studied reward allocation norms are equality, equity, and social responsibility.[14]

The norm of *equality* suggests that everyone should be treated the same. We all share equally in our status as group members; therefore, the rewards that come to the group should be distributed equally to everyone.

The norm of *equity* suggests that the rewards should be allocated on the basis of merit according to each person's contribution to the group. Those who have made the largest contribution to the group's product, either through effort, skill, or ability, should receive a larger share of the rewards.

The norm of *social responsibility* suggests that the rewards should be allocated on the basis of need. People who have special needs, especially those who are disadvantaged or disabled, should receive special consideration and a larger share of the rewards, regardless of their contribution.

Norm of reciprocity:
A widely accepted social norm that insists that if person A helps person B, then person B has an obligation to help others, especially person A.

Norm of Reciprocity. The *norm of reciprocity* suggests that when people make an effort to help you, you should feel an obligation to help them at a later time. Among some people, this norm is a very firmly held expectation, and they keep track of favors and who owes whom. Although some people feel that service should be rendered specifically to those who have helped them, others have a much broader interpretation of whom they should help. For example, a mentor may be very happy to help a new employee, not because the mentor expects help from the new employee in the future, but because of the help that the mentor received as a new employee from someone else in the past.

Norm Violation

Although group norms are a group product, they may not match the private beliefs of all members. Norms are accepted in various degrees by the group members. Some norms may be completely accepted by all group members, while other norms are only partially accepted. Norms vary according to their inclusivity, or the number of people to whom they apply. Some norms are nearly universal in nature, such as the prohibition against theft, which applies to all members of society. Other norms, however, apply only to specific group members. Production norms, for example, may not apply to a lead worker who is expected to spend part of the time training other employees.

For a group norm to be created and maintained, a majority of the active members must agree that the norm specifies appropriate and required behavior. Furthermore, there must be a shared awareness that the group supports a given belief. Although some members may violate the norm, it will continue to survive as long as the majority uphold and accept it. If adherence to the norm continues to erode, it will eventually collapse and no longer serve as a standard for evaluating behavior. Most students have witnessed the disintegration of student conduct norms. One or two students may violate the norm of raising their hands without the norm being destroyed, but when three or four more students begin to violate the norm, the class dissolves into a shouting match where all the students are speaking at once, rather than raising their hands and waiting to be acknowledged.

Conformity to the essential group norms is a requirement for sustained group membership. Group members who do not conform to important norms are excluded, ignored, or ridiculed by the group, as punishment. The ultimate punishment is to be banished from membership in the group.

Because of their status, group leaders are in a better position to violate the norms than are other group members. Indeed, leaders sometimes deviate slightly from accepted group norms as a means of asserting their uniqueness or superiority over other group members. Group members must not come late to work, but managers think they can come when they want as a privilege of being a manager. Studies have shown that highly intelligent group members are also less likely to conform to group norms than less intelligent members are. However, group members with a strong authoritarian personality are more likely to conform to group norms than nonauthoritarians do.[15]

Group norms are difficult to change. Since they were created by the group, they must be changed by the group. Organizational leaders are sometimes successful in helping groups change norms by communicating new expectations of behavior. They are successful to the extent that they can get the group to accept what they say as the new standard of behavior.

CONFORMITY

Group norms provide regularity and predictability to the behavior of group members, but only if members conform to the group norms. Norms do not exist without conformity. Unless the members create pressure to enforce the group norms, these norms will disappear and be replaced by other norms. Conformity means yielding to group influence by doing or saying something you might otherwise choose not to do. To say you have conformed means you have succumbed to social influence and behaved differently from how you would have behaved in the absence of the influence.

Why do people conform? Organizations have been criticized for needless pressures that force people to conform in their thinking, dress, and living habits. Although conformity does reduce variability in the ways people behave, it also increases individual freedom by providing greater predictability and regularity of behavior. Group norms help groups achieve their goals, and as conformity increases, the likelihood of success also increases. Therefore, conformity reduces individuality and personal autonomy, but it also contributes to greater success for both the group and its members.

Pressures to Conform

Groups use two major social influence processes to obtain conformity: reward dependence and information dependence.[16]

Reward dependence:
When group members feel induced to conform to group pressure because there are positive or negative consequences attached to doing so.

Reward Dependence. Groups have the capacity to reward or punish their members. Leaders of formal groups can use organizational rewards and punishments to induce conformity, such as promotions, pay increases, performance evaluations, and job assignments. Informal groups have powerful rewards for inducing conformity among group members, such as praise, recognition, and social approval for good behavior, or criticism, ridicule, and harassment for deviant behavior.

Information dependence:
When group members feel induced to conform to group pressure because they depend on the group to provide important information to help them know what to do.

Information Dependence. Individuals also conform to group pressure because they depend on others for information about the appropriateness of their thoughts, feelings, and behavior. We are particularly dependent on others in novel situations. We rely heavily on others to know how to behave, to interpret our feelings, and to help us understand our emotions.

Levels of Conformity

People conform to social pressure at three very different levels, depending on their motives. Writing your name and address on a check so you can cash it is behavior at a different level of conformity from refusing to accept a bribe from a client because it violates company policy. When driving an automobile, you are expected to obey speed limits, stop at stop signs, and yield the right of way to pedestrians. When you conform to these accepted norms, what are your motives? Conforming to group norms occurs for three significantly different motives: compliance, identification, and internalization.[17]

Compliance
The first level of conformity, in which the individual's motive is to obtain rewards or avoid punishment.

Compliance. At the lowest level of conformity, people comply with social pressure either to obtain rewards or to avoid punishment. Peer pressure and fear of harassment or criticism induce group members to comply. *Compliance*, however, is usually quite temporary and is limited to the specific situation. If a police officer is parked at an intersection, the fear of being ticketed will probably induce compliance to stop for the stop sign. If the fines for overdue library books are exorbitantly high, students will probably return them on time. If supervisors receive a $50 bonus for a good safety rating, they will probably conduct periodic safety inspections, simply to obtain the reward.

Identification:
The second level of conformity, in which the motive to conform is to please or be like others.

Identification. The second level of conformity is called *identification* because the motive is the desire to be accepted by others who are perceived as important. Identification is the process of behaving like "significant others" and adopting their characteristics and personal attributes. Not only do we want to be like them and acquire their attributes, we also want them to think well of us and to approve of our attitudes and actions. Through imitative learning, we tend to model their behavior and accept what they say and how they behave. People who identify with a significant other will stop at stop signs, return library books, and work independently on take-home exams if that is the way they think the significant other expects them to behave.

Internalization. At the highest level of conformity, the standards of behavior are internalized and become part of the person's basic character. At the *internalization* level of conformity norms are followed because the person accepts the beliefs, attitudes, and values supporting the norms. Conformity does not occur because it achieves rewards, avoids punishment, or pleases others; it occurs because the behavior is perceived as morally right and proper. At this level you stop for stop signs, return library books, and avoid cheating on exams not to avoid punishment nor to receive the praise of others, but because you personally believe it is right and you are committed to abide by your own personal standards of right and wrong, which coincide with the group norms.

Internalization: The highest level of conformity, in which the motive to conform is based on the group member's acceptance of the prescribed behavior as a basic principle of right and wrong.

Factors Influencing Conformity

Whether group pressures influence behavior depends on many factors. Research has shown that conformity is influenced by the nature of the group influence, the individual being influenced, and the specific issue at hand.[18]

Group Size. In general, group pressure tends to increase as the size of the majority arrayed against the individual increases. Beyond a certain point, however, additional members do not add appreciably to the effectiveness of the pressure.

Group Composition. The qualifications of other group members influence the likelihood of conformity. Group members who are perceived as experts or as highly qualified or experienced persons exert greater pressures to conform. Conversely, minority group members tend to be more highly influenced by group pressure, especially when they are alone.

Unanimity of Group Consensus. A united group exerts much greater pressure to conform than a group divided by dissension. In some cases, the presence of a single dissenter is enough to destroy the influence of the group.

Ambiguity. Conformity increases as the situation becomes more ambiguous. When people do not know what is expected of them, they become increasingly dependent on the influence of others. Group members can create greater ambiguity as an intentional strategy for inducing conformity by raising irrelevant questions or suggesting immaterial facts to confuse the situation.

Goal Achievement. The pressure to adhere to a social norm increases when conformity is essential to the group's success. As a group gets closer to achieving its goal, the anticipation of success increases the pressure to conform and makes nonconformity less acceptable. During the playoff games at the end of a season, team members experience particularly strong pressures to abide by the group norms. As the probability of a strike increases, unions demand greater conformity among union members as a show of strength to management. Deviation from the group norm becomes absolutely unacceptable at crucial times.

Self-Confidence. Individuals who are highly confident of their skills and abilities are less susceptible to group pressures. When insecure people are faced with a discrepant judgment by a unanimous majority, their first step in seeking to reconcile the difference is to blame their own judgments and perceptions. Individuals who are high in self-confidence, however, generally resist blaming themselves and prefer instead to blame the group for the discrepant judgments.

THE EFFECT OF THE GROUP ON INDIVIDUAL BEHAVIOR

How does the presence of a group influence an individual's performance? Suppose you were laying bricks with four other bricklayers. Would more bricks get laid if the five of you worked together as a group along one side of a wall, or would it be better to assign each of you to different walls on the construction site? Two contrasting processes have been identified to explain the effects of the group on individual performance: social facilitation and social loafing. Another concept, called *deindividuation*, also explains the effects of a group on individual behavior.

Social Facilitation

Social facilitation effect:
The tendency for the presence of other people to increase motivation and arousal, which tends to help the individual perform better.

Evaluation Apprehension:
The concern that people experience when they know they are being observed and evaluated by others.

Social inhibition effect:
The tendency for the presence of other people to disrupt performance and cause them to perform poorly.

Early studies in social psychology noted that people performed better as members of a group than they did when performing alone. It was observed, for example, that cyclists rode faster if they raced in head-to-head competition than they did when they raced alone to beat the clock. Subsequent research showed that the presence of an audience or crowd or simply the presence of other coworkers facilitated the performance of well-learned responses, such as crossing out letters and words, doing multiplication problems, and other simple tasks. This process, called the *social facilitation effect*, is caused by the mere presence of others rather than direct competition between individuals, since a number of studies found that subjects performed better even in front of a passive audience. The social facilitation effect has been observed not only on people, both adults and children, but also on an unusual assortment of other animals including, ants, fish, chickens, rats, and cockroaches.[19]

One explanation for the social facilitation effect is called *evaluation apprehension.* According to this explanation, the presence of others creates a higher level of arousal and motivation because we expect others to evaluate our performance, and their opinions matter to us. When others are watching we want to look good, sometimes for no other reason than that we want others to think well of us.

Although the presence of others may improve performance, it can also inhibit performance on some tasks. This process, called *social inhibition effect*, has been observed on complex learning tasks such as learning a maze or a list of nonsense syllables. Since the social inhibition effect is the opposite of the social facilitation effect, it is important to know when the presence of others will inhibit and when it will facilitate an individual's performance.

Perhaps the best explanation of the contradictory results relies on an important distinction between learning a new task and performing a well-learned task. The presence of others increases our level of arousal and motivation, which helps us perform well-learned responses.[20] Therefore, the presence of others tends to improve our performance on well-learned responses such as walking, running, bicycling, or playing the piano (for a highly skilled pianist). However, if the response has not been well learned, which is the case with all new learning situations, then the presence of others will inhibit performance. Therefore, according to social facilitation, the learning of complex new tasks is best accomplished in isolation, but the performance of well-learned tasks will be facilitated by an audience.

Social Loafing

Social loafing:
The tendency to exert less effort when working as a member of a group than when working alone.

Social loafing occurs when the members of a group exert less effort while working as a group than when working as individuals. Social loafing is the opposite of social facilitation, but it is different from social inhibition. The social inhibition effect is a reduction in the individual's ability to perform because of the presence of others. Social loafing, in contrast, is not attributed to a decline in ability but to a decline in motivation or the amount of effort. One of the earliest studies in social loafing examined how much effort individuals exerted in pulling on a rope, either individually or in a group. The average pressure exerted by each individual was 63 kilograms, which was more than double the average pressure exerted by a group of eight people pulling together (248 kilograms per group, or 31 kilograms per person).[21] Later studies have shown that social loafing also occurs in decision-making groups with cognitive tasks: people in groups exert less effort and less concentration, and they also use less complex judgment strategies than do single judges or judges working in pairs.[22]

Subsequent research has concluded that social loafing occurs because being in a group reduces the individual's identifiability.[23] As members of a group, individuals know their efforts cannot be identified, so they display only mediocre effort. The social loafing effect becomes increasingly apparent in larger groups because of reduced personal identifiability. When individuals cannot be identified, there is no relationship between their efforts and their outcomes; therefore, they cannot be individually rewarded for good effort or punished for poor performance.

Deindividuation

Deindividuation:
The loss of individuality that occurs by being a member of a large crowd.

The issue of identifiability is related to another process of group dynamics: *deindividuation*. Individuals often become lost in crowds and perform acts they would not perform if they were alone. Unruly crowds at rock concerts have produced hysterical screaming and uncontrolled emotions, angry fans at athletic contests have thrown objects at athletes and assaulted referees, and groups of union picketers have destroyed property and committed acts of violence. Stories of lynch mobs illustrate how individuals in a group get carried away and do things they would not have done without the presence of the group. Crowds have the capacity to create a mental homogeneity, referred to as a *collective mind*, that is frequently irrational and often functions at an intellectual level below that of the isolated individual.

Three mechanisms have been proposed to explain the process of deindividuation in groups. First, the individual is anonymous because he or she loses a sense of individual identification. Second, the contagion of the group causes people to act differently by reducing their inhibitions and allowing them to behave like other group members. Third, people become more suggestible in groups where they feel greater pressures to conform.

The loss of individuality has often been associated with rather undesirable social consequences. In a study of the warfare patterns of many cultures, for example, it was found that in cultures where warriors deindividuated themselves by wearing masks and paint, there was a greater tendency to torture captives than in cultures whose warriors were not deindividuated. Another study of trick-or-treaters on Halloween found that they were more likely to steal when they wore masks and remained anonymous than when they were clearly identifiable.[24]

Perhaps the most shocking study of deindividuation was the Stanford Prison study, conducted by Phillip Zimbardo.[25] In this study, 24 male students who were described as mature, emotionally stable, normal, intelligent people were randomly assigned to play the roles of guards or prisoners. Both the prisoners and the guards were given appropriate uniforms, and the prisoners were placed in three-man cells for the duration of the experiment, which was to be two weeks. The guards were instructed to run the prison, and the experimenter served only as a warden. The guards wore silver reflector sunglasses, which increased the level of deindividuation. The prisoners made only meager attempts to escape, and their behavior was described as that of servile, dehumanized robots. The behavior of the guards became tyrannical and brutal, and the situation became so ugly and repressive that the experiment had to be terminated after only six days instead of the two weeks originally planned.

Deindividuation does not necessarily create undesirable social behavior; it can also be positive. Although they don't attract as much attention, many groups have noble purposes and worthwhile social goals that sweep people along in productive activities. Schools, charitable foundations, religious groups, and even business organizations frequently create groups where individuals lose a sense of their own personal identity and are carried along as part of the group in activities that contribute to their own growth and development and to the betterment of society.[26] Therefore, although groups can be destructive and abusive, they don't necessarily need to be that way. Those who have enjoyed the exhilaration of wildly cheering for their favorite athletic teams know how much fun being "lost in the crowd" can be.

Discussion Questions

1. List some examples of additive, conjunctive, and disjunctive tasks. What type of tasks would the following groups most likely have: (a) a semi-autonomous work team in an electronics manufacturing firm, (b) a group of students working on a research project for an organizational behavior class, (c) an executive search committee trying to hire a new manager, (d) a swimming team, and (e) a fraternity.

2. What are the different kinds of role conflict? List some specific instances of role conflict you have experienced recently.

3. What are some of the most important norms regulating your behavior at your residence? How did these norms develop? What forms of social pressure are used to enforce compliance with these norms?

4. Identify at least two examples from your own life that illustrate the three levels of conformity: compliance, identification, and internalization.

5. How does a study group influence individual learning? If you formed a study group with some of your classmates, would you expect the effects of studying together to produce social facilitation, social inhibition, or social loafing?

Notes

1. Stanley Schachter, *The Psychology of Affiliation: Experimental Studies of the Sources of Gregariousness* (Stanford, CA: Stanford University Press, 1959).

2. B. W. Tuckman, "Developmental Sequences in Small Groups," *Psychological Bulletin* 63 (1965): 384–99; M. F. Maples, "Group Development: Extending Tuckman's Theory," *Journal for Specialists in Group Work* 13 (1988): 17–23.

3. Douglas McGregor, *The Human Side of Enterprise* (New York: McGraw-Hill, 1960), pp. 232–40.

4. B. Mullen, C. Symons, L. Hu, and E. Salas, "Group Size, Leadership Behavior, and Subordinate Satisfaction," *Journal of General Psychology* 116 (1989): 155–70.

5. Marjorie Shaw, "A Comparison of Individuals and Small Groups in the Rational Solution of Complex Problems," *American Journal of Psychology* 44 (1932): 491–504.

6. T. J. Allen and D. I. Cohen, "Information Flow in R&D Laboratories," *Administrative Science Quarterly* 14 (1969): 12–25; Robert H. Miles, "Roles Set Configuration as a Predictor of Role Conflict and Ambiguity in Complex Organizations," *Sociometry* 40 (1977): 21–34; Andrew D. Szilagyi and W.E. Holland, "Changes in Social Density: Relationships with Perceptions of Job Characteristics, Role Stress, and Work Satisfaction," *Journal of Applied Psychology* 65 (1980): 28–33.

7. Greg R. Oldham, "Effects of Changes in Workspace Partitions and Spatial Density on Employee Reactions: A Quasi-Experiment," *Journal of Applied Psychology* 73 (1988): 253–58; Eric Sundstrom, *Work Places* (Cambridge, England: Cambridge University Press), 1986; Eric Sundstrom, Robert E. Burt, and Douglas Kamp, "Privacy at Work: Architectural Correlates of Job Satisfaction and Job Performance," *Academy of Management Journal* 23 (1980): 101–07.

8. Kenneth D. Benne and P. Sheats, "Functional Roles of Group Members," *Journal of Social Issues* 2 (1948): 42–47; Hal B. Gregersen, "Group Observer Instructions," in J. B. Ritchie and Paul Thompson, *Organization and People*, 3rd ed. (St. Paul, MN: West, 1984), pp. 231–34.

9. Daniel Katz and Robert L. Kahn, *The Social Psychology of Organizations*, 2nd ed. (New York: Wiley, 1978), chap. 7.

10. Samuel Rabinowitz and Stephen A. Stumpf, "Facets of Role Conflict, Role-Specific Performance, and Organizational Level Within the Academic Career," *Journal of Vocational Behavior* 30 (1987): 72–83; Shaker A. Zahra, "A Comparative Study of the Effect of Role Ambiguity and Conflict on Employee Attitudes and Performance," *Akron Business and Economic Review* 16 (Spring 1985): 37–42.

11. Robert L. Kahn, D. M. Wolfe, R. P. Quinn, J. D. Snoek, and R. A. Rosenthal, *Organizational Stress: Studies in Role Conflict and Ambiguity* (New York: Wiley, 1964).

12. Daniel C. Feldman, "The Development and Enforcement of Group Norms," *Academy of Management Review* 9 (1984): 47–53.

13. Kenneth L. Bettenhausen and Jay Keith Murnighan, "The Development of an Intragroup Norm and the Effects of Interpersonal and Structural Challenges," *Administrative Science Quarterly* 36 (March 1991): 20–35.

14. Jerald Greenberg, "Equity, Equality, and the Protestant Ethic: Allocating Rewards Following Fair and Unfair Competition," *Journal of Experimental Social Psychology* 14 (1978): 217–26; Boris Cabanoff, "Equity, Equality, Power, and Conflict," *Academy of Management Review* 16 (April 1991): 416–31.

15. Bernard M. Bass, C. R. McGehee, W. C. Hawkings, P. C. Young, and A. S. Gebel, "Personality Variables Related to Leaderless Group Discussion," *Journal of Abnormal and Social Psychology* 62 (1953): 120–28; E. B. Nalder, "Yielding, Authoritarianism, and Authoritarian Ideology Regarding Groups," *Journal of Abnormal and Social Psychology* 68 (1959): 408–10.

16. Edward E. Jones and Harold B. Gerard, *Foundations of Social Psychology* (New York: Wiley, 1967), chaps. 3 and 4.

17. H. C. Kelman, "Compliance, Identification, and Internalization: Three Processes of Opinion Change," *Journal of Conflict Resolution* 2 (1958): 51–60; Nail, op. cit.

18. See the literature review by David Krech, Richard S. Krutchfield, and Egerton L. Ballachey, *Individual in Society* (New York: McGraw-Hill, 1962): 512–29.

19. Reviewed by Stephen Worchel and Joel Cooper, *Understanding Social Psychology*, 3rd ed. (Homewood, Ill.: Dorsey Press, 1983): 485–88.

20. Robert Zajonc, "Social Facilitation," *Science* 149 (1965): 269–74.

21. This early study by Ringelmann is reported by J. F. Dashiel, "Experimental Studies of the Influence of Social Situations on the Behavior of Individual Human Adults," in Carl Murchison (ed.), *The Handbook of Social Psychology* (Worcester, MA: Clark University Press, 1935).

22. Kenneth H. Price, "Decisions Responsibility, Task Responsibility, Identifiability, and Social Loafing," *Organizational Behavior and Human Decisions Processes* 40 (December 1987): 330–45; Elizabeth Weldon and Elisa L. Mustari, "Felt Defensibility in Groups of Coactors: The Effects of Shared Responsibility and Explicit Anonymity on Cognitive Effort," *Organizational Behavior and Human Processes* 41 (June 1988): 330–51.

23. Norbert L. Kerr and Steven E. Brunn, "Dispensability of Member Effort and Group Motivation Losses: Free Rider Effects," *Journal of Personality and Social Psychology* 44 (1983): 78–94; Norbert L. Kerr and Steven E. Brunn, "Ringelmann Revisited: Alternative Explanations for Social Loafing Effect," *Journal of Personality and Social Psychology* 7 (1981) 224–31.

24. R. I. Watson, "Investigation into Deindividuation Using a Cross Cultural Survey Technique," *Journal of Personality and Social Psychology* 25 (1973): 342–45; E. Diener, S. Fraser, A. Beaman, and Z. Kellem, "Effects of Deindividualtion Variables on Stealing Among Halloween Trick-or-Treaters," *Journal of Personality and Social Psychology* 33 (1976): 178–83.

25. Phillip Zimbardo, *The Psychological Power and Pathology of Imprisonment*, statement prepared for the U.S. House of Representatives Committee on the Judiciary, (Subcommittee No. 3, Robert Kastemeyer, Chairman, Hearings on Prison Reform). Unpublished paper, Stanford University, 1971.

26. Michael T. Farrell, "Artists' Circles and the Development of Artists," *Small Group Behavior* 13 (1982): 451–74

The College Scholarship Committee Meeting

In this exercise, participants are assigned as members of a college scholarship committee and asked to allocate $10,000 among six applicants.

Directions. Six people should be selected as participants and assigned to represent one of the scholarship applicants. Others should be selected as observers and assigned to observe a specific participant. Each participant should read the description of the scholarship applicant he or she is assigned to represent. However, the participants should not read any information about any of the other applicants.

After the participants have had time to study their applicants and prepare what they want to say, the committee should decide how to allocate the $10,000 among the applicants.

Settings. *To each participant*: You are a member of the scholarship committee of a small private college. This year the school must cut back on the amount of money awarded; only those students with the most crucial needs can be recipients.

Essential costs for the school year include $2,000 for room and board, $4,000 for tuition, and $1,000 for fees and books. Your committee has already awarded several scholarships and has only $10,000 left. The final result of the committee's discussion should be the allocation of this money to one student or to several students.

You have examined the applications and other supporting data and have identified the student who you think should receive a substantial amount of money. Each of the other committee members will also have a student to sponsor. You must try to convince the other members that your proposal suggests the best use of the money. You are aiming to get as much money as possible for this student, while still helping the group to swiftly and fairly accomplish its task. The following material describes the needs of each student. Examine the information for the applicant you will sponsor and decide which points you wish to present.

Applicant A. Kyle Anderson will be a junior next fall. He is a B student majoring in history and minoring in physical education. Kyle plays varsity football, hockey, and golf. Last year he was second in the conference in golf. He plans to coach college football. Kyle is also first vice-president of his fraternity, and is a member of the Interfraternity Council.

Kyle's parent have an above-average income, but they have two other children in college and one son in medical school. They can't afford to send Kyle here. His brothers and sister are at state universities, and Kyle says he will have to transfer to a state school if he doesn't receive financial help from the college. Kyle's application contains a letter from the athletic department describing his contributions to the university and recommending that he receive a scholarship. Kyle works during the summer as a lifeguard, but cannot work during the school year because of all his other activities. He has not received financial aid before.

Applicant B. Larry Bellows will be a sophomore next fall. He is an A student majoring in biology and minoring in chemistry. He was the only first-year student ever taken into the Biology Society. He plans to become a doctor.

Larry's father is dead, and his mother is sending him to school. She has sold their house and has moved into an apartment to try to help with expenses. Larry says his mother is going to cash in her life insurance and sell everything she has of value to help raise money for his education if he doesn't get a scholarship. He doesn't want her to give up everything for him to continue going to school. Larry works during the summer and works in the college library for a few hours a week during the school year. He has received no other financial aid from the school.

Applicant C. Ann Marie Carter will be a senior next fall. She is a C student majoring in English and minoring in speech. Ann Marie is a student senator and varsity debater. Last year she was on the top national-level varsity team and won 15 trophies in debate tournaments all over the country. She hopes to go to graduate school and debate.

Ann Marie's parents have very little money. Her father has quit three jobs in 18 months, and the family is living on the money they have saved for her to go to college. She works during the summer and used to work during the school year, but it became too much for her to handle and she got very ill. She will have to drop debate and work to stay in school if she receives no scholarship. Last year Ann Marie received a scholarship of $1,200 for the second semester after she became ill and had to quit her job.

Applicant D. Alan Dickson will be a first-year student in the fall. He was an A student in high school and made very high scores on his College Boards. He was vice-president of his high school student body, and he won national recognition during high school for his chemistry projects. Alan wants to attend graduate school and eventually go into research.

Alan's parents are very poor. His father is a janitor, and his mother doesn't work. Alan worked this past summer and plans to borrow money, but it still won't be enough. He will be carrying a very difficult course load this year, and he is afraid that he won't be able to keep up with his studies if he finds a job. He plans to continue with this heavy course load and go to summer school while he works so that he can finish in three years. He has a sister three years younger than he who also wants to go to college. She couldn't hope to go, he says, if he is still in school.

Applicant E. Sally Ensley will be a junior next fall. She is a B student majoring in speech and minoring in drama. She is a member of the Drama Honorary, the Forensics Honorary, is Secretary of the Women's Service Sorority, and was treasurer of the sophomore class. On graduation, she wants to work with children's theater and speech correction.

Sally's parents are getting a divorce, and neither will pay for her to finish college. Sally has no other relatives who can finance her next two years here, so she will have to quit school if she receives no scholarship. Sally has not worked in the past because there had never been a need. She has received no previous financial aid.

Applicant F. Diane Fautz will be a senior next fall. She was formerly a low C student, but now is making Bs and a few As. She is majoring in education and minoring in political science. Diane has been a student senator for three years and is a member of the Faculty-Student-Administration Relations Committee. She wants to finish school and join the Peace Corps. Currently, she works weekends and three nights a week as a volunteer for the YMCA's enrichment program for underprivileged children.

Diane's parents have cut her off financially because they strongly disagree with her political and social beliefs. An aunt has agreed to pay her tuition, but can't afford anything else. Diane works summers as a YMCA camp counselor, but makes very little above living expenses. To earn more money, she would have to take another summer job that pays more. She wants to finish school but will quit before she stops working at the YMCA. She has received no previous aid.

Covering the Reception Desk

In their weekly productivity improvement meeting, the 12 committee members listened to a recommendation from Karen Nichols, one of the lead interviewers. The 12 committee members work for the placement division of the Job Service Agency. The purpose of the committee is to improve the performance of the agency by eliminating inefficiencies. Three weeks earlier, the committee identified the problem of inadequate staffing of the reception desk during the heavy midday demand. The busiest part of the day is from 12 to 2, and the receptionist's lunch break is scheduled at noon. Before the recent budget cuts, two receptionists worked at the desk and scheduled their lunch breaks so they were usually both there.

Karen proposed to have the five employer relations representatives assigned to work at the reception desk on a rotating schedule. "You can't expect us to do that," replied Janet Andrus, one of the employer relations representatives. "That's not part of our job. As ER reps we have our own responsibilities."

"So who should do it?" Karen asked. "Do you have a better idea?"

"I think the interviewers should do it. We have 14 interviewers, and one or two of them should be able to handle it," Janet responded.

"But if you take them away from interviewing," Karen persisted, "the whole process slows down. We've got to keep the interviewers talking to the applicants. I think the ER reps could fill in one day a week without hindering their work very much."

"If we have to do it, then I think everyone should have to take a turn, including Barry," said another ER rep. Barry Walker, the placement director, smiled at the suggestion and his smile was all the encouragement Paul and Ernest needed. Suddenly, the meeting degenerated into a comedy as Paul and Ernest began to mimic Barry's voice and facial expressions. "Could ah hep ya pleeze?" "Have ya filled out yer blue card, partner?"

Karen was disappointed that the committee had dismissed her proposal without really considering it. Janet thought the committee was wasting time with silly jokes, but she was glad no one was taking the proposal seriously.

Paul enjoyed making the group laugh at his antics and he tried to have them imagine how Barry would look in a wig, a skirt, false eyelashes, and long fingernails. Louise, the receptionist, was not amused at his humor. After listening to three or four of Paul's comments, Louise quietly left the room.

After she saw Louise leave, Janet decided the group had been clowning long enough. Turning to Paul and Ernest, she announced that it was time to quit fooling around. Stunned by Janet's reproof, they listened quietly as she redirected the group to the reception desk problem. Janet summarized Karen's proposal, explained her objection to it, and suggested they go around the room and each express his or her opinion.

Questions

1. Although Barry is the official leader of this group, who seems to be the real leader in this episode? Why do groups need leaders? What purposes do they serve?

2. What happens to the performance of a group when one or more members begin to act like comedians?
3. What are the other positions or roles that group members played in this episode?

Intergroup Behavior and Conflict

Chapter Outline

Competition and Cooperation
  Differences between Competition and Cooperation
  Effects of Competition and Cooperation
  Organizational Citizenship Behavior
Cohesiveness
  Factors Influencing Cohesiveness
  Consequences of Cohesiveness
Conflict and Organizational Performance
  Functional and Dysfunctional Conflict
  Studies of Conflict
Causes of Intergroup Conflict
  Task Interdependence
  Goal Incompatibility
Consequences of Intergroup Conflict
  Changes within the Group
  Changes between Groups
Resolving Intergroup Conflict
  Avoidance Strategies
  Power Intervention Strategies
  Diffusion Strategies
  Resolution Strategies
Creating Functional Conflict

COMPETITION AND COOPERATION

This chapter examines the causes and consequences of intergroup conflict. The interactions between groups have an enormous influence on the effectiveness and survival of an organization. Individuals and groups depend on each other for information, assistance, and coordinated effort, and this interdependence may foster either a competitive or a cooperative relationship.

The relationship between two groups does not need to be competitive, although it often is; the interaction can just as easily be cooperative, calling for a helping response. This chapter examines the interactions between individuals and groups and the circumstances that determine whether a cooperative or combative relationship will exist between them. When will two groups choose to cooperate or compete? How can intergroup conflict be resolved and be replaced by a cooperative relationship?

Differences between Competition and Cooperation

Interpersonal relationships vary along a continuum representing different degrees of concern for others versus self-interest, as shown in Exhibit 12.1. At one extreme, individuals or groups have a high concern for others and are willing to go out of their way to help them. At the other extreme, individuals are concerned only for their own self-interest, even to the point of attempting to injure or destroy the other party. Four types of interactions can be defined along this continuum: altruism, cooperation, competition, and conflict.

Altruism:
Behavior intended to help someone else, with no expectation of an immediate extrinsic reward for helping.

Altruism. Behavior that is motivated by a regard for others is called *altruism*. Altruism usually involves at least some cost to the helper, such as physical, mental, or emotional effort, for which the helper does not expect to be compensated. Altruism includes both small acts of courtesy, such as holding the door open for the next person, and heroic acts, such as risking your life to rescue someone from danger.

Cooperation:
The relationship that exists between two or more individuals who both benefit from working together and share the benefits of their joint efforts.

Cooperation. *Cooperation* means working together for a joint goal or mutual benefit. Unlike altruism, where no reward is expected, cooperation involves helping another and in so doing helping yourself. A group of doctors and a team of medical technicians cooperate when one group refers patients for medical tests and the other group analyzes the tests. In a cooperative situation, both parties benefit from their combined efforts.

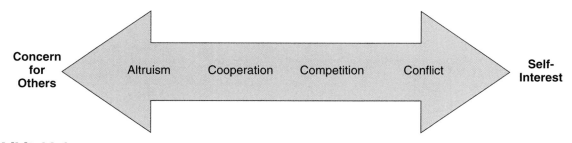

| Concern for Others | Altruism | Cooperation | Competition | Conflict | Self-Interest |

Exhibit 12.1   Continuum of Concern for Others versus Self-Interest

Competition:
An interaction between two or more parties in which the parties cannot meet their goals simultaneously. The success of one individual or group prevents other groups or individuals from being successful.

Competition. *Competition* occurs when two or more parties are striving for a goal that can be obtained by only one of them. Fixed or limited resources is one of the basic characteristics of a competitive situation: the person with the most sales wins the sales contest; the group with the lowest bid is granted the contract; only one individual can be promoted to division manager. Three different types of competition can be created by altering the reward structures.

- *Intragroup competition:* the members of a group compete against each other for a reward.
- *Intergroup competition:* one group is competing against another group for the rewards.
- *Individual competition* (sometimes called *noncompetition):* individuals work independently against an external standard or their own personal record.

If four members of a group ran a race to see who was the fastest, they would be participating in intragroup competition. If they formed a relay and challenged another group to see which team was faster they would be competing in intergroup competition. If they ran individually, however, and measured their times, they would be engaging in individual competition against their own previous records.

Conflict:
Interaction between individuals and groups in which each one attempts to defeat, destroy, or inflict damage on the other because of mutually exclusive goals or values.

Conflict. *Conflict* occurs when two groups have mutually exclusive goals and their interactions are designed to defeat, suppress, or inflict damage on the other. Conflict is not limited to interacting groups, since it can also occur within groups, between individuals, and within and between organizations. For example, conflict usually occurs when labor-management negotiations reach a stalemate and the union decides to strike. Both sides attempt to strengthen their positions by winning public support and weakening their opponents by creating an economic hardship for them.

Effects of Competition and Cooperation

Some of the early research on the effects of competition and cooperation claimed that cooperation produces higher levels of satisfaction and productivity than competition. For example, one classic study compared ten groups of five students each who met weekly to solve puzzles and discuss human relations problems.[1] In the five competitive groups, the members competed with each other to see which member would receive the reward, while the five cooperative groups competed with other groups and all the members of the winning group received a reward. The reward consisted of being excused from writing a term paper and receiving an A on the assignment. The groups were evaluated on how well they performed the tasks, how well they worked together as a unit, and how well each individual contributed to the group. The cooperative groups were judged superior in all three areas.

The harmful effects of competition are not as clear as this study suggests, however. In this study the cooperative groups had a cooperative relationship within the group, but they competed against the other groups. To understand the effects of competition and cooperation, the relationships both within the group and between groups must be carefully evaluated. The effects of competition have been examined on both productivity and satisfaction.

Competition and Productivity. Competition typically increases arousal and motivation, which lead to higher productivity. Workers who compete to finish their job first or to obtain the highest sales generally achieve higher levels of productivity. The enthusiasm and excitement accompanying a contest usually raises performance levels. As a general rule, competition increases productivity.

However, competition is not appropriate for interdependent tasks that require members to work together. A competitive reward system is not compatible with interdependent tasks because it produces behavior that interferes with the task performance. Committee meetings, for example, are interdependent activities in which all members contribute ideas and express opinions. If the committee members compete to see who suggests the most ideas, everyone would talk at once and no one would be listening. Many sales jobs, however, are independent tasks, with sales representatives calling on customers in separate areas. Therefore, competition among the sales representatives should increase their performance.

Competition and Satisfaction. The effects of competition on satisfaction depend largely on the outcome of the situation and whether the competition is so intense that it destroys friendships. Competition tends to destroy interpersonal relationships by creating a feeling of antagonism, distrust, and dislike for the other person, but these negative feelings are often overcome by positive aspects of participating and winning. Many situations, especially athletic contests, are mixed-motive conflicts that combine both competition and cooperation. In a tennis match, for example, both players compete to see who wins, but unless they cooperate, the match will never occur. The cooperation includes agreeing to play, deciding on a time and place, and following a set of consistent rules. If either player decides that the game is dissatisfying or not worth playing, the match will not occur.

Television sportscasting has popularized the phrase "the thrill of victory and the agony of defeat." Obviously, one of the major variables influencing satisfaction in competitive conditions is whether you win or lose. Winning is fun, but the extrinsic rewards are only part of the satisfaction. In addition to the money, prizes, or trophies, there are intrinsic rewards associated with the thrill and elation from excelling in competition.

An important byproduct of competition is personal feedback. In new situations, we don't know how well we are performing, so we compare ourselves with others. In some experimental situations, subjects have voluntarily changed a cooperative situation into a competitive situation just to have a basis for comparing their abilities. An explanation for why people choose a competitive situation is suggested by the theory of social comparison processes, which argues that the absence of information regarding the quality of our performance causes our self-esteem to be unstable. Therefore, we seek a competitive situation to obtain personal feedback. We measure our ability by comparisons with others and establish a level of aspiration from the feedback we obtain.

In summary, the effects of competition on satisfaction are determined primarily by the outcome of the competitive situation.[2] Since competitive situations present such a complex combination of rewards and punishments, it is very difficult to predict the final outcome. Although the winners are usually happy and the losers unhappy, many considerations influence the outcome.

For example, if a work unit competes aggressively to determine which member will be promoted to a new position, both the winner and the losers may be very dissatisfied if the competition destroys the interpersonal relationships within the group. In contrast, Olympic athletes usually report that the competition was exciting and satisfying even though they lost. The thrill of being at the Olympic games and the privilege of representing their country is a satisfying experience in spite of defeat.

Organizational Citizenship Behavior

Organizational citizenship behavior (OCB): When an employee voluntarily helps other employees with no promise of reward. Behaviors directed toward helping individuals are also called *altruism* while behaviors directed toward helping the organization are called *compliance.*

When an employee voluntarily helps other employees with no promise of rewards, this behavior is called *organizational citizenship behavior (OCB)*. It is a form of altruism that consists of going above and beyond the formal job description and doing more than the job normally requires.[3] An example of organizational citizenship behavior is the help a group of high school English teachers voluntarily provided for another teacher who was absent for six weeks after surgery. While she was absent, her colleagues arranged to teach her classes during their preparation periods and they stayed after school to prepare for their own classes. Although altruism is directed toward helping people, it indirectly benefits the organization. Some conditions encourage altruism, such as being treated fairly, feeling accountable, perceiving a need, and observing the example of others.

Leader Fairness and Task Characteristics. Organizational citizenship behaviors are more likely to occur when employees are in a good mood than when they are in a bad mood. Research has consistently found a positive relationship between job satisfaction and the number of citizenship behaviors employees perform as reported by their supervisors.[4] There is some evidence to suggest, however, that OCB is determined by something more fundamental than one's mood. It appears that employees appraise their working relationships and decide whether the conditions are fair enough to allow them to voluntarily help others without fearing others will take advantage of them by expecting them to do more all the time and never reciprocating. To the extent that fairness does not exist, people will choose to contribute less and work according to the rules, doing only what is required.[5]

Similarly, the nature of the task can stimulate organizational citizenship behaviors. Intrinsically motivating tasks create a sense of responsibility that causes people to feel personally accountable for completing the job and doing it well. Their determination to succeed induces them to go beyond the formal job requirements when needed to achieve excellence in their work. Work is meaningful to the extent that it is perceived as personally and socially valuable, especially if it directly improves the quality of life or serves society. The internal satisfaction derived from performing a meaningful job rewards employees for doing more than just what is required.[6]

Personal Responsibility. Research studies on altruism have shown that people are more inclined to render assistance if they feel a personal sense of responsibility for taking action. When other people are present, a person does not feel the same degree of personal responsibility as when others are not present. In one experiment, for example, subjects thought a female experimenter had fallen to the floor and heard her scream in agony, crying out that her ankle had been hurt and she could not get the chair off her. Subjects who were alone responded to the call for help 70 percent of the time. By contrast, only 40 percent of the subjects who came in pairs offered help. Furthermore, if the other individual was actually an experimental confederate who acted as though nothing had happened, the number of subjects who rendered help dropped to only 7 percent.[7]

The presence of other people, however, does not necessarily eliminate the feeling of personal responsibility. A sense of personal responsibility can be created by asking people to be responsible. On a crowded beach, for example, an experimenter placed his blanket and portable radio next to a subject and a few minutes later asked the subject to watch his things while he went to the boardwalk for a few minutes. When another confederate attempted to steal the portable radio, 95 percent of the subjects attempted to intervene in the theft. If the subjects were not asked specifically to watch the experimenter's things, the number who responded directly dropped to only 20 percent.[8]

Character Development. Since altruism requires some degree of self-sacrifice in helping others, it is reasonable to expect that people who behave altruistically are relatively unselfish and emotionally mature. People who are psychologically healthy and whose character is more developed are more inclined to help others. Character development has been shown to influence the motives of men in caring for their families and contributing at work. Men who are at higher stages of personality development are more committed to serving their families and their organization, and they will sacrifice some of their egoistic concerns for the benefit of others.[9] Similarly, research on why people willingly participate in voluntary activities has identified an altruistic motive that seems to apply to many types of voluntary activities. Some people are simply more predisposed than others to volunteer assistance.[10]

Models. The example of others appears to have a particularly strong effect on altruistic behavior. Studies of both children and adults have found that charitable contributions and assistance to others increase when someone observes another person contributing or sharing. One study recorded how many male motorists stopped on a highway to assist a woman who was trying to change a flat tire.[11] The study found that motorists were much more likely to stop if they had recently passed a similar scene in which a male driver had stopped to help a woman change a tire. Those who had observed an altruistic model were more inclined to behave altruistically themselves.

A similar study looked at contributions to a Salvation Army collection box.[12] A much larger percent of the people were willing to contribute if they had observed a model making a contribution. In fact, the percentage of people who contributed was about as high when the model seriously considered the issue, even if he then decided not to contribute.

Perception of Need. People are more inclined to help another if they have a clear perception that the individual needs help. When the situation is ambiguous or uncertain, people tend not to help. Serious situations, in which a helpless victim is in dire need of assistance, may be ignored because people fail to appreciate the situation. However, as the need for assistance becomes increasingly apparent, the likelihood of helping increases. The more serious the plight, the more likely the victim is to receive help.

Studies have found that when people are in a hurry and have important business to perform, they are less likely to behave altruistically.[13] Part of the reason why they fail to help is that they think they are too busy and they assume someone else should lend assistance. But another part of the reason why they don't help is that they simply fail to notice the need for help or appreciate the seriousness of the situation.

Similar People. Since altruism is helping others when we do not anticipate a reward other than our own good feelings, it should not be surprising to learn that people are more inclined to help those whom they like. Indeed, research has shown that greater help is given to those who are liked than those who are disliked. People seem to derive greater satisfaction from helping someone they admire and respect, and for whom they have positive feelings. Since we tend to like people who are similar to us, we would expect people to be more inclined to help others who have similar personal characteristics. Indeed, studies have shown that people are more inclined to render assistance to those of similar race, dress, or appearance.[14]

Implications for Organizations. Studies on altruism and bystander apathy indicate that people are more inclined to behave altruistically when they feel a personal sense of responsibility for providing assistance, when they see others model helping behavior, when they have a clear perception of the need for rendering assistance, and when the person they are helping is someone they like. Managers who want to increase the frequency of altruistic responses should first set a proper example by modeling the behaviors they desire. Managers are usually very visible, high-status models who have a significant influence on the behavior of employees. A manager who makes a concerted effort to assist others communicates an important message that altruism is appropriate and desirable.

In addition to setting a proper example, managers should also communicate a personal responsibility for helping others. Employees can be told that they are specifically expected to go out of their way when necessary to help others in need. They can also be taught to look for specific cues that would indicate that their help is needed. In retail stores, for instance, employees can be encouraged to look for opportunities to help customers.

The effectiveness of an organization is greatly influenced by its ability to obtain altruistic responses from its employees. When employees are willing to go out of their way to help each other, the work is performed more efficiently and the organization maintains a higher level of morale.

COHESIVENESS

To understand conflict, we must examine cohesiveness and explain the causes and consequences of cohesive groups. Cohesiveness is the attraction group members have for each other and for the group as a whole. Some groups have an atmosphere of solidarity with common attitudes and behavior, while in other groups, members possess only minimal interest in one another. Highly cohesive groups provide satisfaction for their members, who may in turn feel an intense loyalty and commitment to the group. Group cohesiveness contributes importantly to the degree of conflict or cooperation in an organization. This section identifies the causes and consequences of cohesive groups.

Factors Influencing Cohesiveness

Cohesiveness:
The degree of interpersonal attraction of group members for each other and for membership in the group.

Group cohesiveness is created by a combination of factors within the group as well as by factors in the external environment beyond the group's control.

Interpersonal Attraction. The most important variable influencing cohesiveness is the interpersonal attraction of members for each other.[15] People are attracted to others who are fun to be with and for whom they feel a mutual trust and respect. Individuals tend to be attracted to those of similar socioeconomic status, religion, sex, and age. Therefore, cohesiveness tends to increase as group members share common interests and attitudes toward religion, politics, and philosophical ideas. The key factor is that cohesiveness increases when people enjoy working with and being with each other.

Frequency of Interaction. Cohesiveness increases as group members have more opportunities to interact with one another. Frequent contact allows people to communicate more openly and develop greater interpersonal attraction for one another. The frequency of interaction can be increased by increasing the number of formal and informal meetings, or by physically moving people closer together.

The size of the group influences opportunities for interaction. As the group gets larger, it becomes increasingly difficult for the members to interact with, or even know, other group members. As group size increases, therefore, cohesiveness tends to decrease. The optimal group size for maximum cohesiveness is probably between six and ten individuals.

Rigor of Initiation. Groups that are more elite in selecting new members and that require more rigorous and severe initiation rites tend to be more cohesive. Some organizations require that new members perform acts that are humiliating, physically exhausting, or perhaps illegal before they are accepted as full members. Fraternities, lettermen clubs, and youth gangs have been particularly noted for their severe initiation rites. Although these practices may be illegal and harmful, they tend to unite group members into a cohesive unit. Military organizations create cohesive groups by their rigorous training of new recruits in basic training. Universities foster a feeling of cohesiveness through a psychological initiation created by advertising rigorous admissions standards. Other organizations attempt to create the same perception by advertising that they accept only the cream of the crop. This practice is designed to make students and new employees feel that they are part of a select group, and that their elite membership elevates their status and prestige for them.

Agreement on Group Goals. Groups tend to be more cohesive when the members agree on the purpose and direction of the group's activities.

Group Success. Successful groups tend to be more cohesive than unsuccessful groups, because people are more attracted to winning groups than they are to losing groups. If two sales units have been competing for a prize and one is declared the winner, the winning team will develop greater cohesiveness, while the losing team may become less cohesive, depending on how they interpret their defeat. If they can blame defeat on an outside force, they may remain a fairly cohesive group, but if they blame other group members, their cohesiveness will decline.

Outside Threats. Groups facing an outside threat will often close ranks and form a more cohesive unit. Intergroup competition usually provides an outside threat, causing the group to become more cohesive. Threat is an effective means of producing cohesiveness when the following conditions exist: (1) the threat comes from outside the group, (2) there is little chance for escape, and (3) cooperation is necessary to resist or overcome the threat.

Sometimes leaders attempt to create a more cohesive group by convincing the members that they face a serious external threat. Coaches and military officers often talk about the power of the enemy as a way to create greater cohesiveness within their unit. For similar reasons, political leaders and business executives talk about the dangers of foreign competition, high interest rates, and a bad economy. Labor union leaders try to develop cohesiveness by convincing union members that management is trying to destroy the union and their jobs.

Consequences of Cohesiveness

Cohesive groups generally achieve better results than non-cohesive groups do. However, the effects of cohesiveness are not universally positive, and need to be examined with respect to four aspects of group functioning: participation, conformity, success, and productivity.

Participation. Cohesive groups elicit greater levels of participation from group members than non-cohesive groups do. Because of their attraction to the group, individuals are willing to devote more time and energy to group activities. A highly cohesive work group, for example, may interact more frequently on the job and even meet informally in recreational activities off the job. For example, some cohesive work groups form bowling teams, softball teams, and other interest groups, which sometimes dominate their lives away from work, particularly when a local tournament is held.

Members of cohesive groups generally spend more time communicating with each other than non-cohesive groups do. This increase in communication and participation further strengthens the cohesiveness within the group. In other words, increased communication and participation increase the interpersonal attraction and cohesiveness the members feel for each other; increased cohesiveness, in turn, leads to greater communication and participation.

Conformity. As discussed in chapter 11, cohesive groups create intense pressures for conformity. Because of the attraction of the group, people value their group membership and are willing to conform to the group's norms and expectations. As groups become more highly cohesive, group norms become more clearly specified, and the behavior of group members conforms more closely to these norms. One of the ways cohesive groups enforce conformity is through greater communication. As they become more cohesive, they communicate more openly and create more explicit expectations regarding acceptable behavior. In non-cohesive groups, members can express deviant views without repercussions or challenges, but in a highly cohesive group, deviant attitudes are not acceptable, and other group members try to reform the deviant members. Those who refuse to change are ostracized.

Success. Successful groups tend to be more cohesive, and cohesive groups also tend to be more successful. On interdependent tasks requiring cooperation, cohesive teams are generally superior because they work well together. Winning athletic teams often attribute their success to teamwork. Although their success is probably due to more than just cohesive teamwork, their cohesiveness contributes greatly to their success.

Productivity. Because cohesive groups tend to elicit more conformity, more participation, and more communication, shouldn't they also be more productive than non-cohesive groups? Studies on the relationship between cohesiveness and performance indicate that highly cohesive groups are not always the most productive. A major review of 34 studies of cohesiveness and productivity found that the relationship was neither direct nor simple.[16] Eleven studies found that cohesiveness and productivity were unrelated; another eleven studies found that productivity was higher in non-cohesive groups; and only twelve studies found that cohesive groups were more productive than non-cohesive groups. These studies involved a wide variety of groups, including radar crews, decision-making groups, basketball teams, combat units, bomber crews, factory workers, college students, nurses, and forest rangers.

There is a good reason why highly cohesive groups are not always the most productive. Cohesive groups would only be expected to be highly productive if the group norms are consistent with the organization's goals and support high productivity. If the group's goals are inconsistent with the organization's goals, a highly cohesive group may be counterproductive; the group may engage in such activities as sabotaging the organization or avoiding work.

The relationship between performance and cohesiveness is illustrated in Exhibit 12.2. The performance of non-cohesive groups tends to be about average, but the performance of highly cohesive groups may be high or low depending on the performance norms of the groups. If a cohesive group has high performance norms, the members will accept the group norms and be highly productive. A cohesive group with low performance norms, however, will have low performance.

Another characteristic of cohesive groups is that there is usually less variation in the performance of individuals. Highly cohesive groups tend to have members who perform at the same level, while non-cohesive groups may have both high and low producers within the group.

Three additional reasons have been suggested to explain why cohesive groups are not necessarily more productive. One reason is that cohesive groups tend to spend more time socializing than working because they enjoy being with each other. If work interferes with visiting, a highly cohesive group may sacrifice some of their working time to spend more time visiting. Another reason why cohesive groups may perform more poorly is because they may be subject to "groupthink," (a phenomenon, described further in chapter 16, that

Exhibit 12.2 Relationship between Performance, Cohesiveness, and Group Norms

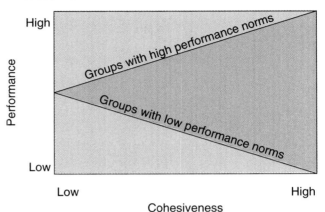

refers to rigid thinking controlled by the group). The desire to maintain a cohesive group may prevent members from challenging ideas and confronting issues, causing cohesive groups to make bad decisions. Furthermore, as groups become more cohesive, they tend to become more conservative in their approach to solving problems, and less willing to take chances. As a result, the group may not produce creative solutions to their problems.

CONFLICT AND ORGANIZATIONAL PERFORMANCE

Like competition, conflict occurs when two or more parties engage in activities that are in some sense incompatible. Both parties cannot win, and the success of one prevents the other from achieving success. Although we often talk about competition and conflict as though they were the same, they differ in the degree of self-interest displayed by each side. This small difference has important consequences for the success of a group or organization.

Competition does not involve direct action by one party to interfere with the activities of the other. With conflict, however, one party tries to prevent or inhibit the success of the other. This difference is clearly illustrated in sports. Track events are examples of competition rather than conflict, since each runner attempts to run faster than the others but no one is allowed to trip or interfere with the others. In contrast, games of football, hockey, and rugby involve both competition and conflict, because each team acts directly to interfere with the activities of the other. The degree of conflict is limited by the rules of the game, and penalties are assessed when players violate the rules.

Conflict designed to destroy the other party is not uncommon in organizations. Price wars involve conflict between organizations, with one company trying to drive its competitors out of business. Conflict between union and management sometimes becomes so intense that the union forces the company to go out of business by making unreasonable demands, or management tries to destroy the union by refusing to accept an agreement or hiring replacements. Conflict between nations that could result in nuclear war probably represents the epitome of conflict.

Social conflict, then, is a struggle in which the aims of the conflicting parties are not only to obtain the desired outcomes, but also to injure or eliminate their rivals. Intense conflict involves not only hindering one's opponents but also injuring and retaliating against them.

Functional and Dysfunctional Conflict

Many people believe that all conflict is dysfunctional and should be eliminated. This common belief is not true, however. Some conflict is inevitable in every organization because of the inherent struggle for organizational survival. Every organization exists within an environment that requires competition for limited resources. Even within friendly work groups there are limited resources that create some degree of conflict, regardless of how cooperatively the members try to allocate resources. Furthermore, all conflict is not bad; some conflict situations produce desirable results. Therefore, we must make a distinction between functional and dysfunctional conflict.

Functional conflict:
Conflict that contributes to the effectiveness of the organization by increasing motivation or improving the quality of decision making.

Functional Conflict. *Functional conflict* is a confrontation between two parties that improves or benefits the organization's performance. For example, two divisions of a public health agency may be in conflict over which one should be allowed to serve a neighborhood. In their attempts to prove that they are better prepared to provide the service, both divisions may create new services and improved methods of delivery that benefit not only the neighborhood in question but other areas as well.

Studies have suggested that some conflict not only helps but may be a necessary condition for creativity. Experimental studies have shown that heterogeneous groups whose members represent a diversity of opinion produce better solutions and more creative ideas than do homogeneous groups.[17] These studies on group decision making have led theorists to conclude that conflict may produce many positive benefits for organizations if it is properly managed. It has been suggested, for example, that functional conflict can lead to the discovery of more effective ways to structure an organization, better recognition of the strategic changes necessary for survival, and a better accommodation and acceptance of the power relationships within and between organizations.[18]

At the individual level, functional conflict can create a number of desirable consequences. Individuals require a certain level of excitement to feel enthusiastic about their work. Within certain limits, conflict produces an element of tension that motivates individuals to action.[19] Channeling this level of tension can produce high levels of productivity and satisfaction. Some have suggested that conflict contributes to personal interest, curiosity, and the full use of individual capacities. To produce the desired results, however, the conflict must somehow be limited or contained to appropriate levels of intensity. Otherwise, dysfunctional consequences occur.

Dysfunctional conflict:
Any interaction between two parties that hinders or destroys the achievement of organizational or group goals.

Dysfunctional Conflict. *Dysfunctional conflict* is any interaction between two parties that hinders or destroys the achievement of organizational or group goals. Some organizations are prepared to handle higher levels of conflict than others, such as professional sports teams, crisis organizations, police

Exhibit 12.3 Relationship between Conflict and Organizational Performance

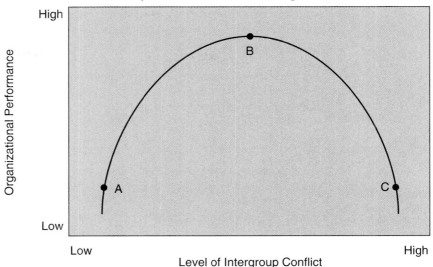

and fire departments, and commodity traders. Most organizations, however, have more conflict than is desirable, and performance would improve if the level of conflict were reduced. When conflict becomes too great, the performance of every organization begins to deteriorate. In research and development companies or universities, for example, intense conflict destroys the working relationships among members and seriously reduces organizational performance.

The relationship between conflict and organizational performance is illustrated in Exhibit 12.3. Organizational performance is low when the level of intergroup conflict is either extremely high or extremely low, while moderate levels of intergroup conflict contribute to high organizational performance. When the level of conflict is too low, such as at point A on the curve, performance suffers because of a lack of stimulation. Individuals are too comfortable and complacent in their environment, and they respond with apathy and stagnation. When they are not challenged and confronted, they fail to search for new ideas, and the organization is slow to adapt to environmental changes. Yet, when the level of conflict is extremely high, performance suffers because of inadequate coordination and cooperation. The organization is in a state of chaos because of disruption to crucial activities. Individuals spend more time defending themselves or attacking others than accomplishing work.

Maximum organizational performance occurs somewhere between these two extremes, where there is an optimal level of intergroup conflict. In this situation, at point B on the curve, there is sufficient conflict to stimulate new ideas and a creative search for solutions to problems, but not so great that it prevents the organization from moving effectively toward its goals. Individuals and groups need to assess their situations and adapt to environmental change. Such adaptation may produce innovation and creativity.

Studies of Conflict

Conflict has been a very popular research topic, and much of the research comes from two research methods: the prisoner's dilemma game and the trucking game. These two designs have been very popular because they allow experimenters to obtain extensive data in a short time from many subjects, and the experimental conditions can be easily varied in a controlled situation. A classic study by Muzafer Sherif called the *Robber's Cave Experiment* has also contributed greatly to our understanding of conflict. The results of these studies will be discussed in later sections after the research methods have been described.

The Prisoner's Dilemma Game. A convenient method for studying conflict between two people is to present them with a two-by-two payoff matrix, similar to the one shown in Exhibit 12.4, and ask them to choose either response 1 or response 2. If person A and person B both choose response 1, B will receive four points while A loses four points. This payoff matrix is called a *zero-sum* or *pure conflict* situation because what one person gains the other loses. Zero-sum conflicts occur in organizations whenever the rewards to one group cause losses to another group, such as budget allocations, territorial assignments, and staffing decisions that reassign employees to different departments.

Many organizational situations, especially interpersonal interactions, are not zero-sum situations because both parties can win by cooperating but one can win more at the expense of the other person by not cooperating. The numbers in the payoff matrix can be changed to create a *mixed-motive* situation. In these situations people can either maximize their own personal gains or maximize the gains for both parties. One mixed-motive situation, called the *prisoner's dilemma game*, concerns two suspects who are taken into custody and placed in separate cells. The district attorney is certain they are guilty of a specific crime but does not have adequate evidence to convict them in a trial. The district attorney tells the prisoners, however, that they have two alternatives: they can confess or not confess. If neither confesses, the district attorney threatens to prosecute them on a minor charge and they will both receive minor punishments. If they both confess, they will be prosecuted but the district attorney will recommend a light sentence. But if one confesses and the other does not, then the confessor will receive lenient treatment for providing evidence, whereas the latter will receive a severe sentence.

The payoff matrix for the prisoner's dilemma is illustrated in Exhibit 12.5. If the prisoners trust each other and neither confesses, they will each receive

Zero-sum conflict:
A type of conflict where the gains to one party represent losses to the other. For one party to win, the other must lose.

Mixed-motive conflict:
A situation in which an individual can either compete to maximize his or her personal gains, or cooperate to maximize the joint gains.

Prisoner's dilemma game:
A method of studying conflict by asking subjects to make either a competitive or a cooperative choice in a mixed-motive game.

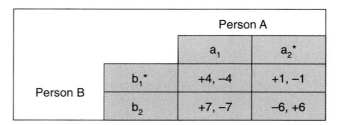

		Person A	
		a_1	a_2*
Person B	b_1*	+4, −4	+1, −1
	b_2	+7, −7	−6, +6

Exhibit 12.4   Payoff Matrix for a Zero-Sum or Pure Conflict Situation

only a one-year sentence. But if only one confesses and testifies against the other, that one will receive an even lighter sentence of only three months while the partner receives a ten-year sentence. The essential features of this and other mixed-motive situations is that one person's gain is not necessarily the other person's loss, and motives of both cooperation (not confess) and conflict (confess) are involved.

The Trucking Game. In the trucking game, pairs of subjects are asked to imagine that they are managers of opposing trucking companies that transport merchandise over a road. One player's company is called Acme and the other's is called Bolt. Both players are told that each time their truck completes a delivery trip they will make sixty cents less their operating expenses, which are determined by the time required to complete the trip (one cent per second). Thus, a trip taking 20 seconds would earn the company forty cents.

The players are then shown a road map, illustrated in Exhibit 12.6, which indicates each player's starting point and destination. Each player has two routes; the main route is clearly shorter but contains a section in the middle wide enough for only one truck at a time. If the two trucks meet in this section, the only way either truck can continue is for the other truck to back up. The alternate route is much longer, and the subjects are told they will lose at least ten cents if they take this route. In playing this game, the two players experience conflict because each knows the only way to win money is to use the one-way pass, but only one person's truck can move down that section at a time. If either player waits to allow the other to pass first, the one who waits makes less money than the one who goes through first.

In some experiments, the trucking game was modified slightly to study the effects of threat. At each end of the one-lane section, a gate was installed. Each gate was controlled by one player, and only that player's truck could pass through the gate. In conditions of unilateral threat, only one player had a gate, while in conditions of bilateral threat, both players had access to a gate.[20]

The trucking game was typically played over twenty trials, which allowed the experimenters to observe the degree of cooperation or conflict of the subjects and the effects of threat on conflict resolution.

The Robber's Cave Experiment. The effects of conflict have been studied extensively by observing the interactions of groups in a natural setting. Some of the best-known studies in conflict were conducted by Carolyn and Muzafer

		Person A	
		Not confess	Confess
Person B	Not confess	One year each	3 months for A 10 years for B
	Confess	10 years for A 3 months for B	4 years for each

Exhibit 12.5 Matrix for the Prisoner's Dilemma Mixed-Motive Payoff

Exhibit 12.6 Diagram of the Trucking Game

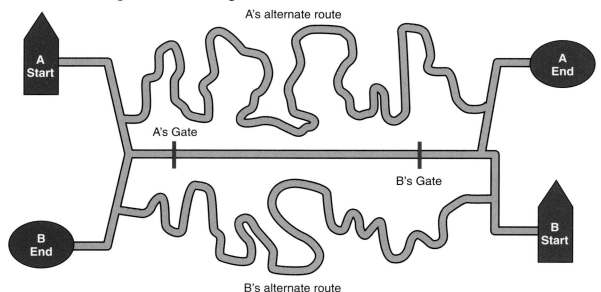

Sherif and their colleagues, who observed the interactions of boys in summer camps in Connecticut (1949), New York (1953), and Oklahoma (1954). The 1954 experiment in Oklahoma is sometimes called the Robber's Cave experiment, referring to the name of the campsite where the two groups of boys stayed.[21]

The boys in each camp were divided into two groups and given a week to develop intragroup cohesiveness. Each group participated in activities that stimulated cooperation. They lived together in bunk houses, cooked their own meals, cleaned their own campsites, and organized their own activities and games. During the first week, each group became a cohesive unit, with its own leadership structure and group norms. The groups were originally assigned the name of a color to differentiate them, such as the Blue Group, but each group quickly coined its own name, such as Eagles, Rattlers, and Bulldogs. After the first week, the two groups were brought together to compete for prizes and participate in games of football, tug-of-war, and baseball. They competed to see which team could have the better skit, have the cleaner cabin, or pitch a tent faster.

The effects of bringing the groups together and introducing competition were striking. The peaceful camp environment quickly turned into a miniature battleground as the two groups began to attack and insult each other. Derogatory terms, such as "pigs," "dirty bums," and "jerks," were used to describe the rival team. Posters were made that insulted the other team, and the opposing team's flags were stolen and mutilated. Incidents of open warfare occurred as food fights erupted in the dining hall and artillery attacks were staged in the surrounding fields, using apples as ammunition. A variety of competitive and cooperative activities were introduced in the boys' camps to examine their effects on stimulating or reducing the level of conflict.

CAUSES OF INTERGROUP CONFLICT

Studies on conflict suggest that conflict can be created by a variety of situations. Some of the most important causes of conflict include task interdependence, goal incompatibility, the use of threats, group identification, and win-lose attitudes.

Task Interdependence

Task interdependence occurs when two or more groups depend on each other to accomplish their tasks, and the potential for conflict increases as the degree of interdependence increases. Three types of task interdependence have been identified: pooled interdependence, sequential interdependence, and reciprocal interdependence.

Pooled interdependence occurs with additive tasks when the performance of different groups is simply combined or added together to achieve the overall performance.

Sequential interdependence occurs with conjunctive tasks when one group cannot complete its task until the preceding group has finished. In assembly line manufacturing, for example, the products must first pass through department A before they can proceed to department B.

Reciprocal interdependence also occurs with conjunctive tasks when each group depends on the performance of the other groups. A depends upon B and C, while B and C depend on each other as well as A. Reciprocal interdependence occurs in many organizations, such as the various departments in a hospital: the x-ray unit, the blood laboratory, the nursing unit, the emergency center, and the anesthesiology staff all depend on each other to provide skilled patient care.

Goal Incompatibility

Although managers try to avoid having incompatible goals for different organizational units, inherent incompatibility sometimes exists between groups because of their individual goals. The goal of a production department is to have low production costs with long production runs, which means fewer models, colors, and styles. These goals conflict with the aim of the marketing department, which attempts to increase sales by promising customers unique products in a unique style and color with a quick delivery. The marketing department also wants to allow customers to pay nothing down and have the first payment postponed for six months. The credit department, however, wants to have cash in hand before the product is shipped.

The likelihood of conflict increases in conditions of scarcity. When resources such as money, space, labor, or materials are limited, the groups are forced to compete for them in a win-lose competition that frequently results in dysfunctional conflict. The Robber's Cave experiment indicated that little conflicts typically lead to larger conflicts. After the competitive sports had concluded, for example, the boys escalated the conflict by food fights, scuffles, and taunting insults.

Pooled interdependence: An additive group task that does not require group members to coordinate their efforts; instead, their individual efforts are simply summed or pooled to form the group product.

Sequential interdependence: Situation in which the task structure is similar to an assembly line in which the performance of later groups depends upon the performance of earlier groups.

Reciprocal interdependence: A conjunctive group task in which each member of the group is mutually dependent upon each of the other members of the group, and successful task completion can be obtained only if each member does his or her part.

Use of Threats. The level of conflict appears to increase when one party has the capacity to threaten the other. The effects of threat were studied in the trucking game by giving one or both players access to a gate. The results indicated quite dramatically that the quickest resolution to the problem and the best payoff for the players occurred when neither player had access to a threat. In fact, the players were able to obtain a profit only in the no-threat condition.[22] The slowest resolution occurred when both players could threaten. Therefore, the absence of threat seems to encourage players to cooperate more and develop a compatible, cooperative relationship. However, when they have access to threats, the evidence seems to show that the players not only communicate the threat, but actually use it.

Group Identification. When two groups are competing for scarce resources, it is easy to understand why conflict would occur. Both groups are striving for the same goal, and only one can obtain it. Research has shown, however, that a competitive situation is not necessary for conflict to exist. Simply assigning people to different groups and allowing them to develop a feeling of cohesiveness are all that is necessary for conflict to result. As the groups become more cohesive, the intergroup conflict increases. One of the major conclusions of the Robber's Cave experiment was that conflict between the groups was a natural outcome of group cohesiveness. The feelings of solidarity and in-group favoritism seem to contribute to unfavorable attitudes and negative stereotypes of the out-group. This suggests that a feeling of hostility and criticism could exist between two groups who work side by side in an organization, even though there is no interaction between the two groups and they do not compete for scarce resources. And as these two groups become more cohesive, the potential for conflict between them increases.

Win-Lose Attitudes. When two groups interact in zero-sum competition, it is easy to understand why conflict occurs. Whatever one group wins, the other group loses. Unfortunately, many situations are perceived as win-lose situations when in reality they are not. Industrial conflict frequently pits union against management, each side bargaining for a larger share of dwindling profits. Rather than fighting for a larger share of a smaller pie, management and union ought to cooperate to increase the size of the profit pie.

Although win-lose situations do not have to occur, they appear frequently when any of these conditions exist:

- someone defines or interprets the situation as a win-lose conflict
- one group chooses to pursue its own goals
- one group understands its needs but publicly disguises them
- one group attempts to increase its power position
- one group uses threats to obtain submission
- one group overemphasizes its needs, goals, and position
- one group adopts an attitude of exploiting the other group whenever possible
- one group attempts to isolate the other group

Getting two groups to change from a win-lose attitude to a win-win attitude is a difficult task, because the groups develop perceptual stereotypes that reinforce their win-lose attitudes. Furthermore, rather than communicating openly, their communication becomes guarded or discontinued, which further reinforces a win-lose attitude. Research using the prisoner's dilemma game found that if the parties were able to communicate before they made their decisions, the level of cooperation increased. Cooperation also increased when the numbers in the payoff matrix were changed to reward players for cooperating.

A very interesting conclusion from the prisoner's dilemma game is that cooperation did not increase just because one player decided to cooperate. Several studies attempted to analyze how subjects would respond to a pacifistic partner who constantly made cooperative choices. The experiments found that subjects tended to exploit a pacifistic partner. This exploitation occurred even when the other player's consistent cooperation was explained in terms of religious convictions or personal morality.[23] At least in the laboratory, unconditional cooperation does not create reciprocal cooperation. Instead, it seems to lead to exploitation.

The most effective strategy for obtaining cooperation was the strategy of conditional cooperation. Here one partner first makes a cooperative move and continues to make cooperative responses as long as the other responds cooperatively. If the cooperative initiative is met with aggression, however, the aggression is reciprocated. Then, on a later trial, a cooperative response may again be tested.

CONSEQUENCES OF INTERGROUP CONFLICT

The consequences of intergroup conflict can be summarized in one simple statement: conflict begets conflict. When conflict occurs, the consequences of this conflict frequently lead to further conflict and create a vicious cycle of spiraling conflict. The consequences of intergroup conflict can be analyzed in terms of the changes that occur both within the group and between groups.

Changes within the Group

When two groups are involved in intergroup conflict, the following changes are likely to occur within each group.

Increased Cohesiveness. Conflict, competition, and external threats usually cause group members to set aside their personal differences and close ranks. Group members become more loyal to the group and committed to its goals. Group norms are followed more closely, and less deviation is tolerated.

Increased Loyalty. When one group is threatened by another group, both groups will demand greater loyalty from their members. Deviant behavior is not tolerated, and friendliness with members of the opposing group is viewed with suspicion, if not hostility. Personal sacrifice for the group is highly rewarded and expected. Group goals take precedence over individual satisfaction because members are expected to demonstrate their loyalty.

Rise in Autocratic Leadership. In normal conditions, democratic leadership methods are popular because they allow group members to participate in making decisions and to satisfy their needs for involvement and affiliation. In extreme conflict situations, however, democratic leadership is generally perceived as time-consuming and ineffective. Members demand strong leadership, and not only tolerate but seem to prefer autocratic leaders.

Activity Orientation. Groups in conflict tend to focus on achieving their goal. Groups are more concerned about identifying what it is they do well and then doing it. Group members are not allowed to visit or waste time if these activities reduce the group's effectiveness in defeating the enemy.

Inflated Evaluation. The perceptions of group members become distorted as they tend to overevaluate their own performance and underevaluate their opponents' performance. Everything within the group is considered good, and a general halo effect tends to bias and inflate the group's perceptions of its members.

Changes between Groups

Intergroup conflict creates three predictable changes between the groups:

Decreased Communication. At the time when the groups have the greatest need of open communication to enable them to discuss the problem and resolve the conflict, the communication processes become most strained. As the conflict increases, communication tends to decrease. Both groups tend to be more guarded in their communication. Rather than openly confronting the problems, each side becomes more cautious and formal. The frequency of communication between the two groups continues to decline until it finally breaks down entirely.

Distorted Perceptions. Conflict creates suspicion and prevents people from accurately perceiving the behaviors and motives of the other party. People think that everything about their own group is good, while everything about the opponent group is perceived as bad. These distorted perceptions are created, in part, by negative stereotypes. The distorted perceptions cause members in each group to misperceive the others' intentions and misinterpret their communications. The performance and success of the other group is underevaluated and minimized. Even simple estimates of factual information, such as time estimates, can be enormously distorted by conflict. In the Robber's Cave experiment, for example, a tug-of-war was declared a tie after 55 minutes. When the members of the group on the verge of victory were asked to estimate the actual time of the tug-of-war, the estimates ranged from 20 to 50 minutes. However, the group that was on the verge of losing the estimated time from 65 to 210 minutes. Many other factual observations were distorted, making the in-group look good and the out-group look bad.

Negative Stereotyping. Group members in one group tend to create negative stereotypes regarding the opposing group. Negative characteristics are used to describe the opposing group, such as greedy, dishonest, unethical, and unfriendly. In a labor-management conflict, for example, management typically views labor leaders as greedy agitators who are out to destroy the company, and union leaders tend to view management as greedy profit grabbers who are trying to exploit labor and keep all the rewards.

RESOLVING INTERGROUP CONFLICT

Since the dynamics of two interacting groups are such that conflict begets conflict, the groups will be the victims of a spiraling escalation of conflict, unless something is done to reverse the process. Conflict causes each group to become more cohesive and task oriented, with a rigid structure and an autocratic leader. Individuality is replaced by loyalty as each group demands greater unity within the group. The cohesiveness, loyalty, and task orientation within each group only contributes to more biased perceptions, negative stereotypes, hostility, and aggression between the groups.

Because conflict is inherent in complex organizations, managers must be capable of resolving it before dysfunctional consequences destroy the organization's effectiveness. The ability to resolve conflict is a valuable managerial skill. The most popular strategies for reducing conflict can be classified into four categories: (1) avoidance, (2) power intervention, (3) diffusion, and (4) resolution. Although the most effective strategy depends in part on the situation and the time available for resolving the conflict, the following strategies are arranged in order from generally least effective to most effective.

Avoidance Strategies

**Avoidance
strategies:**
A method of responding to conflict situations by either ignoring the conflict or separating the conflicting parties.

Avoidance strategies generally disregard the cause of conflict but allow it to continue only under controlled conditions. Two types of avoidance strategies include ignoring the conflict and physical separation.

Ignore the Conflict. If the conflict is mild and the consequences are not very costly, managers may choose to pretend it does not exist. Some managers think conflict reflects badly on the organization, so they ignore the conflict and hope it will eventually resolve itself. Because the sources of conflict are neither identified nor resolved, however, this strategy is seldom effective, and the situation worsens.

Physical Separation. If two combative groups are physically separated, the likelihood of open hostility and aggression is reduced. Unless the source of the conflict is eliminated, however, acts of sabotage and aggression may continue. Physical separation is generally an effective strategy only when the two groups do not need to interact and the separation eliminates the symptom of the conflict. If the two groups are required to interact, however, separating them only contributes to poor performance.

Power Intervention Strategies

**Power intervention
strategies:**
A method of responding to conflict by having higher-level management impose a solution or political maneuvering among the conflicting members to obtain a majority vote.

When two groups cannot resolve the conflict on their own, some form of *power intervention strategies* may be used. The source of power may come from higher levels within the organization in the form of regulated interaction, or the power may come from political maneuvering by either of the groups.

Regulated Interaction. When the conflict becomes too great to ignore, higher-level managers may become irritated and impatient, and try to resolve the conflict by authoritative command. "All right, you guys, that's the end of it, no more!" In addition to the unilateral decree that the conflict will go no further, the command may be accompanied by threats, such as termination or transfer to a different group. Higher-level officers may also establish rules and procedures that limit the conflict to an acceptable level. This procedure, sometimes called *encapsulating* the conflict, occurs when managers establish specific rules and procedures that regulate the interactions between the groups and define their relationship.

Political Maneuvering. The two groups may decide to end the conflict by some form of political maneuvering in which one party attempts to accumulate sufficient power to force compliance on the other party. A democratic process is often used to settle the issue by bringing it to a vote. Both groups try to sway the outcome of the balloting by soliciting outside support and encouraging marginal opponents to defect to their side.

A problem with trying to encapsulate the conflict or vote on the issues is that these strategies typically tend to intensify win-lose situations. The source of the conflict has not been eliminated, and both parties feel more committed to their position. Even after fair elections, the losers may feel resentment and continue to oppose the winners.

Diffusion Strategies

Diffusion strategies:
A conflict resolution method that tries to reduce the emotional anger by either smoothing over the disagreement, developing a compromise, or creating a common enemy to distract attention.

Diffusion strategies try to reduce the level of anger and emotion and buy time until the conflict between the two groups can be resolved. Diffusion strategies generally focus on surface issues rather than strike at the roots of the conflict. Three diffusion strategies have been used to reduce the level of emotion: smoothing, compromise, and identifying a common enemy.

Smoothing. The process of smoothing involves accentuating the similarities and common interests between the two groups and minimizing or rationalizing their differences. Stressing the similarities and common interests helps the groups see that their goals are not so far apart and that there is something to be gained by working together. Although smoothing may help the groups realize they have common interests, it is only a short-term solution when it fails to resolve the basic underlying conflicts.

Compromise. Compromise strategies between two groups involve bargaining over the issues, and they require some degree of flexibility on both sides. If the parties are so inflexible that they are not willing to concede, the negotiation will reach a stalemate and the conflict will continue. Once a compromise solution has been negotiated, the two groups should be able to work together harmoniously. Frequently, however, compromise decisions are inferior solutions, and neither side is happy with the settlement. With labor-management negotiations, for example, both sides may be unhappy with the current labor agreement, and even though they agree to live with it, they criticize each other and try to improve their positions for the next negotiations.

Identifying a Common Enemy. When two groups face a common enemy, they often develop a degree of cohesiveness between them as a means of protection. Differences of opinion and intergroup rivalry may be temporarily suspended while the two groups unite to defeat a common opponent. In the Robber's Cave experiment, the conflict between the two rival boys' groups was temporarily suspended by the challenge from another camp to an all-star baseball game. The best players from both sides were selected to form the all-star team, and the members of both groups directed their attention toward defeating the rival camp. In this experiment, however, it was noted that identifying a common enemy did not reduce the overall level of conflict. A high level of conflict still existed, but now it was directed at another source. When the common enemy was no longer present, the conflict between the two groups once again emerged. The conflict had not been resolved; it had only been suspended. Labor and management, for example, frequently face external threats in the form of foreign competition, government regulation, and declining sales. Although they may work together cooperatively in the face of these outside threats, the basic sources of the conflict have not been resolved, and conflict will soon reappear.

Resolution Strategies

Resolution strategies:
A method of trying to resolve conflict by identifying the cause of the problem through problem solving, removing the cause of the conflict by a structural change, or by creating a higher-level goal that requires cooperation.

The most effective method of resolving conflict is some form of resolution strategy that identifies the source of the conflict and resolves it. Research seems to indicate that resolution strategies are the most effective. One study investigated the conflict resolution styles of 74 managers. The least effective managers tended to ignore the conflict, while the most effective managers confronted the conflict directly by bringing the conflicting parties together to decide how to best meet the overall organizational goals.[24] Four types of resolution strategies include intergroup interaction, superordinate goals, problem solving, and structural change.

Intergroup Interaction. Since one of the consequences of intergroup conflict is a reduction in communication and interaction between groups, it would seem that bringing the groups together and increasing the contact between them would help reduce the conflict. Unfortunately, sometimes it is not good to bring warring groups together. When combative groups are brought together, the members of both groups are likely to use the occasion to demonstrate their loyalty for their own group and dislike for the other. In the Robber's Cave experiment, for example, when the boys were required to eat together, rather than developing new friendships they used the occasion to express their hostility by throwing food.

A better strategy is to bring the leaders of each group together to listen to the other group's position. When these discussions occur in private and the leaders are able to express their own opinions freely, the discussions are usually quite fruitful and represent an important first step in resolving the level of conflict. When the discussions are held in public, however, the leaders are expected to represent their own group. Consequently, the leaders are often more interested in looking good and impressing their constituents by being tough and combative rather than trying to resolve differences of opinion.

Another strategy is to exchange members for a period of time. Three members of the sales force, for example, could trade roles with three members of the credit department for a few weeks to help each group get a better understanding of the problems the other group faces. Another means of developing greater understanding is to share propaganda rather than members. For example, the members of each group could be asked to describe, on paper, their feelings toward the other group, along with a list of criticisms and suggestions. The groups could then exchange lists and respond to any questions or comments. This method of sharing information could continue until the emotional feelings are sufficiently diffused to allow the groups to work together in face-to-face problem solving.

Superordinate goals:
Goals that are highly important to both sides and that cannot be achieved without working together.

Superordinate Goals. A superordinate goal is a goal that is more important to both parties than the relatively minor issues causing the conflict. In labor-management negotiations, for example, both sides may strongly disagree about the work rules and the number of paid vacation days but strongly agree about the survival of the company. If the company is unprofitable and cannot survive, work rules and paid vacations become meaningless issues. Using superordinate goals to resolve conflict involves three conditions. First, the groups must perceive their mutual dependency on each other; second, the superordinate goal must be highly desired by each group; and third, both groups must expect to be rewarded for accomplishing the goal.

Working to achieve a superordinate goal is a powerful motivation for the groups to resolve their basic differences and work together cooperatively. In the Robber's Cave experiment, for example, a series of superordinate goals were created. These goals were important to both groups, and required joint cooperation such as fixing a break in the camp water supply, selecting a movie, pushing a stalled truck supplying camp food, and preparing a joint meal. By cooperating in these tasks, the level of tension and hostility between the two groups was reduced, and feelings of cooperation and friendship were created.

Problem Solving. A joint problem-solving session is an effective resolution strategy if the two groups focus their attention on the problem rather than arguing about who is right or wrong, or using the situation to get even. A problem-solving session usually involves a face-to-face meeting of the conflicting groups to identify the source of the problem and develop alternative solutions for solving it. This strategy is most effective when a thorough analysis of the problem can be made, points of mutual interest are identified, and alternatives are suggested and carefully explored. The disadvantage of this strategy is that it requires a great deal of time and commitment. Furthermore, if the conflict originates from value-laden issues and people are emotionally involved, the tension may prevent them from progressing satisfactorily to an acceptable solution.

Structural Change. Conflicts are frequently caused, or at least encouraged, by the way an organization is structured. Creating a marketing department, for example, means that a group of people will work together to solve marketing problems and plan a marketing strategy. As they become more specialized in their marketing functions, they will focus to a greater extent on marketing goals and disregard the goals of other departments. Other specialized groups in the organization develop an equally narrow focus. Some groups become so highly specialized, in fact, that they lose sight of the organization's goals and focus exclusively on their own group goals. Furthermore, the reward structures in organizations frequently recognize and reward group members for pursuing their group goals rather than organizational goals.

In these situations, an effective strategy for reducing conflict is to change the organizational structure. By emphasizing total organizational effectiveness rather than group effectiveness, cooperation rather than competition can be promoted. Groups can be recognized and rewarded for their contribution to the effectiveness of other groups, and altruistic behavior across group lines can be encouraged. By reorganizing the departments and establishing clear, operational, and feasible goals for the organization, the source of conflict can be removed. For example, members of a marketing department could be assigned to specific projects so that they feel an allegiance not only to the marketing department but also to other departments and programs.

CREATING FUNCTIONAL CONFLICT

While some organizations experience too much conflict, others would be more productive with more conflict. As conflict increases, individuals typically experience greater arousal and levels of motivation. Therefore, in a lethargic organization where ideas have become stale and behavior has become routine, greater conflict may be needed to generate creative ideas and motivate people to higher levels of performance. Four of the most popular methods for creating functional conflict in organizations include altering the communication flow, creating competition, altering the organizational structure, and recruiting outside experts.

Altering the Communication Flow. Information is a source of power in organizations, and conflict can be created by sharing or withholding information, especially if it is evaluative information. Managers rely on the information they receive to assess the performance of their group. This information may or may not be shared with other group members. Higher levels of conflict and concern for the performance of the group can be created by altering the communication flow so that group members know how well they have performed and what is expected of them. Higher performance expectations can be created by showing groups how well they perform relative to other groups in the organization, or by simply suggesting that they should do better. Some managers use the informal grapevine to create conflict by leaking confidential information and false rumors. Leaking false information is not recommended, however, because of its long-term consequence of destroying confidence.

Creating Competition. A competitive environment can be created by offering rewards to the individual or group with the best performance. If they are used properly, financial incentives and other extrinsic rewards can maintain a healthy atmosphere of competition that contributes to functional conflict. The rewards offered to the winners need to be sufficiently attractive and probable to motivate high performance, but not so attractive that those who lose feel that their defeat is a catastrophic loss.

Altering Organizational Structure. Organizations can be restructured to either stimulate or reduce conflict. As a general rule, higher levels of conflict occur when groups become smaller and more highly specialized, because the members tend to focus more exclusively on their group goals. Dividing a large group into smaller, specialized subgroups, for example, would create a situation more conducive to conflict, because each group would be competing for resources, materials, and clients.

Recruiting Outside Experts. Promotion-from-within policies have been criticized as "inbreeding" because new managers tend to follow old procedures that lead to stale thinking and a lack of creativity and imagination. To avoid the problem of inbreeding, organizations should recruit outside experts who will challenge established procedures and stimulate new thinking. Rather than promoting the best faculty member to be the new dean, for example, some business schools have recruited an executive from industry who can think about business education and the role of the business school much differently. An effective program that has been operating for several years allows faculty members and federal government employees to exchange places temporarily to stimulate new ideas both in government agencies and in academic institutions.

Discussion Questions

1. Should managers expect employees to behave altruistically in organizations? What can be done to obtain greater altruism in an organization? Discuss your association with an organization and explain the degree to which you would be willing to act altruistically.
2. How important is cohesiveness to athletic teams? Is cohesiveness important for the effectiveness of work groups? Identify a group to which you belong, and describe your recommendations for making that group more cohesive.
3. Explain the differences between functional and dysfunctional conflict. Describe two situations that illustrate when conflict is functional and when it is dysfunctional.
4. Describe a time when you observed your group unnecessarily creating a win-lose attitude toward an opposing group. What could you do to change your group orientation from a win-lose conflict to a win-win situation?
5. Describe a situation you have observed that demonstrates the spiraling escalation of conflict. The conflict situation could be between two nations, two student groups, or two individuals. How did the conflict start and why is it being perpetuated?
6. Which conflict resolution strategies would you recommend for the following situations: (a) two adjacent fraternities disagree about the use of the parking lot between them; (b) union and management representatives discontinue negotiations, and the union has been on strike for two weeks; (c) two countries, such as Ecuador and Peru or Israel and Syria, have a border dispute between them; (d) roommates disagree about a pile of dirty dishes left in the kitchen.

Notes

1. Morton A. Deutsch, "Experimental Study on the Effects of Cooperation and Competition upon Group Processes," *Human Relations* 2 (1949): 199–231.
2. David J. Cherrington, "Satisfaction in Competitive Conditions," *Organizational Behavior and Human Performance* 10 (1973): 47–71.

3. Larry J. Williams and Stella E. Anderson, "Job Satisfaction and Organizational Commitment as Predictors of Organizational Citizenship and In-Role Behavior," *Journal of Management* 17 (September 1991): 601–17.

4. Jennifer M. George, "State or Trait Affects of Positive Mode on Pro-Social Behaviors at Work," *Journal of Applied Psychology* 76 (1991: 299–308.

5. Jiing-Lih Farh, Philip M. Podsakoff, and Dennis W. Organ, "Accounting for Organizational Citizenship Behavior: Leader Fairness and Task Scope vs. Satisfaction," *Journal of Management* 16 (1990): 705–21; Dennis W. Organ and Mary Konovsky, "Cognitive Vs. Affective Determinants of Organizational Citizenship Behavior," *Journal of Applied Psychology* 74 (1989): 157–64.

6. Jon L. Pearce and Hal B. Gregersen, "Task Interdependence and Extrarole Behavior: a Test of the Mediating Effects of Felt Responsibility," *Journal of Applied Psychology* 76 (1991): 838–44.

7. B. Latané and J. M. Darley, "Bystander Intervention in Emergencies," in J. R. Macaulay and L Berkowitz (eds.), *Altruism and Helping Behavior* (New York: Academic Press, 1970): 13–27.

8. P. Moriarty, "Crime, Commitment, and the Responsive Bystander: Two Field Experiments," *Journal of Personality and Social Psychology* 31 (1975): 370–76.

9. Charlotte O. Phelps, "Caring and Family Income," *Journal of Economic Behavior and Organization* 10 (July 1988): 63–96.

10. Lynette S. Unger, "Altruism as a Motivation to Volunteer," *Journal of Economic Psychology* 12 (March 1991): 71–100.

11. J. H. Bryan and M. A. Test, "Models and Helping: Naturalistic Studies in Aiding Behavior," *Journal of Personality and Social Psychology* 6 (1967): 400–07.

12. J. R. Macaulay, "A Shill for Charity," in J. R. Macaulay and L Berkowitz, *Altruism and Helping Behavior* (New York: Academic Press, 1970): 43–59.

13. J. M. Darley and C. D. Batson, "'From Jerusalem to Jericho': A Study of Situational and Dispositional Variables in Helping Behavior," *Journal of Personality and Social Psychology* 27 (1973): 100–08.

14. D. L. Krebs, "Altruism—An Examination of the Concept and a Review of the Literature," *Psychological Bulletin* 73 (1970): 258–302.

15. A. J. Lott and B. E. Lott, "Group Cohesiveness as Interpersonal Attraction: A Review of Relationships with Antecedent and Consequent Variables," *Psychological Bulletin* 64 (1965): 259–309.

16. Ralph M. Stogdill, "Group Productivity, Drive, and Cohesiveness," *Organizational Behavior and Human Performance* 8 (1972): 26–43.

17. J. Hall and M. S. Williams, "A Comparison of Decision Making Performance in Established and Ad Hoc Groups," *Journal of Personality and Social Psychology* 3 (February 1966): 217–22; L.R. Hoffman and N.R.F. Maier, "Quality and Acceptance of Problem Solutions by Members of Homogeneous and Heterogeneous Groups," *Journal of Abnormal and Social Psychology* 62 (April 1961): 401–07.

18. Jeffrey Pfeffer, *Power in Organizations*, (Marshfield, MA: Pitman, 1981), especially chap. 5.

19. William E. Scott, Jr., "Activation Theory and Task Design," *Organizational Behavior and Human Performance* 1 (1966): 3–30.

20. Morton Deutsch and Robert Krauss, "The Effect of Threat Upon Interpersonal Bargaining," *Journal of Abnormal and Social Psychology* 61 (1960): 181–89.

21. Muzafer Sherif, O. J. Harvey, B. J. White, W. R. Hood, and Carolyn W. Sherif, *Intergroup Conflict and Cooperation: The Robber's Cave Experiment* (Norman, OK: Institute of Group Relations, University of Oklahoma, 1961).

22. See additional studies by Morton Deutsch, D. Canavan, and J. Rubin, "The Effects of Size of Conflict and Sex of Experimenter upon Interpersonal Bargaining," *Journal of Experimental Psychology* 7 (1971): 258–67; S. C. Freedman, "Threats, Promises, and Coalitions: A Study of Compliance and Retaliation in a Simulated Organizational Setting," *Journal of Applied Social Psychology* 11 (1981): 114–36.

23. G. H. Shure, R. J. Meeker, and E. A. Hansford, "The Effectiveness of Pacifist Strategies in Bargaining Games," *Journal of Conflict Resolution* 9 (1965): 106–17; L. Solomon, "The Influence of Some Types of Power Relationships and Game Strategy upon the Development of Interpersonal Trust," *Journal of Abnormal and Social Psychology* 61 (1960): 223–30; Friedel Bolle and Peter Ockenfels, "Prisoners' Dilemma as a Game with Incomplete Information," *Journal of Economic Psychology* 11 (March 1990): 69–84.

24. Ronald J. Burke, "Methods of Resolving Superior-Subordinate Conflict: The Constructive Use of Subordinate Differences," *Organizational Behavior and Human Performance* 5 (1970): 393–411

Who Should Be Moved to the Trailer?

Before the idea of moving to a mobile trailer was proposed, Carol and Marie were hostile co-workers. Carol was hired first and assigned the position of head nurse. Marie was hired two months later and continually challenged Carol's leadership because she had more education and experience. Both women were highly respected nurses who specialized in heart disease before joining Dr. Bachman's cardiology staff. The other four staff members tried to avoid taking sides, but conflicts erupted almost daily.

The conflict between Carol and Marie disappeared almost overnight when it was announced that the cardiology unit would be moved to a mobile trailer to relieve the overcrowded conditions in the clinic. Carol and Marie prepared a joint memo explaining why they opposed the move and convinced the other four staff members to sign it. They threatened to quit if their unit was moved, since they thought a mobile trailer was unprofessional.

Dr. Bachman joined the clinic two years ago with two other doctors: Dr. Adams, a urologist, and Dr. Turner, a dermatologist. The staff members reporting to these two doctors realized that they might be moved to the trailer if the memo by Carol and Marie was convincing. To discredit the cardiology staff memo, the urology and dermatology staffs issued a joint memo, arguing that the cardiology unit should be moved since the basement room that they now used was poorly ventilated and not the best place to conduct stress tests and other examinations.

During the next three weeks, the conflict and antagonism at the clinic became so intense that it reduced the quality of patient care for all nine doctors and their staffs at the clinic.

The problem was resolved when the oncology staff under Dr. Cohen volunteered to move to the trailer. The announcement that they were willing to move surprised the other staff groups because Dr. Cohen was one of the three founders of the clinic and everyone assumed that with her seniority and influence, she and her staff would maintain their position near the front of the clinic. The decision, however, was a consensus decision by Dr. Cohen and her staff and once the trailer was in place, they moved quickly and efficiently. This voluntary move by the oncology staff restored a spirit of cooperation among the other staff groups.

Questions

1. What was the cause of the conflict between Carol and Marie? Why did they decide to unite to issue a joint memo? Has the conflict between them been eliminated?
2. Why did the urology and dermatology staffs form a coalition? Why do coalitions form?
3. What motivated the oncology staff to move voluntarily? What are the motives behind cooperative behavior, and what impact does it have on others?

Conflict and Collaboration Exercise

In many situations, two opposing sides will perpetuate a conflict, even though both sides know that neither side will win and that continued conflict can only increases the costs to both sides. Usually the conflict is perpetuated by a lack of trust in the other side. The purpose of this exercise is to illustrate the difficulty of developing a cooperative relationship between two teams, and to show how difficult it is to establish a spirit of trust once the relationship has been violated. In this exercise, two teams of students have to decide whether the relationship between them will be cooperative or competitive.

Directions. Divide the class into an even number of teams of three or four individuals each; each team should be paired with another team. A referee-timekeeper should be assigned to each pair of teams. Each team establishes its treasury and appoints a treasurer who collects and keeps track of team funds. The referee-timekeeper will collect funds from each team treasurer and establish the bank.

Each team takes 15 minutes to (1) read these directions and ask questions, (2) appoint two negotiators who can be changed at any time by a majority vote, and (3) plan team strategy.

Each team member provides 75 cents; 25 cents is used for the bank and 50 cents is used to help establish the team's own treasury. Your treasury's money will be divided among your team's members at the end of the game. Bank money will *not* be returned at the end of the game.

1. This exercise involves two teams, each trying to win as much money from each other and/or the bank as possible.
2. Each team has ten weapons represented by ten cards. A card with its "X" side up is an active weapon. A card with its "X" side down is an inactive weapon. Each team begins the game with all ten cards in an active state. Cards should never be visible to the opposing team.
3. A total game consists of five moves. During each move a team may change two, one, or no weapons from an active position to an inactive position, or *vice versa*. Two total games are planned for the exercise.
4. A team has two minutes to make each move. If the team fails to decide on a move within that time, no cards will be turned. Referees will signal when moves are to begin and end.
5. At the end of each move, a team may (but does not have to) "attack" the other team. When an "attack" is called, the game ends. The team with fewer active weapons will pay to its opponents five cents per person for each active weapon it has less than the active weapons held by the other team.
6. If neither team is attacked by the end of the fifth move, the game is over.
7. At the end of the game, each team receives two cents per person from the bank for each inactive weapon. Conversely, each team pays the bank two cents per person for each active weapon.

8. Each team should appoint two negotiators who must meet with negotiators from the other team after the first and fourth moves. A team may also request negotiations at the end of any other move. The request may be either accepted or rejected by the other team. Negotiations take place on neutral territory and can last no longer than three minutes. Negotiators may or may not bargain in good faith. Teams are not bound by agreements made by their negotiators. Each team should keep its weapons covered and no one is allowed to see the team's weapons except the team's own members, until the game is over.

CHAPTER 13

Organizational Design

Chapter Outline

Concepts of Organizational Design
Division of Labor
Departmentalization
Span of Control
Delegation of Authority
Coordinating Mechanisms
Matrix Organizational Structures

Universal Design Theories
Mechanistic versus Organic Organizational Structures
Bureaucratic Organizational Design
System Four Organizational Structure

Contingency Theories of Organizational Design
Technology
Environmental Uncertainty
Information Processing

CONCEPTS OF ORGANIZATIONAL DESIGN

Organizations are open social systems that consist of patterned activities. This chapter explains how these patterned activities are structured. The purpose of organizational structure is to create and regulate these activities; organizational structure reduces the variability in human performance, or in other words, it controls behavior by making it coordinated and predictable.

Although some people object to the idea of controlling human behavior because it appears to destroy individuality and autonomy, control is nevertheless essential. An organization cannot survive if its members behave in random, unpredictable ways. Such a situation would produce chaos and disorganization. The difference between a well organized and poorly organized group is as dramatic as the difference between the beauty of an orchestra playing a symphony and the noise the musicians produce when they are tuning their instruments. To produce the necessary patterned activities and thereby create an organization, the variability in human behavior must be reduced so that people behave in predictable patterns. Although organizations vary in the amount of control they require from their members, at least some control is inherent in every organization.

The term *organizational structure* refers to the relatively fixed relationships among the jobs in the organization. The process of creating this structure and making decisions about the relative benefits of alternative structures is called *organizational design*. Creating an organizational structure involves two issues: (1) differentiation, or creating a division of labor; and (2) integration, or coordinating the divisions. Therefore, the study of organizational structure examines the manner in which an organization divides labor into specific tasks and achieves coordination among these tasks. The five major design decisions that must be made are division of labor, departmentalization, span of control, delegation of authority, and coordinating mechanisms.

Organizational Structure:
The arrangement of jobs and relationships among the jobs in an organization.

Organizational design:
The process of deciding on the type of structure appropriate for an organization, particularly regarding its division of labor, departmentalization, span of control, delegation of authority, and coordinating mechanism.

Division of labor:
The process of dividing work into specialized jobs that are performed by separate individuals.

Division of Labor

The term *division of labor* refers to the process of dividing a large task into successively smaller jobs. A related term is *job specialization*. All jobs are specialized to some degree, since one person can't do everything, but some jobs are considerably more specialized than others. One of the major benefits of organized activities is that a group of people working together with a division of labor are able to produce more than they could if they were working alone.

The key issue here is how specialized the work should be. Specialization is low when employees perform a variety of tasks and high when each person performs only a single task. In a word-processing center, for example, the degree of specialization is low if three typists are allowed to edit, type, and proofread the manuscripts they type. However, if each of these functions were assigned to a different individual, the degree of specialization would be high. The degree of specialization can be represented along a continuum.

Division of labor: Specialization

High   Low

Deciding on the appropriate level of specialization is an important design decision because it greatly influences productivity. It is possible to create jobs that are so highly specialized that the organization suffers from a lack of coordination and at times there isn't enough work to keep everyone busy. Highly specialized jobs can also be extremely boring, yet there are definite advantages to highly specialized jobs. The chief advantage is that such jobs contribute to high levels of productivity. Several reasons explain why specialization is more productive:

1. It creates greater proficiency by allowing employees to perform the same repetitive activity.
2. It requires less training to master the job.
3. Less time is lost going from one activity to another.
4. Special tools can be developed that can lead to complete automation of a task.
5. There is better quality control of output.

Departmentalization[1]

Departmentalization:
The process of assigning jobs to units or departments according to one of these common criteria: function, product, geographical area, or clientele.

Functional departmentalization:
Creating departments by grouping jobs that all perform similar functions.

Departmentalization is the process of combining jobs into groups or departments. Managers must decide whether the most appropriate structure is to have a homogeneous department with similar jobs, or a heterogeneous department with unrelated jobs. Jobs can be grouped according to several criteria; the most popular criteria include function, product, territory, and clientele, as illustrated in Exhibit 13.1.

Functional Departmentalization. *Functional departmentalization* involves grouping jobs that perform similar functions into the same department. For example, all the jobs associated with accounting, such as general ledger accountant, accounts payable clerk, accounts receivable clerk, and cost accountant, could all be combined into an accounting department. Organizing the departments by function would be a homogeneous form of departmentalization, since everyone in the department would share the same specialized skills. Other forms of departmentalization tend to be market-based and more heterogeneous.

Functional departmentalization is the most widely used scheme because in most organizations it is the most effective method. This explains why a typical manufacturing company is departmentalized into production, marketing, finance, accounting, research-and-development, and human resource departments. Most hospitals are departmentalized in terms of such functions as surgery, nursing, psychiatry, pharmacy, human resource, and housekeeping.

Functional departmentalization has both advantages and disadvantages. Perhaps the most significant advantage is that it promotes skill specialization by having people who face similar problems and opportunities work together. The functional form also permits the maximum use of resources, and encourages the use of specialists and specialized equipment, thereby eliminating duplication of equipment and effort. Communication and performance are usually improved because superiors share expertise with their subordinates.

The disadvantages of functional departmentalization are that it reduces communication and cooperation between departments and fosters a parochial perspective. This narrow orientation limits managers' capacities for coordination and encourages a short time horizon. Functional departmentalization has

Exhibit 13.1   **Bases of Departmentalization**

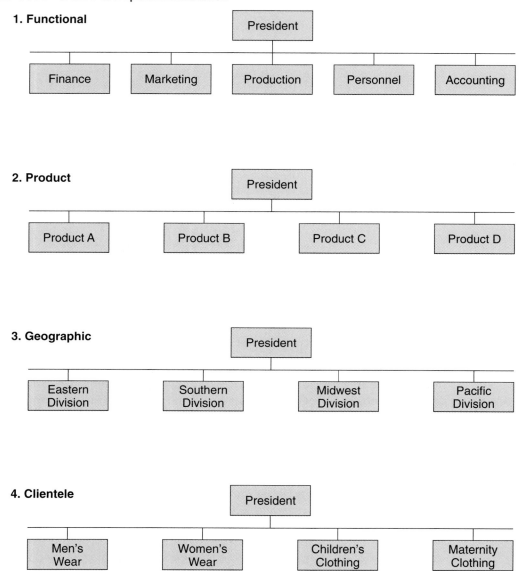

Suboptimizing:
Where one department pursues its self-interest at the expense of the larger organization.

often led to a problem referred to as *suboptimizing*, which occurs when one department pursues its own goals and tries to look good at the expense of other departments or the organization as a whole. Suboptimizing is particularly problematic when departments are rewarded for achieving their own goals. Although departments should be rewarded for helping other departments, many departmental goals can best be achieved when each department pursues its own selfish interests. Custodial departments, for example, could keep the buildings cleaner if no one used the buildings. Likewise, the accounting and human resource departments could generate better reports if managers from whom the information was obtained spent all their time completing lengthy forms. Coordination and support across functional departments are often difficult because departments are separated both geographically and psychologically, and members come to view problems only from their limited functional perspectives.

Product
Departmentalization:
When departments are created by assigning all jobs that produce the same product to a department.

Product Departmentalization. *Product departmentalization* involves grouping jobs that produce similar products, which typically occurs in large firms when it becomes difficult to coordinate the various functional departments. The members of a product-oriented department can develop greater expertise in researching, manufacturing, and distributing a specific product line. Managers have better control over the success or failure of each product if the authority, responsibility, and accountability are assigned according to products. This method is illustrated by the "brand" management structure that Procter & Gamble uses with its major products.

The product form of departmentalization has both advantages and disadvantages, and is often contrasted with the functional form of departmentalization. The major advantage is that it creates greater inter-departmental coordination, and focuses the efforts of each department on producing an effective and useful product. Companies organized by product are generally customer-oriented, and their employees tend to be cohesive and involved in their work.

The major disadvantage of organizing by product is that the resources and skills of the organization are not fully employed unless the organization is extremely large. For example, a computer-driven lathe machine that is used for only one product and sits idle much of the time represents an inefficient use of capital resources. Another disadvantage is that product-oriented departments usually lead to increased costs because of duplication of activities, especially staff functions.

Geographic
departmentalization:
Creating departments by assigning all the jobs in the same geographical region to the same department.

Geographic Departmentalization. Organizations use *geographic departmentalization* when they assign all the activities in an area to the same unit. This method typically occurs when organizations are geographically dispersed and a local manager is assigned to supervise both the functions and products in that area. This method is popular among retail companies that have stores located in many cities. Each store manager is ultimately responsible for recruiting, hiring, training, advertising, selling, and other diverse functions.

The major advantage of geographic departmentalization comes from minimizing problems created by distance, such as difficulties in communicating, observing, and making timely decisions. The disadvantage is that they miss the important advantages of functional and product departmentalization, which would have been superior if distance hadn't precluded them.

Customer
Departmentalization:
Creating departments by assigning all the jobs that serve a particular group of customers to the same department.

Customer Departmentalization. Occasionally the most effective way to combine jobs is to organize them according to the customers who are served. These advantages occur when groups of customers have distinct needs. Many universities, for example, have a separate evening class program or an executive MBA program because the interests of these students are significantly different from those of the regular day-time students. Many department stores have separate departments for men's clothing, women's clothing, maternity clothing, and children's clothing, because the customers served by each department have unique and separate interests.

Each form of departmentalization has both advantages and disadvantages. Therefore, managers are required to balance the strengths and weaknesses of each form and decide which will create the highest efficiency. In most situations, managers use a mixed strategy that combines two or more forms of departmentalization. For example, department stores combine the advantages of customer departmentalization with a functional form of organization among the staff units. The accounting, finance, human resource, and purchasing departments represent functional departmentalization, while the men's clothing, women's clothing, boys' clothing, and maternity departments represent customer departmentalization.

Span of Control

Span of control:
The number of subordinates assigned to a supervisor.

When selecting the *span of control*, managers decide how many people should be placed in a group under one supervisor; the number can vary along a continuum from few to many.

Span of Control: Number

Few   Many

The span-of-control decision has a major influence on the organization's shape and structure. Organizations that use a broad span of control have relatively few hierarchical levels, while a narrow span creates a tall organizational structure, as illustrated in Exhibit 13.2. Each hypothetical structure involves 31 positions. A narrow span of control, with only two subordinates per supervisor, produces a tall organizational structure with five hierarchical levels. However, a span of control of five produces a flat organizational structure with only three hierarchical levels.

A tall organizational structure with a narrow span of control allows for closer control over subordinates and greater personal contact between manager and subordinate. The risk, however, is that a manager with a narrow span of control comes to know only two or three subordinates very well, and fails to become acquainted with others in the hierarchy. Consequently, tall organizations often inhibit interpersonal communication within the organization.

During the 1940s and 1950s, management scholars tried to prescribe the ideal span of control. One scholar calculated the geometric increase in the number of relationships a manager must supervise as the span of control increased, and concluded that the maximum span of control should never exceed three or four subordinates.[2] In actual practice, however, several organizations had spans of control greater than 20, and the groups were supervised quite effectively. Consequently, it was concluded that the appropriate span of control should vary with the nature of the tasks being performed. Although a range of four to six subordinates is often recommended, a much larger span of control may be appropriate, depending on four situational variables:

Exhibit 13.2 Span of Control: Tall versus Flat Organizational Structures

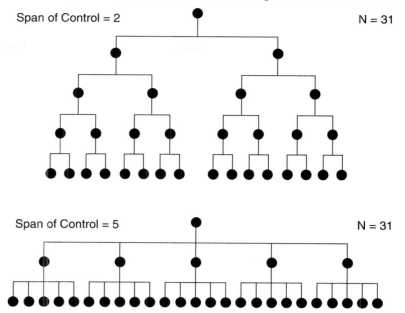

1. *Contact required.* Jobs that require frequent contact and a high degree of coordination between superior and subordinates should use narrower spans of control. For example, jobs in medical technology often require frequent consultation of team members with a supervisor; therefore, a large span of control would preclude the necessary sharing of ideas and information that typically must occur on an informal basis.
2. *Level of subordinates' education and training.* Large spans of control are appropriate for highly skilled employees and professionals who are well trained. They generally require less supervision because they know their jobs well and they largely supervise themselves.
3. *Ability to communicate.* Instructions, guidelines, and policies can be communicated to employees by a variety of methods. If all the necessary instructions can be written and then disseminated, it would be possible for one manager to supervise a large group. However, as communication becomes more difficult and job-related discussions become more important, a narrower span of control is appropriate, to avoid overloading a supervisor.
4. *Nature of the task.* Jobs that are repetitive and stable require less supervision, and are more amenable to wide spans of control. For this reason, some field supervisors are able to supervise as many as 60 to 75 field hands in harvesting agricultural crops. However, when tasks are changed frequently, a narrower span of control is appropriate.

There seems to be a natural tendency for managers to adopt narrow spans of control, which increases the number of hierarchical levels. However, productivity often increases after organizations have eliminated one or more hierarchical levels of administration, so companies are often encouraged to eliminate hierarchical levels by increasing spans of control.

Delegation of Authority

The fourth design issue concerns the delegation of authority. Decentralization involves distributing power and authority to lower-level supervisors and employees. The more decentralized an organization, the greater the extent to which the rank-and-file employees can participate in and accept responsibility for decisions concerning their jobs and the activities of the organization. Decision-making authority can vary along a continuum from *centralized* to *decentralized*.

Centralized authority:
Where the authority to make organizational decisions is retained by top managers in the central office.

Decentralized authority:
Where the authority to make organizational decisions is delegated to lower-level managers and supervisors.

Authority: Delegation

centralized   decentralized

Decentralization often leads to greater organizational effectiveness, since it allows greater autonomy and responsibility among lower-level employees, thereby more effectively using an organization's human resources. Supervisors in decentralized organizations typically report higher levels of job satisfaction and involvement, and they tend to be more productive because of increased autonomy and responsibility. A company that is struggling with declining sales may decide to decentralize its management structure, to make it more responsive to customers and more conducive to new-product development.

In spite of its benefits, however, decentralization is not universally superior and does not always contribute to greater organizational effectiveness. For example, one classic study discovered that decentralized control led to improved performance in research laboratories but caused poorer performance in production departments.[3] Several weaknesses of decentralization have been identified, suggesting that centralized decision making is sometimes superior.

1. Certain shared functions, especially staff functions, are more difficult to execute under decentralization.
2. Decentralization can create jurisdictional disputes and conflicts over priorities, since each unit essentially becomes an independent area.
3. Decentralization requires greater competence and expertise, and greater commitment on the part of decision makers, than centralized control does.
4. Decentralized decisions made by many lower-level managers create problems of coordination and integration. A decentralized organization could be very ineffective, because of inadequate coordination and integration.

To design an effective organizational structure, managers must select the optimal balance between centralized and decentralized authority. Power and authority should be decentralized to the extent that organizations use the knowledge and expertise of lower-level participants while maintaining sufficient centralization to ensure adequate coordination and control. Like the other concepts of organizational design, the ideal policy depends on the situation.

Coordinating Mechanisms

Organizations need to process information and coordinate the efforts of their members. Employees at lower levels need to perform activities consistent with top-level goals, and the managers at the top need to know about the activities and accomplishments of people at lower levels. Five primary methods are available for coordinating the activities of members, and these methods vary according to the amount of discretion workers are allowed.

Coordinating mechanisms: Personal discretion

Direct supervision and rules   Mutual adjustment

1. *Direct supervision.* All work is coordinated by supervisors through rules or specific instructions.
2. *Standardization of work processes.* Jobs that are highly routine, such as assembly-line jobs, can be coordinated through standard operating procedures or by the technology itself.
3. *Standardization of outputs.* When products must be produced according to technical specifications, these specifications may serve as an adequate basis for coordinating the activities. Individual workers are allowed some discretion in performing the work, provided the output meets the required specifications.
4. *Standardization of skills.* Highly skilled and trained employees coordinate their work by performing activities consistent with their technical training. A surgical team or an ambulance crew is often coordinated by having people perform their jobs according to the way they were trained.
5. *Mutual adjustment.* Activities that are constantly changing and uncertain are coordinated through mutual adjustment, which consists of a constant interchange of informal communication. Here, individuals have the greatest discretion and they coordinate their work through informal meetings, personal conversations, and liaison positions, mutually adjusting to one another's needs. Employees communicate with whomever they need to communicate, without regard for formal lines of communication.

A crucial issue in choosing a coordinating mechanism concerns the need for information and the ways in which information is collected, processed, and disseminated. The type of information collected by a driver's license bureau, for example, is mostly routine information that can be coordinated by rules and procedures. Fashion merchandisers, however, require extensive market information that they may obtain from a variety of irregular sources and disseminate informally to anyone who needs to know.

Coordinating mechanisms influence the degree of formalization in an organization. The term *formalization* refers to the degree to which rules and procedures guide the actions of employees. These rules and procedures can be either explicit or implicit. Explicit rules are written in job descriptions, policies and procedures manuals, or office memos. Implicit rules are often unwritten, and develop as employees establish their own ways of doing things over time.

Mutual Adjustment:
A means of achieving organizational coordination by allowing people to coordinate their work through informal processes, mutually adjusting to each other's needs.

Formalization:
The degree to which employee behaviors are guided by formal rules and procedures.

Although they are unwritten, implicit rules often become standard operating procedures with the same effect on employee behavior as explicit rules.[4]

In a highly formal organization, employees are required to follow strict rules and procedures that tell them exactly how to perform their work. Informal organizations have very few rules and procedures; the employees are largely free to structure their own jobs. Formal organizations tend to rely on direct supervision and standardization of work processes, while informal organizations tend to use mutual adjustment and standardization of skills. An example of a formal structure in a university would be an administrative agency, such as the student loans office, while an example of an informal structure would be an academic department, such as the sociology department.

Matrix Organizational Structure

Matrix Organizational Structure:
A combination of two different forms of departmentalization, usually functional and product departmentalization.

Some organizations have found that a combination of functional and product departmentalization provides the best reporting relationships and horizontal linkages. This dual structure, called a *matrix structure*, simultaneously organizes part of the organization along product lines and part of the organization along functional lines to gain the advantages of both, as illustrated in Exhibit 13.3.

In a matrix organization, each department reports simultaneously to both product managers and functional managers, who have equal authority within the organization. For example, a member of the legal department may be assigned to assist with the development of a specific product and assume the responsibility for all the legal activities associated with the development, production, and distribution of the product. This individual would report to both the product manager and the supervisor of the legal department.

Although dual structures are awkward, they can quickly create new products while retaining the benefits of a functional structure. Consequently, a matrix structure is particularly effective when environmental pressures create a demand for both technical quality (functional) and frequent new products (product). These dual pressures require a dual authority structure to deal with them. A matrix structure is particularly useful in an uncertain environment. Frequent external changes and high interdependence between departments require effective linkages between departments within an organization.

The disadvantage of a matrix structure is that it increases role ambiguity, stress, and anxiety, because people are assigned to more than one department. Matrix structures violate the principle of unity of command. The employees who work in a matrix structure often feel that inconsistent demands are made on them, causing unproductive conflicts that call for short-term crisis management. Occasionally, employees abuse the dual-authority structure by playing one manager against another, thereby generating excuses for their incompetence or inactivity.

UNIVERSAL THEORIES OF ORGANIZATIONAL DESIGN

The structure of an organization is determined by its division of labor, departmentalization, span of control, delegation of authority, and coordinating mechanisms. Different combinations of these factors can produce many different organizational structures. Which structure is the most effective? This

Exhibit 13.3 Matrix Organizational Structure

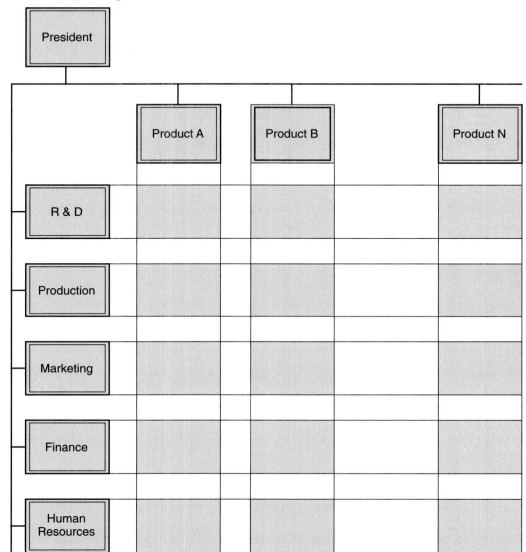

Universal Theories of Organizational Design:
Theories of organizational design that purport to be universally appropriate for every organization. Two widely contrasting universal design theories are bureaucracy and System Four.

section describes *universal theories of organizational design* that were meant to be ideal structures. Unfortunately, a universally superior organizational structure does not exist; the best structure depends on the situation, as explained in the next section.

Mechanistic versus Organic Organizational Structure

Two contrasting types of organizational structure have been recommended as universally appropriate for every organization. These two types differ greatly in the amount of formal structure and control they advocate. Several labels have been used to describe these two types. The labels used in this book are *mechanistic* versus *organic* organizational structures.

Mechanistic and organic organizational structures were first described in a classic study by Burns and Stalker.[5] They observed 20 industrial firms in England and discovered that the external environment was related to the internal organizational structure. When the external environment was stable, the internal organization was managed by rules, procedures, and a clear hierarchy of authority. Most managerial decisions were made at the top, and there was strong centralized authority. Burns and Stalker called this a *mechanistic organizational structure*.

Some organizations, those in rapidly changing environments, had a much different organizational structure. The internal organization was much more adaptive, free-flowing, and spontaneous. Rules and regulations were generally not written, and those that were written were often ignored. People had to find their own way within the system and learn what to do. The hierarchy of authority was not clear, and decision-making authority was broadly decentralized. Burns and Stalker called this an *organic organizational structure*.

The differences between an organic and mechanistic organizational structure are illustrated in Exhibit 13.4. In a mechanistic structure, the work is divided into highly specialized tasks that are rigidly defined by a formal job description. In an organic structure, however, most tasks are not so highly specialized; employees are often expected to learn how to perform a variety of tasks and to frequently adjust and redefine their jobs as the situation changes. In a mechanistic structure, communication patterns follow the formal chain of command between superiors and subordinates. In an organic structure, however, communication is horizontal, and employees talk with whomever they need to in order to do their work.

Mechanistic and organic structures differ in each of the five dimensions of organizational structure, as illustrated in Exhibit 13.5. In addition to having highly specialized jobs, mechanistic structures are characterized by homogeneous departmentalization, a narrow span of control, highly centralized delegation of authority, and coordination through direct supervision and rules. Organic structures are just the opposite. The labor is divided in such a way that the level of specialization is reduced, the jobs are organized into heterogeneous departments, there is a broad span of control, decision-making authority is widely decentralized, and work is coordinated by mutual adjustment.

Bureaucratic Organizational Structure

Perhaps the best description of a mechanistic organizational structure is Max Weber's description of *bureaucracy*.[6] Highly bureaucratic organizations have a very mechanistic organizational structure. Unfortunately, the word bureaucracy is associated with a variety of negative feelings. Many people associate bureaucracy with excessive red tape, procedural delays, and organizational inefficiency. These connotations are not consistent with Max Weber's description of bureaucracy. According to Max Weber, a bureaucracy was a sociological concept that referred to the rational collection of clearly organized activities. The word *bureaucracy* comes from the French word *bureau*, which means "office." In short, a bureaucracy is a collection of carefully organized offices performing specialized functions according to clearly defined rules and procedures. Weber's description of bureaucracy was intended as a description of the ideal form of a large organizational structure. The major attributes of

Mechanistic organizational structure:
A formal organizational structure characterized by highly specialized tasks that are carefully and rigidly defined, with a strict hierarchy of authority to control them. Bureaucracy is a type of mechanistic structure.

Organic organizational structure:
A type of organization structure characterized by people who work together in an informal arrangement, sharing ideas and information, and performing a variety of tasks based on whatever is needed to accomplish the group's task.

Bureaucracy:
An organizational structure that is characterized by an elaborate division of labor based on functional specialization, a hierarchy of authority assigned to different offices, a system of rules explaining how everyone is to perform, and impersonal relationships.

Exhibit 13.4 Mechanistic versus Organic organizational Structures

Mechanistic	**Organic**
1. Tasks are divided into separate, specialized jobs.	1. Tasks may not be highly specialized, and employees may perform a variety of tasks to accomplish the group's task.
2. Tasks are clearly and rigidly defined.	2. Tasks are not elaborately specified: they may be adjusted and redefined through employee interactions.
3. There is a strict hierarchy of authority and control with many rules.	3. There is an informal hierarchy of authority and control with few rules.
4. Knowledge and control of tasks are centralized, and tasks are directed from the top of the organization.	4. Knowledge and control of tasks are located anywhere in the organization.
5. Communication is vertical throughout the formal hierarchy.	5. Communication is horizontal; employees talk to whomever they need to communicate with.

Exhibit 13.5 Structural Differences between Mechanistic and Organic Organizations

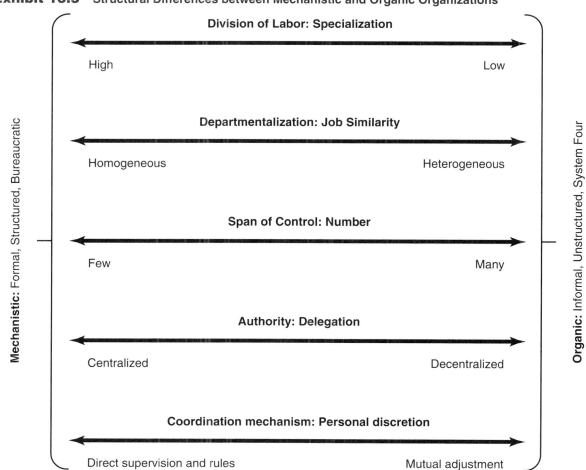

this ideal form were rationality and efficiency. A bureaucratic structure was a well organized collection of offices that combined the efforts of large numbers of people through a system of rules and procedures. Weber's description included the following identifying characteristics.

1. *A division of labor based on functional specialization.* All tasks necessary for accomplishing the goals of the organization are divided into highly specialized jobs. Such job specialization allows jobholders to become expert in their jobs and to be held responsible for the effective performance of their duties.

2. *A well defined hierarchy of authority.* Each officeholder in the organization is accountable to a superior. The authority of superiors is based on expert knowledge and legitimized by the fact that it is delegated from the top of the hierarchy. In this way, a clearly defined chain of command is created.

3. *A system of rules covering the rights and duties of employees.* Each task is performed according to a consistent system of abstract rules to ensure uniformity and coordination of different tasks. Through a system of clearly defined rules, officeholders can eliminate any uncertainty in performing their tasks that is caused by individual differences.

4. *Impersonal relationships.* Each officeholder maintains a social distance from subordinates and clients, and conducts the business of the office in a formal, impersonal manner. Strict adherence to the rules and impersonal relationships ensure that personalities do not interfere with the efficient accomplishment of the office's objectives. There should be no favoritism resulting from personal friendships or ingratiating behaviors.

5. *Promotion and selection based on technical competence.* Employment in a bureaucratic organization is based on technical qualifications, and employees are protected against arbitrary dismissal. Similarly, promotions are based on seniority and achievement. Employment in the bureaucracy is viewed as a lifelong career, designed to create loyalty and commitment.

6. *Written communications and records.* All administrative acts, decisions, and rules are recorded in writing. Since verbal conversations and discussions cannot be filed, all decisions, complaints, and administrative acts are to be written and filed. Record keeping provides an organizational memory, and written documents provide continuity over time.

Many of the characteristics that Weber recommended for an ideal bureaucracy seem quite obvious to us today because we are surrounded by organizations that have rules, a division of labor, written documents, and a hierarchy of authority. These characteristics provide an impersonal means of controlling organizations by guaranteeing that dependable work will be performed by qualified employees under the impartial direction of rational supervisors. These rational characteristics, however, were not so obvious a century ago when there were very few large organizations. Most organizations were family operated, and characterized by nepotism and unfair treatment. Weber's recommendation of a rational, bureaucratic ideal was intended both to eliminate favoritism and increase organizational efficiency.

Advantages of a Bureaucracy. Bureaucracy has survived and even thrived because its advantages outweigh its disadvantages. The advantages of a bureaucracy stem logically from its ideal characteristics. At its best, a bureau-

Exhibit 13.6 Advantages and Disadvantages of Bureaucracies

Advantages	Disadvantages
1. Technical efficiency	1. Rigidity of behavior
2. Elimination of favoritism	2. Bureaucratic personality
3. Predictability of performance	3. Inversion of means and ends
4. Job security	4. Resistance to change
5. Technical competence	5. Peter Principle
6. Minimum direction needed	
7. Avoids impulsive action	

cracy is a smooth-running organization in which decisions and activities are processed efficiently and all members are treated equitably. Seven major benefits have been attributed to bureaucracy, as summarized in Exhibit 13.6.

1. *Technical efficiency.* The chief benefit of a bureaucracy is that the activities and functions have been carefully analyzed and rationally organized in a way that creates maximum efficiency. The process of dividing the labor into highly specialized jobs, assigning them to different offices, and coordinating them through a carefully designed system of rules and procedures produces what has sometimes been called *machine-like efficiency*.

2. *Elimination of favoritism.* By following the correct procedures and administering the rules impartially, clients and officeholders are treated fairly. No one is treated with special favors because of personal friendships or ingratiating behaviors. The rules and procedures are administered without regard to family, wealth, or status. This impartial treatment is consistent with bureaucratic ideals that condemn nepotism, partiality, and capricious judgment.

3. *Predictability in performance.* Strict adherence to clearly defined rules and procedures leads to greater predictability of performance. Both customers and employees know in advance the outcome of a decision. For example, if the vacation policy allows three weeks' paid vacation after five years of service, all employees with at least five years of service can expect to receive a three-week paid vacation.

4. *Job security.* By following the rules and doing what the handbook or procedures manual says they are supposed to do, officeholders are assured that they will not be fired. Such a tenure policy maximizes vocational security. Officeholders tend to view their employment in the organization as a lifelong career. Such an outlook minimizes turnover and engenders a high degree of loyalty and commitment.

5. *Technical competence.* Since officeholders are hired on the basis of their ability rather than on the basis of whom they know, they are highly trained, competent officials.

6. *Minimum direction needed.* Because a bureaucracy has been rationally designed, and the officeholders are trained experts who are expected to follow standard rules and operating procedures, very little day-to-day direction is needed to keep the bureaucracy functioning. Like a carefully designed machine that operates smoothly after it is turned on, a bureaucracy is expected to operate smoothly with little direction or added input.

7. *Avoids impulsive decisions.* Since a bureaucracy operates according to standard operating procedures, it is not possible for an impulsive idea on

the part of one officeholder to immediately disrupt the entire bureaucracy. Since they must be coordinated with other officeholders, new ideas and changes cannot be implemented quickly. Although reducing the possibility of impulsive action is sometimes an advantage, it can also be a disadvantage when change is required, which explains why bureaucracies are often associated with red tape and resistance to change.

Disadvantages of Bureaucracy. Although Weber described bureaucracies as ideal structures, they are not without their problems. Over the years, several dysfunctional consequences have been identified. Some of these dysfunctional consequences are not created because the bureaucracy fails to operate properly. Instead, they are created because the bureaucracy is functioning exactly as it should; the problems are inherent to the bureaucratic structure itself. In other words, these problems cannot be solved by having the bureaucracy operate more effectively; a stricter application of bureaucratic principles would exacerbate the problems.

1. *Rigidity of behavior.* In a bureaucracy, officeholders are expected to know the rules and procedures and to follow them precisely. Bureaucracies control individual behavior by demanding strict rule compliance. However, as employees follow the rules more precisely, their behavior becomes more rigid and more insensitive to individual problems. This rigid behavior inevitably leads to conflict with clients and customers. Many times people think their personal situation represents an exception to the rule, and occasionally they are right. Wise bureaucrats know when to deviate from the rules and accept responsibility for their decisions, but bureaucrats who have been intimidated or threatened seek to protect themselves by following the rules. As the level of conflict rises, the dysfunctional consequences of a bureaucratic structure become more obvious. Instead of responding to the complaints of clients and their demands for individual treatment, bureaucrats respond by following the rules more strictly. By strict adherence to the rules in their handbooks and policy manuals, they are able to defend their actions in the face of conflict, but their client relationships suffer.

2. *Bureaucratic personality.* Employees who work in bureaucratic organizations sometimes develop unhealthy personalities that are excessively power-oriented. Officeholders come to believe that moral decisions of right or wrong are defined by higher-level officers and by the rules they are expected to follow. Following the rules becomes more important than the possibly inhumane treatment required by strict rule compliance. For example, a pregnant student may be required to walk back to her apartment in a storm because she forgot to bring her computer lab pass to show that she is registered in a computer class.

Means-ends inversion:
Where the means of accomplishing a goal become so important that people focus on that activity rather than what the activity is intended to accomplish.

3. *Inversion of means and ends.* Rigid adherence to rules and regulations often results in a situation in which adherence to the rules becomes more important than achieving organizational goals, a condition called ***means-ends inversion***: the means become more important than the end. Although the rules were originally designed to further organizational success, each officeholder comes to see the rules and regulations of that office as the ultimate goal. For example, advertising campaigns, sales

incentives, and other programs are designed to increase sales. But each of these programs can come to be viewed as an end in itself, so that an elaborate awards banquet becomes so important that it dominates everyone's time and attention, and replaces efforts to achieve high sales.

4. *Resistance to change.* As noted earlier, bureaucracies are intentionally designed to resist rapid change. This resistance is created by several aspects of a bureaucracy. First, officeholders tend to avoid responsibility when they are faced with decisions they prefer not to make. By redefining the problem, most officeholders are able to say, "That's not my job." Second, bureaucrats tend to be isolated from external feedback and outside evaluation. Bureaucracies tend to focus on their own internal functioning to the exclusion of external feedback. Their failure to respond to external evaluation prevents them from making corrective adjustments. Third, bureaucracies are not designed to foster setting or accomplishing goals. Rules and procedures focus the efforts of officeholders on activities rather than outcomes. Opportunities to produce innovative products or services tend to be overlooked because of a preoccupation with bureaucratic procedures. Fourth, bureaucracies move at a painfully slow pace when making complex decisions. The delay occurs because of the number of people who must concur before a decision is made about important issues. After the decision is finally made, there is an additional delay while new rules and procedures for each officeholder are created.

5. *The Peter Principle.* The Peter Principle was proposed as a satirical and humorous description of the incompetence that often occurs in bureaucratic organizations.[7] This principle states that in a hierarchy, every employee tends to rise to his or her level of incompetence. In a bureaucracy, promotions are supposed to be based on demonstrated ability; the most competent individual at one level is promoted to the next level. The Peter Principle explains, however, that competence at one level does not guarantee competence at the next level. The skills required for a subordinate position are frequently different from those required for success at the next level. Therefore, the most competent individuals at one level are promoted from level to level within the organization until they reach their level of incompetence, at which time they are no longer considered for promotion. An example of the Peter Principle is the promotion of competent technical or sales personnel into administrative positions for which they are ill-suited by temperament. Outstanding grade school teachers, for example, do not necessarily make outstanding grade school principals. According to the Peter Principle, the only effective work that occurs in bureaucracies is performed by individuals who have not yet reached their level of incompetence.

Peter Principle:
A satirical explanation for incompetence in bureaucracies, suggesting that people rise to their level of incompetence.

System Four Organizational Structure

System Four:
A type of organizational structure that is characterized by responsibility and initiative on the part of members, widely shared decision-making authority, decentralized decision making, and goal setting by employees.

Rensis Likert proposed a theory of organizational design quite different from bureaucracy that is known as a System Four organizational design.[8] Likert recommended his System Four as the ideal way to design an organization, and extensive research by Likert and others has supported his theory. The central premise of Likert's theory is that leaders develop different management systems that can be described along a continuum, from exploitive and authoritative at one end to participative and group-oriented at the other end.

1. The *exploitive-authoritative* style, System One, is characterized by the threat of punishment, hostile attitudes, downward communication, and distrust. Top management makes all the decisions and sets all the goals.
2. The *benevolent-authoritative* style, System Two, is slightly less hostile and threatening, since top management behaves more benevolently, but all decisions, goal setting, and communication are directly under the control of top management.
3. The *consultative* style, System Three, involves greater coordination between upper and lower levels of management. The ideas and interests of lower-level employees are considered, and lower-level employees have a limited opportunity to contribute to the decision making and goal setting.
4. The *participative-group oriented* style, System Four, involves open communication, participative decision making within groups, a decentralized authority structure, broad participation in the goal setting processes whereby realistic objectives are set, and leadership processes that demonstrate a high level of confidence and trust between superiors and subordinates.

Although Likert did not advocate a specific span of control or form of departmentalization (he admitted that these and other design decisions depended on the situation), he argued that higher-level principles should guide management decisions in the design of an organization. Likert advocated three universal principles: (1) the principle of supportive relationships, (2) the use of group decision making, and (3) the creation of high performance goals.

Principle of supportive relationships:
A universal principle that suggests that every interaction between superiors and subordinates should be transacted in a way that builds and encourages each in the performance of their respective duties.

1. The ***principle of supportive relationships*** says that all employees should be treated in ways that build and maintain their sense of personal worth and importance.[9] All interactions between superiors and subordinates must be perceived by subordinates as contributing to their personal worth and increasing their sense of human dignity. Likert assessed the degree to which relationships are supportive by asking such questions as: How much confidence and trust do you feel your superior has in you? To what extent does your boss convey to you a feeling of confidence that you can do your job successfully? To what extent is your boss interested in helping you to achieve and maintain a good income?

Linking Pins:
People who link different organizational units by being a member of one group and the leader of the group below.

2. Likert believed that groups were universally superior to the traditional hierarchical control in decision making and leadership. System Four management involves management by groups and recognizes overlapping group membership; each supervisor of a group also serves as a subordinate in another group at the next level above. Those who hold overlapping memberships are called ***linking pins***. At each hierarchical level, all members of a work group who are affected by the outcome of a decision should be involved in it, and it is the leader's responsibility to build an effective team. This principle has important implications for design decisions, since it encourages greater delegation of authority and coordination through the mutual adjustment of self-managing teams.
3. To achieve high levels of organizational performance, Likert argued that both managers and subordinates must have high performance aspira-

tions. However, these high performance goals cannot be imposed on employees. System Four provides a mechanism through group decision making and overlapping group memberships to set high-level goals that satisfy both individual and organizational aspirations.

CONTINGENCY THEORIES OF ORGANIZATIONAL DESIGN

Contingency design theories:
Organizational design theories that claim that the ideal structure depends on the organization's requirements.

Principles of organizational design have shifted from universal design theories to *contingency design theories* that try to identify the appropriate design features for each situation. Two research studies have contributed greatly to our understanding of contingency design theories. One line of research demonstrates that differences in technology determine the most effective organizational design, while the second suggests that differences in environmental uncertainty and the demands for processing information are the crucial factors.

Technology

Technology:
The knowledge, tools, techniques, and actions that are used to transform organizational inputs into outputs. Essentially, technology is the organization's transformation process.

Technology refers to the organization's transformation process and includes the knowledge, skills, abilities, machinery, and work procedures that are used in the transformation process. Every organization has a unique type of technology, and Joan Woodward, a British industrial sociologist, demonstrated that an organization's technology should determine how it is designed.[10] Her research surveyed 100 manufacturing firms on a wide range of structural characteristics, such as span of control, levels of management, ratios of management to clerical workers, and management style. Her data also included measures of performance regarding economic success.

When she examined the relationships between structure and performance for all 100 companies, she found no relationships. However, when she divided the companies into three categories according to their technology, she found that the successful companies in each category had structures that fit their technology. The three technology groups were small-batch manufacturing, such as a printing company; mass production, such as an assembly-line firm; and continuous process, such as an oil refinery. In each of the three technology groupings, the successful firms had ratios and numbers that were close to the median, while the unsuccessful firms had ratios and numbers that were much higher or lower than the median. Successful small-batch and continuous process organizations tended to have organic structures, while successful mass production organizations tended to have mechanistic structures.

Other research has likewise shown that an organization's structure needs to match the *routineness* of its processes. Routineness refers to the degree of continuity, automation, and rigidity in the production process; the technology would be considered extremely routine if the production process were totally automated and produced a consistent product. The structural variables most frequently analyzed in technology studies are the degree of centralization, formalization, and specialization; all three of these variables are positively related to routineness. According to this research, when the technology is highly routine (1) decision making should be centralized, (2) the rules and procedures should be formalized, and (3) the process should be decomposed and performed by specialized people and equipment.[11]

Environmental Uncertainty

The degree of instability and uncertainty in the environment is another important situational variable that influences the appropriate type of organizational structure. Different organizational structures are required in order to cope with environmental uncertainty. Research fairly consistently indicates that organic structures tend to be most effective in uncertain environments, while mechanistic structures are more effective in stable environments. The classic study examining the effects of environmental uncertainty on organizational structure was conducted by Paul Lawrence and Jay Lorsch of Harvard University.[12]

Lawrence and Lorsch examined organizations in three industries: plastics, packaged food products, and paper containers. These three industries were selected because significant differences were found in the degree of environmental uncertainty. The environment of the plastics firms was extremely uncertain because of rapidly changing technology and customer demand. Decisions about new products were required, even though feedback about the accuracy of the decisions often involved considerable delay. In contrast, the paper container firms faced a highly certain environment. Only minor changes in technology had occurred in the previous 20 years, and these firms focused on producing high-quality, standardized containers, and delivering them to the customer quickly. The consequences of decisions could be ascertained in a short period. Between these two extremes, the producers of packaged foods faced a moderately uncertain environment.

In analyzing how these firms interacted with their environments, Lawrence and Lorsch identified two key concepts: differentiation and integration. *Differentiation* is the degree of segmentation of the organizational system into subsystems, which is similar to the concepts of specialization of labor and departmentalization. However, differentiation also considers the behavioral attributes of employees in highly specialized departments. As noted earlier, members of highly specialized functional departments tend to adopt a rather narrow-minded, department-oriented focus that emphasizes the achievement of departmental rather than organizational goals.

The consequence of high differentiation is that greater coordination among departments is required. More time and resources must be devoted to achieve coordination, since the attitudes, goals, and work orientations among highly specialized departments differ so widely. Lawrence and Lorsch developed the concept of *integration* to refer to this coordinating activity.

Lawrence and Lorsch found that environmental uncertainty was related to the amount of differentiation and integration used in each industry. For example, the firms in the container industry faced a fairly stable environment, so they did not need to be highly differentiated, and they tended to adopt a mechanistic structure. The most successful container companies were organized along functional lines, with a highly centralized authority structure. Coordination was achieved through direct supervision, with formal written schedules. A bureaucratic structure was consistent with the container industry's degree of environmental certainty.

In the plastics industry, however, where companies face an extremely uncertain environment, the most successful plastics companies adopted organic

Differentiation:
The degree of segmentation or division of labor into specialized jobs. It includes the behavioral attributes brought about by creating a narrow, department-oriented focus in the minds of individuals.

Integration:
The coordinating activity that is used to achieve a unity of effort among various subsystems within an organization. The five major methods of integration include direct supervision, standardization of work processes, standardization of outputs, standardization of skills, and mutual adjustment.

structures. A highly unstable environment required that these companies have a highly differentiated structure with highly specialized internal departments of marketing, production, and research and development, to deal with uncertainty in the external environment. Coordination was achieved through mutual adjustment, ad hoc teams that cut across departments, and special coordinators who served as liaisons between departments. The most successful plastics firms achieved high levels of differentiation and high levels of integration to coordinate them.

Lawrence and Lorsch's study contributes to our understanding of organizational design by showing the effects of environmental uncertainty on organizational structure. When the environment is highly uncertain, frequent changes require more information processing to achieve coordination, so special integrators and coordinating mechanisms are a necessary addition to the organization's structure. These integrators are called *liaison personnel, brand managers*, or *product coordinators*. Organizations that face a highly uncertain environment and a highly differentiated structure may have a fourth of their management personnel assigned to integration activities, such as serving on committees, task forces, or in liaison roles. Organizations that face very simple, stable environments may not have anyone assigned to a full-time integration role.

The analysis of Lawrence and Lorsch can be extended from the organizational to the departmental level within an organization. A large firm may need to organize its production department quite differently from its research department. One department may tend toward a mechanistic design and the other toward an organic design. The differences between these two departments are due to the different environments to which the two departments must adapt. For example, if a marketing department of a large firm faced an extremely unstable environment because of transportation problems across international boundaries, the marketing department would need to adopt an organic structure to respond to rapid developments. In contrast, the production department may face a very stable environment that allows for long production runs of standardized products. In this case, a mechanistic structure with formal bureaucratic procedures would be most appropriate for the production department.

Information Processing

The key integrating concept that explains the relationship among environmental uncertainty, technology, and organizational structure is the way the organization processes information.[13] Information flows into the organization from various environmental sectors, and the organization must respond and adapt to this information. The more rapid the changes in the external environment, the greater the need for incoming information. The consequence of environmental uncertainty on managers is an increase in the flow of information, which leads to a communication overload. In essence, the organization becomes inundated with exceptional cases that require individual attention. As a greater number of nonroutine demands are made on the organization from the environment, managers are required to be more and more involved in day-to-day operations. Problems develop as plans become obsolete and the various coordination functions break down. An effective organization requires a structure that allows it to adapt to such a situation.

Organic structures can deal with greater amounts of uncertainty than mechanistic structures can. Organic structures have more highly connected communication networks that permit the efficient use of individuals as problem solvers, and increase the opportunity for feedback. Because highly connected networks do not depend on any one individual, they are less susceptible to information overload or saturation. But while organic structures are able to deal effectively with greater amounts of uncertainty than mechanistic structures, there are costs associated with being able to process more information. Organic structures consume more time, effort, and energy, and are less subject to managerial control. Thus, the benefits of increased efficiency and capacity to process information must be weighed against the costs of less control and greater effort and time.

Organizations in a dynamic and complex environment cannot rely on traditional information processing and control techniques where all information is communicated through a chain of command. Changes in market demand, uncertain resources, and new technology disrupt the organization's plans and require adjustments while the task is being performed. Immediate adjustments to production schedules and job assignments disrupt the organization. Coordination is made more difficult because it is impossible to forecast operations or revise standard operating rules or procedures. Organizations must obtain information that reflects the environmental changes.

Discussion Questions

1. Explain why the functional form of departmentalization tends to be the most efficient, and why product departmentalization tends to be the most customer-oriented. Provide specific examples.

2. It has been suggested that companies should turn their company charts upside down and put power in the hands of the front-line employees who deal directly with customers. What does it mean to turn an organization's chart upside down? Is this change just window dressing in the form of customer service, or does it represent a significant change in decision making and responsibility?

3. What are the advantages and disadvantages of a matrix organizational design? When would you recommend using it or discourage using it?

4. In recent years, some organizations have thrown away their organization charts and disregarded formal lines of authority. These organizations are typically small, innovative companies that appear to be highly successful. Their success has caused some to suggest that all organizations need to get rid of their organization charts and formal structure. Do you agree? How important is organizational structure? Describe a situation in which it would be appropriate to disregard organizational structure.

5. What are the major advantages of a bureaucracy? Does a bureaucracy deserve the negative reaction it provokes in most people? Describe a time in your life when you have experienced one of the dysfunctional consequences of a bureaucracy.

6. Explain why an unstable environment and extensive demands for information processing are more conducive to an organic structure. Provide illus-

trations of contrasting companies that are in stable and unstable environments and therefore need to be organized differently.

Notes

1. An early discussion of departmentalization is found in Luther Gulick and Lyndall Urwick (eds.), *Papers on the Science of Administration* (New York: Institute of Public Administration, 1937).

2. V.A. Graicunas, "Relationship in Organization," *Bulletin of the International management Institute* 7 (March 1933): 39–42; reprinted in Luther H. Gulick and Lyndall F. Urwick (eds.), *Papers on the Science of Administration* (New York: Institute of Public Administration, Columbia University, 1937): 182–187; Arthur G. Bedeian, "Vytautas Andrius Graicunas: A Biographical Note," *Academy of Management Journal* 17 (1974): 347–49; Lyndall F. Urwick, "V.A. Graicunas and the Span of Control," *Academy of Management Journal* 17 (1974): 349–54.

3. Paul R. Lawrence and Jay W. Lorsch, *Organization and Environment* (Boston: Harvard Business School, Division of Research, 1967).

4. Rachid M. Zeffane, "Centralization or Formalization? Indifference Curves for Strategies of Control," *Organization Studies* 10 (Summer 1989): 326–52.

5. T. Burns and G. M. Stalker, *The Management of Innovation* (London: Tavistock Institute, 1961).

6. Max Weber, *The Theory of Social and Economic Organization,* trans. A.M. Henderson and T. Parsons (New York: Free Press, 1947).

7. Lawrence F. Peter and Raymond Hull, *The Peter Principle* (New York: Morrow, 1969); Donald E. Walker, "The Peter Principle: A Simple Put-On About Complex Issues," *Change* 17 (July–August 1985): 11.

8. Rensis Likert, *New Patterns of Management* (New York: McGraw-Hill, 1961); Rensis Likert, *The Human Organization* (New York: McGraw-Hill, 1967).

9. Likert, *New Patterns of Management,* p. 103.

10. Joan Woodward, *Industrial Organization: Theory and Practice* (London: Oxford University Press, 1965).

11. C. Chet Miller, William H. Glick, Yau-De Wang, and George P. Huber, "Understanding Technology-Structure Relationships: Theory Development and Meta-Analytic Theory Testing," *Academy of Management Journal* 34 (1991): 370–99; Stephen R. Barley, "The Alignment of Technology and Structure Through Roles and Networks," *Administrative Science Quarterly* 35 (March 1990): 61–103.

12. Paul R. Lawrence and J. W. Lorsch, *Organization and Environment* (Boston: Harvard Business School, 1967); Paul R. Lawrence and J. W. Lorsch, "Differentiation and Integration in Complex Organizations," *Administrative Science Quarterly* 12 (1967): 1–47.

13. Michael L. Tushman and David A. Nadler, "Information Processing as an Integrating Concept in Organizational Design," *Academy of Management Review* 3 (1978): 613–24.

Bureaucratic Battles and Unorganized Efficiency

During his undergraduate years, Jim Tolman worked three summers for Land Managers, a real estate service company that provided accounting, legal, financial, and computer assistance to real estate investors. When he was hired, Jim was simply told to help some of the other employees or find his own clients to service. He was not assigned to a department, he was not given a job description, and he was not told when to start work. He was given a desk and a list of the five company officers, and told to report to one of them at least monthly to justify what he was doing. The company had almost no formal policies or rules and no standard operating procedures, yet it seemed to function very efficiently.

Because Land Managers functioned so well with a loose structure, Jim could not understand why the university he was attending had so many formal rules and procedures. The formality of the rules was especially troublesome when Jim tried to get a tuition refund for a seminar that was canceled due to insufficient enrollment. When he asked for a refund from the registration office where he originally paid the tuition, he was told they didn't give refunds, only the finance office gives refunds. When he went to the finance office, however, he was told that before they could give him his full refund they would need verification that the course had been canceled, and this verification would need to come from the department that offered the course.

When Jim asked the department chairman to send a memo to the finance office explaining that the course had been canceled, the chairman refused. He said that the cancellation decision was not made by the department but by an "archaic rule" within the college to which he objected. He instructed Jim to go to the dean's office to complain about the canceled course and to get a memo from someone there.

When he got to the dean's office, he learned that the dean was out of town for two weeks and no one else would help him. Both the dean's secretary and the associate dean said course listings were under the direction of the departments and the memo would have to come from the department.

When he returned to make an appointment with the department chairman, Jim was frustrated and angry. He felt trapped in the middle of a bureaucratic battle that was beyond his control, and he expressed his irritation to the department secretary. After learning of his plight, she told Jim that she knew someone who worked in the finance office and offered to call her and say that the course was canceled. Jim waited for her to make the call and then returned to the finance office for his refund.

Questions

1. Should the university be as loosely structured as the real estate company?
2. Are the elaborate rules and procedures in universities either necessary or desirable? Could a university operate with a more loosely organized structure, like that of the real estate company?
3. What are the benefits of rules and formal procedures? When do they make organizations more effective?

Profiling Organizational Characteristics

Purpose. The purpose of this exercise is to improve your skill at diagnosing the effectiveness of an organization. This exercise is based on Rensis Likert's research, which identifies four significantly different management systems and the variables that characterize each system.

Activity. This exercise works best if all class members describe the same organization. However, if some have not experienced the same organization, they should select another organization that they know well enough to describe. Use the scales in Chart 1 to describe this organization. As you describe it, try to think of specific incidents you have personally experienced or illustrations you have heard of.

Discussion. Compare your evaluations with the evaluations of others who described the same organization. To what extent did you agree? If your evaluations were significantly different, talk about the differences and try to identify the specific experiences that led to your disagreements. Likert argued that every organization would be more effective if it moved closer to a System Four organization. How close is your organization to the System Four, and do you think it would be more effective if it were closer? Is it realistic or possible for your organization to become a System Four organization?

Chart 1   Profile of Organizational Characteristics

	Organizational Variables	System 1	System 2	System 3	System 4
Leadership	How much confidence is shown in subordinates?	None	Condescending	Substantial	Complete
	How free do they feel to talk to superiors about their job?	Seldom	Sometimes	Usually	Always
	Are subordinates' ideas sought and used, if worthy?	Seldom	Sometimes	Usually	Always
Motivation	Is predominant use made of 1 fear, 2 threats, 4 punishment, 4 rewards, 5 involvement?	1,2,3 occasionally 4	4, some 3	4, some 3 and 5	5, 4 based on group
	Where is responsibility felt for achieving organizational goals?	Mostly at top	Top and middle	Fairly general	At all levels
	How much cooperative teamwork exists?	None	Little	Some	Great Deal
Communication	What is the direction of information flow?	Downward	Mostly downward	Down and up	Down, up, and sideways
	How is downward communication accepted?	With suspicion	Possibly with suspicion	With caution	With a receptive mind
	How accurate is upward communication?	Often wrong	Censored for the boss	Limited accuracy	Accurate
	How well do superiors know problems faced by subordinates?	Know little	Some knowledge	Quite well	Very well
Decisions	At what level are decisions made?	Mostly at top	Policy at top, some delegation	Broad policy at top, more delegation	Throughout, but well integrated
	Are subordinates involved in decisions related to their work?	Not at all	Occasionally consulted	Generally consulted	Fully involved
	What does the decision-making process contribute to motivation?	Nothing, often weakens it	Relatively little	Some contribution	Substantial contribution
Goals	How are organizational goals established?	Orders issued	Orders, some comments invited	After discussion, by orders	By group action (except in crisis)
	How much covert resistance to goals is present?	Strong resistance	Moderate resistance	Some resistance at times	Little or none
Control	How concentrated are review and control functions?	Highly at top	Relatively highly at top	Moderate delegation to lower levels	Quite widely shared
	Is there an informal organization resisting the formal one?	Yes	Usually	Sometimes	No—same goals as formal
	What are cost, productivity, and other control data used for?	Policing, punishment	Reward and punishment	Reward, some self-guidance	Self-guidance problem solving

Source: From *The Human Organization* by Renis Likert. Copyright © 1967 by McGraw-Hill Companies, Inc. Reproduced with permission of The McGraw-Hill Companies.

CHAPTER 14

Organizational Culture

Chapter Outline

Defining Organizational Culture
  Organizational Climate
  Organizational Culture
Development of Organizational Culture
  Founder Expectations
  Member Contributions
  Historical Accommodations
Maintaining Organizational Culture
  Employee Selection
  Reward Allocations
  Leader Behaviors
  Rites and Ceremonies
  Stories and Symbols
  Reactions to Problems
Effects of Culture
  Worker Attitudes and Behavior
  Culture and Ethical Behavior
  International Cultural Differences
Changing Organizational Culture

DEFINING ORGANIZATIONAL CULTURE

Organizational culture consists of those socially acquired rules of conduct that are shared by members of the organization. Some researchers believe that some aspects of an organization's culture are so intangible and pervasive that even the members of the organization cannot be expected to describe them accurately. Nevertheless, an understanding of organizational culture is essential to building effective organizations. Like the powerful undercurrents of ocean tides and rivers that move mighty ships, or the hidden icebergs that can destroy these ships, an organization's culture affects the entire organization.

Culture defines the basic organizational values, and communicates to new members the correct ways to think and act and the ways things ought to be done. Culture enhances the stability of the organization and helps members interpret organizational activities and events. The focus of culture is to provide members with a sense of identity and to generate within them a commitment to the beliefs and values of the organization. In this chapter we define culture and explain how it develops, how it is maintained, how it affects organizational events, and how it can be changed.

Organizational Climate

Organizational Climate:
The characteristics describing an organization that are relatively visible and stable, but amenable to change.

Organizational Culture:
The shared beliefs and expectations among the members of an organization that are relatively enduring and resistant to change.

Each organization has its own unique constellation of characteristics and properties. *Organizational climate* and *organizational culture* are two terms that have been used to describe organizations and their subunits. Although these two terms are used interchangeably and refer to similar phenomena, a subtle distinction is often made regarding their permanence: *culture* generally refers to organizational rules and beliefs that are relatively enduring and resistant to change, whereas *climate* is used to describe characteristics that are temporary and capable of being changed. Climate typically refers to people's attitudes and how they feel about the organization. For example, we might characterize an organization's climate as "supportive," "trusting," or perhaps "fearful" or "hostile." These attitudes and feelings are often a function of the organization's culture. The weather has been used as a popular analogy to explain the differences between culture and climate. Like daily weather patterns, organizational climate (employee attitudes) can fluctuate from time to time because of organizational changes. Culture, however, is like the seasons of the year, which change slowly over time. The seasons are associated with stable and enduring weather characteristics that transcend daily variations.

Organizational Culture

The people who study culture have tried to make a clear distinction between culture and climate. *Culture* refers to something that is more stable and enduring than climate, and it is more difficult to define and evaluate. While climate can be measured quantitatively by asking employees to complete a climate survey, culture is usually measured qualitatively using the ethnographic research methods from anthropology.[1]

Levels of Organizational Culture. Organizational culture is difficult to understand because it includes virtually every aspect of the organization, and the most important elements of culture are not visible. Culture can be studied from four levels of analysis:

Cultural Artifacts:
The visible symbols and objects that are unique to an organization and that suggest the kinds of shared beliefs and expectations of members.

1. *Cultural Artifacts.* The most superficial and visible level of organizational culture consists of artifacts and symbols. Artifacts are those tangible aspects of culture—the behaviors, language, and physical symbols—that we can perceive with our senses and that represent the rules and core beliefs of the organization's culture. Many of these symbols are readily apparent to anyone who visits an organization and observes its surroundings. The furnishings in the buildings and the appearance of the people at a police station are very different from those of the people at a corporate headquarters, a factory, or a university. The uniforms, badges, and other symbols of authority at a police station are intended to convey a much different message from the comfortable chairs and lavish surroundings of a corporate headquarters. Common behavioral patterns and rituals also reflect the rules governing behavior in the organization. For example, at NuSkin Enterprises, the regular conventions that they hold for the distributors of their products are designed to recognize and reward those distributors who have been successful. These recognition ceremonies reinforce the company's core values, and much of the convention is devoted to articulating the "rules" for getting ahead as distributors of the company's products.

Shared Norms:
The common expectations that guide the behavior of organizational members.

2. *Shared Norms.* The next level of culture consists of shared norms of the organization. These norms, or situation-specific rules, are often not directly visible but can be inferred from the organization's artifacts. Key norms can often be determined by the degree of consistency in how group members act. For example, if students raise their hands and wait to be recognized before commenting in class, we can infer that there is a norm of hand raising. If the majority of team members report to committee meetings five or ten minutes late, we can infer that being on time is not important. Some norms are explicitly spelled out, either verbally or in writing, for the organization's members, often with penalties for not complying with the norms. Thus we can also look to formal documents such as employee manuals to glean some information regarding norms.

Cultural Values:
The social values that are shared among the members of an organization and tend to regulate their individual behaviors and induce collective conformity.

3. *Cultural Values.* The next level of culture consists of values that represent the collective beliefs, ideals, and feelings of members about what things are good, proper, valuable, rational, and right. Values are the broader rules that we can see applied across situations, and such values are often written down in statements of corporate values or management philosophy. For example, the Boy Scouts of America list their values as "trustworthy, loyal, helpful, friendly," and so on, in their scout law. The Boy Scouts assume that each scout leader is attempting to instill in their boys these "values," or general rules, that would guide their behavior in a variety of situations. Of course, there is almost always a discrepancy between the "ideal values" and the "real values." Not all members of the organization behave in ways consistent with the values. Not all 12 year-old and 13 year-old scouts follow all the values in the scout oath. Thus, when studying an organization's values, we must be careful to articulate what people say they believe and what they actually do. In some organizations, the discrepancy between stated ideals and actual behavior is so great that

it causes people to become disillusioned with the organization, and has a negative impact on morale. For example, if a company publicly states that it values "serving the customer," but fails to provide employees with the necessary training or resources to serve customers well, then there will likely be significant cynicism and low morale in the workforce.

4. *Shared Assumptions.* The deepest level of culture consists of shared assumptions that provide a foundation for how people think about what happens in organizations. These assumptions represent beliefs about reality and human nature that are taken for granted and embedded in the way we understand and interpret daily life. Consequently, shared assumptions are the most difficult to study.

Shared Assumptions:
The foundation beliefs that impact how people think about and respond to organizational events, but that are mostly subconscious.

Core Shared Assumptions. Although the shared assumptions in an organization are extremely difficult to identify and describe, these assumptions are the most interesting aspect of culture to study because of their pervasive impact on how people behave, and their implications for improving organizational effectiveness. Efforts to understand organizational cultures have identified some of the most significant categories of shared assumptions:[2]

1. *The Nature of Relationships.* Are relationships among members of society assumed to be primarily hierarchical, collateral, or individualistic in nature? Is there a caste system, and does organizational hierarchy impact relationships?

2. *Human Nature.* Are humans considered to be basically good, basically evil, or neither good nor evil? Can people be trusted? What is the value of a human life, and do people care for one another?

3. *The Nature of Truth.* Is truth revealed by external authority figures, or is the accuracy of information determined by a process of personal investigation and testing?

4. *Our Fit with the Environment.* What is our relationship with the environment? Do members believe they have the capacity to master the environment? Are they supposed to live in harmony with it? Do they think they are controlled by it?

5. *Time Orientation.* Are members of the organization primarily oriented to the past, the present, or the future?

6. *Assumptions about Activity.* Assumptions about the nature of human activity can be divided into three approaches: (1) a "doing" orientation, where people are basically active and evaluated according to what they produce; (2) a "being" orientation, where people are passive and unable to alter existing circumstances; and (3) a "becoming" orientation, where people are continually developing and becoming an integrated whole.

7. *Universalism/Particularism.* Do we treat all members of the organization the same regardless of their background (universalism), or do we treat people differently based on certain criteria such as race, age, religion, family affiliation, etc. (particularism)?

These assumptions, while often unspoken, form the foundation of the culture and are reflected in the artifacts, norms, and values. For example, suppose a manager decided to organize his department around the assumption that his employees were lazy and couldn't be trusted to do their work. We might find a variety of control mechanisms—time sheets, spot checks, harsh punishment for mistakes—to be key artifacts of such a culture. These artifacts would reflect norms and values of distrust and high control on the part of the manager. The culture of the department would likely be quite different, however, if it were based on the assumption that all employees could be trusted to work hard and make significant contributions to the organization. Uncovering these tacit assumptions is an important part of cultural analysis.

DEVELOPMENT OF CULTURE

Since culture refers to the complex configuration of shared artifacts, norms, values, and assumptions, it cannot simply be dictated by top management. Indeed, many researchers argue that the pronouncements and speeches of top management do very little to create the fundamental beliefs and values that are both created by and reflected in the ceremonies, stories, symbols, and slogans within the organization.[3] An organization's culture is not created by any single person or event, but by a complex combination of forces that include the visions of the founders, the expectations of leaders, the contributions of organizational members, and the way the organization has historically responded to problems of internal integration and external adaptation.

Expectations of Founders and Leaders

Founders have a large influence on the culture of an organization, especially in the beginning. Their expectations, their decisions, how they treat people, how they spend their time, and what they value have a major impact on what employees value and how outsiders perceive the organization. Unless the founder's influence becomes institutionalized, however, the impact of a founder diminishes as the organization grows. Later in the life of the organization, its culture will reflect a complex mixture of the assumptions, values, and ideas of the founder or other early top managers and the subsequent experiences of managers and employees. The impact of a founder is recognized by the kinds of questions that are typically included in a culture audit:[4]

1. Why was the organization started? What was the founder trying to achieve?
2. What problems did the founder encounter in managing the business? How were they solved?
3. What are the founder's values and assumptions concerning how the organization should be managed?

Leaders can have a significant impact on creating or changing an organization's culture. Great transformational leaders have the capacity to create a new vision and inspire members to change how they think about the organization.

Member Contributions

The members of an organization bring with them their own personal cultures, which come from their families, their communities, their religions, any professional associations to which they belong, and their nationalities. The members of the organization have been raised in a particular society and thus bring the dominant values of the society into the firm. For example, the culture of the United States is much different from the culture in Egypt. In the United States, individuals learn to place a high value on freedom of speech, respect for individual privacy, and acceptance of new technology, for example. Egyptians place a high value on fundamental Islamic teachings and perpetuating traditional practices both at home and at work. Therefore, the culture of a company with mostly Americans would likely be very different from the culture of a company with mostly Egyptians.

Historical Accommodations

External Adaptation:
How the organization responds to the external environment and the changes that occur in it.

Every organization has to confront two major challenges that impact the development of its culture: (1) external adaptation, and (2) internal integration.[5] *External adaptation* and survival refer to the way an organization secures its place in industry and the way it copes with a constantly changing external environment. As members of an organization attempt to solve various problems posed by the organization's environment, they develop "solutions" to these problems (e.g., how to find and treat customers, what products customers want, how we deal with downturns in the economy, etc.), which then form the rules that members of the organization will follow in the future. External adaptation requires the organization to face the following issues associated with its mission and strategy:

1. What major crises has the organization confronted? How did it deal with these crises?
2. What major changes have been made in its strategy, structure, technology, size, and leadership? How and why were the changes made? How did these changes affect the organization?
3. What are the specific goals the organization is striving to achieve? What problems has the organization solved that have allowed it to achieve its mission and goals?

Internal Integration:
How the organization coordinates its internal systems and processes.

Internal integration is concerned with establishing and maintaining effective working relationships among the members of an organization. Internally, organizational culture helps to define the criteria for the allocation of power and status. Every organization establishes a pecking order and rules for how members acquire, maintain, and lose power. These rules help members manage their expectations and feelings of aggression. The criteria for allocating rewards and punishments are also defined by the organizational culture. The legends and myths let members know which behaviors are heroic or sinful—what gets rewarded with status and power and what gets punished through withdrawal of rewards or excommunication. Internal integration is concerned with the following kinds of issues:

1. How does the organization reward and control its members?
2. Are decisions made participatively or autocratically?
3. Are the relationships among employees close and friendly, or distant and individualistic?
4. What criteria are used for finding new recruits for the organization? How are these new recruits socialized and trained?
5. What does an employee need to know or do to become an accepted member of the organization and be successful?

An organization's culture emerges when members and leaders share ideas, values, aspirations, and assumptions as they discover ways to cope with issues of external adaptation and internal integration. The creation of a culture appears to be a complex combination of forces that involve members and leaders striving to adjust to internal and external demands.

MAINTAINING ORGANIZATIONAL CULTURE

Organizational cultures are maintained by a combination of many forces, especially (a) the selection and retention of employees, (b) the allocation of rewards and status, (c) the reactions of leaders, (d) the rites and ceremonies, (e) the stories and symbols, and (f) the reactions to crises.

Employee Selection and Discipline

Organizations tend to hire people who match their culture. They want employees who will fit in and adapt to the organization's culture. The recruitment and selection procedures in a company are designed to identify not just the specific skills and talents of job applicants, but also their personalities and interests. The organization then maintains its culture by disciplining or even terminating employees who consistently deviate from accepted norms and practices. Thus, discipline procedures also become an important instrument for maintaining cultural values.

Other human resource practices also help to reinforce the organization's culture. For example, the assumptions, values, and beliefs of a company can be controlled and reinforced by those who establish the criteria for evaluating employees, decide which managers get promoted, set the standards that determine how pay increases are granted, and develop and present the orientation training. These practices become known throughout the organization, and serve to maintain or change an existing culture.

Reward and Status Allocation

An organization's reward system can either maintain or change its culture. The rewards and punishments attached to various behaviors convey to employees the priorities and values of both individual managers and the organization. A dramatic change in an organization's reward system can make a significant change in its culture almost overnight. For example, the creation and implementation of a profit sharing plan almost immediately changed the culture of a company in the agricultural industry from one of distrust and disregard for employees to a culture of caring and fairness. Rather than having all year-end bonuses distributed by managers to the assistant managers based on personal relationships, a fixed percent of the profit was distributed to all employees according to a formula that combined base pay and years of service. The plan was greeted with suspicion when it was first announced, but after the first profit share was distributed, a new culture emerged that had a dramatic impact on the degree of cooperation, interpersonal relationships, patterns of communication, involvement in decision making, styles of leadership, distribution of power, and feelings of respect for all members.

Leader Reactions

Although it is rather subtle, what managers pay attention to is one of the more powerful methods of maintaining organizational culture. Administrators perform a variety of symbolic activities that influence the power relationships in organizations. The following is a list of symbolic actions that explain what leaders can do to increase their personal power and exert greater influence in an organization.

1. *Spend time on activities that are important.* The amount of time an administrator spends on an activity communicates a message regarding the importance of that goal or function.
2. *Change or enhance the setting.* A new setting conveys the feeling that something new is happening. An enhanced setting with more elaborate furnishings generally means that the activity is more consequential and important. Changing the meeting from the lunchroom to the boardroom communicates a message of significance to the attendees.
3. *Review and interpret history.* Events have meaning only through our interpretations of them. The most important interpretations are those derived from a historical analysis that demonstrates a consistent line of meaning and direction. If current events appear to be consistent with historic trends, it is easier to obtain a consensus on a chosen course of action. For example, wage cuts and extra hours are more acceptable if it can be shown that the employees have always responded with loyalty and sacrifice during hard times.
4. *Establish a dominant value expressed in a simple phrase.* A simple phrase, one that reflects a dominant value and is easily remembered, can influence the behavior of organizational members by creating a consensus about appropriate behavior. For example, a simple slogan such as "Pride in performance brings excellence in service" can mobilize support for greater organizational commitment and dedication to work.

Rites and Ceremonies

Rites and Ceremonies: The special events in organizations that recognize individuals and the ways they are treated.

Ceremonies are planned events that have special significance for the members and are conducted for their benefit. Ceremonies serve the same purpose for organizations that ordinations and initiations do for religious groups and social clubs. Ceremonies are special occasions when managers can reinforce specific values and beliefs. These occasions provide an opportunity to recognize heroes and induct them into the organization's hall of fame. For example, McDonald's Corporation conducts a nationwide contest to determine the best hamburger-cooking team in the country. Competition occurs among local teams and gradually progresses until the best teams from the company compete at the national level. The teams are judged on subtle details that determine whether the hamburger is cooked to perfection. This ceremony communicates to all McDonald's employees the value of hamburger quality. It also requires store managers to become very familiar with the 700-page policy and procedures book.

Rites and ceremonies provide opportunities to reward and recognize employees whose behavior is congruent with the values of the company. Six kinds of rites in organizations have been identified:[6]

1. *Rites of passage* show that an individual's status has changed, such as a promotion or a retirement.
2. *Rites of enhancement* reinforce the achievement of individuals, such as recognition awards.
3. *Rites of renewal* emphasize change in the organization and commitment to learning and growth, such as opening a new store or launching a new product.
4. *Rites of integration* unite diverse groups or teams within the organization and renew commitment to the larger organization, such as annual picnics and company newsletters.
5. *Rites of conflict reduction* focus on dealing with conflicts or disagreements that arise naturally in organizations, such as grievance hearings or union contract negotiations.
6. *Rites of degradation* are used by organizations to publicly punish or demean persons who fail to adhere to the accepted values and norms of behavior, such as a demotion or dissemination of a public apology.

Stories and Symbols

Organizational Myths:
Significant stories that are told about an organization's earlier years that impact the way members think about its history, even if they are not true.

Organizational stories have a profound impact on culture regardless of whether they are true or false. Most stories are narratives based on true events that are shared among employees and told to new members to inform them about the organization. Some stories are considered legends because the events are historic, but may have been embellished with fictional details. Other stories may be myths, not supported by facts, but directionally consistent with the values and beliefs of the organization. Stories are important because they preserve the primary values of the organization and promote a shared understanding among all employees.

An excellent illustration of the effects of organizational culture is the "H-P way" at Hewlett-Packard Corporation. The H-P way consists of a constellation of attitudes and values, among which is an insistence on product quality, the recognition of achievement, and respect for individual employees. New employees are viewed with suspicion until they have demonstrated that they understand and follow the H-P way. Questions about sloppy work or careless performance are resolved immediately because sloppy work is inconsistent with the H-P way. A classic story that serves to symbolize and preserve the H-P way at Hewlett-Packard involves one of the founders, David Packard. One evening, as Packard was wandering around the Palo Alto lab after work hours, he discovered a prototype constructed of inferior materials. Packard destroyed the model and left a note saying, "That's not the H-P way. Dave."

A symbol is something that represents something else. In one sense, ceremonies, rites, and stories are symbols because they represent the deeper values and assumptions of the organization. Physical symbols are often used in organizations to represent and support organizational culture because they focus attention on a specific item and because they are so powerful. The value of physical symbols is that they communicate important cultural values. If the physical symbols are consistent with the ceremonies and stories, they are a powerful facilitator of culture.

Many organizations give 10- and 20-year service pins as a form of recognition to employees who stay with the organization. Although these service pins are attractive pieces of jewelry, their significance to the employees far exceeds their economic value. Part of their value comes from the elaborate awards banquets at which they are presented. Such elaborate ceremonies and rites often contribute to the significance of physical symbols.

Almost every organization develops its own jargon and abbreviations, and these communication devices contribute to a unique organizational culture. Some companies use a specific slogan, metaphor, or saying to convey special meaning to employees. Metaphors are often rich with meaning, and convey an entire sermon in only a short sentence. Slogans can be readily picked up and repeated by employees as well as customers of the company. "IBM means service," Hallmark's "When you care enough to send the very best," and "Everybody at Northrup is in marketing" are examples of slogans that symbolize what the company stands for to both employees and the external public.

Reactions to Problems

The way managers and employees respond to a crisis reveals much about an organization's culture. When problems arise and employees do not have standard operating procedures telling them what to do or an opportunity to consult upper management to seek direction, they are forced to rely on their understanding of the organization's culture to do what they think is best. Such was the case with the employees of Johnson & Johnson when cyanide was found in some Tylenol capsules. Without waiting for direction from upper management or an order from the FDA, these employees acted quickly to remove all potentially harmful bottles from the shelves and to preserve customer confidence. Their actions were dictated by the company's credo and a culture that left no uncertainty about how they should act.

The way managers and employees respond to a crisis also has the potential to create or change an organization's culture. The way in which a crisis is handled can either reinforce the existing culture or generate new values and norms that change the culture in some way. For example, a company facing a dramatic reduction in demand for its products might react by laying off or firing employees. This reaction would communicate an important message that people are not very highly valued, regardless of how reasonable the terminations were or how well they were explained. Or the company might reduce employee hours or pay and ask employees to sacrifice temporarily while the company experienced an economic correction. Such a situation occurred at Lincoln Electric during the recessions of the 1980s, when employees in the arc welding and electric motor departments were reduced to 30 hours per week because of declining demand. Terminations were avoided and year-end bonuses were paid. However, some employees were reassigned and the overall workforce was reduced through normal retirement and attrition.

EFFECTS OF ORGANIZATIONAL CULTURE

Worker Attitudes and Behavior

A classic illustration of the effects of organizational culture on worker attitudes and behavior is the culture of "family, fun, and LUV" at Southwest

Airlines. The walls of the corporate headquarters are covered with pictures of people at parties. These people are the Southwest family and they have frequent employee parties. Although Southwest employees believe work is important and that they must perform their jobs with excellence, they also believe that work can be fun. Humor is used throughout the company to help anxious travelers remain calm and make work fun for the Southwest family. When you fly on Southwest Airlines, you may hear the traditional instructions to passengers sung to the tune of "Under the Boardwalk" or "I Heard it Through the Grapevine." An in-flight contest may be held to see which passenger has the biggest holes in his socks or bald spot on his head. When leaving the gate area, pilots have been heard to ask passengers next to the aisles to hold in their elbows so they can see to back up. When approaching the gate, the pilots have said over the intercom, "Whoa big fella, whoa!"

Southwest's culture is reinforced by its CEO, Herb Kelleher, who has been seen at parties dressed as a chicken or Elvis. He frequently hugs and kisses his employees, and his commitment to affection is demonstrated by Southwest's ticker symbol of LUV on Wall Street. His commitment to efficiency is manifested by his willingness to help load luggage and serve peanuts and drinks to passengers. Herb also arm-wrestled a potential litigant to forestall a possible lawsuit.

Southwest's corporate culture is highly visible and it translates into unsurpassed customer service and efficiency. Through effective teamwork, Southwest succeeds in turning around most of its 2300 daily fights within 20 minutes at the gate. It has also created an extremely desirable place to work—Southwest has been ranked number one on the list of America's 100 Best Companies to work for.[7]

Culture and Ethical Behavior

Every organization faces the challenge of creating ethical norms that are understood and accepted. Employee theft, cheating, and embezzlement are common temptations in every company and seem to grow unchecked unless the organization has a vigorous program to counter them and tries to create a culture of honesty.

A culture that endorses ethical behavior has a profound influence on the honesty of employees and the profitability of the company. A moral culture exists when the group norms and social expectations in a company endorse the importance of honesty. In organizations where such a culture exists, employees feel a personal responsibility to behave honestly and expect others to do likewise. Saying things that are knowingly untrue, taking things that belong to others, giving false impressions, withholding relevant information, and mistreating others are widely recognized as unacceptable behaviors. When there is a culture of honesty, the suggestion to hide a defective part in the middle of a batch would be perceived as a joke—everyone knows that such an act would be unacceptable, and no one would seriously consider doing it. In a culture of dishonesty, however, the same suggestion would be perceived as an expedient way to dispose of a defective part.

Whether a company's culture endorses honesty or dishonesty has a significant impact on the attitudes and behaviors of its members. A survey of 22 retail stores demonstrated that the norms regarding honesty within each store

were positively related to the personal honesty of employees and negatively related to inventory shrinkage rates.[8]

A culture of honesty depends on establishing general standards of acceptable behavior and a clear perception that everyone accepts them. The following strategies have been suggested for creating a culture that endorses
ethical behavior:

1. As a rule, visible moral acts speak louder than company communications.
    When executives are forced to make tough moral choices and they decide
    to act ethically in spite of the consequences, these decisions communicate
    a powerful message throughout the company about the importance of eth-
    ical behavior. For example, one CEO described how his company refused
    to pay an illegal bribe and walked away from a lucrative foreign contract,
    even though the state departments of both countries encouraged them to
    negotiate the deal and one government agency even offered to pay the
    bribe for them.[9] This moral decision became widely known throughout the
    company and served as a pattern for negotiating other contracts. This
    company found that its reputation for being open and honest contributed
    to its financial success; but, executives must be willing to make moral de-
    cisions that are right even if they do not seem expedient.

2. What employees do off the job influences how they are perceived at work.
    The degree to which employees are perceived as having firm commit-
    ments to honor and fidelity in their personal lives is an indication of the
    integrity that can be expected from them at work. The culture of honesty
    is enhanced when a significant number of employees, and especially top
    managers, are perceived as individuals who are devoutly religious or
    committed to a similar high moral code.

3. Develop and publish a code of ethics. Some companies have effectively
    solicited extensive input from employees as they developed their codes of
    ethics. Having employees participate in the development appears to in-
    crease their commitment to it and compliance afterwards. To ensure that
    the employees know the code and agree to abide by it, some organiza-
    tions require employees to sign a statement saying that they understand
    the code, they agree to abide by it, and any deviations in their past have
    been discussed with management. Although a written code does not ap-
    pear to have much impact on creating a culture of honesty, it has consid-
    erable impact when it is endorsed by management decisions and
    practices.

4. Company communications can contribute to a culture of ethical behavior
    by discussing the importance of integrity. The most frequently used in-
    formation is statistical data showing how current levels of theft threaten
    the economic health of the company. Other helpful information includes
    reports of ethical conduct and statements endorsing integrity. The media
    may include company newsletters, posters on walls, bulletin boards, TV
    monitors, comments added to payroll check stubs, public address an-
    nouncements, and even paid advertisements in the public media.

5. Encourage employees who observe unethical behaviors to report them,
    and then protect them from retribution. People who report corporate
    misdeeds are called whistle blowers, and the most difficult problem they
    face is being fired or mistreated for blowing the whistle. Employees

should be encouraged to report unethical behaviors internally first and seek outside help only if internal efforts have been unsuccessful. To encourage whistle blowing within the federal government, Congress passed the Whistle Blowers Protection Act to protect employees from being fired and to reward them financially.

International Cultural Differences

While we have discussed the characteristics of organizational culture, we must also remember that national cultures have an impact on organizational effectiveness. Hofstede has studied cross-cultural comparisons among different nationalities and the way these differences affect business operations in an attitude survey of IBM employees from 50 countries.[10] He identified four cultural values that he used to explain differing reactions to problems in organizational life: power distance, uncertainty avoidance, individualism versus collectivism, and masculinity versus femininity. He found that these work-related values are related to societal norms that are embedded within countries and influence the functioning of families, education systems, and business organizations.

Power differences:
The acceptability of status differentials between members of a society.

1. Power distance refers to the acceptability of power differentials within a society. In every society there are those who are powerful and those who are powerless, such as rich versus poor or leaders versus followers. Societies differ with respect to whether this *power difference* is considered acceptable or unacceptable. In low power distance countries, high power distance is considered undesirable and illegitimate, such as Scandinavian and European countries. Inequality exists, but it is perceived as something that should be minimized. In high power distance countries, such as the Philippines, Mexico, India, and Singapore, power differences are perceived as neither legitimate nor illegitimate. In these countries, powerful individuals are entitled to privileges, inequality is a fact of life, and the way to gain power is to overthrow those who have it.

Uncertainty Avoidance:
The degree of ambiguity and uncertainty people are willing to tolerate.

2. *Uncertainty avoidance* refers to the degree of tolerance people have for ambiguity and whether they feel threatened by uncertain situations. People use various coping styles dictated by their culture to respond to the uncertainties of life. On a societal level this coping may be accomplished through the use of technology, laws, and religion. Countries and cultures strong on uncertainty avoidance, such as Greece, Japan, and Peru, attempt to structure risky situations in order to avoid risk and promote security. Other cultures see risk as unavoidable and have a greater tolerance for ambiguity, such as Singapore, Denmark, and Sweden.

Individualism versus collectivism:
The degree to which people are willing to act individually as a unique person versus as a uniform member of a group.

3. *Individualism versus collectivism* refers to the relationship between the individual and the larger society. People in individualistic cultures, such as the United States and Canada, prefer to act as individuals; they believe in self-reliance and do not build strong ties to other people. People in collectivistic cultures, such as Asian and South American countries, assume they are automatically members of a cohesive in-group to which they have belonged since birth. Loyalty to that group is not to be questioned. Someone outside the in-group will remain outside unless included by unusual circumstances. Individualistic countries have a tradition of more

individualistic thinking and action, power is more evenly distributed, and there is greater occupational and economic mobility. Collectivistic societies tend to focus more on strong ties among individuals within their in-group, and differentiate between themselves and out-group members.

Masculinity versus femininity:
The degree to which gender role differences are emphasized in terms of valuing assertive and aggressive male roles over more tender feminine attributes.

4. *Masculinity versus femininity* addresses how a society perceives role differences between men and women, and how these differences should impact their roles and activities. Low masculinity countries, such as the Scandinavian countries, minimize this distinction, so that there is a blurring or overlap of social roles; high masculinity countries, such as Japan, Austria, and Italy, assume that social gender roles are clearly distinct and that there should be specific occupations for males and females. In high masculinity societies, "tough" values such as assertiveness, accomplishment, success, and competition prevail over more "tender" values such as empathy, supportiveness, and maintaining relationships.

While Hofstede's dimensions are just one approach to comparing cultures, his research emphasizes the importance of understanding cultural differences in today's global economy. Managers must be aware of and sensitive to these cultural differences. There are many examples of organizations failing because they violated some cultural value in a foreign country with the result being disgruntled employees, upset customers, or alienated suppliers.

CHANGING ORGANIZATIONAL CULTURE

Most cultural interventions are actually attempts to clarify the culture of the organization. These interventions are typically conducted with top-level managers in the organization in a series of group discussions that focus on such questions as: What is our unique mission? What do we want to be known for? What are the ten commandments of this organization?[11]

Changing an organization's culture is considerably more dramatic and difficult than modifying other parts of a system. Acquiring new artifacts and symbols may not be too difficult; it may even be possible to change some group norms and patterns of behavior. But at the deepest level, a culture change requires alteration of the basic assumptions of the organization in its essential character. The following steps have been suggested for changing an organization's culture.[12]

1. *Conduct a Culture Audit.* The first step in the change process involves diagnosing the culture and subcultures within the organization. What are the assumptions, values, behaviors, and artifacts currently in the organization, and are there discrepancies between espoused beliefs and actual behavior? The goal of the diagnosis is to develop an accurate "map" of the culture, which generally requires extensive interviewing rather than written surveys.

2. *Assess the Need for Change.* Cultural change is needed if the current culture is not solving problems of integration or adaptation, or if it is producing negative consequences for individuals in the organization. As organizations grow and evolve, their cultures may become incompatible with the changing circumstances. Values and beliefs that may have been appropriate for a smaller company may be dysfunctional in a larger company.

3. *Unfreeze the Current Culture.* Change efforts are much more successful when there is a perceived need for change that compels people to be open to influence and willing to consider something new. Thus, an organization's culture will be more receptive to change if the current assumptions, values, and beliefs have been called into question, producing a high degree of tension. Most instances of significant cultural change are not planned; they accompany sudden and cataclysmic events, such as the death or retirement of the founder, a decision to merge or sell the business, dramatic changes in growth or profitability, major technological changes, or fundamental changes in the strategy or structure. These events tend to "unfreeze" or destabilize the entire cultural system and prepare it to consider a major restructuring of the assumptions, values, and beliefs. Sharing data about the impact of the organization's culture—both positive and negative—can also create the impetus for change.

4. *Elicit Support from the Cultural Elite.* Top management and other opinion leaders compose the "cultural elite" in an organization; they are the ones who interpret events for members and establish the rules of conduct. Because successful change may be impossible without their assistance, a strategy for locating them and enlisting their support is essential. Another option is to hire a completely new leadership team that holds beliefs consistent with the organization's new direction.

5. *Implement an Intervention Strategy.* A variety of interventions are possible for changing the organization's culture, such as conducting team-building meetings, revising the training and development activities, installing new reward systems, changing the organizational structure, rewriting the mission statement, and negotiating new roles. The replacement of key individuals who hold the "old" beliefs may also be necessary.

6. *Monitor and Evaluate.* Cultural change is incremental, and rarely occurs quickly. A system for monitoring and evaluating the transition to a new set of values and beliefs can provide an ongoing process of transitional change.

Leadership succession has a major impact on an organization's culture. A new leader with different assumptions and values has great potential to alter the prevailing pattern of culture. Business history is replete with stories of cultures formed by remarkable organizational founders such as Henry Ford, John D. Rockefeller, Thomas Watson, Andrew Carnegie, Hewlett and Packard, James Cash Penney, and Willard Marriott. In his early examination of bureaucracies, Max Weber discusses the challenges of organizational change, and suggests that a charismatic leader whom others perceive as having extraordinary powers, could change the culture of an organization. From a position of power that is derived from respect and admiration, a new leader can articulate new patterns and values that are voluntarily accepted by members throughout the organization.

Cultural interventions that focus on changing shared values should explain the need for the change, identify the new value, and generate enthusiasm for its acceptance. For example, one organization sought to create a culture that was centered around a commitment to excellence. This intervention involved a series of meetings attended by all employees in which the top administrators presented talks on the theme, "What it means to me to have a commitment to excellence." People in the organization were asked to identify everyday common practices that did not reflect a commitment to excellence. Department supervisors and division heads were asked to analyze careless and sloppy practices that failed to conform to the commitment to excellence, and eliminate them.

An important element in creating a new culture is creating cultural artifacts that support the new culture, such as the language, metaphors, stories, labels, and other supporting systems. For example, British Rail conducted a three-year development project designed to change its bureaucratic culture and relied greatly on being able to eliminate dysfunctional modes of thinking by negatively labeling them ("isms").[13] Similarly, General Mills used a label, "Company of Champions," to describe the new culture it wanted to create and used three words to define it: innovation, speed, and commitment. To implement and reinforce its new culture, General Mills made corresponding changes in its reward systems, its recognition program, and its education and training programs.[14] The words used by General Electric to support its new culture were *simplicity, self-confidence,* and *speed.*[15]

Metaphors can play an important role in cultural change. New ways of thinking require a departure from an *old world* view to a new set of ideas, values, and beliefs that are reflected in a new language. Metaphors can refocus familiar images in a new light and provide a shared vision that guides future actions and gives its members meaning and purpose. Metaphors from war, religion, and sports are common in business (and some of these metaphors have been criticized because they are associated with a predominantly male language that women feel uncomfortable using).[16] An important part of Jack Welch's success in changing the culture of General Electric to a leaner and more adaptable company was his frequent criticism of bureaucratic inefficiencies. Like fat on a bloated bureaucracy, these inefficiencies had to be eliminated in what were called "Work-Out" sessions. A six-inch stack of manuals was replaced with a one-page statement. The metaphor of an exercise program helped overcome resistance to removing layers of management and departmental boundaries. The metaphor also made employees think the company would ultimately be in better shape, which ultimately provided an acceptable foundation for building trust and cooperation. Metaphors are an essential medium through which reality is constructed, and they help to encourage and control change.[17]

Discussion Questions

1. Identify an organization and use examples from it to explain the differences between organizational climate and organizational culture.
2. Select an organization and use it to explain the different levels of culture: cultural artifacts, shared norms, cultural values, and shared assumptions. How can you know what the shared assumptions of an organization are?
3. Explain the concepts of external adaptation and internal integration, and describe how these concepts contribute to our understanding of an organization's culture. Provide illustrations of these concepts.
4. Identify a group, preferably one that you lead, and explain what you could do as the leader of that group to preserve or alter the group's culture.

Notes

1. Robert A. Cooke and Denise M. Rousseau, "Behavioral Norms and Expectations: A Quantitative Approach to the Assessment of Organizational Culture," *Group and Organization Studies* 13 (September 1988): 245–73; W. Gibb Dyer, Jr., and Alan L. Wilkins, "Better Stories, Not Better Constructs, to Generate Better Theory: A Rejoinder to Eisenhardt," *Academy of Management Review* 16 (1991): 613–19; Kathleen M. Eisenhardt, "Better Stories and Better Constructs: The Case for Rigor and Comparative Logic," *Academy of Management Review* 16 (1991): 620–27.

2. Edgar H. Schein, *Organizational Culture and Leadership*, (San Francisco: Josey-Bass, 1985).

3. Terrence E. Deal and Allan A. Kennedy, *Corporate Cultures* (Reading, MA: Addison Wesley, 1982); Harrison M. Trice and Janice M. Beyer, "Studying Organizational Cultures Through Rites and Ceremonials," *Academy of Management Review* 9 (1984): 653–69.

4. The questions in this section come from W. Gibb Dyer, Jr. "Organizational Culture: Analysis and Change" In William G. Dyer, *Strategies for Managing Change*, (Reading, MA: Addison-Wesley, 1984), ch. 20.

5. Edgar H. Schein, "Coming to a New Awareness of Organizational Culture," *Sloan Management Review* 25 (Winter 1984): 3–16.

6. H. M. Trice and J. M. Beyer, "Studying Organizational Cultures through Rites and Ceremonials," *Academy of Management Review* 9 (1984): 653–69.

7. T. A. Stewart, "America's Most Admired Companies: Why Leadership Matters." *Fortune Magazine* (March 2, 1998): 70 +.

8. David J. Cherrington and J. Owen Cherrington. "The Climate of Honesty in Retail Stores." In William Terris (ed.) *Employee Theft: Research, Theory, and Applications.* (Park Ridge, IL: London House Press, 1985): 3–16.

9. Coleman Raphael, "The Ethical Dimensions of America's Corporate Practices: A Reexamination." In the Donald S. MacNaughton Symposium Proceedings, 1986, 31–42.

10. Geert Hofstede, *Culture's Consequences: International Differences in Work-related Values* (Beverly Hills, CA: Sage Publications, 1980).

11. David Bradford, "Cultural Interventions" (Paper presented at the 1984 Organizational Behavior Teaching conference, Boise, Idaho, May 1984); Larry B. Meares, "A Model for Changing Organizational Culture," *Personnel* 63 (July 1986): 38–42.

12. W. Gibb Dyer, Jr. "Organizational Culture: Analysis and Change. In William G. Dyer, *Strategies for Managing Change* (Reading, MA: Addison-Wesley, 1984), ch. 20.

13. Paul Bate, "Using the Culture Concept in an Organization Development Setting," *Journal of Applied Behavioral Science* 26 (1990): 83–106.

14. Stephanie Overman, "A Company of Champions," *HR Magazine* 35 (Oct 1990): 58–60.

15. John F. Welch, Jr., "Working Out of a Tough Year," *Executive Excellence* 9 (Apr 1992): 14–16.

16. Catherine Cleary, Thomas Packard, Achilles Armenakis, Arthur Bedeian, Laurie Larwood, and W. Warner Burke, "The Use of Metaphors in Organizational Assessment and Change: The Role of Metaphors in Organi-

zational Change," *Group and Organization Management* 17 (Sept 1992): 229–59; Fiona Wilson, "Language, Technology, Gender and Power," *Human Relations* 45 (Sept 1992): 883–904.

17. Stratford P. Sherman and Cynthia Hutton, "Inside the Mind of Jack Welch," *Fortune* (27 Mar 89): 39–49.

Johnson's Foods: Honoring the Sabbath Day

Robert Johnson, the chief executive officer of Johnson's Foods, faces a serious question about whether his supermarkets should open on Sundays. Johnson's Foods was started by Robert's father 57 years ago and there are now 15 stores located in two western states. The stores are highly respected in their communities because they have contributed generously to many civic projects and community events. But, they have never been open on Sundays. Over the years, the stores have been highly profitable, with revenues increasing each year until about six years ago, when they started to decline. The decline has been quite noticeable the past three years due to the emergence of several competitors that are open seven days a week.

Johnson and his family are devout Christians who believe that their stores should not be open on Sunday, the Lord's "day of rest." His employees appreciate the fact that they can spend Sundays with their families and they admire Johnson for his strong, ethical values. However, Johnson knows that he is losing business to his competitors who are open on Sunday. A growing number of customers are not seeing Sundays as days of rest and worship, but as days to do shopping and engage in recreation. Consumer surveys in the communities where stores are located indicate that 26 percent of grocery shopping is done on Saturdays and 24 percent on Sundays. By closing on Sunday, Johnson's Foods is forfeiting the second-most active shopping day of the week. More seriously, however, the data indicate that the location where people do their major shopping on the weekends is also where they tend to shop for extra items during the week.

Johnson is concerned that his revenues will continue to decline until his supermarkets are eventually unprofitable. He also recognizes, however, that many of his customers are loyal to his stores because they share his religious beliefs and appreciate the way he allows his employees to honor the Sabbath day. This is a very difficult decision. Should he change his policy and open on Sunday, or continue to observe the Sabbath day?

Questions

1. Should Johnson open his stores on Sunday? What would be the reaction of his family, his customers, and his employees if he decided to open on Sunday?
2. Does having strong values help or hinder company performance?
3. If Johnson did decide to change his policy, how should it be implemented? How should he go about announcing the change?

Wilson Electronics: When Values Collide with Actions

Peter Thompson had only been on his new job a few weeks at Wilson Electronics when he faced his first serious dilemma. As a quality control inspector for Wilson's new disk drives, Peter discovered a possible flaw in the design of the drives that could cause many of them to fail in the field. He brought this issue to the attention of Fred James, the quality control manager, who quickly dismissed Peter's concern as "trivial" saying, "We've got more important fish to fry. We're behind in our schedule already this month and don't have time to go back and look at something that may or may not be a problem."

Peter was attracted to Wilson Electronics in the first place by the company's values statement which read, in part: "We believe in creating valuable products for our customers and ensuring the highest quality. Our customers deserve the best, and we give it to them!"

His conversation with Fred James left him doubting whether the company really had the best interests of its customers at heart. If the company actually wanted the best products for its customers, why didn't his manager take his concerns seriously? This question bothered Peter for several days. Finally he came to the conclusion that either he would have to go over his manager's head and report the problem to the vice-president of quality control, or he would have to resign from the company, even though he liked his job, his salary, and the security the job provided for his family. Peter felt that it would be difficult to work for a company where the managers lacked integrity and violated the company's stated values.

Questions

1. What should Peter Thompson do?
2. Is it important for organizations to have values statements?
3. What should be done if employees don't follow the values of the company?

What are the key processes leading to organizational effectiveness?

Organizational processes refer to the flow of information and the activities associated with how it flows, including how it is generated, how it is transmitted, how it is used to make decisions, who makes these decisions, and how people use information to influence the behavior of people and organizations. Formal organizations have highly structured processes for gathering, disseminating, and using information, and many individuals are involved in the communication loops. Informal organizations have much more flexible processes for handling information.

Section V describes the central processes that are involved in disseminating information and using it in organizations. Chapter 15 presents the basic interpersonal communications model that is used in sharing information between two people. Organizational communication systems are based on this model, but are much more complex. Chapter 16 explains how information is used to make decisions and how various individual, group, and organizational factors influence decision making and occasionally contribute to inferior decision making. Chapter 17 describes leadership, and explains when leaders should use a particular style of leadership for making a decision depending on the nature of the decision, the characteristics of the followers, and the demands of the situation. Chapter 18 presents a different model for making decisions and explains why most decisions are based on power relationships rather than on rational decision making.

CHAPTER 15
Communication

CHAPTER 16
Decision Making

CHAPTER 17
Leadership

CHAPTER 18
Power and Influence

15

Communication and Interpersonal Skills

Chapter Outline

Interpersonal Communication
    The Communication Process
    Persuasive Communication
    Supportive Communication
    Listening
    Nonverbal Communication
Organizational Communication
    The Effects of Organizational Structure
    Direction of Communication Flow
    Communication Roles
Improving Communication
    Barriers to Effective Communication
    Reactions to Communication Overload

INTERPERSONAL COMMUNICATION

Communication is the exchange of information between a sender and a receiver. The information may be something other than verbal or written messages, and the senders and receivers may be other than people. For example, an airplane instrument panel (sender) sends messages to the pilot (receiver), and a smoke detector (sender) notifies the fire department (receiver) of a fire. In today's organizations, many messages are sent by complex management information systems, where data are input from numerous sources, analyzed by computer, and then electronically transmitted to receivers.

Communication is the lifeblood of an organization; it is the thread that holds the various interdependent parts of an organization together. An organization is a stable system of patterned activities where people work together to achieve common goals through a hierarchy of assigned roles and a division of labor. These patterned activities depend on communication for coordination and integration. If the communication flows could somehow be removed from an organization, the organization would cease to exist. The patterned activities of organizations depend on the exchange of information.

The Communication Process

Symbolic interaction:
The idea that communication consists of the transmission of messages through symbols that must be properly encoded and decoded to convey the intended meaning.

Symbolic Interaction. The communication process is a *symbolic interaction* between two people. For example, when a customer orders a turkey club sandwich and a strawberry milkshake at a fast-food restaurant, the customer is using words as symbols to indicate what he wants to eat. A symbol is something that represents something else. The words "turkey sandwich" are made from letters of the alphabet, but they are used to represent something made from slices of turkey and bread. The customer selected a turkey club sandwich after looking at a nonverbal representation showing a picture of the sandwich. The person behind the counter used other symbols to inform the kitchen what to prepare—"One turkey deluxe, one strawberry."

Although some symbols are quite clear, such as a hat or a chair, other symbols are much more ambiguous and difficult to explain, such as loyalty and diligence. Our ability to use symbols allows us to learn from the experience of others. People who lived many centuries ago can communicate their experiences to us symbolically through writing and art. Highly complex messages can be effectively communicated because of our ability to use symbols even though receivers have not experienced the same events as the senders. For example, someone who has never experienced a tropical storm may not know exactly what such an event might be like, but a skilled communicator who has experienced such an event should be able to describe it vividly enough for the receiver to appreciate how powerful and frightening a tropical storm can be. A symbolic presentation using words, however, is almost always only a rough approximation of what actually occurred. Even when we are communicating information about physical objects, the meaning may be ambiguous and incomplete because of our inability to find a common ground in communication.

Elements of the Communication Process. The basic elements of the communication process are diagramed in Exhibit 15.1.

Exhibit 15.1 The Communication Process

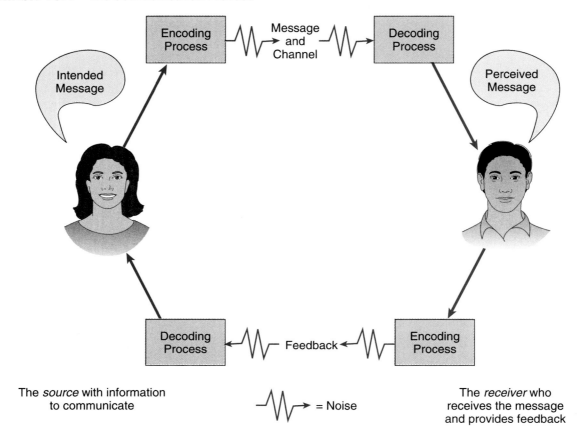

The *source* with information to communicate

⟋⟍⟋⟍⟋⟍ = Noise

The *receiver* who receives the message and provides feedback

1. The *source* or *sender* is the originator of the message and may be one person or several people working together, such as a musical group or a television news team.
2. The *message* is the stimulus the source transmits to the receiver and is composed of symbols designed to convey the intended meaning, such as words, body language, Morse code, sign language, winks, gestures, or electronic impulses.

Encoding:
The process of translating the intended message into symbols that can be used to transmit the message.

3. The *encoding process* transforms the intended message into the symbols used to transmit the message.
4. The *channel* is the means by which the message travels from a source to a receiver, which could include personal conversations, mass media (such as radio, television, and newspapers), or electronic media (such as the Internet, fax machines, voice mail, videotape, teleconferencing, and email).
5. The *receiver* is the person who receives the message and has the responsibility to interpret it.

Decoding:
The process of translating the symbols contained in a message into meaning and interpreting the message.

6. The *decoding process* involves translating the message and interpreting it.
7. *Feedback* from the receiver back to the sender is actually another message indicating the effectiveness of the communication. One-way communication does not provide an opportunity for feedback.

Noise:
Any type of interference in the transmission of a message, either actual noise or interference within the channel.

8. *Noise* refers to anything that disrupts the transmission of the message or feedback, which includes everything from ambiguous wording of a message to a poor telephone connection or static from a poor TV antenna.

The accuracy of communication depends on the successful completion of each step in the communication process. It is not enough to carefully prepare and transmit a message and then simply assume that effective communication has occurred. The encoding, transmitting, decoding, and feedback processes are all essential for effective communication.

Persuasive Communication

Changing attitudes and swaying public opinion are important issues for many organizations, such as political parties, religious organizations, business groups, and neighborhood committees. Consequently, persuasive communication has been investigated by scholars for many years; Aristotle was one of the first to construct a basic outline of the elements of persuasive communication. In his classic work, *Rhetoric,* Aristotle identifies the three important dimensions for analyzing persuasive communication: the source, the message, and the audience.[1] Some of the characteristics associated with these three dimensions are summarized in Exhibit 15.2.

Credibility:
The degree of expertise and trustworthiness in the source.

Characteristics of the Source. Extensive research has shown that the effectiveness of a message is largely influenced by the receiver's perception of the source's *credibility*. When changing attitudes, a highly credible communicator is more effective than one with low credibility.[2] Countless TV commercials attempt to get viewers to buy products because of recommendations by doctors or the American Dental Association or a panel of leading experts. Presumably, these authorities know the facts and should be listened to.

Communicators acquire credibility largely by possessing two characteristics: expertise and trustworthiness. Research scientists, for example, are more believable because they are considered experts who know the facts and are well informed. The fact that a doctor endorses a particular medication on television is effective both because doctors supposedly know what they are talking about

Characteristics of the Source
Credibility: expertise and trustworthiness
Similarity or dissimilarity from the receiver

Characteristics of the Message
Logical and reasonable
Pleasant versus fear appeal
One-sided versus two-sided arguments
Primacy versus recency
Overheard messages

Characteristics of the Audience
Level of intelligence
Initial position

Exhibit 15.2 **Characteristics of Persuasive Communication**

and because they supposedly have nothing to gain by recommending the product. The credibility of a communicator is destroyed, however, if he or she has an ulterior motive, or if the recommendation appears to be self-serving.

Several studies have shown that the effectiveness of a highly credible source lasts for only a short time. When measures of attitude are obtained immediately after the persuasion attempt, the studies show that highly credible sources produce significantly greater attitude change than low-credibility sources do. If the measures are obtained four to six weeks later, however, the credibility of the source appears to have no impact; both groups show essentially equal degrees of attitude change.[3]

Another variable associated with the source is the similarity or dissimilarity of the communicator with the audience. People are more persuaded by communicators who share similar backgrounds and personality characteristics. If you want to sell a computer to a word-processing center, it may be better to get the endorsement of other users rather than a computer expert. Whether a communicator is more persuasive because of similarity or expertise depends largely on whether the issue in question is one of values or facts. If the persuasive message is a value issue, such as accepting new technology, learning new skills, or increasing productivity, the most effective communicator is one who shares similar characteristics with the audience. However, if the persuasive message concerns facts, such as which printer is the fastest and most reliable, the most effective communicator is one who possesses high credibility as a trustworthy expert.[4]

Characteristics of the Message. In general, the most persuasive communications consist of logical, well reasoned presentations delivered in an eloquent, organized fashion. To persuade others, messages must be reasonable and logical. However, some attitudes are not changed very easily by logic or reason because they are based on emotion and feeling.[5]

In preparing a persuasive communication, you need to know whether to present one or both sides of an issue, and if both, which side should be presented first. Should you reach a conclusion, or let the receivers draw their own conclusion? Several studies have examined the relative effectiveness of one-sided versus two-sided presentations. Most of the evidence seems to indicate that they are almost equally effective. One-sided presentations may be superior if listeners are not aware that a reasonable case could be made for the other side, yet two-sided communications were found to produce change that could withstand a counterattack.[6]

If a communicator is going to present both sides of an argument, which side should be presented first—pro or con? Studies suggest that the order of presentation does not seem to make much difference as long as both messages are presented about the same time. If there is a long time span between the two messages, and attitudes are measured immediately following the second presentation, a recency effect typically occurs, in which the most recent message is accepted.[7]

Messages that make the receivers feel good tend to be more persuasive. Messages that evoke happy feelings and pleasant associations seem to attract attention and evoke a favorable response from the receiver. Favorable surroundings, such as pleasant music, good food, and beautiful scenery, also contribute to the persuasiveness of communications,. The persuasive effect of pleasant surroundings explains why many TV commercials use beautiful scenery and pleasant music, and people who look as though they are having fun.

However, studies have also shown that communications tend to be more persuasive when they arouse the listener's level of fear. For example, advertisements about the effects of cigarette smoking on health tend to be more effective when they specifically describe the harmful effects of cancer and emphysema. Similarly, messages about tetanus injections, safe driving standards, and dental hygiene tend to be more effective when the listeners are told specifically about possible serious consequences.[8] However, the level of arousal can be too intense if the listeners are shown vivid portrayals of accidents, disease, or other repulsive scenes. The relationship between the degree of fear and the amount of attitude change appears to be an inverted-U relationship. As the level of fear increases, there is initially an increase in attitude change. As the level of fear becomes too intense, however, people cannot cope with the problem, and respond by avoiding or denying the information.[9]

Another variable influencing the credibility of a message is whether the listeners believe it was intended for them. Overheard messages tend to be very persuasive because the listeners are not worried about being intentionally manipulated; thus the source is more credible. People are also influenced by messages that appear to be censored or kept from them. The effect of censorship, whether it be movies, books, or magazine articles, generally stimulates greater interest in obtaining the censored material, which then has a more persuasive impact than would have been realized had the material not been censored.

In interpersonal communication, the total message is more persuasive when both the verbal and nonverbal messages are consistent. When they are inconsistent, however, the effectiveness of the verbal message is diminished. In fact, when the verbal and nonverbal communications are inconsistent, the listeners are usually influenced more by the nonverbal behavior, such as facial expressions, physical posture, and body language, rather than by the words. Furthermore, nonverbal cues portraying emotion are recognized more easily and remembered longer than inconsistent verbal messages.[10]

Video-taped messages, such as television, are generally considered the most persuasive form of mass communication, because they combine the visual picture of the communicator with the verbal message. Audio messages, such as tape or radio, are generally second in effectiveness, and the printed word, such as newspapers and magazines, is third. Studies indicate, however, that the relative effectiveness of video-taped, audio, and written messages depends on the complexity of the message. Highly complex messages are more effective in a written form, which allows the receiver to reread and analyze the content of the message. Simple messages are more effectively and persuasively communicated through video-tape, where they are presented in living color.[11]

Characteristics of the Audience. The effectiveness of a persuasive communication is limited by the receiver's ability to understand the message. A highly educated audience would be expected to understand complex arguments. The relationship between intelligence and persuasiveness, however, appears to be mixed. Although highly intelligent people are more receptive to communications than less intelligent people, they are more resistant to influence. Therefore, people with moderate intelligence are generally the most easily influenced by the average communication. Those with very low intelligence do not understand the influence attempt, while those at very high levels of intelligence tend to resist the influence.[12]

Latitude of acceptance:
The range of attitudes or opinions that are sufficiently close to the receiver's opinion that the receiver is willing to attend to the message.

The initial attitudes of the receivers influence the effectiveness of persuasive communication. People tend to have a *latitude of acceptance* that includes a range of attitudes slightly more or less favorable than their own. Their latitude of rejection consists of attitudes that differ significantly from their personal position. Persuasive communications are more successful when they advocate a position that falls within the listener's latitude of acceptance. When the message falls outside the latitude of acceptance, the listeners typically respond by changing their attitudes in the *opposite* direction. The results are quite different, however, if the source is a highly credible expert. Persuasive communication has a greater impact when the expert's position is significantly different from the listener's initial position. The wider the discrepancy, the greater the distress listeners have about the differences between their opinions and the expert's. If the communicator is not an expert, the listeners are inclined to disregard such a discrepant communication: only a fool could have such a far-out position. But if the source is an expert, the wide discrepancy cannot be so easily dismissed, and the listeners are more prone to change their opinions.[13]

Supportive Communication

Supportive communication:
Communication designed to help both parties maintain open and congruent communication by avoiding defensiveness.

While the goal of persuasive communication is to change attitudes, *supportive communication* is designed to avoid defensiveness. When defensiveness occurs, people feel anger and hostility toward the other person, and communication breaks down. Defensiveness on the part of the sender results in incongruent messages, in which there is a mismatch between what the sender thinks and communicates. People are congruent when their feelings are consistent with their behavior. Defensive communicators feel irritated and angry, but refuse to express their feelings and attempt to deny them. Rather than dealing with their upset feelings openly, they allow their hostility to be expressed covertly through sarcasm and insincerity. When defensiveness occurs on the part of the listener, the message is typically not received. Defensive listeners do not listen effectively, and important elements of the message are either ignored or distorted. To the extent that a defensive communication is received, it usually results in a defensive response that further aggravates the problem of ineffective communication. Defensiveness is avoided, or at least reduced, by supportive communication. This type of communication is descriptive, problem-oriented, flexible, and owned rather than disowned.

Descriptive. Supportive communication is descriptive and specific rather than evaluative or general. When people are told that their ideas or behaviors are good or bad, the evaluation process causes them to feel defensive. Evaluative statements create defensiveness and often result in arguments. For example, telling a cashier, "You did a terrible job handling that customer's complaint," would be an evaluative comment that creates defensiveness and antagonism. A descriptive comment, such as "The customer became upset because you interrupted him several times and raised your voice at him," would be less threatening and more supportive.

Descriptive communication allows the situation to be discussed without arousing the need to defend or argue. Descriptive communication consists of three elements: (1) describing the event as objectively as possible, (2) describing your feelings about the event or consequences of the event, and (3) suggesting an alternative that would be more acceptable to you.

As a general rule, communication becomes more useful and arouses less defensiveness as it becomes more specific. For example, "You are a poor cashier," is not a helpful comment because it does not indicate what behaviors need to be changed. In contrast, "You interrupted the customer three times and spoke louder each time," is a specific statement telling the cashier what was wrong.

Problem-oriented. Supportive communication focuses on the specific problem rather than the personalities or status of the members. For example, the statement "You are too hotheaded when a customer comes in with a complaint," is a criticism of the cashier's personality. Problem-oriented communication focuses on the problem and its solution rather than on personal traits or blame. Focusing on the problem rather than personalities is particularly appropriate during performance appraisals, since employees need to understand how to improve their performance, not how to change their personalities. "You are unreliable, and we can't trust you to do your job," is a person-oriented statement that will generate defensiveness and hostility; "Your weekly reports have been late, and some of the information is so inaccurate that we can't use it" is a problem-oriented statement that helps the individual know exactly what is wrong.

Problem-oriented communications also help to avoid making the listener feel inferior. The solution to a problem should be generated by a careful analysis of the problem, not by the invocation of status or power. Defensiveness results when one person attempts to create an impression that says, "I know and you don't," or "I am right and you are wrong," or "I have more power, so we'll do it my way." These statements are examples of win-lose conflict, where one individual attempts to win at the expense of another, or to look good by making others look inferior.

Flexible. Supportive communication is flexible, not rigid. When one person adopts a know-it-all attitude and behaves in a dogmatic manner, the other person becomes defensive, and effective communication is inhibited. "That sales projection has got to be wrong; I know it can't be that high" is a very rigid statement. A much more flexible statement is "It seems to me that the sales projection is wrong; I don't see how it can be that high." People who are dogmatic in their conversation generally prefer to win an argument than to solve a problem, and winning is more important than building a relationship. The consequence of such rigid communication is reciprocal rigidity, defensiveness, and interpersonal conflict.

Flexible communication means that the communicator is willing to accept additional information, and acknowledges that other alternatives may exist. Being flexible is not synonymous with being insecure or easily influenced; it indicates a willingness to learn and grow by considering the contributions of others. Attitudes and opinions are stated provisionally rather than as firm facts. One consequence of flexible communication is that it affirms and acknowledges the potential contribution of other people. Other individuals are encouraged to share their attitudes and opinions because they are led to feel that they can make a significant contribution to the conversation.

Owned. Supportive communication is owned, which means that the communicator takes responsibility for what is said. An example would be "After reviewing your qualifications, I have concluded that you have not satisfied the entrance requirements." Disowning communication, in contrast, is indicated by speaking in the third person or using plural pronouns, such as "We think," or "They said," or "We've heard." By attributing the source of a communication to some unknown party or external source, the communicator avoids responsibility for the message and avoids becoming invested in the communication: "The feeling of the committee is that you have not satisfied all the requirements and should not be admitted." One result of disowning communication is that the listener does not know whose point of view the message represents, and often feels frustrated by not being able to pursue the problem further. Furthermore, disowned communications contain an implicit message that a certain psychological distance should be maintained rather than offering a close, interpersonal relationship.

Listening

Although listening is essential for effective communication, it is probably the most overlooked process in interpersonal communications. Reading, writing, and public speaking are taught in our educational system, and students spend many hours developing these skills, but students are usually left to falter along on their own when it comes to listening. Listening skills are developed to some extent by teaching students how to read and speak; but listening skills are different from reading and speaking skills, and students who are good at reading and speaking may still be very poor listeners.

Studies on listening indicate that most people are at best only mediocre listeners. One study found that most people remember less than half of what they hear immediately after hearing it, no matter how carefully they thought they listened. Two months after listening to a person talk, the average listener will remember less than one fourth of what was said. Listening tests likewise indicate that people usually recall only about 25 percent of a conversation. Furthermore, when asked to rate the extent to which they are skilled listeners, 85 percent rate themselves as average or worse.[14] Clearly, listening is an important skill that needs to be more carefully developed. Effective listening comes from developing empathy and using effective listening skills.

Empathic listening:
Active listening that requires you to project yourself into the speaker's frame of reference to comprehend the full impact of the message.

Empathy. Effective listeners have been called ***active listeners, reflective listeners***, and ***empathic listeners***. Each of these labels implies that the listener must have the ability to listen to another's message empathically. Empathy is the capacity to participate in another's feelings or ideas; it involves understanding and relating to another's feelings. Empathic listeners imaginatively project themselves into the speaker's frame of reference and comprehend the full impact of the message. ***Empathic listening*** involves accurately perceiving the content and also understanding the emotional components and unexpressed meanings contained in the message.

Expressed level of empathy:
The level of understanding at which the listener paraphrases, restates, or summarizes the content of the communication as it was stated.

Implied level of empathy:
A more advanced level of listening in which the listener attends not only to what the communicator expresses, but also to what was implied or left unstated.

Empathic listening involves being able to reflect or restate the communicator's message on two levels. The first level is called the *expressed level of empathy*, in which the listener simply paraphrases, restates, or summarizes the content of the communication. The second level, called the *implied level*, is more advanced, and involves attending not only to what the communicator expresses but also to what was implied or left unstated.

The differences between the expressed and the implied levels can be illustrated by comparing alternative responses to a student who complains about not performing very well on a test. "I read and outlined every chapter in the text and spent 20 hours reviewing my notes and still scored 10 points lower than my roommate, who didn't even read all the chapters." At the expressed level of empathy, the listener responds to the content and emotion of what was expressed: "You feel frustrated because you tried so hard to learn and still didn't do as well as your roommate." At the implied level of empathy, however, the listener responds not only to what was said but also to the implied or unstated component: "You sound discouraged about trying so hard and not doing as well as your roommate. It can be very frustrating when you try so hard and not do as well as you expected. When that happens, it's easy to get depressed and feel sorry for yourself."

Good empathizers need to know when to display each level of empathy. At the beginning of an interaction, listeners need to use the expressed level. The implied level is not appropriate until a feeling of trust and acceptance has been created. If the listener continues to use the expressed level as the relationship advances, the expressed level will appear superficial and insincere. If the listener uses the implied level of empathy too early in the interaction before a feeling of trust and acceptance has been developed, the communicator may feel threatened, as though he or she were being psychoanalyzed.

Effective Listening Skills. Many listeners believe listening is just a matter of sitting back and absorbing information like a sponge. Effective listening does not just happen, however; it requires much effort and hard work.

Different situations call for different kinds of listening. In a classroom, for example, students listen to obtain information and comprehend the most important concepts. In a political debate, the public often listen to confirm previously held biases supporting their points of view. In a courtroom, the opposing lawyer listens for faults, weaknesses, and contradictions in the testimony. In building a relationship, an empathic listener tries to understand the content and feeling of the message to enhance personal growth for both the communicator and the listener.

Several lists of guidelines have been proposed to explain the principles of good listening. Ten principles of effective listening are summarized in Exhibit 15.3. These ten principles identify the major differences between good and bad listeners. Good listeners look for areas of interest, overlook errors of delivery and objectionable personal mannerisms, postpone judgment until they understand the central point, listen for ideas and identify the main points, take careful notes to help them remember, are actively responsive in trying to listen, resist distractions, challenge their minds by trying to learn difficult material, capitalize on mind speed, and assist and encourage the speaker by asking for clarifying information and paraphrasing the ideas.[15]

Exhibit 15.3 Principles of Effective Listening

Principle	The Good Listener	The Bad Listener
1. Look for areas of interest	Seeks personal enlightenment; entertains new topics as potentially interesting	Tunes out dry subjects; narrowly defines what is interesting
2. Overlook errors of delivery.	Attends to meaning and content; ignores delivery errors while being sensitive to any messages in them	Ignores if delivery is poor; misses messages because of personal attributes of the communicator
3. Postpone judgement.	Avoids quick judgments; waits until comprehension of the core message is complete	Quickly evaluates and passes judgement; inflexible regarding contrary messages
4. Listen for ideas.	Listens for ideas and themes; identifies the main points	Listens for facts and details
5. Take notes	Takes careful notes using a variety of methods depending on the speaker	Takes incomplete notes using one system
6. Be actively responsive.	Responds frequently with nods, "uh-huhs," etc.; shows active body state	Passive demeanor; few or no responses; little energy output
7. Resist distractions.	Resists being distracted; has a long attention span; puts loaded words in perspective	Easily distracted; focuses on loaded or emotional works; short attention span
8. Challenge your mind.	Uses difficult material to stimulate the mind; seeks to enlarge understanding	Avoids difficult material; does not seek to broaden knowledge base
9. Capitalize on mind speed.	Uses listening time to summarize and anticipate the message; attends to implicit as well as explicit messages	Daydreams with slow speakers; becomes preoccupied with other thoughts
10. Help and encourage the speaker	Asks for examples or clarifying information; rephrases the idea	Interrupts; asks trivial questions; makes distracting comments

Source: Developed by Kim Cameron.

Making Appropriate Responses. An important element in effective listening is responding to the communicator by making appropriate responses. Some responses stimulate the communicator to discuss the issue more extensively and expand to related areas of interest. Other responses tend to restrict the topic of communication or terminate the conversation.

The appropriateness of a response depends largely on the purpose of the communication and the goal of the interaction. If the purpose of the conversation is to evaluate performance, an evaluative or confrontive response is generally best. However, if the purpose of the interaction is to help another individual solve a problem or make a decision, a reflective or probing response is generally most appropriate. Six response types have been identified that range from directive responses, which close communication, to nondirective, which tend to open additional topics for consideration, as shown in Exhibit 15.4. Each of these six responses is appropriate for different purposes.[16]

Nonverbal Communication

Face-to-face communication involves more than just the words we use. The verbal portion actually constitutes only a small part of the total message. The way

Exhibit 15.4   Six Alternative Types of Responses

These six responses illustrate different ways of responding to an irate customer who states, "I ordered that part last month, and you said it would be here in a week. I think you're trying to take advantage of me."

1. Evaluative responses: Pass judgment, express agreement or disagreement, or offer advice; for example, "We are not trying to take advantage of you. You need to be patient longer." Evaluative responses are useful after a topic has been explored in depth, and it is appropriate for the responder to express an opinion.

2. Confrontive responses: Challenge the other person to clarify the message and identify points of inconsistency or contradiction; for example, "Just because we haven't been able to deliver the part yet doesn't mean we're taking advantage of you. No one else feels that way." Confrontation is useful for helping people clarify their thoughts and feelings or to think more broadly about the issue.

3. Diverting responses: Change the focus of the communicator's problem to a problem selected by the responder; for example, "Your comment reminds me of a problem I had last summer. I remember when . . ." Diverting responses often involve changing the subject and are helpful when a point of comparison is needed and the communicator needs to know that someone else has experienced a similar event.

4. Probing responses: Ask the communicator to clarify what was said or to provide additional information or illustration; for example, "Yes, our deliveries are late, but could you tell me specifically why you think we're trying to take advantage of you?" Probing responses are useful when the respondent needs specific information to understand the message or the communicator needs to respond to another topic in order to make the communication clearer.

5. Pacifying responses: Reduce the intensity of emotion associated with the message and help to calm the communicator; for example, "There's no need to think that we're trying to take advantage of you; the delay is simply out of our control." Pacifying responses are useful when the communicator needs to be reassured that discussing the message is acceptable or when the intensity of feeling being experienced is inhibiting good communication.

6. Reflective or reinterpretive responses: Reflect back to the communicator what was heard, but in different words; for example, "You're saying that we intentionally misrepresented our delivery date and are treating you unfairly." Reflective responses help communicators know they have been both heard and understood. Reflective responses should not simply mimic the communicator or be a direct restatement of what was said. Instead, they should contribute understanding, meaning, and acceptance to the conversations.

in which the words are arranged and presented, including the tone, rate of speech, inflection, pauses, and facial expressions, actually provide most of the message's content for the receiver. The words themselves do not stand alone but depend on nonverbal components for their true meaning. To illustrate, the expression "Isn't this just great!" could be used as an honest expression of happiness and joy, but if it is used with the appropriate facial expression and intonation, it becomes a sarcastic comment conveying disgust and contempt. The study of nonverbal communication has identified five major variables that influence the meaning of messages. These five variables include physical distance, posture, facial cues, vocal cues, and appearance.

Physical Distance. The study of the way people structure their space and the distances between people in daily interactions is called *proxemics*.[17] The physical distance between the source and the receiver communicates a message in itself, in addition to influencing the interpretation of what is said. We tend to stand closer when talking with people we know and like, and farther away from people we do not know or do not like. Shaking hands and touching is

Proxemics:
A study of the physical distance between two people during communication.

another way to communicate to people that you like them and have an interest in them. Physical distance is also an indication of status, and subordinates tend to maintain greater distance between themselves and people of higher status. Elevation can also be used as an indication of status, particularly in some cultures, such as Tonga. People of higher status are seated on higher-level platforms than people of lower status.

Kinesics:
A study of the posture of people while speaking.

Posture. The study of posture and other body movements, including facial expressions and gestures, is called *kinesics*.[18] Posture, or body language, can be used to indicate numerous things, including liking or status. We tend to relax by leaning backward, maintaining an open-arm posture, and directly facing those we like. However, we tend to become rigid and tense around those of high status or those whom we perceive as threatening. Higher-status individuals are generally more relaxed in posture than those of lower status. Standing, pacing, and putting your hands on your hips are all nonverbal cues of high status. When talking to another individual, we can communicate an element of responsiveness and interest in what they have to say by making spontaneous gestures, shifting our posture from side to side, and moving closer to the individual.

Facial Cues. Although some people tend to be rather expressionless, others are very expressive and communicate many messages just using facial cues. In a job interview, for example, eye contact is an important indicator of an applicant's competence and strength of character. A pleasant facial expression also communicates a feeling of liking for another individual. We tend to maintain eye contact with people we like and avoid contact with those we dislike. High-status people tend to display less eye contact than do those of lower status. Smiling, furrowing one's eyebrows, and other facial expressions also indicate a degree of responsiveness to the communicator.[19]

Paralinguistics:
A study of the meaning of vocal cues during communication.

Vocal Cues. The study of the human voice, including range, pitch, rhythm, resonance, and tempo, is called *paralinguistics*.[20] Interpersonal attraction and concern for another individual can be expressed through vocal cues. Speaking in a pleasant tone of voice at a moderate rate of speed indicates a desire to communicate with the other individual. Anger is usually expressed in a loud, high-pitched tone of voice, while boredom is expressed with a deep, lethargic tone of voice. Lower-status people tend to have a lower voice volume than do those of higher status. Speaking loudly, rapidly, and in a moderate tone of voice generally conveys a sense of intensity and enthusiasm.

Appearance. Physical appearance, especially clothing, sends surprisingly strong nonverbal messages. High-status people often display appropriate ornaments, such as the badges and bars used in the military or police units. "Dress for success" seminars emphasize the importance of appearance in manipulating one's personal power and status in a group. For example, it is suggested that men wear long-sleeved rather than short-sleeved shirts if they want to increase their personal power and have greater influence on the outcome of a committee meeting.[21]

Although listeners may be unaware of it, they often look for nonverbal indicators as they listen to the message. The evidence suggests that women are more effective than men at both encoding and decoding nonverbal messages.[22]

If the nonverbal component supports the verbal message, it can reinforce the intended meaning of the message and assist the receiver in properly decoding the message. However, if communicators say one thing but nonverbally transmit a different message, the receiver tends to give more credence to the nonverbal components. For example, if supervisors use an apathetic, monotonic voice to say, "Thanks, I really appreciate what you've done," their vocal cues destroy their intended message.

In a courtroom, jurors may ignore the testimony of a witness whose verbal testimony is inconsistent with his or her nonverbal behavior. Post-trial interviews with jurors have revealed that the testimony of a key witness may be discounted because the paralinguistic behaviors of the witness overwhelm the content of the testimony.[23]

ORGANIZATIONAL COMMUNICATION

The Effects of Organizational Structure on Communication

There is a common misperception about communication problems in organizations. The "myth of open communication" suggests that organizational problems are caused by inadequate communication, and the solution is to make all information universally available. In fact, just the opposite is true. An important function of organizational structure is to *restrict* communication flows and thus *decrease* problems of confusion and information overload. Some organizational problems are solved not by increasing but by restricting the flow of communication and clearly specifying how information is to be gathered, processed, and analyzed.

Consider the situation of 60 people who gather informally in an auditorium. As long as they interact with whomever they choose, they will remain a disorganized collection of people regardless of their purpose for meeting. Unless the communication channels become organized and constraints are placed on the flow of information, this group will find it virtually impossible to accomplish anything, whether they are a state legislature, a college fraternity, or a group of concerned citizens. With an unorganized group of 60 people visiting at random, the number of potential communication links between two people is $N(N - 1)/2$, or 1,770. However, if they are organized into six groups of ten with a formally appointed leader, the number of communication channels is reduced to just nine in each group.

The situation is similar to that of an orchestra. If 60 musicians play whatever they want, such as they do when they are warming up, the result is unpleasant noise rather than beautiful music. To make beautiful music, the members must play exactly what they are supposed to play at exactly the right time. The same is true of communication patterns in organizations. To move from an unorganized state to an organized state requires that restrictions be placed on the flow of communication. People must use the appropriate communication channels, and only job-relevant information should be transmitted. Unrestricted communication produces noise and confusion in the organization. Without precision and timing, there may be sound but no music. Likewise, without structure and regulations, there may be conversations but no meaning.

Direction of Communication Flow

One way to analyze organizational communication is to study the direction of information flow, that is, who communicates with whom. The three most important directions of formal communication flow are downward, upward, and horizontal. Informal communication is circulated through the grapevine.

Downward Communication. Downward communication follows the organizational hierarchy, and flows from higher-level people to those in lower levels. The most common downward communication includes explanations of organizational policies and practices, instructions about how to do the job, the rationale for the job's importance, feedback to subordinates about their performance, and explanations of the goals of the organization. This information teaches subordinates how to perform their jobs properly and makes them feel part of the organization. However, organizational members frequently complain that the information they receive is both inadequate and inaccurate. A typical complaint is "We have absolutely no idea what's happening." Although managers usually communicate job instructions adequately, they fail to provide an adequate rationale for the job or sufficient feedback to subordinates.

A problem in downward communication is inaccuracy as the information is passed from level to level. Orders are typically expressed in a language appropriate for the next level down rather than the lowest level, where the message is aimed. Therefore, as the information travels down the organizational structure, it needs to be adapted to the members at each successive level. A classic study of downward communications in 100 organizations estimated that 80 percent of the information was lost after passing through five levels of the organization.[24]

Upward Communication. Upward communication is designed to provide feedback on how well the organization is functioning. Lower-level employees are expected to provide upward communication about their performance and the organization's practices and policies. The most common forms of upward communication include memos, written reports, suggestion boxes, group meetings, and grievances.

The most serious upward communication problem is filtered information. Since it is typically used to monitor the organization's performance, upward communication can best be described as what subordinates want the supervisors to hear rather than what the supervisors need to know. Another problem with upward communication is that organizations typically rely on lower-level members to initiate it. Instead of actively soliciting information and providing channels for receiving it, managers frequently adopt an open-door policy and assume that people who have something to say will voluntarily express it.

Horizontal Communication. Horizontal communication is lateral communication between peers; it does not follow the formal organizational hierarchy. Formal bureaucratic structures do not provide for horizontal communication, and one of the challenges in creating an effective organization is providing acceptable channels for lateral communication. Adhering strictly to a formal chain of command is inefficient, and creates a serious communication overload for upper-level executives. However, unrestricted horizontal communication detracts from maximum efficiency. Organizations must provide for horizontal communication channels where they are necessary, while restricting unnecessary channels.

In addition to helping people coordinate their work, horizontal communication among peers furnishes emotional and social support. Horizontal communication contributes to the development of friendships and informal work groups.

Grapevine:
The informal communication system through which messages are passed in an organization, especially rumors and myths.

Informal Communication. Informal communication is called *grapevine communication,* and it exists in every organization. The *grapevine* is created by informal associations, and cuts across formal lines of communication. Some of the major characteristics of grapevine information are as follows:

1. Grapevines are found in every organization, and they are virtually impossible to eliminate. It is only natural for employees to discuss matters of mutual concern, and even the closest monitoring of their conversations will not prevent them from talking.
2. Information usually travels more rapidly through the grapevine than through official communication channels.
3. The grapevine is a more spontaneous form of expression, hence more intrinsically gratifying and credible than formal communication.
4. In situations where official censorship and filtering occur, grapevine information is more informative.
5. On noncontroversial topics related to the organization, most of the information communicated through the grapevine (estimated to be at least 75 percent) is correct. Emotionally charged information, however, is more likely to be distorted.
6. The number of people who serve as actual links in the grapevine is generally relatively small (estimated to be less than 10 percent of the group).[25]

Occasionally grapevines benefit the organization, and managers use them as a regular substitute for formal communication. For example, the grapevine can be used to test reactions to a proposed change without actually making a formal commitment. Managers have been known to leak ideas to the grapevine just to test their acceptability before implementing them.

Grapevines tend to cause trouble in organizations that are characterized by a lack of trust and confidence among managers and workers. The unfortunate irony is that organizations most in need of an effective grapevine are usually plagued by a grapevine prone to distortion. Grapevines provide a disservice when they become a constant source of false rumors. Rumors seem to spread fastest and farthest when the information is ambiguous, when the content of the rumor is important to those involved, and when the people are emotionally aroused.

Although rumors can be destructive to an organization, it has been shown that some stories and myths perpetuated in organizations contribute greatly to the organization's effectiveness by preserving valuable aspects of the organization's culture. At Hewlett-Packard Corporation, for example, feelings of job security among employees are perpetuated by a story describing how the workers at one point years ago went on a reduced workweek to avoid layoffs and preserve jobs.[26]

Communication Roles

Communication integrates and coordinates the various activities of an organization and helps it function more effectively. If communication were eliminated, the organization would cease to exist. Studies of communication networks in real organizations have identified four communication roles that disseminate information within the organization and help it communicate with the outside world.

Gatekeeper:
A communication role in an organizational structure that controls the flow of information, especially between lower and upper levels in the organization.

Liaison:
A communication role within an organizational structure in which an individual serves as a communication link between two groups.

Opinion leader:
A communication role in an organizational structure in which noted personalities become the opinion leaders who receive information from the mass media and interpret it for other organizational members.

Boundary spanners:
Individuals who perform the role of communicating with the organization's environment by sensing environmental changes and selling the organization to the environment.

Gatekeepers. A *gatekeeper* is someone who controls the flow of messages between two people or two groups in an organization structure. A gatekeeper in a communication network acts like a valve in a water pipe. One function of the gatekeeper is to decrease information overload by filtering the flow of messages from one group to another. An example is a quality control clerk who collects daily reports, summarizes them, and presents them to the plant manager.

Liaisons. A *liaison* is someone who connects two or more cliques within a system without belonging to either clique. Liaisons are the cement, or the linking pin, that holds the groups of an organization together. Liaisons are somewhat similar to gatekeepers, but while gatekeepers typically govern the flow of upward communication, liaisons are typically positioned between two groups that are not arranged hierarchically. An example of a liaison between a football team and the faculty is a sports writer who tells the faculty about the team and its travel schedule, and tells players how they are doing in class.

Opinion Leaders. *Opinion leaders* fill an important role in what is called the two-step flow model of attitude change. Persuasive messages flow from the mass media to opinion leaders, who interpret the information and pass it on to the public audience.[27] Within a group, opinion leaders are able to influence the attitudes of group members by helping them interpret new information and define situations.

Boundary Spanners. *Boundary spanners* are people who communicate with the organization's environment. These people are typically top executives who travel widely and enjoy many types of contact with other organizations. They help the organization gain acceptance in society and sense social changes that could influence the organization. In one sense, boundary spanners are a special type of gatekeeper because they control the communication flows by which new ideas enter the organization. Boundary spanners help the organization predict future changes and cope with its environment.

IMPROVING COMMUNICATION EFFECTIVENESS

Improving communication in organizations involves more accurate encoding, transmitting, decoding, and feedback at the interpersonal level, and at the organizational level, creating and monitoring appropriate communication channels. Several strategies can be used to help managers communicate more effectively.

Increasing Feedback. Adequate feedback lets communicators know whether their messages need to be revised or repeated, thus reducing the frequency and severity of misunderstanding. Feedback mechanisms are just as important for organizational communication as they are in interpersonal communication. Top managers should not issue orders or policy statements and assume they have been understood. Feedback mechanisms and reporting systems need to be established, so managers know whether their messages have been understood, accepted, and followed.

Regulating Information Flow. Managers who want everyone to "see the big picture" often create a serious communication overload. Rather than trying to keep everyone involved, top-level managers need to follow the *"need-to-know" principle* when transmitting downward communication. Managers should ask whether lower-level positions need this information to perform their tasks effectively. If the answer is no, the message should not be transmitted. Another useful principle in regulating the flow of information is the *exception principle.* This principle states that only significant deviations from standard policies and procedures should be brought to the attention of superiors. As long as performance falls within the acceptable range, regular procedures are followed.

Repetition. Repetition helps listeners interpret messages that are ambiguous, unclear, or too difficult to understand the first time. Repetition also reduces the problem of forgetting. Since forgetting is such a serious problem, many managers adopt the policy of having very important messages repeated at least three or four times. Effective communicators build repetition into their presentations by expressing the same idea in different ways. A popular strategy in both writing and speaking to help the audience remember the main point is to tell them what you're going to tell them, then tell them, then tell them what you've told them.

Simplifying Language. Complex language, technical terms, and jargon make communication difficult to understand and frustrating to the listener. Complex ideas do not require complex terms to explain them. Almost every idea can be explained in relatively simple language. When it is important that listeners understand the message, communicators should make certain that the language they use is clear and easily understood.

There are times when complex language using jargon and technical terms is appropriate. When a message is communicated to an audience that understands them, technical terms and jargon are useful. Scientific research reports, for example, are written for an audience of scientists who understand the technical terms that are used. One advantage of using technical terms is that they have a precise meaning that conveys precise information without using many words. Although simple language tends to increase comprehension, complex language tends to save time and make communication more efficient for those who comprehend it.

One of the best ways to simplify an explanation is to provide an example or illustration. Complex ideas are not only difficult to understand but also difficult to remember. A simple illustration helps the listener comprehend the idea and remember it. Sometimes when listeners feel baffled and confused, the most effective thing they can do is simply ask, "Can you give me an example to help me understand that?"

Effective Timing. A useful strategy for improving communication is to manage the timing of messages so that they are received in an orderly manner. Speakers often begin to speak before the listeners are ready to listen. Many managers find that messages come to them in a disorganized fashion, and they cannot switch effectively from one topic to another as rapidly as they need to. This principle is similar to the procedure many executives use in responding to their in-baskets. Incoming mail is sorted into related topics. A similar procedure can be used, to some extent, with verbal communication where time periods are scheduled for discussing a specific topic. Organizations can schedule conferences, meetings, and retreats to focus on identified problems without the influence of other distractions.

Barriers to Effective Communication

The following are nine of the major barriers to effective communication.

Omission. The transmitted message is almost always an abbreviated representation of the intended meaning. Listeners may hear a message and feel secure thinking they understood the communication, but what they may not realize is that what they heard was neither complete nor what the sender really intended to say.

Filtering. Filtering is the manipulation of information so that selected data, especially negative comments, are either removed or altered before they are transmitted to the next individual.

Time Pressures. Limited time, which is a reality in every aspect of life, causes vital information to be distorted or deleted. Occasionally people who should be included in the formal communication channel are overlooked, creating a situation called *short-circuiting.*

Jargon. Jargon consists of abbreviated words or simplified phrases summarizing more complex concepts that convey a unique meaning to other group members. Consequently, jargon tends to increase the speed and accuracy of communication within groups, and strengthen cohesiveness. But it creates a difficult barrier for members outside the group. New group members typically feel confused and alienated from the group until they master the jargon.

Value Judgments. While the source is speaking, the receiver should be listening. However, many receivers assign an overall worth to the message based on small samples of it and then begin to develop a rebuttal. Effective listening requires that the listener suspend judgment until the entire message has been received, and only then evaluate the worth or accuracy of the message.

Differing Frames of Reference. Accurate communication requires that the encoding and decoding processes be based on a common field of experience that the sender and receiver may not share. For example, two people will have difficulty talking about living in the mountains of Idaho if snowy winters mean skiing, snowmobiling, and ice skating to one while the other thinks about wet feet, cold hands, icy roads, and cars that won't start.

Selective Listening. The problem of selective listening is part of the larger problem of selective perception, in which people tend to listen to only part of a message and ignore other information. We hear only what we want to hear and tend to disregard information that creates cognitive dissonance or threatens our self-esteem. We try to ignore information that conflicts with established beliefs or values.

Semantic Problems. Occasionally people who speak the same language discover that the symbols they use do not have a common meaning. Semantic problems are particularly troublesome in communicating abstract concepts or technical terms. Words such as "discounted present value," "exercise option," and "trusts" have special meanings to a finance executive that they do not have to someone in production.

Information Overload. When people receive more messages than they can possibly handle, they experience communication overload. New and innovative communication channels, such as facsimile, voice mail, Internet, teleconferencing, and electronic mail, are making communication easier, faster, and more convenient, but they are also causing a severe information overload. Organizations are being forced to create usage guidelines for the effective use of communication channels.

Reactions to Communication Overload

Organizational processes are frequently responsible for generating excessive amounts of communication. Too much communication can be just as troublesome as inadequate communication. Individuals and organizations use a variety of reactions to communication overload; some are more adaptive than others. Adaptive responses focus on solving the problem, whereas dysfunctional responses do not, although they may delay the collapse of the system momentarily.

Disregarding involves ignoring what cannot be easily absorbed, which is a dysfunctional response, since information is disregarded on an irrational basis. The information that is typically ignored is usually the information that seems the most difficult to comprehend or the least pleasant to attend to.

Queuing consists of collecting the information in a pile, with the expectation of processing it at a later time. Queuing is only appropriate for recorded information such as letters, phone mail, and memos. Telephone calls and other verbal messages cannot be conveniently placed in a queue. Queuing, or delaying the processing of information, can be either an adaptive or dysfunctional response, depending on the amount of overload. If messages continue to arrive faster than they can be processed, the queue becomes infinitely long. However, if there is adequate time between the surges of incoming messages to process them, queuing may be an effective way to respond.

Filtering involves screening information that appears to be irrelevant, and it can also be either adaptive or dysfunctional, depending on whether useful guidelines have been created for deciding what to screen. People tend to screen information that they do not readily understand or that does not make them look good.

Approximating consists of processing a sample of the information and using it to make inferences regarding the rest of the information. Approximation is typically an adaptive response, because most information is highly redundant, and a random sample usually provides a good estimate of the total message.

Multiple Channels involves assigning different people or departments to be responsible for collecting and analyzing portions of the information. It is a highly adaptive response in terms of organizational effectiveness. An example of this decentralized process of handling information is to have employee complaints sent to the employee relations department, questions about stock options referred to the finance department, and issues regarding product quality submitted to the quality control department.

Discussion Questions

1. What are the principles of supportive communication, and how does it differ from persuasive communication? Provide some illustrations of when you would want to use supportive communication, and describe what you would say.
2. How good are your listening skills? What can you do to be a better listener? What are the principles involved in being a good listener?
3. Why must communication be restricted in an organization? Can you provide any examples, fictitious or real, that illustrate how the free flow of communication can disrupt an organization?
4. What are the major conditions that contribute to information overload? Explain the methods of responding to an information overload, and provide illustrations of them to indicate when they are functional or dysfunctional.

Notes

1. Aristotle, *Rhetoric*. See also Annette N. Shelby, "The Theoretical Bases of Persuasion: A Critical Introduction," *Journal of Business Communication* 23 (Winter 1986): 5–29.
2. Carl I. Hovland and W. Weiss, "The Influence of Source Credibility on Communication Effectiveness," *Public Opinion Quarterly* 15 (1952): 635–50.
3. H. C. Kelman and C. I. Hovland, "'Restatement' of the Communicator in Delayed Measurement of Opinion Change," *Journal of Abnormal and Social Psychology* 48 (1953): 326–35.
4. Roobina Ohanian, "Construction and Validation of a Scale to Measure Celebrity Endorsers' Perceived Expertise, Trustworthiness, and Attractiveness," *Journal of Advertising* 19, 3 (1990): 39–52; Roobina Ohanian, "The Impact of Celebrity Spokespersons' Perceived Image on Consumers'

Intention to Purchase," *Journal of Advertising Research* 31 (February–March 1991): 46–54.

5. David Kipnis and Stuart Schmidt, "The Language of Persuasion; Hard, Soft, or Rational: Our Choice Depends on Power, Expectations, and What We Hope to Accomplish," *Psychology Today* 19 (April 1985): 40–45.

6. R. A. Jones and J. W. Brehm, "Persuasiveness of One-and Two-Sided Communications as a Function of Awareness: There Are Two Sides," *Journal of Experimental Social Psychology* 6 (1970): 47–56.

7. N. Miller and D. Campbell, "Recency and Primacy in Persuasion as a Function of the Timing of Speeches and Measurements," *Journal of Abnormal and Social Psychology* 59 (1959): 1–9.

8. H. Leventhal and P. Niles, "Persistence of Influence for Varying Duration of Exposure to Threat Stimuli," *Psychological Reports* 16 (1965): 223–33; H. Leventhal and R. Singer, "Affect Arousal and Positioning of Recommendation in Persuasive Communications," *Journal of Personality and Social Psychology* 4 (1966): 137–46; H. Leventhal, R. Singer, and S. Jones, "The Effects of Fear and Specificity of Recommendation upon Attitudes and Behavior," *Journal of Personality and Social Psychology* 2 (1965): 20–29.

9. Irving L. Janis and Semour Feshbach, "Effects of Fear-Arousing Communications," *Journal of Abnormal and Social Psychology* 48 (1953): 78–92.

10. Paula T. Hertel and Alice Narvaez, "Confusing Memories for Verbal and Nonverbal Communication," *Journal of Personality and Social Psychology* 50, 3 (1986): 474–81.

11. S. Chaiken and A. H. Eagly, "Communication Modality as a Determinant of Message Persuasiveness and Message Comprehensibility" *Journal of Personality and Social Psychology* 34 (1976): 605–14.

12. Reviewed by Everett Rogers and Rekha Agarwala-Rogers, *Communication in Organizations* (New York: Free Press, 1976).

13. E. Aronson, J. Tumer, and I. M. Carlsmith, "Communicator Credibility and Communicator Discrepancy as Determinants of Opinion Change," *Journal of Abnormal and Social Psychology* 67 (1963): 31–36; Marvin E. Goldberg and Jon Hartwick, "The Effects of Advertiser Reputation and Extremity of Advertising Claim on Advertising Effectiveness," *Journal of Consumer Research* 17 (September 1990): 172–79.

14. Ralph Nichols, "You Don't Know How to Listen," *Colliers Magazine* (July 1953): 16–17; Lyman K. Steil, "Your Listening Profile" (Sperry Corporation, 1980).

15. Steven Golen, "A Factor Analysis of Barriers to Effective Listening," *Journal of Business Communication* 27 (Winter 1990): 25–36.

16. David Whetten and Kim Cameron, *Developing Management Skills* (Glenview, IL: Scott, Foresman, 1984), chap. 5.

17. Philip V. Lewis, *Organizational Communication,* 3rd ed. (New York: Wiley, 1987), chap. 5.

18. R. H. Birdwhistell, *Kinesics and Context* (Philadelphia: University of Pennsylvania Press, 1970).

19. A. Mehrabian, "Communication Without Words," *Psychology Today* (1968): 52–55; Neil R. Anderson, "Decision Making in the Graduate

Selection Interview: An Experimental Investigation," *Human Relations*, 44 (April 1991): 403–17.

20. Lewis, op. cit.

21. John T. Malloy, *Dress for Success* (New York: Warner Books, 1975).

22. Gerald H. Graham, Jeanne Unruh, and Paul Jennings, "The Impact of Nonverbal Communication in Organizations: A Survey of Perceptions," *Journal of Business Communication* 28 (Winter 1991): 45–62.

23. Aaron Abbott and Adam Davis, "Pre-Trial Assessments Make Witness Testimony Pay Off," *Risk Management* 36 (June 1989): 22–29.

24. Reported in Rogers and Agarwala-Rogers, op. cit., p.93.

25. Harold Sutton and Lyman W. Porter, "A Study of the Grapevine in a Governmental Organization," *Personnel Psychology* 21(1968): 223–30.

26. Alan Wilkins, "The Culture Audit: A Tool for understanding Organizations," *Organizational Dynamics* 12, 2 (Autumn 1983): 24–38.

27. V. O. Key, Jr., *Public Opinion and American Democracy* (New York: Knopf, 1961).

Use Open Communication in Troubled Times

Because of an economic recession, Hugh Aaron, the CEO of a small closely held plastics manufacturer, told his employees that the company must eliminate overtime, wage increases, quarterly bonuses, and the purchase of new equipment; even his own salary was being cut. This announcement was spurned with suspicion and resentment. To counter the snickers of doubt and innuendo, management decided to share the company's entire financial records with its employees.

The decision to open the company's records was difficult, because such information is usually kept from employees. But the biggest problem was helping employees understand how to interpret a profit-and-loss statement. A manager who enjoyed teaching held daily sessions with small groups of employees to explain basic accounting and finance.

Some employees were still skeptical, and accused the company of keeping two sets of books for ulterior motives. In response, the company's outside accountant and auditor attended the next session to validate the figures and to explain their fiduciary responsibilities.

Gradually the employees' skepticism changed from questioning the profits to questioning the costs. They wanted to know, for example, why the company spent $4,000 each quarter on laundry expenses. When they were told it was for the uniforms they carelessly tossed into a laundry heap each night, they suggested buying washers and dryers and laundering their own uniforms. They also questioned why the company spent several thousand dollars on a Christmas party and suggested that it be eliminated. Each employee was given direct responsibility for making policy decisions that affected him or her, including the janitor, who chose the most efficient and economical broom to buy.

Although some employees could not see beyond their own narrow interests, open communication helped most of them see and accept the company's financial crisis. Open communication helped the company survive in difficult times.

Questions

1. Why are a company's financial records not usually open to all employees?
2. If sharing financial information with all employees made this company more efficient, is this something other companies should also consider? Why, or when?
3. The myth of universal information suggests that every group functions better when everyone knows everything. What are the problems with this idea, and do they arise here?

Part I: Information Dissemination

Purpose. The purpose of this exercise is to determine how accurately information is passed from one individual to another. It is also designed to examine the kinds of distortion that occur and why.

Instructions. Five individuals should be selected from the class for this exercise, and four of them should be asked to leave the room. While they are out, the remaining person (person 1) receives a message by looking at a picture or listening to the description of an incident. Person 2 is then invited back into the room, and person 1 describes the message to person 2 in front of the class. Person 3 is invited back into the room, and person 2 then describes the message to person 3, who describes it to person 4, who describes it to person 5. While this information is being passed from person 1 to person 5, other class members identify the information that was added, deleted, or changed.

Part II: Nonverbal Communication

Purpose. The purpose of this exercise is to help you see how information is communicated through body language, and to help you be more sensitive to nonverbal messages.

Instructions. For this exercise, the class should be divided into groups of six to ten members. Two individuals in each group should be identified as actors, preferably one male and one female. The ten emotions shown below should be listed on the board for class members to see. The actors will rearrange the order of the ten emotions and then try to portray them to the group without saying anything. Each actor will have 3-4 minutes to portray all ten emotions, about 20 seconds per emotion. The members of the group should try to identify the emotions and record them without any group interaction.

Anger	Jealousy
Fear	Sympathy
Boredom	Infatuation
Happiness	Embarrassment
Enthusiasm	Despair

CHAPTER 16

Decision Making

Chapter Outline

Individual Decision Making
- The Decision-Making Process
- Cognitive Limits of Rationality
- Psychological Limitations

Group Decision Making
- Individual versus Group Decision Making
- Group Influences on Decisions

Decision Making in Organizations
- Types of Decisions
- Decision-Making Techniques

INDIVIDUAL DECISION MAKING

The Decision-Making Process

The basic elements of the rational decision-making process consist of establishing goals and objectives, identifying problems, developing and evaluating alternatives, choosing an alternative and implementing it, and evaluating its results. This model is derived from classical decision theory, which assumes that people are rational decision makers who have immediate access to all relevant information, who can identify all feasible solutions and evaluate them, and who will always select the best alternative.

```
┌─────────────────────────────────────┐
│  Establish goals and objectives      │
└─────────────────────────────────────┘
                 │
                 ▼
┌─────────────────────────────────────┐
│  Identify the problem                │
└─────────────────────────────────────┘
                 │
                 ▼
┌─────────────────────────────────────┐
│  Develop alternative solutions       │
└─────────────────────────────────────┘
                 │
                 ▼
┌─────────────────────────────────────┐
│  Evaluate the alternatives           │
└─────────────────────────────────────┘
                 │
                 ▼
┌─────────────────────────────────────┐
│  Choose an alternative               │
└─────────────────────────────────────┘
                 │
                 ▼
┌─────────────────────────────────────┐
│  Implement the decision              │
└─────────────────────────────────────┘
                 │
                 ▼
┌─────────────────────────────────────┐
│  Evaluate and control                │
└─────────────────────────────────────┘
```

This model outlines the elements in the normal decision-making process and identifies some of the obstacles to effective decision making. Knowing the elements in this decision-making process can help you avoid feelings of frustration and uncertainty when problems arise. For example, if the person who normally drives you to work tells you that you will need to find other transportation, you might feel temporarily overwhelmed by this problem until you systematically go through the decision-making process. Your objective is to be to work on time every day without spending much money on transportation, and your problem is that you do not have a way to get there. Alternatives might include taking public transportation, finding a new car pool, making a new friend at work who could drive you, or buying a new car or bicycle. You would need to evaluate the pros and cons of each of these alternatives relative to your goals and objectives, and then select the best one. After you implement your decision you may reevaluate it and conclude that you did not choose the best alternative. For example, if you decided to take the bus but found that it was too slow, you might change your mind and get a bicycle.

Cognitive Limits of Rationality

This rational decision-making model is somewhat misleading because it implies that decision making follows a fixed series of logical steps and that people are purely rational decision makers. In reality, individual decision making is far less orderly or systematic than this process suggests. We typically do not make completely rational and well informed decisions.

Bounded rationality:
The idea that there are limits to our capacity to think rationally because of our inability to gather infinite information and process it accurately. Therefore, there are cognitive limits to our rationality based on limits in our ability to think, reason, and process information.

Bounded Rationality. The model of the perfectly rational decision maker was challenged by Herbert Simon, a Nobel Prize winner, who suggested that administrators exhibit *bounded rationality* rather than perfect rationality.[1] Bounded rationality implies that people are forced to make decisions under a number of external and psychological constraints. People do not have perfect information regarding the problem, nor are they aware of all feasible solutions. And even if this information were available, they would probably not have the mental ability to understand and remember it all, nor would they want to even if they could. The decision maker's ability to analyze only a few things at a time is referred to as *cognitive limits of rationality*. Contrary to the rational decision-maker model, most people explore very few alternatives and make decisions after considering only a small amount of information.

Satisficing:
Rather than evaluating every alternative and selecting the optimal one, decision makers look until they find the first satisfactory alternative that achieves a minimum level of outcome.

Maximizing:
The unrealistic notion that decision makers carefully consider all possible alternatives and select the one that maximizes their rewards.

Suboptimizing:
Making decisions that do not provide an optimal solution for everyone simultaneously. While a decision may optimal according to one criterion, it is suboptimal or inferior according to other criteria.

Escalation of commitment:
The willingness to invest additional time and resources to achieve a successful outcome as a result of having already invested considerable time and resources on it.

Maximizing versus Satisficing. A major implication of bounded rationality is that decision makers are *satisficers* rather than *maximizers*. *Satisficing* means establishing a minimum level of acceptability for a solution and then evaluating the alternatives until one reaching the minimum level is found. Once we find an alternative that meets the minimum level, we accept it and stop searching. The rational decision maker model implies that decision makers are *maximizers*, who evaluate all possible solutions against a unitary goal and select the alternative that produces the maximum benefit.

Another implication of bounded rationality is that people limit their search for information to the most convenient and inexpensive data. Obtaining additional information is a double problem: it takes time and resources to obtain and process it. Decision makers may be inundated with too much information.

Optimizing versus Suboptimizing. Most decision-making situations involve multiple goals and objectives. For example, the decision to purchase a new machine can be examined in terms of its impact on profitability, employee morale, or environmental contamination. If all the objectives cannot be optimized simultaneously, some will be *suboptimized*. For example, a new machine could improve the profitability of the company at the expense of employee morale or environmental pollution. In organizations, work groups frequently adopt practices that optimize the rewards to the group but suboptimize the organization's objectives, such as restrictive work rules and the careless use of company resources.

Escalation of Commitment. Once people have made a decision, they tend to feel emotionally committed to their decision and want it to succeed. Most decision makers become ego-invested in the projects they endorse, and they are willing to invest additional effort and resources if necessary to assure their success. This process, which has been referred to as "throwing good money after bad," is also known as the *escalation of commitment.*

An example of commitment escalation is when a drug company invests money to develop a new medication. If the first allocation is spent without successfully developing a new product, there is a tendency to allocate more money. Studies suggest that in these situations the more people have already invested, and the closer they believe they are to a new discovery, the more they are willing to invest in further research. The danger is that decision makers can become so ego-invested in their decisions that they are blind to contrary information and incapable of objectively evaluating the possibility of failure.[2]

The escalation of commitment does not appear to occur quite as much in group decision making when the group is asked to make a consensus decision. Apparently consensus decision making tends to diffuse the responsibility for the decision onto other group members, thereby reducing the feelings of personal responsibility and the need for self-justification.[3]

Psychological Limitations

Another implication of bounded rationality is that the search for alternative solutions and the process of evaluating them are influenced by the decision maker's attitudes, values, and thought processes. Some of the most important psychological forces that influence the way people think include the following:[4]

1. *Social Position.* Our thought processes are influenced by our social position in an organization, the family, the community, or society. Our social position influences the information we allow ourselves to be exposed to, what alternatives we consider, and how we evaluate them. Upper-level managers are conditioned to focus on different problems and analyze them according to different criteria from those used by lower-level managers.

2. *Reference Groups.* Our thinking is influenced by the imaginary or actual groups that we use as a basis for evaluating our ideas. Studies have indicated, for example, that the family unit is a very powerful reference group that influences an individual's work habits.[5]

3. *Projection of Attitudes and Values.* We tend to project our own attitudes and values onto others and assume that their attitudes and values are similar to ours. This tendency causes us to make errors when we falsely assume that others have the same interests and desires we do.

4. *Global or Undifferentiated Thinking.* Undifferentiated thinking is thinking about a concept or an object as one homogeneous idea without appreciating that the concept may actually consist of numerous subconcepts that should be considered separately. Russia, for example, is not one large, homogeneous country, but a very diverse nation with many ethnic groups who possess a vast array of political, economic, and religious views.

5. *Dichotomized Thinking.* People tend to view the world in terms of opposites—good or bad, right or wrong, high or low—without realizing that some issues are both good and bad, or perhaps neutral. For example, most people have firmly entrenched attitudes that labor unions are either good or bad, without realizing that in some situations, for specific problems, unions can be either good or bad.

6. *Cognitive Nearsightedness.* Most people tend to respond to what is most urgent, immediate, and visible, and neglect the problems that may be more significant but are removed in time and place.

7. *Oversimplified Explanations of Causation.* When diagnosing problems, we consider only a limited number of variables without remembering that some events are caused by many forces. Simple linear thinking, such as A causes B, can create serious decision-making problems if A, B, C, and D all influence each other.

Personality Determinants

Our decisions are also influenced by the following personality orientations:[6]

1. *Ideology versus Power.* Some people base their decisions on ideology—a coherent philosophy or set of principles. Others base their decisions on what appears to be politically expedient and increases their personal power. Social reform movements typically have leaders with a very strong ideological orientation, while politicians tend to be influenced more by

power. Significant organizational contributions are typically made by leaders who have a strong ideological orientation.

2. *Emotionality versus Objectivity.* Some people make decisions with their hearts, based on feelings and emotions, while others make decisions with their heads, using objective facts. The first would hire a friend who applied for a job, while the second would offer the job to the friend only if the friend were the most qualified candidate.

3. *Creativity versus Common Sense.* Some people try to redefine each problem and discover new relationships and creative solutions to it. Other people tend to focus more on what has worked in the past and what seems to make good sense.

4. *Action Orientation versus Contemplation.* Some people have a propensity for action and want to make things happen. Others are more prone to contemplation and have a greater interest in exploring the possible solutions and implications.

GROUP DECISION MAKING

A common method for making organizational decisions is to delegate the task to a group and ask the members to reach a group decision. As a general rule, the most complex problems in organizations are assigned to committees, task forces, and other decision-making groups for a solution. Since so many decisions are made by groups, it is important to understand the effects of groups on the decision-making process and know how to improve it.

Individual versus Group Decision Making

If a manufacturing company needed to know where to locate a new production facility, it could delegate the problem to one person, but would more likely assign it to a committee. Group decisions are expected to be superior because:

1. They are more accurate since they have a larger reservoir of insight and knowledge than a single individual has.
2. They produce greater commitment to and acceptance of the decision.
3. They are implemented more quickly, since everyone understands the decision.
4. They are more consistent with the democratic values espoused by our society.

However, committee decision making has also been criticized because:

1. Committee meetings can be a waste of time for the members who attend them.
2. Group decisions are notoriously slow; indeed, some executives assign unpopular issues to a committee, knowing that the issue will die before the committee ever reaches a decision.
3. Group recommendations can be biased by one or two dominant people who manipulate the group.
4. The decision may be an irrational compromise for which no one is willing to accept responsibility.

Exhibit 16.1   Assets and Liabilities of Groups in Making Decisions

Assets of Groups	Liabilities of Groups
1. Greater knowledge and information	1. Social pressures to conform
2. Greater variety of approaches to a problem	2. Loss of valuable time of group members
3. Increased acceptance of the decision	3. Hasty convergence on a solution
4. Reduced communication problems	4. Possibility of control by a dominant individual
	5. Distraction by hidden agenda and secondary goals
	6. Insufficient time to reach a decision
	7. Problems with disagreement and interpersonal conflicts
	8. Possibility that the final decision will be an irrational compromise

Just because several people have participated in making the decision does not mean that the decision is more effective or brilliant than what any member could have produced alone. Some of the assets and liabilities of groups are listed in Exhibit 16.1. Group size is relevant, since larger groups enhance the value of the assets and exacerbate the liabilities. Although groups generally are superior to individuals in making decisions, their superiority is not universal. A comparison of individual versus group decision making must consider four criteria: accuracy and judgment, creativity, commitment and acceptance, and time and cost.

Accuracy and Judgment. As a general rule, group decisions tend to be more accurate than individual decisions, but for only certain kinds of problems. Group decisions tend to be superior when (1) the problems have multiple parts, allowing for a division of labor among the group members; (2) group members have complementary skills and information; (3) the problem involves estimation rather than creativity; or (4) the problem involves remembering information.

Individual decision making tends to be superior when (1) the situation requires a sequence of multiple stages, (2) the problem is not easily divided into separate parts, and (3) the correctness of the solution cannot be easily demonstrated.

For example, a group decision would normally be superior to an individual decision in developing a new product. This decision requires information from several functional departments within the organization, including accounting, finance, marketing, production, and legal. It is virtually impossible for any single individual to comprehend adequately all these areas of knowledge, and experts from each area would need to be consulted even if individuals tried to make the decision alone. A committee composed of experts from each area has the potential to make a more accurate decision.

The mere presence of complementary information does not guarantee a superior decision. Various group dynamics may inhibit a group from effectively sharing information or using it to make a good decision. The status and expertise of group members can interfere with the deliberations of the group. For example, the presence of a perceived expert or a higher-level manager tends to create an autocratic rather than a democratic group atmosphere.

Exhibit 16.2 Guidelines for Achieving Consensus in Group Decisions

1. Avoid arguing for your position. Present your position as lucidly and logically as possible, but listen to other members' reactions and consider them carefully before you press your point.
2. Help others share their ideas, even if you don't agree. Summarize their arguments even more eloquently and forcefully than they presented them so they know their ideas have been fairly presented.
3. Do not assume that someone must win and someone must lose when the discussion reaches a stalemate. Instead, look for the next-most-acceptable alternative for all parties involved.
4. Do not change your mind simply to avoid conflict and reach agreement and harmony. When agreement seems to come too quickly and easily, be suspicious. Explore the reasons, and be sure everyone accepts the solution for basically similar or complementary reasons. Yield only to positions that have objective and logically sound foundations.
5. Avoid conflict-reducing techniques such as a majority vote, averages, coinflips, and bargaining. When dissenting members finally agree, don't feel that they must be rewarded by having their way on some later point.
6. Differences of opinion are natural and expected. Look for them and try to involve everyone in the decision process. Disagreements can help the group's decision because a wide range of information and opinions increases the chance that the group will find an adequate solution.

Their presence inhibits the open exchange of ideas, and their comments are usually not challenged or reviewed as critically as the comments of others.

In the decision-making process, group members need to challenge the information and assumptions of other members and strive to reach a consensus. Guidelines for effective group decision making are presented in Exhibit 16.2.

Group decisions are generally more accurate than individual decisions on estimation problems. Estimating the size of an audience, forecasting the demand for next year's sales, and guessing how many items of inventory are in a large container are examples of problems for which groups produce superior results. The group decision is generally more accurate than the average of the individual decisions.

An example of a problem that is more conducive to individual decision making than group decision making is a problem that involves complex computations, such as developing an inventory-control model or a cost-benefit analysis. Such problems cannot be easily subdivided and delegated to group members, and they involve a sequence of multiple stages that require the concentration of one individual rather than many.

Through experience and training, group members can learn how to make more effective decisions. Effective groups make consensus decisions that are typically superior to the group average or the level of the most knowledgeable member. Consensus decisions are superior to other techniques, such as majority votes, coin tosses, or autocratic pronouncements. A longitudinal study of student groups who worked together for a semester on class projects and exams found that the group outperformed the most proficient member 97 percent of the time. The average improvement of the group's score over the most knowledgeable member's score was 8.8 percent. Therefore, on tasks that require analyzing, synthesizing, and remembering information, the optimal decision-making strategy appears to be consensus group decision making.[7]

Creativity. As a general rule, individual decision making generates higher levels of creativity than group decision making does. Research shows that group decision making tends to inhibit creativity, and individuals working alone produce ideas of higher quantity and quality than individuals working in a group do.[8] These conclusions, however, are not consistent with common belief: most people believe that groups are more creative than individuals.

The myth about the superiority of group creativity originated with a technique called *brainstorming*.[9] The purpose of this technique was to enhance creativity through group discussions, and it was particularly recommended to help advertising executives develop new promotional ideas. In a group brainstorming session, individuals are instructed to concentrate on a topic and express every idea that comes to mind, regardless of how outlandish or absurd the thought may be. Criticizing another's ideas is not allowed; in fact, members are encouraged to think about absurd ideas with the hope that they will eventually stimulate a totally novel and creative solution.

Although brainstorming continues to be used quite frequently, some of the enthusiasm for it declined when studies failed to support its claims. One study compared the creativity of four individuals working together versus four individuals working separately.[10] Four problems were used in this study: one concerning the problems of handling increased school enrollments in subsequent decades, one seeking ways to increase tourism in America, one assessing the advantages and disadvantages of being born with an extra thumb on each hand, and one assessing the consequences to society if the average adult height increased by ten inches. Each group worked together on two of these problems and separately on the other two.

The results indicated that individuals consistently generated a greater number of nonredundant ideas when working alone than they did when working in a group. A panel of judges evaluated the quality of each idea, and the results indicated that individuals working alone not only produced more ideas, but their ideas were superior to those they produced when working in a group. These results are consistent with the results of other studies indicating that group processes inhibit creativity. Even though people in a brainstorming group are instructed to ignore the influence of the group, they cannot entirely ignore the presence of others. Generating new ideas is apparently an individual thought process that requires concentration and insight, and it seems to be inhibited by the presence of others.

One reason why brainstorming continues to be used is because it at least forces people to think about the problem. If they were by themselves concentrating on the problem, they might be more creative, but they would probably think about something other than the problem. A second reason why brainstorming might be helpful is because it teaches members how to engage in divergent thinking. A brief experience in a brainstorming group might help newcomers grasp the freewheeling nature of divergent thinking.

One technique designed to minimize the distraction of the group in brainstorming sessions is to require people to speak in sequence or to pass if they have no ideas to contribute. This technique prevents one individual from dominating the discussion and helps timid members participate more openly. One study reported an 80 percent increase in the number of ideas using this technique over the normal brainstorming technique.[11]

Commitment and Acceptance. When people participate in making a decision, they feel greater commitment and loyalty to the decision and are willing to commit more of their own time and energy to implement it successfully.

Brainstorming:
A group technique for generating creative ideas in a freewheeling session in which ideas are proposed without being evaluated or criticized.

Furthermore, there is a greater chance that the solution will be implemented properly, since people will have a better understanding of the situation.

The powerful influence of participative decision making was revealed in an early series of studies on the food selections of homemakers. During World War II, several food items were in short supply because the country was committed to providing one pound of meat per day for every American soldier. There was a shortage of desirable cuts of meat, but a surplus of undesirable items, especially brains, kidneys, and tripe, which are an excellent source of protein and minerals. Although these undesirable animal parts are nutritious, and Europeans considered them edible and even delicacies, American consumers refused to eat them.

Government food experts asked Kurt Lewin, a leader in the field of group dynamics, to study the conditions necessary for changing eating habits. He believed that participating in a group discussion would influence the level of commitment and acceptance of the group members. Using groups of homemakers and Red Cross volunteers as participants, Lewin had some women participate in a group decision while others listened to a persuasive communication.[12] In the persuasive sessions, the women listened as panels of experts described the value of the undesirable products and exhorted them to support the government's efforts. In the group decisions, experts were available to answer questions, but the women were expected to discuss the pros and cons of eating the undesirable animal parts and reach a consensus.

The effects of these conditions were assessed by observing what the women actually purchased and consumed two and four weeks after the session. The results indicated that the group discussions had a much greater influence than the lectures. After four weeks, the consumption of kidneys, brains, and hearts increased by 32 percent among those who participated in the group decisions, but only 3.7 percent among those who attended the lectures. The group discussions also had a much greater impact than the lectures on the consumption of other products, such as evaporated milk and cod liver oil. Subsequent research has produced similar results, and helped to identify the factors in group decision making that contribute to commitment and behavior change. Group decisions reached by consensus create intense social pressures for individuals to accept the group decision and follow it. Unlike the individuals who attend a lecture, group members are forced to reach a decision and publicly declare their intention. Furthermore, their decision to change is reinforced by observing the change in others.[13]

Time and Cost. Although group decision making has the advantage of creating greater acceptance and commitment, these benefits are not free: group decisions can be very time-consuming. If the decision is accompanied by conflict, some groups never reach a decision. A management strategy for delaying an issue or avoiding it altogether is to delegate it to a committee without appointing a leader. If the committee is large enough, there is a good chance it will never succeed in recommending a solution.

The enormous cost associated with committee assignments can be estimated by counting the number of employee hours executives spend in committees and calculating the total cost of a meeting based on the hourly rate of the members in attendance. As the size of the committee increases, both the length of time needed to reach a decision and the cost of the meeting increase dramatically. When speed in reaching a decision is a major factor, large groups should be avoided.

Group Influences on Decisions

The presence of others has a significant influence on the way people make decisions. Although the combined efforts of several people should increase the acquisition, retention, and recall of relevant information, studies of group remembering and decision making have found that the dynamics of the group often prevent it from making a good decision. Decision-making groups have often been observed to fumble in search of relevant information until one member claims to recall it. If the information, right or wrong, is asserted with enough conviction, it may be accepted by the group, who then confers expert status on the individual who provided the information. Groups also have a tendency to selectively recall information supporting only one side of an issue, and suppress or ignore information consistent with an opposing position. The influence of the group can be analyzed by examining changes in risk taking and a phenomenon called **groupthink.**

Risk Taking. Decision making typically involves some degree of risk and uncertainty, and an important question is whether group decisions tend to be more risky or conservative than the decisions of individuals. For example, a traditional principle of military leadership is that individuals, not groups, should make decisions because groups are not capable of the boldness and courage needed for a successful military strategy. This principle assumes that group decisions tend to be conservative.

Early research found just the opposite, however: group decisions tended to be more risky than individual decisions. Individuals were asked to review hypothetical cases involving career choices, investment decisions, and medical operations. In each case they faced a dilemma requiring them to choose between a relatively safe alternative with a moderate payoff and a riskier alternative with a higher potential payoff, such as a secure job with a big corporation or an uncertain job with a new but potentially more rewarding and exciting company and a larger salary. Individuals were asked to determine the highest level of risk they would tolerate before rejecting the uncertain alternative. After reaching their individual decisions, they were formed into groups where they discussed each case and reached a consensus decision. The early results indicated that groups were willing to make more risky decisions, and this effect was called the **risky-shift phenomenon.**[14]

Early attempts to explain why groups made more risky decisions focused on the **diffusion of responsibility**. According to this explanation, individual decision makers are more conservative because they are totally responsible for their decisions. If the consequences are bad, the individual must bear full responsibility. However, groups need not be so conservative, since criticism for a bad decision can be shared by the entire group.

Although diffusion of responsibility was a reasonable explanation, additional studies found that some groups produced conservative shifts in which the group decisions were less risky than the individual decisions. It is now clear that group discussion can produce both risky and conservative shifts in a wide variety of settings, such as investment, purchasing, and termination

Risky-shift phenomenon:
A phenomenon that occurs when a group discussion causes a group to choose a more risky alternative than the group members would have been willing to accept on their own.

Diffusion of Responsibility:
The loss of personal accountability for the outcome of a decision when the decision is made by a group.

decisions. In addition to the diffusion of responsibility, two additional explanations have been proposed to explain the effects of groups on risk taking: the polarization explanation and the cultural values explanation. The *polarization* explanation suggests that the group discussion seems to polarize or exaggerate the initial positions of group members. While the initial positions of individuals tend to be only slightly conservative or risky, they tend to move toward the nearest end of the continuum as a result of the group discussion. Thus, individuals who are only slightly risky before the group discussion adopt a much more risky position afterward, while people who are only a little conservative become much more conservative after the discussion. If the majority of the group members are slightly risky, the discussion will produce a risky shift, while a conservative shift will occur if the majority of the group members are slightly conservative.

The *cultural values* explanation for changes in risk taking suggests that the group discussion tends to reinforce the dominant cultural values. If the dominant social value tends to be conservative, such as saving the life of the mother when there are childbirth complications, then the group discussion tends to produce a conservative shift. However, if the dominant social value tends to be risky, such as developing new technology or investing in a new product, the group decision tends to produce a risky shift.[15]

Groupthink. Although group decision making provides several potential advantages, one of the most serious disadvantages is the phenomenon identified by Irving Janis as *groupthink*. Groupthink occurs in highly cohesive groups when group pressures lead to reduced mental effort, poor testing of reality, and careless moral judgments. Janis has used the phenomenon of groupthink to study several of the major fiascoes involving high-level decisions, such as the Bay of Pigs incident of the Kennedy administration, the decision to escalate the war in Vietnam during the Johnson administration, and the failure to adequately protect Pearl Harbor against the Japanese attack during World War II.[16] The destruction of the *Challenger* spacecraft disaster also appears to illustrate groupthink. Public testimony has suggested that NASA officials failed to heed relevant warnings in their decision to launch another space shuttle mission.[17] Although groupthink does not necessarily occur with all cohesive groups, Janis identified eight of the main symptoms of groupthink.

1. *Illusion of invulnerability.* Group members develop an illusion of invulnerability that leads them to ignore obvious dangers. As a result, they become overconfident and are willing to assume greater risks.
2. *Rationalization.* Problems and counter arguments that should not be ignored are rationalized away. Group members collectively construct rationalizations to discount warnings or other sources of information that challenge their thinking. Therefore, negative information is discredited in the group discussion.
3. *Illusion of morality.* Group members believe unquestioningly in the inherent morality of their position and ignore the ethical or moral consequences of their decisions. The decisions adopted by the group are perceived not only as sensible, but also morally correct.
4. *Shared stereotypes.* Members develop stereotyped views about leaders of outside groups. Opposing leaders, for example, are viewed as evil, stupid,

Polarization: The tendency for groups to become more risky or more conservative in their decisions depending on the positions of dominant group members.

Cultural Values: Where the dominant values in society induce a group's decision to become more risky or more conservative after the group discussion.

Groupthink: The tendency for a highly cohesive group to agree with what appears to be a unanimous group consensus without challenging the consensus or realizing that it may not represent the group.

or too weak to deal effectively with whatever the group decides. Such stereotypes effectively block any reasonable negotiations between differing groups.

5. *Pressure for conformity.* Members pressure each other to conform with the group views and accept the group consensus. Dissenting views among the members are not acceptable.

6. *Self-censorship.* Group members convince themselves that they should avoid expressing opinions contrary to the group. Personal reservations and doubts are self-censored by members who do not want to "rock the boat."

7. *Illusion of unanimity.* Because no one expresses doubt or disagreement, members perceive unanimous support for the group decision. The group falsely assumes that because no one says otherwise, everyone in the group is in full agreement.

8. *Mind guards.* Just like bodyguards who protect people from physical harm, mind guarding occurs when individual members adopt the role of protecting the group from information that contradicts its decision.

The Bay of Pigs fiasco was a serious embarrassment to President John F. Kennedy and his new administration. On April 17, 1961, a brigade of about 1,400 Cuban exiles, aided by the U.S. military, invaded the coast of Cuba at the Bay of Pigs. The planning for this event was seriously flawed. On the first day, none of the four ships containing reserve ammunition and supplies arrived. By the second day the brigade was completely surrounded by 20,000 Cuban troops, and by the third day those who had not been killed were captured and led to prison camps. This embarrassing event forced Kennedy and other top administration officials to carefully review the poor method by which their group decisions had been made.

A careful review of their failure enabled them to respond much more effectively eighteen months later to the Cuban missile crisis, when Soviet missile sites were being constructed in Cuba. This time Kennedy took several precautions to avoid the problem of groupthink. He assigned each cabinet member the role of critical evaluator responsible for voicing objections and doubts; he did not state his personal preferences and expectations at the beginning; he invited outside experts to share information and challenge the views of the group; and he divided the group into subgroups to consider issues separately. By avoiding the problems of groupthink, the Kennedy administration was able to handle the Cuban missile crisis much more successfully than it did the Bay of Pigs invasion.

Abilene Paradox:
The dysfunctional organizational consequences of compliance and agreement.

Very similar to the groupthink phenomenon is the Abilene Paradox. The *Abilene Paradox* occurs when members of an organization take an action contrary to what they really want to do and, as a result, defeat the very purposes they are trying to achieve. This label comes from the story of a father, mother, daughter, and son-in-law who endured a miserable trip to Abilene and ate a terrible Sunday dinner, only to discover when they returned home that none of them had wanted to go, even though they had all expressed interest when the idea was first proposed. The Abilene Paradox occurs in organizations when members fail to communicate their true ideas and desires because they think it is better to be agreeable.[18]

To prevent groupthink and the Abilene Paradox, groups should create a climate that tolerates disagreement and accepts debates. Leaders can reduce groupthink if they refrain from expressing their desires, encourage criticism, assign members to express dissenting views, and recruit outside experts to review and assist in decision making.

Programmed conflict:

Conflict that is intentionally created to force a group to think more objectively and to defend its decision.

Programmed Conflict. The Abilene Paradox and the groupthink phenomenon occur when group members feel a need to be agreeable and they want to maintain harmony in their deliberations. Conflict threatens the unity of the group, and members often want to avoid any appearance of disrupting the group. But conflict can also be functional. Knowing that contrasting viewpoints can improve the quality of a group decision, some groups use a form of programmed conflict in which opposing arguments are presented in a structured format. The two most prominent forms of programmed conflict are the devil's advocacy and dialectical inquiry.

The *devil's advocacy* technique gets its name from the traditional practice used by the Catholic Church when the College of Cardinals considers someone for sainthood. One person is assigned the role of devil's advocate and is expected to expose and examine all possible objections to the person's canonization. When this technique is used in organizations, one member of the group is assigned the role of critic and expected to criticize every proposal and decision. A good devil's advocate challenges and exposes bad ideas, thereby reducing the likelihood of groupthink.

The method of *dialectical inquiry* traces its beginnings to the dialectic school of philosophy in ancient Greece. Plato and his followers developed the art of logically examining issues by discussing a principle (thesis) and then considering its opposite (antithesis). When this approach is used in organizations, the assumptions underlying a proposal are identified, and then a counter-proposal is presented using different assumptions. Different teams usually represent each side. Advocates of each position present the merits of their arguments to help a decision maker make an informed decision. This method is used extensively in the legal systems of most countries.

Although the devil's advocacy and dialectical inquiry techniques are slightly different, research indicates that they have about the same effect.[19] Both methods help groups produce better decisions than the average produced by individual members. It is usually a good idea to rotate the role of critic so no one person or group develops a reputation of being negative and uncooperative. Furthermore, learning to challenge assumptions is good training for developing better analytical skills.

DECISION MAKING IN ORGANIZATIONS

The structure of an organization largely determines who is involved in the decision-making process and what kinds of decisions they will make. Whether an organization has a centralized or decentralized organizational structure depends on whether the decision making rests primarily with top-level managers or whether important decisions have been delegated to lower levels in the organization.

To analyze organizational decision making, we need to understand what kinds of decisions need to be made, who should make them, and what organizational procedures are necessary to gather information, evaluate alternatives, and implement a decision.

Types of Decisions

Many kinds of decisions are made in organizations. Top administrators make policy decisions that influence the entire organization. Other decisions are made lower in the organization and involve very few people, such as scheduling a committee meeting. After analyzing the kinds of decisions made in organizations and the individuals who make them, Herbert Simon suggested a useful classification that distinguishes between programmed and nonprogrammed decisions.[20]

Programmed decisions:
Highly structured decisions that can be made by following established rules of thumb or procedures created for handling them.

Programmed Decisions. *Programmed decisions* are repetitive, routine decisions for which a simple decision-making procedure can be developed. They are appropriate when people know how to achieve the desired consequences because the problems are well structured and their solutions are noncontroversial. College students observe dozens of programmed decisions as they interact with the university staff. These decisions are made by lower-level staff members as students register for classes, buy a parking permit, purchase an activity card, request a copy of their grade transcript, apply for graduate school, and try to appeal a parking ticket.

Many complex business decisions are reduced to programmed decisions by the use of mathematical formulas, statistics, and operations research. These methods have helped decision makers identify the relevant information and process it in a way that produces a straightforward decision. In some situations, very complex conditions involving a large volume of information can be effectively reduced to a simple programmed decision.

Nonprogrammed decisions:
Unstructured decisions in response to new or unique problems requiring decision makers to go carefully through the decision-making process in order to reach a solution.

Nonprogrammed Decisions. *Nonprogrammed decisions* are novel, unstructured decisions. Procedures cannot be established for handling certain problems, either because they have not occurred in exactly the same manner or because they are extremely complex and important. Nonprogrammed decisions are not well structured, either because the current conditions are unclear, the methods of obtaining the desired results are unknown, or there is disagreement about what constitutes a desired result. An example of an unstructured problem that many students experience as they near graduation is deciding whether to attend graduate school and, if so, where. Deciding whether to go to graduate school is not a decision students make every day, and they cannot refer to rules of thumb or standard operating procedures to make this decision. In fact, most students don't even have clear criteria to help them make the decision; is their goal to maximize their future earnings, acquire knowledge, secure a better job, achieve higher social status, or something else?

Nonprogrammed decisions have typically been handled by general problem-solving processes involving intuition, judgment, and creativity. The group decision-making techniques were primarily developed to help make nonprogrammed decisions. Because nonprogrammed decisions are typically unique, complex, and without a clear criterion, they are usually surrounded by controversy and political maneuvering. An interesting irony is that while modern decision theory has created many decision rules to help with programmed decisions, very few exist to help with nonprogrammed decisions, and yet nonprogrammed decisions have the greatest impact on the survival and effectiveness of an organization.

Ideally, top management should be primarily concerned with nonprogrammed decisions, while first-level managers should be more concerned with programmed decisions. Unfortunately, many top-level managers spend inordinate amounts of time on programmed decisions that should be made much more rapidly and efficiently, leaving themselves time to contemplate significant nonprogrammed decisions. Herbert Simon referred to an important principle of organizational decision making called Gresham's Law of Planning. This law suggests that programmed activity tends to replace nonprogrammed activity. If a leader's job involves both programmed and nonprogrammed decisions, programmed decisions tend to be emphasized at the expense of nonprogrammed decisions. Therefore, managers need to identify which decisions should be treated as programmed decisions and develop a procedure for handling them quickly and efficiently.

The variables that should determine whether a decision is programmed or not are the nature of the problem, the frequency with which it occurs, and the degree of certainty involved. To the extent that problems are routine, easily categorized, and frequently observed, and exist within fairly stable conditions, they should be treated as programmed decisions for which standard operating procedures or policies have been created. For example, deciding whether to contribute to the purchase of new band uniforms for the local high school or allowing an employee to have two weeks off with pay for military duty may be treated as nonprogrammed decisions the first time they occur. If organizations receive numerous requests for charitable contributions or personal leave time, policies should be created that allow members of the finance and human resource departments to make these decisions without referring them to upper-level managers. Organizational effectiveness suffers when top managers spend considerable time and effort on programmed decisions. The unfortunate consequence of this practice is the neglect of long-range planning. Top managers cannot attend to the long-range issues of survival and change if they are overly preoccupied with day-to-day programmed decisions.

Decision-Making Techniques

Three decision-making techniques can help organizations make effective decisions: brainstorming, the Delphi technique, and the nominal group technique.

Brainstorming. The purpose of brainstorming is to enhance creativity in group discussions by creating an environment that stimulates the generation of new ideas. The four basic rules of brainstorming include:

1. No ideas are criticized.
2. Freewheeling, or the free association of ideas, is encouraged. The more far-fetched an idea, the better.
3. The quantity of ideas is stressed. The larger the number of ideas, the greater the probability of getting a winner.
4. "Hitchhiking" is encouraged; that is, participants are urged to improve on the ideas of others and combine ideas to form new and more complex solutions.

Although brainstorming looks like an effective method for generating creative ideas, empirical results have forced the proponents of brainstorming to be a bit more cautious in their enthusiasm. Consequently, although brainstorming continues to be a rather popular method for generating new ideas, research suggests that other methods are superior.

Delphi technique:
A method of group decision making in which information is individually gathered from the group members, summarized, and then redistributed to the group members to see if any of them would like to change their evaluations. Group members are not brought together in a face-to-face interaction.

The Delphi Technique. The *Delphi technique* was developed by employees at the Rand Corporation as a method of combining the information and insights of a group of people without suffering the adverse effects of face-to-face interaction. The Delphi technique consists of the following steps:

1. After the problem has been identified, several experts are asked to participate in the project.
2. The basic problem is presented to each expert, but the experts are not brought together.
3. Each expert, independently and anonymously, answers the problem and provides comments, suggestions, and justifications for the proposed solution.
4. The experts' comments are compiled at a central location, summarized, and reproduced.
5. Each expert receives a summary of the group's answers along with comments and explanations.
6. Each expert evaluates and comments on the justifications provided by the other experts, and revises his or her decision if necessary as a result of the comments of others.
7. The explanations and revised estimates of the experts are once again compiled at a centralized location, summarized, and redistributed. Several iterations of compiling and disseminating information may be used until a consensus is reached.

The Delphi technique has two advantages over typical group decision making. First, the absence of face-to-face interaction prevents the group from being swayed by a dominant individual or succumbing to groupthink. The second advantage is its ability to combine the expertise and wisdom of several people without incurring the cost of meeting at a common location.

The disadvantages of the Delphi technique include time and motivation. Going through successive iterations of collecting information, submitting it to experts, and compiling their revised estimates require a great amount of time. Without the pressures of face-to-face interaction, some experts tend to procrastinate in responding, and the long gaps of time between each iteration tend to dilute the experts' enthusiasm for participating.

Nominal group technique:
A group decision-making method that structures the way group members propose solutions, discuss them, and select and alternative.

Nominal Group Technique. The *nominal group technique* incorporates some of the features of brainstorming and the Delphi technique. As in brainstorming, individuals work together as a group on a problem, but, as with the Delphi technique, the process for generating alternatives and evaluating them is intended to protect individuals from group biases. The procedure for conducting a nominal group technique consists of the following steps:

1. After the problem has been clearly identified, individual members are asked to develop their own solutions to the problem or task. This step is accomplished silently and independently and may even occur before the individuals are brought together in a group.

2. A recorded round-robin procedure is followed in which group members, one at a time, present one of their ideas to the group without discussion. The ideas are summarized and recorded on a blackboard or sheet of paper.
3. After all the initial ideas have been presented, the group discusses the ideas, clarifying and evaluating them.
4. The meeting concludes with a silent, independent vote in which each member ranks the solutions. The idea with the highest ranking is the group decision.

Since the nominal group technique provides a more structured method for eliciting ideas and evaluating them, larger groups can be used effectively with this technique. Although a group of five or six individuals tends to be the maximum size for typical discussion groups, nominal groups of ten members have been found to be optimal when both productivity and satisfaction are considered.

A high-tech adaptation of the nominal group technique involves electronically compiling information. Group members have access to a computer keypad and during the group discussion the facilitator can ask them to type their ideas into their computers, which are then shown on a screen. The facilitator can examine each idea by asking the participants to evaluate it anonymously, using multiple-choice questions. Computer software programs can compile the group decisions instantaneously so all members know the feelings of the group without the biasing effect of strong personalities and powerful individuals.[21]

Studies have examined the effectiveness of the Delphi technique, nominal group technique, and traditional interaction groups. These studies have generally revealed that the nominal and Delphi groups generate significantly more unique ideas than traditional groups, and satisfaction tends to be highest using the nominal group technique than either of the other two.[22]

Discussion Questions

1. How well does the decision-making process outlined in the chapter correspond with the actual way you make decisions? Identify a major decision you have made in the past few months, and look for each of these decision-making steps in your behavior.
2. What is bounded rationality? Provide two or three illustrations from your own experience of the concept of bounded rationality.
3. What are the reasons that groups sometimes make bad decisions? Identify a time when you were a member of a group that made a bad decision and explain the dynamics that contributed to the process of making a bad decision.
4. What guidelines would you recommend to improve group decision making? Apply these guidelines to a group in which you have participated to explain how it could have functioned better.

Notes

1. James G. March and Herbert A. Simon, *Organizations* (New York: Wiley, 1959); Herbert A. Simon, *Behavioral Economics and Business Organization* 2 (Cambridge, Mass.: MIT Press, 1982).

2. Howard Garland, "Throwing Good Money After Bad: The Effect of Sunk Costs on the Decision to Escalate commitment to an On-Going Project," *Journal of Applied Psychology* 75 (1990): 728–31.

3. Glen Whyte, "Diffusion of Responsibility: Effects on the Escalation Tendency," *Journal of Applied Psychology* 76 (1991): 408–15.

4. This section is based largely on Daniel Katz and Robert L. Kahn, *The Social Psychology of Organizations*, 2nd ed. (New York: Wiley, 1978), chap. 15.

5. David J. Cherrington, *The Work Ethic: Working Values and Values That Work* (New York: AMACOM Publishing, 1980), chap. 7.

6. Based on Katz and Kahn, op. cit.

7. Larry K. Michaelson, Warren E. Watson, and Robert H. Black, "A Realistic Test of Individual Versus Group Consensus Decision Making," *Journal of Applied Psychology* 74 (1989): 834–39; Warren Watson, Larry K. Michaelson, and Walt Sharp, "Member Competence, Group Interaction, and Group Decision Making: A Longitudinal Study," *Journal of Applied Psychology* 76 (1991): 803–9.

8. Donald W. Taylor, Paul C. Berry, and Clifford H. Block, "Does Group Participation When Using Brainstorming Facilitate or Inhibit Creative Thinking?" *Administrative Science Quarterly* 3 (1958): 23–47; Terry Connolly, Leonard M. Jessup, and Joseph S. Valacich, "Effects of Anonymity and Evaluative Tone on Idea Generation in Computer-Mediated Groups," *Management Science* 36 (June 1990): 689–703.

9. Alex F. Osborn, *Applied Imagination* (New York: Scribners, 1957).

10. John P. Campbell, Marvin D. Dunnette, and Kay Jaastad, "The Effect of Group Participation on Brainstorming Effectiveness for Two Industrial Samples," *Journal of Applied Psychology* 47 (1963): 30–37.

11. T. J. Bouchard. "Whatever Happened to Brainstorming?" *Journal of Creative Behavior* 5, 3 (1971): 182–89.

12. Kurt Lewin, "Group Decision and Social Change," in E. E. Maccoby, T. M. Newcomb, and E. C. Hartley (eds.), *Readings in Social Psychology*, 3rd ed. (New York: Holt, Rinehart and Winston, 1958).

13. Betty W. Bond, "The Group-Discussion-Decision Approach: An Appraisal of Its Use in Health Education," *Dissertation Abstracts* 16 (1956): 903–4.

14. J. A. F. Stoner, "A Comparison of Individual and Group Decisions Involving Risk" (Master's thesis, MIT, Sloan School of Industrial Management, 1961); J .A. F. Stoner, "Risky and Cautious Shifts in Group Decisions: The Influence of Widely Held Values," *Journal of Experimental Social Psychology* 4 (1968): 442–59.

15. D. G. Marquis and H. Joseph Reitz, "Effects of Uncertainty on Risk Taking in Individual and Group Decisions," *Behavioral Science* 4 (1969): 181–88.

16. Irving L. Janis, *Victims of Groupthink* (Boston: Houghton Mifflin, 1972).

17. Gregory Moorhead, Richard Ference, and Chris P. Neck, "Group Decision Fiascoes Continue: Space Shuttle Challenger and a Revised Groupthink Framework," *Human Relations* 44 (1991): 539–50; Glen Whyte, "Groupthink Reconsidered," *Academy of Management Journal* 14 (January 1989): 41–56.

18. Jerry B. Harvey, Rosabeth Moss Kanter, and Arthur Elliott Carlisle, "The Abilene Paradox: The Management of Agreement," *Organizational Dynamics* 17 (Summer 1988): 16–43; Daphne Gottlieb Taras, "Breaking

the Silence: Differentiating Crisis of Agreement," *Public Administration Quarterly* 14 (Winter 1991): 401–18.

19. David M. Schweiger and William R. Sandberg, "The Utilization of Individual Capabilities in Group Approaches to Strategic Decision Making," *Strategic Management Journal* 10 (January–February 1989): 31–43; Charles Schwenk, "A Meta-Analysis on the Comparative Effectiveness of Devil's Advocacy and Dialectical Inquiry," *Strategic Management Journal* 10 (May–June 1989): 303–6.

20. Herbert A. Simon, *The New Science of Management Decision* (New York: Harper & Row, 1960), p. 5.

21. Michael Finley, "Welcome to the Electronic Meeting," *Training* 28 (July 1991): 28–32.

22. N. C. Dalkey and Olaf Helmer, "An Experimental Application of the Delphi Method to the Use of Experts," *Management Science* 9 (1963): 458–67; A. H. Van de Ven and Andre L. Delbecq, "The Effectiveness of Nominal, Delphi, and Interacting Group Decision Making Processes," *Academy of Management Journal* 17 (1974): 605–32.

Outstanding Faculty Award Committee

Several years ago I served on the Outstanding Faculty Award committee for the College of Business. This award is the most significant honor that our college bestows on a faculty member, and it represents a great personal honor for the recipient and an important ceremony for our college. The award is presented at a formal banquet for the entire faculty and their spouses at the end of the school year.

At the first meeting, our committee discussed the nomination process and decided to use our traditional practice of inviting nominations from both the faculty and students. During the next month, we received six completed files with supporting documentation. Three of the nominations came from department chairs, two from faculty who recommended their colleagues, and one from a group of 16 graduate students.

At the second meeting, we discussed the six applicants and discovered that we didn't know them as well as we needed. Finally, we decided that we each needed to read the applications on our own and rank them. We did not identify any ranking criteria; I think we assumed that we shared a common definition of *outstanding*.

Our lack of a common definition became very evident at the third meeting, at which we expected to make a final decision. The discussion was polite, but there was very little agreement. We disagreed about whether this was an award for teaching, or research, or service to the college, or scholarly textbook writing, or consulting, or service to society, or some combination of these. After three hours we were no closer to a decision than when we started. Finally, we decided to identify five criteria and independently rate each candidate on them, using a five-point scale.

When we reconvened the next day, our discussion was much more focused as we tried to achieve a consensus regarding how we judged each candidate on each criteria. After a lengthy discussion, we finally completed the task and summed the ratings. The top two scores were 21 and 20 and the lowest score was 12. I assumed the person with the highest total would receive the award and was surprised to see the debate continue over the relevance of our five criteria. We tested different weights for the criteria and found that the top two candidates remained at the top, but not always in the same order. But, more importantly, Dr. H was always on the bottom.

After we had met for almost two hours, the Associate Dean dropped a real bomb. Turning to one committee member, he said, "Dolan, I sure would like to see Dr. H in your department receive this honor. He retires next year and this would be a great honor for him and no one has received this honor in your department recently."

Dolan agreed, "Yes, this is Dr. H's last year with us and it would be a great way for him to go out. I'm sure he would feel very honored by this award."

I sat there stunned at the suggestion while Dolan retold how Dr. H had been active in public service, his only real strength on our criteria. I was even more stunned when another committee member said, "Well, I so move." and Dolan seconded it.

The Associate Dean, who was conducting the meeting, said, "Well, if the rest of you think this is a good idea, all in favor say Aye." A few members said Aye, and he quickly proceeded to explain what we needed to do to advertise the winner and arrange the ceremony without calling for nays.

During my conversations with other committee members over the next two weeks, I learned that everyone was as shocked as I was at the outcome of our committee, even two who said Aye. I thought we made a terrible decision and I was embarrassed to be a member of the committee. I felt we were appropriately punished when Dr. H gave a 45 minute acceptance speech that started poorly and got worse.

Questions

1. What problems did this committee face in making a decision? How can these problems be resolved?
2. How do you explain why the lowest-rated candidate received the award? What were the dynamics in this group that allowed for such an event?
3. What should you do as a member of such a committee to avoid making a bad group decision?

Individual versus Group Decision Making

Purpose. The purpose of the exercise is to identify the times when individuals are superior at making decisions and when groups are superior.

Activity. For this exercise the class should be divided into groups of three to five individuals. On some of the problems, the groups should work as *interacting* groups sharing ideas and feedback. On other problems, however, the group should be a *nominal* group; that is, a group in name only, and the members should work individually without any interaction. The decision regarding which groups will be interacting groups for the various problems should be decided by the instructor for the class as a whole.

Problem 1 Collecting and Synthesizing Factual Information

On a blank sheet of paper, draw a map of the United States, showing each of the forty-eight contiguous states. Label each state and identify its capital city.

Problem 2 Generating Creative Ideas

Suppose you were Robinson Crusoe and one day you saw a Coke bottle float ashore. In 20 minutes, list the possible uses that could be made of the Coke bottle, regardless of how outlandish they are.

Problem 3 Solving Problems

Solve the following problems:

1. Suppose you were given nine coins, identical in every respect, except that one is counterfeit and slightly heavier than the genuine coins. Using only a sensitive balance scale, one with two pans and no weights, how would you identify the counterfeit coin by making only two weighings?
2. The Big Chew Bubble Gum Company has ten bubble gum machines that normally produce gum balls weighing 1 ounce each. However, one of the ten machines is defective and makes hollow gum balls weighing only 1/2 ounce. Using a scale, how could you find the defective machine in only one weighing? An unlimited number of gum balls is available from each machine.
3. Two friends had an eight-quart jug of cider that they wanted to share equally. They had two empty jars, a five-quart jar and a three-quart jar. They were able to divide the cider equally without spilling a drop. How were they able to do this?
4. Sam and Jim, who live two and a half miles apart, decide to meet for a visit. Jim walks two miles per hour, Sam walks three miles per hour, and Sam has a pet swallow that flies twenty-six miles per hour. When the two men begin walking toward each other, Sam's swallow flies to meet Jim and then returns immediately to Sam and continues to fly back and forth between the two men until they meet. Assuming the swallow does not lose any time in reversing directions, how far does the swallow fly?

17

Leadership

Chapter Outline

Leadership
Managers versus Leaders
Transformational Leadership
Leadership Traits
Physical Traits
Intelligence
Personality Traits
Leader Behaviors
Authoritarian, Democratic, and Laissez-faire Leadership
Initiating Structure and Consideration
Production-centered and Employee-centered Leader Behaviors
The Leadership Grid®
Leader Behaviors as Leadership Roles
Situational Leadership
Leader Behavior Styles
Follower Characteristics
Environmental Factors
Determinants of Leadership Effectiveness
Strategies for Improving Leadership
Reciprocal Influence of Leader and Follower

LEADERSHIP

Leadership is an extremely popular topic in organizational behavior, because of the role we assume it plays in group and organizational effectiveness. We assume that the success of a group depends primarily on the quality of leadership. A winning season requires a good coach, a military victory requires a great commander, and a productive work group requires a competent supervisor. Whether they deserve it or not, leaders are usually credited for the group's success and blamed for its failure. When a team has a losing season, the coach is fired, not the team.

The most useful definition of leadership is to view it as the *incremental influence* one individual exerts on another beyond mechanical compliance with routine directives. Leadership occurs when one individual influences others to do something voluntarily rather than because they were required to do it or they feared the consequences of noncompliance. It is this voluntary aspect of leadership that distinguishes it from other types of influence, such as power and authority. Although leaders may use force or coercion to influence the behavior of followers, they must also have the ability to induce voluntary compliance. By this definition, anyone in the organization can be a leader, whether or not that individual is formally identified as such. Indeed, informal leaders are extremely important to the effectiveness of most organizations.

Incremental influence: The influence one individual exerts on others above and beyond their normal role requirements.

Managers versus Leaders

Although leadership is similar to management, some writers make a clear difference between these topics to highlight the importance and distinctive nature of leadership.

Managing Things versus Leading People. One contrast between management and leadership focuses on what is influenced: managers manage *things*, while leaders lead *people*.[1] Managers focus their efforts on inanimate objects, such as budgets, financial statements, organization charts, sales projections, and productivity reports. Leaders focus their efforts on people as they encourage, inspire, train, empathize, evaluate, and reward. Leaders build organizations, create organizational cultures, and shape society. Managers focus on internal organizational issues as they maintain bureaucratic procedures and keep organizations running smoothly by solving problems.

It has also been said that *managers are people who do things right, and leaders are people who do the right thing.* This statement suggests that leaders and managers focus on different issues. To manage means to direct, to bring about, to accomplish, and to have responsibility for. The functions of management are planning, organizing, directing, and controlling. The successful manager is viewed as someone who achieves results by following the prescribed activities and maintaining behaviors and products within prescribed limits.

To lead, however, is to inspire, to influence, and to motivate. Effective leaders inspire others to pursue excellence, to extend themselves, and to go beyond their perfunctory job requirements by generating creative ideas. This distinction is somewhat overstated, because effective leaders do a lot of managing, and effective managers need to lead. But it serves to emphasize an important organizational outcome: We desperately need leaders who can create an energetic and highly committed work force that is successfully adapting to the demands of a changing environment and competently producing viable products and services.

Controlling Complexity versus Producing Change. Another contrast between management and leadership focuses on maintaining stability versus creating change.[2]

- *Management* focuses on *controlling complexity*—creating order in the organization, solving problems, and ensuring consistency.
- *Leadership* focuses on *creating change*—recognizing the dynamic environment, sensing opportunities for growth, and communicating a vision that inspires others.

Both management and leadership involve influencing others through four common roles: planning, organizing, directing, and controlling. As they perform each of these roles, managers and leaders behave very differently, because they focus on different outcomes, as summarized in Exhibit 17.1.

Planning—Deciding What Needs to Be Done. Managers decide what to do by planning and budgeting—setting targets and goals for the future, establishing detailed steps for achieving them, and allocating resources to accomplish those plans. Planning and budgeting are the processes managers use to control complexity and produce orderly results; they are not used to create change.

Leadership involves helping an organization achieve constructive change, which requires setting a direction—developing a vision of the future and strategies for producing the changes needed to accomplish the vision.

Organizing—Creating Networks and Relationships to Get Work Done. Managers perform a variety of organizing and staffing activities to create a structure for getting work done. These activities include dividing the work into distinct jobs, staffing the jobs with qualified workers, structuring jobs in defined units, establishing reporting relationships, and delegating authority for following the assigned procedures. By organizing and staffing, managers control a complex environment and create a stable structure for getting work done.

Management: Doing things right; controlling complexity by solving problems.

Leadership: Doing the right things; creating essential change by communicating a vision that inspires others.

Focus	Leadership Producing useful change	Management Controlling complexity
Role 1. Deciding what needs to be done	Setting direction Creating a vision and strategy	Planning and budgeting
Role 2. Creating a structure of networks and relationships to get work done	Aligning people with a shared vision Communicating with all relevant people	Organizing and staffing Structuring jobs Establishing reporting relationships Providing training Delegating authority
Role 3. Directing productive work	Empowering people	Solving problems Negotiating compromises
Role 4. Ensuring performance	Motivating and inspiring people	Implementing control systems

Exhibit 17.1 Comparison between Leadership and Management

The corresponding leadership activity involves aligning people behind a shared vision of how the organization needs to change. Aligning people involves communicating a new direction to the relevant people who can work unitedly and form coalitions with a common vision and sense of direction. Change is not an orderly process, and it will be staggered and chaotic unless many people coalesce and move together in the same direction.

Directing Productive Work. Managers are problem solvers. They tend to view work as an enabling process, involving people with multiple talents and interests that may not coincide with each other or with the interests of the organization. They strive to create an acceptable employment exchange by negotiating agreements that satisfy the expectations of workers and the demands of the organization. Bargaining and compromise are used to establish an agreement, and rewards and punishment are used to maintain it.

Leaders rely on empowering people and letting them work autonomously according to their shared vision. Free to exercise individual initiative and motivated by a sense of ownership, people throughout the organization respond quickly and effectively to new opportunities and problems.

Controlling—Ensuring Performance. Managers ensure performance by implementing control systems—establishing measurable standards, collecting performance data, identifying deviations, and taking corrective action.

Leaders ensure performance by motivating and inspiring people to go above and beyond the formal job expectations. Motivation and inspiration energize people, not by monitoring their behavior as control mechanisms do, but by satisfying basic human needs for fulfillment: accomplishment, recognition, self-esteem, a feeling of control over one's life, and the ability to achieve one's ideals. These feelings touch people deeply and elicit a powerful response.

Control systems are supposed to ensure that normal people perform their work in normal ways, day after day. Managing routine performance is not glamorous, but it is necessary. Leadership that inspires excellence and helps organizations thrive in an uncertain world is glamorous, but it may not be any more necessary than management.

In this theory of leadership, leadership is not necessarily better than management, nor is it a replacement for it. Both functions are necessary in organizations, and some believe that the skills for both functions can be acquired by everyone. Others believe that managers and leaders require very different skills and personalities, because they focus on almost opposite behaviors that must therefore be performed by different individuals. This issue is not resolved, and there are data supporting both views.

Transformational Leadership

Transactional leadership:
A style of leadership that focuses on accomplishing work by relying on contingent rewards, task instructions, and corrective actions.

Another contrast used to highlight a particular kind of leadership is transformational versus transactional leadership.[3] *Transactional leaders* are managers who manage the transactions between the organization and its members; they get things done by giving contingent rewards, such as recognition, pay increases, and advancement for employees who perform well. Employees who do not perform well are penalized. Transactional leaders frequently use the man-

Exhibit 17.2 Characteristics of Transactional and Transformational Leadership

Transactional Leadership

- Establishes goals and objectives
- Designs work flow and delegates task assignments
- Negotiates exchange of rewards for effort
- Rewards performance and recognizes accomplishments
- Searches for deviations from standards and takes corrective action

Transformational Leadership

- *Charismatic:* Provides vision and sense of mission, gains respect and trust, instills pride
- *Individualized consideration:* Gives personal attention, treats each person individually, coaches and encourages followers
- *Intellectually stimulating:* Promotes learning, shares ideas and insights, encourages rationality, uses careful problem solving
- *Inspirational:* Communicates high performance expectations, uses symbols to focus efforts, distills essential purposes, encourages moral behavior

Transformational leadership:
A style of leadership that focuses on communicating an organizational vision, building commitment, stimulating acceptance, and empowering followers.

agement-by-exception principle to monitor the performance of employees and take corrective actions when performance deviates from the standard.

Transformational leadership focuses on changing the attitudes and assumptions of employees and building commitment for the organization's mission, objectives, and strategies. Transformational leaders are described as charismatic, inspirational, and intellectually stimulating, and they show individual consideration for each member. This form of leadership occurs when leaders broaden and elevate the interests of their employees, when they generate awareness and acceptance of the purposes and mission of the group, and when they stir their employees to look beyond their own self-interest for the good of the group. The major differences between transactional and transformational leaders are shown in Exhibit 17.2.

Empowerment:
A condition created by leaders that stimulates followers to act on their initiative and perform in a highly committed, intelligent, and ethical way.

A result that is attributed to transformational leadership is the empowerment of followers, who are capable of taking charge and acting on their own initiative. *Empowerment* involves providing the conditions that stimulate followers to act in a committed, concerned, and involved way. The kinds of conditions that contribute to empowerment include providing relevant factual information; providing resources such as time, space, and money; and providing support such as backing, endorsement, and legitimacy. Empowered followers make things happen without waiting for detailed instructions or administrative approvals.

Charismatic leadership:
A type of leadership attributed to outstanding and highly esteemed leaders who gain the confidence and trust of followers.

Charismatic leadership is a special kind of influence that is attributed to outstanding and gifted individuals. Followers not only trust and respect charismatic leaders, they also idolize them as great heroes or spiritual figures. Charismatic leadership is evidenced by the amount of trust that followers have in the correctness of the leader's beliefs, their unquestioning acceptance of the leader, their willing obedience, and their affection for the leader.

Charismatic leaders are described as people who have a high need for social power, high self-confidence, and strong convictions about the morality of their cause. They establish their influence most importantly by the example they model in their own behavior for followers. They maintain their status by managing their charismatic perception (impression management) to preserve the followers' confidence, by articulating an appealing vision of the group's goals in ideological terms, communicating high expectations for followers, and expressing confidence in their followers.

Transformational leaders seek to raise the consciousness of followers by appealing to higher ideals and values such as liberty, justice, equality, peace, and humanitarianism, rather than baser emotions such as fear, greed, jealousy, or hatred. This kind of leadership should be viewed as a priceless national treasure that is sorely needed to rejuvenate society and reform institutions. Many writers have suggested that many social and economic problems, including unemployment and the decline in international competitiveness, stem from insufficient transformational leaders who dream inspired visions and are able to motivate followers to pursue them.

Studies of transformational leadership indicate that it can be learned and that it is greatly influenced by the kind of leadership modeled in an organization. Leaders at all levels can be trained to be more charismatic, to be more intellectually stimulating, and to show more individual consideration. Successful training programs have been conducted for a variety of groups, such as first-level supervisors in high-tech computer firms, senior executives of insurance firms, and officers in the Israeli military.[4]

LEADERSHIP TRAITS

Leadership has been studied at three different levels—the individual, the group, and the organization.

- At the individual level of analysis, leadership studies have focused on the traits of successful leaders.
- At the group level, leadership studies have focused on leadership behaviors of both formal and informal leaders.
- The organizational level of analysis has examined how organizational effectiveness is determined by the interactions among the leader, the follower, and the situation.

Trait Studies:
A stream of research that tried to identify the essential personality traits that contributed to effective leadership.

The traits of successful leaders have been studied for more than a century. World War I highlighted the need for selecting and training effective leaders, and for the quarter century between World War I and World War II, numerous studies investigated the characteristics of good leaders. These studies are generally referred to as *trait studies*, because their primary goal was to identify the personal traits of effective leaders.

In general, the trait studies were quite disappointing. Although several traits were frequently associated with effective leaders, the research was weak and sometimes contradictory, because of methodological problems associated with identifying good leaders, measuring leader traits, and measuring group effectiveness. Because of weak results, the focus of leadership research shifted from trait studies to contingency studies, which examined more than just the traits of the leader.

The research on leadership traits should not be dismissed too quickly, however. Although the trait studies were disappointing, they were not worthless. Several traits produced a significant difference in leadership effectiveness, but they did not act alone. Four major reviews have surveyed the trait studies, and the results can be summarized in three categories: physical traits, intelligence, and personality traits.[5]

Physical Traits

Trait studies examined such physical factors as height, weight, physique, energy, health, and appearance. To the extent that anything can be concluded regarding the relationship among these factors and leadership, it appears that leaders tend to be slightly taller and heavier, have better health, a superior physique, a higher rate of energy output, and a more attractive appearance.

To illustrate, one early study on the effects of height found that executives in insurance companies were taller than policyholders, that bishops were taller than clergymen, that university presidents were taller than college presidents, that sales managers were taller than sales representatives, and that railway presidents were taller than station agents.[6] Results of this sort, however, have not always been consistent. While one literature review found nine studies showing that leaders tend to be taller, it reported two studies showing that leaders tended to be shorter. Attractiveness and a pleasant appearance were found to be highly correlated with leaders among Boy Scouts, but among groups of delinquent youth, leaders were rated as more slovenly and unkempt than other members.[7]

In summary, studies of personal characteristics are not particularly interesting or useful. The results are generally too weak and inconsistent to be useful in selecting leaders, nor are they useful for training purposes, because very little can be done to change most of these physical traits. The results seem to say more about cultural stereotypes than they do about leadership.

Intelligence

Many studies have investigated the relationship between leadership and general intelligence, and they generally agree that leaders are more intelligent than nonleaders. The relationship between intelligence and leadership probably stems from the fact that so many leadership functions depend on careful problem solving. One review of leadership studies reported 23 experiments showing that leaders were brighter and had greater levels of intelligence than did their followers. Only five studies reported that intelligence made no difference. In general, it appears safe to conclude that leaders are more intelligent than nonleaders, but again the correlations are small. Obviously, many variables other than intelligence influence leadership effectiveness.[8]

An interesting conclusion from these studies is the suggestion that leaders should be more intelligent than the group, but not by too wide a margin. Members who are significantly brighter than other group members are seldom selected as leaders. Because of their superior intellect, it appears that other group members tend to reject them; they are too different from the rest of the group. People with high IQs tend to have different vocabularies, interests, and goals from those of other group members, which create communication and interpersonal relations problems.

Leadership effectiveness also appears to be related to scholarship and knowledge. Leaders generally excel scholastically and receive better-than-average grades. General information, practical knowledge, and simply knowing

Exhibit 17.3   Personality Factors Most Frequently Associated with Effective Leadership

Capacity	Achievement	Responsibility	Participation	Status
Intelligence	Scholarship	Honesty	Activity	Socioeconomic
Alertness	Knowledge	Dependability	Sociability	Position
Verbal facility	Athletic accomplishment	Initiative	Cooperation	Popularity
Originality	Personality adjustment	Persistence	Adaptability	
Judgment		Aggressiveness	Humor	
		Self-confidence		
		Desire to excel		

how to get things done appear to be important for effective leadership, and several studies have shown a positive relationship between general knowledge and leadership ability.

Personality Traits

Other personality traits appear to be related to leadership, although most of the relationships are not especially strong. A list of the personality traits most frequently associated with leadership is shown in Exhibit 17.3. This list is based on the 1948 review of 124 studies of leadership traits by Ralph Stogdill. This list suggests that the average leader is more social, displays greater initiative, is more persistent, knows how to get things done, is more self-confident, displays greater cooperativeness and adaptability, and possesses greater verbal skills than the average person does.

Studies examining emotional adjustment quite consistently found that leaders are more emotionally mature than nonleaders. Rather consistent support was also found for the relationship between leadership and self-confidence or self-esteem. Indeed, the relationship between self-confidence and leadership generally produced some of the highest correlations of any of the personality traits tested. Honesty or integrity is another characteristic attributed to good leaders. Several studies of the characteristics people admire most in leaders report that honesty is the most important trait.[9]

Consequently, it is not correct to conclude that personal characteristics are unrelated to leadership; some characteristics are important, but their relationships are rather complex. Four major reviews have concluded that effective leadership does not depend solely on personality traits. Situational variables are also important, and the situation often determines whether a personality characteristic will be positively or negatively associated with effective leadership. Each review concluded that leadership must be examined as an interaction of three variables: characteristics of the leader, characteristics of the subordinate, and the nature of the task.

LEADER BEHAVIORS

A second line of leadership research examined leader behaviors in the context of the group, and attempted to describe what leaders actually do. These studies examined whether certain ways of behaving were more effective than others: How do effective leaders behave differently from other group members? Most of these studies started in the 1940s and have continued since then.

Authoritarian, Democratic, and Laissez-Faire Leadership

The contrasting political systems in the United States and Germany preceding World War II inspired one of the early classic studies of leadership that compared the effects of three leadership styles: authoritarian, democratic, and laissez-faire. Ten-year-old boys who were organized into groups of five participated in after-school activities under the leadership of a graduate student trained to provide democratic, autocratic, or laissez-faire leadership. Every six weeks the leaders were rotated among groups so that each group experienced each type of leadership. Under the *democratic leaders,* group decisions were made by majority vote in which equal participation was encouraged, and criticism and punishment were minimal. Under the *autocratic leader,* all decisions were made by the leader and the boys were required to follow prescribed procedures under strict discipline. Under the *laissez-faire leader,* the actual leadership was minimized and the boys were allowed to work and play essentially without supervision.[10]

During the 18 weeks of this study, the performance of the boys was observed in order to assess the effects of the three leadership styles. Laissez-faire leadership produced the lowest levels of satisfaction and productivity, while autocratic leadership produced the highest levels of aggressive acts. Democratic leadership seemed to produce the most satisfied groups, who also functioned in the most orderly and positive manner, which is what the researchers hoped to find. However, the effects of the leadership styles on productivity were somewhat mixed, although actual measures of productivity were not obtained. Under autocratic leadership, the groups spent more time in productive work activity and had more work-related conversations, but appeared to be more productive only when the leader was present. When the leader left the room, the amount of work-related activity dropped drastically.

The results of this study were somewhat surprising to the researchers, who had expected the highest satisfaction and productivity under democratic leadership. This study was conducted under the direction of Kurt Lewin, a behavioral scientist who came to America from Germany just prior to World War II. Lewin believed that the repressive, autocratic political climate he had left in Germany was not as satisfying, productive, or desirable as a democratic society. He expected the results of the experiment to confirm his hypothesis. Although the boys preferred a democratic leader, they appeared to be more productive under autocratic leadership.

Other studies have also shown that democratic leadership styles are not always the most productive. In fact, some studies have found that both the satisfaction and the productivity of group members are higher under directive leaders than democratic leaders. For example, a study of 488 managers in a consumer loan company found that employees who had high authoritarianism scores (high acceptance of strong authority relationships) were more satisfied and productive when they worked for supervisors who had little tolerance for freedom.[11] Greater satisfaction with an authoritarian leader was also found in another study of over one thousand workers. This study found that employees who worked independently but were required to have frequent interaction with their superior preferred and were more satisfied with an autocratic leader. Some examples of such employees are fire fighters, police officers, and administrative aides.[12]

Initiating Structure and Consideration

Initiating structure:
Leader behavior that focuses on clarifying and defining the roles and task responsibilities for subordinates.

Consideration:
Leader behavior that focuses on the comfort, well-being, satisfaction, and need fulfillment of subordinates.

Following World War II, a team of researchers at Ohio State University collected extensive data that were used to identify two leadership factors called *initiating structure* and *consideration*.[13] ***Initiating structure*** consisted of leader behaviors associated with organizing and defining the work, the work relationships, and the goals. A leader who initiated structure was described as one who assigned people to particular tasks, expected workers to follow standard routines, and emphasized meeting deadlines. The factor of ***consideration*** involved leader behaviors that showed friendship, mutual trust, warmth, and concern for subordinates.

Survey data indicated that initiating structure and consideration are independent dimensions of leadership behavior. Therefore, a leader could be high on both dimensions, low on both dimensions, or high on one and low on the other. Since both factors are important leader behaviors, the early studies assumed that effective leaders would be high on both dimensions; however, subsequent research failed to support this expectation. The most effective leaders are usually high on both dimensions, but not always. Occasionally other combinations have produced the highest levels of satisfaction and performance, including being high on one scale and low on the other, or being at moderate levels on both dimensions.[14]

Production-Centered and Employee-Centered Leader Behaviors

Production-centered leadership:
Behaviors that focus on performing the group's goals.

Employee-centered leadership:
Behaviors that focus on helping group members feel satisfied and willing to contribute to the group.

About the same time that the Ohio State University researchers were discovering the dimensions of initiating structure and consideration, a similar research program at the University of Michigan identified two similar dimensions of leadership behavior which they labeled *production-centered* and *employee-centered* behaviors. ***Production-centered*** behaviors were similar to initiating structure, in which leaders established goals, gave instructions, checked on performance, and structured the work of the group. ***Employee-centered*** behaviors were similar to the dimension of consideration, in which the leader developed a supportive personal relationship with subordinates, avoided punitive behavior, and encouraged two-way communication with subordinates.[15]

Studies on the relationship between production-centered and employee-centered behaviors also found them to be independent dimensions of leadership. A review of 24 studies dispelled a popular myth suggesting that supervisors focus on either production or people, and to the extent that they focus on one they ignore the other. These studies indicated instead that supervisors can be interested in both production and employees. Therefore, a leader who has a strong production orientation is not necessarily uninterested in the employees.[16]

The Leadership Grid®

Another theory that combines concern for task accomplishment and a concern for people was created by Robert Blake and Jane Mouton using a 9x9 matrix called the Leadership Grid. The concern for production dimension is measured on a nine-point scale and represented along the horizontal dimension,

Leadership Grid®
(formerly
Managerial Grid®):
A matrix that combines
two factors: concern
for people and con-
cern for production.
Each factor is mea-
sured with a nine-point
scale.

while the vertical dimension measures an individual's concern for people, again using a nine-point scale. Blake and Mouton assume that the most effective leadership style is a 9,9 style, demonstrating both concern for production and concern for people.[17]

By responding to a questionnaire, individuals place themselves in one of the 81 cells on the Leadership Grid. Five different grid positions at the four corners and in the middle are typically used to illustrate different leadership styles:

1,9 Style—Country Club Management: a maximum concern for people with minimum concern for production. This individual is not concerned whether the group actually produces anything, but is highly concerned about the members' personal needs, interests, and interpersonal relationships.

9,1 Style—Authority-Compliance Management: primarily concerned with production and task accomplishment and unconcerned about people. This person wants to get the job done and wants to follow the schedule at all costs.

1,1 Style—Impoverished Management: minimal concern for both production and people. This person essentially abdicates the leadership role.

5,5 Style—Middle-of-the-road Management: a moderate concern for both people and production. This person organizes production to accomplish the necessary work while maintaining satisfactory morale.

9,9 Style—Team Management: a maximum concern for both production and people. This leader wants to meet schedules and get the job done, but at the same time is highly concerned about the feelings and interests of the group members.

The Leadership Grid is popular among managers, and it has been used extensively in management training to help managers move toward a 9,9 style. In spite of its popularity, however, the usefulness of the Leadership Grid has not been consistently supported by research. Most of the available research consists of case analyses that have been loosely interpreted to support it. Empirical research has failed to show that a 9,9 leadership style is universally superior. The demands of the situation, the expectations of other group members, and the nature of the work being performed interact in complex ways that call for a variety of leadership styles. Consequently, the 9,9 leadership style is not always the most effective.

Leader Behaviors as Leadership Roles

Research on leader behaviors helps us understand effective leadership in groups. Rather than thinking of leadership strictly in terms of how a formal leader behaves, it is helpful to think of leadership as essential roles performed within a group. This line of thinking implies that leadership consists of essential leader behaviors that can be performed by any group member. The leadership roles of initiating structure and consideration are similar to the work roles and maintenance roles in groups.[18] These two roles are necessary for a group to be effective, and can be performed either by the formally appointed leader or by other group members.

If a task is already highly structured, or if other group members adequately structure the task, then efforts by the leader to add additional structure are unnecessary and ineffective. Likewise, the maintenance roles of showing consideration and concern for group members may be performed by other group members, thereby eliminating the need for the formal leader to perform this role. Summarizing research on consideration and initiating structure, one review concluded that when the formally appointed leaders fail to perform either of these leader behaviors, an informal leader will emerge and perform them if they are necessary for success.

SITUATIONAL LEADERSHIP

Contingency theories of leadership:
Leadership theories that recognize the influence of situational variables in determining the ideal styles of leadership.

Research on leader traits and behaviors failed to find one style of leadership that was universally superior. Extensive reviews concluded that effective leadership depended on more than the leader alone; what worked well in one situation would not necessarily work well in other situations. These studies concluded that effective leadership depended on a combination of leadership styles, follower characteristics, and environmental factors. This approach to leadership is referred to as *situational leadership theory* or *contingency theories of leadership*.

Five situational leadership theories have received primary attention: (a) Paul Hersey and Ken Blanchard's life cycle theory of leadership, (b) Fred Fiedler's contingency theory of leadership, (c) Robert House's path-goal leadership theory, (d) Victor Vroom and Philip Yetton's decision-making model of leadership, and (e) Robert Tannenbaum and Warren Schmidt's model for choosing a leadership pattern.[19] Rather than describing the development and results of each of these theories, they are combined into an integrated model of leadership effectiveness, and only the summary conclusions and applications are presented here. These theories all suggest that leader effectiveness depends on a combination of leader behavior styles, follower characteristics, and environmental factors, as illustrated in Exhibit 17.4.

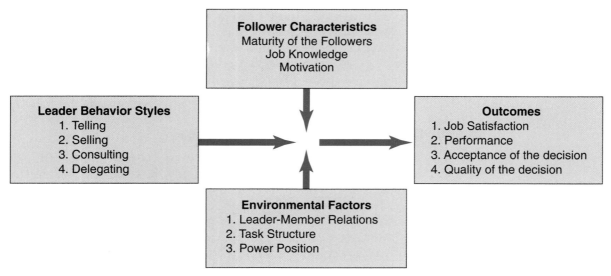

Exhibit 17.4   Situational Leadership Model

Leader Behavior Styles

Leaders can select from among many different styles of leadership, and these styles can involve varying levels of interpersonal sensitivity, affiliation, appreciation, and even humor. The most important variable influencing a person's leadership style is the degree to which the leader is willing to allow subordinates to participate in making decisions and directing their own actions. At one extreme is autocratic leadership, where all decisions and influence come from the leader, and at the other end of the continuum is democratic leadership, where the leader delegates authority to decide and act to the members of a group. This decision is influenced by the leader's value system, especially the value the leader places on participation and involvement by subordinates. The amount of confidence leaders have in their subordinates and the leader's ability to handle uncertainty are also relevant considerations in selecting a leadership style.

When selecting a leadership style, a leader could choose any one of the following patterns that illustrate increasing levels of participation:

1. *Telling:* The leader makes all decisions; he or she simply announces them and tells subordinates what to do. This leadership style is the most autocratic and generally the least preferred by most subordinates. However, it may be appropriate when time is limited and an immediate decision is necessary.
2. *Selling:* The leader presents a tentative decision subject to change, and attempts to sell the decision to subordinates. The leader may present ideas and invite questions so that subordinates feel that their ideas are heard. Most subordinates want their feelings and ideas to be considered; they like having an opportunity to ask questions.
3. *Consulting:* The leader presents the problem to the group and obtains their suggestions and preferences before making the decision. Group participation often yields higher-quality ideas than when the leader acts alone, and lower resistance when implementing the decision.
4. *Delegating:* The leader may delegate the decision and its implementation to the group and let them handle it on their own, or the leader may join the group and participate as any other member in making and implementing the decision. This style requires great confidence in the ability and motivation of the group, and usually requires much more time to make a decision. However, the acceptance of the decision is usually much faster and the implementation is much smoother when the entire group participates.

To decide which is the most appropriate level of participation, a leader may want to consider the following questions:

- As long as it is accepted, does it make any difference which decision is selected? Are some decisions qualitatively superior to others?
- Do I have enough information to make a high-quality decision, or do subordinates have additional information that must be considered?
- Is acceptance of the decision by subordinates crucial to effective implementation? If I make the decision by myself, will they accept it?
- Can I trust subordinates to base their decisions on the best interests of the organization?

- Will subordinates agree on the preferred solution, or will there be conflict?
- How much time do we have to make this decision, and what are the costs of delaying a decision to involve others?

Follower Characteristics

When selecting a leadership style, the leader should consider such follower characteristics as whether followers have high needs for independence, whether they are ready to assume responsibility for decision making, whether they are interested in the problems, and whether they have enough experience to deal with them. As subordinates gain greater skill and competence in managing themselves, leaders ought to give them more autonomy.

The appropriate leadership style depends primarily on the maturity of the followers. Maturity is defined as the ability and willingness of people to take responsibility for directing their own behavior as it relates to the specific task being performed. An individual or group may demonstrate maturity on some tasks and immaturity on others. Maturity is determined by two components: job maturity (ability) and psychological maturity (willingness). Job maturity is the ability to successfully perform a task, and is a function of the follower's job knowledge, training, experience, and skills. Psychological maturity refers to the willingness or motivation to perform the job, and is a function of the follower's commitment and confidence.

Telling is an appropriate leadership style for subordinates who have low maturity and are both unable and unwilling to perform the job. Selling is appropriate for followers who are able but unwilling, while consulting is well suited for followers who are willing but unable to do the job. Delegation requires followers who are both able and willing.

Environmental Factors

Many environmental forces influence the appropriate leadership style, including the culture of the organization and its history of allowing subordinates to exercise autonomy; cohesiveness of the group and the degree to which the members work together as a unit; the nature of the problem itself and whether subordinates have the knowledge and experience needed to solve it; and the pressures of time, since group decision making is time-consuming and ineffective in a crisis situation.

Extensive research by Fred Fiedler demonstrated that the following environmental factors had an important impact on how leaders should act:

1. *Leader-member relations:* whether the natural relationships in the situation are friendly and pleasant or unfriendly and unpleasant.
2. *Task structure:* whether the task is relatively structured and followers know what to do without being told, or unstructured so that the leader must clarify the goals, identify how the task is to be accomplished, and defend the selected solution.
3. *Power position:* whether the leader has a strong power position because of official recognition and the ability to administer rewards and punishments, or the leader has a weak power position that is not recognized or accepted.

The combination of these three environmental factors determines whether the leader's situation is favorable or unfavorable. The most favorable position for a leader is to have positive leader-member relations, a structured task, and a strong power position. Conversely, the leader is in a very unfavorable situation when the leader-member relations are unpleasant, the task is unstructured, and the leader's power position is insecure. Between these two extremes, of course, are situations of moderate favorableness, which are very important in Fiedler's contingency theory because they call for a very different style of leadership from those of extremely favorable or unfavorable situations.

Fiedler conducted extensive research studies that examined the most effective leadership style in certain situations. His research demonstrated that in extremely favorable situations, task-oriented leaders achieve the best results because they focus on getting the work done without worrying too much about their relationships with followers. In these situations, the personal needs of followers are apparently already satisfied, and interpersonal sensitivity is unnecessary because there is already a friendly and comfortable situation.

Likewise, when the situation is extremely unfavorable, the same task-oriented style of leadership achieves the best results because the job must get done, and efforts to act friendly and concerned about followers will not make any difference. A task-oriented leader who simply focuses on getting the work done is more effective than a relationship-oriented leader who spends time fruitlessly trying to build good relationships in an impossible situation.

At intermediate levels of favorableness, however, a much different style of leadership is superior. Here, the ideal style is one that is sensitive to the feelings and interests of followers. Interpersonal sensitivity and involvement are important at intermediate levels, since followers need to feel included and relevant. Concern for the group members is apparently a necessary prerequisite for motivating them to perform well.

DETERMINANTS OF LEADERSHIP EFFECTIVENESS

Strategies for Improving Leadership

Since the quality of leadership contributes so greatly to the effectiveness of an organization, knowing how to increase leader effectiveness is a serious issue. Improved leader behavior is not a panacea for all organizational problems, but quality leadership is so important that improving the quality of leadership should be an ongoing effort in every organization. Four of the most popular methods of increasing leadership effectiveness include leadership training, managerial selection and placement, organizational redesign, and rewarding leader behavior.

Leadership Training. Leaders can benefit from training in interpersonal skills and management functions—planning, organizing, directing, and controlling. Leaders need to know the differences between transactional and transformational leadership, and have an opportunity to practice the skills involved in each kind of leadership. Although training can help leaders acquire better leadership skills, it is doubtful that such training will change a leader's basic leadership orientation or personality structure.

Managerial Selection and Placement. Since basic leadership orientations are not easily changed, companies should select leaders who have leadership styles that fit the situation. Biographical information examining a person's previous leadership experiences can help to predict future leadership effectiveness. Effective leadership depends far more on good selection than on training.

Organizational Engineering. When people are placed in situations inconsistent with their leadership style, they are generally unsuccessful and feel very frustrated until they are reassigned. Fiedler recommends that organizations engineer the job to fit the manager.[20] This approach is particularly useful when a specific individual is necessary to the organization, yet that person does not possess a compatible leadership style. The job can be changed most easily by changing the degree of task structure or the power position of the leader.

Rewarding Leader Behavior. Leaders can acquire new leadership skills and learn different leader behaviors if they are sufficiently motivated to experiment and learn. A variety of incentives can reward leaders for learning and developing. Pay increases and promotions are popular incentives that encourage leaders to improve. However, the most powerful incentive is probably the intrinsic satisfaction that comes from greater self-confidence and improved interpersonal relationships between leaders and members.

Reciprocal Influence of Leader and Follower

With thousands of books and articles written about leadership, it is surprising that so little has been written about "followership." We seem to assume that leadership is a one-way process in which leaders influence followers; we overlook the influence in the opposite direction. Only meager efforts have attempted to describe the influence of the group on the leader.

The discussion to this point has assumed that leaders influence followers —that the satisfaction and performance of the followers is caused by the leader's behavior. There are good reasons to reverse this statement, however, and argue that the behavior of the leaders is caused by the performance and satisfaction of the followers. When we acknowledge the leader's capacity to reward the behavior of followers, we should not overlook the capacity of the followers to reward the leader by the ways they perform. For example, organizations reward managers according to the performance of their group. Consequently, the managers of high-performing groups are highly rewarded because of their group's success.

One study has demonstrated the reciprocal nature of influence between leaders and subordinates. In this study, data were collected from first-line managers and two of the supervisors who reported to them. Leaders who were more considerate created greater satisfaction among their subordinates; at the same time, the performance of the subordinates caused changes in the behavior of the leaders. Employees who performed well caused their supervisors to reward them and treat them with greater consideration. Although research on the reciprocal influence between leaders and followers is still rather limited, it is important to remember that leadership may be significantly constrained by the followers.[21]

Some observers contend that the leadership crisis in society is not really caused by bad leaders, but by incompetent or uncooperative followers who fail to complete their work in an active, intelligent, and ethical way. Effective followers are characterized as having (1) personal integrity that demands loyalty to the organization and a willingness to follow their own beliefs, (2) an understanding of the organization and their assigned roles, (3) versatility, and (4) personal responsibility.

Constraints on Leader Behavior. Leaders do not have unlimited opportunities to influence others. Leadership effectiveness is constrained by a variety of factors, such as the extent to which managerial decisions are preprogrammed because of precedent, structure, technological specifications, laws, and the absence of available alternatives. Leadership can also be constrained by a variety of organizational factors limiting the leader's ability either to communicate with or reinforce the behavior of subordinates. The constraints imposed on leaders include external factors, organizational policies, group factors, and individual skills and abilities.

1. *External factors.* Leaders are constrained in what they can do because of economic realities and a host of state and federal laws. For example, leaders are required to pay at least the minimum wage and they are required to enforce safety standards. Leaders who have unskilled followers will have difficulty leading regardless of their leadership style, and the availability of skilled followers is influenced by the external labor market. Some locations have a better supply of skilled employees than others.
2. *Organizational policies.* The organization may constrain a leader's effectiveness by limiting the amount of interaction between leaders and followers, or by restricting the leader's ability to reward or punish followers.
3. *Group factors.* Group norms are created by the dynamics of the group. If the group is highly cohesive and very determined, it can limit the leader's ability to influence the group.
4. *Individual skills and abilities.* The leader's own skills and abilities may act as constraints, since leaders can only possess so much expertise, energy, and power. Some situations may simply require greater skills and abilities than the leader may possibly hope to possess.

Substitutes for leadership:
Subordinate, task, or organizational factors that decrease the importance of a leader's influence; forces within the environment that supplant or replace the influence of the leader.

Substitutes for Leadership. While some situations constrain leaders, other situations make leadership unnecessary. These variables are referred to as *leader substitutes* because they substitute for leadership, either by making the leader's behavior unnecessary or neutralizing the leader's ability to influence subordinates. An example of a variable that tends to substitute for leadership is training. Subordinates who have extensive experience, ability, and training tend to eliminate the need for instrumental leadership. Task instructions are simply unnecessary when subordinates already know what to do.

Realizing that there are constraints on a leader's behavior and that other factors may serve to neutralize or substitute for the influence of a leader helps explain why the research on leadership has produced such inconsistent results. The inconsistency does not mean that leadership is unimportant; rather, it illustrates the complexity of the world in which leaders are required to function. Leadership is an extremely important function that has an enormous influence on the effectiveness of groups and organizations. The complexity of the situation, however, may prevent us from knowing in advance which leadership behaviors will be the most effective.

Discussion Questions

1. Identify someone who is a great transformational leader and someone who is a great transactional leader. How are they different? What are the effects of these differences?
2. Studies of the relationship between physical traits and leadership in men suggest that leaders tend to be tall, intelligent, and handsome. How do you account for these results?
3. What is the relationship between the two leader behaviors—initiating structure and consideration—and the two group roles—work roles and maintenance roles? What does this association suggest in terms of essential activities for group functioning?
4. Apply Fiedler's contingency theory of leadership by identifying two situations, one extremely favorable and the other extremely unfavorable, and explain why a task-oriented leader is most effective in each situation. Also, identify a situation of moderate favorableness and explain why a relations-oriented leader would be best.
5. The relationship between the leader and the group involves a reciprocal influence. Who do you think exerts the greatest influence—the leader or the group? Using the principles of operant conditioning, describe how a group would need to behave in order to create a punitive, authoritarian supervisor or a rewarding, participative supervisor.

Notes

1. Warren Bennis, *On Becoming a Leader* (Reading, MA: Addison-Wesley, 1989); Warren Bennis, "Why Leaders Can't Lead, *Training and Development Journal* 43 (April 1989): 35–39.
2. John P. Kotter, "What Leaders Really Do," *Harvard Business Review* 68 (May–June, 1990): 103–11; Abraham Zaleznik, "Managers and Leaders: Are They Different?" *Harvard Business Review* 70 (March–April 1921): 126–35.
3. Bernard M. Bass, "From Transactional to Transformational Leadership: Learning to Share the Vision," *Organizational Dynamics* 18 (Winter 1990): 19–31; James M. Burns, *Leadership*, (New York: Harper & Row, 1978); Bruce J. Avolio, David A. Waldman, and Francis J. Yammarino, "Leading in the 1990s: The Four I's of Transformational Leadership," *Journal of European Industrial Training* 15, 4 (1991): 9–16.
4. Bernard M. Bass and Bruce J. Avolio, "Developing Transformational Leadership: 1992 and Beyond," *Journal of European Industrial Training* 14, 5 (1990): 21–27; Micha Popper, Ori Landau, and Ury M. Gluskines, "The Israeli Defense Forces: An Example of Transformational Leadership," *Leadership and Organization Development Journal* 13, 1 (1992): 3–8; Francis J. Yammarino and Bernard Bass, Transformational Leadership and Multiple Levels of Analysis," *Human Relations* 43 (October 1990): 975–95.

5. Bernard M. Bass, *Leadership, Psychology, and Organizational Behavior* (New York: Harper & Row, 1960); Cecil A. Gibb, "Leadership," in G. Lindzey and E. Aronson (eds.), *The Handbook of Social Psychology*, 2nd ed., vol. 4 (Reading, Mass.: Addison-Wesley, 1969); R. D. Mann, "A Review of the Relationships Between Personality and Performance in Small Groups," *Psychological Bulletin* 56 (1959): 241–70; Ralph M. Stogdill, "Personal Factors Associated with Leadership: A Survey of the Literature," *Journal of Psychology* 25 (1948): 35–71.

6. E. B. Gowin, *The Executive and His Control of Men* (New York: Macmillan, 1915).

7. Stogdill, op. cit.

8. Stogdill, op. cit.

9. Shelley A. Kirkpatrick and Edwin A. Locke, "Leadership: Do Traits Matter?" *Academy of Management Executive* 5 (May 1991): 49–60.

10. Kurt Lewin, R. Lippitt, and R. K. White, "Patterns of Aggressive Behavior in Experimentally-Created Social Climates," *Journal of Social Psychology* 10 (1939): 271–301.

11. Henry Tosi, "Effect of the Interaction of Leader Behavior and Subordinate Authoritarianism," *Proceedings of the Annual Convention of the American Psychological Association* 6, 1 (1971): 473–74.

12. Victor H. Vroom and Floyd C. Mann, "Leader Authoritarianism and Employee Attitudes," *Personnel Psychology* 13 (1960): 125–40.

13. John K. Hemphill, *Leader Behavior Description* (Ohio State Leadership Studies Staff Report, 1950); Ralph M. Stogdill, *Handbook of Leadership* (New York: The Free Press, 1974), chaps. 11 and 12.

14. E. A. Fleishman, "Twenty Years of Consideration and Structure," in E.A. Fleishman and J. G. Hunt (Eds.), *Current Developments in the Study of Leadership* (Carbondale: Southern Illinois University Press, 1973): 1–40; E. A. Fleishman and E. F. Harris, "Patterns of Leadership Behavior Related to Employee Grievances and Turnover," *Personnel Psychology* 15 (1962): 43–56.

15. Daniel Katz, N. Maccoby, and N. C. Morse, *Productivity, Supervision, and Morale in an Office Situation* (Ann Arbor: University of Michigan Survey Research Center, 1950).

16. Peter Weissenberg and M. H. Kavanagh, "The Independence of Initiating Structure and Consideration: A Review of the Evidence," *Personnel Psychology* 25 (Spring 1972): 119–30.

17. Robert R. Blake and Anne Adams McCanse, *Leadership Dilemmas—Grid Solutions* (Houston, TX: Gulf Publishing, 1991).

18. Kenneth D. Benne and Paul Sheats, "Functional Roles and Group Members," *Journal of Social Issues* 4 (Spring 1948): 42–47.

19. Paul Hersey and Ken Blanchard, *Management of Organizational Behavior*, 4th ed. (Englewood Cliffs, NJ: Prentice-Hall, 1982) chap. 4; Fred E. Fiedler and Martin M. Chemers, *Leadership and Effective Management* (Glenview, IL: Scott, Foresman, 1974); Robert J. House and Terrence R. Mitchell, "Path-Goal Theory of Leadership," *Journal of Contemporary Business* (Autumn 1974): 81–98; Victor H. Vroom and Philip W. Yetton, *Leadership and Decision-Making* (Pittsburgh: University of Pittsburgh Press, 1973); Robert Tannenbaum and Warren H. Schmidt, "How to Choose a Leadership Pattern," *Harvard Business Review* 51 (May–June, 1973).

20. Fred E. Fiedler, "Change the Job to Fit the Manager," *Harvard Business Review* 43 (1965): 115–22.

21. Charles N. Green, "The Reciprocal Nature of Influence Between Leader and Subordinate," *Journal of Applied Psychology* 59 (April 1975): 187–93; Ifechukude B. Mmobousi, "Followership Behavior: A Neglected Aspect of Leadership Studies," *Leadership and Organizational Development Journal* 12, 7 (1991): 11–16.

Leading with Vision

Part 1: Confronting Success

The department of Business Education at Brigham Young University was one of the most successful departments in the College of Business. It had a faculty of about 20 professors who were highly trained and nationally recognized in their field. The department offered a bachelor's degree for undergraduate students who wanted to learn shorthand and typing and who planned to work in offices. This degree was popular on campus and the department had an excellent record of placing its graduates in successful careers after graduation. At the graduate level, the department offered master's and doctorate degrees for those who wanted to teach business education at the high school or college level and, again, the demand for these graduates was strong. This doctorate degree was the only one offered in the College of Business. The alumni from this department were scattered across the nation and their outstanding performances contributed greatly to the department's outstanding national reputation.

During his third year as dean of the College of Business, William G. Dyer questioned whether the Business Education Department should continue as in the past or whether it needed to change its focus. Personal computers were growing in popularity and the future of shorthand and typing was not clear. Although the department had an excellent faculty, high-quality degree programs, outstanding students, and a nationally recognized alumni, Dean Dyer thought that some kind of change would be needed in the future.

Because of his training as an organizational consultant, Dean Dyer decided to appoint a task force to study the Business Education Department and make a recommendation about how it should be changed in the future. This task force was comprised of two faculty who taught business education, someone from the dean's office, plus faculty representatives from other departments. They interviewed faculty, students, and alumni, and returned two months later with the recommendation to stay the course. Based on their interviews, they concluded that the department currently had excellent degrees, a dedicated faculty, and outstanding students, and there was a strong demand for its graduates. Consequently, there was no need to change.

Questions

1. Was appointing a task force a good idea? What are the strengths and weaknesses of delegating an important decision to a committee?
2. What other options were available to the dean for examining this problem? What are their strengths and weaknesses?

Part II: A Bold Decision

Dean Dyer was surprised at the recommendation that the Business Education Department continue unchanged. He expected the task force to recommend major changes in the department, or at least some alteration in its focus. Instead, it recommended that no changes be made: "If it isn't broke, don't fix it." Now the dean faced another problem: how could he reject the recommendations of a committee he appointed to study the issue after they had spent two months working on it?

After considerable thought and discussion with his staff, Dean Dyer decided to reject the recommendations of the committee and disband the department. He announced that the College of Business was no longer in the business of training secretarial students; rather, it would begin to train students in management information systems. His unilateral decision was shocking to the entire faculty and many questioned whether he had the authority to act unilaterally. Nevertheless, he met with the faculty members and told them they would need to either find new employment or retool and prepare to teach information systems courses.

The announcement generated considerable animosity between the dean and the faculty at first. Each faculty member was forced to make a major career change, since teaching shorthand and typing is very different from teaching computer technology and information systems. Rather quickly, however, most of them recognized the need for change and they began to learn a new discipline. Within two years, the faculty who remained had created a new management information systems program with bachelor's and master's degrees that were quickly gaining a national reputation. Twenty years later, a faculty member who left described the decision as the greatest mistake ever made at the university, while another faculty member who remained described it as a courageous decision that could never have been made by a committee.

Questions

1. Was unilateral action necessary or desirable in this situation? When should leaders act unilaterally in forcing change on an organization? What are the potential benefits and dangers of taking arbitrary action?
2. Transformational leadership has been described as a lonely experience. What are the leadership challenges of acting unilaterally?

Leadership Orientation

Directions: The following statements describe aspects of leadership behavior. Think about the way you usually act when you are the leader of a group. Respond to each item according to the way you would most likely act if you were the leader of a work group. Circle whether you would most likely behave in the described way: *always* (A), *frequently* (F), *occasionally* (O), *seldom* (S), or *never* (N).

A	F	O	S	N	1. I would consult the group before making any changes.
A	F	O	S	N	2. I would encourage the group to set specific performance standards.
A	F	O	S	N	3. I would trust the group to exercise its own good judgment.
A	F	O	S	N	4. I would urge the group to beat its previous record.
A	F	O	S	N	5. I would try to make certain all group members were comfortable and happy.
A	F	O	S	N	6. I would assign group members to specific tasks.
A	F	O	S	N	7. I would represent the group and defend them at outside meetings.
A	F	O	S	N	8. I would be the one to decide what should be done and how it should be done.
A	F	O	S	N	9. I would permit group members to use their own judgment in solving problems.
A	F	O	S	N	10. I would try to keep the work moving at a rapid pace.
A	F	O	S	N	11. I would invite group members to share their personal concerns with me.
A	F	O	S	N	12. I would carefully plan how to do the work most efficiently.
A	F	O	S	N	13. I would eliminate conflicts and make certain there were friendly feelings in the group.
A	F	O	S	N	14. I would encourage overtime work.
A	F	O	S	N	15. I would allow members complete freedom in their work.
A	F	O	S	N	16. I would encourage members to follow the standard procedures.
A	F	O	S	N	17. I would encourage members to get to know each other.
A	F	O	S	N	18. I would establish a schedule for getting the work done.
A	F	O	S	N	19. I would encourage members to share their ideas with me.
A	F	O	S	N	20. I would emphasize quality and insist that all mistakes be corrected.

Scoring: These 20 items measure two leadership orientations: the odd-snumbered items measure concern for people and the even-numbered items measure concern for the task.

The responses to each item are scored as follows: A = four points, F = three points, O = two points, S = one point, and N = zero points. Calculate your score for both leadership orientations by adding the points for the odd items and then adding your points for the even items. Your score for each variable will be a number between 0 and 40.

Sum of the odd items: _____ Concern for People score

Sum of the even items: _____ Concern for the Task score

Source: Adapted after *The Leader Behavior Description Questionnaire* by the Ohio State Leadership Studies, published by the Bureau of Business Research, College of Commerce & Administration, The Ohio State University, Columbus, Ohio, 1962.

Evaluating Your Leadership Style: To help you evaluate your style of leadership, mark your Concern for People score on the left arrow of the diagram below and your Concern for the Task score on the right arrow. Draw a straight line between the two points on the two arrows. The point at which that line crosses the team leadership arrow in the middle indicates your score on that dimension. Shared leadership comes from the balanced concern for the task and a concern for people.

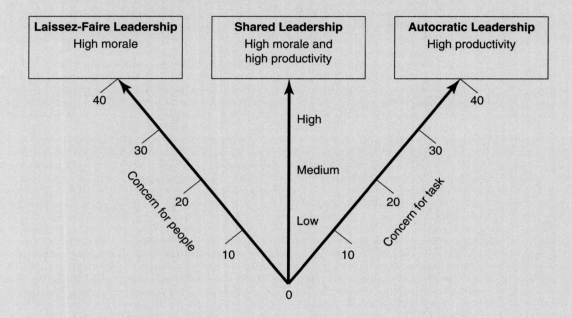

Power and Influence

Chapter Outline

Political versus Rational Decision Making
  Power Orientation: A Way to View Organizations
  Types of Influence
  Conditions Necessary for the Use of Power
  Authority versus Power
  Power Indicators
Interpersonal Power
  Five Bases of Power
  Acquiring Interpersonal Power
  Perpetuating Personal Power
Group and Subunit Power
  Acquiring Subunit Power
  Institutionalizing Subunit Power
Organizational Politics
  Political Strategies
  Influence Strategies

POLITICAL VERSUS RATIONAL DECISION MAKING

Power and organizational politics make people feel uncomfortable. Power is a word that has an emotional tinge. When people use politics to accomplish something they want, their behavior is often described as immoral or unethical. Nevertheless, power, influence, and political activity exist in organizations, and some have argued persuasively that the use of power is not only inevitable but often beneficial to both organizations and individuals. An important objective of this chapter is to show that power and politics are not only inevitable but are important parts of administrative activity. It is important to recognize when power is being used by ourselves or others, and to know how to use it more effectively and ethically.

Power Orientation: A Way to View Organizations

The effects of power can be seen in almost every aspect of organizational life, such as (1) when budgets are allocated to organizational subunits, (2) when promotion and hiring decisions are made, and (3) when organizational structures are redesigned. We typically dislike admitting that politics plays an important role in making organizational decisions because we think our behavior should be based on socially accepted values of rationality and effectiveness. We want to believe that budget allocations are based on a rational assessment of departmental needs rather than the political power of the department managers.

Exorbitant executive salaries illustrate the use of power. The golden rule of power states that those who have the gold get to rule; in other words, those who have power can successfully manipulate situations to retain power and increase their share of the rewards. The major reason why executive pay is so enormous is because executives have the power to play a central role in deciding their own pay. Technically, executive pay is determined by the board of directors, and someone who doesn't know better might think executive pay is based on an impartial evaluation of their performance. It sounds good, but it's not true. This naive belief fails to recognize (1) how top managers manipulate and control the information presented to the board, and (2) the fact that in many corporations the top executives are members of the board. Although executives may not comprise a majority of the board, they control both the kind of information seen by the board and many of the comparisons the board uses to make salary and bonus decisions.

Rational decision making assumes that decision makers define the organization's objectives and select good alternatives. This process assumes that everyone agrees on the objectives and, after a careful review, everyone will also agree on the ideal alternative. Two of the leading researchers on power, Jeffrey Pfeffer and John Kotter, argue that in reality the rational decision-making model is seldom used.[1] Pfeffer argues that rational decision-making models fail to account for the diversity of interests and goals within organizations, and concludes that the decision-making processes in organizations must be understood from the perspective of power and organizational politics. This does not necessarily mean that most decisions are contrary to the best interest of the organization. Indeed, Pfeffer argues that political decision making is often beneficial, if not necessary, for organizational effectiveness because it provides a mission and direction for the organization. Trying to achieve a consensus about the organization's objectives and which alternatives best serve its interests would be extremely time-consuming and ineffective, particularly in today's large, complex organizations with diverse cultures and interests.

Although power may be necessary for organizational decision making, the prevalence of politics among top management teams is associated with poor firm performance. Political decision making is not necessarily the most effective.[2]

Organizational politics and power provide a way of conceptualizing organizational behavior that is different from the open-systems model that has been used throughout most of this text. Open-systems theory describes organizations as a set of patterned activities that are structured in a variety of effective or ineffective ways. Political models view organizations as pluralistic collections of people and subcultures competing for scarce resources and the right to determine the organization's strategy and objectives. Conflict is viewed as normal, or at least as a customary part of the organization. The activities of individuals and groups are not viewed as goal-directed behaviors but as games among players who are pursuing their own individual or subunit objectives. Political models of organizations assume that when the interests of people conflict, decisions will be determined by the relative power of the individuals or subunits involved. Those who possess the greatest power receive the greatest rewards as a result of the interplay of organizational politics. Power is used to overcome the resistance of others and to get one's way in the organization.

Types of Influence

Power:
The capacity to influence the behavior of others; the probability that one actor within a social relationship can carry out his or her own will despite resistance.

Democratic alternative:
A political strategy that allows everyone in the organization to participate equally in making decisions and approving policies.

The need for influence in organizations stems from the need to reduce the variability of human behavior. In every organization, people must behave in prescribed ways; employees cannot behave however they please. The need to do the right thing at the right time is particularly visible in such groups as athletic teams, orchestras, and assembly-line workers. In these groups, the need for influence to reduce the variability of human behavior is quite evident. The definitions of power, authority, control, leadership, and politics are summarized in Exhibit 18.1.

Most organizations are arranged hierarchically, with power and authority concentrated at the top. An alternative to this hierarchical structure, called the *democratic alternative*, separates the functions of management into the legislative and executive functions, similar to the branches of government. In a democratic system, the executive function is performed by leaders who are

Influence	Definition
Power	The capacity to influence the behavior of others; the ability of one party to overcome resistance in others to achieve a desired objective.
Authority	The legitimate exercise of power, where *legitimate* means relevant to one's role.
Control	The capacity to determine acceptable behavior and prevent someone from behaving unacceptably.
Leadership	Incremental influence; the ability to induce voluntary compliance by inspiring and motivating others.
Politics	The use of power in organizations to obtain one's preferred outcomes.

Exhibit 18.1 **Types of Influence**

either appointed or elected to their offices, and the power they exercise has been granted to them by the vote of the membership. The legislative function is performed by everyone in the organization, including lower-level members who participate equally with top management in deciding the organization's policies and rules. Labor unions are supposed to operate democratically—each union member should participate equally, expressing opinions and ratifying contracts.

Although this democratic alternative is rather appealing, it is not the most effective power structure. In fact, studies on the structure and distribution of power in society have identified what is called the *irony of democracy*.[3] Briefly stated, this irony is that the basic democratic values of our society are not preserved by the masses of population they are intended to protect. Instead, our basic democratic values are preserved by small elitist groups who exercise tremendous power even though they are not formally elected as leaders. Important freedoms protecting political, social, and economic interests are preserved by the efforts of these small, elite groups who are willing to be involved in social issues.

Conditions Necessary for the Use of Power

Some situations are more susceptible to the use of power than others. For example, in a physical exercise program there is no reason for one jogger to exert power over other joggers because all the joggers are independent—they can run whenever they want, wherever they want, and as far as they want. The scheduling of tennis courts, however, provides many opportunities for conflict; the use of power may be necessary for resolving the conflict. Three conditions are necessary for the use of power: interdependence, scarcity, and heterogeneous goals.[4]

Interdependence. A state of interdependence provides an opportunity for conflict and a corresponding need for some method to resolve it. *Interdependence* arises from joint activity in which the work of one individual or group affects the work of others. Interdependence ties the activities of organizational members together: each member becomes concerned with what others do and what they obtain. In the absence of interdependence, there would be no basis for conflict and no reason for one individual to exert influence over others.

Scarcity. When resources are ample and people have everything they want, conflict tends to be eliminated. When resources are scarce, however, choices must be made concerning their allocation. The greater the *scarcity* relative to the demand, the greater the opportunity for power and influence to be used in resolving the conflict.

Heterogeneous Goals. When everyone agrees on the goals of the organization and how to achieve them, conflict is reduced. However, most organizations experience considerable disagreement because they have heterogeneous goals and incompatible beliefs about how these goals should be achieved. Managers may strongly disagree about which products should be promoted or which innovations will be the most profitable. They may also disagree about the long-term effects of organizational policies and human resource practices.

Irony of democracy:
The irony that democratic values and freedoms are preserved more by the political actions of a small number of elites than by the actions of the entire population.

Interdependence:
Where the work or activities of people depend on one another.

Scarcity:
When insufficient resources are available for everyone.

Heterogeneous goals:
When individuals disagree about the organization's goals and objectives and the means that should be used to achieve them.

Exhibit 18.2 Conditions Necessary for the Use of Power

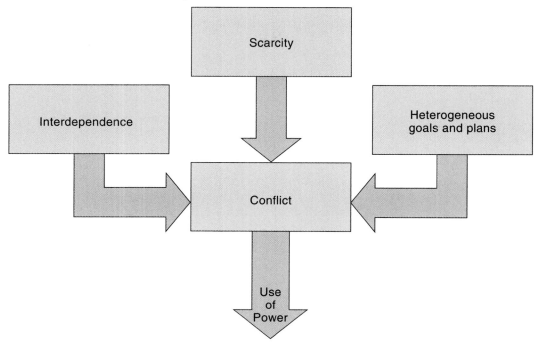

When interdependence, scarcity, and heterogenous goals are present, as illustrated in Exhibit 18.2, the likelihood that some form of power will be exerted is very high. Indeed, Pfeffer argues that under these conditions the use of power is virtually inevitable; essentially it is the only way to arrive at a decision. The use of power is inevitable because there is no rational way to determine whose preferences should prevail or whose beliefs about the goals or the methods of achieving them should guide the decision.

Prolonged discussions using rational decision-making processes will generally heighten the awareness of goal incompatibility. In these situations, social customs, traditions, and group norms may be called on to guide the decision, but in actuality they are only used by the most powerful to make the use of power appear less obtrusive and more legitimate. In many situations, power can be used so effectively by those who are powerful that others are not even aware that it is happening and they feel no conflict or resistance. By manipulating the situation, redefining the objectives, and using other political tactics, high-power people can make low-power people believe they are engaged in a cooperative situation. Here the use of power is perceived by everyone as contributing to greater effectiveness. People who are adept at manipulating power can successfully achieve their own ends without causing resentment or unhappiness. Indeed, others can be so seduced by the skilled use of power that they approve of the actions and willingly comply.

Authority versus Power

It is important to distinguish between power and authority. Power represents the capacity of one person to secure compliance from another person, while

Authority:
The legitimate use of power, where legitimate is defined as role relevant.

authority represents the *right* of this person to seek compliance by others. Therefore, **authority** is defined as legitimate power and is conferred upon an individual by the organization or social customs. Authority is backed by legitimacy.

Here, **legitimate** is defined as "role relevant" or, in other words, "related to one's job or position within the organization." Behaviors, attitudes, and even manners of dress and grooming, if they are related to successful job performance, are considered role relevant. However, behaviors and attitudes that have nothing to do with job performance are not role relevant, such as food preferences, choice of friends, or hairstyles.

If a manager asks an assistant to prepare a report, this request would be role relevant, and the manager would be exercising authority. However, if the manager asks the assistant to perform personal errands during the lunch hour, this would not be a role relevant request and would not constitute an exercise of authority. If the assistant performed the personal errands, it would not be because of legitimate power but because of some other form of power. Sometimes managers admit that some of their directives are not role relevant. Usually they say that their directives are requests or suggestions rather than orders or commands.

Max Weber used a historical perspective to contrast three types of authority: traditional, charismatic, and rational-legal.[5]

Traditional authority:
Authority that is derived from inheritance or social custom.

1. **Traditional authority.** *Traditional authority* is the influence exerted by an individual who has rightfully inherited a position of status. This form of authority is characteristically found in cultures where kings or chiefs occupy a position of status that is widely accepted within the society. The authority possessed by the king or chief is based on inheritance or a natural order that has always been followed and presumed to have always existed. In some family businesses, the children of the founder exert considerable influence on others even though they do not occupy a formal position in the company.

Charismatic authority:
The authority derived from the magical or mystical, personal qualities of a highly respected and revered leader.

2. **Charismatic authority.** *Charismatic authority* stems from the alluring and mystical quality of a leader who is highly respected and revered. A true charismatic leader possesses a special quality of leadership that captures the popular imagination and inspires unwavering allegiance and devotion. Charismatic leaders are able to exert influence because of the respect and devotion others have for them. Their directives are seen as legitimate because the followers assume that a charismatic leader has the vision or inspiration to know what must be done.

Rational-legal authority:
A type of authority that is derived from the hierarchical structure of the organization granting office holders the right to exert influence over others.

3. **Rational-legal authority.** The authority that comes from a person's formal position within an organizational hierarchy is called *rational-legal authority*. Weber's description of rational-legal authority was derived from his definition of a bureaucracy in which office holders had the authority to issue official directives and sanctions based on the rules and official procedures associated with their offices.

An important question is why people respond to authority. Why do people submit to the influence of others? One reason is that obedience is usually necessary for continued membership—if you want to play the game you have to follow the rules. Another reason is that everyone realizes that rule compliance is necessary for the organization to survive. Most people say they feel "a duty" to obey accepted authorities.

Finally, obedience to authority is a central part of our training from early childhood through adulthood. People have been taught to obey authority figures as part of the basic socialization process. This willingness has been illustrated in a series of surprising studies conducted by Stanley Milgram showing that experimental subjects willingly obeyed the instructions of an experimenter even when they thought they were inflicting intense pain on another person.[6]

In Milgram's study, volunteers were assigned to teach a "learner" (actually a confederate actor) a series of word association pairs and to administer increasingly intense levels of electrical shock for each mistake. Milgram was surprised with his subjects' obedience to authority and he claimed that his subjects were not acting blindly without feeling. Instead, they exhibited considerable anxiety caused by conflicts of conscience and sympathy for the learners. Although they were critical of the study, the experimenter, and the research organization, they continued to obediently administer shocks.

Power Indicators

Sometimes it is difficult to tell when power is being used. Those who use power typically do not want others to know about it. Indeed, power is most effective when it is not visible. People tend to resist the use of power when they see themselves being influenced contrary to their own desires. However, if the influence attempt appears to be legitimate and rational, we are more willing to comply and subject ourselves to the wishes of others.

Frequently, individuals who are using power fail to recognize what they are doing. They honestly feel that they are exerting rational influence that can be justified for legitimate reasons other than just their own personal wishes. They sincerely think their influence is rational rather than political. There is often considerable disagreement about when power is actually being used.

A good illustration of political versus rational decision making comes from research on university budget allocations. Most department heads, deans, and administrators believe their budgets are determined by rational criteria based on the relative importance and needs of the different departments. Consequently, some directors are extremely incensed by the suggestion that budget allocations are determined more by political influence than by rational criteria. Nevertheless, research has found that the best predictors of who gets the most money are political variables, especially the number of department members serving on the budget committee or other important university committees.[7]

Five indications that power is being exerted are shown in Exhibit 18.3. Diagnosing whether decisions are based on power or reason involves looking for a convergence of these indicators of power.

INTERPERSONAL POWER

One of the greatest concerns about power is its effects on those who use it. The more people use power, the more they tend to perceive situations in terms of power relationships, and the more they are inclined to use power for personal

Exhibit 18.3 Indicators of Power

Indicator	Examples
1. Determinants of power	The capacity to use any of the bases of power: reward power, coercive power, referent power, legitimate power, or expert power. How many of these bases of power does each individual possess?
2. Consequences of power	Budget allocations, win-loss record on debated issues, ability to authorize exceptions to policy, authority to hire and fire others. Since power is used to influence decisions, those with the greatest power should be the ones who obtain the most favorable decisions.
3. Symbols	Size, location, and furnishings of one's office. Invitations to attend social events and seating at those events. Special parking privileges or eating facilities. The use of company automobiles or airplanes.
4. Reputation	Comments by others acknowledging one's power. Seeking one's advice. Asking for one's opinion. Requesting that person's endorsement.
5. Representation on committees	The number and status of committee memberships: boards of directors, advisory councils, presidential task forces, and executive committees.

ends. This danger is expressed in the statement, "Power corrupts; absolute power corrupts absolutely." The addictive effects of power have been recognized for many years. Plato was convinced that power would continue to corrupt unless philosophers became rulers and rulers were philosophers.[8]

When is it appropriate to use power? Using one's position to inflict physical or psychological damage on others is an abuse of power; but is it wrong to require employees to perform their jobs the way they agreed to when they joined the company? People who adopt political strategies ought to be aware of the moral implications of their behavior. Political activities and the use of power are not necessarily good or bad. Although we typically think political activities are bad because they are defined as the self-serving use of power, the consequences may also be desirable for the organization and society.

A survey of 428 managers provides some interesting insights about their perceptions of political behavior in organizations. Almost 90 percent of them agreed that successful executives must be good politicians, and 70 percent agreed that managers have to behave politically to advance their careers. Nevertheless, 55 percent of the managers said that politics in organizations is detrimental to efficiency, and almost 50 percent agreed that top management should try to get rid of organizational politics.[9]

Five Bases of Power

Where does power come from? Why can some individuals prevail over others in the allocation of resources or in the hiring and promotion of personal friends? In a classic article, John R.P. French, Jr. and Bertram Raven described five bases of power: reward power, coercive power, legitimate power, referent power, and expert power.[10]

Reward power:
Power derived from one person's ability to reward others.

Reward Power. Person A has *reward power* over person B to the extent that A controls desired rewards that B wants. These rewards include any form of incentives, such as pay increases, promotions, desirable job assignments, an opportunity to work overtime, or time away from work. Person B must value the reward and think that A has the ability to either provide or withhold it.

Coercive power:
Power obtained because one person has the ability to punish others or deprive them of rewards.

Coercive Power. Person A has *coercive power* over person B to the extent that A can administer some form of punishment to B. The punishment can be in the form of inflicting pain, such as public humiliation or a physical beating, or it can be administered by removing reinforcers, such as firing an employee, taking a player out of the game, or removing an employee from a training program. The punishment must be important to person B, who must also see A as having the ability to administer or withhold it. Coercive power is the opposite of reward power, and followers typically comply because of fear.

Legitimate power:
Power that is derived from one's position in the organizational hierarchy.

Legitimate Power. Person A has *legitimate power* over person B to the extent that person B perceives that person A has the right to influence person B. Legitimate power is typically based on the formal organizational hierarchy in which superiors have the right to influence subordinates. Legitimate power may also exist outside the organizational hierarchy when the right to influence is prescribed by cultural values. For example, social values say it is legitimate for adults to influence children, and a voting district chairman has the legitimate right to conduct a public mass meeting. Legitimate power can be acquired through assignment, election, or some other form of formal recognition. Subordinates play a major role in the exercise of legitimate power, since their compliance depends on whether they perceive the use of power as legitimate.

Referent power:
Power that is derived from the interpersonal attraction that one person has for another because of the latter's personal qualities, reputation, and charismatic leadership.

Referent Power. Person A has *referent power* over person B when person B admires the personal qualities, characteristics, or reputation or person A. Referent power has also been called ***charismatic power*** since allegiance is based on the inner personal attraction of one individual for another. People who are highly admired and respected can exert referent power because other people seek their approval and want to please them.

Expert power:
Power derived from the special knowledge and ability an individual possesses.

Expert Power. Person A possesses *expert power* over person B to the extent that person A has more knowledge or expertise relevant to a particular problem or situation than person B does. To possess expert power, a person must be perceived as credible and trustworthy. Person B must believe that person A actually possesses the crucial information and skills. This power is generally limited to specific situations where the information is relevant and needed.

Interactions among the Bases of Power. The five sources of power are not independent of each other; one base of power can be used effectively to increase the availability of the others. For example, the wise use of reward power can increase your referent power, since people are attracted to those whom they admire and who reward them. In contrast, the use of coercive power tends to decrease referent power for the same reason—people tend to avoid and dislike those who punish them. By properly administering or withholding rewards for legitimate reasons, people can increase their referent power. The appropriate use of legitimate power also influences referent power. Because organizational leaders are typically respected, their legitimate power helps to increase their referent power when they perform their jobs competently. Referent power is also influenced by expert power, since people tend to be impressed by those who possess valuable knowledge and skills. Therefore, to the extent that people have greater knowledge and use it at appropriate times, they are well liked and admired, and their referent power increases.

Guidelines have been proposed to explain how managers should use each of these five bases of power to obtain favorable responses.[11] Person B may respond to person A's influence with either commitment, compliance, or resistance, depending upon the influence attempt. Commitment means that person B accepts and is highly motivated to carry out the wishes of person A. Compliance means that person B is willing to fulfill person A's wishes, but only as long as the extra effort and energy are adequately rewarded. Resistance, however, means that person B opposes person A's wishes, and will try to deliberately neglect or sabotage the request. The guidelines proposed in Exhibit 18.4 explain how to obtain commitment rather than resistance. These guidelines assume that the goals of employees are in harmony with the goals of the leader and the organization. When the employee's goals do not match the organization's goals, the employee may or may not comply, depending on whether the supervisor is perceived as genuine and concerned or arrogant and insulting.

Acquiring Interpersonal Power

People want to have power because of what it allows them to do. Powerful people have quick access to top executives to obtain early information about policy changes, they can hire a talented replacement or reinstate a terminated employee, they can approve expenditures exceeding the budget or grant above-average salary increases for subordinates who are excellent performers. Some individuals clearly receive more than their share of the organization's resources and exert great influence on decisions and activities. Why are some people more powerful than others? How can a person acquire power? Two methods of acquiring personal power are (1) doing the right things and (2) cultivating the right people.[12]

Doing the Right Things. Many employees are good workers, but methodical and dependable role performance does not necessarily increase one's power. To increase one's power, a person needs to perform activities that are extraordinary, visible, and relevant.

1. *Extraordinary Activities.* Routine job performance does not contribute much to personal power even when the performance is excellent. To be truly powerful, people need to perform unusual or nonroutine activities that commonly involve an element of risk. Examples of extraordinary activities include negotiating a new contract, developing a new program, or designing a new product.
2. *Visible Activities.* Extraordinary activities will not generate much power if no one knows about them. Therefore, the extraordinary activities must be visible to others in the organization, preferably without the individual's

Exhibit 18.4 Guidelines for Using Power

Bases of Power	Guidelines for Use
Reward Power	Verify compliance.
	Make feasible and reasonable requests.
	Make only ethical and proper requests.
	Offer rewards desired by subordinates.
	Offer only credible rewards.
Coercive Power	Inform subordinates of rules and penalties.
	Warn before punishing.
	Try to administer punishment consistently.
	Try to administer punishment uniformly.
	Understand the situation before acting.
	Maintain credibility.
	Fit punishment to the infraction.
	Punish in private.
Referent Power	Treat subordinates fairly.
	Defend subordinates' interests.
	Be sensitive to subordinates' feelings.
	Select subordinates similar to oneself.
	Engage in role modeling.
Expert Power	Promote image of expertise.
	Maintain credibility.
	Act confident and decisive.
	Stay informed.
	Recognize employee concerns.
	Do not threaten subordinates' self-esteem.
Legitimate Power	Be cordial and polite.
	Be confident.
	Delegate clearly with timely follow-up.
	Make certain that requests are appropriate.
	Explain reasons for requests.
	Follow proper channels of communication.
	Exercise power discreetly.
	Enforce compliance with reasonable force.
	Be sensitive to subordinates' concerns.

Source: Adapted from Gary A. Yukl, *Leadership in Organization*, 1981. Prentice-Hall, Inc., Englewood Cliffs, N.J., pp. 44-58.

having to "toot his or her own horn." People who advertise their own extraordinary activities do not gain as much power as those whose activities are announced by top management or influential people outside the organization.

3. *Relevant Activities.* Besides being extraordinary and visible, the activities need to be seen as relevant to the mission of the organization or to the solution of important problems. Trivial activities do not produce the same degree of personal power as activities that are central to the survival of the organization.

Cultivating the Right People. In addition to doing the right things, people can increase their personal power by developing informal relationships with the right people. If the interpersonal relationships are properly managed, virtually everyone can contribute to the development of the individual's personal power, including superiors, subordinates, and peers.

1. *Superiors.* Higher-level managers can significantly increase an individual's personal power, as suggested by the phrase "It's not what you know but who you know that counts." Superiors who show a special interest and willingness to help a promising subordinate are referred to as *mentors* or *sponsors*. These individuals may be immediate supervisors or any higher-level officers. They can be extremely helpful in increasing personal power by speaking favorably of subordinates, recommending them for new assignments, and providing introductions to other influential people.

2. *Subordinates.* Although it may seem unusual for subordinates to have the capacity to increase their superiors' power, they may indeed play a very significant role by making their superior look good or by endorsing their superiors' views and recommendations. Professors who train brilliant doctoral students and managers who train outstanding new leaders are able to exert greater influence, not only because of their reputation as outstanding trainers but also because of their continuing relationships with their former subordinates.

3. *Peers.* An individual's personal power can be enhanced or destroyed by favorable or unfavorable relationships with peers. People cannot succeed alone. They depend on support and cooperation from their peers. An antagonistic relationship with peers can destroy personal power and prevent people from being effective within the organization.

Perpetuating Personal Power

People who have power usually become more powerful because they can manipulate the situation and engage in political strategies to perpetuate their own personal power. Once they have achieved a position of power, most people either intentionally or unintentionally structure the situation so that they increase their control over the outcomes for others.

Some strategies are so subtle that they go unrecognized. Powerful people can enhance their power position through such simple acts as creating new jargon or telling jokes. For example, a study of humor in the workplace revealed how certain group members are more frequently chosen as the target, or butt, of the jokes and how their jokes tend to be rejected.[13] Humor can be used to "keep people in their place." When their jokes are rejected, their ideas and suggestions are also ignored.

Reward power, coercive power, and legitimate power are conferred by the organization. Consequently, maintaining organizationally based power depends largely on continued organizational support. If the organization withdraws support by terminating an individual or refusing to endorse that person's use of rewards and punishment, the person's power may suddenly end.

Individuals whose personal power is based on expert or charismatic power do not depend on the organization for their ability to influence others, and they can use a variety of strategies to help them maintain their power position.

Three conditions are necessary to maintain expert power: maintaining one's expertise, making certain the organization continues to need one's expertise, and avoiding being replaced by other experts. In short, expert power can be maintained only if there is a crucial need for the skills and knowledge of the expert that cannot be conveniently obtained elsewhere.

Charismatic power typically develops when a group of people are feeling uncertainty or anxiety, particularly at a time of crisis, and a leader emerges who provides a sense of direction and inspiration. As long as the crisis continues and the leader can provide inspiration and a sense of mission, the charismatic influence of the leader will be maintained. Once the crisis ends and operations return to normal, however, the power of a charismatic leader will depend on whether the charismatic power has become institutionalized. If so, the leader will remain in power and continue to lead the group.

The story of Fidel Castro illustrates the ability of a charismatic leader to perpetuate his power. In the late 1950s Fidel Castro led a revolution in Cuba as a young charismatic rebel. Today he still heads the government and relies heavily on his charismatic power to maintain his position. Castro's success in institutionalizing his charismatic power is a result of his using these four methods of maintaining charismatic power:

1. *Perpetuate the charismatic image.* By emphasizing the symbols associated with the rise of the charismatic leader, the perception of charisma can be maintained. Pictures of Castro are displayed everywhere in Cuba, and his physical appearance is similar to what it was during the revolution—he keeps his beard and continues to dress in battle fatigues.
2. *Control interactions with others.* Charismatic leaders are able to set themselves apart from the rest of society and rise above the crowd by controlling their interactions with others and regulating their public contact. Castro is typically seen in controlled settings such as speeches, rites, or ceremonies that allow him to look "presidential."
3. *Recall past atrocities.* Remembering how bad it used to be helps people think kindly of the charismatic leader. Positive feelings for a charismatic leader are particularly strong when specific negative images of atrocities and injustices are recalled.
4. *Provide a general vision of the future.* By speaking in general terms about the future, a charismatic leader can help people acquire a sense of meaning and direction. If the future is described in only general terms, people can interpret the message consistent with their own specific goals. Believing that the future will be better often helps people endure the frustrations and injustices of the present.

GROUP AND SUBUNIT POWER

In examining the issues of power within groups, we are largely concerned with the acquisition of subunit power and the ways in which this power becomes institutionalized or perpetuated. The term *subunit* applies to any organizational department, such as finance, nursing, intensive care, marketing, human resources, research and development, or word processing.

Acquiring Subunit Power

Why can some groups exert greater power than others? Five strategies for acquiring group power are controlling resources, controlling strategic contingencies, coping with uncertainty, being irreplaceable, and being central to the organization.[14]

Controlling Resources. The most powerful subunits of an organization are those that control, or have the capacity to provide, crucial organizational resources. Resource control largely explains the "golden rule of power"—those who have the gold are able to rule. Because they control the resources, they can exert greater influence, and other groups will look to them for direction, and respond to their directives. Critical organizational resources include anything of value to the organization, such as money, time, materials, patents, expertise, or market survey information.

A study of the power relationships among the departments of a university found that the most important variable influencing the relative power was the ability to secure outside funds for the university in the form of contracts and research grants.[15] Contracts and research grants are valuable resources to a university, and the department that provides the most resources exerts the greatest influence.

Power differentials among groups are magnified when resources become scarce. When resources are plentiful, groups tend to spend less time maneuvering for an advantageous political position. During lean times, however, weak subgroups are either reduced or eliminated from the organization. Because of their weak power position, weak subunits are perceived as irrelevant and superfluous to the basic mission of the organization.

Strategic contingencies:
The critical interactions and workflow interdependencies within organizations that make one subunit dependent on another. Subunits are able to increase their power by controlling the most critical of these contingencies.

Control of Strategic Contingencies. Controlling *strategic contingencies* means having control of activities or functions that other subunits depend on. When one department cannot perform its function until another department has done its job, the first part is contingent on the second. For example, the sales department in an engineering company has far more power than their limited expertise and training would suggest in a high-tech organization. In spite of their limited educational background, the sales force wield enormous power because others with more training and expertise cannot perform their function until the sales have been made. Thus, a contingency represents a source of uncertainty in the decision-making process, and a contingency becomes strategic when it has the potential to change the balance of power between subunits in such a way that one unit depends on another.

An example of power derived from controlling strategic contingencies comes from the classic study by Lawrence and Lorsch of the plastics, food processing, and container manufacturing industries.[16] In the most successful firms, power was distributed according to the strategic contingencies for that industry. That is, the units that possessed the greatest power were those units on which other units depended. For example, in the food processing firms, where the strategic contingencies focused on expertise in food sciences and marketing, the major power of the most successful firms rested in the sales and research units. However, in the container manufacturing companies, where the strategic contingencies were customer delivery and product quality, the major power resided in the sales and production staffs. In other words, the departments that held the power in the most successful firms were those units that performed vital functions for the organization in terms of its survival. The subunits that were the most important for organizational success were controlled by the most powerful decision makers. In the less successful firms, however, power was not distributed according to these strategic contingencies.

Ability to Cope with Uncertainty. Subunits are able to acquire power when they have the capacity to help other departments cope with uncertainty or minimize the consequences of uncertainty. For example, if department A is able to help reduce some of department B's uncertainties, then department A has power over department B. The uncertainty itself does not give power; the power comes from helping another department reduce the uncertainty or cope with it.

A study of two departments in a French factory illustrates how a group of maintenance workers exerted considerable power over the production workers because they controlled the major uncertainty—machine breakdowns.[17] Because the production workers were entitled to employment under French law, one would expect the production workers to exert considerable power over the maintenance people, who were expected to keep the machines in working order. The power relationships, however, were just the opposite of what one would expect. In the routine of the factory, machine stoppages were the only major events that could not be predicted or programmed. The production workers were clearly dependent on the salaried maintenance workers, who in their turn were not dependent on the production workers. Consequently, the maintenance workers not only controlled a strategic contingency within the factory, but they also helped the production workers cope with the uncertainties of their jobs.

One subunit can reduce another subunit's uncertainty in a variety of ways. One method is by providing information so the other subunit can predict its future and prepare for change. A second method is to forestall the uncertainty by preventing unwanted events from occurring. Finally, a third method is to absorb the pressures by helping the subunit deal with its problems after they occur.

Irreplaceability:
A method of acquiring power that comes from being the only one capable of performing a critical function or providing a critical resource.

Substitutability:
The capacity of not having to depend upon a particular subunit for resources or the performance of critical functions. To the extent that a subunit is not substitutable it is irreplaceable and, therefore, more powerful.

Irreplaceability. Individuals or departments who provide a crucial resource or perform a vital function and who cannot be readily replaced are able to exert greater power. This power is destroyed by *substitutability,* which refers to the ability of other subunits to perform the activities of a particular subunit. If an organization can obtain alternative sources of skill, information, or resources to perform the job of another subunit, that subunit's power will be diminished. The training department loses its power if training can be provided by line managers, and the computer department loses its power over the accounting department if the accountants know enough computer programming to revise the management information systems.

A strategy for maintaining a subunit's irreplaceability involves monitoring the company's hiring policies to prevent the hiring of individuals with the same scarce skills. If a subunit can maintain a monopoly on certain types of expertise and the capacity to cope with uncertainty, it becomes increasingly irreplaceable and powerful within the organization. For example, studies of the distribution of power in hospitals indicate that physicians gain their power because they are perceived to be irreplaceable. Nurses, however, are not irreplaceable, but their power comes from reducing uncertainty and from being central to the work of the hospital.[18]

Centrality. Subunits that are the most central to the workflow in an organization typically acquire the greatest power. Although all of the subunits are

Centrality:
A method of acquiring subunit power by occupying an important role in the workflow of an organization, particularly within the communication network.

interdependent, some subunits contribute more directly to the final output of the organization and therefore have greater *centrality*. The power that comes from centrality was discovered in some of the earliest communication network experiments. In the wheel structure, for example, the person in the center, who communicated with each of the other members, was the one who occupied the most central role and was usually perceived as the leader of the group and the most powerful figure. This individual's power stemmed largely from the ability to control the flow of information. Subsequent research on technological gatekeepers, those who control the flow of crucial technological information in an organization, has shown that these people have great power within an organization. Physical centrality can be just as important as work flow centrality in increasing a subunit's power.

Institutionalizing Subunit Power

The power structure in most organizations is fairly constant over time because powerful subunits can do many things to maintain their supremacy even though the people change. Studies of power usually find that the best predictor of which subunit will emerge as the most powerful during times of change is the amount of power it had before the change.[19] Power relationships in organizations can be perpetuated by maintaining the subsystem relationships and the organizational culture that support the current power positions. Four of the best ways to institutionalize power come from controlling the organization's business strategy, controlling the selection of new personnel, controlling who gets promoted, and controlling training and socialization activities.

Influencing Strategy. Powerful subunits can use their power to keep the organization focused on critical contingencies that they control. For example, if the marketing department is the most powerful subunit, it may decide to block the acquisition of a new company that would give greater power to the finance department or to oppose the development of a new product that would transfer power to the engineering department.

Personnel Selection. By defining the selection criteria and controlling the hiring of new applicants, powerful subunits can increase their relative power within organizations. If one department succeeds in acquiring the best and brightest new employees, the status and power of that department increases.

Personnel Promotion. Unless the organizational culture changes, it is difficult for power to shift to other subunits, and the culture is not likely to change if the values and perspectives of people at the top stay the same. Subunits can secure employees who have the right perspective by influencing the advancement and promotion policies. Even if a selection error is made, it can be corrected by passing over the person who failed to meet expectations when it comes time for promotions. If those who are in powerful positions can succeed in defining the required competence and the right perspective, they can protect their power position and reinforce the present power structure. Individuals who rock the boat by challenging those in power can be kept in lower-level positions or transferred to a weak subunit.

Training and Socialization. Training activities instill important values and expectations in employees. Orientation programs are particularly crucial in the socialization process, because new employees learn which behaviors and attitudes are acceptable to the organization. Because of their position, powerful subunits are better able to control the content of training and present their interpretation of the topics. Consequently, the norms and values transmitted through organizational training programs tend to reflect those of the key power groups. For example, in a manufacturing company whose safety department is the most powerful subunit, a major part of the new employee orientation and other training programs would emphasize the importance of safe operating procedures.

ORGANIZATIONAL POLITICS

Politics:
The use of power in organizations to allocate resources or make decisions.

Organizational politics refers to activities in organizations designed to acquire, develop, or use power in a conscious way to obtain one's preferred outcomes or to manipulate a situation for one's own purposes. Individuals and subunits who want to exert political influence can select from a fairly long list of political strategies. Which strategy is the most effective depends on the situation.

Political Strategies

Suppose a company was trying to decide which of five new products it should develop. If the marketing vice-president has a clear preference for one product over the others, a variety of political strategies are available to this vice-president to make certain that the preferred product is the one selected.

Control the Agenda. Committee decisions depend not only on the opinions of the members but also on whether the committee has time to make a decision. Decisions can be stalled by removing items from the agenda, or they can be manipulated by placing them at the beginning or end of the agenda. The items at the beginning of an agenda are typically discussed in greater detail, allowing greater tolerance for ambiguity and broader consideration of empirical information than for items placed at the end of an agenda. Many items at the end of the agenda are either superficially decided or completely overlooked.

Select the Decision Criteria. Decision making can be manipulated by changing the criteria. In any decision-making situation, multiple criteria are available for assessing alternatives. Rather than arguing for one's preferred alternative, a more effective political strategy is to simply suggest that the decision should be based on the criteria favoring the preferred alternative.

Control Access to Information. Information is a powerful weapon in a fight for power, and those who have access to information or who have the capacity to filter or manipulate information can often succeed in controlling decisions. Sales projections, salary information, quality reports and many other items of information are frequently treated as confidential information to increase the political power of those privy to it. Although information may be intentionally manipulated as a political power strategy, it can also occur innocently. Through the process of selective perception, people show differential attention to and retention of facts that favor their position on an issue. In an early study of a company's decision to purchase a computer, it was found that people selectively collected and used information in the decision-making process that provided support for the decision they already favored.[20] Selective perception and manipulation of information are illustrated by a remark attributed to Peter Drucker that anyone over age 21 should be able to find enough facts to support his or her position.

Use Outside Experts. Outside experts can usually be found to support any point of view, regardless of the issue. Individuals can influence the outcome of the decision by carefully selecting the right outside expert and providing a forum for that individual to express an opinion. The use of outside experts as a political strategy is particularly obvious in jury trials, where the names and reputations of the experts are more important than the substance of their testimony.

Control Access to Influential People. Many great ideas and quality suggestions are killed or ignored because they never reach the people who have the capacity to do anything with them. New ideas often rock the boat and threaten people's jobs. Middle managers often succeed in preventing lower-level members from submitting creative ideas or constructive criticisms by preventing them from communicating with top management. Being able to communicate regularly with members of top management increases one's ability to use power, whether the interaction comes from a scheduled meeting, a weekly game of golf, or commuting to work together.

Form a Coalition. When groups of people discover they lack the power to influence the decision process, they can increase their power by forming a coalition with other groups. Coalitions are typically formed to maximize the rewards or outcomes to the group and its members. Therefore, most coalitions comprise the minimum number of members required to achieve a successful decision. Coalitions tend to be unstable and temporary unless there are philosophical or ideological commonalities that keep the parties together.

Co-optation:
A strategy of bringing opposition members into the organization to obtain their support and cooperation.

Co-opt the Opposition. The strategy of co-opting is similar to the strategy of forming a coalition. However, *co-optation* generally refers to an enduring relationship rather than a temporary alliance of a coalition. Co-opting occurs, for example, when members of a subunit ask a local critic to join their group and work with them in solving their problems. School systems, hospitals, and other civic organizations use a co-opting strategy of placing influential citizens on their board of directors as a conscious strategy of reducing their uncertainty and minimizing outside criticism.

Manipulate Symbols. Politics, either in organizations or in government, has a language of its own that is designed to rationalize and justify decisions by using the appropriate symbolic labels. Without this legitimization, the exercise of power would be unacceptable and would thus create resistance. If people use the appropriate language and symbols when their decisions are made on the basis of power, their decisions can often be made to appear as though they resulted from rational decision making.

The "right to work" section of the Taft-Hartley Act (1947) illustrates the power of a label. Section 14b of the Taft-Hartley Act allows states to pass a law guaranteeing workers the right to refuse to join a union even though the majority of the workers vote in favor of it. This section has been labeled the "right to work," which portrays the idea of personal rights and freedom. Union leaders complain that this law allows workers to refuse to join the union even though they benefit from the negotiations and sacrifices of their co-workers. It is doubtful that the "right to work," provision would enjoy the same degree of popularity if it carried a negative label, such as the "freeloader bill."

Use Interpersonal Manipulation. Perhaps the most blatant political strategy occurs when people directly pursue their goals through persuasion, manipulation, or ingratiation. Persuasion is an overt attempt to influence others by asking for cooperation and by providing information that supports the request. There is no effort to conceal the intentions of the persuader, and for the most part, the information is considered accurate.

There is an important difference between persuasion and manipulation. Both involve the presentation of information designed to obtain one's desired goal. In manipulation, however, the intent of the person is concealed from the other person, and crucial information is either distorted or withheld to influence the decision.

Ingratiation is a form of interpersonal manipulation that is accomplished through flattery and a display of sincerity. Flattery is a form of positive reinforcement designed to alter the target person's perception of the flatterer. The most direct form of ingratiation occurs when person A goes to person B and makes flattering comments. However, the effectiveness of this strategy is limited, because person B may be skeptical of person A's motives. A more effective strategy is for person A to make flattering comments about B to someone else who could be expected to report the comments back to B. Flattering comments by person A do not create suspicion if they come through person C.[21]

Influence Strategies

Managers can exert power in three directions: on their subordinates, on their superiors, and on their peers. To effectively use power, managers need to know how to exert influence in all three directions.[22]

Influencing Subordinates. Because supervisors have the legitimate right to hire, fire, and discipline subordinates, we often overestimate the power of supervisory jobs. What we typically overlook is the power that subordinates *as a group* have over their bosses. Subordinate power comes in many forms and is based on (1) skills that are difficult to replace quickly or easily; (2) specialized information and knowledge that others do not have; (3) good personal relationships that prevent a supervisor from reprimanding or replacing a subordinate without alienating other employees; and (4) the centrality of the subordinate's job, which may be crucial to the performance of the supervisor's job.

The combination of these factors creates a situation in which the power of subordinates is greater than the power of the supervisor despite the formal power that comes from the organization. Consequently, supervisors need to expand their power base beyond the legitimate power conferred by the organization. Effectively leading subordinates demands that supervisors bring additional sources of power to the job. The following suggestions have been made for supervisors to increase their clout during their early tenure as supervisors:

1. *Acquire the relevant interpersonal skills and abilities.* Being a good supervisor and successfully exerting power requires good interpersonal skills, persuasiveness, and the ability to identify and resolve conflicts quickly. Good verbal skills in listening and communicating are essential for influencing subordinates.

2. *Establish good working relationships.* Good working relationships are based on a combination of respect, admiration, obligation, and friendship. To be perceived as effective and a credible source of influence, supervisors need to maintain good relationships not only with subordinates but with superiors and others outside the chain of command.

3. *Acquire information.* Knowledge is power, but the most important knowledge in leadership jobs is detailed information about the social reality in which the job is embedded. Supervisors need to know who the relevant parties are, their several perspectives, and when these perspectives may be in conflict.

4. *Maintain a good track record.* Being perceived as a successful supervisor contributes to the supervisor's power position. A credible track record and the reputation it earns can help a supervisor obtain compliance in a fraction of the time that is required if credibility is lacking. Success breeds success, and the successful application of power in one situation increases the supervisor's potential power for the next occasion.

Influencing Superiors. Successful employees need an effective boss to provide them with the necessary job opportunities, resources, organizational protection, and job security. Although we typically think of power being exerted downward in an organization, it is equally important for subordinates to effectively exert power upward. To obtain sufficient resources, support, and encouragement, subordinates must develop and maintain good working relationships with their superiors. The following principles have been suggested for exerting influence upward and developing good relationships with superiors.

1. Creative, competent subordinates take some of the load off their boss's shoulders. Effective subordinates solve problems rather than create them, and whenever possible they bring good news of successful solutions to the boss, rather than failures and problems.

2. Change your boss's bad behavior with rewards. Catching your boss doing something good and rewarding this behavior are far more effective than criticizing or complaining. If your boss has traits you would like to change, reward positive behavior with thanks or sincere praise.

3. Look beyond the boundaries of your job description to let others benefit from your ideas and efforts. Bosses enjoy being told by outsiders that they have an exemplary subordinate. Take advantage of opportunities outside work to make yourself visible, and manage your own public relations without devoting too much time and effort to it.

4. Recognize your boss's weaknesses and let them be your strengths. If the boss hates to attend meetings, offer to go instead and give a briefing later.

If the boss hates to write reports, be a ghost writer and prepare a first draft. If the boss relates badly with certain people, perform those functions yourself that entail meeting those people. By becoming a representative of your boss, you will be given the knowledge and stature to do so properly.

5. Maintain a good working relationship by keeping the boss informed, behaving dependably and honestly, and using the boss's time and resources very selectively. Subordinates who are undependable or dishonest, or who waste their boss's limited time and energy, are certain to destroy their relationship with their boss.

Influencing Peers. Almost everyone depends on people outside the formal chain of command. Our success is influenced by how well we manage these outside relationships. Being able to influence one's peers is often the difference between effective and ineffective performance. Four suggestions have been offered for managing peer relationships.

1. Identify all of the relevant lateral relationships, both inside and outside the organization.
2. Assess who among these people may resist cooperation, why, and how strongly.
3. Wherever possible, develop a good relationship with these people to facilitate the communication, education, and negotiation processes required to reduce or overcome resistance. A good working relationship requires dependability and reciprocity from both parties.
4. When a good working relationship cannot be developed, some additional type of power intervention that is more subtle and more forceful should be developed to deal with the resistance.

Discussion Questions

1. What are the determinants of personal power, and how can you increase your personal power? If you were the secretary of a pre-professional student club, such as the dental club, what could you do to increase your personal power?
2. Subunits within an organization can increase their power by controlling strategic contingencies. Choose an organization and identify which strategic contingencies are being controlled by which subunits, and with what effect.
3. If you were a member of a graduate school admissions committee and you wanted to admit a friend who had inferior grades and test scores, what political strategies could you use, and how would you use them? Which strategies would make the other committee members not only agree but think they had made the best possible decision?
4. How can you manage your boss? Describe one of your leaders or supervisors, and explain what you can do to increase your power position relative to this person.

Notes

1. Jeffrey Pfeffer, *Power in Organizations*, (Marshfield, MA: Pitman, 1981); John P. Kotter, *Power and Influence*, (New York: The Free Press, 1985); Jeffrey Pfeffer, *Managing With Power* (Boston: Harvard Business School Press, 1992).

2. Kathleen M. Eisenhardt, "Politics of Strategic Decision Making in High-Velocity Environments: Toward a Midrange Theory," *Academy of Management Journal* 31 (1988): 737–70.

3. Thomas R. Dye and L. Harmon Zeigler, *The Irony of Democracy: An Uncommon Introduction to American Politics*, (Belmont, CA: Wadsworth, 1970).

4. Pfeffer, op. cit., chap. 3.

5. Henderson and Parsons, op. cit.

6. Stanley Milgram, *Obedience to Authority*, (New York: Harper & Row, 1973); Stanley Milgram, "Behavioral Study of Obedience," *Journal of Abnormal and Social Psychology* 67 (1963): 371–78.

7. Jeffrey Pfeffer and Gerald R. Salancik, "Organizational Decision-making as a Political Process: The Case of a University Budget," *Administrative Science Quarterly* 19 (1974): 135–51.

8. Quotation is by John Emrich Edward Dalberg, Lord Acton, in a Letter to Bishop Mandell Creighton, 1887. Cited in John Bartlett, *Familiar Quotations*,. 12th ed., edited by Christopher Morley and Louella D. Everett (Boston: Little, Brown, 1949), p. 1041; Manfred F. R. Kets De Vries, "Whatever Happened to the Philosopher-King? The Leader's Addiction to Power," *Journal of Management Studies* 28 (July 1991): 339–51.

9. Jeffrey Gandz and Victor Murray, "The Experience of Work place Politics," *Academy of Management Journal* 23 (1980): 237–51.

10. John R. P. French, Jr., and Bertram Raven, "The Bases of Social Power," in Dorwin Cartwright (ed.), *Studies of Social Power* (Ann Arbor: Institute for Social Research, University of Michigan, 1959): 150–65.

11. Gary A. Yukl, *Leadership in Organizations* (Englewood Cliffs, NJ: Prentice-Hall, 1981): 44–58.

12. Rosabeth Moss Kanter, *Men and Women of the Corporation*, (New York: Basic Books, 1977).

13. W. Jack Duncan and J. Philip Feisal, "No Laughing Matter: Patterns of Humor in the Workplace," *Organizational Dynamics* 17 (Spring 1989): 18–30.

14. Pfeffer, op. cit., chap. 4.

15. Pfeffer and Salancik, op. cit.

16. Paul R. Lawrence and Jay W. Lorsch, *Organization and Environment* (Boston: Harvard University Graduate School of Business Administration, 1967).

17. M. Crozier, *The Bureaucratic Phenomenon* (Chicago: University of Chicago Press, 1964).

18. Genevieve E. Chandler, "Creating an Environment to Empower Nurses," *Nursing Management* 22 (August 1991): 20–23; Bruce J. Fried, "Power Acquisition in a Health Care Setting: An Application of Strategic Contingencies Theory," *Human Relations* 41 (December 1988): 915–27;

Jennifer E. Jenkins, "Professional Governance: The Missing Link," *Nursing Management* 22 (August 1991): 26–30.

19. Ron Lachman, "Power from What?" A Reexamination of Its Relationships with Structural Conditions," *Administrative Science Quarterly* 34 (June 1989): 231-51.

20. Richard M. Cyert, Herbert A. Simon, and Donald B. Trow, "Observation of a Business Decision," *Journal of Business* 29 (1956): 337-48.

21. Edward E. Jones, *Ingratiation: A Social Psychological Analysis* (New York: Appleton-Century-Crofts, 1964).

22. John P. Kotter, *Power and Influence* (New York: Free Press, 1985)

Chapter 18 Case Study

Student Power

When the course outline was distributed the first day of class, the students were surprised to discover that it was very different than they expected. The course was a required graduate-level class titled "Research Methods in Organizational Diagnosis" that had been taught as a case course the previous two years by a former faculty from Harvard University who used Harvard Business School cases as the basis for class discussions. This year, however, a new faculty member from Indiana University had been hired to teach the class and he was instructed to teach a research methods class that included both quantitative and qualitative methods of analysis.

As they reviewed the course outline, they discovered that there were at least three major assignments that would require them to know and apply statistics. A selection validation assignment would require them to calculate correlation coefficients to examine whether a selection procedure was correlated with performance measures. A training evaluation study would require them to calculate T-tests to determine which training method was the most effective. And a job redesign study would require them to use analysis of variance to examine the effects of three different job designs over four time periods. Other assignments also looked rather challenging, such as designing questionnaires and interpreting the data from them.

Some students thought these assignments were unreasonable, "Statistics was not listed as a prerequisite for this course and these assignments are unfair." "I took statistics four years ago in an undergraduate class and I don't remember any of it now." "The reason why I'm majoring in organizational behavior is because I wanted to get away from quantitative stuff. If I wanted to do these kinds of assignments I would have stayed in finance."

Two students decided to hold a meeting to discuss the course requirements, and twenty of the twenty three students attended. Jim, the informal group leader, told the group that they could force the professor to change the course requirements if they all acted in unison. He noted that the professor was a new faculty member who did not have tenure. Therefore, his teaching performance was very important to him and his department. If they all dropped the course in protest against unreasonable assignments this action would be viewed as a serious criticism of the professor and his ability to teach. Jim argued that all they would have to do to eliminate the quantitative assignments and replace them with case analyses is to announce in class that they were all planning to drop the course in unison. Jim prepared a petition announcing their intentions and eighteen students signed it.

The next morning in class, Jim interrupted the lecture at the beginning of class and announced, "We need to talk about the course requirements. This course isn't covering the kinds of things we want to learn. We want to study cases rather than quantitative methods and if you refuse to change the direction of this class, we plan to drop it. I have a petition that everyone has signed and if we can't negotiate a different course, we will leave."

The professor paused for a moment and then responded, "I have been asked to teach a research methods class and research methods involves more than case discussions. This is the same kind of research methods class that I would expect at any other major university. If it doesn't fit your expectations, you are free to drop. But, I'm not willing to rewrite the course requirements to eliminate the quantitative section." The professor then proceeded with his lecture and Jim and four students stood up and walked out of class.

Jim called another meeting and all twenty three students attended. He assured them that they controlled the power and said the next move was for everyone to drop the course. Most of the students, however, thought the professor had greater power and they were not willing to drop the class. They claimed that the professor had called their bluff and they didn't think they would ever have enough power to force him to change. But, Jim assured them that if they acted together they would have more power than the professor and they could still force him to change.

Questions

1. Is Jim right? If the students act in unison do they have more power than the professor? Can students ever have more power than the professors?
2. What other alternatives do the students have for exerting pressure on the professor other than dropping the course?
3. What would be the long-term consequences of giving students sufficient power to force professors to change their course requirements?

Personal Power Profile

Instructions: Listed below are statements that describe how supervisors can influence their subordinates. Read each statement and decide how you would prefer to influence your subordinates if you were appointed to be their supervisor.

To influence others and have them do what I want, I would prefer to	Strongly Disagree	Disagree	Agree	Strongly Agree
1. Offer them a pay increase	0	1	2	3
2. Threaten to cut their pay	0	1	2	3
3. Just tell them what to do and expect them to do it	0	1	2	3
4. Share my experience and training as an expert	0	1	2	3
5. Make them feel important	0	1	2	3
6. Promise them a bonus or award	0	1	2	3
7. Give them an undesirable job assignment	0	1	2	3
8. Explain what the organization requires of them	0	1	2	3
9. Give them good technical advice	0	1	2	3
10. Help them feel valued and approved	0	1	2	3
11. Recommend that they be promoted	0	1	2	3
12. Make working unpleasant if they resist me	0	1	2	3
13. Rely on my authority to give commands	0	1	2	3
14. Make certain they have the best information	0	1	2	3
15. Let them know that I care about them	0	1	2	3

Scoring: Use the matrix below to calculate your score for each of the five bases of power. Your score for each source of power can range from zero to nine; this is your power profile. A score of six or greater suggests that you prefer to influence others by using that particular form of power. Your personal power profile is not determined by the sum of all five bases of power, but by the contrast between each power source. Some combinations of power bases are synergistic. For example, referent power tends to enhance the impact of reward, legitimate, and expert power because these influence attempts are coming from a respected person. Likewise, reward power often increases the impact of referent power because people generally tend to like those who give them positive rewards.

Reward	Coercive	Legitimate	Expert	Referent
1 _____	2 _____	3 _____	4 _____	5 _____
6 _____	7 _____	8 _____	9 _____	10 _____
11 _____	12 _____	13 _____	14 _____	15 _____
_____ total	_____ total	_____ total	_____ total	_____ total

VI

How do you improve organizational effectiveness?

Every organization contains the seeds of its own destruction, and every organization must change periodically to retain its effectiveness. Organizational processes are designed to create stability and predictability by establishing patterned activities that everyone can expect. But organizations exist in an ever-changing world that requires them to adapt to new people, new technologies, and new environments. Companies that refuse to change or fail to change fast enough will not survive. On the other hand, those that successfully adapt can survive and grow, even in turbulent times, and even if they have to change industries or markets.

CHAPTER 19
Organizational Change

CHAPTER 20
Organizational Development

CHAPTER 21
Improving Your Own Effectiveness

The final chapters in Section VI explain the change process for individuals and organizations. Chapter 19 describes the theories of change and explains what must occur to achieve lasting change. Chapter 20 applies these theories to different organizational change interventions. Many change efforts have been tried in organizations to help them adapt to new demands, and organizational development interventions need to focus on the appropriate target of change. Chapter 21 discusses the problems of obsolescence and describes what you can do to achieve career success. This chapter also explains the causes of job stress, and suggests ways to manage it.

19

Organizational Change

Chapter Outline

Organizational Survival and Adaptation
  Forces of Change
  Resistance to Change
Organizational Change
  Kinds of Change
  Targets of Change
  Theories of Change
  Action Research Model
  Re-energizing the Mature Organization

ORGANIZATIONAL SURVIVAL AND ADAPTATION

Forces of Change

Organizations live in an ever-changing environment, and their survival depends on their ability to adapt to new demands and opportunities. As shown in Exhibit 19.1, organizations are required to change because of a broad variety of both internal and external forces.

Internal Forces of Change. Several forces within the organization may require it to change:

1. *New Technology.* The rate of technological change seems to increase every year with new machines, new manufacturing processes, and scientific discoveries. New jobs are created and old jobs are deleted because of technological change. Advances in computer technology and communication systems are probably the most significant technological changes in recent years. The use of computers and the Internet will continue to increase, influencing every industry. Communication is facilitated by mobile phones that people carry with them at all times.

2. *Work values.* Organizations are forced to respond to the changing values of their members. Some of the most significant changes include an increase in those who put family responsibilities ahead of work, a decline in the moral obligation to have a job, a decline in the sense of organizational loyalty, greater indifference toward promotions and advancement,

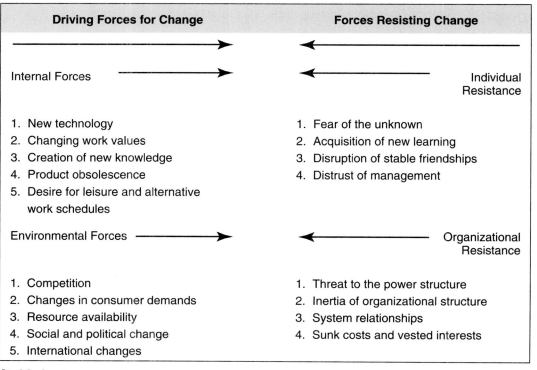

Exhibit 19.1 Forces of Change

greater variety in lifestyle and work schedules, and greater career mobility. Many managers are asking, "Why should I be loyal to the company if the company is not loyal to me?" Years of dedicated service seem to be ignored as layers of managerial jobs are deleted from the organizational chart after a merger or acquisition.

3. *Knowledge management.* The creation of new knowledge requires that organizations operate differently, and new knowledge is being created at a very rapid rate. Managers must find methods for assimilating, storing, and converting information to profitable products and services.

4. *Product obsolescence.* Technological advances and the explosion of knowledge combine to make many products obsolete in a very short time. In an average supermarket, for example, approximately 55 percent of the items sold today did not exist ten years ago. Of the products sold then, about 40 percent are no longer produced. When the first pocket calculator was sold in the early 1970s, it was priced at approximately $250. Ten years later, a pocket calculator that was more complex and compact could be purchased for less than a tenth of its earlier price. In recent years, calculators have been built into wallets, watches, and even matchbooks, and have been given away as party favors at luncheons. Rapid product obsolescence requires that organizations shorten production lead times and develop the capacity to adjust rapidly.

5. *Alternative work schedules.* More attractive opportunities for leisure and hobbies have encouraged employees to place greater demands on the organization for alternative schedules of work, such as job sharing and flextime, plus time away from work. With the increasing use of email and fax machines, some people avoid commuting to work by working at home on a computer connected to the Internet.

Environmental Forces of Change. Organizations cannot control the environment, but astute managers can identify the external forces for change and respond appropriately to them.

1. *Competition.* Changes in the marketplace can destroy a company's profitability. Managers need to know when their competitors introduce new products, change their advertising, reduce their prices, or improve their customer service. Although competition creates uncertainty, it contributes to the development of better consumer products and services. The benefits of competition are illustrated most dramatically when we compare the cost and quality of consumer goods in competitive economies to the limited consumer goods available in regulated socialist economies.

2. *Consumer demand.* Managers must be concerned about changes in consumer tastes and preferences because a firm's products may lose their appeal for very trivial and superficial reasons. Fashions change frequently, regardless whether the previous style was functional or comfortable. Rumors that a product causes cancer, high blood pressure, or some other health hazard can destroy consumer products even if the rumors are false.

3. *Resource availability.* Organizations depend on the external environment for raw materials and other resources. Disruptions in the supply of crucial resources can force organizations to drastically alter their operations,

as was illustrated by the oil embargo in the mid-1970s and the shortages during World War II. Uncertainty in obtaining resources has prompted many organizations to extend their boundaries in an attempt to reduce this uncertainty. For example, electric power companies have purchased their own coal mines, steel companies produce their own coke, and food industries have purchased their own trucking lines.

4. *Social and political change.* As social and political changes occur, organizations are required to adapt. The Civil Rights Act of 1964, for example, had a very powerful impact on reducing discrimination by requiring organizations to eliminate discriminatory employment practices. Federal regulations regarding environmental pollution, toxic wastes, and safety hazards require organizations to either comply or cease doing business.

5. *International forces.* International economic forces, such as wars, balance-of-payments problems, and lower labor rates in foreign countries, exert an ever-increasing influence on organizations. Managers are learning that the flow of oil from the Middle East, monetary transactions in Switzerland, the war in Central Europe, and low wages in Asian nations are having as large an impact on the success of their organization as are their competitors down the street.

Organizational effectiveness depends in part on balancing flexibility and structure. Organizations can improve their effectiveness by creating a highly structured organization with clearly defined rules and procedures. If the environment remains constant, a stable structure contributes to effectiveness, but conditions do not remain constant. Highly structured organizations that are rigid and inflexible are doomed to inefficiency and will eventually disappear. Hence, organizations face a perpetual dilemma—being sufficiently organized to operate efficiently, versus being sufficiently adaptable to respond to change.

Resistance to Change

Although change is inevitable, people tend to resist it. Some evidence of resistance to change is overt, such as wildcat strikes, work stoppages, turnover, and protests to proposed change. Resistance to change may also be subtle and indirect, such as dissatisfaction, grievances, requests for transfers, absenteeism, excessive damage to machines, and conflict among members of a work crew. The reasons for resistance to change can be divided into individual and organizational forces of resistance, as shown in Exhibit 19.1.

Individual Resistance. People resist change for a variety of reasons. Before implementing change, managers should try to understand why people are likely to object.

1. *Fear of the unknown.* Although change may improve life, the outcome is not certain, and fear of the unknown causes a powerful resistance to change. Significant change presents a realistic possibility that jobs will be terminated and employees laid off. These fears can be very frightening and persist in spite of management's attempt to assure employees that jobs will not be eliminated.

2. *Acquisition of new learning.* Learning a new task or procedure requires a conscious effort and is not as comfortable as doing it the "same old way." Some changes are small; others are far more significant, requiring people to learn a new language, develop a new technology, learn how to operate a computer, or adjust to a totally new culture. Although learning new ideas can be exciting, most people report that the excitement comes after the learning, not before.

3. *Disruption of stable friendships.* By working together, employees develop stable friendships. When these social interactions are disrupted, the resulting dissatisfaction is quite understandable. Almost any organizational change has the potential to destroy stable interactions and create uncomfortable feelings of social isolation and loneliness.

4. *Distrust of management.* Employees often suspect that change is intended to make them work faster for the same pay. Management usually has difficulty assuring employees of their motives because too many times in the history of labor relations, managers have exploited labor. Workers on piece-rate incentive plans, for example, have learned by sad experience that if they work rapidly to earn more money, their jobs are likely to be re-timed, requiring them to work at the same speed for less money.

Organizational Resistance to Change. The organizational structure itself resists change. Necessary changes may be resisted even when the survival of the organization depends on it.

1. *Threats to the power structure.* Most changes have the capacity to disrupt the organization's power structure. Participative changes may be particularly threatening to managers because group decisions tend to restrict the manager's influence. Decentralized decision making may be a welcomed improvement for lower-level employees, but a threat to higher-level employees.

2. *Inertia of organizational structure.* Organizational control systems are overdetermined in the sense that they are designed to produce stability. Organizational structures are designed to maintain a stable pattern of interactions among people. Job assignments, selection procedures, training programs, performance and reward systems, and many other aspects of the organizational structure are designed to maintain stable interactions—thus resisting change. To the extent that an organization is more highly structured, it tends to be resist to change.

3. *System relationships.* Since organizations are complex collections of interacting subsystems, it is difficult to make a change in one subsystem without affecting other subsystems. A change in the accounting department may influence the methods of reporting and record keeping of every other department. A revised regulation in a labor contract may require that supervisors throughout the organization behave differently.

4. *Sunk costs and vested interests.* "Sunk costs" are investments in fixed assets, such as equipment, land, and buildings. "Vested interests" are the personal commitments of individuals to programs, policies, or other people. Vested interests may be as difficult for individuals to abandon as sunk costs are difficult for an organization to recoup. Sunk costs and vested interests make it difficult to assess objectively the benefits of doing things differently.

A principle that seems rather well accepted among change agents is that significant change only occurs when people are feeling pain. Unless their present conditions create enough discomfort, there is no motive for change. Change agents usually try to assess how much emotion people feel regarding the change issues before they try to initiate a change strategy.

ORGANIZATIONAL CHANGE

A common mistake in initiating change is assuming that because an organization is a collection of people it can be changed by changing each individual. This assumption is wrong because it overlooks the complexity of individual behavior and the influence of organizational processes. Organizational change is a complex process, and many strategies have been proposed for creating change. In the field of psychology, most change strategies focus on changing the behavior of a single individual. In organizational behavior, efforts to change a single personality are rare because organizational problems are seldom problems of isolated people. Most problems are caused by the interactions of individuals within groups and between interacting groups. Consequently, successful change strategies require the active involvement of many people.

Kinds of Change

Organizations are constantly involved in change, but not all change is the same. Although some organizations make minor adjustments to take advantage of new opportunities, other organizations are devoured in corporate takeovers that move them into entirely different industries: some changes have a larger impact on people and are more difficult to implement than others. Three kinds of change have been categorized according to degree of complexity and potential for resistance to change, as shown in Exhibit 19.2: developmental, transitional, and transformational.[1]

Developmental change:
Gradual improvement in the skills, methods, and current processes of an organization.

Developmental Change. *Developmental change* is incremental improvement in skills, methods, or processes to help an organization function more efficiently. This kind of change might be considered fine-tuning, because it is usually a small adjustment that helps to raise individual productivity, reduce conflict, improve communication, eliminate wasted motions, or otherwise contribute to organizational effectiveness. Developmental change improves what is currently happening rather than form an entirely new process. This kind of change could be incorporated into the company's training and development programs and reviewed as part of its performance evaluation. Resistance to developmental change is usually not manifested in open opposition but as a subtle refusal to learn new skills or adopt new procedures.

Transitional change:
Changes that involve adopting new methods, revising the organization's processes, or producing new products; these changes occur in a series of defined stages.

Transitional Change. *Transitional change* is having an organization evolve slowly from an old state to a new state. The change occurs gradually, but it involves more than improving what is already there, as in developmental change. Transitional change involves new processes, new activities, new products, and sometimes a new organizational structure. This kind of change usually occurs in defined steps such as a series of delineated stages, pilot projects, phase-in operations, temporary arrangements, and reorganizations.

Exhibit 19.2   Kinds of Organizational Change

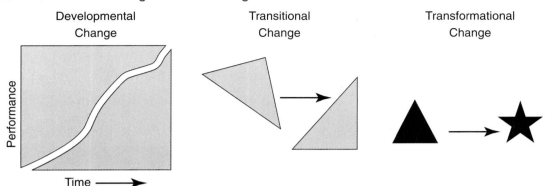

Developmental
Change

Transitional
Change

Transformational
Change

Performance

Time ———▶

Low ◀——————————————————————————————▶ High

Degree of complexity, cost, uncertainty, and frustration
Potential for resistance to change

Transformational change:
Change that is highly disruptive and chaotic and usually results in the adoption of significantly different products, processes, or relationships.

Transformational Change. The most dramatic kind of change is *transformational change*, characterized by a radical reconceptualization of the organization's mission, culture, products, leadership, or structure. This kind of change occurs in companies that have become stagnant and need to be rejuvenated. A typical candidate for this kind of change is a mature company whose sales reached a plateau several years ago and that has recently experienced chaos because of declining sales and a loss of market share due to foreign competition.

It is possible for an entire industry to be threatened by technological improvements that make the old ways of doing business obsolete, such as the shift in the steel industry from large, integrated steel mills with their open-hearth furnaces to small minimills with electric furnaces. The minimills produce about four times as many tons of steel per employee hour, and their process is superior in terms of safety, speed, and reduced environmental pollution.

Paradigm change:
A change in the basic assumptions and ways of structuring an issue or thinking about a problem. Paradigm changes typically create significant change throughout an industry.

Transformational change often occurs because of a significant *paradigm change* within the industry. The word *paradigm* comes from the Greek word for "pattern," and the new paradigm is a new pattern of behavior or a new way of looking at the world. Paradigm changes often result from a new set of assumptions, a new way of structuring an issue, a new way of thinking about a problem, or a new technological innovation that makes the former technology obsolete. [2]

Paradigm changes within an industry affect every organization in that industry. For example, the efficiency of electric furnaces influences all steel mills worldwide—minimills and large, integrated mills. Organizations that cannot or choose not to change usually die. The industrial graveyard is filled with organizations that dissolved because their success kept them from recognizing the paradigm shift and the need to change. If an organization recognizes a paradigm shift early enough, it can plan for gradual systematic transitional change. Organizations that fail to recognize the need for change until they are in the middle of chaos and turmoil are forced into transformational change that is usually associated with frustration, uncertainty, and crisis planning.

Another way to describe transformational change is ***punctuated equilibrium***, which refers to an alternation between periods of incremental adjustments and brief periods of revolutionary upheaval. During periods of calm, only developmental changes are happening. But every so often, massive restructuring or realignment occurs that fundamentally alters the structure and direction of the organization. Punctuated equilibrium has been observed not only in organizational change, but also in other domains, such as individual development, group dynamics, biological evolution, and the history of science.[3] Punctuated equilibrium is illustrated by the paradigm changes in the computer industry.

Targets of Change

Organizational change strategies are designed to create change at a specific level in an organization. The seven most common targets of change are as follows:

Individual Personality. Occasionally, organizational difficulties stem from the personality of a specific individual. For example, a supervisor could be excessively punitive and dictatorial, or a worker might be constantly critical, negative, or otherwise offensive. Key individuals who work in administrative or executive positions are often criticized because of their supervisory style.

Dyad:
Two people and the relationship between them.

Dyad. The term *dyad* refers to the relationship between two people, such as two co-workers or a married couple. Occasionally the problems between two people are not specifically caused by either person; they are caused by the relationship between them. In an interdependent relationship, both members develop expectations regarding one another. When these expectations are violated, serious conflicts can occur. The cause of the problem may have nothing to do with inadequacy or immaturity on the part of either individual. Both may be healthy individuals, but they may have unrealistic or inconsistent expectations regarding their relationship. Here the problem is not people, but the relationship between them.

Group. Work groups are probably the most popular target of organizational development interventions. These change strategies can focus on conflict within the group or on changing group norms. Each group develops its own goals and norms that influence member behavior. Occasionally the group norms are inconsistent with the goals of the organization or unacceptable to members of the group. Groups may also develop a hostile climate in which some group members are not accepted.

Family group:
A work group composed of a supervisor and his or her immediate subordinates.

Family Groups. Family groups consist of a supervisor and the immediate subordinates who report to that supervisor. Specific problems can exist within family groups in addition to the typical problems that occur in peer groups. Issues regarding leadership style, authority, delegation of work assignments, and performance evaluations are sources of potential conflicts.

The Entire Organization and Its Divisions. Greater cohesiveness within groups usually inspires more conflicts between groups. Change strategies may need to focus on the relationships between groups and the ways in which the major divisions of a company coordinate their efforts. The contributions of all the separate departments should result in a carefully balanced and highly integrated organization.

Organizational Structure. Occasionally the structure of the organization must change to meet new demands or provide greater efficiency. Change strategies may focus on a variety of structural characteristics, such as the division of labor, the pattern of departmentalization, the span of control, or the reporting relationships.

Organizational Strategy. Significant changes in technology or competition may require organizations to alter their strategic direction. The target of some change efforts is clarifying the mission of the organization and determining what it must do to survive. The outcome of this change could be something as simple as adding or deleting product lines, or as drastic as moving into a different industry or merging with another company.

Theories of Change

One of the earliest theories of change was the force field analysis proposed by Kurt Lewin. Although this model was derived from the physical sciences, it continues to provide a valuable framework for thinking about change and diagnosing problems. Other change models have come from psychology, social psychology, and group dynamics.

Kurt Lewin's Force Field Analysis. Kurt Lewin's theory of change was derived from the laws of physics, which state that the position and direction of an object are determined by the forces operating on it. Change occurs when the forces pushing in one direction are greater than the forces pushing in the opposite direction. A state of balance exists when the restraining forces acting to prevent change are equal to the driving forces attempting to produce change. The equilibrium point is determined by the resultant forces operating in different directions, as shown in Exhibit 19.3. According to Kurt Lewin, planned change occurs in three stages: unfreezing, change, and refreezing.[4]

1. *Unfreezing* occurs when people see a need for change. The status quo is disturbed by unsettling forces that challenge current values, attitudes, and behaviors.
2. *Change* is the action-oriented stage, in which the situation is diagnosed, improved patterns of behavior are selected, and a new equilibrium is created. As a result of change, people develop new values, attitudes, and/or behaviors.
3. *Refreezing* stabilizes the change and solidifies the new patterns of behavior. Refreezing requires continued management of the change process beyond the immediate implementation. Refreezing also requires that people have positive experiences to strengthen their continuing commitment to the change. The new state then becomes the status quo for future behavior.

Force field analysis:

A method for analyzing a change situation by looking at the driving and restraining forces operating on a situation.

According to Lewin's *force field analysis,* managers create planned change by altering the restraining and driving forces. A careful analysis is necessary to determine how the restraining forces can be reduced and how the driving forces can be strengthened. Lewin's force field analysis has been a popular model for analyzing change programs and predicting the effects of future changes.

Change Processes. Most change efforts do not produce lasting change. Even when a change effort succeeds in reaching its target, the likelihood that the new behavior will persist for more than six months is very small. Weight-loss programs illustrate the challenge of producing lasting change. Most people who start a diet never reach their target weight, and less than 5 percent of those who do will maintain their target six months later. The percentage of people who quit smoking and are still smoke-free six months later is less than half, even when they suffer a serious health problem and are told that their quality of life depends on avoiding tobacco. Therefore, we should not be surprised to learn that change interventions in organizations often fail to produce lasting change.

Gene Dalton has developed a model that explains what must occur during the unfreezing, change, and refreezing processes in order to ensure lasting change. He argues that change will not occur unless there is sufficient pain and tension to motivate it. Unless people feel a need for change, they will con-

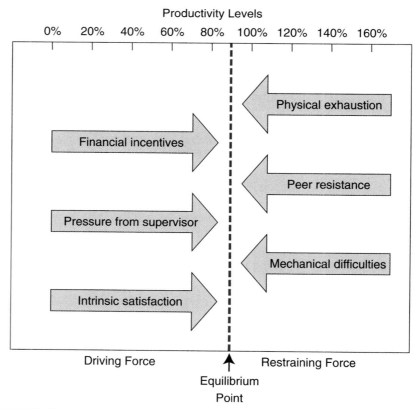

Exhibit 19.3 An Illustration of Kurt Lewin's Force Field Analysis

tinue to display the same behavior. Change also needs to be supported by a credible source. Those who initiate change in organizations must be perceived as trusted and respected facilitators. Two precursors to change, then, are a felt need for change and support for it by significant others. Dalton's model identifies four processes that involve movement away from one state to an opposite state to ensure that a change persists:[5]

1. *Generalized goals → Specific objectives*. During the change process, people need to move from general goals and intentions to specific objectives and measurable targets. For a change strategy to successfully produce lasting change, people need to know exactly what they need to do differently and what is expected of them. To the extent that their goals are only general and nonspecific, or to the extent that there is uncertainty in how they should behave or think, the change will not persist.

2. *Former Social Ties → New Relationships*. The most lasting change efforts involve moving people into different social settings with new members. It is doubtful that people who remain with their former social ties, where their behavior patterns were built around their previous associations, will ever create new and lasting behavior patterns. Lasting change requires new relationships that support the intended changes in behavior and attitudes. This condition is best achieved by associating with a completely new peer group. Achieving lasting change while remaining with the same peer group is unlikely unless there is a significant change in the relationships. New attitudes and behaviors must be accepted and even encouraged by the previous group in order for the change to endure.

3. *Self-Doubt → Heightened Self-Esteem*. One of the most important conditions for the successful initiation of lasting change is a sense of tension or a felt need for change. Unless people feel a sense of pain and discomfort, they are not motivated to change. This pain and discomfort tends to cause self-doubt and decreased self-esteem. As improvement occurs during the change process, people begin to feel better about themselves and acquire a heightened sense of self-esteem and self-confidence. Thinking that the change was good and feeling greater self-esteem tend to reinforce the change effort and cause it to endure.

4. *External Motives for Change → Internal Motive for Change*. Change efforts that are motivated by external pressures tend to persist only as long as the external pressures persist. Lasting change is more likely when people have good reasons for it (cognitive justifications), which they have internalized as their own. This new belief system can be taught by others, such as an influential change agent, but at some point people need to apply it to their personal lives and verify it through their own experiences.

Three theoretical explanations, based on different underlying motives for behavior, have been proposed to explain why change occurs: education, reinforcement, and peer group influences.[6] These strategies can also be viewed as methods for dealing with resistance to change. Exhibit 19.4 summarizes when each method is most effective, and the advantages and disadvantages of each method.

Education and Communication. Many change efforts are based on the assumption that new information creates change. People are expected to behave differently after they acquire new attitudes, insights, or self-awareness. This theory of change has been called a ***rational-empirical*** change strategy, because it assumes that people are rational and will follow their self-interest once this is identified for them.[7]

Because we assume that people are rational and motivated by self-interest, it is reasonable to assume that they will adopt a proposed change if we can rationally justify it and show that they will gain by the change. For example, salesclerks would be expected to lock their lockers after they are told that their personal items may be stolen, and they would be expected to be less "pushy" after they discover that customers are offended by their behavior.

New information is not always effective in changing behavior, however. The relationship between attitudes and behaviors is usually extremely weak. Changing a person's attitudes will not necessarily change the person's behavior. The effectiveness of empirical evidence or new information in changing behavior depends largely on whether there was a lack of information to begin with. New information is a powerful force for change in ambiguous situations. For example, new-employee orientations are particularly effective in changing the behavior of new employees, because they wouldn't have known how to behave otherwise. However, new information is not an effective impetus for change when people already know the correct way of behaving but fail to conform. For example, employees already know that absenteeism and sloppy work are wrong, and training programs discussing attendance and careful work will do little to create new knowledge. Likewise, many people continue to smoke in

Method of Change	When it Should Be Used	Advantages	Disadvantages
1. *Education and Communication:* Explain the need for change, what will happen, and how it will affect each person. Help them see the logic and rationale for change.	When there is a lack of information or when the situation is novel or uncertain. It should normally accompany other change methods.	Highly effective in ambiguous situations. It provides cognitive support for other change methods. Once persuaded, people help to implement the change.	New information seldom motivates a change in behavior. Providing new knowledge or rational justifications can be very time consuming.
2. *Reinforcement:* a. *Incentives*: Offer additional incentives for compliance and negotiate agreement.	When the incentives are highly valued but not too costly, and when it is important for the employees to perceive a fair exchange.	A fair exchange helps to preserve dignity and equity. It can be a relatively easy way to avoid resistance.	It can be very costly and the costs may escalate in future encounters.
b. *Coercion:* Force employees to change using threats, such as pay cuts, job loss, or undesirable tasks.	When speed is essential and management has sufficient power to enforce the threats.	It takes little time and allows the company to begin rebuilding faster.	If it makes people angry, they may retaliate or leave.
3. *Peer Group Influence:* Allow groups of people to participate in the change process by discussing issues, recommending creative ideas, and implementing the change.	When insight or cooperation are needed. When group norms impede the group. When people are contemplating changes in their attitudes or values.	People who participate in change are more prepared to implement it and more committed to its success. Group influence is a powerful impetus for change.	Can be very time-consuming, and it is possible the group may decide to oppose the change.

Exhibit 19.4 **Methods for Overcoming Resistance to Change**

spite of frequent warnings and mounting evidence showing the health hazards of tobacco use. Information alone is often not adequate to change behavior.

Reinforcement. Another explanation for change is that people do what they are reinforced for doing. This method has been called a ***power coercive*** change strategy because it involves the application of power in which people with less power are forced to comply with the plans, directions, and leadership of those with greater power.[8] People tend to change quite quickly when there are sufficient incentives or punishments. The reinforcement may be overt, such as bribes, payoffs, and bonuses, or subtle, such as social approval, self-esteem, and peer group pressure.

People can be forced to accept change under implicit or explicit threats, such as job loss, pay cuts, demotions, or undesirable transfers. Coercion can be effective when speed is essential and the change agents have considerable power, but it is not highly recommended—people tend to be uncooperative if they feel abused or ignored. A lack of cooperation may lead to periodic sabotage and prevent even good ideas from succeeding.

Peer Group Influence. Another theory of change recognizes the influence of social norms, especially at the level of the group. This method of change has been called a ***normative-reeducative*** change strategy, because it is based on the assumption that change occurs as people learn new normative orientations that result in new attitudes, values, and interpersonal relationships.

Peer pressure is perhaps the most subtle and powerful impetus for change, which partially explains why group discussion is one of the most frequently used change methods in organizational development. A classic study in a garment factory illustrated the advantages of peer group discussions on overcoming resistance to change. When job changes had to be introduced, a control group received the conventional explanation, which simply told them their jobs had to be changed. A second group received an elaborate explanation of the need for change and then selected representatives from the group to help make the change. Two other experimental groups also received a careful explanation of the need for change and then participated as a total group in redesigning the new jobs. After the changes were implemented, the control group showed hardly any improvement over its earlier efficiency ratings, and the hostility of this group toward management resulted in a 17-percent turnover within the first 40 days. The group that selected representatives relearned quickly and was able to reach standard performance within 14 days, as well as continued improvement thereafter. The two groups that were allowed total participation showed the greatest performance improvement and the highest levels of morale. Only in the control group did any of the employees quit.[9]

Four reasons have been proposed to explain why group discussions are so effective in changing the attitudes and behavior of their members:

1. People who are contemplating a change in their attitudes or behavior are reinforced by seeing other group members make the same change.
2. The group discussion forces members to come to a decision point. Rather than just passively considering the issue, they are required to decide whether they accept or reject the change.

3. As they talk about the change and arrive at a group consensus, members are forced to make a public commitment to change their behavior. If they fail to follow through after the group discussion, there is a sense of dishonesty and loss of self-esteem.

4. Some aspect of the decision-making process itself helps people accept the change, such as the risky-shift phenomenon or emotional catharsis.

Action Research Model

Action research model:
A strategy of organizational development that typically involves the processes of problem identification, data gathering, feedback of the data to the client group, data discussion and diagnosis, action planning, action, and reevaluation. These processes are recycled as needed to increase organizational effectiveness.

A useful model describing the basic approach of most organizational change activities is the ***action research model.***[10] This model is consistent with the scientific method of inquiry and its reliance on data gathering and analysis to solve problems. This model has also been called the ***action learning model,*** to emphasize the collective involvement of members to discover and adopt new behaviors.[11] Exhibit 19.5 illustrates the six basic steps in this model: data gathering, feedback of the data to the target group, data discussion and diagnosis, action planning, action, and recycling. Each of these six processes is important to successful change efforts.

Data Gathering. When evidence of a problem exists and is serious enough to merit attention, the first step is to gather information about the problem. Data may be collected about the causes of the problem and its seriousness from a variety of sources, including interviews, observations, questionnaire surveys, and archival data. Each method contains advantages and disadvantages, and successful change agents develop the ability to use all four methods rather than rely on one or two. Interviews are very time-consuming, but they contain "rich" information for diagnosing problems. Conversely, questionnaires can quickly measure the opinions of many people, but they provide answers only to the questions that were asked.

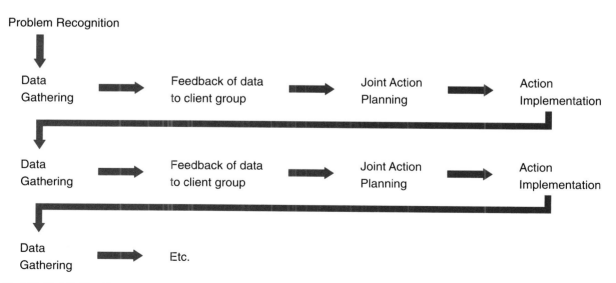

Exhibit 19.5 The Action Research Model for Organizational Development

Target of change:
The focus of a change effort that could be either an individual personality, a dyad, a group, a family group, the entire organization, or the organizational structure.

Feedback of Data to Target Group. After the data have been collected and summarized, they are presented to the *target of change*. The target group includes those who are involved in the problem, which could be an individual, a group, or the entire organization. The data are not simply reported to top management and kept locked in confidential files. The data should be open to anyone for whom it is relevant. Information about group conflicts should be shared with the group; information about the entire organization should be open to the entire organization, but not criticisms about a particular supervisor.

Data Discussion and Diagnosis. The data should be used to identify and diagnose organizational problems. A careful analysis is necessary to identify the real problems rather than just surface symptoms. This analysis generally involves a group discussion by the target group. To reduce the likelihood of misinterpreting the data, the group should explore alternative causes of the problem. The diagnosis may focus on either a specific problem or a general issue. Insufficient supplies, incorrect reports, and scheduling problems are examples of specific problems that need to be resolved. Declining sales, high turnover, and low morale are indications of a general problem that requires a more careful diagnosis.

Action Planning. After the cause of the problem has been identified, the target group should develop an action plan to solve the problem. The action plan may involve more than just the target group because corresponding changes in other parts of the organization may be necessary to avoid dysfunctional consequences. A variety of change strategies that are described in the next chapter are typically used in the action-planning process.

Action. After the change has been carefully planned, it is implemented. Some organizational development interventions are very narrow and shallow; others are broad and deep. The change may involve something as simple as having supervisors complete a new form, or as complex as restructuring the entire organization or revising the compensation system.

Recycling. Organizational development is not a one-shot event; it is an iterative process. After the change has been implemented, the situation is reassessed to see if the original problem has been eliminated and if new problems have appeared. This iterative process involves recycling through the previous steps, as shown in Exhibit 19.5. Each recycling is in essence an evaluation of the previous cycle.

Reenergizing the Mature Organization

Organizations evolve through a lifecycle. Each stage is characterized by a dominant issue and a specific change challenge that must be faced before it advances to the next stage.

Entrepreneurial stage:
Focuses on developing new products.

In stage one, the *entrepreneurial stage,* organizations focus on identifying and developing new products. During this stage, the organization revolves around the creative efforts of an entrepreneur and the dominant issue is establishing a market niche.[12]

Collectivity or growth stage:
Focuses on creating a division of labor and becoming efficient.

Formalization or maturity stage:
Focuses on establishing formal policies and procedures with additional support staff to perform them.

Elaboration stage:
When bureaucratic procedures and controls have proliferated and are often excessive and inefficient and need to be revitalized.

The change challenge that moves the organization to stage two, the *collectivity* or *growth* stage, is the need for leadership. Directing an organization through a growth period requires managerial direction and control. The dominant issue at stage two is delegating responsibilities and providing clear direction, so that the collective efforts of many people will combine effectively to produce the desired product or services.

The change challenge that moves an organization to stage three, the *formalization* or *maturity* stage, is the need for delegation and control. The establishment of formal procedures contributes to predictable, patterned activities. As responsibilities are delegated, internal control systems are required to integrate diverse activities. The dominant issue is selecting the most appropriate control systems.

The change challenge that organizations face as they move to stage four, the *elaboration* stage, is the need to control bureaucratic inefficiencies. As organizations enter the elaboration stage, they usually begin to decline as a result of excessive bureaucratic procedures: unnecessary reports, useless meetings, needless approvals, and meaningless activity measures. At this stage, organizations will continue to decline unless they can be revitalized.

It is very unlikely that a mature organization can maintain its size and market domination for an extended period without some form of revitalization. Even large and once-powerful organizations, such as General Motors, General Electric, and International Business Machines, have found they cannot continue to produce the same products with the same technology and the same organizational structure year after year. The process of revitalizing mature organizations occurs in five stages: restructuring, bureaucracy "bashing," employee empowerment, continuous improvement, and cultural change.[13]

Restructuring. The first stage of renewal generally begins with a significant restructuring effort focused on downsizing or delayering the organization. Complacent organizations usually have more employees than they need. The leadership challenge at this stage is knowing which positions to eliminate, and having the courage to make difficult but fair termination procedures.

Bureaucracy "Bashing." The next step is to remove bureaucratic inefficiencies, such as unnecessary reports, approvals, meetings, policies, and other activities that waste effort or impede productive work. Reducing bureaucratic inefficiencies involves getting rid of work that fails to add value to customers. Unless they are essential for coordinating work, activity reports and productivity measures result in wasted time preparing them and wasted time reading them.

Employee Empowerment. Employees should be free to identify better work procedures, and implement them. Self-directed work teams, employee involvement activities, and job redesign help to remove barriers between people and give them the authority to act. In a bureaucracy, only the top managers are empowered. By reducing bureaucratic inefficiencies, all employees are empowered to suggest process improvements and new product ideas. Empowerment allows the organization to benefit from the creativity and ingenuity of employees.

Continuous Improvements. After the organization is restructured, bureaucratic inefficiencies are eliminated, and employees are empowered, renewal efforts should focus on achieving continuous improvements in the value chain. These improvements could involve better relationships with upstream suppliers or downstream customers in the value chain. Barriers between suppliers and customers should become more permeable, allowing for a smoother flow of products and information. Problems are identified, complexities are simplified, and delays are eliminated to improve the quality of the product or service.

Cultural Change. The final renewal stage, cultural change, is a consequence of the previous stages if they have been successful. Employees will not think of themselves as part of a mature organization, but will feel enthusiasm for trying new approaches and looking for better ways to serve customers. How they think about their work and the company will form a new mind-set that amounts to a fundamental cultural change. With an involved and committed workforce, the organization will achieve a sustained competitive advantage in its industry.

Discussion Questions

1. Describe the major theories of change. What is your theory about how you get groups or organizations to change? Describe the action research model, and illustrate how you would use it to resolve a problem in a student dormitory.
2. Explain the processes involved in producing lasting change. Use an example from your own life that may or may not have been a successful change effort to illustrate these processes.
3. If organizations are collections of people, why can't you change an organization by simply changing each individual? Explain why most change efforts involve groups, and explain the benefits of using groups in change strategies. Describe a change effort that has involved a group of which you were a member.

Notes

1. Linda Ackerman, "Development, Transition or Transformation: The Question of Change in Organizations," *O.D. Practitioner* (December 1986): 1–8; Dexter C. Dunphy and Doug A. Stace, "Transformation and Cohesive Strategies for Planned Organizational Change: Beyond the O.D. Model," *Organizational Studies* 9 (1988): 317–34.
2. Joel Barker, "Discovering the Future: The Business of Paradigms," (video-tape produced by Public Media Inc., 1989); Joel Barker, "Discovering the Future: The Power of Vision," (video-tape produced by Public Media Inc., 1990).
3. Connie J.G. Gersick, "Revolutionary Change Theories: A Multilevel Exploration of the Punctuated Equilibrium Paradigm," *Academy of Management Review* 16 (1991): 10–36.
4. Kurt Lewin, *Field Theory in Social Science*, (New York: Harper and Row, 1951), pp. 228–29.

5. Gene W. Dalton, "Influence and Organizational Change." In Anant R. Negandhi (ed.) *Modern Organizational Theory*. (Kent, OH: Kent University Press,): 343–72.

6. Robert Chin and Kenneth D. Benne, "General Strategies for Effecting Changes in Human Systems," in *The Planning of Change*, 3rd ed., ed. W.G. Bennis, K.D. Benne, R. Chin, and K.E. Corey (New York: Holt, Rinehart and Winston, 1976): 22–45.

7. Ibid.

8. Ibid.

9. Lester Coch and John R.P. French, "Overcoming Resistance to Change," *Human Relations* 1 (1948): 512–33.

10. Wendell French, "Organization Development Objectives, Assumptions, and Strategies," *California Management Review* 12 (Winter 1969): 23–34; Chris Lee, "Action Research: Harnessing the Power of Participation," *Training: The Magazine of Human Resources Development* 27 (1990): 85–87.

11. Rafael Ramirez, "Action Learning: A Strategic Approach for Organizations Facing Turbulent Conditions," *Human Relations* 36 (1983): 725–42.

12. Robert E. Quinn and Kim Cameron, "Organizational Life Cycles and Some Shifting Criteria of Effectiveness: Some Preliminary Evidence," *Management Science* 29 (1983): 33–51.

13. Richard W. Beatty and David O. Ulrich, "Re-energizing the Mature Organization," in Todd D. Jick *Managing Change: Cases and Concepts* (Homewood, IL: Erwin, 1993): 60–74

Increasing Work Standards

Scott Condie is a union steward. It was not a job he really wanted, but after he was elected he decided to do his best. Scott has worked for the company for eight years, and as long as he can remember, a full day's work in the mixing building has been thirty-six pallets with fifty-six sacks on each pallet. He assumed this standard was negotiated with management many years ago. Everyone knows, however, that it is a loose standard, and one night two college students on summer employment proved it convincingly.

The work in the mixing building is performed by seven men: five sackers, a machine operator, and a chemical mixer. The five sackers alternate working on the sacking machine since only two can work at the same time. When the other three are not sacking, they prepare the next pallet and wait for their turn to sack.

One night the two college students boasted that with the cooperation of the operator and mixer, they could meet an eight-hour quota in the first two and a half hours all by themselves. Since they worked on the night shift with little supervision, the other three sackers called their challenge. Without any help from the other three, they made the full quota of 36 pallets in just two and one quarter hours. They used a slightly different procedure that required more effort. When one sack was filled, they pulled it off the machine with one hand and started the next sack with the other hand so that it was filling while they stacked the first one. Since each sack weighs 50 pounds, this procedure requires more effort but is considerably faster.

The rest of the crew went on to produce an additional 36 pallets that night. Subsequently, the new standard became 50 pallets. When the day shift heard about the night shift's new standard, some members stayed after work to get the night shift "straightened out." The meeting was mostly a shouting match of accusations and threats. After it was over, the night shift decided they would raise the standard to 60 pallets just to make the day shift look bad.

When the production superintendent learned about the night shift's new quota, she instructed the day shift supervisor, Carlos Romero, to have 60 pallets become the standard for the day shift also. Carlos knew this would be a very unpopular change, but he thought most of the crew would cooperate. However, those opposed to the change were able to unite the group against the new standard.

Since Scott is the union steward, the day shift crew warned him that they would pull a wildcat strike and shut the entire plant down if the standards are changed. To add to the problem, Scott has also been asked to warn the day shift about alleged acts of violence. Two night shift workers claim their cars were damaged in the company parking lot by members of the day shift. Day shift members have threatened additional violence if the night shift doesn't return to the original standard.

Because of these threats, Scott carefully checked the labor agreement and discussed the issue with management. He was surprised to find that nothing is written about 36 pallets being the standard. The contract only says that management will direct the employees in the performance of their work, and unfair treatment should be handled through the grievance procedure. The 36-pallet standard is simply an informal quota that has never been questioned.

Scott informed both the day and night crews about the right of management to determine the work standards.

Carlos thinks the problem would be resolved if the workers had an economic incentive to change. He has proposed a gainsharing incentive that would set 50 as the standard for each shift and pay a bonus for producing anything more than that. Scott agrees that this is a good idea, but he argues that a new incentive system cannot be implemented unless it is part of the bargaining agreement.

Questions

1. Why does the day shift oppose the new standards if they are reasonable?
2. What will likely happen if Carlos tries to enforce new work standards? How should Carlos and Scott react to the acts of violence?
3. What is the best way for Carlos to change the group norms and increase the work standards?

Force Field Analysis

Kurt Lewin developed a model of change, called the Force Field Analysis, that was derived from the laws of physics. The central idea of this model is that the position and direction of an object are determined by the forces operating on it. To move it to a different position, one must increase the forces pushing it in that direction or reduce the forces from the opposite direction.

This model was used effectively to increase the productivity at an oil refinery by a former football player who used a football metaphor in a series of team-building exercises. At the beginning of a three-day retreat, the facilitator drew a football field on the blackboard and labeled one end zone the 100 percent level of efficiency. He asked the participants to identify their current line of scrimmage, meaning their current level of productivity. After a lengthy discussion, the group concluded they were about 70 percent as effective as they could be and the facilitator drew a line at the opponent's 30-yard line, saying they had 30 yards to go for a score. Next they spent several hours identifying the things they were doing well and making them as effective as they were, and even more hours identifying the forces that were preventing them from doing better. By the end of the three-day session, the group emerged with an action plan designed to improve the refinery's efficiency by strengthening the driving forces and eliminating the restraining forces.

Directions:

Use Lewin's force field analysis to help you improve in something that matters to you, such as getting better grades, exercising, losing weight, or improving your spiritual or moral life.

1. Identify the objective you want to achieve. Choose something that is important and that matters to you.
2. Describe the situation as it now exists and mark this point on a model football field, such as is shown below.
3. Describe your ultimate goal or the situation as you would like it to be.
4. List all of the driving forces that are moving you in the direction of your objective.
5. List all of the restraining forces that keep you from moving toward your objective.
6. Classify the strength of each of the driving forces as either strong, medium, or weak, and consider what could make them stronger.
7. Do a similar analysis of the restraining forces, and focus especially on how much control you have on these forces.
8. Make an action plan for achieving your objective, and share your plan with someone who will encourage you. Be specific; focus on observable behaviors and establish a definite timetable.

Current Situation:	Situation as you would like it to be:
Driving Forces: →	← Restraining Forces:

Organizational Development

Chapter Outline

The Organizational Development Process
   Historical Stems
   Assumptions of OD
   Change Agents
   Transfer and Diffusion of Change
   Evaluating OD
OD Interventions
   Interpersonal Interventions
   Group Interventions
   Intergroup Interventions
   Organizational Interventions

THE ORGANIZATIONAL DEVELOPMENT PROCESS

Unless they continually adapt to a changing environment, all organizations begin to deteriorate and will eventually die if they are not revitalized. Organizational development (OD) is a process of preparing for and managing a planned change effort. However, not all change efforts are organizational development, because OD is typically differentiated from management training and other educational interventions. Organizational development involves a collaborative diagnosis and problem-solving approach for avoiding organizational decay and encouraging organizational renewal.

Historical Stems

The foundations of OD began with some of the early change strategies that started in the 1940s and 1950s: laboratory training, survey feedback, quality management, and sociotechnical systems.[1] By the early 1970s, several successful OD interventions had occurred, and many managers recognized the benefits of OD.

T-group:
T-group ("T" for "training") is another name for sensitivity training group.

Laboratory Training. Laboratory training, also called *T-group* training or *sensitivity training*, was started by Kurt Lewin and others in the 1940s. Lewin found that informal discussions with small groups of participants were very effective in helping members learn more about themselves and about interpersonal relations. He found that discussions about individual and group behavior, combined with feedback at the end of each day, appeared to produce more insight and learning than lectures and seminars. Kurt Lewin died in 1947, but the basic design of sensitivity training was continued by other behavioral scientists. For many years, organizational development specifically meant sensitivity training. Today, organizational development is defined much more broadly, and sensitivity training is only one of many OD interventions.

Survey Feedback. Survey research and feedback were started by the Survey Research Center founded in 1946 at the University of Michigan by Rensis Likert and others. This group pioneered the development and use of carefully constructed questionnaires, rigorous probability sampling, and information feedback to managers and supervisors. They found that when managers shared their results with subordinates and involved them in discussing the problems, substantial improvement occurred. Today, survey feedback is another valuable OD intervention that is used to diagnose and resolve organizational problems.

Quality Management. During the reconstruction of Japan after World War II, W. Edwards Deming, a management consultant from the United States, was invited to share his ideas about continuous quality improvement. He designed a four-day seminar for Japanese executives in 1950 and subsequently became a national hero to Japanese industry. To honor his contributions, Japanese industry created the Deming Prize in 1951. This annual prize, highly esteemed in Japan, recognizes the company that attains the highest level of quality for that year. Deming's ideas attracted little attention in America until an NBC documentary in 1980 featured the work of Deming and other colleagues in Japan.

Demonstrations of dramatic quality improvement in Japanese manufacturing attracted considerable interest, and drew attention to the problems of poor quality in the United States. Deming taught that poor quality is 85 percent a management problem and 15 percent a worker problem. Management must plan for quality, and quality must be built into the product rather than inspected into it. In 1987, the United States started the Malcolm Baldrige National Quality Award to recognize U.S. companies that excel in quality achievement and management.

Sociotechnical Systems. Sociotechnical system design emphasizes the need to balance the technological factors associated with machines and work processes with the social needs of workers for interesting work and meaningful social interactions. This OD intervention originated in the early 1950s when researchers from England's Tavistock Institute redesigned the hazardous work of coal miners in Great Britain. For many years miners had worked in groups of six, performing all the functions of extracting coal. A new longwall method, with conveyors and coal-cutting machinery, was more productive because it created specialized jobs, but it destroyed the stable work group culture and caused considerable resistance. To combine the advantages of the new machines with the essential social support of work groups, the researchers used a "composite longwall" system in which 41 miners worked as a team performing all the necessary functions. Workers were trained to perform multiple tasks, and they were paid as a group. The group was responsible for selecting and training new members, making job assignments, scheduling work, and rotating the shifts. The performance of the composite longwall system was far superior to the traditional longwall system: voluntary absenteeism was only a tenth as much, output per person-shift was 5.3 tons versus 3.5 tons, operating potential was 95 percent versus 78 percent, and the company was saved the salary of a supervisor, because the group managed itself.[2]

Assumptions of OD

OD interventions are based on a number of underlying assumptions and values concerning people, groups, and organizations. These assumptions and values play a large role in understanding the processes that are used in OD. Most of these processes depend heavily on individual involvement and effective group functioning for success.

Assumptions about People. OD interventions are based on the assumption that most people want to make, and are capable of making, a greater contribution to the organization than they are normally permitted to make. Many people feel constrained in their present environment, unable to exert constructive energy toward the attainment of organizational goals. OD attempts to unleash the energy and enthusiasm of employees and provide a means for channeling this constructive energy into creative and insightful avenues.

Assumptions about Groups. OD interventions recognize the powerful influence of peer groups on individual behavior. Small groups are generally considered the basic building blocks of excellent companies. To help the group function effectively, most interventions assume that a formal leader cannot perform all the leadership and maintenance functions necessary for group effectiveness; hence, other group members must act to supplement the leadership functions. Many interventions try to improve the effectiveness of groups because they cannot function effectively when there is a lack of interpersonal trust, support, and cooperation.

Assumptions about Organizations. Most OD interventions assume that organizational conflict need not be viewed as an us-against-them confrontation. Instead, conflict is reinterpreted from a win-lose situation to a win-win strategy by approaching it in terms of "how can we all win?" OD interventions reject the idea that the goals of individuals are incompatible with organizational goals. Instead, the goals of individuals and the organization are viewed as consistent: individuals can pursue their own best interests while working to help the organization become successful.

Another important assumption about organizations, derived from open-systems theory, is that a change in one subsystem of an organization will impact other subsystems. Therefore, organizational development efforts need to be sustained by appropriate changes in every subsystem of the organization.

Values in OD. OD interventions place a high value on two aspects of human behavior: the dignity and worth of a human being, and personal growth and development of each person. Individuals do not exist to serve the organization; organizations are created to serve people. Even though individual behavior must be controlled to some extent for the organization to exist, OD is based on the premise that excessive control should be changed or eliminated to preserve the dignity of the individual. OD interventions view the individual as a growing and developing person progressing toward self-actualization and self-improvement. Helping people to attain high levels of maturity and growth is an important aspect of OD interventions.

Change Agents

OD interventions are typically supervised and guided by a person or group of people who serve as facilitators to the process. These facilitators are typically referred to as *change agents.* They may be either internal or external to the organization, each with its advantages and disadvantages.

Change agent:
A person or persons who serve as a catalyst facilitating an OD intervention.

External Change Agents. An external change agent is typically a consultant or team of consultants who are asked to intervene and help bring about change. Coming from outside the organization allows change agents to see problems objectively, and they can contribute valuable insights from other organizations. Another advantage is that after a feeling of trust has been established, employees are usually more willing to speak openly about sensitive problems and difficulties with an external change agent.

The disadvantage is that external change agents sometimes have difficulty establishing a feeling of trust, and their lack of experience with the organization may prevent them from identifying the root causes of the problems. Coal miners, for example, typically feel that no one can truly understand their problems until they have spent time working underground. Another disadvantage of external change agents is that they are typically inclined to recommend more drastic changes, which may be overly disruptive to the organization.

Managers use external change agents for a variety of purposes to help them perform their work. Normally, external change agents are expected to provide technical assistance and information, or assist in diagnosing and resolving problems. But external change agents are sometimes employed by a company to make unpopular decisions, such as recommending that a branch office be closed, or to perform undesirable chores, such as terminating an employee. Consequently, external change agents are justifiably viewed with suspicion by employees until their motives are clear.

Internal Change Agents. Internal change agents are typically staff employees who have been specifically trained in organizational development. Some companies hire people with graduate degrees in organizational behavior to assist with their change and redesign efforts, but managers and supervisors can be trained as change agents and conduct OD interventions that are designed to improve the functioning of their own units. Internal change agents have the advantage of being familiar with the organization and its personnel, and they can develop long-term, trusting relationships sometimes necessary for successful change. The disadvantage of internal change agents is that they are often viewed as agents of management who are primarily interested in the good of the company rather than the good of the workers.

Transfer and Diffusion of Change

All organizational development interventions must contend with two troublesome problems that have limited their usefulness: the transfer-of-training problem, and the intervention-diffusion problem.

Transfer of training:
When the learning that occurs during training transfers back to the actual job setting.

Transfer of Training. The *transfer-of-training* problem refers to the difficulty of transferring the learning and changes in behavior that are achieved during the training situation back to the work environment. Training programs, for example, may teach employees new insights and help them acquire new skills, but if they fail to use these skills when they return to the job, the training is ineffective. The transfer-of-training problem was a serious problem that limited the success of early sensitivity training programs. Participants returned from their sensitivity training and quickly reverted back to their former behavior patterns.

OD interventions and training experiences need to be designed to reduce the transfer-of-training problem. Evidence indicates that positive transfer is most likely to occur in the following situations:

1. When the learning environment is similar to the actual work environment.
2. When the new skills, attitudes, and behaviors are supported and modeled by other individuals.
3. When the new learning is perceived as useful in the work environment.
4. When participants are allowed to practice their new behaviors in the training.
5. When participants are evaluated and rewarded for their new behavior on the job.

Diffusion:
Extending a change in
one part of the organi-
zation to additional
areas and arranging
for complementary
changes in these areas
to facilitate the change.

Diffusion. The *diffusion* of an OD intervention refers to the extent to which the initial change spreads throughout the organization and produces complementary changes in other individuals or programs. It may be possible, for example, for an OD intervention to have a large impact in one unit without benefitting other units of the organization or making the organization more effective. An otherwise useful intervention may die if diffusion does not occur. The problem of limited diffusion may occur because of resistance within other parts of the organization, or because the sequential process linking one change with subsequent changes was never clearly specified in the beginning. An excellent team-building meeting, for example, may help one group produce more efficiently, but unless corresponding changes can be made in adjacent groups, there may be conflict and no increase in organizational effectiveness.

Several factors contribute to the problems of diffusing of OD interventions:

1. The intervention lacks the support and commitment of top management.
2. Other departments are content with the status quo and feel no pain or dissatisfaction motivating them to accept a change.
3. The reward system does not recognize or reinforce the change.
4. Structural and technological changes necessary to support the change are not made.
5. Other problems are perceived as more pressing.

Evaluating OD

Most of the literature evaluating the effectiveness of OD interventions, especially the early reports, relied on anecdotal observations rather than sound empirical assessments. The literature largely consisted of case studies that were reported by the same people who served as the change agents. One study, reviewing 574 case studies of OD, found that the vast majority were considered successful.[3] These studies included a wide variety of OD interventions, including team building, conflict resolution, survey feedback, and process consultation. In contrast, fewer than half of the senior executives in Fortune 500 companies reported in a survey that their change initiatives were successful. Not surprisingly, they said the major barrier to success was employee resistance to adopting new ways. They also said that the main impetus for achieving successful change was a change in management, which was not something they were likely to recommend.[4]

Over the years, the quality of the research evaluating OD has improved, and a growing number of change efforts have been evaluated with acceptable experimental or quasi-experimental designs. One study examined the results of almost 100 research studies and concluded that the results were quite encouraging.[5] Eleven types of OD interventions were included in this review, and they all had generally positive effects on various performance measures, such as output, turnover, absenteeism, and grievances. This review concluded that the average improvement, expressed statistically, was an increase of almost one half of a standard deviation unit.

Although most evaluations suggest that OD improves both job performance and worker satisfaction, several studies have found that the perceived changes in the quality of work-life are negative when the change focuses on work redesign and productivity improvements. One review of 56 studies that measured both productivity changes and changes in the self-perceived quality of work-life found substantial positive effects on performance measures but almost uniformly negative changes in quality of work-life.[6] These negative effects were attributed to the performance pressures placed on the workers as a result of the *action levers* and control mechanisms implemented as part of the change.[7]

A crucial question concerning the favorable conclusions regarding OD research is whether the change is caused by the OD intervention itself or by the self-fulfilling prophecy. OD interventions are implemented with the expectation that they will improve organizational functioning; therefore, positive results should be obtained, because of the self-fulfilling prophecy, even if the intervention is worthless. At least one study has found that an OD intervention improved actual performance measures when those involved were led by the experimenter to expect it to, whereas the same intervention failed when organizational members were led not to expect strong positive results.[8] Very few studies have attempted to control for the effects of the self-fulfilling prophecy, but it seems safe to conclude that it has contributed importantly to the positive results of OD.

A study of the benefit of team building in the Israeli military controlled for the effects of the self-fulfilling prophecy by creating success expectations for both the experimental and control groups. The results indicated that the team-building intervention significantly improved the teamwork and conflict handling of the experimental groups more than the control groups.[9] Therefore, even though the self-fulfilling prophecy may contribute importantly to the success of OD interventions, it appears that the interventions also make an important contribution to organizational functioning.

OD INTERVENTIONS

OD Intervention:
A series of structured activities designed to improve the functioning of an organization or subgroup.

An *OD intervention* is a set of structured activities designed to improve some aspect of organizational functioning. The set of activities does not have to be a rigid procedure; most OD interventions involve only a loosely defined sequence of activities that are adapted to the situation. A convenient way to classify OD interventions is according to the group for which they are intended. The major targets to be considered here are (1) interpersonal relationships, (2) group processes, (3) intergroup processes, and (4) the total organization. Some interventions are appropriate for more than one target, but most interventions are specifically designed to create change at one of these target areas. Some of the most prominent interventions for each target are described here, but many additional interventions are described in the literature.

Interpersonal Interventions

Interpersonal interventions are directed primarily toward individual learning, insight, and skill building. They are designed to improve the effectiveness of individuals and to contribute to personal growth and adjustment.

Coaching and Counseling. An organization's formal performance appraisal system should provide feedback to employees regarding their performance.

This information, however, is often inadequate because it does not tell a person what to do differently. A skilled observer is needed to identify problems and to suggest new behaviors. Usually the skilled observer is an external consultant who is able to take a fresh look at the situation. The consultant must be highly trained in observing human behavior, and must know which behaviors are inappropriate. The role of the consultant is to respond to such questions as "What do you think I should do in this instance to improve my performance?" or "Now that I can see some areas for improvement, how can I change my behavior?" Management education programs could be viewed as OD interventions of *coaching and counseling.*

Sensitivity Training. Sensitivity training (or T-groups, with "T" standing for training) basically consists of unstructured group discussions by a small face-to-face group of not more than 12 to 15 people. The focus of the discussions is on the "here and now" as opposed to what has happened in the past. The here and now consists mostly of the feelings and emotions of the group members. Group members share their perceptions of each other and describe the attributes they admire in one another and the things that irritate them.

A trainer is usually present during sensitivity training, but not in a leadership role. The trainer usually refuses either to lead the group or to recognize other forms of leadership or status among group members, such as organizational position. Typically, no activities or topics of discussion are planned, although short questionnaires are sometimes used at the beginning to encourage participants to think about themselves and reveal their feelings to others. When the participants are asked to respond to a questionnaire as a means of facilitating the session, these sessions are referred to as *instrumented T-group* sessions.

The lack of structure in a T-group often creates feelings of frustration and expressions of hostility, and some members attempt to organize the group. These attempts usually fail, however, and the group ultimately discusses why some members felt the need for structure. The ambiguity and frustration created in a T-group are not undesirable, since they force the participants to respond to new situations and help them obtain greater self-insight. The primary objectives of sensitivity training are improved self-insight and self-awareness, increased sensitivity to the feelings and behaviors of others, and greater awareness of the processes that facilitate or inhibit group functioning.

Because of its popularity during the 1960s, T-group training stimulated much research and controversy. The research generally indicated that T-group training had a significant influence on changing interpersonal behavior, but the direction of the change was unclear.[10] Some participants said the change they experienced was not desirable. Empirical research found both positive and negative results. Most participants indicated that their T-group experience increased their interpersonal skills and made them more aware of others. However, some described it as a threatening experience that left them feeling inadequate and destroyed their self-confidence.

Sensitivity training continues to be used to help people improve their interpersonal competence, but it is generally not appropriate when the target of change is the organization or intergroup processes. Other interventions are more effective at creating change at those levels.[11] The transfer-of-training problem, a serious problem that limits the value of sensitivity training, has

Coaching and counseling:
An interpersonal OD intervention that provides feedback and insights to help individuals in their personal development.

Sensitivity training:
Unstructured group discussions in which group members share their perceptions and feelings of each other and of what is happening in the organization.

Instrumented T-group:
Sensitivity training that uses a questionnaire to facilitate the discussion.

already been noted. To overcome this problem, "stranger T-groups" were replaced by "family T-groups" where the participants were members of an organizational family (a supervisor and his or her immediate subordinates).

Process Consultation. No organization operates perfectly, and managers often realize that there are problems but don't know precisely what caused them or how to solve them. Consultants are frequently asked to help managers diagnose organizational problems and evaluate alternative solutions. *Process consultation* refers to activities on the part of a consultant that help the client perceive, understand, and alter the processes occurring in the organization.

Like sensitivity training, process consultation assumes that organizational effectiveness can be improved by resolving interpersonal problems. However, process consultation is much more task-oriented than sensitivity training. A process consultant observes the interactions between the client and other people and helps the client understand these interactions. The consultant does not solve the organization's problems but serves as a coach advising the client on the processes and interpersonal relationships that need improvement.

One major role of a successful process consultant is to teach the client how to diagnose group activities and interpersonal relationships. Process consultation is a joint effort in diagnosing and solving problems with the goal of helping managers acquire problem-solving skills they can use after the consultant is gone. Process consultation often occurs as a one-on-one coaching process in which the consultant observes the interactions of a manager in meetings, interviews, and conversations, and tries to help the manager understand what occurred, and how the interactions could be improved.

Process consultation:
An interpersonal intervention in which a consultant helps to diagnose and improve organizational processes.

Group Interventions

The OD interventions that focus on group functioning receive the most attention, because of the significant influence that groups exerts on the behavior and attitudes of group members, and because much of the work in today's organizations is accomplished through groups. Both organizational effectiveness and the quality of work life are influenced greatly by how well a group functions.

Studies in group dynamics have identified some of the characteristics of an effective work group. In an effective group, there is a norm of cooperation and teamwork. The members communicate with each other openly, without defensiveness. Everyone participates in task-relevant discussions, and members listen well to one another. Decisions are usually based on consensus rather than organizational position or a majority vote. The decisions and group goals are widely accepted. Conflict and disagreement are not necessarily eliminated, but they are focused on ideas and methods rather than on personalities; and they stimulate creative problem solving.

Effective teams help their members satisfy their personal needs while cooperating to achieve the group's goal. Sometimes employees want to improve their groups but do not know what to do. Individual efforts to create a more effective group are often resisted by other group members and only create more antagonism and conflict. Successful group interventions usually require the involvement of all group members. Four of the most popular group interventions include (1) the group diagnostic meeting, (2) the team-building meeting, (3) the role analysis technique (RAT), and (4) responsibility charting.

Group diagnostic meeting:
A group meeting that allows members of the group to identify problems confronting the group, and prioritize them.

Group Diagnostic Meetings. *Group diagnostic meetings* are usually held by organizational "family" groups consisting of a supervisor and his or her immediate subordinates. The purpose of the diagnostic meeting is not to solve problems but simply to identify them and decide which are the most crucial. Solutions come later, and may involve further interventions.

Group diagnostic meetings usually require an outside consultant to facilitate the discussion; however, supervisors can serve just as well if they possess adequate interpersonal skills and are not overly defensive. Being able to conduct a group diagnostic meeting is a valuable supervisory skill, but it is easy for a supervisor to feel defensive during the meeting, since the discussion focuses on such questions as: "What are we doing right?" "What are we doing wrong?" "Are we taking advantage of our opportunities?" "What problems do we need to address?" "How good are our relationships with each other?"

A group diagnostic meeting consists of an open discussion of the group's problems. If there are intense hostilities or the group is too large for everyone to participate, the group may be divided into small subgroups. The subgrouping could be as small as peers who interview each other and then report to the total group. Typically, the problems are written on a chalkboard or on large pieces of paper taped to the walls. The group members discuss the problems, sharing their feelings about the cause of each problem and its seriousness.

The outcome of a group diagnostic meeting should be a careful analysis of the group's problems and a priority list that shows which problems are the most crucial. Later interventions may involve the group in generating and implementing solutions to the problems, but the goal of the diagnostic meetings is simply diagnosis. If the group members discuss the problems, sharing their feelings about the cause of each problem and its seriousness, many problems can be resolved without further interventions.

Team building:
An OD intervention that attempts to build a more cohesive work group by having the group create better communication, better decision making, improved personal interactions, and greater goal accomplishment.

Team-Building Meetings. The goal of a *team-building meeting* is to build a better functioning team. This goal includes greater goal accomplishment and improved group processes, such as better communication, decision making, personal interactions, and problem solving. Group processes tend to improve as a byproduct of learning to solve problems that prevent the group from achieving its goals.[12]

Most team-building meetings involve getting the work group together, away from the workplace, for an extended period of time, such as one to three days. The group identifies the important problems, usually with the help of a consultant or an outside facilitator. As these problems are discussed, alternative solutions are developed and evaluated. The outcome of the meeting should be a carefully planned procedure that identifies the action steps and specifies who will do what and when. This plan should be a realistic solution that is acceptable to all group members. If the meeting is dominated by a leader, the action plan probably will not be accepted by the group, nor will the group function as a coordinated team. All team members should be involved in the discussions, and all the decisions should be reached by consensus rather than majority vote.

Role Analysis Technique. An organizational role consists of the task assignments and responsibilities of a particular job. A role also involves relationships with other jobs, and these relationships must be understood if the roles are to

RAT intervention (Role analysis technique):
An intervention designed to clarify the roles and responsibilities of key employees.

Focal role:
The central role being evaluated in a role analysis technique intervention.

Responsibility charting:
An intervention that clarifies the responsibilities of group members for each decision in terms of initiating action, approving or vetoing, providing resources, or being informed.

be performed effectively. The *role analysis technique (RAT)* is designed to reduce the uncertainty surrounding an employee's task assignments and responsibilities. Although the RAT intervention is used most frequently for managerial jobs, it can be used to clarify the responsibilities of any job. It is particularly applicable when new teams are created or when a new member is added to an established team. The result of an effective RAT intervention should be the creation of well written job descriptions that are understood by all group members.

The RAT intervention defines the requirements of a *focal role*, that is, the role being examined. This intervention basically has two steps. The first step consists of the person in the focal role defining the essential functions of his or her job—what it entails, why it exists, and what its place is in achieving the organization's goals. The specific duties are listed on a chalkboard and discussed by the entire group. Responsibilities are added and deleted until the role incumbent and the group are satisfied with the description. The second step consists of clarifying the expectations that the focal role person has of others. These expectations are likewise listed and discussed until the group and the role incumbent agree on them. RAT interventions focus on one role at a time, and it is usually wise to repeat the process until all crucial roles in the group have been clarified. Role confusion can be a serious cause of conflict in a work group.

Responsibility Charting. The effectiveness of a work group depends on the quality of decisions that are made, how carefully they are implemented, and whether task assignments and other responsibilities are carefully delegated and clearly understood. *Responsibility charting* is an intervention that helps to clarify who is responsible for which decisions and actions.

The first step in responsibility charting is to construct a matrix. The types of decisions and classes of actions that need to be taken are placed along the left side of the matrix, and the group members are listed across the top of the matrix, as shown in Exhibit 20.1. The second step is to determine how each actor should be involved in each of the decisions. If a group member is totally removed from a particular decision, such noninvolvement is indicated by a dash in that cell of the matrix.

| R | Responsibility (initiates) | | S | Support (put resources against) | | |
| A-V | Approval (right to veto) | | I | Inform (to be informed) | | |

Decisions	Karen	Jill	Ken	Bob	Dick	Janet
Advertise jobs	R	I	—	S	—	A-V
Screen applicants	I	R	I	I	—	A-V
Interview applicants	I	I	R	—	S	S
Contact references	—	I	R	—	S	S
Make job referrals	I	I	—	I	S	R
Update data files	—	R	—	—	—	A-V
Administer tests	—	I	—	—	R	S

Exhibit 20.1 **Responsibility Chart for an Employment Office**

Most decisions should be the responsibility of only one person, in order to maintain personal accountability. The authority to approve or veto a decision should also be limited, because it is too time-consuming to get approval from a large group. Furthermore, if one individual is involved in too many approval-veto roles, that person could become a bottleneck inhibiting the group's progress. One of the immediate insights that usually comes from responsibility charting is the realization that many decisions are not adequately supported by enough people. People like having the authority to approve or veto decisions, but providing the necessary support is not as popular.

Intergroup Interventions

Conflict and tension between two groups typically produce undesirable consequences for an organization. Each group pursues its self-serving goals, with little regard for the success of the other groups or the total organization. Communication between the two groups becomes distorted or is completely severed. Each group blames the other for problems and justifies its own actions. Gradually the other group is viewed as an enemy and perceived in terms of negative stereotypes. The groups may even resort to acts of sabotage or violence, and each group may become more interested in damaging the other group than in pursuing its own goals. The typical conflict between union and management is an excellent example of intergroup conflict. The causes and consequences of intergroup conflict and some of the strategies for resolving it were discussed in an earlier chapter.

Finding a Common Enemy. This strategy involves finding an outside object or group that both groups dislike. Fighting a common enemy forces the groups to coordinate their efforts in order to achieve success. An example of a common enemy in union-management conflict is government regulation that threatens to eliminate jobs, or foreign competition that threatens to dominate the industry.

Joint Activities. In pursuing joint activities, the groups are required to interact and communicate with each other. Although the initial interaction may be a bit strained, increased interaction under favorable conditions tends to create positive feelings toward members of the other group. Pursuing joint activities is especially effective in reducing conflict when there is a goal that both groups desire to achieve that neither can obtain without the help of the other. Some examples of joint activities that have helped to resolve labor-management conflicts are quality-of-work-life programs.

Rotating Membership. This strategy consists of moving members from one group to the other. The expectation is that the transferred members will be able to share their feelings with the new group and help the groups understand each other better. This strategy has helped to improve international relationships by having foreign student exchanges. In union-management relations, this strategy has been limited mostly to promoting union members into management. A small number of managers have also been demoted to union member status. The evidence indicates that employee attitudes are strongly influenced by their group membership. When they were union members, they held pro-union attitudes; when they became managers, they adopted pro-management attitudes; and when they were demoted back to union status, they reverted again to pro-union attitudes. Apparently, the forces that create intergroup conflict can be very powerful.[13]

Conflict Resolution Meetings. Another strategy for resolving intergroup conflict involves a series of steps that gradually bring the groups together to share feelings and to engage in joint problem solving. The first step usually involves bringing the leaders of both groups together to give them instructions and to gain their commitment to seek better cooperation. In the second step, the two groups meet alone to develop two lists. Each group describes its feelings about the other group in one list, and then indicates what it thinks the other group is saying about it in the other list. In the third step, the groups come together and share lists. Discussion is limited to questions for clarification; justifications and explanations are not allowed. In the fourth step, the groups move toward a joint problem-solving session if they are ready for it. The number of steps in this intervention should be influenced by the degree of conflict. The groups should not be brought together in open discussion until they are ready to focus on the issues without having to defend themselves or blame one another. They continue to share lists until the hostility is diffused.

Group conflict may be caused by substantive issues, emotional issues, or both. Substantive issues are disagreements over policies and practices, competition for scarce resources, or differing expectations about role relationships. Emotional issues include negative feelings caused by resentment, distrust, and anger. The conflict resolution meetings should focus on the relevant issues. If conflict exists over substantive issues, the meeting should include problem solving and negotiation. If conflict exists over emotional issues, the meeting should focus on restructuring attitudes and discussing negative feelings.

Organizational Interventions

The preceding interventions can be used throughout a company to change the entire organization. Sensitivity training and team-building sessions, for example, could start with top management groups and cascade down to successively lower levels in the organizational hierarchy until every member has participated. In a family group, everyone would participate as both a subordinate and as a supervisor except for the lowest levels, which would participate only as subordinates. These sessions could focus on goal setting, task redesign, role clarifications, group processes, performance evaluation, or whatever the problems happen to be. If they were successfully held at each level of the organization, these sessions could greatly increase the effectiveness of the organization by identifying problems, resolving conflicts, creating shared goals, and clarifying accountability for individuals and groups.

Vision and mission statements facilitate organizational change by providing guidance and direction. Organizational change frequently requires people to do things differently—to change directions, to pursue other goals, or to perform different functions. To get people to march to the beat of a different drummer, it helps to have a clear signal coming from the new drummer. Vision and mission statements provide a shared direction that helps align the efforts of many members behind a common idea that energizes and excites them.

Organizational interventions do not necessarily have to start at the top. An alternative is to start at the periphery and move toward the corporate core by putting employees into a new corporate context that imposes new roles and responsibilities on them. This approach to change focuses on task alignment and the development of a shared vision. A new corporate culture emerges over time as new policies and systems become institutionalized.

Although most interventions can be implemented throughout the entire organization, some interventions are considered company-wide interventions. These interventions are called *comprehensive interventions* because they usually involve the entire organization and are implemented throughout a company. Five of the most widely known comprehensive interventions include (1) survey feedback, (2) structural interventions, (3) sociotechnical system design, (4) total quality management, and (5) cultural interventions.

Survey Feedback. Survey feedback interventions consist of two activities. The first is administering the attitude survey to assess the opinions of employees. The second is reporting the data back to members of the organization, analyzing what they say, and using them to design corrective actions.

When survey feedback is used as an OD intervention, everyone participates in providing information and reviewing the data (rather than just top management, as with the typical opinion survey). Each group is the first to receive a report on its own group attitudes; the data are used to identify problems and diagnose the organization. During the feedback session, the groups engage in problem-solving activities to correct problems and to increase organizational effectiveness.

Survey feedback interventions have been used successfully by many organizations, but their success depends primarily on three factors. The first factor is the commitment of organizational members to each other and the success of the organization. They must be willing to share their feelings and participate openly in the feedback and problem-solving sessions. Second, top management must support the intervention and create an open environment so that employees feel their efforts are worthwhile. Finally, the questionnaire must address the major issues and accurately assess employee feelings. The development of a good questionnaire is a creative endeavor that usually requires some preliminary interviewing to make certain it focuses on relevant employee concerns. Part of a questionnaire used in survey feedback is shown in Exhibit 20.2.

A questionnaire developed by Rensis Likert measuring System One versus *System Four* managerial styles is especially useful for survey feedback interventions because it focuses on vital organizational variables. Likert argued that an autocratic, exploitative, System One management style was not as effective as a participative, democratic, employee-centered System Four management style. Likert collected extensive data to support his argument that organizations become more effective as they move from a System One to a System Four style of management.[14] Members of the organization are asked to describe the current style of management using a questionnaire. This questionnaire focuses specifically on the dimensions of management style that Likert's research indicates are important determinants of organizational effectiveness, such as leadership, motivation, communication, decision making, goal setting, and control.

Comprehensive interventions:
Interventions that influence the entire organization, such as survey feedback or a structural change.

Survey feedback intervention:
Collecting survey data from the members of an organization and letting them use this information to make appropriate changes.

Exhibit 20.2 Questionnaire Used for Survey Feedback

	Strongly Disagree			Neither			Strongly Agree
1. Considering everything about the company, I'm very well satisfied with it.	1	2	3	4	5	6	7
2. People in top management respect my personal rights.	1	2	3	4	5	6	7
3. The company frequently expects me to do things that are not reasonable.	1	2	3	4	5	6	7
4. I have a lot of confidence in the business judgment of top management.	1	2	3	4	5	6	7
5. There's a friendly feeling between the employees and management.	1	2	3	4	5	6	7
6. Management usually keeps us informed about the things we want to know.	1	2	3	4	5	6	7
7. The company tries to unfairly take advantage of its employees.	1	2	3	4	5	6	7
8. This company is a good one for a person trying to get ahead.	1	2	3	4	5	6	7
9. The company offers good opportunities for self-improvement.	1	2	3	4	5	6	7
10. Management is not very interested in the feelings of the employees.	1	2	3	4	5	6	7
11. I know exactly what's expected in my job.	1	2	3	4	5	6	7
12. The employees frequently don't know what they're supposed to be doing.	1	2	3	4	5	6	7
13. This company is a better place to work than most companies around here.	1	2	3	4	5	6	7
14. The jobs in this company are well organized and coordinated.	1	2	3	4	5	6	7
15. There is a lot of time and effort wasted in this company because of poor planning.	1	2	3	4	5	6	7

Structural changes: Such changes as altering the departmentalization, span of control, or reporting relationships.

Structural Change. Perhaps the easiest and fastest way to change an organization is to alter its structure. Structural changes include such changes as altering the span of control, changing the basis of departmentalization, revising the authority system by creating a different hierarchical reporting relationship, or revising the organization's policies. These changes often have an enormous and relatively permanent impact on individual behavior and organizational functioning. A structural change is often suggested as part of the problem solving and action planning of other OD interventions, but it could also be a unilateral decision of top management. Some examples of structural changes include:

■ Moving a job from one department to another
■ Reducing a supervisor's span of control
■ Dividing a large department into two smaller departments
■ Transferring an entire department to a different division (such as taking security out of the human resource department and assigning it to the operations division)
■ Creating a new department to centralize a particular function (such as creating a word-processing center rather than allowing managers to have personal secretaries)

- Reorganizing an entire organization along different lines (such as eliminating the management, finance, accounting, and economics departments within a college of business and assigning the faculty instead to undergraduate or graduate degree programs)

In recent years some companies have experimented with new structural arrangements to respond to a rapidly changing environment. Many companies have used a project structure in which employees are assigned to work on special projects under the direction of the project leader, but they retain their memberships in their original departments while they work on the project. During this time, they report to two supervisors.

Because an organization's structure has a strong influence on its effectiveness, structural changes can have a significant and immediate impact. Therefore, the structure of an organization must be periodically evaluated. Frequent changes in the structure can create confusion, but an obsolete structure can place a serious constraint on organizational effectiveness.

Sociotechnical system redesign:
A type of work redesign that recognizes the importance of balancing the social needs of employees with the technical demands of the work process, such as creating autonomous work groups that manage themselves.

Greenfield:
A startup company with a new plant and equipment and a new workforce.

Sociotechnical System Design. A sociotechnical system intervention could involve any change in either the social or technical systems of an organization; however, sociotech interventions typically involve organizing workers into teams and allowing them to structure their work in the optimal way. Sociotech redesign is especially popular in middle-sized manufacturing and service companies that must be highly responsive to changing customer demands.

Although sociotech interventions can be started in an existing workforce, they are best implemented in a *greenfield*, which is a startup operation with new plant and equipment and a new workforce. The advantage of a greenfield is that the new work environment can be designed to maximize both productive efficiency and optimal social interaction. Machines, desks, partitions, and other physical design features can be arranged to facilitate the flow of work and the needs of employees.

Sociotech redesign typically involves the formation of autonomous or semiautonomous groups who supervise themselves. The responsibilities of these teams may include selecting and training their own team members; disciplining and terminating team members; administering salary and benefits; ensuring adequate multicultural diversity through affirmative action; budgeting, planning and distributing materials; shipping the end product; evaluating performance; engineering changes; monitoring product quality; maintaining equipment; providing safety and first aid; setting goals; solving problems; and scheduling work.

In most sociotech systems, a strong emphasis is placed on training and skill development. Team members are encouraged to learn how to perform all the jobs in the team so they can rotate freely. Multiskilling is rewarded by the compensation system, which is typically based on a philosophy of pay for knowledge rather than pay for performance. The base rate of pay for each employee is determined by how many skills and work functions the employee can perform.

Research evaluating the effectiveness of sociotechnical system designs has generally been positive.[15] A survey of 17 studies found that sociotech interventions generally increase productivity and the increases are greater when they involve the formation of autonomous rather than semiautonomous groups, when they include increases in monetary incentives, and when they occur in countries other than the United States.[16] However, many sociotech interventions have also failed, and they have been criticized for lacking a clear conceptual focus and for not maintaining a consistent direction or application. There is no model to follow in designing a sociotech system, and sometimes a better balance in the social and technical systems of a company fails to improve productivity or satisfaction.[17]

Total quality management (TQM):

A change strategy that emphasizes flawless quality productivity, continuous improvement, and being responsive to customers.

Total Quality Management (TQM). *Total quality management* is characterized by three primary principles: doing things right the first time, striving for continuous improvement, and being responsive to the interests of customers. TQM interventions involve making quality a major responsibility of all employees. Continuous improvement usually includes working with suppliers to improve the quality of incoming parts and ensuring that manufacturing processes are capable of consistently high quality. Statistical process control (SPC) is a popular TQM technique. SPC involves carefully measuring the production process and using the data to identify problems and monitor quality improvement.

The steps that might be used in a TQM intervention include:

1. Defining the major functions and services that must be performed
2. Determining the customers and suppliers of these services
3. Identifying the customers' requirements, and developing quantitative measures to assess customer satisfaction regarding these requirements
4. Identifying the requirements and measurement criteria that the suppliers to the process must meet
5. Mapping, or flow-charting, the processes that occur within each department and between departments
6. Continuously improving the process with respect to effectiveness, quality, cycle time, and cost

TQM interventions are often combined with other production management interventions, such as just-in-time inventory (JIT) and advanced manufacturing technology (AMT). *Just-in-time inventory control* is a set of practices for reducing lead time and inventory. Its name derives from the practice of receiving or producing each subcomponent just in time for it to be used in the next step of production. JIT is usually associated with a "kanban" replenishment system. A kanban is a ticket in a container of parts that initiates the production of more parts so they will arrive just before the container is empty.

Advanced manufacturing technology includes a variety of computerized technologies, such as computer-aided manufacturing (CAM) and computer-aided process planning (CAPP). These technologies have facilitated the use of robots in the assembly process and have greatly increased both productivity and quality.

TQM interventions have produced mixed results. Some companies have reported tremendous success, and credited TQM for their competitive advantage, such as Motorola, Xerox, Federal Express, and Harley-Davidson. In other companies, however, TQM failed to produce the anticipated spectacular results. Florida Power & Light implemented what appeared to be a successful TQM project and won Japan's Deming Prize for quality management. However, worker complaints of excessive paperwork prompted Florida Power to slash its program. Likewise, the Wallace Company, a Houston oil supply company that won the Commerce Department's Malcolm Baldrige National Quality Award, found the honor did not protect it from economic hard times—it had to file for bankruptcy.[18]

Many authors have tried to explain why TQM succeeds or fails, but the advice is mostly anecdotal. The most popular suggestions call for employee training and the support of top management, but these suggestions did not guarantee success for Douglas Aircraft. After two years, Douglas Aircraft's TQM program was in shambles in spite of extensive preparation and training, which included two-week training seminars for its 8,000 employees.[19] These failures highlight the need for more information about how to involve employees in a successful quality program. The total quality movement is important to organizational success, and better research is needed to identify when and how to implement TQM interventions.

Cultural interventions:

An intervention that attempts to diagnose the current culture of the organization and either clarify it or change it.

Cultural Interventions. It has been suggested that significant changes in organizational structures or processes require concurrent changes in the organization's culture, and that formal change in the way the organization operates will endure only if consistent changes occur at the informal level of interpersonal relations and social expectations. Unless there is a cultural change, formal changes will be resisted. Organizational stories and myths that legitimize and rationalize a change strategy have been shown to contribute greatly to the acceptance of change, because these stories (1) create a new organizational image and identity, (2) reward new behaviors, (3) facilitate organizational diagnosis, (4) establish new standards of behavior, and (5) serve as an effective source of social control.

Cultural interventions are the most difficult interventions to implement, and some scholars question whether organizational culture can even be changed by a conscious change strategy. The culture of an organization consists of the shared feelings, beliefs, and expectations of members within the organization. These variables are not physically observable and can only be inferred indirectly by observing members of the organization and talking with them. Nevertheless, it is possible to change an organization's culture even though the process is slow and the desired outcome may be an evolving target. The steps of a cultural change intervention were explained in chapter 14.

Discussion Questions

1. What is a team-building meeting? Identify a group in which you are a member and explain how you would conduct a team-building meeting for this group. Develop an agenda and list the issues you would discuss.
2. Explain one of these OD interventions: Role Analysis Technique or Responsibility Charting. Apply one of these interventions to a position you hold in a group by making a list of your duties (for a RAT intervention) or responsibilities (for Responsibility Charting). Comment on how much agreement you think there would be regarding your list among other members of your group.

Notes

1. Wendell L. French and Cecil H. Bell, Jr., "A Brief History of Organization Development," *Journal of Contemporary Business* (Summer 1972): 1–8.
2. Eric L. Trist and Kenneth W. Bamforth, "Some Social and Psychological Consequences of the Longwall Method of Co-getting," *Human Relations* 4 (1951): 3–38; Eric L. Trist, "The Assumptions of Ordinariness as a Denial Mechanism: Innovation and Conflict in a Coal Mine," *Human Resource Management* 28 (Summer 1989): 253–64.
3. R.T. Golembiewski, C.W. Proehl, and D. Sink, "Estimating the Success of OD Applications," *Training and Development Journal* 36 (April, 1982).
4. William A. Schienann, "Why Change Fails," *Across the Board* 29 (April 1992): 53–54.
5. R.A. Guzzo, R.D. Jette, and R.A. Katzell, "The Effects of Psychologically Based Intervention Programs on Worker Productivity: A Meta-Analysis," *Personnel Psychology* 38 (1985): 275–91.
6. B.A. Macy, H. Izumi, C.C.M. Hurts, and L.W. Norton, "Meta-Analysis of United States Empirical Organizational Change and Work Innovation Field Experiments" (Paper presented at the National Academy of Management Meetings, Chicago, 1986).
7. See Marshall Sashkin and W. Warner Burke, "Organization Development in the 1980's," *Journal of Management* 13 (1987): 393–417.
8. A.S. King, "Expectation Effects of Organizational Change," *Administrative Science Quarterly* 19 (1974): 221–30.
9. Dov Eden, "Team Development: Quasi-Experimental Confirmation Among Combat Companies," *Group and Organization Studies* 11, 3 (1986): 133–46.
10. John P. Campbell and Marvin D. Dunnette, "Effectiveness of T-Group Experiences in Managerial Training and Development," *Psychological Bulletin* 70, 2 (August 1968): 73–104.
11. Eric Berne, *Games People Play* (New York: Grove Press, 1964); Eric Berne, *Transactional Analysis and Psychotherapy* (New York: Grove Press, 1961).
12. William G. Dyer, *Team Building: Issues and Alternatives*, 2nd ed. (Reading, MA: Addison-Wesley, 1987).
13. Seymour Liberman, "The Effects of Changes in Roles on the Attitudes of Role Occupants," *Human Relations* 9 (1956): 385–402.
14. Rensis Likert, *New Pattern of Management* (New York: McGraw-Hill, 1961); Rensis Likert, *The Human Organization* (New York: McGraw-Hill, 1967).
15. Rupert F. Chisholm, "Introducing Advanced Information Technology into Public Organizations," *Public Productivity Review* 11 (Summer 1988): 39–56.
16. Rafik I. Beekun, "Accessing the Effectiveness of Sociotechnical Interventions: Antidote for Fad?" *Human Relations* 42 (1989): 877–97.
17. Bob Maton, "Socio-technical Systems: Conceptual and Implementation Problems," *Industrial Relations* 43 (1988): 869–87.
18. J. Matthews and Peter Katel, "The Cost of Quality: Faced With Hard Times, Business Sours on 'Total Quality Management,'" *Newsweek*, (7 Sept 92), pp. 48–49.
19. Ibid.; Gilbert Fuchsberg, "'Total Quality' is Termed only Partial Success," *The Wall Street Journal*, (1 Oct 92), p. B1

Tomahawk Industries

Tomahawk Industries manufactures motor boats primarily used for water skiing. During the summer months, a third production line is normally created to help meet the heavy summer demand. This third line is usually created by assigning the experienced workers to all three lines and hiring college students who are home for summer vacation to complete the crews. In the past, however, experienced workers resented having to break up their teams to form a third line. They also resented having to work with a bunch of college kids, and complained that they were slow and arrogant.

The foreman, Dan Jensen, decided to try a different strategy this summer and have all the college students work on the new line. He asked Mark Allen to supervise the new crew because Mark claimed that he knew everything about boats and could perform every job "with my eyes closed." Mark was happy to accept the new job and participated in selecting his own crew. Mark's crew was called "the Greek Team" because all the college students were members of a fraternity or sorority.

Mark spent many hours in training to get his group running at full production. The college students learned quickly, and by the end of June their production rate was up to standard, with an error rate that was only slightly above normal. To simplify the learning process, Dan Jensen assigned the Greek Team long production runs that generally consisted of 30 to 40 identical units. Thus the training period was shortened and errors were reduced. Shorter production runs were assigned to the experienced teams.

By the middle of July, a substantial rivalry had been created between the Greek Team and the older workers. At first, the rivalry was good-natured. But after a few weeks, the older workers became resentful of the remarks made by the college students. The Greek Team often met its production schedules with time to spare at the end of the day for goofing around. It wasn't uncommon for someone from the Greek Team to go to another line pretending to look for materials just to make demeaning comments. The experienced workers resented having to perform all the shorter production runs, and began to retaliate with sabotage. They would sneak over during breaks and hide tools, dent materials, install something crooked, and in other small ways do something that would slow production for the Greek Team.

Dan felt good about his decision to form a separate crew of college students, but when he heard reports of sabotage and rivalry, he became very concerned. Because of complaints from the experienced workers, Dan equalized the production so that all of the crews had similar production runs. The rivalry, however, did not stop. The Greek Team continued to finish early and flaunt their performance in front of the other crews.

One day the Greek Team suspected that one of their assemblies was going to be sabotaged during the lunch break by one of the experienced crews. By skillful deception, they were able to substitute an assembly from the other experienced line for theirs. By the end of the lunch period, the Greek Team was laughing wildly because of their deception, while one experienced crew was very angry with the other one.

Dan Jensen decided that the situation had to be changed and announced that the job assignments between the different crews would be shuffled. The employees were told that when they appeared for work the next morning, the names of the workers assigned to each crew would be posted on the bulletin board. The announcement was not greeted with much enthusiasm, and Mark Allen decided to stay late to try to talk Dan out of his idea. Mark didn't believe the rivalry was serious enough for this type of action, and he suspected that many of the college students would quit if their team was broken up.

Questions

1. Is the relationship between the teams healthy competition or unhealthy conflict?
2. What are the reasons for the conflict, and how could the conditions be changed to reduce the conflict?
3. Is reassigning members to the different teams a useful way to resolve the conflict? What types of consequences will this likely create?

Group Effectiveness

The simplest way to evaluate group effectiveness is to simply ask each member, "How well does your group function as a percentage of how well you think it could function?" Group problems could then be diagnosed by asking members to explain why their estimates were not higher or lower.

A more sensitive method of assessing a group is to ask members to evaluate it according to the characteristics of an effective group. Use the following scale to evaluate your group on each of the 11 characteristics below.

Strongly Agree	Agree	Neutral	Disagree	Strongly Disagree
4	3	2	1	0

1. The relationships between group members are close and friendly and they are loyal to the group.
2. Everyone participates equally in the group activities and there is a supportive atmosphere.
3. All group members accept the objectives of the group and are committed to them.
4. Group members are willing to listen to each other and they are not afraid to offer ideas.
5. Conflict and disagreement are used to improve the group and conflict is dealt with and resolved.
6. Everyone has an opportunity to participate in making group decisions.
7. Group members receive accurate and timely feedback about their performance and use it to improve.
8. Members feel free to express their feelings openly on all relevant topics.
9. Task assignments are clearly delegated and willingly accepted.
10. Leaders are selected by the group and leadership functions are shared among group members.
11. The group is conscious of its own operations, and monitors and improves these processes.

Scoring: Add the points for these 11 items to obtain a score for your group. Scores greater than 35 indicate highly effective groups. Scores below 20 indicate dysfunctional groups. What can your group do to become more effective?

Improving Your Own Effectiveness

Chapter Outline

Managing Yourself
    Career Success
    Career Choice
    Maintaining Your Competence
    Work and Family
Stress Management
    Mental Health
    Physiology of Stress
    Stress Management Methods

MANAGING YOURSELF

All of us are responsible for managing our own careers and maintaining our competence. A useful metaphor is to view ourselves as the chief executive officer of a one-person company responsible for our own strategy formulation, product development, manufacturing, marketing, and public relations. As the environment around us changes we must be prepared to adapt to assure the survival of our company.

Career Success

Career:

Each individual's work-related experiences.

A *career* is best viewed as a process of work-related experiences that include both paid and unpaid work in one or more organizations or self-employed. In essence, everyone who works has a career. Some people join an organization early in their careers and remain until retirement. Others make significant changes by either changing companies or changing their entire vocations. Nevertheless, everyone experiences a unique sequence of work activities.

Everyone wants to be successful. Career success or failure is best evaluated by the person whose career is being considered rather than by the opinions of others. Deciding whether we have achieved success is difficult because career effectiveness can be measured in many ways. The most popular methods of measuring career success are career performance, satisfaction, adaptability, and identity.

1. *Career performance.* Career performance is measured by the popular symbols of success: money and position. Financial indicators include salary, pay increases, bonuses, and executive perks. Evidence of position and status includes the number of people you supervise, the size of the budget you manage, the revenue generated by the organizational unit you supervise, and the level of your position on the organizational chart.

2. *Satisfaction.* Since you make your own career decisions, you should decide whether you like what you do. This criterion is entirely subjective. You decide for yourself whether you are satisfied.

3. *Adaptability.* Since jobs are continually changing, another measure of career success is how well you adapt to the new demands. According to this criterion, career success is measured by maintaining the technical competence needed to adapt to new changes. Adaptability comes from acquiring new skills and knowledge through such activities as self-training, continuing education seminars, job rotation, and independent study.

4. *Career Identity.* Career identity refers to the integration of your work activity and your self-esteem. Each of us has a sense of identity that defines who we are. Therefore, an important measure of career success is whether your daily occupation is consistent with your identity. A woman who thinks of herself as an interior decorator and is working in such a position would feel that she has a successful career. On the other hand, an individual would be considered to have an unsuccessful career if, when he was asked what he did, said, "I'm a clarinet player but I don't have time to join an orchestra because I have to work at the mill." The enormous influence of work on self-identity is reflected in the fact that most people, when asked who they are, describe themselves in terms of their occupation.

Individuals differ in terms of how well they plan their careers. Some individuals develop elaborate career plans with specific timetables and clearly defined goals, while others do essentially no planning at all. During the last three or four weeks of spring semester, college placement offices are typically flooded with students who have failed to plan what they want to do after graduation. Other students do an excellent job of managing their careers. They know which careers they want to pursue and they arrange their educational training to prepare them for their careers. Long before graduation they conduct an aggressive job search to find which organizations offer them the best opportunities to fulfill their career aspirations.

The responsibility for career planning belongs to each person. Finding a good job does not just happen; individuals make it happen. People should be responsible for managing their own careers regardless of economic factors influencing the supply and demand of labor. A major ingredient of successful career planning is looking ahead. Finding a good job involves a careful process of assessing one's abilities and interests, becoming aware of job opportunities, preparing an effective resume, locating job opportunities, interviewing prospective employers, and then assessing the job offers. Each of these activities takes time. An individual should begin to look for a job before graduation or before terminating other employment.

Effective career planning benefits both you and your company. For you, the most immediate benefits include a better job, more money, increased responsibility, greater mobility, better use of your skills, and higher productivity. It also provides less tangible benefits, such as increased satisfaction and self-esteem. The development of a career orientation rather than a job orientation is another valuable byproduct of career planning that leads to increased involvement in work, greater exposure and visibility to top management, a better understanding of what is expected, and a broader knowledge of additional areas of career interest.

Career planning benefits organizations by identifying and developing future managers. When competent replacements are available, an organization can adopt a policy of promotion from within that motivates aspiring managers. Career planning activities are designed to nurture employees and increase their capacity to achieve organizational goals. Employees who remain in the same position for an extended period typically become obsolete. Career planning helps to avoid the problems of obsolescence by training employees and stimulating their desires to maintain their job skills.

Career Choices

As their careers unfold, people make numerous career choices. Some of these decisions are irreversible, since early decisions can eliminate options later in life. For example, deciding to drop out of high school virtually eliminates many professional and technical jobs from consideration. However, most career decisions are not permanent—there is little need for anyone to feel locked into a dead-end job. People who are not satisfied with the work they are doing are free to pursue something more suitable.

It is not unusual for individuals to make a significant career change and pursue a totally different line of work. In fact, it has been estimated that the average person will pursue at least three careers during his or her lifetime.

Making a significant career change usually helps individuals acquire new skills, avoid obsolescence, and become more enthusiastic about life and work. A gardening metaphor is used to explain the rejuvenating effects of changing careers in mid-life: individuals who change careers mid-life are called "repotters." The most common motivation for changing careers is to find more meaningful work.[1]

Career decisions involve many choices. Three of the most important choices include (1) occupational choice—selecting a vocation or profession; (2) organizational choice—deciding which company to work for; and (3) job choice—selecting a desirable job.

Occupational Choice. The selection of an occupation is not a decision that is made once and for all at one dramatic point in life. Instead, occupational choices are made and revised repeatedly throughout a person's life. The following variables have been found to influence the kinds of occupations individuals select.

1. *Socio-economic status.* The socio-economic status of parents influences the occupations their children select. Children from higher socio-economic families are more likely to choose careers in law, medicine, or business management than in non-salary professions.[2] Children raised in higher socio-economic level families receive more information about the educational opportunities and professional training required for higher professional occupations. Furthermore, their parents communicate higher expectations about the amount of discipline and study necessary for success.

2. *Race.* Although considerable progress has been made in providing more equal-employment opportunities, a larger proportion of minorities than of whites enter lower-status occupations. This discrepancy occurs even though the vocational preferences (the ideal jobs they would like to have) of minorities and whites are similar. Apparently, minorities are forced to compromise their eventual career choices more often than whites.[3]

3. *Gender.* For many years, certain jobs were classified as either male or female jobs. For example, mining and construction jobs were considered male occupations, while nursing and grade school teaching jobs were considered female occupations. Although significant efforts have been made in recent years to eliminate these stereotypes, cultural norms, child-rearing practices, and other social expectations continue to perpetuate the feeling among many people that certain jobs are primarily intended for a particular gender.

4. *Communities.* Occupational choice is influenced by the occupational structure found in a community. Significant differences have been found between rural and urban locations.[4] Individuals who are reared in rural communities generally aspire to occupations with lower prestige than those from urban communities. These differences have been attributed to the limited educational opportunities found in rural areas and the lack of career information.

5. *Intelligence.* A relationship has been observed between average intelligence levels and occupational choice.[5] For example, taken as a group, individuals in accounting, mechanical engineering, medicine, chemistry,

and electrical engineering have intelligence levels that are slightly above average. Teamsters, miners, farmworkers, and lumberjacks have below-average intelligence, when considered as a group. It should be noted, however, that a broad range of intelligence is found in every occupation.

6. *Aptitudes and interests.* Probably the greatest determinants of occupational choice are aptitudes and interests. Often, we allow our vocational interests to override considerations about our aptitudes and abilities. What we want to do becomes more important than what we are capable of doing best. Indeed, asking young adults what occupation they want to enter is generally the best predictor of their eventual occupation.

These factors have contributed to the occupational preferences of job applicants for a long time; their implications should not be overlooked. Long-term career choices can limit an organization's ability to attract and retain new employees and can influence the effectiveness of recruiting activities. Before a recruiter tries to sell a job opening, the applicants may have already decided that they are not willing to consider it. Consequently, these background variables may represent formidable obstacles to organizations attempting to achieve their affirmative-action goals of hiring a larger percentage of minorities and females. For example, a decision by AT&T to employ women in outdoor crafts jobs was found to be more difficult to execute than anticipated. To achieve its goals, the company had to launch an aggressive educational program in the public schools to convince women that outdoor crafts jobs were a legitimate female occupation.

People who possess special aptitudes and abilities typically try to find occupations where they can use these skills to achieve success in their work. Since occupational success often depends on having the necessary skills, individuals should carefully assess their aptitudes and use this information to make a wise occupational choice. The evidence shows, however, that many individuals do not make very accurate assessments of their abilities. One study found mainly low correlations between the self-evaluations of a group of adolescents and how these individuals were measured on a battery of tests.[6]

Organizational Choice. In addition to choosing an occupation, individuals also choose the organization in which their occupation will be performed. Three characteristics seem to influence organizational choice: the organization's mission, its image, and its culture or personality.

1. *Organizational mission.* Organizations serve a variety of social purposes, and individuals may be attracted to an organization because of its mission. People tend to select companies whose missions are consistent with their career interests. For example, individuals with social interests may prefer occupations in teaching and helping others, such as a mental hospital or a government welfare agency. Individuals who have intellectual interests may prefer scientific occupations and choose to work for a university or a research institute.

2. *Organizational image.* Some individuals are attracted to an organization because of the status and prestige associated with the company or its industry. For example, chemical companies have had a reputation for polluting the environment, government agencies have had a reputation for bureaucratic inefficiencies, and railroads have had an image of financial

decline. Although these reputations are not entirely accurate and some organizations are quite different from their industry's image, individuals' perceptions of an organization influence their employment decisions. An organization's image also influences the status and social life of employees and their families off the job. Employees tend to transfer the status and prestige of the organization onto their own self-esteem. A study examining the reasons why employees decided to remain with or leave an organization found that the decision was greatly influenced by the prestige of the organization as viewed by an employee's spouse.[7]

3. *Organizational personality.* Some evidence demonstrates that individuals are attracted to organizations that manifest personalities or styles similar to their own. In one study, the personalities of a group of subjects were measured on a number of dimensions and the subjects were then asked to describe the personalities of the organizations in which they would most prefer and least prefer to work. The results of this study indicated that the same dimensions of personality were used for describing both the personality of the individual and the personality of their preferred organization. The better the match of personalities, the more highly the organization was preferred.[8] These results are consistent with other studies showing that people choose vocations consistent with their self-esteem and self-concept.

Job Choice. Several factors associated with the job itself influence an individual's job choice. The most important factors seem to be pay and benefits, geographical location, opportunities for service and responsibility, flexibility and autonomy, and the friendliness of supervisors and co-workers.

Studies of the relative importance of these job factors generally show that pay and benefits are the most important factors in choosing a job.[9] However, the results are not entirely consistent, and the evidence seems to suggest that the results are influenced greatly by the method used to collect the information. When individuals are asked to rank the job factors in order of importance, they usually rank responsibility, opportunities for growth, and the opportunity to provide essential services as the most important factors. However, when they are shown job descriptions and asked to select between several pairs of jobs, their preferences seem to be most strongly influenced by pay and benefits.[10]

A hierarchical decision framework has been proposed to explain the relative importance of these job choice factors. This framework suggests that applicants first consider *objective factors* associated with alternative job offers such as salary, benefits, location, and the job requirements. These factors can be objectively evaluated and, in some cases, a dollar figure can be assigned to them. Objective job factors that can be easily measured, such as one job having a $200 higher starting salary or being 200 miles closer to home, appear to be the most important factors involved in choosing a job.

If the objective factors are roughly comparable, applicants are likely to turn to *subjective factors* and base their decisions on such things as the organization's image and the opportunity to serve society. Subjective factors are concerned with how well alternative jobs will satisfy personal needs and career goals; they may include such things as organizational prestige, responsibility, freedom from supervision, and the opportunity to benefit society. These subjective factors tend to be emotional and intuitive rather than objective.

If both the objective and subjective factors are roughly comparable, new recruits tend to base their decision on *critical contacts* with the organization. Recruits are influenced by how they feel about their interview and the interviewer, how speedily the organization handled the correspondence, and how hospitable the company representatives were during visits to the company offices. Critical contacts with the company are usually influential only if the objective and subjective factors are comparable, or when the recruits do not know enough about the organization to rate one above the other.

Maintaining Your Competence

Obsolescence refers to a reduction in effectiveness because of a lack of knowledge or skill, and it is a serious problem that is getting worse. The deficiency is sometimes due to forgetfulness, but more often it results from the creation of knowledge and technologies that replace old knowledge. Obsolescence among professionals has become so serious that several states require professionals to return to school. In some states, lawyers must return to school periodically or they are limited to representing only a full-time employer or members of their family. Similar requirements for medical doctors also have been enacted. A number of medical boards require periodic recertification every six years. Several states require physicians to take 50 to 60 hours of continuing education annually to maintain their licenses. Other professions, including accounting and human resource management, also require their members to obtain continuing education units (CEUs) to maintain their professional certification.

The quantity of knowledge is expanding in every occupation. Furthermore, new knowledge is being created at an accelerated pace, especially in occupations that disseminate or use new information, such as engineering and teaching. The creation of knowledge, however, does not necessarily mean that people will become obsolete. Even though a study of engineering firms showed that the average performance of older engineers declined, the researchers were quick to note that some older engineers were extremely competent and productive. Through study, work assignments, and training, these older engineers were able to maintain high rates of performance.[11]

Managerial obsolescence is not necessarily a function of age. The inevitable physiological changes that come with aging have little effect on executive performance. Mental abilities, as measured by intelligence tests, can actually improve over time, and particular improvement is often observed in verbal and conceptual skills that involve the assembly of objects and designs. Creativity, which involves a synthesis of concepts and experience, is also little affected by aging. The effects of aging on vitality and energy levels, however, are more variable. While some older people are physically incapacitated, others have remarkable strength and endurance. Nevertheless, reduced stamina is seldom the major cause of obsolescence. There is no reason to assume that age is an automatic indicator of obsolescence; managerial incompetence is not a function of aging.

There are many ways to maintain one's competence and avoid obsolescence. Companies provide their employees with a variety of programs to help them learn. Most of these programs are rather expensive, but because the costs of obsolescence are also high, they are usually cost-effective.

1. Continuing education appeals to many employees, the most popular form being evening classes at a local college or university. Tuition and other expenses are normally paid by the company if the course is relevant to an employee's job and the employee receives a passing grade.
2. Training and development programs can be held at the company on company time or at some other site on weekends or evenings. These programs can be taught by competent members of the organization, by outside consultants, or by someone like the service representative who sold the new equipment.
3. Training materials can be purchased by the company and made available to employees. The materials might include reference books, manuals, professional periodicals, films, video-tapes, and textbooks.
4. Periodic seminars and conferences can be held at which experts present information to professional groups or groups of employees.
5. Education sabbaticals can be arranged for managers and engineers, similar to those for college professors. Many executives think going to school full-time for a semester is more profitable than going to evening school forever. Sabbaticals help employees acquire better job skills, and organizations benefit from greater creativity and loyalty.
6. Job rotation and new project assignments can help employees gain new skills and knowledge. Although some lost time and frustration usually are associated with beginning a new assignment, the benefits of new learning frequently outweigh the lost time and effort.
7. Supervisors can encourage employees to maintain their competence by providing performance feedback, career counseling, opportunities for updating their skills, rewards for updating, and goal setting.

Company-sponsored training opportunities do not really focus on the root of the obsolescence problem, which is personal motivation. The motivation to learn and retain information must come from within an individual. If people are motivated to learn, they will do so, regardless of whether opportunities are provided by a company. If employees attend a training program only because someone else wants them to be there and not because they want to be there, the training will not be of much value. Organizations need to create healthy attitudes toward learning. They should emphasize that the successful workers of tomorrow need to develop positive outlooks toward learning, overcome resistance to change, understand their own shortcomings as learners, and be more open to experiences and ready to learn from them. In essence, successful workers have to learn how to learn.

Another important strategy for helping to combat the problem of obsolescence is to foster in employees favorable attitudes toward the importance of work. To combat obsolescence and to help employees in their current career development, a company should strive to strengthen the meaning of work for employees and to provide opportunities for them to be of service. Obsolescence is avoided more by promoting strong work values than by sponsoring company training programs.

Work and Family

Most people feel a constant tension between the demands of work and family responsibilities. Maintaining a comfortable balance between these two forces has become increasingly difficult because of changes in the traditional family structure, the increase in female employment, and the shortage of skilled workers in some industries. Dual-career families, where both husband and wife pursue full-time employment, present special challenges to both organizations and individuals, especially when employees are responsible for the care of young children or aging parents.

Dual-career family:
A family where both father and mother are pursuing careers outside the home.

Dual-Career Families. Following World War II, the dominant employment trend was to release women from the workforce, where they had supported the war effort, and allow them to remain at home raising the baby-boom generation. This trend was reversed in the 1960s, however, as increasing numbers of women joined the labor force. From 1960 to 2000 the percent of women in the 25-to-34 age category who joined the labor force increased from 36 percent to 79 percent.[12] This increase in female employment represents a profound social trend that requires families and organizations to develop new patterns of accommodation.

The most difficult problems accompanying this change concern the care of young children and balancing other family responsibilities when both parents work. While some couples have joint career aspirations and both want to pursue careers outside the home, many couples prefer having one partner stay at home or only work part-time when there are young children in the home.

The percentage of children living in dual-career families and single-parent families continues to increase. From 1975 to 2000 the number of dual-career families increased from 30 to 64 percent and single-parent families increased from 16 to 27 percent. Forecasts indicate that the percent of dual-career and single-parent families will continue to increase because of two primary reasons: career fulfillment and money.

Money is usually an important reason why both partners decide to work; having two incomes is perceived to be an economic necessity for some couples. The average income of a dual-career family is about 25 percent higher than a traditional family.[13] But while the incomes of dual-career families are higher, so are the costs: spending patterns indicate that dual-career families spend more on services and nondurable goods.[14] Consequently, the average disposable incomes of a dual-career family may not be much different from that of traditional families, if they have to pay more for taxes, child care, elder care expenses, household services, clothing, and prepared foods.

Studies on the effects of dual-career families indicate that the lives of both parents and children are impacted by the decision to have both parents work full-time. Having a second source of income creates greater financial security for both partners, and the feelings of freedom and professional self-determination are especially pronounced in men.[15] However, other results are not so positive.

The growth in dual-career families has been accompanied by an increase in physical and social problems for women that were once dominated by men, such as heart disease, heart attacks, ulcers, hypertension, and white-collar crime. Dual-career partners typically experience greater stress as they try to balance housework and childcare, and this burden falls unevenly on women in most families. Significant feelings of guilt are reported by both dual-career partners, with women usually reporting slightly higher levels.[16] In dual-career families, wives spend more hours doing housework than husbands, although dual-career husbands do more than traditional husbands. Daughters in dual-career families do 25 percent more housework than the daughters in traditional homes. The sons of dual-career families, however, only do about one third as much housework as sons in traditional families and they often develop very chauvinistic attitudes.[17] Men in dual-career families report lower job satisfaction than men in traditional families.[18]

Quality childcare facilities help to relieve some of the tension for dual-career parents, but child care can never replace the constancy and love of a parent in the home. There is little doubt that some dual-career families experience intense stress that reduces the quality of life for all family members, both at home and at work. There is also evidence, however, that these problems are not universal in all dual-career families, and the stress can be reduced by satisfactory childcare facilities and flexibility in work schedules. Employers are being asked to provide greater flexibility to accommodate family demands of workers.

Accommodation:
The process of achieving a balance between family demands and responsibilities at work. The most accommodative individuals are those who place the highest priority on family responsibilities.

Balancing Work and Family. Adapting work demands to family responsibilities has been referred to as ***accommodation.*** Individuals who give the highest priority to family responsibilities, while work and other outside interests remain secondary, are said to be the most accommodative. Those who are the most nonaccommodative are those whose work and career interests are always a higher priority than family responsibilities. In the past, the most accommodative individuals were the wives and mothers in traditional families who assumed responsibility for the family needs; the most nonaccommodative were career-oriented male executives who focused their interests and attention almost exclusively on work.

In recent years, new patterns of accommodation have emerged, largely because husbands are becoming more accommodative. Most women who are employed outside the home think their husbands should share household responsibilities. To achieve a successful marriage, dual-career couples need to decide who is responsible for such things as child care, meal preparation, housecleaning, shopping, yard work, and other family responsibilities. Unplanned events and emergencies often present special problems of accommodation, such as deciding which spouse remains home with a sick child or who should arrange for the repair of a household appliance.

The trend toward greater accommodation in our society on the part of husbands is indicated by the number of successful managers who, at mid-career, reject advancement opportunities because their new responsibilities would interfere with family commitments.

Mommy Track:
A career choice of women who are willing to sacrifice career advancement for greater flexibility to handle their responsibilities as a mother.

Organizations have been encouraged to develop alternative career tracks for mothers and fathers that allow them to sacrifice career advancement for the opportunity of spending more time with their families. A separate ***"mommy"*** or ***"daddy" track*** allows parents to hold flexible jobs with less travel and time demands while they have responsibilities for young children at home.[19] When their parenting demands ease, they once again pursue a fast-track path. A separate mommy track has been severely criticized, however, by those who fear it will be used as a pretext for discrimination against women or as proof that it means women can't have it all—motherhood and a career.[20]

A major problem for dual-career couples and their companies is job relocations, because they are so disruptive to family life. Some organizations offer to help the employee's spouse find a job when it wants to relocate an employee. Some dual-career couples find it necessary to live in metropolitan areas to increase the career opportunities of both partners.

Many couples have decided that the benefits of dual careers are not worth the costs, and a growing number of women have decided that the joys of mothering justify interrupting their careers. The process of leaving the workforce to raise a family and returning later is called *sequencing,* and an informal survey indicates that a growing number of career women are choosing sequencing as a means of balancing career and family interests.[21] Women who elect to sequence their careers first complete their education and work a short time, usually two to eight years in their chosen careers, then leave full-time work during the years they bear and mother their young children, and then, as their children grow, gradually incorporate professional activities back into their lives so that mothering and profession do not conflict.

Employment gaps by women, especially for purposes of child rearing, are generally perceived as acceptable career decisions that do not seriously damage their career advancement. An investigation of employment gaps among MBA graduates revealed that discontinuous employment histories had less impact on women than men. While an employment gap for women who return to work reduces their income 9 percent below what it would have been with continuous employment, a corresponding gap for men reduces their income by 21 percent.[22]

Some of the innovative ways women become reincorporated in the work force include job sharing, permanent part-time employment, flexible work hours, work-at-home programs, relocation assistance for the spouse of a transferred employee, childcare and day care assistance, time- and stress-management workshops, and employee assistance programs.

Organizations can help employees cope with the stress of dual-career families by legitimizing boundaries between work and home. For example, when professional employees are home in the evenings, are they still on call, or can they dedicate themselves to home and family? Some organizations help create boundaries by stating that evenings and weekends are family time, and employees and their supervisors should not allow work to encroach on family time. A consequence of this policy is that people who work late are not seen as super-achievers, but as poor time managers.

STRESS MANAGEMENT

A major component of adapting to work is learning to manage stress. Everyone experiences stress, and its effects can be either positive or negative. Individuals who achieve an optimal level of stress tend to work at peak efficiency, report high levels of job satisfaction, and experience a sense of accomplishment and well-being. Unfortunately, many people experience levels of stress that are either too high or too low. When stress is too low we tend to feel lethargic, lazy, and bored. However, excessive levels of stress can produce a loss of efficiency, excessive accidents, ill health, drug abuse, alcoholism, and other undesirable physical consequences.

Many of the physical and emotional problems college students experience are partially created by unhealthy levels of stress that they don't understand and don't know how to control. Too many individuals who are experiencing high stress levels make the mistake of associating stress with mental illness, and are unwilling to recognize the causes or consequences of stress.

Mental Health

The mental health of employees is just as important as their physical health. Mental illness is caused by many factors both on and off the job, including child abuse and other traumatic childhood experiences, marital conflicts and an unhappy family life, peer pressure and social ridicule, and a stressful work environment. Everyone occasionally feels frustrated, depressed, and a bit insecure, but most people can cope with temporary setbacks.

Maintaining good mental health requires a healthy environment, just as the maintenance of good physical health requires good hygiene. Mental illness sometimes involves serious emotional problems that require professional psychiatric help. However, the emotional problems of most people are not that severe. Most employees can adjust to everyday problems and live reasonably healthy, normal lives. A stressful, unpleasant work environment can cause severe trouble for some employees by destroying their self-esteem and making them feel inadequate. Creating a healthier work environment can make a big difference in their mental health.

Anxiety:
An intense feeling of fear and apprehension that is not associated with a specific threatening situation.

Anxiety and Depression. Two of the most common mental disorders are anxiety and depression. *Anxiety* refers to a state of tension associated with worry, apprehension, guilt, and a constant need for reassurance. Anxiety is more than the ordinary fear and apprehension that is consistent with reality. If a person is scheduled to speak to an executive board, some fear and apprehension are normal and even desirable. Moderate tension improves performance. Without some degree of concerned anticipation, an individual might be indifferent and apathetic. Anxiety, however, refers to a general state of fear and apprehension that is abnormally high and is not associated with a specific cause.

Depression:
A feeling of intense gloom and despair that is not associated with a specific unpleasant event.

Depression is a mood characterized by dejection and gloom, and usually contains feelings of worthlessness, guilt, and futility. Depression is more than just being unhappy or sad. Unhappiness is usually associated with a specific unpleasant event. Depression is an intense sadness that has lost its relationship to a specific series of events. Depression may be mild or severe. When it is severe, an individual may be unable to make even simple decisions or to respond to customary, everyday situations. In its extreme form, depression occasionally leads to suicide.

Both anxiety and depression are accompanied by a host of physiological effects. Anxiety usually leads to profuse perspiration, difficulty breathing, gastric disturbances, rapid heartbeat, frequent urination, muscle tension, diarrhea, or high blood pressure. Depression is usually associated with a series of biochemical disturbances that may be linked to a genetic predisposition. Both anxiety and depression have been treated chemically. However, drug treatments are not an ideal long-term solution, since they often have undesirable side effects and usually do not solve emotional problems in the long run. Various forms of psychiatric counseling are recommended for severe cases. For mild forms, a good book, a vacation, or talks with close friends are highly recommended.

Burnout:

The inability to handle continued stress on the job, and the feeling of psychological exhaustion.

Burnout and Boredom. An inability to handle continued stress on the job that results in demoralization, frustration, and reduced efficiency, has been called *burnout*. Some occupations are particularly prone to burnout, primarily occupations that require a large investment of personal commitment and involvement. Burnout was first observed as a general problem among people who work in the helping professions, especially psychiatrists, social workers, and counselors, and since then it has also been used to explain the frustration and apathy of other professionals. The concept of burnout is popular because it helps to explain why people who are constantly asked to give of themselves can come to feel emotionally drained.

Boredom refers to the psychological responses of workers to repetitive jobs. All repetitive activities, however, are not boring. For example, playing a slot machine is a very repetitive activity that some people find very interesting. Jobs that have short work cycles and require the workers to do the same thing again and again are usually described as boring. Assembly-line jobs are frequently described as the most boring jobs.

Although boredom and burnout are different problems, they are both caused in part by a lack of meaning in work. Burnout occurs on jobs that usually provide a considerable amount of variety, significance, skill, and responsibility. At first, employees feel excited about their work and their opportunities to make a significant contribution. They invest themselves in their jobs and often work extra hours. After a while, however, the excitement wears off but the job still demands much in the way of effort and commitment. The jobs are no longer meaningful to the employees and they feel unwilling to exert the effort that is needed. Periodic vacations are usually recommended for professionals, to take time to reassess the meaning and importance of their work. But like blue-collar workers who are bored with their work, some professionals feel they have to find a different job.

Stress:

The nonspecific physiological response of the body to a stressor.

Stress. *Stress* refers to the nonspecific response of the body to stressors in the environment. Stressors can appear in a variety of forms and almost any physical or psychological demand can serve as a stressor. Some examples of stressors include a barking dog about to attack you, a speeding auto about to hit you, an executive committee you are planning to address, or a disciplinary hearing. The variety of potential stressors is shown in Exhibit 21.1.

All these stressors have one thing in common: They represent a potential demand that may exceed the person's ability or capacity to respond. Thus, stress involves an interaction between the person and the environment. It should be remembered, however, that all individuals do not perceive the environment similarly, and an extremely stressful situation for one person may not be stressful for another. Stressful events are not necessarily negative; a passionate kiss and receiving an award are positive experiences even though they create the same physiological responses as negative stressors.

Exhibit 21.1   Typical Stressors

Physical environment stressors
- Hazardous jobs and toxic substances
- Busy highways and bad driving conditions
- Stormy weather and violent storms

Individual stressors
- Type A personality
- Low tolerance for ambiguity

Job stressors
- Time pressures and deadlines
- Pressure to perform and exposure to public
- Limited control over important matters
- Responsibility for the well-being of others
- Too much or too little work to do

Organizational stressors
- Inefficient work procedures
- Unfair policies and inequitable practices
- Office politics
- Role conflict

Life stressors
- Death of a spouse or serious illness
- Divorce or family conflicts
- Financial problems
- Pregnancies and childbirth
- Marriage and falling in love

Physiology of Stress

The proper understanding of stress requires an understanding of the physiological changes that occur during stress. The same series of changes occur during periods of extreme stress, regardless whether the stressors are positive or negative.

General adaptation syndrome:
A process that describes how individuals respond to stress.

Alarm reaction:
The first stage of stress, in which the body prepares for a "fight or flight" response by activating the endocrine system.

Resistance stage:
The second stage of stress, in which individuals attempt to re-establish a state of balance after first responding to stress.

Exhaustion stage:
The final stage of stress, where physical damage occurs because the individual cannot adapt to the stress.

General Adaptation Syndrome. Our understanding of stress comes largely from the pioneering research of Dr. Hans Selye, a famous endocrinologist who described the general adaptation syndrome in 1936.[23] Selye defined stress as the nonspecific response of the body to any demand that is placed on it, and he made a clear distinction between stress and a stressor. When a stressor is present, a sequence of biological events occurs. Because the same syndrome of physiological responses is elicited by many different situations, Selye called it the *general adaptation syndrome*, which consists of three stages: alarm, resistance, and exhaustion.

1. The *alarm reaction* occurs when a stressor is recognized. A biochemical message is sent from the brain to the pituitary gland, which is a small gland just below the brain. The pituitary gland, the master control of the endocrine system, secretes adrenocorticotrophic hormone (ACTH), which causes the adrenal gland to secrete corticosteroids such as adrenaline. Immediately, the entire endocrine system is engaged in the secretion of complex hormones, and a general alarm is sent to all systems of the body.

2. During the *resistance* stage the body tries to return to a state of equilibrium once the immediate threat has passed. The physiological changes in this stage are mostly the exact opposite of those that characterize the alarm reaction. The body tries to regain a state of balance, even if the stressor is present.

3. The *exhaustion* stage occurs if the stressor continues and the body exhausts its ability to adapt. The symptoms of the exhaustion stage are similar to the alarm reaction. If the stress persists unduly, severe wear and tear will occur, resulting in damage to a local area or death to the organism as a whole.

Exhibit 21.2 Physiological Responses to an Alarm Reaction

1. The breath rate increases to provide more oxygen.
2. Red blood cells flood the bloodstream to carry more oxygen to the muscles.
3. The heart beats faster, and blood pressure soars to provide blood to needed areas.
4. Stored sugar and fats are converted to blood glucose to provide fuel for quick energy.
5. Blood-clotting mechanisms are activated to protect against possible bleeding.
6. Digestion ceases so that blood may be diverted to muscles and brain.
7. Perspiration and saliva increase.
8. Bowel and bladder muscles loosen.
9. Muscles tense in preparation for strenuous activity.
10. The pupils dilate, allowing more light to enter the eye.
11. The endocrine system increases the production of hormones.

The alarm reaction has been called the fight-or-flight response. In this stage, the autonomic nervous system makes dozens of immediate responses to prepare the body for physical action. When pedestrians are crossing the street and suddenly see a car speeding toward them, the alarm reaction prepares their bodies to quickly get out of the way. Some of the major responses that the body makes during the alarm reaction are listed in Exhibit 21.2.

The alarm reactions are very useful when a physical threat demands an immediate physical response. If you attempted to flee from a dog that was about to bite you or a car about to hit you, and your body failed to make the appropriate alarm reactions, you would very quickly become unconscious because of a lack of oxygen or blood glucose. However, the stressors most people face do not call for an immediate physical response. The most typical kind of alarm reactions are such things as taking exams, being called on in class, speaking before an executive committee, or seeing another motorist cut in front of you. A strenuous physical response is not appropriate in such situations, even though the alarm reaction prepares your body to make such a response.

The alarm reaction is a major source of distress when it is constantly turned on without being used for its intended purpose. When the alarm reaction is fired too often or for too long, the body may remain in a constant state of mobilization. The alarm reaction can become classically conditioned to inappropriate conditioned stimuli. The body may remain in a state of chronic tension with high blood pressure, rapid heart beat, and disrupted digestion. The consequences are usually very serious. Damage can occur to the nervous system itself or to many vital organs. The results may range from simple hypertension to fatal heart disease.

The consequences of excessive stress may lead to a wide variety of health problems. A useful analogy is to think of a chain that is subjected to increasing levels of tension until it breaks. The increasing tension will cause the chain to break at its weakest link. Likewise, excessive levels of stress will result in injury to the weakest system of the body. Some individuals will respond to excessive stress by experiencing coronary heart disease, others by digestive problems such as ulcers, while others experience nervous disorders and hypertension. During periods of intense pressure, such as the week of midterms and final exams, students may experience a variety of physiological problems, especially sore throats, indigestion, and headaches.

Eustress:
Pleasant or curative stress that contributes to interest, enthusiasm, and a zest for living.

Distress:
Unpleasant stress that is destructive to physical and mental well-being.

Stress versus Distress. Not all stress is unpleasant. Selye described stress as the spice of life and said that the absence of stress is death. He differentiated between positive stress, which he called *eustress*, and negative, harmful stress which he called *distress*.[24] Some examples of eustress are falling in love, winning a contest, and receiving an award. Since stress is the nonspecific response of the body to any demand, the physiological responses of distress and eustress are virtually the same. However, eustress causes much less damage to the body because the person is more inclined to successfully adapt to the change. How the individual chooses to respond to a stressor has a large influence on how much damage is likely to occur. If the stressor is viewed as an opportunity, the situation is much more likely to produce a growth enhancing reaction.

A common assumption is that top executives experience the most stressors. However, a study of 270,000 male employees in major corporations showed that the rate of coronary disease was lower at successively higher levels of the organization, probably because upper-level executives have greater control and predictability over their own situations than those in lower levels.[25] Rather than feeling stress themselves, they are more inclined to create stress for others. Those who have more perceived control over their environments experience less stress and fewer somatic disorders.

Individual Differences. Large individual differences have been observed in the way people respond to stressors. Speaking before a large audience is a frightening and stressful experience for most people, but some individuals enjoy speaking to large audiences and would gladly accept the opportunity, even though they might feel a little nervous. Individual differences such as these are caused by many factors including biochemistry, physical strength, psychological and emotional makeup, past experience, and personal values.

Research suggests that the negative effects of stress have been more evident in the lives of men than women. Women have a longer life expectancy than men, and at certain ages men are four times more likely to die of coronary heart disease and five times more likely to die of alcohol-related disease than women. While these differences may be partially attributed to biological sex differences, they are also caused by role differences. Men have historically held occupations involving higher levels of stress and limited opportunities for physical exercise to manage the stress. Today, however, the differences between male and female occupational roles are being reduced as more women move into the mainstream of organizational life. Consequently, an increasing number of women are now beginning to experience stress-related health problems. As the occupational differences between male and female roles have narrowed, so also have the differences in stress-related health problems. For example, peptic ulcers and coronary disease among females below age 45 are increasing.[26]

Self-esteem appears to moderate the effects of stress. Individuals with high self-esteem have greater confidence and can deal successfully with stressors. These people are more inclined to perceive a stressful situation as a challenge or opportunity than a threat. Individuals with high self-esteem have been found to experience fewer coronary heart disease risk factors. Even when the situation is beyond their control, individuals with high self-esteem are influenced less by stressful events. Research on the survivors of wartime prison camps found that high levels of self-esteem helped the prisoners endure the stress of captivity.

Type A versus Type B behavior patterns:
A personality dimension related to the way people respond to stressors. Type A individuals are intense, high-strung, and impulsive, while Type B individuals are contemplative and relaxed.

The personality characteristic most closely associated with stress is the Type A versus Type B behavior pattern. This behavior pattern was discovered by two medical practitioners who found that the traditional coronary heart risk factors such as diet, cholesterol, blood pressure, and heredity could not totally explain or predict coronary heart disease.[27] Through their interviews and observations they found that a certain personality characteristic that they called Type A predisposes some people to coronary heart disease. In fact, Type A individuals have approximately twice the risk of developing coronary heart disease as Type B individuals. The person with a Type A behavior pattern has these characteristics:

- Chronically struggles to get as many things done as possible in the shortest time period.
- Speaks explosively.
- Rushes others to finish what they're saying.
- Is always in a struggle with people, things, and events.
- Is preoccupied with deadlines and task accomplishment.
- Is impatient, hates to wait. Considers waiting a waste of precious time.
- Is aggressive, ambitious, competitive, and forceful.

On the other hand, the Type B behavior pattern is characterized by an individual who is contemplative and feels no need to hurry or race against the clock. Although Type B people may have considerable drive and want to accomplish things, they tend to work at a steady pace and do not feel the intense pressures of time and deadlines. Type B people are not as easily angered or disappointed by their own work or the work of others. They tend to be more relaxed and noncompetitive. Because of their contemplative approach to problem solving, Type B people tend to be more creative than Type A.[28]

Events that force us to change our daily routine and face new challenges contribute to feelings of stress. The greatest stress comes from major changes such as divorce, marriage, or the death of a family member. But even positive events such as vacations and Christmas can contribute to stress levels because of the excitement, time pressures, and self-imposed deadlines associated with them. A scale for measuring the amount of change in a person's life, called the Social Readjustment Rating Scale, was developed from a study of over 5,000 patients suffering from stress-related illnesses. People who score high on this scale because of many life-changing events are encouraged to reduce the number of changes in their lives and to adopt some form of stress management exercise to manage their stress.[29]

Stress Management Methods

Since stress cannot be eliminated from daily life (nor should it be), the solution is to manage it effectively. If it is managed effectively, stress can enhance rather than diminish individual productivity, interpersonal relationships, and a general zest for living. The basic principle in managing stress is to reverse the stress response when it occurs inappropriately. The alarm reaction needs to be extinguished when it occurs at the wrong time. For pedestrians who see a car speeding toward them, the alarm reaction is appropriate, but it is not appropriate for motorists caught in heavy traffic. Several techniques have been proposed for controlling stress: eliminating the stressor, relaxation, social support, and physical exercise.

Eliminating the Stressor. In some cases, the easiest way to manage stress is to avoid it. All stress cannot and should not be avoided, but much unnecessary stress can be avoided by changing your environment or altering your interpretation of the stressor. Some executives avoid the stress of traffic jams by being driven in a chauffeured car. Supervisors can avoid the stress of criticizing an employee face to face by writing the criticism in a memo. Students avoid the stress of difficult exams by taking easy classes and not applying to graduate school. Some parents avoid the stress of having children around during the summer by sending them to summer camp.

Sometimes the stressor can be eliminated psychologically by changing the meaning of the situation. The goal here is to reassess the seriousness of the situation by thinking about the worst consequences that could possibly occur and then deciding how serious they really would be. "If I don't get this project finished by the deadline, will I die? No. Will my family leave me? No. Will I lose my job? Well, maybe. So how bad is that? It would be a real blow and I don't want that to happen, but I could get another job."

Much of the stress students experience in preparing for final exams can be handled quite effectively by this form of reassessment. "If I'm not prepared, will I fail the exam? No, but I'll probably get a low score. So, how bad is that?" Generally, the worst possible consequence does not happen, yet seriously thinking about it helps individuals to remove the stress psychologically. This method is particularly useful for those who suffer from vague premonitions of disaster. When two or three problems occur simultaneously, we often feel overwhelmed and think everything is crumbling around us. These vague premonitions of disaster can often be relieved by making a written list of our specific responsibilities or problems and prioritizing them.

Relaxation techniques:
Techniques that use relaxation to reverse the alarm reaction and avoid stress, such as abdominal breathing, transcendental meditation, and biofeedback.

Relaxation Techniques. Since muscle tension is a classically conditioned response to stress, relaxation techniques attempt to extinguish these responses.

1. Abdominal breathing involves taking long, deep breaths, which cause the body to relax and counteract the stress responses associated with an alarm reaction. This is an especially effective technique for most stress situations because it can be done without breaking a person's routine. A few deep breaths can effectively calm a person but go unnoticed in a committee meeting or during a phone call.
2. Muscle massage also relieves tension. The recommended procedure is to start at the top of the head, massaging slowly, and move down the neck to the arms, back, legs, and feet. However, some other sequence or even part of a sequence that allows the body enough time to relax and regain a state of equilibrium should be helpful. Several organizations hire on-site massage therapists to help employees manage job stress more effectively.
3. Transcendental Meditation (TM) is a relaxation technique derived from the ancient traditions of India that uses a meaningless sound called a "mantra." The mantra is individually assigned to the meditator by a

trained instructor. Proper use of the mantra is said to automatically reduce the level of excitation and disorderly activity of the nervous system and to quiet the mind while maintaining its alertness. Evidence evaluating TM indicates that metabolic changes occur during meditation that move the body toward a deep state of rest. Employees who practice TM have high levels of satisfaction and productivity and good relationships with supervisors and co-workers. The mantra is classically conditioned to evoke a state of calm and quiet within the nervous system, which replaces the conditioned responses that evoke stress.

Biofeedback:
Using electronic monitoring equipment to measure internal body functions, such as blood pressure and muscle tensions, which allows individuals to sense them and control them.

4. *Biofeedback* uses sophisticated equipment to monitor internal body processes, such as muscular tension, skin temperature, blood pressure, and brain waves. When people are able to observe their brain waves or blood pressure, they can begin to control them by observing the internal and external conditions that caused them to change. Once they are aware that their internal body responses are in a state of stress, they can begin to make adjustments by altering their environment or their frame of mind to reduce the levels of stress. Some people even develop the skill to reduce their stress responses by conscious thought processes.

Social Support. Another method of managing stress is to develop a network of people with whom you can interact. A wide variety of people may be part of a social support system, including a spouse, family members, other relatives, friends, neighbors, work supervisors, co-workers, members of self-help groups, and health and welfare professionals. Since people spend such a large part of their lives at work, the amount of social support they obtain from work associates represents a major part of their total social support. An effective social support system may provide four major types of supportive behaviors:

1. *Emotional support:* Providing empathy, love, caring, and trust.
2. *Instrumental Support:* Providing direct help to people who are in need, such as doing their work, taking care of them, or helping them pay their bills.
3. *Informational Support:* Providing knowledge or information to help people cope with their personal or environmental problems.
4. *Appraisal Support:* Providing specific evaluative information to help individuals with their self-evaluations.

Each form of social support serves a useful function, but the most important form is emotional support. When individuals think of people being supportive toward them, they usually think of emotional support—providing empathy, love, caring, and trust. Most of the research showing that social support reduces occupational stress and improves health has focused specifically on emotional support.

The evidence indicates that the most important source of social support comes from the family unit, especially from one's spouse. The death of a spouse is usually a traumatic experience that influences both the physical and mental health of the surviving partner. The trauma is much less severe, however, if individuals have other social supports that can help them, such as an understanding supervisor, co-workers who are willing to listen and empathize, and a counselor who can provide supportive nondirective counseling.

Exhibit 21.3   Benefits of Regular Exercise

General Benefits to Overall Health

1. Strength and endurance are increased.
2. Energy is used more efficiently, even in mental tasks.
3. Proper circulation is maintained.
4. Grace, poise, and appearance improve.
5. Posture and muscle tone improve.
6. Chronic tiredness and tension are reduced.
7. Ideal weight is more effectively maintained.
8. Aches, pains, and stiffness are reduced.
9. Degenerative risk factors decline.

Specific Benefits to the Heart

1. Resting heart rate is lowered, meaning that the heart does not have to work as hard to circulate blood to the body.
2. Cardiac output is increased, meaning that under stress the heart is better able to distribute blood.
3. Number of red blood cells is increased, meaning that more oxygen can be carried per pint of blood.
4. Elasticity of the arteries is increased.
5. Blood cholesterol and triglyceride levels are lowered.
6. Adrenal secretions in response to emotional stress are lowered.
7. Lactic acid causing fatigue is more effectively eliminated.
8. Heart muscle is strengthened, and additional blood vessels within it are formed.

Physical Exercise. Exercise enthusiasts argue that the best technique for managing stress is a regular program of physical exercise. They claim that exercise prevents many physical and mental health problems and significantly reduces the seriousness of others. Although these claims may be a bit overstated, a flood of studies has shown that a well designed physical exercise program can significantly improve both physical and emotional health.[30] Some of the major benefits are listed in Exhibit 21.3

Many kinds of exercise programs exist. Some isometric routines are very brief, and can be done sitting in a chair or standing in an office. An isometric routine involves tightening the different muscle groups and holding them tight for a short time, such as ten seconds. These exercises are designed to maintain good muscle tone and strengthen the ligaments and tendons.

Almost any form of physical activity can provide good exercise if it is done properly. Basketball, football, and tennis are good activities for staying in shape, but they are not recommended for getting into shape because of the potential harm from jarring and abrupt movements. A common mistake in exercising is overdoing it and tearing the body down rather than building it up. Exercise should be systematic and regular, and never too much at one time. People who have been inactive for several years should start slowly when they begin exercising again.

Aerobic exercises are extremely valuable because they contribute to cardiovascular conditioning. *Aerobic exercises* refer to regular rhythmic activities that raise the heart and breath rate to a training range and keep them within that range for a period of time. (A simple formula for calculating one's training range heart rate is between 70 and 85 percent of 220 minus your age, which would be between 140 and 170 beats per minute for a 20-year-old.) Some of

Aerobic exercise:
Regular, rhythmic exercise that uses the large muscle systems to raise the heart rate to a training range and maintain it for a period of time. Aerobic exercise contributes to cardiovascular conditioning.

the best aerobic exercises are jogging, cycling, swimming, brisk walking, and aerobic dancing, because they involve a constant level of activity. It is recommended that aerobic exercise be done a minimum of three times each week for at least 12 to 15 minutes each time. More exercise is better, but the gains are not very large for exercise beyond 45 minutes daily.

Many large corporations have some form of in-house physical fitness facilities. A growing number of organizations encourage everyone to participate, and some organizations even offer financial incentives to participating employees. For example, the Hospital Corporation of America gives its employees four cents a mile for cycling, sixteen cents per mile for walking or jogging, and sixty-four cents per mile for swimming. Some organizations spend a considerable amount of money providing physical fitness centers for their employees but claim that these centers more than pay for themselves by reduced health insurance costs and benefits claims.[31] Students who are reluctant to begin a physical exercise program, especially those who claim to be too busy with the pressures of exams and research papers, should memorize the following lament of a graduating doctoral student: "For we labored all our days to stuff a million-dollar mind into a ten-cent body."

Discussion Questions

1. What is meant by the term *career success*? What criteria do you use to measure your own personal career success?
2. What are the major challenges in balancing work and family responsibilities? How were these challenges handled in your family as a child, and how do you plan to balance them in your family as a parent?
3. What are the typical situations in a student's life that can create alarm reactions? Which of these do you experience and how can you manage them appropriately?
4. What are the advantages and disadvantages of different stress-management techniques? Which stress-management techniques do you prefer personally?

Notes

1. O. C. Brenner and Marc G. Singer, "Career Repotters: To Know Them Could be to Keep Them," *Personnel* 65 (November 1988): 554–58.
2. Donald Robertson and James Symons, "The Occupational Choice of British Children," *Economic Journal* 100 (September 1990): 828–41; Robert F. Sherer, Janet S. Adams, Susan S. Carley, and Frank A. Wiebe, "Role Model Performance Effects on Development of Entrepreneurial Preference," *Entrepreneurship: Theory and Practice* 13 (Spring 1989): 53–71; Milton Rosenberg, *Occupations and Values* (Glencoe, IL: Free Press, 1957).
3. J. J. Kirkpatrick, "Organizational Aspirations, Opportunities, and Barriers." In K.S. Miller and R.M. Dreger (eds.), *Comparative Studies of Blacks and Whites in the United States* (New York: Seminar Press, 1973); Jeffrey H. Greenhaus, Saroj Parasuraman, and Wayne M. Wormley, "Effects of Race on Organizational Experiences, Job Performance Evaluations, and Career Outcomes," *Academy of Management Journal* 33 (March 1990): 64–86.

4. W. H. Sewell and A.M. Orenstein, "Community of Residence and Occupational Choice," *American Journal of Sociology* 70 (1965): 551–63.

5. Naomi Stewart, "Sources of Army Personnel Grouped by Occupation," *Occupations, the Vocational Guidance Journal* 20, 1 (1947): 5–41; George D. Dreher and Robert D. Bretz, "Cognitive Ability and Career Attainment: Moderating Effects of Early Career Success," *Journal of Applied Psychology* 76 (June 1991): 392–97.

6. R. P. O'Hara and D. V. Tiedman, "Vocational Self-Concept in Adolescence," *Journal of Counseling Psychology* 6 (1959): 292–301.

7. Benjamin Schneider and L. K. Olson, "Effort as a Correlate of Organizational Reward System and Individual Values," *Personnel Psychology* 23 (1972): 313–26.

8. V. R. Tom, "The Role of Personality and Organizational Images in the Recruiting Process," *Organizational Behavior and Human Performance* 16 (1971): 573–92.

9. Daniel C. Feldman and U. J. Arnold, "Position Choice: Comparing the Importance of Organizational and Job Factors," *Journal of Applied Psychology* 63 (1978): 706–10; Abraham E. Haspel, "A Study in Occupational Choice: Managerial Positions," *Southern Economics Journal* 44 (April 1978): 958–67; Sara L. Rynes, "Compensation Strategies for Recruiting," *Topics in Total Compensation* 2 (Winter 1987): 185–96; A. G. Peppercorn and G. A. Skoulding, "How Do Managers Position Themselves?" *Industrial Management and Data Systems* (September/ October 1987): 12–16.

10. Moshe Krausz, "A New Approach to Studying Worker Job Preferences," *Industrial Relations* 17 (February 1978): 91–95.

11. Dalton and Thompson, "Accelerating Obsolescence;" Asya Pazy, "The Threat of Professional Obsolescence: How Do Professionals at Different Career Stages Experience It and Cope With It?" *Human Resource Management* 29 (Fall 1990): 251–69.

12. From the Bureau of Labor Statistics published in the *Monthly Labor Review.*

13. Howard V. Hayghe, "Children in Two-Worker Families and Real Family Income," *Monthly Labor Review* (December 1989): 48–52.

14. Stephanie Shipp, Eva Jacobs, and Gregory Brown, "Families of Working Wives Spending More on Services and Nondurables," *Monthly Labor Review* 112 (February 1989): 15–21; Paul N. Strassels, "It's Your Money; A Spouse's Income Costs as Well As Pays," *Nation's Business* 77 (March 1989): 66; Mary Rowland, "Can You Afford Not to Work?" *Women's Day* (March 28, 1989), pp. 54–56.

15. Hazel M. Rosin, "Consequences for Men of Dual Career Marriages: Implications for Organizations," *Journal of Managerial Psychology* 5 (No. 1, 1990): 3–8.

16. "Housework Gap," *Executive Female* 12 (September–October 1989): 8; Jack L. Simonetti, Nick Nykodym, and Janet M. Goralske, "Family Ties: A Guide for HR Managers," *Personnel* 65 (January 1988): 37–41; Uma Sekaran, "Understanding the Dynamics of Self-Concept of Members in Dual-Career Families," *Human Relations* 42 (February 1989): 97–116.

17. Thomas Exter, "Everybody Works Hard Except Junior," *American Demographics* 13 (May 1991): 14.

18. Saroj Parasuraman, Jeffrey H. Greenhaus, Samuel Rabinowitz, Arthur G. Bedeian, and Kevin W. Mossholder, "Work and Family Variables as Mediators of the Relationship Between Wives' Employment and Husbands' Well-Being," *Academy of Management Journal* 32 (March 1989): 185–201.

19. Felice Schwartz, "Management Women and the New Facts of Life," *Harvard Business Review* (January–February, 1989): 65–76; Douglas T. Hall, "Promoting Work/Family Balance: An Organization-Change Approach," *Organizational Dynamics* 18 (Winter 1990): 4–18.

20. Joani Nelson-Horchler, "Derailing the Mommy Track," *Industry Week* 239 (August 6, 1990): 22–26.

21. Daniel F. Jennings, "Special Problems of Married Women at Work," *Baylor Business Review* 8 (Summer 1990): 9–11.

22. Joy A. Schneer and Frieda Reitman, "Effects of Employment Gaps on the Careers of MBA's: More Damaging for Men Than for Women?" *Academy of Management Journal* 33 (June 1990): 391–406.

23. Hans Selye, *The Stress of Life*, (New York: McGraw-Hill, 1956, 1976).

24. Ibid, p. 74; Hans Selye, *Stress Without Distress*, (New York: J.B. Lippincott, 1974).

25. Philip Goldberg, *Executive Health*, (New York: McGraw-Hill, 1978), p. 29.

26. M. A. Chesney and R. H. Rosenman, "Type A Behavior in the Work Setting." In C. Cooper and R. Payne (eds.), *Current Concerns in Occupational Stress* (New York: John Wiley and Sons, 1980), pp. 187–212.

27. Meyer Friedman and Ray H. Rosenman, *Type A Behavior and Your Heart*, (New York: Alfred A. Knopf, 1974).

28. Muhammad Jamal, "Relationship of Job Stress and Type-A Behavior to Employees' Job Satisfaction, Organizational Commitment, Psychosomatic Health Problems, and Turnover Motivation," *Human Relations* 43 (August 1990): 727–38.

29. Thomas H. Holmes and Richard H. Rahe, "The Social Readjustment Rating Scale," *Journal of Psychosomatic Research* 11 (1967): 213–17.

30. Some of the best references summarizing the benefits of physical exercise programs are Goldberg, Executive Health, chapter 6; Kenneth H. Cooper, *The Aerobics Way*, (New York: J. B. Lippincott, 1977); Kenneth H. Cooper, *The New Aerobics*, (New York: J. B. Lippincott, 1970); Valerie DeBenedette, "Getting Fit for Life: Can Exercise Reduce Stress?" *The Physician and Sports Medicine* 16 (June 1988): 185–91.

31. David Clutterbuck, "Executive Fitness Aids Corporate Health," *International Management* 35, (February 1980): 18–22.

Being an Emergency Medical Technician

I always planned to be a doctor; I remember announcing in the first grade that some day I would be a doctor. I still felt that way when I started college, but I didn't get the kind of grades I needed to go to medical school. My first two years were horrible; I just didn't take my career very seriously. But back then it didn't seem like anyone else did either, with all the protests and demonstrations.

A major turn in my career path was when I spent time in the Army and served as a medic in Vietnam. I got some good training in the military and I started to take my career seriously again. I really liked that work; there was something very exciting about patching people up and saving their lives. When I got home I got a job as an emergency medical technician and finished my college degree. I was married and didn't have enough money for graduate school. Besides, my grades weren't good enough anyway. I've been doing the same thing ever since then.

We moved out of the city 10 years ago when this community decided to start an emergency ambulance service. I was hired to manage the service, and it sounded like a good opportunity. But now I'm not sure what I want. I don't like being an administrator; that just means headaches and ulcers. Besides, it keeps from doing what I like to do. I still like putting accident victims together; that's still my first love. But I've started to think that ambulance running is for the young. Sure, it's exciting, but it's also emotionally draining and physically taxing. No doubt it's a high-stress job. Sometimes I think that if I don't change careers soon it's going to be me lying in that ambulance.

Questions

1. What is this person's career? How would you evaluate this person's career success? What constitutes a "successful career"?
2. What career advice would you give this person?

Stress and Adaptation: Self-Assessment

This exercise provides an opportunity to examine the levels of stress in your life. The type A versus Type B personality patterns were described by two San Francisco cardiologists, Meyer Friedman and Ray Rosenman, who were investigating the relationship between behavior and heart disease. (See M. Friedman and R. Rosenman, *Type A Behavior and Your Heart*, New York: Alfred A. Knopf, 1974.) Their observations led them to suspect that the effects of competition and job deadlines were more damaging than had been previously imagined. From their research, they concluded that people who had what they called type A personalities were more susceptible to coronary heart disease. Before studying more about type A versus type B personalities, complete a questionnaire measuring your personality.

Directions

Each of the following items contains two alternatives. Indicate which of the two alternatives is more descriptive of you. In some items you may feel that the alternatives are equally descriptive; for other items you may feel that neither is descriptive. Nevertheless, try to determine which alternative fits you best. For each item you may distribute a total of five points between the two alternatives in any way you choose. For instance, if X is totally descriptive of you and Y is not at all descriptive, place a 5 by the X and a O by the Y. If Y is slightly more descriptive of you than X is, place a 3 by the Y and a 2 by the X. There are six possible combinations for responding to each pair of alternatives. Whatever combination you use, be sure that the points you allocate to each item add up to 5. Remember, answer on the basis of what you honestly feel *is* descriptive—not how you feel you *should* be or how you would like to be.

Behavior Activity Profile Questionnaire

X Y

1. __ __ X. I guess I'm just interested in what other people have to say—I seldom find my attention wandering when someone is talking to me.
   Y. Often when someone is talking to me I find myself thinking about other things.
2. __ __ X. When I talk, I tend to accent words with increased volume, and my delivery is staccato, but rapid.
   Y. My speech usually flows slowly in a smooth amplitude, without changes in speed.
3. __ __ X. I like to enjoy whatever it is I'm doing; the more relaxed and noncompetitive I can be, the more I enjoy the activity.
   Y. In just about everything I do, I tend to be hard-driving and competitive.
4. __ __ X. I prefer being respected for the things that I accomplish.
   Y. I prefer being liked for whom I am.

5. __ __ X. I let people finish what they are doing or saying before I respond in any way—no use in jumping the gun and making a mistake.

Y. I usually anticipate what a person will do or say next; for example, I'll start answering a question before it has been completely asked.

6. __ __ X. My behavior is seldom or never governed by a desire for recognition and influence.

Y. If I were really honest about it, I'd have to admit that a great deal of what I do is designed to bring me recognition and influence.

7. __ __ X. I often get upset or angry with people, even though I may not show it.

Y. I rarely get upset with people; most things simply aren't worth getting angry about.

8. __ __ X. I frequently feel impatient with others, either for their slowness or for the poor quality of their work.

Y. While I may be disappointed with the work of others, I don't let it frustrate me.

9. __ __ X. My job provides me with my primary source of satisfaction, I don't find other activities nearly as gratifying.

Y. Although I like my job, I regularly find satisfaction in other things, such as spectator sports, hobbies, friends, and family.

10. __ __ X. If I had to identify one thing that really frustrates me, it would be having to stand in line.

Y. I find it kind of amusing the way some people get upset about waiting in line.

11. __ __ X. I don't have to control my temper; it's just not a problem for me.

Y. I frequently find it hard to control my temper, although I usually manage to do so.

12. __ __ X. I work hard at my job because I have a very strong desire to get ahead.

Y. I work hard at my job because I owe it to my employer, who pays my salary.

13. __ __ X. It's very unusual for me to have difficulty getting to sleep because I'm excited, keyed up, or worried about something.

Y. Many times I'm so keyed up that I have difficulty getting to sleep.

14. __ __ X. I may not be setting the world on fire, but I don't really want to, either.

Y. I often feel uncomfortable or dissatisfied with how well I am doing in my job or career.

15. __ __ X. It really bothers me when, for some reason, plans I've made can't be executed.

Y. Few plans I make are so important that I get upset if something happens and I can't carry them out.

16. __ __ X. Such things as achieving peace of mind or enjoyment of life are as worthy ambitions as a desire to get ahead.

Y. People who do not want to get ahead professionally or career-wise simply don't have any ambition.

Scoring

Calculate and interpret your score on the Behavior Activity Profile using the following information. Add your responses to 1Y, 2X, 3Y, 4X, 5Y, 6Y, 7X, 8X, 9X, 10X, 11Y, 12X, 13Y, 14Y, 15X, and 16Y. The average score for a group of 364 male students aged eighteen to twenty five was 49, while the average score of a sample of 397 female students was 42.

71-80	Hard-core Type A
56-70	Strong Type A
47-55	Moderate Type A
41-46	Low Type A
40	A and B tendency
32-39	Low Type B
24-31	Moderate Type B
12-23	Strong Type B

Although people cannot be easily categorized as having either type A or type B personalities, the research of Friedman and Rosenman indicates that the incidence of coronary heart disease is more prevalent among people whom they categorized as having type A personalities. The following is true of type A people:

- They chronically struggle to get as many things done as possible in the shortest amount of time.
- They are aggressive, ambitious, competitive, and forceful.
- They speak explosively, hurrying others to finish what they are saying.
- They are impatient, and they consider waiting a waste of precious time.
- They are preoccupied with deadlines and are highly work-oriented.
- Their lives always seem to be a struggle with people, things, and events.

AAP, 116
Abdominal breathing, 534
Abilene Paradox, 410
Ability problem, 257
Ability tests, 76
Abusive discharges, 254
Accommodation, 526
Achievement tests, 76–77
Action learning model, 485
Action research model, 485–486
Active listeners, 382
Active participation, 97
Adaptive subsystem, 14
Additive tasks, 272
ADEA, 70, 122
Adjourning, 270
Adolescent stage, 91
Adulthood stage, 92
Advanced manufacturing technology
    (AMT), 510
Advertising, 52–53
Aerobic exercise, 536
Aerospace industry, 52
Affirmative action, 116–117
Affirmative action plans (AAP), 116
Age discrimination, 121–122
Age Discrimination in Employment Act
    (ADEA), 70, 122
Aggressor, 275
Aims of Scientific Management, 197
Alarm reaction, 530, 531
Aligning the organization, 41
Alternative dispute resolution, 248
Alternative work schedules, 208–213
    compressed workweek, 211–212
    flextime, 209
    job sharing, 210–211
    organizational change, 474
    permanent part-time, 210
    telecommuting, 212–213

Altruism, 296, 299–301
Americans with Disabilities Act, 79, 123
AMT, 510
Analyzing the firm, 41–45
Anticipatory socialization, 89
Anxiety, 161, 528
Application blank, 75
Appraisal support, 535
Apprentice, 94
Apprenticeship, 98
Approximating, 394
Aptitude tests, 76
Arbitration hearing, 247–248
Archival data, 26
Aristotle, 377
Arsenal of Venice, 196
Artifacts, 355
Assembly line work, 202
Assessment center, 80
Assigned goals, 184
Assigned roles, 274
Assimilation, 138
Assistantship, 98
Athletic teams, 267
Atkinson, John, 147
AT&T, 80, 202, 521
Attention, 131–132
Attribution theory, 141–142
Attrition, 70
Authoritarian leader, 431
Authority, 450
Authority-Compliance Management
    style, 433
Authorization cards, 110
Autocratic leader, 431
Automobile companies, 51
Autonomy, 205
Aversive stimuli, 167
Avoidance behavior, 275
Avoidance contingency, 171–172

Avoidance strategies, 315
Awards banquets, 362

Babbage, Charles, 198
Back strain, 198
Balanced scorecard, 62
Bandura, Albert, 164
Barney, Jay, 44
BARS, 224, 226
Base rate of success, 81
Bay of Pigs, 409, 410
Behavioral contingency management
    (BCM), 176
Behavioral interviews, 75
Behavioral science research, 21.
    See also Theories
Behaviorally anchored rating scales
    (BARS), 224, 226
Benevolent-authoritative management
    style, 344
Benmark Inc., 39
BFOQ, 115
Binding arbitration, 247
Bingo, 173
Biodata forms, 75
Biofeedback, 535
Biographical information blanks, 75
Biotechnology, 198
Blake, Robert, 432
Blanchard, Ken, 434
Blocking roles, 275
Board of directors, 52
Body language, 386
Bona fide occupational qualifications
    (BFOQ), 115
Bonus plans, 236–237
Boredom/burnout, 529
Boundary role occupants, 277
Boundary spanners, 390
Boundary-spanning activities, 13
Bounded rationality, 400
Boy Scouts of America, 355
Brainstorming, 406, 413–414
Brand managers, 347
Breathing techniques, 534
British Rail, 368
Budgeting, 67
Bureaucracy, 338–343
Bureaucratic inefficiencies, 487
Bureaucratic personality, 342

Burnout, 529
Burns, T., 338
Business drivers, 236
Business necessity, 115
Business planning, 64–65
Business simulations, 100
Business statement, 35
Bystander apathy, 299–301

California Psychological Inventory (CPI), 77
CAM, 510
Canadian Tire, 38
CAPP, 510
Career, 518
Career choices, 523
Career development, 91–94
Career identity, 518
Career management
    anxiety, 528
    boredom/burnout, 529
    career choices, 523
    career planning, 523
    career success, 518–523
    depression, 528–529
    dual-career families, 525–526
    job choice, 522–523
    maintaining competence, 523–524
    mental health, 528–537
    occupational choice, 520–521
    organizational choice, 521–522
    stress, 529–537. *See also* Stress
    work-family balance, 526–527
Career performance, 518
Career planning, 523
Career success, 518–519
Carpal tunnel syndrome, 198
Case discussions, 100
Case studies, 24
Cash plans, 235
Castro, Fidel, 457
Catholic Church, 11
CBT, 100
Central tendency effect, 223
Centrality, 460
Centralization, 344, 345
Ceremonies, 360
Chaining, 163
Challenger spacecraft disaster, 409
Change, 480. *See also* Organizational change
Change agents, 496–501

Character development, 300
Charismatic authority, 450
Charismatic leadership, 425
Charismatic power, 453
Cheaper by the Dozen (Gilbreth/Gilbreth), 198
Civil Rights Act of 1866, 114
Civil Rights Act of 1964, 119, 475
Civil rights laws, 114–116
Clarifier, 275
Classical conditioning, 160–161
Classification procedures, 224
Classification systems, 232
Climate, 354
Clinical judgment, 79
Closed-system logic, 8
Closure, 133
Co-optation, 462
Coaching and counseling, 99, 499–500
Coal miners, 495, 496
Coalition, 462
Code of ethics, 364
Coercion, 483, 484
Coercive power, 453, 455
Cognitive complexity, 135
Cognitive distortion, 181
Cognitive limits of rationality, 400–401
Cognitive nearsightedness, 402
Cognitive structuring, 252
Collaboration, 269
Collective bargaining, 112–113
Collective mind, 286
Collectivity stage, 487
Comedian, 275
Commitment escalation, 401
Committee assignments, 98
Committee decision making, 403. *See also* Group decision making
Common enemy, 316–317, 504
Communicate the problem, 255–256
Communication and interpersonal skills, 374–398
  barriers to communication, 392–393
  communication overload, 393–394
  communication process, 375–377
  communication roles, 390
  improving effectiveness, 390–394
  listening, 382–384
  myth of open communication, 387
  nonverbal communication, 384–387
  organizational communication, 387–390

Communication and interpersonal skills—*cont.*
  persuasive communication, 377–380
  supportive communication, 380–382
Communication overload, 393–394
Communication process, 375–377
Communication roles, 390
Company-wide incentives, 235–236
Compensation maxim, 231
Compensation package, 231–239
  base pay, 231–233
  bonuses, 236–237
  gainsharing, 236
  intrinsic *vs.* external rewards, 238–239
  monetary incentives, 233–237
  profit-sharing plan, 235–236
  recognition awards, 237–238
  Scanlon plan, 236
Compensation programs, 170
Competition, 297, 474
Competitive advantage, 34
Competitor analysis, 49–50
Competitor intelligence, 50
Complaint procedures, 248–250
Complex ideas, 391
Compliance, 282, 299
Composite long wall system, 495
Comprehensive interventions, 506
Compressed workweek, 211–212
Compromise, 316
Compromiser, 275
Computer-aided manufacturing (CAM), 510
Computer-aided process planning (CAPP), 510
Computer-based training (CBT), 100
Computer simulations, 100
Conciliation, 116
Conditioned response (CR), 160
Conditioned stimulus (CS), 160
Conferences, 99
Conflict, 297. *See also* Intergroup conflict
Conflict resolution meetings, 505
Conflict-resolution strategies, 315–319
Conformity, 281–284, 303–304
Confrontation, 269
Confrontive responses, 385
Conjunctive tasks, 272
Consensual validation, 13
Consensus decisions, 405
Consensus tester, 275
Consideration, 432
Constituency approach, 17–18

Construct, 23
Constructive discharge, 122
Constructive ideas, 220
Consultative management style, 344
Consulting, 433, 434
Consumer demand, 474
Consumer markets, 46
Contacts and referrals, 72
Container industry, 346
Contingency design theories, 345
Contingency theories of leadership, 434
Contingent labor force, 73
Contingent workers, 73
Continuing education, 524
Continuous improvement, 488
Contrast, 138
Contrast effect, 223
Contrived consequences, 251
Control systems, 424
Controlling behavior, 21
Conviction records, 118
Cooperation, 220, 296
Cooperative education project, 98
Cooptation, 52
Coordinating mechanisms, 337–338
Core capability, 45
Core competency, 40
Core job dimensions, 205, 206
Core period, 209
Core shared assumptions, 356
Correlational studies, 25
Cost leadership, 38
Cost reduction, 59
Counter-attitudinal role playing, 100
Counter-proposal, 113
Country Club Management, 433
CPI, 77
CR, 160
Creativity, 523
Credibility, 377–378
Crowds, 285–286
CS, 160
Cuban missile crisis, 410
Cultural artifacts, 355
Cultural change, 366–368, 488
Cultural elite, 367
Cultural interventions, 367, 510–511
Cultural values, 355, 409
Culture, 43, 354. *See also* Organizational
    culture

Culture audit, 366
Customer departmentalization, 329, 331–332

Daewoo Group, 36
Dalton, Gene, 94, 481
Dalton's model of change, 481–482
Data collection methods, 26–27
Debasement techniques, 89
Decentralization, 334
Decision making, 399–400
    brainstorming, 413–414
    cognitive limits of rationality, 400–401
    decision-making process, 400
    Delphi technique, 414
    Gresham's law of planning, 413
    group, 403–411. *See also* Group decision
        making
    nominal group technique, 414–415
    personality determinants, 402–403
    psychological limitations, 402
    techniques, 413–415
    types of decisions, 412–413
Decision-making process, 400
Decision-making techniques, 413–415
Decision rules, 66
Decoding, 376
Defensive communicators, 380
Deferred compensation plans, 235–236
Deindividuation, 285–286
Delayed reinforcement, 172
Delegating, 433, 434
Delegation of authority, 334
Dell Computer, 13
Delphi technique, 414
Delta Airlines, 38
Deming, W. Edwards, 494–495
Deming Prize, 494
Democratic alternative, 447
Democratic leader, 431
Demotion, 253–254
Departmentalization, 329–332
Dependable role performance, 220
Dependent variable, 26
Depression, 528–529
Describing the situation, 255–256
Descriptive communication, 380–381
Descriptive essays, 224
Design. *See* Organizational design
Despair, 92
Detailed position-replacement chart, 69

Determinism, 165
Development, 95
Developmental change, 477
Devil's advocacy, 411
Diagnosing the problem, 256–257
Dialectical inquiry, 411
Dichotomized thinking, 402
Differentiation, 10, 38, 269, 346
Diffusion, 498
Diffusion of responsibility, 408
Diffusion strategies, 316–317
Direct threat, 123
Disability discrimination, 123
Discharge, 253
Discipline, 246–254. *See also* Employee
    discipline
Discipline procedure, 246
Disclaimer (employee handbook), 63–64
Discrimination
    age, 121–122
    disability, 123–124
    gender, 119–121
    national origin, 117–118
    prejudice, 137–139
    prohibited questions, 117–118
    racial, 114–118
    religious, 121
    reverse, 117
    systemic, 117
Discriminative stimulus, 163
Discussions, 99, 100
Disjunctive tasks, 272
Disney, 45
Disowning communication, 382
Disposal subsystem, 14
Disregarding, 393
Dissatisfiers, 201
Distinctive competence, 45
Distributive bargaining, 112, 113
Distrust of management, 476
Diversification strategy, 45
Diverting responses, 385
Division of labor, 328–329
Do-your-best goals, 184
Domain, 45
Dominator, 275
Douglas Aircraft, 510
Downward communication, 388
Dress code, 280
Dress for success seminars, 386

Drucker, Peter, 224
Drug screening, 78–79
Dual-career families, 525–526
Due process, 253
DuPont, 41
Dyad, 479
Dysfunctional conflict, 306–307

Economic forecasting, 52
Economics sector, 47
Education, 95
Education sabbaticals, 524
EEOC, 116
Effectiveness, 14. *See also* Organizational
    effectiveness; Career management
Efficacy perceptions, 144–145
Efficiency, 13
Effort, 179
Ego and esteem needs, 145
Ego integrity, 92
Elaboration stage, 487
Emergent problems, 260
Emergent roles, 274
Emotional support, 535
Empathic listening, 382–383
Employee-centered leadership, 432
Employee discipline, 246–254
    complaint procedures, 248–250
    grievance procedures, 246–248
    progressive discipline, 253–254
    punishment, 250–252
    rule enforcement, 250–254
    wrongful discharge, 254
Employee empowerment, 487
Employee handbook, 63–64
Employee profile, 66
Employment-at-will doctrine, 254
Employment discrimination. *See*
    Discrimination
Employment forecasting, 67
Employment interviews, 75
Employment law, 107–128
    affirmative action, 116–117
    BFOQ, 115
    business necessity, 115
    discrimination. *See* Discrimination.
    equal employment opportunity, 114–117
    fair employment practices, 108–109
    labor relations legislation, 109–110
    unions. *See* Labor unions.

Employment testing, 76–77
Empowerment, 425, 487
Enactive mastery, 144
Encapsulating, 316
Encoding, 376
Encourager, 275
Entrepreneur, 3
Entrepreneurial stage, 486
Entropy, 10
Environment, 6–7
Environmental complexity, 50
Environmental determinism, 165
Environmental forces of change, 474–475
Environmental scanning, 40, 64
Environmental sectors, 45–47
Environmental stability, 51
Environmental stressors, 530
Environmental uncertainty, 50–53, 346–347
Equal employment opportunity, 114–117
Equal Employment Opportunity Commission (EEOC), 116
Equal Pay Act, 119
Equality, 280
Equity, 280
Equity theory, 180–183
Ergonomics, 198
Erikson, Erik H., 91
Erikson's theory of development, 91–93
Escalation of commitment, 401
Escape contingency, 171–172
Ethical Bill of Rights, 108
Ethics
    compensation, 231
    fair employment practices, 108–109
    illegal activities, 53
    intelligence-gathering techniques, 50
    organizational abuse, 18–19
    organizational culture, 366–368
Evaluating performance. *See* Performance evaluation
Evaluation apprehension, 284
Evaluative responses, 385
Evaluative statements, 380
Exaggerated advertising claims, 38
Exception principle, 391
Executive bonus, 236
Executive Order 11246, 116
Executive pay, 446
Exercise (physical activity), 536–537
Exhaustion stage, 530

Expectancy (E_P), 178
Expectancy theory, 178–180
Expectancy/valence theory, 178
Experiential learning, 21, 100
Expert power, 453, 455
Exploitive-authoritative management style, 344
Expressed level of empathy, 383
External adaptation, 358
External change agents, 496–497
External locus of control, 142
External recruiting, 71, 72–73
Extinction contingency, 171–172
Extrinsic rewards, 168–169, 238–239
Eye contact, 386

Face-to-face communication, 384–387
Facial expression, 386
Fact finding, 249–250
Fair Credit Reporting Act, 78
Fair employment practices, 108–109
False negative error, 81
False positive error, 81
Family groups, 479
Fast-track employees, 221
Favorable attitudes, 220
Federal Express, 510
Feedback
    communication effectiveness, 391
    communication process, 376
    competition, 298
    core job dimensions, 205, 206
    learning, as requisite of, 97
    organizational change, 11
    performance, 97, 164
    survey feedback interventions, 506-507
Fiedler, Fred, 434–436
Fiedler's contingency theory, 434–435
Field experiment, 25
Field studies, 24–25
Figure-ground separation, 133
Filtering, 392, 394
Final interview, 79
Financial incentives, 233–237
Financial resources sector, 46
Fine-tuning compensation, 237
Firm resources, 44
First impressions, 137
Five forces model, 47–49
Fixed interval schedule, 174

Fixed ratio schedule, 173
Flat organizational structure, 332, 333
Flattery, 463
Flexible communication, 381–382
Flexible manufacturing systems, 196
Flextime, 209
Florida Power & Light, 510
Flow centrality, 460
Focal person, 276
Focal role, 503
Focus strategy, 39
Followership, 434, 436–437
Force field analysis, 480–481
Ford Motor Company, 208
Forecasting
    economic, 52
    employment needs, 67
    planning, and, 52
Formal groups, 267
Formalization, 337
Formalization stage, 487
Forming, 269
Founders, 357, 367
4/40 alternative, 211
Fraternities, 302
Fraternity pledges, 89
Fraudulent promise, 254
Freedom of speech, 18
Freemasonry, 11
Freewheeling, 413
French, John R. P., Jr., 452
Functional authority, 61
Functional conflict, 306, 319–320
Functional departmentalization, 329–331

Gainsharing, 236
Gamblers, 174
Games of chance, 173
Gatekeeper, 275, 390
Gay rights movement, 119
Gender discrimination, 119–121
General adaptation syndrome, 530
General Electric (GE), 60, 207, 368, 487
General Mills, 368
General Motors (GM), 41, 60, 487
Generativity, 92
Generic strategies, 36
Geographic departmentalization, 329, 331
Gilbreth, Frank, 198
Gilbreth, Lillian M., 198

Glass ceiling, 119
Globalization, 47
GM, 41, 60
Goal acceptance, 185
Goal commitment, 185
Goal difficulty, 184
Goal setting, 13–14, 183–185
Goal specificity, 184
Golden rule of power, 446
Good-faith bargaining, 113
Government sector, 47
Grand strategies, 37–39
Grapevine, 389
Graphic rating scales, 224, 225
Greenfield, 508
Gresham's law of planning, 413
Grievance appeal procedure, 249
Grievance committee, 248–249
Grievance procedures, 246–248
Group decision making, 403–411
    Abilene Paradox, 410
    accuracy and judgment, 406–407
    commitment and acceptance, 406–407
    consensus, 405
    creativity, 405
    groupthink, 409–410
    programmed conflict, 411
    pros/cons, 403–408
    risk taking, 408–409
    time and cost, 407–408
Group development, 267–270
Group diagnostic meetings, 502
Group discussion, 99
Group dynamics, 266–294
    cohesiveness, 301–305
    competition/cooperation, 296–301
    conflict, 305–320. See also Intergroup
        conflict
    conformity, 281–284, 303–304
    decision making, 403–411. See also Group
        decision making
    deindividuation, 285–286
    effective groups, characteristics, 270–271
    group development, 267–270
    group formation, 267–271
    group norms, 278–281
    group roles, 274–278
    group size, 271–273
    group structure, 271–274
    OD interventions, 502–505

Group dynamics—*cont.*
  organizational citizenship behavior, 299–301
  organizational development
      interventions, 479
  outside threats, 303
  peer pressure, 484–485
  power, 461–647
  productivity, 298, 304
  satisfaction, 298–299
  social density, 273
  social facilitation, 284–285
  social loafing, 285
Group formation, 267–271
Group incentives/bonuses, 234–235
Group interventions, 502–505
Group level of analysis, 6
Group norms, 278–281
Group roles, 274–278
Group size, 271–273
Group structure, 271–274
Groupthink, 408, 409–410
Growth stage, 487

H-P way, 363
Hallmark, 362
Halo effect, 136, 223
Harley-Davidson, 510
Harmonizer, 275
Hawthorne effect, 26
Hayes, Jack L., 45
Hayes International, 45
Hazing, 101
Healthy organizations, 3
Hersey, Paul, 434
Herzberg, Frederick, 201
Herzberg's hygiene-motivator theory, 201–202
Heterogeneous goals, 448
Hewlett-Packard (HP), 35, 363, 389
Hierarchal authority structure, 19
High-need achievers, 148
Hiring process
  discrimination. *See* Employment.
  equal employment opportunity, 114–117
  recruitment, 70–73
  selection, 73–81. *See also* Selection
Historical accommodations, 358
Hitchhiking, 413
Hofstede, Geert, 365
Honesty tests, 76
Horizontal communication, 388–389

Horizontal expansion, 201
Horizontal loading, 205
Hospital Corporation of America, 537
Hostile environment harassment, 120
Hot stove rule, 251
House, Robert, 434
HP, 35, 363, 389
HR planning, 64–70
HRIS, 66
HRM. *See* Hiring process; Human resource
      management (HRM)
Human relations movement, 22
Human resource information system
      (HRIS), 66
Human resource management (HRM), 58–86.
      See also Hiring process
  balanced scorecard, 62
  economic contribution, 62
  forecasting employment needs, 68
  HR/line management relationship, 60–63
  HRIS, 66
  planning, 64–70
  policies, 63–64
  recruitment, 70–73
  selection, 73–81. *See also* Selection
  strategic alignment of, 59–60
  strategic partner, as, 61
  succession planning, 68–69
  surplus personnel, 70
Human resource plan, 59
Human resource planning, 64–70
Human resource planning system, 65–66
Human resource policies, 63–64
Human resource sector, 46
Human-resource subsystem, 14
Hygiene-motivator theory, 201–202
Hygienes, 201
Hyperbole, 38
Hypothesis, 23, 24

I/O model, 47
IBM, 60, 362, 487
Ideal bureaucracy, 340
Identification, 282–283
Identity, 92
Ignoring problems, 255
Illegal activities, 53
Imitative behavior, 97
Imitative learning, 165–166, 283
Immediate reinforcement, 172

Imperfect competition, 36, 37
Implicit personality theories, 136
Implied contract, 254
Implied level of empathy, 383
Implied promise, 63
Imposed consequences, 259
Impoverished Management, 433
In-house physical fitness facilities, 537
Inbreeding, 71, 320
Incentive systems, 233–237, 483
Incorporation, 89
Incremental influence, 422
Independent contributor, 94
Independent self-study, 99
Independent variable, 26
Individual competition, 297
Individual incentives, 233–234
Individual level of analysis, 5
Individual stressors, 530
Individual wage decision, 232
Individualism *versus* collectivism, 365
Industrial organization model (I/O model), 47
Industry sector, 47
Inequity, 181
Influence. *See* Power and influence
Influence strategies, 463–465
Informal communication, 389
Informal groups, 267
Information dependence, 282
Information flows, 347
Information overload, 393
Information processing, 347–348
Informational support, 535
Informer, 275
Ingratiation, 463
Initiating structure, 432
Initiation, 89
Initiation ceremonies, 302
Initiator, 275
Institutional function, 13
Instrumental conditioning, 162
Instrumental support, 535
Instrumentality (P_R), 178
Instrumentality theory, 178
Instrumented T-group, 500
Insubordination, 257
Integration, 10–11, 346
Integrative bargaining, 112–113
Intelligence-gathering techniques, 50
Inter-role conflict, 278

Interdependence, 448
Interest inventories, 77
Intergroup competition, 297
Intergroup conflict, 305–330
    avoidance strategies, 315
    causes, 311–313
    changes between groups, 314
    changes within group, 313–314
    conflict resolution meetings, 505
    defined, 297
    diffusion strategies, 316–317
    functional/dysfunctional conflict, 306–307, 319–320
    power intervention strategies, 315–316
    prisoner's dilemma game, 308–309
    programmed conflict, 411
    resolution strategies, 317–319
    Robber's Cave experiment, 309–310
    trucking game, 309
Intergroup interventions, 504–505
Interlocking directorate, 52
Intermittent reward schedule, 173
Internal change agents, 497
Internal integration, 358
Internal locus of control, 142
Internal recruiting, 72
Internalization, 283
Internship, 98
Interpersonal interventions, 499–502
Interpersonal manipulation, 463
Interpersonal power, 452–457
Interpersonal sensitivity and involvement, 434
Interpersonal skills. *See* Communication and interpersonal skills
Interrater reliability, 223
Intersender role conflict, 277
Interval schedules, 174
Interview
    behavioral, 75
    data collection, as method of, 26
    employment, 75
    final (hiring), 79
    nondirective, 26
    patterned, 26
    performance, 229–231
    sandwich, 230
Intimacy, 92
Intragroup competition, 297
Intrasender role conflict, 277

Intrinsic rewards, 168–169
Intrinsic satisfaction, 97
IQ test, 23
Irony of democracy, 448
Irreplaceability, 459
Isolation, 92
It Ain't Disney, 208

Janis, Irving, 409
Jargon, 392
JIT, 510
Job bidding, 72
Job breadth, 202
Job characteristics model, 203–206
Job depth, 202
Job design programs, 196
Job Diagnostic Survey, 205
Job enlargement, 201
Job enrichment, 201–207
Job instruction training, 98, 101
Job interview, 75
Job knowledge test, 77
Job maturity, 434
Job pairing, 210
Job posting and bidding, 72
Job redesign methods, 205–206
Job rotation, 98
Job sample test, 77
Job scope, 202, 213
Job sharing, 210–211
Job specialization, 196–200, 328–329
Job stressors, 530
Job tryout test, 77
Johnson, Lyndon B., 116
Johnson & Johnson, 362
Joint venture, 52
Junior boards, 98
Just cause, 253
Just-in-time inventory control, 510

Kelleher, Herb, 363
Kennedy, John F., 410
Kinesics, 386
Knowledge management, 474
Kotter, John, 446

Labor relations legislation, 109–110
Labor unions
    certification, 110
    collective bargaining, 112–113

Labor unions—*cont.*
    constitution, 112
    decertification, 110
    grievance procedures, 246–248
    negotiating an agreement, 112–113
    organizing campaign, 110–112
    pros/cons, 110
    work stoppage, 113–114
Laboratory experiment, 26
Laboratory training, 494, 500–502
Laissez-faire leader, 431
Landrum-Griffin Act, 109
Latitude of acceptance, 380
Lawrence, Paul, 346–347, 458
Layoffs, 70
Leader behaviors, 430–433, 437
Leader substitutes, 437
Leadership, 421–444
    behaviors, 430–433, 437
    defined, 423
    followers, 434, 436–437
    improving, 435–436
    intelligence, 429–430
    Leadership Grid, 432–433
    management, compared, 422–424
    personality traits, 430
    situational, 434–435
    substitutes for, 437–438
    traits, 426–430
    transactional, 424, 425
    transformational, 424–426
Leadership Grid, 432–433
Leadership succession, 367
Leadership training, 434
Leadership traits, 426–430
Learned needs theory, 147–151
Learning, principles of, 97–98
Learning new ideas, 476
Lecture, 99
Legitimate power, 453, 455
Leniency-strictness effect, 223
Letter of recommendation, 77
Letterman clubs, 302
Levels of analysis, 5–7
Lewin, Kurt, 407, 431, 494
Lewin's force field analysis, 480–481
Liaison, 390
Liaison personnel, 347
Life cycle theory of leadership, 434
Life stressors, 530

Likert, Rensis, 343–344, 494, 507
Lincoln Electric, 362
Line authority, 60–61
Linking pins, 344
Listening, 382–384
Locke, Edwin A., 183
Lockout, 114
Locus of control, 142–143
Logical consequences, 251
Long-range business planning, 64
Lorsch, Jay, 346–347, 458
Lynch mobs, 285

Maintenance factors, 201
Maintenance roles, 275
Malcolm Baldridge National Quality
     Award, 495
Management, 423
Management by objectives (MBO), 224–226
Managerial obsolescence, 523–524
Managerial subsystem, 14
Managers, 3, 422–424
Manipulation, 463
Mantra, 534–535
Marathon Oil, 41
March of Dimes, 16
Marine Corps recruits, 89
Mary Kay Cosmetics, 38
Masculinity *versus* femininity, 366
Maslow, Abraham, 145
Maslow's need hierarchy, 145–147
Matrix organizational structure, 338, 337
Matsushita Electric, 44
Maturity, 92, 434
Maturity stage, 487
Maximizing, 401
Maytag, 38
MBO, 224–226
McClelland, David, 147
McClelland's learned needs theory,
     147–151
McDonald's Corporation, 52, 360
McGregor, Douglas, 135
Means-ends inversion, 342
Mechanistic organizational structure,
     338, 339
Mental health, 528–537
Mentor, 94, 102
Mergers and acquisitions, 52, 60
Merit pay, 233

Metaphors, 362, 368
Method of successive approximations, 164
Mid-life crisis, 93
Middle-of-the-road Management, 433
Middle-range business planning, 64–65
Milgram, Stanley, 451
Mind guards, 410
Minnesota Multiphasic Personality Inventory
     (MMPI), 77
Mission statement, 34–35
Mixed-motive conflict, 308
MMPI, 77
Mommy track, 526
Monetary incentives, 233–237
Money, 168
Moral dilemmas, 18
Motivating employees, 185–187
Motivating potential score (MPS), 205
Motivation, 159–193
     classical conditioning, 160–161
     cognitive theories, 178
     employees, of, 185–187
     equity theory, 180–183
     expectancy theory, 178–180
     goal setting, 183–185
     operant conditioning, 162–164
     reinforcement, 167–177. *See also*
        Reinforcement
     social cognitive theory, 164–167
     theories of learning and reinforcement,
        160–167
Motivation problems, 257–260
Motivators, 201
Motor response learning, 97
Motorola, 510
Mouton, Jane, 432
MPS, 205
Multidivisional structure, 42
Multiple channels, 394
Multiple constituencies, 17–18
Multiple cutoff, 79
Muscle massage, 534
Muscular Dystrophy Association, 16
Musical groups, 267
Myth of open communication, 387

nAch, 147–150
nAff, 150
Narrow span of control, 332
National Association of Manufacturers, 53

National Labor Relations Act, 109
National Labor Relations Board (NLRB), 109
Natural consequences, 251, 258–259
Need for achievement (nAch), 147–150
Need for affiliation (nAff), 150
Need for power (nPow), 150–151
Need-to-know principle, 391
Negative entropy, 10
Negative reinforcement contingencies, 171
Negative reinforcers, 167
Negative transfer of training, 98
Negligent hiring, 78
Nepotism, 72
New information, 483
Niche strategy, 39
9,9 leadership style, 433
NLRB, 109
Noise, 377
Nominal group technique, 414–415
Noncompetition, 297
Nondirective interview, 26
Nonmonetary reward systems, 237–238
Nonprogrammed decisions, 412
Nonverbal communication, 384–387
Nordstrom, 38
Norm of reciprocity, 280
Normative-reeducative change strategy, 484
Norming, 269
Norms, 278–281, 355
Norris-LaGuardia Act, 109
Northrup, 362
nPow, 150–151
Numbers fetish, 223
NuSkin Enterprises, 355
N.V. Philips, 44

OB Mod, 176–177
Obedience to authority, 451
Objective job factors, 522
Observational learning, 166
Observational studies, 24
Observations, 23–24, 26
Obsolescence
    adulthood stage, 92
    managerial, 523–524
    product, 474
OCB, 299–301
OD. *See* Organizational development (OD)
OD interventions, 499–511
OFCCP, 116

Off-the-job training, 99–100
Office of Federal Contract Compliance
    Programs (OFCCP), 116
Official goals, 13
Olympic athletes, 299
Ombudsman, 248
On-the-job training, 98–99
Open-door policy, 249
Open social systems, 8–9
Open-systems model of organization, 9
Open-systems theory, 7–13
Operant conditioning, 97, 162–164
Operant responses, 162, 163
Operational definition, 23
Operations subsystem, 14
Operative goals, 13
Opinion leader, 390
Organic organizational structure, 338, 339
Organization, 8
Organizational abuse, 18–19
Organizational analysis, 20
Organizational behavior modification
    (OB Mod), 176–177
Organizational change, 366–368, 472–490
    action research model, 485–486
    Dalton's model of change, 481–482
    education and communication, 482–484
    force field analysis, 480–481
    forces of change, 473–475
    kinds of change, 477–479
    peer group influence, 484–485
    reengineering the mature organization,
        486–488
    reinforcement, 484
    resistance to change, 475–477
    targets of change, 480–485
    theories of change, 480–485
Organizational citizenship behavior (OCB),
    299–301
Organizational climate, 354
Organizational communication, 387–390
Organizational culture, 43–44, 353–372
    changing the culture, 366–368
    defined, 43, 354
    development of culture, 357–359
    effects of, 362–366
    employee selection/discipline, 359
    ethical behavior, 363–365
    expectations of founders and leaders, 357
    historical accommodations, 358

Organizational culture—*cont.*
  international cultural differences, 365–366
  leaders, 357, 360
  levels of, 354–356
  maintaining the culture, 359–362
  member contributions, 357–358
  reactions to problems, 362
  reward and status allocation, 359
  rites and ceremonies, 360–363
  stories and symbols, 363–362
  worker attitudes/behavior, 362–363
Organizational design, 327–352
  bureaucracy, 338–343
  contingency theories, 345–348
  coordinating mechanisms, 337–338
  delegation of authority, 334
  departmentalization, 329–332
  division of labor, 328–329
  environmental uncertainty, 346–347
  information processing, 347–348
  matrix structure, 336
  mechanistic/organic structure, 337–338
  span of control, 332–333
  System Four, 343–345
  technology, 345
  universal theories, 336–345
Organizational development (OD), 491–515
  assumptions, 495–496
  change agents, 496–497
  coaching and counselling, 499–500
  common enemy, 504
  conflict resolution meetings, 505
  cultural interventions, 510–511
  defined, 494
  diffusion, 498
  evaluating, 498–499
  group interventions, 502–505
  historical overview, 486–495
  intergroup interventions, 504–505
  interpersonal interventions, 499–502
  organizational interventions, 506–509
  process consultation, 502
  RAT intervention, 503
  responsibility charting, 503–504
  sensitivity training, 500–502
  sociotechnical system design, 508–509
  structural change, 507–508
  survey feedback intervention, 506–507
  TQM, 509–510
  transfer-of-training problem, 497, 502–502

Organizational development (OD)—*cont.*
  values, 496
Organizational effectiveness
  balancing flexibility and structure, 475
  goal-setting, 13–14
  job enrichment, 207
  measuring, 14–18
Organizational engineering, 436
Organizational founders, 357, 367
Organizational goals, 13–14
Organizational image, 521–522
Organizational integration, 88
Organizational interventions, 506–509
Organizational level of analysis, 6
Organizational lifecycle, 486
Organizational mission, 521
Organizational myths, 363
Organizational personality, 522
Organizational politics, 461–465
Organizational processes, 44
Organizational resistance to change, 476
Organizational stories, 363
Organizational stressors, 530
Organizational structure, 41–42, 51, 328.
  See also Organizational design
Organizational subsystems, 11–13
Organizational uncertainty, 50–51
Orientation, 269
Orientation training, 101–102
Otherwise qualified, 123
Output approach, 16
Over-socialization, 89
Overheard messages, 379
Owned communication, 382

Pacifying responses, 385
Packaged food products, 346
Packard, David, 363
Paradigm, 22
Paradigm change, 478
Paradigm shift, 22
Paralinguistics, 386
Parent-teacher associations (PTAs), 11
Part-time employment, 210
Participant observation, 24
Participative goals, 184
Participative-group oriented management style, 344
Path-goal leadership theory, 434
Patterned activities, 9–10

Patterned interview, 26
Pavlov, Ivan, 160
Pay for knowledge, 234
Payoff matrix, 308–309
Pearl Harbor, 409
Peer evaluations, 228
Peer group influence, 483, 484–485
Peers, 456, 464
PEO, 73
People with disabilities, 123–124
Perception, 131–140
    defined, 132
    discrimination and prejudice, 137–139
    perceptual errors, 136–137
    perceptual process, 131–136
    self-fulfilling prophecy, 139–140
    theory X/theory Y, 135–136
Perceptual errors, 136–137
Perceptual inferences, 132
Perceptual organization, 133
Perceptual process, 131–136
Perceptual tendency, 138
Perfect competition, 37
Performance appraisal. *See* Performance
    evaluation
Performance evaluation, 220–231
    behaviorally based rating scales, 224
    classification procedures, 224
    criticisms, 221–222, 223
    descriptive essays, 224
    graphic rating scales, 224
    MBO, 224–226
    performance feedback, 226–227
    performance interviews, 229–231
    ranking procedures, 223–224
    results-oriented appraisals, 224–226
    role, 220–221
    360 degree appraisal, 228
    who should do the evaluation, 227–229
Performance feedback, 97, 164, 226–227
Performance interviews, 229–231
Performance management, 219–243. *See also*
    individual subject headings
    discipline, 246–254
    evaluating performance, 220–231
    rewarding performance, 231–239
    solving performance problems, 254–260
Performance measures, 13
Performance norms, 280
Performing, 269

Permanent part-time, 210
Person-role conflict, 278
Personal feedback, 298
Personal power, 151
Personal responsibility, 299–300
Personality, 141–151
    attribution theory, 141–142
    defined, 141
    locus of control, 142–143
    Maslow's need hierarchy, 145–147
    McClelland's learned needs theory, 147–151
    self-efficacy, 144–145
    self-esteem, 143–144
Personality dimensions, 142–145
Personality tests, 77
Personnel testing, 76–77
Persuasion, 463
Persuasive communication, 377–380
Peter Principle, 343
Pfeffer, Jeffrey, 446
P&G, 331
Philips, 44
Physical appearance, 386
Physical centrality, 460
Physical disabilities, 123
Physical distance, 385–386
Physical exercise, 536–537
Physical symbols, 363
Physiological needs, 145
Piece-rate incentives, 233–234
Planning
    HR, 64–70
    recruitment, 70–72
    uncertainty, and, 52
Plant closings, 70
Plastics industry, 346–347
Plato, 452
Point method, 232
Polarization, 409
Political activity, 53
Political maneuvering, 316
Political strategies, 461–463
Politics, 461–465
Pooled interdependence, 272, 311
Porter, Michael, 37, 47
Position-replacement chart, 69
Positive correlation, 25
Positive reinforcement contingency, 169–170
Positive reinforcers, 167
Positive transfer of training, 98

Posture, 386
Power and influence, 445–470
   authority vs. power, 449–451
   bases of power, 452–454
   conditions for, 448–449
   definitions, 447
   golden rule of power, 446
   indicators of power, 451, 452
   interpersonal power, 452–457
   organizational politics, 461–465
   subunit power, 457–461
   types of influence, 447–448
Power coercive change strategy, 484
Power difference, 365
Power distance, 365
Power intervention strategies, 315–316
Power needs, 151
Practice and repetition, 97
Practice of Management, The (Drucker), 224
Preemployment medical examination, 124
Prejudice, 137–139
Preliminary screening interview, 75
Prepotency, 146
Price wars, 305
Primacy effect, 137
Primary rewards, 167, 168
Principle of supportive relationships, 344
Principles of learning, 97–98
Prisoner's dilemma game, 308–309, 313
Privacy and Security Act, 78
Probing responses, 385
Problem-solving session, 318
Process consultation, 502
Process losses, 273
Process time, 272
Processes, 44
Procter & Gamble (P&G), 331
Procurement subsystem, 11–12
Product coordinators, 347
Product departmentalization, 329, 331
Product obsolescence, 474
Production-centered leadership, 432
Production subsystem, 14
Professional career stages, 94
Professional employer organization (PEO), 73
Profit-sharing plan, 235–236
Programmed conflict, 411
Programmed decisions, 412
Programmed instruction, 100
Progressive discipline, 253–254

Projection, 136
Promotion from within, 71, 72, 320
Protective acts, 220
Proxemics, 385
Proximity, 133
Psychological maturity, 434
PTAs, 11
Public relations, 52–53
Punctuated equilibrium, 479
Punishment, 170–171, 250–252
Punishment contingencies, 170–171
Punitive damages, 254
Pure conflict, 308
Purpose statement, 35
Pygmalion effect, 139

Qualified privilege doctrine, 78
Quality, 59–60
Quality management, 494–495, 509–510
Quality of work-life programs, 206
Questionnaire, 26
Queuing, 393
Quid pro quo harassment, 120

Racial discrimination, 114–117
Ranking procedures, 223–224
RAT intervention, 503
Ratification, 112
Ratio reinforcement schedule, 173
Rational-empirical change strategy, 483
Rational-legal authority, 450
Raven, Bertram, 452
Raw materials sector, 46
Realistic job preview (RJP), 90
Reality shock, 71, 89
Reality tester, 275
Reasonable accommodation, 123
Recency effect, 223
Reciprocal determinism, 165
Reciprocal interdependence, 311
Recognition awards, 237–238
Recruiting sources, 72–73
Recruitment, 70–73
Recruitment planning, 70–72
Recycling approach, 17
Reduced hours, 70
Reengineering the mature organization, 486–488
Reference checks, 77–78
Reference group, 402

Referent power, 453, 455
Referrals, 72
Reflective listeners, 382
Reflective responses, 385
Reflexive conditioning, 160
Reflexive responses, 160
Refreezing, 480
Regression analysis, 67
Reinforcement, 167–177, 484
     behavior modification, 174–177
     contingencies, 169–173
     interval schedules, 174
     reinforcers, 167–169
     reward schedules, 172–174
Reinforcement contingencies
     avoidance contingencies, 172
     defined, 167
     escape contingencies, 171–172
     extinction contingencies, 172–173
     positive, 169–170
     punishment contingencies,
        170–171
Reinforcers, 167–169
Reinterpretive responses, 385
Reliability, 74
Religious discrimination, 121
Replacement chart, 68
Replacement planning, 68
Repotters, 520
Research methods, 24–26
Resistance stage, 530
Resistance to change, 343, 475–477
Resolution strategies, 317–319
Resource acquisition approach, 15–16
Resource availability, 474–475
Resource-based theory of the firm, 44
Respondent behaviors, 160
Respondent conditioning, 160
Response repertoire, 163
Responsibility charting, 503–504
Restrictive hiring, 70
Restructuring, 487
Results-oriented appraisals, 224–226
Retaliatory discharges, 254
Retrenchment, 60
Reward allocation norms, 280
Reward dependence, 282
Reward power, 453, 455
Reward schedules, 172–174

Rewarding performance. *See* Compensation
     package
Rhetoric (Aristotle), 377
Risky-shift phenomenon, 408
Rites and ceremonies, 360–361
Rites of conflict reduction, 361
Rites of degradation, 361
Rites of enhancement, 361
Rites of integration, 361
Rites of passage, 89, 361
Rites of renewal, 361
RJP, 90
Robber's Cave experiment, 309–310, 311,
     312, 314, 317, 318
Role, 274
Role ambiguity, 276–277
Role analysis technique (RAT), 503
Role conflict, 277–278
Role confusion, 92
Role episode, 276
Role learning, 97
Role overload, 278
Role playing, 100
Role readiness, 276
Role sender, 276
Role transition process, 88–90
Rule enforcement, 250–254

Sabbaticals, 524
Safety and security needs, 145
Sales representatives, 174
Salvation Army collection box, 300
Sandwich interview, 230
Sandwiching, 255
Satisficing, 401
Satisfiers, 201
Scanlon, Joseph, 236
Scanlon plan, 236
Scarcity, 448
Schmidt, Warren, 434
Scientific management, 22, 183, 197
Scientific method, 22–24
Scientific research methods, 24–26
Screening interview, 75
Secondary rewards, 168
Section 1981, 114
Selection, 73–81
     application blank, 74
     basic principles, 73–74
     decisions, 79–81

Selection—*cont.*
  drug screening, 78–79
  employment testing, 76–77
  evaluating the procedure, 80–81
  final interview, 79
  interview, 75
  preliminary screening interview, 74
  reference checks, 77–78
  steps in process, 74
Selection decisions, 79–81
Selection process, 74
Selection ratio, 80
Selective listening, 393
Selective perception, 136
Self-actualization, 146–147
Self-concept, 143
Self-confidence, 284
Self-efficacy, 144–145
Self-esteem, 143–144, 532
Self-evaluation, 229
Self-fulfilling prophecy, 139–140, 499
Self-study, 99
Self-training, 220
Selling, 433, 434
Selye, Hans, 530
Seminars and conferences, 524
Sensation, 131
Sensitivity training, 494, 500–502
Separation, 89, 270
Sequencing, 527
Sequential interdependence, 311
Service pins, 361
Sexual harassment, 120–121
Sexual orientation, 119
Shaping, 164
Shared assumptions, 356
Shared norms, 355
Sherif, Carolyn and Muzafer, 309–310
Short-circuiting, 392
Short-range business planning, 64–65
Short-term employment forecasting, 67
Sickout, 114
Similarity, 133
Simon, Herbert, 400, 413
Simplifying language, 391–392
Simulations, 100
Single-business strategy, 42
Situational leadership, 434–435
Sixteen Personality Factor Questionnaire
  (16PF), 77

Skill-based pay, 234
Skill variety, 205
Skinner, B. F., 162
Slogans, 362
Slot machines, 173, 174
Smith, Adam, 196, 198
Smoking, 20–21
Smoothing, 316
Social and political change, 475
Social cognitive theory, 164–167
Social conduct norms, 279–280
Social conflict, 306
Social density, 273
Social facilitation, 284–285
Social facilitation effect, 284
Social inhibition effect, 284
Social loafing, 285
Social needs, 145
Social organizations, 11
Social position, 402
Social power, 151
Social readjustment rating scale, 533
Social responsibility, 280
Social systems, 8
Socialization process, 88–89
Socio-economic status, 520
Sociotechnical system design, 495, 508–509
Solving ability problems, 257
Solving performance problems, 254–260
  describing the situation, 255–256
  diagnosing the problem, 256–257
  emergent problems, 260
  motivation problems, 257–260
  solving ability problems, 257
Southwest Airlines, 38, 363
Span of control, 332–333
SPC, 509
Sponsor, 94, 102
Spontaneous and innovative behaviors, 220
Spontaneous recovery, 161
Staff authority, 60–61
Staffing model, 65
Stage I-IV professionals, 94
Stagnation, 92
Stakeholders, 17
Stalker, G. M., 338
Stanford Prison study, 286
STAR interviewing technique, 75
Statistical process control (SPC), 509
Stereotyping, 137

Stimulus generalization, 161, 163
Stimulus-response bonds, 162
Stogdill, Ralph, 430
Storming, 269
Strategic alignment, 59
Strategic contingencies, 458
Strategic management process, 39–40
Strategy
    defined, 34
    formulation, 39–41
    grand, 37–39
    role of, 36–37
    selecting, 35–41
Strategy formulation, 39–40
Stress, 161
Stress management methods, 533–537
Stressors, 530
Strike, 113–114
Structural change, 507–508
Structure, 42
Subjective job factors, 522
Submission agreement, 247
Suboptimizing, 330, 401
Subordinate appraisals, 228
Subordinate power, 463
Subordinates, 456, 463–464
Substitutability, 459
Substitutes for leadership, 437–438
Subsystem activities, 42
Subsystems, 11–13
Subunit power, 457–461
Succession planning, 68–69
Summarizer, 275
Summary motivation model, 186
Sunk costs, 476
Superiors, 456, 464
Superordinate goal, 318
Supervisors, 464, 524
Supportive communication, 380–382
Supportive relationships, 344
Surplus personnel, 70
Survey feedback interventions, 494,
    506–507, 508
Suspension, 253
Swearing, 257
SWOT method of strategy development,
    39–41
Symbol, 361–362
Symbolic interaction, 375
Symbolic label, 462–463

Symbolic learning, 166
System, 8, 42
System One, 344
System Two, 344
System Three, 344
System Four, 343–345, 507
Systems model of training, 95–96

T-group training, 494, 500–497
Taft-Hartley Act, 109, 463
Tall organizational structure, 332, 333
Tannenbaum, Robert, 434
Target of change, 486
Task identity, 205
Task interdependence, 311
Task-oriented leader, 434
Task significance, 205
TAT, 147
Taylor, Frederick W., 183, 197, 198, 233
Team-building meeting, 502–503
Team Management, 433
Technical terms, 391
Technology, 345, 473
Technology sector, 47
Telecommuting, 212–213
Teleconferencing, 99
Telling, 433, 434
Testable hypothesis, 24
Thematic Apperception Test (TAT), 147
Theories, 19–27
    data collection methods, 26–27
    defined, 21
    developing, 21–22
    good, 21–22
    research methods, 24–26
    testing, 22–27
Theories of change, 480–485
Theories of learning and reinforcement,
    160–167
Theory X, 135
Theory Y, 135–136
Therblig, 198
Thompson, Paul, 94
3/36 alternative, 211
358 degree appraisal, 228
Title VII, 115
TM, 534–535
Tobacco companies, 45
Total quality management (TQM), 494–495,
    509–510

Toyota, 38
TQM, 494–495, 509–510
Trade associations, 53
Traditional authority, 450
Training, 95
Training and development, 95–102
   definitions, 95
   off-the-job training, 99–100
   on-the-job training, 98–99
   orientation training, 101–102
   principles of learning, 97–98
   systems model, 95–96
Trait studies, 426
Transactional leadership, 424, 425
Transcendental meditation (TM), 534–535
Transfer, 253
Transfer of training, 98, 497, 497–502
Transformation approach, 16
Transformational change, 478–479
Transformational leadership, 424–426
Transitional change, 477
Trend projections, 67
Trucking game, 309, 310
Tylenol cyanide capsules, 362
Type A behavior pattern, 533
Type B behavior pattern, 533

UCS, 160
Uncertainty, 50–53, 346–347, 459
Uncertainty avoidance, 365
Unconditioned stimulus (UCS), 160
Under-socialization, 89
Undifferentiated thinking, 402
Unfair policies, 18
Unfreeze the current culture, 367
Unfreezing, 480
Unions. *See* Labor unions
Unit demand forecasting, 67
Universal theories of organizational
   design, 337
Unobtrusive measures, 26
Upward appraisals, 228
Upward communication, 388
U.S. Gypsum, 20
U.S. Steel, 41
USX, 41

Valence, 179
Valence-instrumentality-expectancy (VIE)
   theory, 178

Validity, 74
Validity coefficient, 80
Value chain, 13
Values statement, 35
Variable interval schedule, 174
Variable ratio schedule, 173
Verbal persuasion, 144–145
Verbal reprimand, 253
Verbal warning, 253
Vertical loading, 206
Vested interests, 476
Vestibule training, 99, 101
Vicarious experience, 144
Vicarious learning, 165–166
VIE theory, 178
Visibility, 138
Visible moral acts, 364
Visual presentations, 99
Vocal cues, 386
Vroom, Victor, 432

Wage level decision, 232
Wage-structure decision, 232
Wal-Mart, 37, 38
Wallace Company, 510
Walt Disney, 45
Wealth of Nations, The (Smith), 196
Weber, Max, 338, 339, 367, 450
Weight-loss programs, 481
Weighted application blanks, 75
Weighted composite, 79
Welch, Jack, 368
Whistle Blowers Protection Act, 365
Wildcat strike, 114
Win-lose attitude, 312–313
Women
   gender discrimination, 119
   glass ceiling, 119
   life expectancy, 532
   sexual harassment, 120–121
   stress-related health problems, 532
Woodward, Joan, 345
Work design, 195–217
   alternative work schedules, 208–213. *See
     also* Alternative work schedules
   job breadth, 202
   job characteristics model, 203–206
   job depth, 202
   job enlargement, 201
   job enrichment, 201–207

Work design—*cont.*
    job scope, 202
    job specialization, 196–200
Work-family balance, 526–527
Work roles, 275
Work slowdown, 113
Work values, 473
Worker Adjustment and Retraining
        Notification Act, 70
Workload analysis, 67
Written reprimand, 253
Wrongful discharge, 254
Wrongful termination claims, 63

Xerox, 510

Yellow dog contract, 109
Yetton, Philip, 432
Yield ratio, 71
Young adulthood stage, 91
Youth gangs, 302

Zero-sum conflict, 308
Zero-sum problem, 223
Zimbardo, Phillip, 286